HUMAN BEHAVIOR AT WORK
Organizational Behavior

McGRAW-HILL SERIES IN MANAGEMENT

Fred Luthans and Keith Davis, Consulting Editors

Allen:	The Management Profession
Arnold and Feldman:	Organizational Behavior
Benton:	Supervision and Management
Buchele:	The Management of Business and Public Organizations
Cascio:	Managing Human Resources: Productivity, Quality of Work Life, Profits
Cleland and King:	Management: A Systems Approach
Cleland and King:	Systems Analysis and Project Management
Dale:	Management: Theory and Practice
Davis and Newstrom:	Human Behavior at Work: Organizational Behavior
Newstrom and Davis:	Organizational Behavior: Readings and Exercises
Del Mar:	Operations and Industrial Management: Designing and Managing for Productivity
Dobler, Lee, and Burt:	Purchasing and Materials Management: Text and Cases
Dunn and Rachel:	Wage and Salary Administration: Total Compensation Systems
Feldman and Arnold:	Managing Individual and Group Behavior in Organizations
Finch, Jones, and Litterer:	Managing for Organizational Effectiveness: An Experential Approach
Flippo:	Personnel Management
Frederick, Davis, Post:	Business and Society: Management, Public Policy, Ethics
Gerloff:	Organizational Theory and Design: A Strategic Approach for Management
Hampton:	Management
Hampton:	Inside Management: Readings from *Business Week*
Hicks and Gullett:	Management
Hicks and Gullett:	Modern Business Management: A Systems and Environmental Approach
Hicks and Gullett:	Organizations: Theory and Behavior
Hodgetts:	Effective Supervision: A Practical Approach
Jauch and Glueck:	Business Policy and Strategic Management
Jauch and Glueck:	Strategic Management and Business Policy
Jauch and Townsend:	Cases in Strategic Management and Business Policy
Johnson, Kast, and Rosenzweig:	The Theory and Management of Systems
Karlins:	The Human Use of Human Resources
Kast and Rosenzweig:	Experiential Exercises and Cases in Management
Knudson, Woodworth, and Bell:	Management: An Experiential Approach
Koontz, O'Donnell, and Weihrich:	Essentials of Management
Koontz and Weihrich:	Management
Kopelman:	Managing Productivity in Organizations: A Practical, People-Oriented Perspective
Levin, McLaughlin, Lamone, and Kottas:	Production/Operations Management: Contemporary Policy for Managing Operating Systems

Luthans: Organizational Behavior
Luthans and Thompson: Contemporary Readings in Organizational Behavior
McNichols: Executive Policy and Strategic Planning
McNichols: Policymaking and Executive Actions
Maier: Problem-Solving Discussions and Conferences: Leadership Methods and Skills
Margulies and Raia: Conceptual Foundations of Organizational Development
Mayer: Production and Operations Management
Miles: Theories of Management: Implications for Organizational Behavior and Development
Miles and Snow: Organizational Strategy, Structure, and Process
Mills: Labor-Management Relations
Mitchell and Larson: People in Organizations: An Introduction to Organizational Behavior
Molander: Responsive Capitalism: Case Studies in Corporate Social Conduct
Monks: Operations Management: Theory and Problems
Newstrom, Reif, and Monczka: A Contingency Approach to Management: Readings
Parker: The Dynamics of Supervision
Pearce and Robinson: Corporate Strategies: Readings from Business Week
Porter, Lawler, and Hackman: Behavior in Organizations
Prasow and Peters: Arbitration and Collective Bargaining: Conflict Resolution in Labor Relations
Quick and Quick: Organizational Stress and Preventive Management
Reddin: Managerial Effectiveness
Rue and Holland: Strategic Management: Concepts and Experiences
Rugman, Lecraw, and Booth: International Business: Firm and Environment
Sartain and Baker: The Supervisor and the Job
Sayles: Leadership: What Effective Managers Really Do . . . and How They Do It
Schlesinger, Eccles, and Gabarro: Managing Behavior in Organizations: Text, Cases and Readings
Schroeder: Operations Management: Decision Making in the Operations Function
Sharplin: Strategic Management
Shore: Operations Management
Steers and Porter: Motivation and Work Behavior
Steinhoff and Burgess: Small Business Management Fundamentals
Sutermeister: People and Productivity
Vance: Corporate Leadership: Boards, Directors, and Strategy
Walker: Human Resource Planning
Weihrich: Management Excellence: Productivity through MBO
Werther and Davis: Personnel Management and Human Resources
Wofford, Gerloff, and Cummins: Organizational Communications: The Keystone to Managerial Effectiveness

HUMAN BEHAVIOR AT WORK

EIGHTH EDITION

KEITH DAVIS, Ph.D. *Arizona State University*

JOHN W. NEWSTROM, Ph.D. *University of Minnesota, Duluth*

McGRAW-HILL PUBLISHING COMPANY

New York St. Louis San Francisco Auckland Bogotá Caracas
Hamburg Lisbon London Madrid Mexico Milan Montreal
New Delhi Oklahoma City Paris San Juan São Paulo
Singapore Sydney Tokyo Toronto

Human Behavior at Work: Organizational Behavior

4 5 6 7 8 9 0 DOC DOC 9 3 2 1

ISBN 0-07-015574-7

This book was set in Caledonia by Better Graphics, Inc. (CCU). The editors were Kathleen L. Loy, Cynthia L. Phelps, and Larry Goldberg; the production supervisor was Janelle S. Travers. The design was done by Betty Binns Graphics. New drawings were done by Accurate Art.
R. R. Donnelley & Sons Company was printer and binder.

Library of Congress Cataloging-in-Publication Data

Davis, Keith, (date)
Human behavior at work.

Includes index.
1. Organizational behavior. 2. Industrial sociology.
I. Newstrom, John W. II. Title.
HD58.7.D36 1989 658.3 88-13189
ISBN 0-07-015574-7

ABOUT THE AUTHORS

KEITH DAVIS is Professor Emeritus of Management in the College of Business Administration at Arizona State University. He is the author of prominent books on management and a past consulting editor for approximately eighty books in the McGraw-Hill Book Company's Series in Management. He is a Fellow in both the Academy of Management and the International Academy of Management. Prior to entering the teaching field, Davis was a personnel specialist in industry and a personnel manager in government.

Davis received his Ph.D. from Ohio State University and has taught at the University of Texas and Indiana University. His fields of work are organizational behavior, personnel management, and social issues in management. He has been visiting professor at a number of universities, including the University of Western Australia and Georgia Institute of Technology. In addition, he has served as consultant to a number of business and government organizations, including Mobil Oil Company, Texaco, the U.S. Internal Revenue Service, and the state of Hawaii.

Davis is a former president of the Academy of Management, and he received the National Human Relations Award from the Society for Advancement of Management. He also has been a National Beta Gamma Sigma Distinguished Scholar. He is an Accredited Senior Professional in Human Resources.

Two other popular books by Davis are (with William B. Werther, Jr.) *Personnel Management and Human Resources* (3d ed., 1989) and (with William C. Frederick and James E. Post) *Business and Society: Corporate Strategy, Public Policy, Ethics* (6th ed., 1988), both published by McGraw-Hill Book Company. He also has contributed chapters to over 100 other books, and he is the author of over 150 articles in journals such as *Harvard Business Review*, *Academy of Management Journal*, *Management International*, and *California Management Review*. Four of his books have been translated into other languages.

JOHN W. NEWSTROM is Professor of Human Resource Management in the School of Business and Economics at the University of Minnesota, Duluth. He previously taught at Arizona State University after receiving his Ph.D. from the University of Minnesota. His fields of interest are management development and the transfer of training to the work site, alternative work schedules, and group dynamics.

Newstrom is a former chairperson of the Management Education and Development Division of the Academy of Management, and was a member of the board of directors for the American Society for Training and Development. He has served on the editorial review boards for the *Academy of Management*

Journal, Academy of Management Review, Journal of Management Development, and *Personnel Administrator*. He also has been a training consultant to numerous government organizations at the federal, state, and city level, as well as to firms in the utility, paper products, health care, and heavy machinery industries.

Newstrom is the coauthor (with Keith Davis) of *Organizational Behavior: Readings and Exercises* (8th ed., 1989) and three earlier books published by McGraw-Hill Book Company. Two other popular books jointly prepared by Newstrom include (with Jon L. Pierce) *The Manager's Bookshelf: A Mosaic of Contemporary Views* (1988) and (with Jon L. Pierce, Randall B. Dunham, and Alison Barber) *Alternative Work Schedules* (1989). He also has written over fifty articles that have appeared in journals such as *Personnel Psychology, Journal of Management, Academy of Management Journal, Personnel Journal,* and *Training*.

To my wife Sue,
son Charles,
and daughter Jean

KEITH DAVIS

To my wife Diane,
son Scott,
and daughter Heidi

JOHN W. NEWSTROM

CONTENTS

PART 3 Leadership and organizational change

PART 4 *Organizational environment*

PART 6 Conclusion

PART 7 Case problems

PREFACE

This book provides rich insights about people at work in all kinds of organizations, and suggests how they may be motivated to work together more productively. This exciting study of human behavior at work is called organizational behavior, and it is an integration and application of social science knowledge. Management, labor, behavioral researchers, and others can take justifiable credit for advances in the field of organizational behavior during this century, but much opportunity for improvement still remains. This book summarizes current knowledge and also suggests some areas in which further progress is still required.

All people who work in organizations will find this book helpful in understanding and guiding the behavior of others. It is designed primarily for college and university courses in organizational behavior, human behavior in organizations, and similar topics. Earlier editions have been used worldwide; and international editions include one published in Japan for the Asian market, an edition in India, and translations into three other languages.

The book has been tested on the firing line in university classrooms and in organizations for more than thirty years, and many ideas offered by users of earlier editions have been incorporated into this new one. We actively invite comments from both faculty and students to help us make the book even more useful. *We listen, and we care.* In response to recommendations by readers, we have expanded features such as figures and examples from actual practice to illustrate ideas.

The authors' roles

Overall, we have several key roles as authors of this book. We begin by immersing ourselves in the thinking, research, and practice of organizational behavior to provide ourselves with an in-depth understanding of it. This requires continuous reading of professional journals and books, as well as regular interaction with managers in a variety of organizations. Then we develop a logical and interesting organizational framework, and proceed to identify the most important elements for inclusion. Finally, we seek to present the information in ways that will help readers learn and retain the ideas.

Our final objective is to produce a book that is both accurate and useful. We emphasize content and substance, and present the material in an organized fashion that will enable readers to integrate the various parts of this discipline into a whole philosophy of organizational behavior. The eighth edition has been upgraded by thorough citations to recent research to indicate the data basis for our conclusions.

Where appropriate, we include alternative viewpoints on a subject (while attempting to screen out trivial issues and fads). This indicates that there are no simple answers to complex behavioral issues, and also encourages readers to do their own thinking on the subject. In addition, it challenges them to integrate a variety of perspectives. Consequently, we believe that this book will serve as a valuable reference book for a long period of time, as well as providing a stimulus for readers to enrich their knowledge by continued study of organizational behavior.

Features of the book

One of the most notable features of this book is its careful blending of theory with practice, so that basic theories come to life in a realistic context. Readers learn that concepts and models will apply in the real world and will help to build better organizations and a better society. The ideas and skills they learn in an organizational behavior course can help them cope better with life.

Another popular feature, widely recognized, is the hundreds of examples of real organizational situations. They illustrate how actual organizations operate and how people act in specific situations. The majority of major concepts in this book are illustrated with one or more of these examples.

A feature liked by both faculty and students is the book's readability. Following the concepts of both Flesch and Gunning, we have maintained a moderate vocabulary level and a readable style. Variety enhances the readability by inclusion of the many change-of-pace examples mentioned earlier.

Other features of the book include:

1 A widely accepted framework of four models of organizational behavior that extends throughout the book

2 Strong coverage of employee communication, much of it based on the authors' own research

3 Two comprehensive chapters on motivational theories and another on their application to reward systems in organizations

4 A chapter on participation that is unique among organizational behavior books in its focus on this contemporary approach

5 A detailed Table of Contents to indicate the location of major topics, margin notes to highlight key concepts within the text, and provocative quotes at the beginning of each chapter to stimulate thought and discussion

6 A list of classic and contemporary books at the end of each chapter that provides suggestions for in-depth additional reading

7 A comprehensive glossary of terms at the end of the book

New or expanded features in the eighth edition include:

1 A new emphasis on the important role of organizational culture

2 A revised structure, placing the discussion of communication early in the book because of its essential role in motivation, leadership, and other behavioral processes

3 An upgraded discussion of motivational theories, including sections on the equity model and Alderfer's classification of needs

4 A new chapter on international organizational behavior, highlighting some of the ways that human behavior at work varies in different cultures

5 New coverage of gain sharing, telecommuting, organizational citizenship, the leader-member exchange model of leadership, and the visionary role of leaders

6 A new section (in Chapter 22) on the contributions of theory, research, and practice to the field of organizational behavior

7 Several new cases at the end of the book, representing a variety of organizational settings and behavioral issues

Learning aids

Major features included in each chapter are chapter objectives, introductory quotations and incidents, a chapter summary, terms and concepts for review, true case incidents for analysis in terms of chapter ideas, and a thorough and up-to-date set of references that provide a rich source of additional information for the interested reader. There are also numerous discussion questions, many of which require thought, encourage insight, or invite readers to analyze their own experiences in terms of the ideas in the chapter. Other questions suggest appropriate group projects. A number of experiential exercises are also included for classroom use.

Instructional aids

Since this book has been used in classrooms for seven editions, several classroom-proven instructional aids have been developed and refined over the years.

1 *Readings and experiential exercises.* The eighth edition of *Organizational Behavior: Readings and Exercises,* by John W. Newstrom and Keith Davis, has over sixty readings from a rich variety of sources to give students a broader view of organizational behavior. There are also several experiential exercises designed to allow students to compare their own thoughts with those of other classmates in the application of organizational behavior ideas.

2 *Study guide.* The study guide, by Jon L. Pierce and John W. Newstrom, provides a valuable tool to help students learn and assess their progress as they work through the text. It includes a brief chapter summary and objectives, plus a variety of multiple-choice, true-false, matching, and essay questions arranged in assignments for each chapter. New features include chapter outlines, key terms, and crossword puzzles.

3 *Test bank.* There is an extensive test bank to help instructors prepare examinations. It is available to instructors through McGraw-Hill Book Company.

4 *Instructor's manual.* The instructor's manual, prepared by Gaber Abou El Enein, contains sample course assignment sheets, various types of questions for each chapter, notes on the incidents and end-of-text cases, and sample examinations. In addition, there is a film and videotape list for each chapter.

5 *Transparency masters.* A full set of transparency masters is supplied for each chapter with the instructor's manual.

6 *Transparencies.* A set of professionally prepared color transparencies, representing the important figures in the text and many others, is available to adopters.

Acknowledgments

Many scholars, managers, and students have contributed to this book, and we wish to express our appreciation for their aid. In a sense, it is their book, for we are only the agents who prepared it. We are especially grateful for thorough and competent reviews of the book by Dennis G. Allen, Grand Rapids Junior College; Lloyd Baird, Boston University; Richard Hill, Indiana University; Jim Keenan, St. Mary's College of California; Gerald McCarthy, Purdue University; Gerald Parker, St. Louis University; Garth S. Thompson, SUNY at Fredonia; Judith Vogt, University of West Florida; George Wagman, Texas A & M University; and Paul Wilkens, Florida State–Tallahassee. Many of our colleagues have provided valuable insights, support, and encouragement, and for that we wish to thank Larry E. Penley and Angelo Kinicki of Arizona State University and Jon L. Pierce, Greg Fox, Steve Rubenfeld, and Cynthia and Mark Lengnick-Hall of the University of Minnesota, Duluth. We also appreciate the help of many McGraw-Hill employees who worked with the book, especially Kathy Loy, Cynthia Phelps, Laura Warner, and Larry Goldberg. Finally, we are grateful to Joe Murphy for his role in the production of technically excellent prior editions of this book.

Keith Davis
John W. Newstrom

HUMAN BEHAVIOR AT WORK

Organizational Behavior

PART 1

Fundamentals of organizational behavior

CHAPTER 1

Working with people

If you dig very deeply into any problem, you will get "people."

J. WATSON WILSON[1]

But the big gap is in the way human beings are being utilized—or more accurately, under-utilized.

ROBERT H. GUEST[2]

CHAPTER OBJECTIVES

To understand

The meaning of organizational behavior

The key elements with which it is concerned

High points in its early history

Basic concepts of organizational behavior

Major approaches of this book

How organizational behavior affects organizational performance

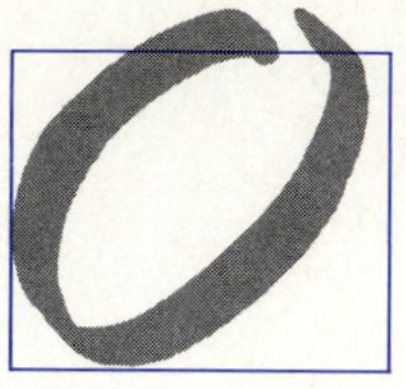

rganizations are social systems. If one wishes to work in them or to manage them, it is necessary to understand how they operate. Organizations combine science and people—technology and humanity. Technology is difficult enough by itself, but when you add people you get an immensely complex social system that almost defies understanding. However, society must understand organizations and use them well because they are necessary to achieve the benefits of civilization. They are necessary for world peace, successful school systems, and other desirable goals that people seek. The progress of our society depends on effective organizations.

Human behavior in organizations is rather unpredictable. This is because it arises from people's deep-seated needs and value systems. However, it can be partially understood in terms of the frameworks of behavioral science, management, and other disciplines; and that is the objective of this book. There are no simple formulas for working with people. There is no perfect solution to organizational problems. All that can be done is to increase our understanding and skills so that human relationships at work can be upgraded. The goals are challenging and worthwhile.

No simple formulas

We can work effectively with people if we are prepared to think about them in human terms. Consider the following situation in which a manager's motivation was increased after years of passive, minimum performance.

John Perkins, age about fifty, worked as assistant manager of a branch bank in a large banking system. He had been an assistant manager for eleven years. His work was so mediocre that no branch manager wanted him. Usually his current manager would arrange to move him out of the way by transferring him to a new branch that was opening; so John worked in eight branches in eleven years. When he became assistant manager at his ninth branch, his manager soon learned of his record. Although tempted to transfer John, the manager decided to try to motivate him. The manager learned that John had no economic needs because he had a comfortable inheritance and owned several apartment houses. His wife managed the apartments. His two children were college graduates and had good incomes. John was contented.

The manager made little headway with John and twice considered discharging him. Occasionally John developed a drive for a few weeks, but then he lapsed into his old ways again. After a careful analysis of John's situation, the manager concluded that although John's needs for tangible goods were satisfied, he might respond to more recognition; so the manager started working in that direction. For example, on the branch's first birthday the manager held a party for all employees before the bank opened. He had a caterer prepare a large cake and write on top an important financial ratio that was under John's jurisdiction and was favorable at the moment. John was emotionally inspired by the recognition and the "kidding" that his associates gave him about the ratio. His behavior substantially changed thereafter, and with further recognition he improved to become a successful manager of another branch within two years. In this instance John's performance was improved because his manager carefully analyzed the situation and used behavioral skills, such as recognition, to achieve a result beneficial to both parties. That is the essence of organizational behavior, which we will now define.

UNDERSTANDING ORGANIZATIONAL BEHAVIOR

Definition

Organizational behavior is the study and application of knowledge about how people act within organizations. It is a human tool for human benefit. It applies broadly to the behavior of people in all types of organizations, such as business, government, schools, and service organizations. Wherever organizations are, there is a need to understand organizational behavior.[3]

Key elements

The key elements in organizational behavior are people, structure, technology, and the environment in which the organization operates. When people join together in an organization to accomplish an objective, some kind of structure is required. People also use technology to help get the job done, so there is an interaction of people, structure, and technology, as shown in Figure 1-1. In addition, these elements are influenced by the external environment, and they influence it. Each of the four elements of organizational behavior will be considered briefly.

PEOPLE People make up the internal social system of the organization. They consist of individuals and groups, and large groups as well as small ones. There

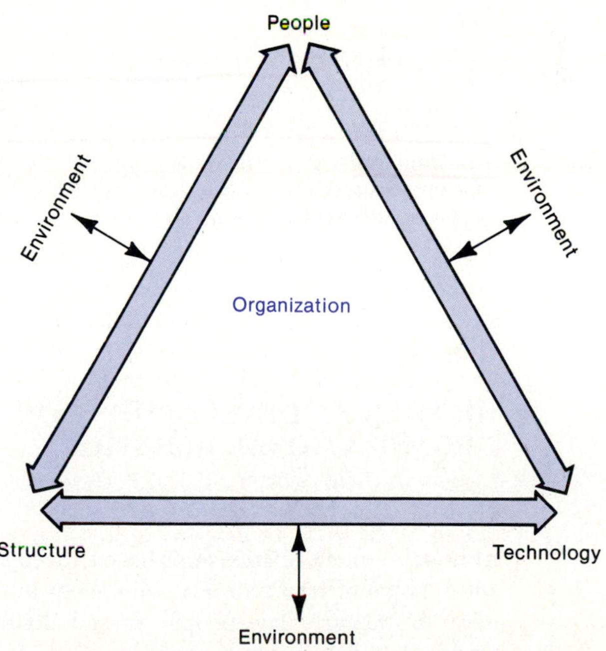

FIGURE 1-1
Key elements in organizational behavior

are unofficial, informal groups and more official, formal ones. Groups are dynamic. They form, change, and disband. The human organization today is not the same as it was yesterday, or the day before. People are the living, thinking, feeling beings who work in the organization to achieve their objectives. Organizations exist to serve people, rather than people existing to serve organizations.

STRUCTURE Structure defines the formal relationships of people in organizations. Different jobs are required to accomplish all of an organization's activities. There are managers and employees, accountants and assemblers. These people have to be related in some structural way so that their work can be effectively coordinated. These relationships create complex problems of cooperation, negotiation, and decision making.

TECHNOLOGY Technology provides the resources with which people work and affects the tasks that they perform. They cannot accomplish much with their bare hands, so they build buildings, design machines, create work processes, and assemble resources. The technology used has a significant influence on working relationships. An assembly line is not the same as a research laboratory, and a steel mill does not have the same working conditions as a hospital. The great benefit of technology is that it allows people to do more and better work, but it also restricts people in various ways. It has costs as well as benefits.

ENVIRONMENT All organizations operate within an external environment.[4] A single organization does not exist alone. It is part of a larger system that contains many other elements, such as government, the family, and other organizations. All of these mutually influence each other in a complex system that creates a context for a group of people. Individual organizations, such as a factory or a school, cannot escape being influenced by this external environment. It influences the attitudes of people, affects working conditions, and provides competition for resources and power. It must be considered in the study of human behavior in organizations.

HISTORICAL DEVELOPMENT OF ORGANIZATIONAL BEHAVIOR

Historical origins

Although human relationships have existed since the beginning of time, the art and science of trying to deal with them in complex organizations is relatively new. In the early days people worked alone or in such small groups that their work relationships were easily handled. It has been popular to assume that under these conditions people worked in a Utopia of happiness and fulfillment, but this assumption is largely a nostalgic reinterpretation of history. Actual conditions were brutal and backbreaking. People worked from dawn until dusk under intolerable conditions of disease, filth, danger, and scarcity of resources. They had to work this way to survive, and very little effort was devoted to their job satisfactions.

Robert Owen

Then came the industrial revolution. In the beginning the condition of people did not improve, but at least the seed was planted for potential improvement. Industry expanded the supply of goods and knowledge that eventually gave workers increased wages, shorter hours, and more work satisfaction. In this new industrial environment Robert Owen, a young Welsh factory owner, about the year 1800, was one of the first to emphasize human needs of employees. He refused to employ young children. He taught his workers cleanliness and temperance and improved their working conditions. This could hardly be called modern organizational behavior, but it was a beginning. He was called "the real father" of personnel administration by an early writer.[5]

Andrew Ure

Andrew Ure incorporated human factors into his *The Philosophy of Manufactures*, published in 1835.[6] He recognized the mechanical and commercial parts of manufacturing, but he also added a third factor, which was the human factor. He provided workers with hot tea, medical treatment, "a fan apparatus" for ventilation, and sickness payments. The ideas of Owen and Ure were accepted slowly or not at all, and they often deteriorated into a paternalistic, do-good approach rather than a genuine recognition of the importance of people at work.

Early development

Frederick W. Taylor

Interest in people at work was awakened by Frederick W. Taylor in the United States in the early 1900s. He is often called "the father of scientific management," and the changes he brought to management paved the way for later development of organizational behavior. His work eventually led to improved recognition and productivity for industrial workers. He pointed out that just as there was a best machine for a job, so were there best ways for people to do their jobs. To be sure, the goal was still technical efficiency, but at least management was awakened to the importance of one of its neglected resources.

Taylor's major work was published in 1911.[7] It was followed in 1914 by Lillian Gilbreth's *The Psychology of Management*, which primarily emphasized the human side of work.[8] Shortly thereafter the National Personnel Association was formed, and later, in 1923, it became the American Management Association, carrying the subtitle "Devoted Exclusively to the Consideration of the Human Factor in Commerce and Industry." During this period Whiting Williams was studying workers while working with them, and in 1920 he published a significant interpretation of his experiences, *What's on the Worker's Mind*.[9]

Research studies

In the 1920s and 1930s Elton Mayo and F. J. Roethlisberger at Harvard University gave academic stature to the study of human behavior at work. They applied keen insight, straight thinking, and sociological backgrounds to industrial experiments at the Western Electric Company, Hawthorne Plant. They concluded that an organization is a social system and the worker is indeed the most important element in it.[10] Their experiments showed that the worker is not a simple tool but a complex personality interacting in a group situation that often is difficult to understand.

Development of research

To Taylor and his contemporaries, human problems stood in the way of production and so should be minimized. To Mayo, human problems became a broad new field of study and an opportunity for progress. He is recognized as the father of what was then called *human relations* and later became known as *organizational behavior.* Taylor increased production by rationalizing it. Mayo and his followers sought to increase production by humanizing it.

Human relations

The Mayo-Roethlisberger research has been strongly criticized as being inadequately controlled and interpreted,[11] but its basic ideas, such as a social system within the work environment, have stood the test of time. The important point is that it was substantial research about human behavior at work, and its influence was widespread and enduring.

In the 1940s and 1950s other major research projects developed in a number of organizations, including the Research Center for Group Dynamics, University of Michigan (especially leadership and motivation); Personnel Research Board, Ohio State University (leadership and motivation); Tavistock Institute of Human Relations in London (various subjects); and the National Training Laboratories in Bethel, Maine (group dynamics). As the results of this research began to filter into the business and academic communities, it stimulated new interest in the behavior of people at work. An "age of human relations" had begun.

A fad

The new emphasis on people at work was a result of trends that had been developing over a long period of time. It helped bring human values into balance with other values at work. Unfortunately, human relations grew so fast that it was not well understood, and some shallowness developed. Some practitioners began to emphasize "being nice to people," while subtly trying to manipulate employees. This approach is illustrated by the cartoon in Figure 1-2. One humorist observed, "We have moved from the 'invisible hand' of Adam Smith's economics to the 'glad hand' of human relations." These practices led to well-deserved criticisms.[12]

The term "human relations" gradually lost favor, although it continues to be used—especially at the operating level—because of its appropriateness. An example is the statement "The supervisor is effective with human relations." As the field became more mature and research-based, the new term that arose to describe it was "organizational behavior."[13]

Interdisciplinary

A major strength of organizational behavior is its interdisciplinary nature, as it integrates behavioral sciences and other social sciences that can contribute to

FIGURE 1-2
The cooperative approach can be overdone.
Source: *United Features Syndicate; copyright © 1956. Used with permission.*

PEANUTS® Charles M. Schulz

the subject. It applies from these disciplines any ideas that will improve the relationships between people and organizations. Its interdisciplinary nature is similar to that of medicine, which applies physical, biological, and social sciences into a workable medical practice.

The interest of various social sciences in people is sometimes expressed by the general term "behavioral science," which represents the systematized body of knowledge pertaining to why and how people behave as they do. Organizational behavior then integrates behavioral science with formal organizations. It has been said that the formal organization view sees "organizations without people," while behaviorists speak of "people without organizations." However, organizations must have people, and people working toward goals must have organizations; so it is desirable to treat the two as a working unit, as organizational behavior does.

FUNDAMENTAL CONCEPTS

Every field of social science (or even physical science) has a philosophical foundation of basic concepts that guide its development. In accounting, for example, a fundamental concept is that "for every debit there will be a credit." The entire system of double-entry accounting was built on this philosophy when it replaced single-entry bookkeeping many years ago. In physics, a basic belief is that elements of nature are uniform. The law of gravity operates uniformly in Tokyo and London, and an atom of hydrogen is identical in Moscow and Washington, D.C. But the same cannot be said for people.

As shown in Figure 1-3, organizational behavior starts with a set of six fundamental concepts revolving around the nature of people and organizations. A summary of these ideas follows, and they are developed further in later chapters.

The nature of people

With regard to people, there are four basic concepts: individual differences, a whole person, motivated behavior, and value of the person (human dignity).

The nature of people
- **Individual differences**
- **A whole person**
- **Motivated behavior**
- **Value of the person (human dignity)**

The nature of organizations
- **Social systems**
- **Mutual interest**

Result
- **Holistic organizational behavior**

FIGURE 1-3 Fundamental concepts of organizational behavior

INDIVIDUAL DIFFERENCES People have much in common (they become excited, or they are grieved by the loss of a loved one), but each person in the world is also individually different. On the hills of Greenland lie billions of tiny snowflakes; yet we are reasonably sure that each is different. On the planet Earth are billions of complex people who are likewise all different (and we expect that all who follow will be different)! Each one is different from all others, probably in millions of ways, just as each of their fingerprints is different, as far as we know. And these differences are usually substantial rather than meaningless. Think, for example, of a person's billion brain cells and the billions of possible combinations of connections and bits of experience that are stored inside. All people are different. This is a fact supported by science.

The idea of individual differences comes originally from psychology. From the day of birth, each person is unique, and individual experiences after birth tend to make people even more different. Individual differences mean that management can get the greatest motivation among employees by treating them differently. If it were not for individual differences, some standard, across-the-board way of dealing with employees could be adopted, and minimum judgment would be required thereafter. Individual differences require that a manager's approach to employees should be individual, not statistical. This belief that each person is different from all others is typically called the *Law of Individual Differences.*[14]

Law of Individual Differences

A WHOLE PERSON Although some organizations may wish they could employ only a person's skill or brain, they actually employ a whole person, rather than certain characteristics. Different human traits may be separately studied, but in the final analysis they are all part of one system making up a whole person. Skill does not exist apart from background or knowledge. Home life is not totally separable from work life, and emotional conditions are not separate from physical conditions. People function as total human beings.

For example, a supervisor wanted Margaret Townsend to work overtime Wednesday night on a rush report. Townsend had the necessary knowledge and skill for the job. She also wanted the overtime pay. However, from her point of view a social obligation made it impossible for her to work that night. The date was her tenth wedding anniversary, and an anniversary party was scheduled with a few friends at her house. This anniversary was important to her, so her supervisor had to consider her needs as a whole person, not just a worker.

Better person

When management practices organizational behavior, it is trying to develop a better employee, but also it wants to develop a better *person* in terms of growth and fulfillment. Jobs shape people somewhat as they perform them, so management needs to be concerned about its effect on the whole person. Employees belong to many organizations other than their employer, and they play many roles inside and outside the firm. If the whole person can be improved, then benefits will extend beyond the firm into the larger society in which each employee lives.

MOTIVATED BEHAVIOR From psychology we learn that normal behavior has certain causes. These may relate to a person's needs and/or the consequences that result from acts. In the case of needs, people are motivated not by what we think they ought to have but by what they themselves want. To an outside observer a person's needs may be unrealistic, but they are still controlling. This fact leaves management with two basic ways to motivate people. It can show them how certain actions will increase their need fulfillment, or it can threaten decreased need fulfillment if they follow an undesirable course of action. Clearly a path toward increased need fulfillment is the better approach.

Motivation is essential to the operation of organizations. No matter how much technology and equipment an organization has, these things cannot be put to use until they are released and guided by people who have been motivated.

Think for a minute in terms of a modern locomotive sitting in a railroad station. All the rails and equipment are in order; the schedule and routes are prepared; the destination is set; tickets are sold; and the passengers are on board. No matter how well all this preliminary work has been done, the train cannot move an inch toward the next station until the energy is usefully applied—that is, until the motive power is supplied. Similarly, in an organization motivation turns on the power to keep the organization going.

VALUE OF THE PERSON (HUMAN DIGNITY) This concept is of a different order from the other three because it is more an ethical philosophy than a scientific conclusion. It asserts that people are to be treated differently from other factors of production because they are of a higher order in the universe. It recognizes that because people are of a higher order, they want to be treated with respect and dignity—and should be treated this way. Every job, however simple, entitles the people who do it to proper respect and recognition of their unique aspirations and abilities. The concept of human dignity rejects the old idea of using employees as economic tools.

Ethics

Ethical philosophy is reflected in the conscience of humankind confirmed by the experience of people in all ages.[15] It has to do with the consequences of our acts to ourselves and to others. It recognizes that life has an overall purpose and accepts the inner integrity of each individual. Since organizational behavior always involves people, ethical philosophy is involved in one way or another in each action. Human decisions cannot, and should not, be made apart from values.

The nature of organizations

With regard to organizations, the two key concepts are that they are social systems and that they are formed on the basis of mutual interest.

SOCIAL SYSTEMS From sociology we learn that organizations are social systems; consequently, activities therein are governed by social laws as well as psychological laws. Just as people have psychological needs, they also have social roles and status. Their behavior is influenced by their group as well as by their individual drives. In fact, two types of social systems exist side by side in organizations. One is the formal (official) social system, and the other is the informal social system.

The existence of a social system implies that the organizational environment is one of dynamic change, rather than a static set of relations as pictured on an organization chart. All parts of the system are interdependent and subject to influence by any other part. Everything is related to everything else.

The effects of the broader social system can be seen in the experience of a supervisor, Glenda Ortiz. Ortiz disciplined an employee for a safety violation. The action was within the rules and considered routine by Ortiz. However, the local union already was upset because of what it considered to be unfair discipline for safety violations in another branch of the company. It wanted to show sympathy for its fellow members in the other branch, and it also wanted to show management that it would not accept similar treatment in this branch. In addition, the union president, Jimmie Swallen, was running for reelection, and he wanted to show members that he was protecting their interests.

The union encouraged the employee to file a grievance about Ortiz's action, and the simple disciplinary matter became a complex labor relations problem that consumed the time of many people.

The idea of a social system provides a framework for analyzing organizational behavior issues. It helps make organizational behavior problems understandable and manageable.

Superordinate goal

MUTUAL INTEREST Mutual interest is represented by the statement "Organizations need people, and people also need organizations." Organizations have a human purpose. They are formed and maintained on the basis of some mutu-

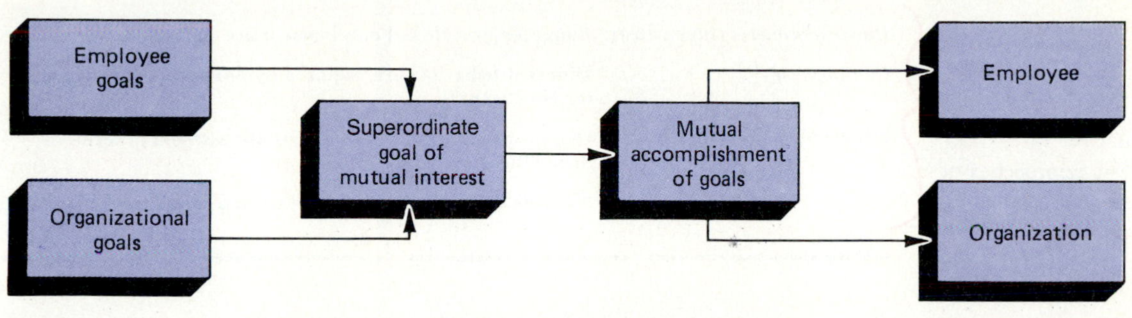

FIGURE 1-4
Mutual interest provides a superordinate goal for employees and the organization.

ality of interest among their participants. People see organizations as a means to help them reach their goals, while organizations need people to help reach organizational objectives.[16] If mutuality is lacking, it makes no sense to try to assemble a group and develop cooperation, because there is no common base on which to build. As shown in Figure 1-4, mutual interest provides a superordinate goal that integrates the efforts of individuals and groups. The result is that they are encouraged to attack organizational problems rather than each other!

Holistic organizational behavior

When the six fundamental concepts of organizational behavior are considered together, they provide a holistic concept of the subject. *Holistic organizational behavior* interprets people-organization relationships in terms of the whole person, whole group, whole organization, and whole social system. It takes an across-the-board view of people in organizations in an effort to understand as many as possible of the factors that influence their behavior. Issues are analyzed in terms of the total situation affecting them rather than in terms of an isolated event or problem.

The holistic concept is illustrated by the story of John Perkins, bank manager, at the beginning of this chapter. Perkins's problems could not be understood in terms of the job he currently held. His manager had to examine his job history, career needs, investments outside the bank, children's status, and other factors. In this way Perkins could be helped to become effective again. This was holistic organizational behavior.

BASIC APPROACHES OF THIS BOOK

Organizational behavior seeks to integrate the four elements of people, structure, technology, and the environment. It rests on an interdisciplinary foundation of fundamental concepts about the nature of people and organiza-

Human resources (supportive)	**Employee growth and development are supported.**
Contingency	**Different behaviors are required by different environments for effectiveness.**
Productivity	**Organizational behavior programs are assessed in terms of their efficiency.**
Systems	**All parts of an organization interact in a complex relationship.**

FIGURE 1-5
Basic approaches of the book

tions. In addition, this book accents four basic themes that will be woven throughout subsequent chapters, as shown in Figure 1-5.

A human resources (supportive) approach

The human resources approach is developmental. It is concerned with the growth and development of people toward higher levels of competency, creativity, and fulfillment, because people are the central resource in any organization and any society. The nature of the human resources approach can be understood by comparing it with the traditional management approach in the early 1900s. In the traditional approach, managers decided what should be done and then closely controlled employees to ensure task performance. Management was directive and controlling.

The human resources approach, on the other hand, is supportive. It helps employees become better, more responsible persons, and then it tries to create a climate in which they may contribute to the limits of their improved abilities.[17] It assumes that expanded capabilities and opportunities for people will lead directly to improvements in operating effectiveness. Work satisfaction also will be a direct result when employees make fuller use of their abilities. Essentially, the human resources approach means that better people achieve better results. It is somewhat illustrated by this ancient proverb:

Give a person a fish, and you feed that person for a day;
Teach a person to fish, and you feed that person for life.

Supportive approach

Another name for the human resources approach is the *supportive* approach, because the manager's primary role changes from control of employees to active support of their growth and performance. The supportive model of organizational behavior is discussed in a later chapter.

A contingency approach

Traditional management relied on principles to provide a "one best way" of managing. There was a correct way to organize, to delegate, and to divide work. The correct way applied regardless of the type of organization or situation involved. Management principles were considered to be universal. As the field of organizational behavior developed, many of its followers also supported the concept of universality. Behavioral ideas were supposed to apply in any type of situation. For example, employee-oriented leadership should consistently be better than task-oriented leadership, whatever the circumstances. An occasional exception might be admitted, but the early ideas were more or less universal.

The more accepted view now is that there are few across-the-board concepts that apply in all instances. Situations are much more complex than first perceived, and the different variables may require different behavioral approaches. The result is the *contingency approach to organizational behavior*, which means that different situations require different behavioral practices for effectiveness.[18]

No one best way

No longer is there a one best way. Each situation must be analyzed carefully to determine the significant variables that exist in order to establish the kinds of practices that will be more effective. The strength of the contingency approach is that it encourages analysis of each situation prior to action while at the same time discouraging habitual practice based on universal assumptions about people. The contingency approach also is more interdisciplinary, more system-oriented, and more research-oriented than the traditional approach. Thus it helps to use in the most appropriate manner all the current knowledge about people in organizations.

A productivity approach

Productivity

Most organizations try to be productive, so this idea is a common thread woven through organizational behavior.[19] *Productivity* is a ratio that compares units of output with units of input. If more outputs can be produced from the same amount of inputs, productivity is improved. Or if fewer inputs can be used to produce the same amount of outputs, productivity has increased. The idea of productivity does not imply that one should produce more output; rather, it is a measure of how efficiently one produces whatever output is desired. Consequently, better productivity is a valuable measure of how well resources are used in society. It means that less is consumed to produce each unit of output. There is less waste and better conservation of resources.

Multiple inputs and outputs

Productivity often is measured in terms of economic inputs and outputs, but human and social inputs and outputs also are important. For example, if better organizational behavior can improve job satisfaction, a human output or benefit occurs. In the same manner, when employee development programs lead to a by-product of better citizens in a community, a valuable social output occurs. Organizational behavior decisions typically involve human, social, and/or economic issues, so productivity usually is a significant part of these decisions and will be discussed throughout this book.

Four equations

A FORMULA The role that organizational behavior plays in creating productive organizations is illustrated by a set of equations. Let us look first at a worker's ability. It is generally accepted that knowledge and one's skill in applying it constitute the human trait called "ability." This is represented by the equation

Knowledge × skill = ability

Let us look now at motivation. It results from a person's attitudes reacting in a specific situation. This is represented by the equation

Attitude × situation = motivation

Motivation and ability together determine a person's potential performance in any activity.

Ability × motivation = potential human performance

We now have a series of equations as shown by items 1 to 3 of Figure 1-6. The scope of organizational behavior is represented by the second equation (attitude × situation = motivation). This book will emphasize attitudes and how they are affected by situational factors to determine motivation.

The importance of organizational behavior is shown by the third equation (ability × motivation = potential human performance). Organizational behavior, as represented by the term "motivation," is one of two factors in the equation. Furthermore, organizational behavior plays a part in motivating workers to acquire the other factor, ability. Thus organizational behavior is part and parcel of the whole equation of potential human performance.

Human performance has to be mixed with resources such as tools, power, and materials to get organizational productivity,[20] as indicated by the fourth equation:

Human performance × resources = organizational productivity

Even in this last equation, the role of organizational behavior is major, because it is a significant contributor to "human performance." "Resources," on the other hand, relate primarily to economic, material, and technical factors in an organization.

FIGURE 1-6
Equations showing the role of organizational behavior in work systems

1 Knowledge × skill	**=**	**ability**
2 Attitude × situation	**=**	**motivation**
3 Ability × motivation	**=**	**potential human performance**
4 Human performance × resources	**=**	**organizational productivity**

A systems approach

A system implies that there are many variables in organizations and that each of them affects all the others in a complex relationship. An event that appears to affect one individual or one department actually may have significant influences elsewhere in the organization. This means that managers in taking actions must look beyond the immediate situation in order to determine effects on the larger system.

All people in organizations should be concerned with improving organizational behavior. The clerk, the machinist, and the manager all work with people and thereby influence the behavioral quality of life in an organization. Managers, however, tend to have a larger responsibility, because they are the ones who make decisions affecting many people throughout an organization, and most of their daily activities are people-related. Managers represent the *administrative system* and their role is to use organizational behavior to improve people-organization relationships, as shown in Figure 1-7. Managers try to build a climate in which people are motivated, work together productively, and become more effective persons.

Triple reward system

When organizational behavior is applied with a systems approach, it creates a *triple reward system* in which human, organizational, and social objectives are met. People find more satisfaction in work when there is cooperation and teamwork. They are learning, growing, and contributing. The organization also is more successful, because it operates more effectively. Quality is better and costs are less.[21] Perhaps the greatest beneficiary of the triple reward system is society itself, because it has better products and services, better citizens, and a climate of cooperation and progress. There is a three-party win-win-win result in which there need not be any losers.

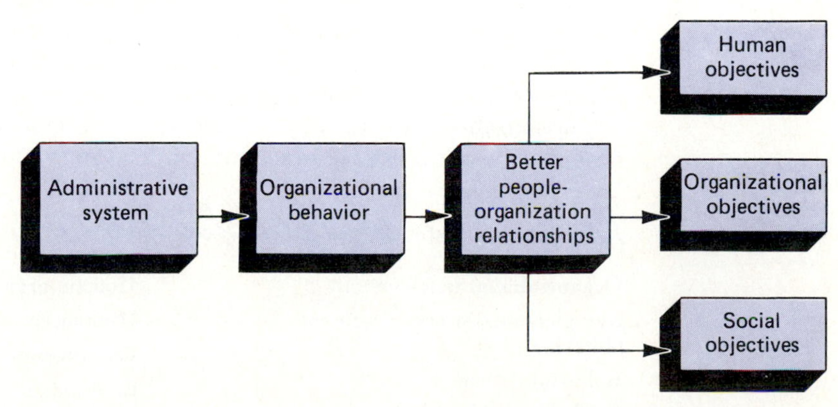

FIGURE 1-7
The administrative system in organizational behavior

Cost-benefit analysis

However, negative effects as well as positive effects sometimes result from a behavioral action, so it is necessary to make a *cost-benefit analysis* to determine whether an action will produce a net positive or a net negative effect. No longer is it sufficient to look at only benefits, because there may be costs in other parts of the system. This is illustrated in the following experience of a supervisor:

> **In the upholstery department of a furniture factory, a supervisor refused to allow an employee to take leave without pay to attend the funeral of a second cousin in a city 200 miles away. The employee claimed that special family relationships with this cousin required her attendance and took two days off without permission. When she returned, the supervisor disciplined her by giving her one day off without pay. Employees in other departments heard about the incident, and they felt that the discipline was unfair; so all plant employees walked off the job in a wildcat strike, threatening to remain off the job until the supervisor withdrew her penalty. The supervisor had failed to realize that actions in her department could have effects beyond that department in the larger factory system.**

The systems approach applies especially to the social system and the idea of organizational culture discussed in Chapter 3.

SUMMARY

Organizational behavior is the study and application of knowledge about how people act in organizations. Key elements are people, structure, technology, and the external environment. Previously known as human relations, organizational behavior has emerged as an interdisciplinary field of value to managers. It builds on a research foundation begun in the 1920s by Mayo and Roethlisberger at the Western Electric Company, and draws upon useful ideas in the behavioral sciences.

Fundamental concepts of organizational behavior relate to the nature of people (individual differences, a whole person, motivated behavior, and the value of the person) and to the nature of organizations (social system and mutual interest). The collective result is a holistic view of organizational behavior. Managerial actions to attain superordinate goals of interest to both employees and organizations are aided by the managers' understanding and use of human resources, contingency, productivity, and systems approaches.

Terms and concepts for review

Organizational behavior

Key elements in organizational behavior

Behavioral science

Law of Individual Differences

Mutuality of interest

Holistic organizational behavior

Human resources approach

Contingency approach

Elements of organizational productivity

Systems approach

Discussion questions

1 Define organizational behavior in your own words. Ask a friend or work associate to do the same. Identify and explore the nature of any differences between the two definitions.
2 Assume that a friend states, "Organizational behavior is selfish and manipulative, because it serves only the interests of management." How would you respond?
3 As you trace the early history and evolving nature of organizational behavior, why do you think it has become a popular field of interest?
4 Consider the statement "Organizations need people, and people also need organizations." Is this equally true in all types of organizations? Give examples where it is, and probably isn't, true.
5 Review the fundamental concepts that form the basis of organizational behavior. Which concepts do you think are more important than the others? Explain.
6 Select one of your work associates or friends. Identify the qualities that make that person substantially different from you. In what ways are you basically similar? Which dominates, the differences or the similarities?
7 Discuss the major features of the social system in an organization where you have worked. In what ways did that social system affect you and your job performance (either positively or negatively)?
8 Review the four approaches to organizational behavior. As you read this book, begin keeping a list of the ways in which those themes are reflected in each major topic.
9 Examine the formulas leading to effective organizational productivity. Which of the factors do you think have the greatest potential for making a difference between organizations? What can be done to affect the other ones?

Incident

THE TRANSFERRED SALES REPRESENTATIVE

Harold Burns served as district sales representative for an appliance firm. His district covered the central part of a Midwestern state, and it included about 100 retail outlets. He had been with the company twenty years and in his present job and location for five years. During this time he met his district sales quota each year.

One day Burns learned through local friends that the wife of a sales representative in another district was in town to try to rent a house. She told the real estate agency that her family would be moving there in a few days because her husband was replacing Burns. When Burns heard this, he refused to believe it.

Two days later, on January 28, he received an airmail letter, postmarked the previous day, from the regional sales manager. The letter read:

Dear Harold:

Because of personnel vacancies we are requesting that you move to the Gunning District, effective February 1. Mr. George Dowd from the Parsons District will replace you. Will you please see that your inventory and property are properly transferred to him?

I know that you will like your new district. Congratulations!

Sincerely yours,
(Signature)

In the same mail he received his twenty-year service pin. The accompanying letter from the regional sales manager read:

Dear Harold:

I am happy to enclose your twenty-year service pin. You have a long and excellent record with the company. We are honored to give you this recognition, and I hope you will wear it proudly.

Our company is proud to have many long-service employees. We want you to know that we take a personal interest in your welfare because people like you are the backbone of our company.

Sincerely yours,
(Signature)

Harold Burns checked his quarterly sales bulletin and found that sales for the Gunning District were running 10 percent below those in his present district.

Questions

1 Comment on the events in this case as they relate to organizational behavior.
2 Was a human resources approach to Burns applied in this instance? Discuss.

References

1 J. Watson Wilson, "The Growth of a Company: A Psychological Case Study," *Advanced Management Journal*, January 1966, p. 43. Entire quotation italicized in the original.
2 Robert H. Guest, "Management Imperatives for the Year 2000," *California Management Review*, Summer 1986, p. 63.
3 For additional discussion, see L. L. Cummings, "Toward Organizational Behavior," *Academy of Management Review*, January 1978, pp. 90–98.
4 For further discussion of the external social system, see William C. Frederick, Keith Davis, and James E. Post, *Business and Society*, 6th ed., New York: McGraw-Hill Book Company, 1988.
5 Lee K. Frankel and Alexander Fleisher, *The Human Factor in Industry*, New York: The Macmillan Company, 1920, p. 8; and Frank Podmore, *Robert Owen*, New York: Augustus M. Kelly, 1968.
6 Andrew Ure, *The Philosophy of Manufactures*, London: Charles Knight, 1835.
7 Frederick W. Taylor, *The Principles of Scientific Management*, New York: Harper & Brothers, 1911. Most of Taylor's insights are supported as being valid in Edwin A. Locke, "The Ideas of Frederick W. Taylor: An Evaluation," *Academy of Management Review*, January 1982, pp. 14–24.
8 Lillian Gilbreth, *The Psychology of Management*, New York: Sturgis and Walton Company, 1914.

9 Whiting Williams, *What's on the Worker's Mind,* New York: Charles Scribner's Sons, 1920; and Whiting Williams, *Mainsprings of Men,* New York: Charles Scribner's Sons, 1925. More recent, similar studies are Studs Terkel, *Working: People Talk about What They Do All Day and How They Feel about What They Do,* New York: Pantheon Books, a division of Random House, 1974; and Robert Schrank, *Ten Thousand Working Days,* Cambridge, Mass.: The MIT Press, 1978.

10 Elton Mayo, *The Human Problems of an Industrial Civilization,* Cambridge, Mass.: Harvard University Press, 1933; F. J. Roethlisberger and W. J. Dickson, *Management and the Worker,* Cambridge, Mass.: Harvard University Press, 1939; and F. J. Roethlisberger, *The Elusive Phenomena: An Autobiographical Account of My Work in the Field of Organizational Behavior at the Harvard Business School,* Cambridge, Mass.: Harvard University Press, 1977. The symposium on the fiftieth anniversary of the Western Electric Company, Hawthorne Studies, is reported in Eugene Louis Cass and Frederick G. Zimmer (eds.), *Man and Work in Society,* New York: Van Nostrand Reinhold Company, 1975. Recollections of the participants are reported in Ronald G. Greenwood, Alfred A. Bolton, and Regina A. Greenwood, "Hawthorne a Half Century Later: Relay Assembly Participants Remember," *Journal of Management,* Fall–Winter 1983, pp. 217–231. The earliest general textbook on human relations was Burleigh B. Gardner and David G. Moore, *Human Relations in Industry,* Chicago: Irwin, 1945.

11 For example, see Alex Carey, "The Hawthorne Studies: A Radical Criticism," *American Sociological Review,* June 1967, pp. 403–416; and Richard Herbert Franke and James D. Kaul, "The Hawthorne Experiments: First Statistical Interpretations," *American Sociological Review,* October 1978, pp. 623–643.

12 An example of criticism is Malcolm P. McNair, "Thinking Ahead," *Harvard Business Review,* March–April 1957, pp. 15ff.

13 The history of organizational behavior was traced by Keith Davis, "Human Relations, Industrial Humanism, and Organizational Behavior," in a presentation to the Southern Division of the Academy of Management, Nov. 13, 1986.

14 Erwin S. Stanton, *Reality-Centered People Management,* New York: AMACOM, 1982, pp. 30–35.

15 The payoff for respect for human dignity is reflected in the statement by former U.S. Labor Secretary William E. Brock, in a speech to the 1986 World Congress on Human Resources. He said, "Success is going to come to those . . . who put a primary emphasis on human values." *Resource,* American Society for Personnel Administration, October 1986, p. 3.

16 One author suggests that a dozen different organizational behavior models all assume that it is possible to achieve both employee satisfaction and organizational performance at the same time through this mutuality of interest. See Barry M. Staw, "Organizational Psychology and the Pursuit of the Happy/Productive Worker," *California Management Review,* Summer 1986, pp. 40–53.

17 Early emphasis on the human resources approach to organizational behavior was provided in Raymond E. Miles, "Human Relations or Human Resources?" *Harvard Business Review,* July–August 1965, pp. 148–163; it was later presented in his book *Theories of Management: Implications for Organizational Behavior and Development,* New York: McGraw-Hill Book Company, 1975.

18 For an example, see Fiedler's contingency model of leadership in Chapter 8. Early books on contingency management were Donald Hellriegel and John W. Slocum, Jr., *Management: Contingency Approaches,* 2d ed., Reading, Mass.: Addison-Wesley, 1978; and John W. Newstrom, William E. Reif, and Robert M. Monczka, *A Contingency Approach to Management: Readings,* New York: McGraw-Hill Book Company, 1975.

19 Productivity was one among several problems facing General Motors in the late 1980s, as reported by William J. Hampton and James R. Norman, "General Motors:

What Went Wrong," *Business Week*, Mar. 16, 1987, pp. 102–110. It is one of the four "most heavily researched outcomes" in research on organizational behavior, as reported in Mark R. Rosenzweig and Lyman W. Porter (eds.), *Annual Review of Psychology, Volume 35, 1984*, Palo Alto, Calif.: Annual Reviews, Inc., 1984.

20 Another "resource"—the opportunity to perform work—is discussed in Melvin Blumberg and Charles D. Pringle, "The Missing Opportunity in Organizational Research: Some Implications for a Theory of Work Performance," *Academy of Management Review*, October 1982, pp. 560–569. Several of the obstacles to employee productivity are presented in Wayne L. Wright, "Overcoming Barriers to Productivity," *Personnel Journal*, February 1987, pp. 28–34.

21 Examples of how companies such as Corning, Kodak, Westinghouse, and Mellon Bank have engaged in quality improvement through systematic programs are presented in a special supplement called "The Quality Imperative," *Fortune*, Sept. 29, 1986, pp. 61ff.

For additional reading

Beer, Michael, Bert Spector, Paul R. Lawrence, D. Quinn Mills, and Richard E. Walton, *Managing Human Assets*, New York: Macmillan Company (Free Press), 1984.

Brief, Arthur P. (ed.), *Productivity Research in the Behavioral and Social Sciences*, New York: Praeger, 1984.

Eden, Dov, *Pygmalion in Management: Productivity as a Self-Fulfilling Prophecy*, Lexington, Mass.: Lexington Books, 1987.

Mayo, Elton, *The Human Problems of an Industrial Civilization*, Cambridge, Mass.: Harvard University Press, 1933.

Pastin, Mark, *The Hard Problems of Management: Gaining the Ethics Edge*, San Francisco: Jossey-Bass Inc., Publishers, 1986.

Roethlisberger, F. J., and W. J. Dickson, *Management and the Worker*, Cambridge, Mass.: Harvard University Press, 1939.

Staw, Barry M., and L. L. Cummings (eds.), *Research in Organizational Behavior*, Greenwich, Conn.: JAI Press (annual), vol. 1 (1979) to present. Order of editors varies with each volume.

Toffler, Alvin, *The Adaptive Corporation*, New York: McGraw-Hill Book Company, 1985.

Tjosvold, Dean, *Working Together to Get Things Done*, Lexington, Mass.: Lexington Books, 1986.

Weihrich, Heinz, *Management Excellence: Productivity through MBO*, New York: McGraw-Hill Book Company, 1985.

Werther, William B., Jr., William Ruch, and Lynne McClure, *Productivity through People*, St. Paul, Minn.: West Publishing Company, 1986.

CHAPTER 2

Models of organizational behavior

Only a small fraction of U.S. workplaces today can boast of a comprehensive commitment strategy, but the rate of transformation (to them) continues to accelerate.

RICHARD E. WALTON[1]

The Japanese philosophy is to make people an important item, as opposed to the typical U.S. philosophy that workers are just an extension of machines.

D. WILLIAM CHILDS[2]

CHAPTER OBJECTIVES

To understand

An organizational behavior system

Alternative models of organizational behavior

Trends in the use of these models

Allocative versus incremental values

Theory Z systems

One of the authors recently boarded a plane on a winter day in Duluth and flew to Phoenix to visit his coauthor. The differences between the two geographical areas were easily apparent. One was cold, damp, and windy; the other was warm, dry, and calm. As a matter of fact, the temperature differential between the two cities on that day was over 100°!

Organizations differ.

The differences between organizations can sometimes be equally extreme. A look at the factory rules of Amasa Whitney in Figure 2-1 shows that organizations have undergone tremendous changes during the last 160 years. Although employers in early days had no systematic program for managing their employees, the existing rules still exerted a powerful influence on them. Many of the old rules are now out of date, but some are still relevant today (note the current trend to create smoke-free work environments, much like rule 11). Some organizations today are experimenting with exciting new ways to attract and motivate their workers, as indicated by the introductory quotation. A century from now, though, people may look back upon these practices and consider them outdated, too. This is the price—and the reward—of progress.

Amasa Whitney's reference to employees as "hands" was a natural reflection of the prevailing model of organizational behavior at that time. Employers took a narrow economic view that they were purchasing the commodity of labor—that is, the skill of the *hands* of employees. Continuing the holistic view presented in Chapter 1, this chapter will present alternative models of organizational behavior that reflect more progressive approaches. We will see that even the words by which one refers to employees (such as "hands," as contrasted to the usage in some organizations of the term "associates" to convey equality) tells a lot about the underlying model in use.

This chapter builds on fundamental concepts presented in Chapter 1 by showing how all behavioral factors can be combined to develop an effective organization. We discuss the interrelated elements of an organizational behavior system, present alternative models of organizational behavior, and conclude with an overview of Theory Z organizations.

AN ORGANIZATIONAL BEHAVIOR SYSTEM

Organizations achieve their goals by creating, operating, and communicating an organizational behavior system, as shown in Figure 2-2. Major elements of this system are introduced on the following pages and presented in detail throughout the book. These systems exist in every organization, although they have a greater chance of being successful if they have been consciously created by drawing upon the constantly growing behavioral science base of knowledge mentioned in the previous chapter.

RULES & REGULATIONS To Be Observed By All Persons Employed In The Factory Of AMASA WHITNEY

FIRST : The Mill will be put into operation 10 minutes before sunrise at all seasons of the year. The gate will be shut 10 minutes past sunset from the 20th of March to the 20th of September, at 30 minutes past 8 from the 20th of September to the 20th of March. Saturdays at sunset.

SECOND : It will be required of every person employed, that they be in the room in which they are employed, at the time mentioned above for the mill to be in operation.

THIRD : Hands are not allowed to leave the factory in working hours without the consent of their Overseer. If they do, they will be liable to have their time set off.

FOURTH : Anyone who by negligence or misconduct causes damage to the machinery, or impedes the progress of the work, will be liable to make good the damage for the same.

FIFTH : Anyone employed for a certain length of time, will be expected to make up their lost time, if required, before they will be entitled to their pay.

SIXTH : Any person employed for no certain length of time, will be required to give at least 4 weeks notice of their intention to leave (sickness excepted) or forfeit 4 weeks pay, unless by particular agreement.

SEVENTH : Anyone wishing to be absent any length of time, must get permisison of the Overseer.

EIGHTH : All who have leave of absence for any length of time will be expected to return in that time; and, in case they do not return in that time and do not give satisfactory reason, they will be liable to forfeit one week's work or less, if they commence work again. If they do not, they will be considered as one who leaves without giving any notice.

NINTH : Anything tending to impede the progress of manufacturing in working hours, such as unnecessary conversation, reading, eating fruit, &c.&c., must be avoided.

TENTH : While I shall endeavor to employ a judicious Overseer, the help will follow his direction in all cases.

ELEVENTH : No smoking will be allowed in the factory, as it is considered very unsafe, and particularly specified in the Insurance.

TWELFTH : In order to forward the work, job hands will follow the above regulations as well as those otherwise employed.

THIRTEENTH : It is intended that the bell be rung 5 minutes before the gate is hoisted, so that all persons may be ready to start their machines precisely at the time mentioned.

FOURTEENTH : All persons who cause damage to the machinery, break glass out of the windows, &c., will immediately inform the Overseer of the same.

FIFTEENTH : The hands will take breakfast, from the 1st of November to the last of March, before going to work—they will take supper from the 1st of May to the last of August, 30 minutes past 5 o'clock P.M.—from the 20th of September to the 20th of March between sundown and dark—25 minutes will be allowed for breakfast, 30 minutes for dinner, and 25 minutes for supper, and no more from the time the gate is shut till started again.

SIXTEENTH : The hands will leave the Factory so that the doors may be fastened within 10 minutes from the time of leaving off work.

AMASA WHITNEY

Winchendon, Mass. July 5, 1830.

FIGURE 2-1
Factory rules in 1830

Source: *Samuel H. Adams, Sunrise to Sunset, New York: Random House, Inc., 1950.*

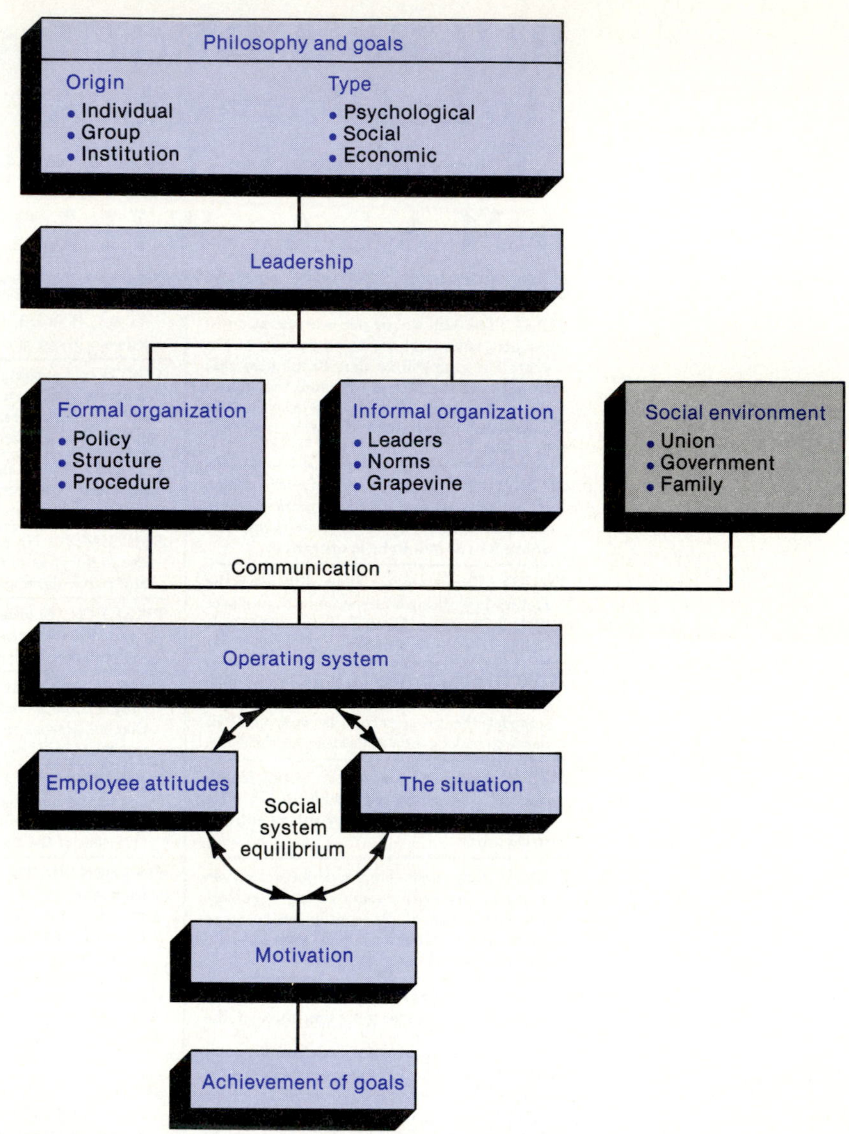

FIGURE 2-2
An organizational behavior system

Elements of the system

Fact premises

An important basis for the system resides in the philosophy and goals of those who join together to create it. The philosophy of organizational behavior held by a manager derives from both fact and value premises. *Fact premises* represent our descriptive view of how the world behaves, and are drawn from both behavioral science research and personal experiences. For example, you would not throw an expensive camera from a ten-story building, because you believe gravity will pull it downward and crush it against the ground, and you don't wish this to happen. Fact premises, then, are acquired through lifelong learning and are very useful to guide our behavior.[3]

Value premises

Value premises, on the other hand, represent our view of the desirability of certain goals. If you were very unhappy with the camera's performance, then you might choose to throw it off the ten-story building. You still accept the fact premise of gravity, but now your value premises have changed. As this illustration shows, value premises are variable beliefs we hold and are therefore under our control. Many organizations have sought to identify and state the values they cherish, as shown in the following illustration:

Philosophy is important.

A group of 800 professional staff in the FMC Corporation were given the goal of creating "user satisfaction" with the services they provided to the firm's 28,000 employees. The key to achieving this goal, however, lay in a four-day meeting that produced a statement of philosophy (see Figure 2-3). This clarification of values, coupled with other organizational changes and skill-building sessions, resulted in dramatic improvements in employee satisfaction and service to clients, with a 50 percent reduction in turnover of valued employees.[4]

People also bring their psychological, social, and economic goals with them to an organization, which they express individually and collectively. All these different interests come together and are combined into a working social system.

The organizational philosophy and goals are implemented by leadership (discussed in Part Three), which has become increasingly participative in recent years. Leaders create formal policies, structures, and procedures to help attain the goals. They also need to be aware of the informal organization (discussed in Part Four) and work with its members to create positive norms. Together, the formal and informal organizations provide the "glue" that binds the institution into an effective working team.

Each organization is affected by the other institutions it comes in contact with, which constitute its social environment. In Figure 2-2, these institutions are shown as separate from the employing institution but may be very much involved with it through laws, contracts, and public pressure. For example,

FIGURE 2-3
Selected elements of a philosophy statement

Source: *Adapted from FMC Corporation's management information systems' "Mission, Values, and Policies," as reported in Edmund J. Metz, "Managing Change toward a Leading-Edge Information Culture,"* Organizational Dynamics, *Autumn 1986, pp. 28–40.*

- **We are committed to quality, cost-effectiveness, and technical excellence.**
- **People should treat each other with consideration, trust, and respect.**
- **Each person is valuable, is unique, and makes a contribution.**
- **All employees should be unfailingly committed to excellent performance.**
- **Teamwork can, and should, produce far more than the sum of individual efforts. Team members must be reliable and committed to the team.**
- **Innovation is essential.**
- **Open communications are important for attaining success.**
- **Decisions should be reached participatively.**

union Local 3146 represents workers in companies A, B, and C. It is a separate legal organization but is very much involved in the success of each of the three companies. Similarly, local, state, and federal laws create restrictions on organizations, and they also must respond to the demands of various public-interest groups. This social environment is discussed primarily in Part Five.

The philosophy, goals, leadership style, and character of the formal and informal organizations are communicated to employees so that they will know what is expected of them and receive feedback on their performance. These influences lead to an operating system that guides employee behavior and lends predictability to organizations. A part of this system is the process of appraising and rewarding workers for their contributions (Part Two).

The social system at work

The operating system in an organization interacts with employee attitudes and with specific situational factors to produce a specific motivation for each employee at a certain time. If any one of the three—operating system, attitudes, or situations—is changed, the motivation will also be different. Because of this interaction, leaders need to learn to manage employee motivation contingently. For example, if a procedure is arbitrarily changed but attitudes and the situation remain the same, motivation may change and produce different results. The social equilibrium has been upset, and its effects will show up sooner or later.

Contrasting effects of operating-system changes were seen in some of the efforts to revitalize airline companies in the 1980s. Despite hostile takeovers by corporate raiders, employees in some firms accepted the necessity of drastic cost-saving actions and responded with increased efforts to save their company and jobs. Employees in other firms, fearful for their jobs and resentful of imposed changes, strongly resisted attempts to change work rules and pay systems.

The result of an effective organizational behavior system is motivation which, when combined with employee skills and abilities, results in human productivity (as we saw in the formulas in Chapter 1). Successful motivation can get above-average performance out of average people. It builds two-way relationships that are mutually supportive, meaning that manager and employee are jointly influencing each other and jointly benefiting. This is power *with* people rather than power over them, and this is consistent with present human values regarding how people wish to be treated.

MODELS OF ORGANIZATIONAL BEHAVIOR

Organizations differ in the quality of organizational behavior that they develop. These differences are substantially caused by different *models of organizational*

Why are models important?

behavior that dominate management's thought in each organization. The model that a manager holds usually begins with certain assumptions about people and leads to certain interpretations of events. Underlying theory, therefore, is an unconscious but powerful guide to managerial behavior. Managers tend to act as they think. Eventually this means that the underlying model that prevails in an organization's management (especially in the firm's chief executive officer) extends throughout that firm. For this reason, models of organizational behavior are highly significant.

We highlight in this chapter a discussion of the following four models: autocratic, custodial, supportive, and collegial. (Earlier models, such as those of feudalism and slavery, are bypassed.) These four models are summarized in Figure 2-4. In the order mentioned, they represent an approximate historical evolution in management practice during the last 100 years or more. One model tends to dominate a particular time in history, but at the same time each of the other models is practiced by some organizations.

Just as organizations differ among themselves, so practices may vary within the departments or branches of one organization. The production department may work within a custodial model while the supportive model is being tried in the research department. And, of course, the practices of individual managers may differ from their organization's prevailing model because of their personal preferences or different conditions in their department. The point is that no one model of organizational behavior is sufficient to describe all that happens in an organization, but it can help distinguish one way of life from another.

The autocratic model

The autocratic model has its roots deep in history, and certainly it became the prevailing model of the industrial revolution. As shown in Figure 2-4, it

FIGURE 2-4
Four models of organizational behavior

Source: *The four models of organizational behavior were originally published in Keith Davis,* Human Relations at Work: The Dynamics of Organizational Behavior, *3d ed., New York: McGraw-Hill Book Company, 1967, p. 480.*

	AUTOCRATIC	CUSTODIAL	SUPPORTIVE	COLLEGIAL
Basis of model	**Power**	**Economic resources**	**Leadership**	**Partnership**
Managerial orientation	**Authority**	**Money**	**Support**	**Teamwork**
Employee orientation	**Obedience**	**Security and benefits**	**Job performance**	**Responsible behavior**
Employee psychological result	**Dependence on boss**	**Dependence on organization**	**Participation**	**Self-discipline**
Employee needs met	**Subsistence**	**Security**	**Status and recognition**	**Self-actualization**
Performance result	**Minimum**	**Passive cooperation**	**Awakened drives**	**Moderate enthusiasm**

Power and authority are used.

depends on *power*. Those who are in command must have the power to demand, "You do this—or else," meaning that an employee who does not follow orders will be penalized.

In an autocratic environment the managerial orientation is formal, official *authority*. This authority is delegated by right of command over the people to whom it applies. Management believes that it knows what is best and that the employee's obligation is to follow orders. It assumes that employees have to be directed, persuaded, and pushed into performance, and this is management's task. Management does the thinking; the employees obey the orders. This conventional view of management leads to tight control of employees at work.

Under autocratic conditions the employee orientation is *obedience* to a boss, not respect for a manager. The psychological result for employees is *dependence* on their boss, whose power to hire, fire, and "perspire" them is almost absolute. The boss pays minimum wages because *minimum performance* is given by employees. They are willing to give minimum performance—though sometimes reluctantly—because they must satisfy *subsistence* needs for themselves and their families. Some employees give higher performance because of internal achievement drives, because they personally like their boss, because the boss is "a natural-born leader," or because of some other factor; but most of them give only minimum performance.

Autocratic model works.

The autocratic model is a useful way to accomplish work. It is not a complete failure. The picture of the autocratic model just presented has been an extreme one, but actually the model exists in all shades of gray from rather dark to rather light. This view of work built great railroad systems, operated giant steel mills, and produced the dynamic industrial civilization that developed in the United States. It does get results, but usually only moderate results. *Its principal weakness is its high human costs.*

The autocratic model was an acceptable approach to guide managerial behavior when there were no well-known alternatives, and it still can be useful under some conditions (such as organizational crises[5]). However, the combination of emerging knowledge about the needs of employees and changing societal values suggested that there were better ways to manage organizational systems. A second step in the ladder of progress was needed, and it was soon forthcoming.

The custodial model

As managers began to study their employees, they soon recognized that although autocratically managed employees did not talk back to their boss, they certainly "thought back." There were many things they wanted to say, and sometimes they did say them when they quit or lost their tempers! Employees were filled with insecurity, frustrations, and aggressions toward their boss. Since they could not vent these feelings directly, sometimes they went home and vented them on their families and neighbors; so the entire community might suffer from this relationship.

An example of the effects of management-induced frustration on the behavior of employees occurred in a wood-processing plant. Managers treated workers crudely, sometimes even to the point of physical abuse. Since employees could not strike back directly for fear of losing their jobs, they found another way to do it. They *symbolically* fed their supervisor to a log-shredding machine! They did this by purposely destroying good sheets of veneer, which made the supervisor look bad when monthly efficiency reports were prepared.[6]

It seemed rather obvious to progressive employers that there ought to be some way to develop better employee satisfactions and security. If the insecurities, frustrations, and aggressions of employees could be dispelled, they might feel more like working. In any case, they would have a better quality of work life.

To satisfy the security needs of employees, a number of companies began welfare programs in the 1890s and 1900s. In their worst form these welfare programs later became known as paternalism. In the 1930s welfare programs evolved into a variety of fringe benefits to provide employee security. Employers—and unions and government—began caring for the security needs of workers. They were applying a custodial model of organizational behavior.

Employee security remains a high priority for millions of workers in today's job market where lifetime employment is seldom promised to any employee. IBM, however, goes out of its way to stabilize its work force and preserve jobs. To avoid layoffs, it constantly retrains employees, reduces overtime, freezes hiring, encourages both job transfers and relocations, provides early retirement incentives, and reduces subcontracting to adjust to slowdowns in the computer industry.[7]

As shown in Figure 2-4, a successful custodial approach depends on *economic resources.* If an organization does not have the wealth to provide pensions and pay other benefits, it cannot follow a custodial approach. The resulting managerial orientation is toward *money* to pay wages and benefits. Since employees' physical needs are already reasonably met, the employer looks to *security* needs as a motivating force.

Employees become dependent.

The custodial approach leads to employee *dependence on the organization.* Rather than being dependent on their boss for their weekly bread, employees now depend on organizations for their security and welfare. Perhaps more accurately stated, an organizational dependence is *added* to a reduced personal dependence on the boss. If employees have ten years of seniority under the union contract and a good pension program, they cannot afford to quit even if the grass looks greener somewhere else!

A current example of a program consistent with a custodial environment is the provision of child-care centers at the workplace. At Dominion Bankshares Corporation, studies showed that employees had enormous problems arranging for quality child care, and this resulted in absenteeism, turnover, and stress problems. The company now subsidizes an on-site day-care center, which is filled to capacity. The program requires economic resources—$85,000 per year— and creates organizational dependence, as illustrated by the employee who said it would take an "awesome" job offer to induce him to leave Dominion.[8]

Employees working in a custodial environment become psychologically preoccupied with their economic rewards and benefits. As a result of their treatment, they are well maintained, happy, and contented, but they are not strongly motivated, so they may give only *passive cooperation*. The result tends to be that they do not produce much more vigorously than under the old autocratic approach.

The custodial model is described in its extreme in order to show its emphasis on material rewards, security, and organizational dependence. In actual practice, the model has various shades of gray from dark to light. Its great benefit is that it brings security and satisfaction to workers, but it does have substantial flaws. The most evident flaw is that most employees are not producing anywhere near their capacities, nor are they motivated to grow to the greater capacities of which they are capable. Though employees are happy, most of them really do not feel fulfilled or motivated. In confirmation of this condition, a series of studies at the University of Michigan in the 1940s and 1950s reported that "the happy employee is not necessarily the most productive employee."[9] Consequently, managers and academic leaders started to ask again, "Is there a better way?"

The search for a better way is not a condemnation of the custodial model as a whole but rather a condemnation of the assumption that this is "the final answer"—the one best way to motivate employees. The error in reasoning occurs when people perceive the custodial model as so desirable that there is no need to build on it toward something better. A reasonable amount of the custodial model is desirable to provide security. It is the foundation for growth to the next step.

The supportive model

The supportive model of organizational behavior had its origins in the "principle of supportive relationships" as stated by Rensis Likert, who said, "*The leadership and other processes of the organization must be such as to ensure a maximum probability that in all interactions and all relationships with the organization each member will, in the light of his* [or her] *background, values, and expectations, view the experience as supportive and one which builds and maintains his* [or her] *sense of personal worth and importance*."[10] It is similar to the human resources approach to people mentioned in Chapter 1.

The supportive model depends on *leadership* instead of power or money. Through leadership, management provides a climate to help employees grow and accomplish in the interests of the organization the things of which they are capable. The leader assumes that workers are not by nature passive and resistant to organizational needs but that they are made so by an inadequately supportive climate at work. They will take responsibility, develop a drive to contribute, and improve themselves if management will give them a chance. Management's orientation, therefore, is to *support* the employee's *job performance*, rather than simply supporting employee benefit payments as in the custodial approach.

Employees are supported.

Since management supports employees in their work, the psychological result is a feeling of *participation* and task involvement in the organization. They may say "we" instead of "they" when referring to their organization. They are more strongly motivated than by earlier models because their status and recognition needs are better met. Thus they have *awakened drives* for work.

Supportive behavior is not the kind of behavior that requires money. Rather, it is a part of management's lifestyle at work, reflected in the way that it deals with other people. The manager's role is one of helping employees solve their problems and accomplish their work. Following is an example of a supportive approach.

Juanita Salinas, a young divorcée with one child, had a record of frequent tardiness as an assembler in an electronics plant. Her supervisor, Helen Ferguson, scolded her several times about her tardiness, and each time Salinas improved for two or three weeks but then lapsed back into her normal habit pattern. At about this time Ferguson attended a company training program for supervisors, so she decided to try the supportive approach with Salinas.

The next time Salinas was tardy, Ferguson approached her with concern about what might have caused her tardiness. Rather than scolding her, Ferguson showed a genuine interest in Salinas's problems, asking, "How can I help?" and "Is there anything we can do at the company?" When the discussion focused on delays in getting the child ready for school early in the morning, Ferguson arranged for Salinas to talk with other mothers of children in the department. When Salinas talked about the distance she had to walk to catch a bus, Ferguson worked with the personnel department to get her into a dependable car pool.

Although the new car pool undoubtedly helped, an important point was that Salinas seemed to appreciate the recognition and concern that was expressed, so she was more motivated to come to work on time. She also was more cooperative and interested in her job. It was evident that the supportive approach influenced Salinas's behavior. An important by-product was that Ferguson's job became easier because of Salinas's better performance.

Are theory and practice consistent?

The supportive model works well with both employees and managers, and it has been widely accepted by managers in the United States. One survey of middle managers reported that 90 percent agreed with many of the basic ideas of a supportive approach to organizational behavior.[11] Of course, their verbal agreement with supportive ideas does not necessarily mean that all of them practice those approaches regularly or effectively. *The step from theory to practice is a difficult one.* Nevertheless, there are more and more reports of companies that reap the benefits of a supportive approach, as this example illustrates:

When computer sales slowed at Hewlett-Packard, CEO John Young ordered all workers in the affected divisions to take two days off without pay each month. (This was done to avoid layoffs.) Many employees continued to work on the payless days anyway. Even more dramatically, managers in another profitable division voluntarily took 10 percent pay cuts to show their solidarity with other Hewlett-Packard employees.[12] This suggests that a supportive approach, if practiced consistently in profitable times, represents an investment that can pay high dividends when the firm needs them.

The supportive model of organizational behavior tends to be especially effective in affluent nations because it awakens employee drives toward a wide array of needs. It has less immediate application in the developing nations, because their employees' current needs and social conditions are often quite different. However, as those needs for material rewards and security become satisfied, and as employees become aware of managerial practices in other parts of the world, we may also expect employees in those countries to demand a more supportive approach.

The collegial model

A useful extension of the supportive model is the collegial model. The term "collegial" relates to a body of persons having a common purpose. It is a team concept. The collegial model especially is useful in research laboratories and similar work environments, and gradually it is evolving into other work situations as well.[13]

The collegial model is less useful on assembly lines, because the rigid work environment makes it difficult to develop there. A contingency relationship exists in which the collegial model tends to be more useful with unprogrammed work, an intellectual environment, and considerable job freedom. In other environments management often finds that other models may be more successful.

As shown in Figure 2-4, the collegial model depends on management's building a feeling of *partnership* with employees. The result is that employees feel needed and useful. They feel that managers are contributing also, so it is easy to accept and respect their roles in the organization. Managers are seen as joint contributors rather than as bosses.

The feeling of partnerships can be built in many ways. Some organizations have abolished the use of reserved parking spaces for executives, so every employee has an equal chance of finding one close to the workplace. Some firms have tried to eliminate the use of terms like "bosses" and "subordinates," feeling that those terms simply create perceptions of psychological distance between managers and nonmanagers. Other employers have removed time clocks, set up "fun committees," sponsored company canoe trips, or required managers to spend a week or two annually working in field or factory locations.[14] All of these approaches are designed to build a spirit of mutuality, in which every person makes contributions and appreciates those of others.

Teamwork is required.

The managerial orientation is toward *teamwork*. Management is the coach that builds a better team. The employee response to this situation is *responsibility*. For example, employees produce quality work not because management tells them to do so or because the inspector will catch them if they do not, but because they feel inside themselves an obligation to provide others with high quality. They also feel an obligation to uphold quality standards that will bring credit to their jobs and company.

The psychological result of the collegial approach for the employee is *self-discipline.* Feeling responsible, employees discipline themselves for performance on the team in the same way that the members of a football team discipline themselves to training standards and the rules of the game. In this kind of environment employees normally feel some degree of fulfillment, worthwhile contribution, and *self-actualization,* even though the amount may be modest in some situations. This self-actualization will lead to *moderate enthusiasm* in performance.

The collegial model tends to produce improved results in situations where it is appropriate. One study covered scientists in three large research laboratories. Laboratories A and B were operated in a relatively traditional hierarchical manner. Laboratory C was operated in a more open, participative, collegial manner. There were four measures of performance: esteem of fellow scientists, contribution to knowledge, sense of personal achievement, and contribution to management objectives. All four were higher in laboratory C, and the first three were significantly higher.[15]

Conclusions about the models

Several conclusions will now be made about the models of organizational behavior. They are, in practice, subject to evolutionary change; they are based on incremental values; they are a function of prevailing employee needs; there is a trend toward the newer models; and any of the models can be successfully applied in some situations. In addition, the models have been modified and extended in a variety of ways.

EVOLVING USAGE Managerial use of these models tends to evolve over time, and this is also true on a broader scale for organizations. As our individual or collective understanding of human behavior increases or as new social conditions develop, we move somewhat slowly to newer models.[16] It is a mistake to assume that one particular model is a "best" model that will endure for the long run. This mistake was made by some managers about both the autocratic model and the custodial model, with the result that they became psychologically locked into these models and had difficulty altering their practices when conditions demanded it. Eventually the supportive model may also fall to limited use. There is no one permanently "best" model, because what is best is contingent on what is known about human behavior in whatever environment exists at that time.

Effectiveness of current models

The primary challenge for management is to *identify the model it is actually using and then assess its current effectiveness.* Some observers suggest that this self-examination is a difficult task for managers, who tend to profess publicly one model (e.g., the supportive or collegial) yet practice another.[17] In effect, a manager has two key tasks—to acquire a new set of values as models evolve and to learn and apply the behavioral skills that are consistent with those values.

The challenge of changing the values and behaviors of intact management teams has been successfully addressed by the Norwegian Center for Organizational Learning in Oslo.[18] The fifteen top managers from a single institution experience an intense week-long simulation of a relevant organizational crisis (e.g., an oil spill in the North Sea). Through continual questioning and feedback, the managers discover how their colleagues perceive their behavior and its consequences. The rich data provided to them create a potent stimulus for reexamination and change of their underlying model.

INCREMENTAL VALUES The human values that result from the models are quite different from economic values in an organization. Economics deals with the allocation of scarce resources—those that must be given up by someone in order for another to have them. For example, if you have automobile A, I cannot have it; if you have budget B, those funds are not available to my department. Economic values are, therefore, mostly *allocative*, but human values are mostly *incremental*. These are resources, such as education, that a person may receive without the necessity of another person's giving them up. Incremental values are self-generated, being created within individuals and groups as a result of their attitudes and lifestyles.

The difference between allocative and incremental values is illustrated by a dollar bill and an idea. If Mary has dollar bill L95484272A and she gives it to you, you have it and she does not. Either you or she can have it, but not both of you. However, if you have an idea and give it to her, both of you have it. What was one unit becomes two units; and though she has it, she took nothing of like kind away from you. You can give the idea away fifty times, but you do not lose it. All you do is spread it.

Human values are incremental.

Human values, such as fulfillment and growth, are mostly of this incremental type. In order to build job satisfaction in employee A, it is not necessary to take it from employee B. In order to build satisfaction in department C, one does not have to take it from department D. Likewise, human dignity can be built without taking it from anywhere else.

There are exceptions to the incremental nature of human values because many events in an organization are allocative. In the main, however, organizational behavior models produce incremental effects. For example, there is enough job satisfaction for everybody. In fact, some organizations have achieved high cooperation and job satisfaction for nearly every member through careful application of the supportive or collegial model.

RELATION OF MODELS TO HUMAN NEEDS A second conclusion is that the four models discussed in this chapter are closely related to human needs. New models have been developed to serve the different needs that became important at the time. For example, the custodial model is directed toward the satisfaction of employees' security needs. It moves one step above the autocratic model, which reasonably serves subsistence needs but does not meet needs for security. Similarly the supportive model is an effort to meet employees' other needs, such as affiliation and esteem, which the custodial model is unable to serve.

Effect of satisfied needs

A number of people have assumed that emphasis on one model of organizational behavior is an automatic rejection of other models, but comparison suggests that *each model is built upon the accomplishments of the other.* For example, adoption of a supportive approach does not mean abandonment of custodial practices that serve necessary employee security needs. What it does mean is that custodial practices are given secondary emphasis, because employees have progressed to a condition in which newer needs dominate. In other words, the supportive model is the appropriate model to use because subsistence and security needs are already reasonably met by a suitable structure and security system. If a misdirected modern manager should abandon these basic organizational needs, the system would move back quickly to seek structure and security in order to satisfy these needs for its people.

INCREASING USE OF SOME MODELS A third conclusion is that the trend toward the supportive and collegial models will probably continue. Despite rapid advances in computers and management information systems, top managers of giant, complex organizations cannot be authoritarian in the traditional sense and be effective.[19] Because they cannot know all that is happening in their organization, they must learn to depend on other centers of power nearer to operating problems. In addition, many employees are not readily motivated toward creative and intellectual duties by the autocratic model. Only the newer models can offer the satisfaction of their needs for esteem, autonomy, and self-actualization.

CONTINGENT USE OF ALL MODELS A fourth conclusion is that, though one model may be most used at any point in time, some appropriate uses will remain for other models. Knowledge and skills vary among managers. Role expectations of employees differ, depending upon cultural history. Policies and ways of life vary among organizations. Perhaps more important, task conditions are different. Some jobs may require routine, low-skilled, highly programmed work that will be mostly determined by higher authority and will provide mostly material rewards and security (autocratic and custodial conditions). Other jobs will be unprogrammed and intellectual, requiring teamwork and self-motivation. They generally respond best to supportive and collegial approaches. Therefore, probably all four models will continue to be used, but the more advanced models will have growing use as progress is made.

In general, each new model of organizational behavior opens up an opportunity for a more advanced model to be proposed as an improvement. There is no limit to the possibilities. In 1969, for example, Abraham Maslow published a Theory Z, which he presented as a fifth model to accompany Davis's four models of organizational behavior that were explained earlier in this chapter.[20] However, Maslow's model is theoretical and philosophical, so it has not been widely used. A more applied Theory Z, which was published in a national best-selling book, *Theory Z* (1981), is discussed in the next section.

A hybrid model: Theory Z

An integrative model of organizational behavior, proposed by William Ouchi, provides a useful example of the way in which behavioral prescriptions for management must be woven together with the organization's environment. The Theory Z model adapts the elements of effective Japanese management systems to the U.S. work force.[21] The distinguishing features of Theory Z companies are listed in Figure 2-5, and these are believed to foster close, cooperative, trusting relationships among workers, managers, and other groups. The central notion is the creation of an industrial team within a stable work environment where employee needs for affiliation, independence, and control are met while the organization's needs for high-quality work are satisfied. The first step in this direction is to create and publicize a humanistic statement of corporate philosophy, which will guide the firm's policies. Many corporate giants, such as Eli Lilly, Rockwell International, and Dayton-Hudson, claim to hold Theory Z values.

Some of the most visible illustrations of Japanese management practices in action have occurred in the automotive assembly plants operated in the U.S. by Toyota, Honda, and Nissan. By accenting quality, teamwork, just-in-time production, and nonadversarial labor relations, Japanese managers at the Toyota–General Motors joint venture in Fremont, California, attained results dramatically different from the previous GM operation. Production levels of new autos were attained with one-half the previous work force, outstanding grievances dropped from 5000 to 2, and absenteeism rates plummeted from 20 percent to under 2 percent. "The Japanese philosophy is to make people an important item," concludes the general manager of human resources[22] and the evidence seems to support that contention.

Pros and cons of Theory Z

Evaluations of Theory Z approaches suggest that there are both positive and negative features. On the positive side, Theory Z organizations have made a commendable attempt to *adapt* (not transplant) Japanese ideas into their firms. Theory Z is also based on a shared concern for multiple employee needs, and it clearly typifies the trend toward supportive and collegial approaches by its use of consensus-oriented decisions. Further, there is some evidence that Theory Z firms have been, and can be, productive (as seen in the above example at the Fremont plant).[23]

FIGURE 2-5
Typical features of Theory Z organizations

- **Long-term employment**
- **Nonspecialized careers**
- **Individual responsibility**
- **Concern for the total person**
- **Control systems that are less formal**
- **Consensus decision making**
- **Slower rates of promotion**

Ouchi's Theory Z has not been immune to criticism.[24] It has been suggested that Theory Z is not new, but merely an extension of earlier theories that received less popular acclaim. Other critics have concluded that the research supporting its effectiveness is limited. Perhaps the most damaging criticism is the idea that Theory Z fails to provide useful (contingency) criteria for helping managers decide when to use it and when not to use it. Some firms in volatile industries such as electronics have difficulty balancing their desire to provide lifetime employment with the need to adjust their work forces to meet market demands. Finally, U.S. employees, accustomed to frequent promotions in rapid-growth industries, may become frustrated with the much slower rates of promotions in Theory Z firms. Despite these initial problems, Ouchi's Theory Z model has served a very important function by stimulating many managers to examine the nature and probable effectiveness of their current model of organizational behavior.

SUMMARY

Every firm has an organizational behavior system. It includes the stated or unstated philosophy and goals, quality of leadership, nature of the formal and informal organizations, and the influence of the social environment. These items combine in an operating system that interacts with personal attitudes and situational factors to produce motivation in employees.

Four models of organizational behavior are the autocratic, custodial, supportive, and collegial models. The supportive and collegial models are more consistent with contemporary employee needs and, therefore, will predictably obtain more effective results in many situations. Managers need to examine the model they are using and determine if it is the most appropriate one.

Ouchi's Theory Z is a hybrid model that blends elements of successful Japanese managerial practice with an assessment of U.S. workers' needs. It focuses heavily on a humanistic philosophy, teamwork, and consensus decisions. It has, however, been the object of some criticism.

The idea of organizational behavior models will be extended in Chapter 3, as we discuss social systems, roles, and status. Specifically, we will look at the creation and impact of organizational cultures, which help employees sense what organizational behavior model is in use.

Terms and concepts for review

Organizational behavior system
Fact premises
Value premises
Autocratic model
Custodial model
Supportive model
Collegial model
Allocative values
Incremental values
Theory Z

Discussion questions

1 Distinguish between fact and value premises. What are their implications for managers?

2 Consider an organization where you now work or have worked. What model of organizational behavior does (did) your supervisor follow? Is (Was) it the same as top management's model?

3 Discuss similarities and differences among the four models of organizational behavior.

4 What model of organizational behavior would be most appropriate in each of the fllowing situations? (Assume that you must use the kinds of employees and supervisors currently available in your local labor market.)

   a Long-distance telephone operators in a very large office

   b Accountants with a small certified professional accounting firm

   c Food servers in a local restaurant of a prominent fast-food chain

   d Salesclerks in a large discount department store

   e Circus laborers temporarily employed to work the week that the circus is in the city

5 Discuss why the supportive and collegial models of organizational behavior are especially appropriate for use in the more affluent nations.

6 Interview a supervisor or manager to identify the model of organizational behavior that person believes in. Explain why you think that the supervisor's or manager's behavior would or would not reflect those beliefs.

7 Examine the trends in the models of organizational behavior as they have developed over a period of time. Why have the trends moved in this direction?

8 Assume that a friend of yours contends, "The collegial model is obviously 'best' to use with all employees, or it wouldn't have been placed on the right side of the figure." How would you respond?

9 Theory Z appears to be a hybrid model of organizational behavior. Identify the ways in which it appears to draw from each of the other models presented.

10 Examine the characteristics of the Theory Z model. Assuming that employees had previously been supervised under an autocratic or custodial approach, what satisfactions and frustrations do you predict will result for them when the Theory Z model is implemented?

Incident

THE NEW PLANT MANAGER

Toby Butterfield worked his way upward in the Montclair Company until he became assistant plant manager in the Illinois plant. Finally his opportunity for a promotion came. The Houston plant was having difficulty meeting its budget and production quotas, so he was promoted to plant manager and transferred to the Houston plant with instructions to "straighten it out."

Butterfield was ambitious and somewhat power-oriented. He believed that the best way to solve problems was to take control, make decisions, and use his authority to carry out his decisions. After preliminary study, he issued orders for each department to cut its budget 5 percent. A week later he instructed all departments to increase production 10 percent by the following month. He required several new reports and kept a close watch on operations. At the end of the second month he dismissed three supervisors who had failed to meet their production quotas. Five other supervisors resigned. Butterfield insisted that all rules and budgets should be followed and he allowed no exceptions.

Butterfield's efforts produced remarkable results. Productivity quickly exceeded standard by 7 percent, and within five months the plant was within budget. His record was so outstanding that he was promoted to the New York home office near the end of his second year. Within a month after he left, productivity in the Houston plant collapsed to 15 percent below standard, and the budget again was in trouble.

Questions

1 Discuss the model of organizational behavior Butterfield used and the kind of organizational climate he created.
2 Discuss why productivity dropped when Butterfield left the Houston plant.
3 If you were Butterfield's New York manager, what would you tell him about his approach? How might he respond?

Experiential exercise

THE RAPID CORPORATION

The Rapid Corporation is a refrigeration service organization in a large city. It has about seventy employees, mostly refrigeration service representatives. For many years the company's policies have been dominated by its president and principal owner, Otto Blumberg, who takes pride in being a "self-made man."

Recently Otto and his office manager attended an organizational behavior seminar in which the value of a written corporate philosophy for employees was discussed. Both men agreed to draft one and compare their efforts.

1 Divide the class into two types of groups. One set of groups should draft policy statements for the Rapid Corporation based on the autocratic model; the other groups should create comparable statements of philosophy using the supportive model as a basis.
2 Ask representatives of each group (autocratic and supportive) to read their statements to the class. Discuss their major differences. Have the class debate the usefulness of policy statements for guiding the organizational behavior system in a firm of this type.

References

1 Richard E. Walton, "From Control to Commitment in the Workplace," *Harvard Business Review,* March–April 1985, p. 84.
2 D. William Childs, as quoted in Aaron Bernstein et al., "The Difference Japanese Management Makes," *Business Week,* July 14, 1986, p. 49.

3 A fascinating tale, written in the form of a novel, about teaching managers to sharpen their observational and deductive skills throughout their careers is presented in Eliyahu M. Goldratt and Jeff Cox, *The Goal: A Process of Ongoing Improvement*, rev. ed., Croton-on-Hudson, N.Y.: North River Press, 1986.

4 Edmund J. Metz, "Managing Change toward a Leading-Edge Information Culture," *Organizational Dynamics*, August 1986, pp. 28–40.

5 For a description of the crises that sometimes confront organizations, and suggested managerial preparation for such events, see Steven Fink, *Crisis Management: Planning for the Inevitable*, New York: AMACOM, 1986.

6 "The Law of the Hog: A Parable about Improving Employee Effectiveness," *Training*, March 1987, p. 67.

7 Aaron Bernstein, Scott Ticer, and Jonathan B. Levine, "IBM's Fancy Footwork to Sidestep Layoffs," *Business Week*, July 7, 1986, pp. 54–55.

8 Cathy Trost, "Child-Care Center at Virginia Firm Boosts Worker Morale and Loyalty," *Wall Street Journal*, Feb. 12, 1987, sec. 2, p. 25.

9 An example of this early research is a study of the Prudential Insurance Company in Daniel Katz, Nathan Maccoby, and Nancy C. Morse, *Productivity, Supervision, and Morale in an Office Situation*, part 1, Ann Arbor, Mich.: Institute for Social Research, University of Michigan, 1950. The conclusion about job satisfaction and productivity is reported on p. 63.

10 Rensis Likert, *New Patterns of Management*, New York: McGraw-Hill Book Company, 1961, pp. 102–103. Italics in original.

11 Joel K. Leidecker and James L. Hall, "The Impact of Management Development Programs on Attitude Formation," *Personnel Journal*, July 1974, pp. 507–512.

12 Kathleen K. Wiegner, "John Young's New Jogging Shoes," *Forbes*, Nov. 4, 1985, pp. 42–44.

13 This evolution toward collegial models is supported by the study conducted by the President's Council on Management Improvement, as reported in L. James Harvey, "Nine Major Trends in HRM," *Personnel Administrator*, November 1986, pp. 102ff.

14 A wide array of experimental approaches to building partnerships is discussed in Gene Stone and Bo Burlingham, "Workstyle," *INC.*, January 1986, pp. 45–54.

15 Frank Harrison, "The Management of Scientists: Determinants of Perceived Role Performance, *Academy of Management Journal*, June 1974, pp. 234–241.

16 A related movement to (and a call for) newer models of leadership is portrayed in Robert Terry, "The Leading Edge," *Minnesota*, January–February 1987, pp. 17–22.

17 Chris Argyris, "The Executive Mind and Double-Loop Learning," *Organizational Dynamics*, Autumn 1982, pp. 11–26.

18 Kjell R. Knudsen, "Management Subcultures: Research and Change," *Journal of Management Development*, vol. 1, no. 4, 1982, pp. 11–26.

19 "Some Chief Executives Bypass, and Irk, Staffs in Getting Information," *Wall Street Journal* (Midwest edition), Jan. 12, 1983, pp. 1, 24.

20 Abraham H. Maslow, "Theory Z," *Journal of Transpersonal Psychology*, vol. 2, no. 1, 1969, pp. 31–47. See also A. H. Maslow, *The Farther Reaches of Human Nature*, New York: Viking Press, 1971.

21 William Ouchi, *Theory Z: How American Business Can Meet the Japanese Challenge*, Reading, Mass.: Addison-Wesley Publishing Company, 1981.

22 Aaron Bernstein, Dan Cook, Pete Engardio, and Gregory L. Miles, "The Difference Japanese Management Makes," *Business Week*, July 14, 1986, pp. 47–50. For similar reports on Japanese management practices in U.S. industries, see Bill Powell et al., "Where the Jobs Are," *Newsweek*, Feb. 2, 1987, pp. 42–46.

23 Charles W. Joiner, Jr., "Making the 'Z' Concept Work," *Sloan Management Review*, Spring 1985, pp. 57–63. An interesting speculation on the compatibility of Theory Z and office automation efforts is presented in Paul S. Licker, "Will Office Automation Provide the Theory Z Organization?" *Human Systems Management*, Spring 1985, pp. 11–20.

24 See, for example, Jeremiah J. Sullivan, "A Critique of Theory Z," *Academy of Management Review*, January 1983, pp. 132–142; and Edgar H. Schein, "Does Japanese Management Style Have a Message for American Managers?" *Sloan Management Review*, Fall 1982, pp. 55–68.

For additional reading

Lewis, James, Jr., *Excellent Organizations: How to Develop and Manage Them Using Theory Z*, San Francisco: Jossey-Bass Inc., Publishers, 1985.

Lombardo, Michael M., *Values in Action: The Meaning of Executive Vignettes*, (Technical Report No. 28), Greensboro, North Carolina: Center for Creative Leadership, 1986.

Ouchi, William, *Theory Z: How American Business Can Meet the Japanese Challenge*, Reading, Mass.: Addison-Wesley Publishing Company, 1981.

Pascale, Richard T., and Anthony G. Athos, *The Art of Japanese Management: Applications for American Executives*, New York: Simon & Schuster, Inc., 1981.

Sethi, S. Prakash, Nobuaki Namiki, and Carl L. Swanson, *The False Promise of the Japanese Miracle: Illusions and Realities of the Japanese Management System*, Marshfield, Mass.: Pitman Publishing Inc., 1984.

CHAPTER

3

Social systems and organizational culture

In fact, there is a possibility... that the only thing of real importance that leaders do is to create and manage culture.

EDGAR H. SCHEIN[1]

Corporate cultures powerfully affect employee behavior.

MYRON MAGNET[2]

CHAPTER OBJECTIVES

To understand

The operation of a social system

The psychological contract

Social cultures and their impact

The work ethic

Role and role conflict in organizations

Status and status symbols

Organizational culture

Stanley Pedalino graduated from the university in the top 10 percent of his graduating class. He decided that he needed some manual labor experience before entering his chosen profession of marketing, so he went to work as a construction laborer for a year. He found that his college education was not valued by the other construction workers. Many of them looked down on college graduates, and some of them inquired what "a college dude" like Pedalino was doing working as a construction laborer. A year later, when Pedalino joined the market research staff of a national firm, he found that his education was favorably received. Unlike the construction crew, the research staff respected education and even encouraged pursuit of a master's degree.

Pedalino never stopped to analyze the situation, but he had experienced two social systems, and they had a significant influence on many parts of his job. Similarly, many college students have held a variety of part-time and summer jobs, and encountered different social systems in each organization. These systems reflect the cultural beliefs and values of other individuals surrounding the employee, and powerfully influence the way that people work together. In this chapter we introduce ideas about a social system, such as social equilibrium, the effects of system changes, psychological contracts, and the impact of role and status. Then we examine the effects of both societal and organizational culture.

UNDERSTANDING A SOCIAL SYSTEM

A *social system* is a complex set of human relationships interacting in many ways. Possible interactions are as limitless as the stars in the universe. Each small group is a subsystem within larger groups that are subsystems of even larger groups, and so on, until the world's population is included. Within a single organization, the social system includes all the people in it and their relationships to each other and to the outside world.

Mutual interdependence

It is a complex task to understand the interactions among people in a social system. The behavior of any one member can have an impact, directly or indirectly, on the behavior of any other. Although these impacts may be large or small, all parts of the system are mutually interdependent. Simply stated, a change in one part of a system affects all other parts. Furthermore, any social system engages in exchanges with its environment, receiving input from it and providing input to it. Consequently, members of a system should be aware of both their environment and their own impact on other members within the system.

Social equilibrium

A system is said to be in *social equilibrium* when there is a dynamic working balance among its interdependent parts. Equilibrium is a dynamic concept, not a static one. Despite constant movement in every organization, the system's working balance is retained. The system is like a sea in which there is continuous motion, but the sea's basic character changes very little.

Tendency of change to cause disequilibrium

When minor changes occur in a social system, they are absorbed by adjustments within the system and equilibrium is retained. On the other hand, many changes or a series of rapid changes may throw an organization out of balance, seriously reducing its vigor until it can reach a new equilibrium. In a sense, when it is in disequilibrium, its parts are working against one another instead of in harmony. Here is an example:

In a South American factory, accidents were high. The six native jefes, or supervisors, were not following management's instructions for accident prevention. They seemed agreeable but failed to "get the message" of accident prevention; consequently their employees were careless too. This was disequilibrium, with groups working at cross-purposes.

Finally, management had three-dimensional faces of the six jefes molded and colored, with the idea that each week these faces would be arranged into a "totem pole" in the order of the weekly safety rank of each department. No jefe wanted to be low on the safety totem pole, so the accident problem was quickly corrected.

Functional and dysfunctional actions

The effects of change

A change such as the factory totem pole is considered *functional* when it is favorable for the system. When a change creates unfavorable effects (such as a productivity decline) for the system, it is *dysfunctional.* A major management task is to appraise both actual and proposed changes in the social system to determine their possible functional or dysfunctional effects, so that appropriate responses can be made.

For example, American business has been sharply criticized for investing too little in human resources development. Instead, managers have emphasized the attainment of short-term profits.[3] In essence, decisions that appear to be functional for an organization in the short run may undermine its capacity to survive and prosper in the long run.

Psychological and economic contracts

When employees join an organization, they make an unwritten psychological contract with it, although generally they are not conscious of doing so. As shown in Figure 3-1, this contract is in addition to the economic contract for wages, hours, and working conditions. The *psychological contract* defines the conditions of each employee's psychological involvement with the social system. Employees agree to give a certain amount of work and loyalty, but in return they demand more than economic rewards from the system. They seek security, treatment as human beings, rewarding relationships with people, and support in fulfilling expectations.

Psychological contract

If the organization honors only the economic contract and not the psychological contract, employees tend to have low job satisfaction and performance because their expectations are not met. On the other hand, if both their psychological and economic expectations are met, they tend to be satisfied, stay with the organization, and become high performers.

Observers have criticized the absence of effective psychological contracting by the military forces in their recruitment and placement programs.[4] The problem is twofold—young men and women often approach their service with vague job expectations and unrealistic views of military life, while recruiters under pressure to fill quotas lack the time and data necessary to match people to jobs. Both sides need to clarify their expectations with the aid of skilled counselors before an effective psychological contract can be created.

As shown in Figure 3-1, an employer responds in a similar way to the economic and psychological contract that it sees. It expects responses such as high performance and cooperation. When these results occur, an employee is retained and may earn a promotion. However, if cooperation and performance do not meet expectations, corrective action and even separation may occur.

SOCIAL CULTURE

Whenever people act in accordance with the expectations of others, their behavior is social, as in the case of an employee we will call Maria. Like all other workers, Maria grows to be an adult in a *social culture*, which is her environment of human-created beliefs, customs, knowledge, and practices.

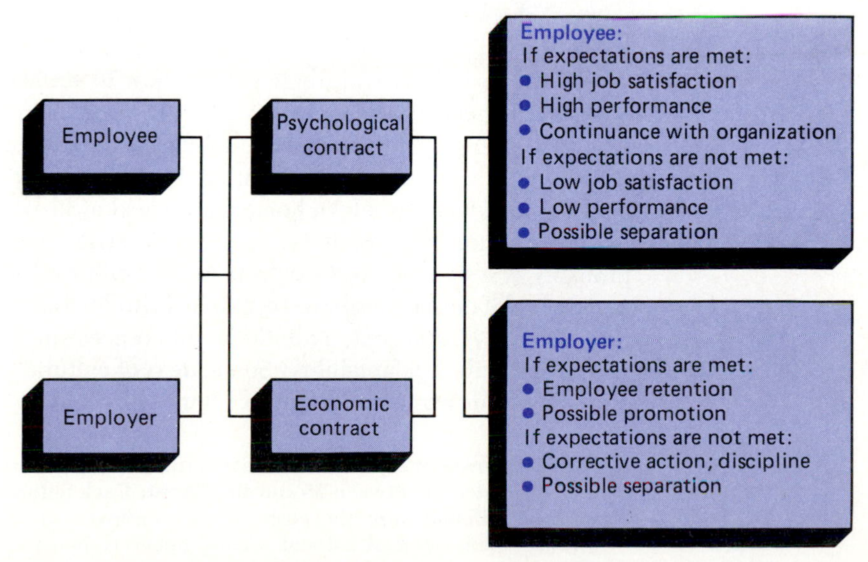

FIGURE 3-1
The psychological contract and the economic contract

Impact of culture

Culture is the conventional behavior of her society, and it influences all her actions even though it seldom enters her conscious thoughts. Maria drives to work on the right or left side of the road, depending on the culture of her society, but she seldom consciously stops to think of this. The car she drives, the drama she attends, and the organization that employs her are evidence of her social culture. Some of the important ways in which culture affects work are discussed in the following paragraphs.

Cultural change

People learn to depend on their culture. It gives them stability and security, because they can understand what is happening in their community and know how to respond. However, two types of cultural change may confront employees. One involves a move to a new location and its culture, the other a gradual change in their existing environment. Employees need to learn to adapt to both situations in order to avoid possible negative consequences.

What is cultural shock?

NEW CULTURE Companies frequently transfer employees between different cities for new job assignments. The employees who move to new job locations often experience various degrees of *cultural shock,* which is a feeling of confusion, insecurity, and anxiety caused by a strange new environment. They are concerned about not knowing how to act and about losing their self-confidence when the wrong responses are made.

A cultural change does not have to be dramatic to cause some degree of shock. For example, when an employee moves from a small town to the Boston or Chicago home office, both the employee and family are likely to suffer cultural shock. A similar shock may occur when a Boston or Chicago employee is transferred to a small town in an isolated rural area. The whole family may not know what to do with their time or how to act and dress.

Cultural shock is even greater when there is a move from one nation to another, especially if the language is different. For unprepared employees, the environment can appear to be chaos. They become disoriented, retreat into isolation, and want to return home on the next airplane. But a different culture is not behavioral chaos; it is a systematic structure of behavioral patterns, probably as systematic as the culture in the employee's home country. It can be understood if employees have receptive attitudes and receive advance preparation. But it is different, and these differences are a strain on newcomers regardless of their adaptability. Some areas of cultural differences both at work and away from work are shown in Figure 3-2.

The failure rate of expatriate managers (those sent to work in foreign countries) has been estimated at between 25 and 40 percent. Each failure may cost the employer as much as $85,000, and the costs to the employee in lost self-confidence, family tensions, and reduced esteem among peers is inestimable. The answer to this difficulty in cultural adaptation may lie in two areas: better *selection* of candidates for international assignments on the basis of factors other than just technical compe-

WORK RELATED	NOT WORK RELATED
□ **Patterns of acceptable initiation of contact with supervisor**	□ **Recreational activities**
□ **Patterns of working hours**	□ **Music**
□ **Expected pace of work**	□ **Food**
□ **Communication practices**	□ **Transportation systems**
□ **Decision-making approaches**	□ **Housing conditions**
	□ **Clothing styles**

FIGURE 3-2
Areas of possible cultural differences across nations

tence, and improved *orientation and training* of the employees and their families long in advance of their transfer.[5]

CULTURAL EVOLUTION A second type of cultural change occurs when the environment around an employee evolves to a different form. Even though employees have remained in the same location, the changing culture may have dramatic effects on them. Examples of such changes are evolving moral values, technological advances, or changes in the composition of the work force. Alert employees will monitor these changes and attempt to adapt to the emerging culture around them.

An example of evolutionary change is the trend toward a service economy in the United States.[6] **The majority of labor hours are now employed in service industries, such as retailing, banking, insurance, and education. The United States was the first major country to shift from an agricultural to an industrial base and on to a service economy in just one century. The computer revolution of the 1980s and 1990s is magnifying the pace of this change and increasing the difficulties of employee adjustment to cultural change.**

Dual-career couples are now common.

Another example of cultural evolution has been the rapid emergence of *dual-career couples*, in which each spouse in a relationship has a separate career. As many as 75 percent of married couples will have both individuals working by the 1990s, according to some estimates.[7] As a result of the two careers, both the couple and the employer are required to adapt to new conditions. An advantage to employers is that they now have a larger labor market to draw from and a greater array of skills available to choose from. However, geographical transfers of an employee often have become especially difficult. Since both spouses hold jobs, one may want to accept the transfer while the other does not. Consequently, a substantial minority of dual-career couples turn down transfers when they are offered.

Some organizations have begun to offer help in the form of spouse employment assistance programs. Some of the options include making direct employment contacts for the spouse, hiring the spouse at the new job site, offering job-seeking aid in résumé preparation and interview skills, fee payment at employment agencies, or

financial support for a job-finding trip to the new locale. Under these conditions, the dual-career couple generally is more willing to accept the transfer.

The work ethic

Work as a desirable life goal

For many years the culture of much of the Western world has emphasized work as a desirable and fulfilling activity. This attitude also is strong in parts of Asia, such as Japan. The result is a *work ethic* for many people, meaning that they view work as a central life interest and a desirable goal in life. They tend to like work and derive satisfaction from it. They usually have a stronger commitment to the organization and its goals than do other employees. These characteristics of the work ethic make it highly appealing to employers.

Religious origins

ORIGINS OF THE WORK ETHIC The work ethic has its origins in both religious and secular values. The Calvinists during the Protestant Reformation, and later the Puritans in the United States, strongly supported the work ethic. Because of its religious origins, it has been called the "Protestant ethic," although it is held by people of various religions. The religious view of the work ethic is that work is an act of service to God and to other people because it builds a better society to help fulfill God's plan. Human talents have been given to people by their Maker for the purpose of use, so hard work and lack of waste become moral obligations. Studies in various organizations confirm that employees who have the work ethic usually feel a moral commitment about the ethic rather than viewing it as a rational, businesslike choice.[8]

Secular origins

The secular origins of the work ethic probably arose from the hard necessities of pioneer life. People had to work hard to stay alive, and therefore they found reason to glorify work. It was a central fact of their environment. It also was the only way they could possibly improve their standard of living, so they viewed it as a desired ideal whereby each generation could contribute something to the generations that were to follow.

An interesting example of the impact of the work ethic emerged in the results of a survey of lottery winners. Over 60 percent of the *million-dollar* winners continued working, and nearly 90 percent of *all winners* kept their jobs. Most of those surveyed, concluded the researcher, showed "strong adherence to the work ethic."[9] Apparently their jobs, and the satisfactions they derived from them, were strong influences in their lives.

TRENDS IN THE WORK ETHIC The work ethic often is a subject of controversy. Some observers claim it is healthy, some contend that it is declining, and others suggest that it is dead or should be laid to rest. The available research indicates that there are wide variations across groups. The proportion of employees with a work ethic varies sharply among sample groups, depending on factors such as personal background, type of work, and geographical location. The ratio of employees in different jobs who report that work is a central life interest may range from 15 to 85 percent.

Decline of the work ethic

In addition to differences among groups, the general level of the work ethic also has declined gradually since the 1930s. The decline is mostly evident in the different attitudes between younger and older workers. Predictably, since their backgrounds differ sharply, younger employees are not as supportive of the work ethic. This is shown in studies such as the following:

College students are surveyed annually by the research firm of Yankelovich, Skelly, and White, Inc. In the mid-1960s over 70 percent believed that "hard work always pays off." A decade later, only 40 percent held that view.[10] What will the figure be by the year 2000?

Dramatic social changes in the latter half of the twentieth century have brought about the work ethic's decline. Competing social values have emerged, such as a leisure ethic, desire for closer personal relationships, and a belief in being entitled to rewards without work. In addition, changes in social policy and tax laws have reduced incentives to work and occasionally even penalized hard work and success. These represent additional illustrations of complex social relationships in action, and they show how an employee's work ethic is contingent on factors in the larger social system.

Managing the work ethic

An example is the underground coal-mining industry. Interviews with managers reveal that miners are productive when three conditions exist: a feeling of certainty at work, some competition between crews or shifts, and conditions that seem to make time pass quickly.[11] When management creates these conditions, the workers mine coal safely and continuously. This study suggests that the work ethic will emerge if a proper social context is created.

Social responsibility

From the 1950s through the 1970s, new cultural values arose out of an awareness of the interdependence of organizations, society, and the environment. People began to realize that organizational actions passed costs to the external society along with their benefits, and there was a strong drive to improve this cost-benefit relationship. In this way, society could receive additional net benefits from organizations, and these benefits would be more fairly distributed.

These new values generally go by the name of social responsibility, social responsiveness, or social involvement. *Social responsibility* is the recognition that organizations have significant influence on the social system and that this influence must be properly considered and balanced in all organizational actions. It simply means that organizations must function as part of a larger social system because they are, in fact, a part of that system.

These social values apply to all organizations, whether they are involved in business, labor, government, or some other activity. Each affects society in both positive and negative ways. For example, the employment policy of a construction company may discriminate against women, handicapped employees, or other groups. The labor-union strike of the municipal transit agency may inconvenience thousands of commuters, reduce attendance at schools, increase consumption of scarce energy, and so on. And when a naval ship dumps its wastes into the sea, marine life may be harmed. The essential philosophy of social responsibility is, "We are all part of one social system, and we all live together on one planet. We must act according to those facts."

One bit of evidence that organizations have increasingly become more socially responsible lies in the area of corporate philanthropy. Both as a product of their own social values and in response to the sharp budget cutbacks in federal spending for social causes, corporations across the country donate several billion dollars annually to various programs such as the American Red Cross, Boy Scouts, and Public Broadcasting Service. The newest thrust is to manage these donations strategically, by setting objectives, establishing special staffs, and tieing the level of their financial support to the extra revenue received.[12] As a result, both the organization and society are winners.

Socioeconomic model of responsiveness

A SOCIOECONOMIC MODEL Most organizations in the past, whether they were business or government, made their decisions on the basis of economic analysis and technical factors. The new emphasis on social responsiveness has led to a *socioeconomic model of decision making* in which social costs and benefits are considered along with the traditional economic and technical values in decision making. Organizations are developing a broader outlook of the social system and its interdependence. They are learning to be more human and to operate more in harmony with the earth's environment. They are being socially responsive.

The effect on leaders of business, labor unions, and government has been to operate with a more holistic view of organizational behavior and other areas of management. Executives are increasingly aware that they must monitor and manage their social responsibilities.

Figure 3-3 presents a chart of a chemical company's responsiveness to the social system. It was meeting expectations reasonably well in pay, fringe benefits, and working conditions. It was showing social responsibility.

On the other hand, it was being less responsive in some other areas, because large gaps existed between social expectations and company practices. For example, its employment practices had some elements of discrimination, even though much improvement had been made. Consumer protection in the use of its products had been largely ignored, and it was polluting the environment unnecessarily in a number of ways. Its community relations also were poorly developed. It needs to take major action to be more socially responsive.

ROLE

Roles define expected behaviors.

A *role* is the pattern of actions expected of a person in activities involving others. Role reflects a person's position in the social system, with its accompanying rights and obligations, power and responsibility. In order to be able to

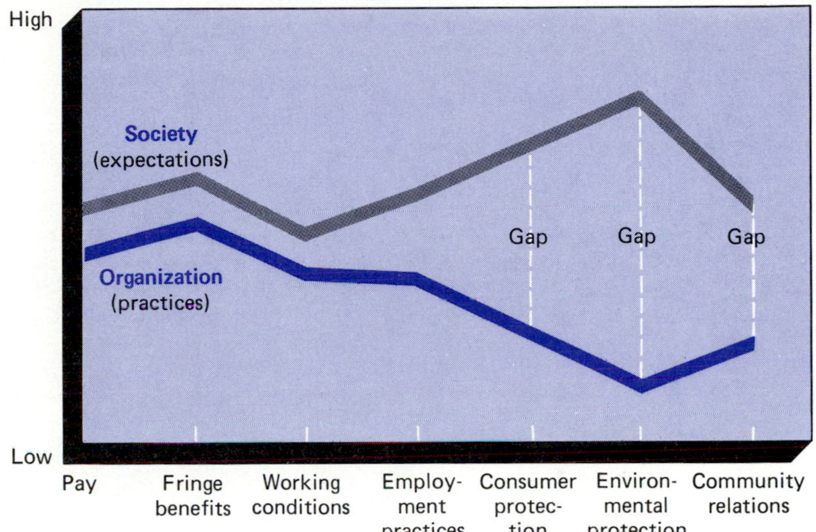

FIGURE 3-3
Comparison of social expectations and social responsiveness for a chemical company

interact with each other, people need some way to anticipate others' behavior. Role performs this function in the social system.

A person has roles both on the job and away from it, as shown in Figure 3-4. One person performs the occupational role of worker, the family role of parent, the social role of club president, and many others. In those various roles, a person is both buyer and seller, supervisor and subordinate, and giver and seeker of advice. Each role calls for different types of behavior. Within the work environment alone, a worker may have more than one role, such as a worker in group A, a subordinate to supervisor B, a machinist, a member of a union, and a representative on the safety committee.

Role perceptions

Activities of managers and workers alike are guided by their *role perceptions,* that is, how they think they are supposed to act in their own roles and how others should act in their roles. Since managers perform many different roles, they must be highly adaptive (exhibiting role flexibility) in order to change from one role to another quickly. Supervisors especially need to change roles rapidly as they work with subordinates and superiors and with technical and non-technical activities.

Multiple role perceptions

When two people such as a manager and an employee interact, each one needs to understand at least three role perceptions, as shown in Figure 3-5. For a manager, the three roles are as follows (three similar roles exist for the employee): First there is the manager's role as required by the job being performed. Then there is the role of the employee being contacted. Finally

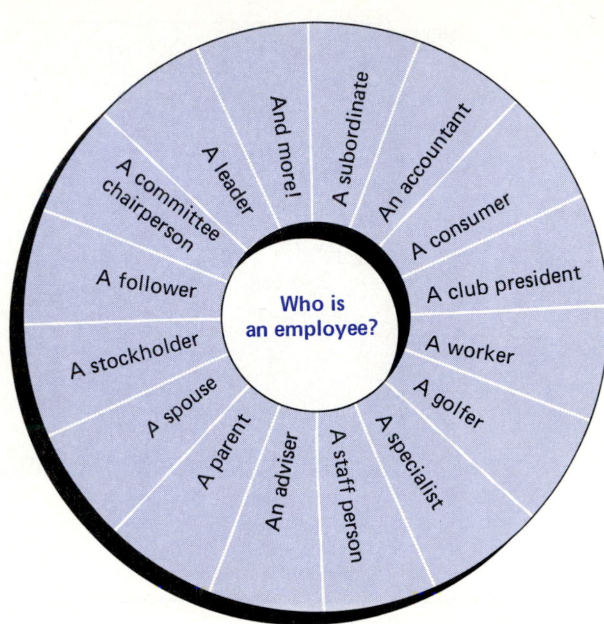

FIGURE 3-4
Each employee performs many roles.

there is the manager's role as seen by the employee. Obviously one cannot meet the needs of others unless one can perceive what they expect.

A study of 887 industrial managers examined (1) their own role expectations, (2) their perceptions of their superiors' expectations for them, and (3) their superiors' actual expectations for them.[13] The results indicated that the subjective differences in role expectations *within* the managers (comparing perceptions 1 to 2) was more strongly related to their job dissatisfaction, low confidence in higher management, and job-related stress than other comparisons. However, since only moderate overall differences in role expectations between managers and their superiors were found, the researchers speculated that managers rather quickly adapt their own perceptions to reality. This illustrates again the need to accurately perceive the surrounding work situation.

Mentors

Mentors are role models for protégés.

Where can employees get information regarding their work-related roles, so that they will have accurate role perceptions? In addition to traditional sources of information such as job descriptions and orientation sessions, many organizations have formal or informal mentorship programs. A *mentor* is a role model who guides another employee by sharing valuable advice on roles to play and behaviors to avoid. Some organizations actually assign protégés to various mentors; other firms simply allow employees to seek out their own role models.

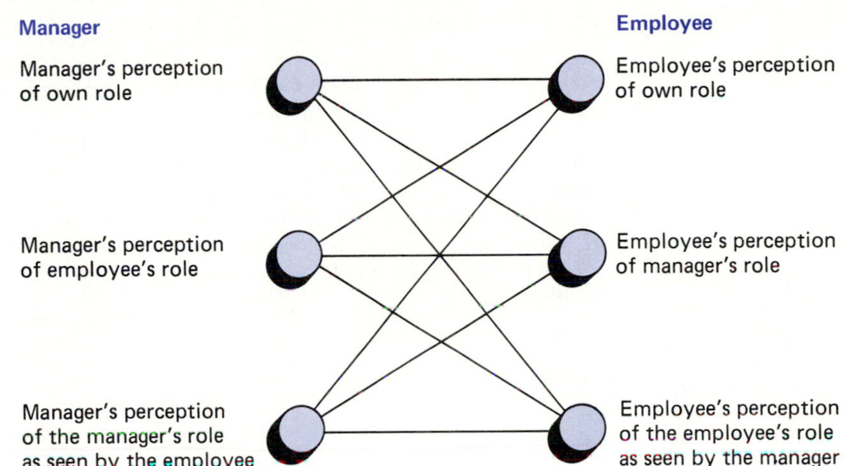

FIGURE 3-5
The complex web of manager-employee role perceptions

Mentors are usually older, successful themselves, respected by their peers (and therefore influential), and willing to commit time and energy to help another person move up the corporate ladder. Mentors are often *not* the employee's direct supervisor, and therefore can provide additional support to aid an employee's career progress.

Several problems can arise in mentoring programs, however.[14] Some mentors are more effective role models than others, or simply more interested in being good mentors. In other cases, a mentor might assign to a protégé routine tasks that don't substantially aid the employee's development. In addition, a protégé's career might be stifled abruptly if the mentor leaves the organization. For these and other reasons, common practice is to have more than one mentor for each protégé, which provides multiple inputs to the employee's role perceptions. Nevertheless, attempts to establish mentor relationships sometimes fail, as in the following example:

In an office, Kenneth Benton, an older employee, tried to play the role of adviser and helper with a new employee, Ben Grossman. Grossman misinterpreted Benton's initiatives and felt that he was being "bossed" by someone who had no right to give him orders. Rebuffed as a mentor, Benton later refused to share his insights with Grossman, even when asked.

Role conflict

When others have different perceptions or expectations of a person's role, that person tends to experience *role conflict*, because it is difficult to meet one set of expectations without rejecting another. A company president faced role conflict, for example, when she learned that both the controller and the personnel director wanted her to allocate the new organizational planning function to their departments.

Role conflict is common.

Role conflict at work is fairly common. A national sample of wage and salary workers reported that 48 percent experienced role conflict from time to time and 15 percent said that role conflict was a frequent and serious problem.[15] Role conflict was most difficult for employees with many job contacts outside the organization, that is, with boundary roles. They found that their external roles placed different demands on their jobs than their internal roles, so role conflict resulted. When people were classified according to the number of their outside job contacts, those with few contacts had the least role conflict and those with frequent contacts had the most conflict.

Role ambiguity

Role ambiguity causes problems.

When roles are inadequately defined or are substantially unknown, *role ambiguity exists,* because people are not sure how they should act in situations of this type. When role conflict and ambiguity exist, job satisfaction and organizational commitment will likely decline. On the other hand, employees tend to be more satisfied with their jobs when their roles are clearly defined by job descriptions and statements of performance expectations. A better understanding of roles helps people know what others expect of them and how they should act. If any role misunderstanding exists when people interact, then problems are likely to occur.

For example, a factory employee, Bryce Bailey, was a union steward. He came to his supervisor, Shelly Parrish, for guidance on a work problem. Parrish thought Bailey was approaching in his role as union steward and was trying to challenge her authority. Because of the misunderstood roles, the two people were not able to communicate, and the problem remained unsolved.

STATUS

Status is the social rank of a person in a group. It is a mark of the amount of recognition, honor, and acceptance given to a person. Within groups, differences in status apparently have been recognized ever since civilization began. Wherever people gather into groups, status distinctions are likely to arise, because they enable people to affirm the different characteristics and abilities of group members.

Individuals are bound together in *status systems,* or *status hierarchies,* which define their rank relative to others in the group. If they become seriously upset over their status, they are said to feel *status anxiety.*

Status is important.

Loss of status, sometimes called "losing face" or *status deprivation,* is a serious event for a typical person. People, therefore, become quite responsible in order to protect and develop their status. One of management's pioneers, Chester Barnard, stated, "The desire for improvement of status and especially the desire to protect status appears to be the basis of a sense of general responsibility."[16]

Since status is important to people, they will work hard to earn it. If it can be tied to actions that further the company's goals, then employees are strongly motivated to support their company.

A laundry manager formerly gave negative attention and reprimands (low status) to workers whom he found idle, even when they had finished their work and were waiting for more from another operator. He wanted them to help other operators, but he found that his approach simply caused them to work more slowly. Upon reexamining his approach, he decided to try to build the status of his "idle" employees who finished their work ahead of others.

He visited with them in a friendly way as he walked through his shop. He permitted them to go to any other workstation to talk and visit or to get soft drinks for themselves or others. The slow workers began to work faster to achieve this status, and the fast workers improved in order to preserve their relative position. As the fast workers visited other workstations, they developed friendships and did much informal training and helping of the slow workers. The manager later commented, "I am amazed by the changed attitudes of the workers and their increased productivity."

Status relationships

High-status people within a group usually have more power and influence than those with low status. They also receive more privileges from their group and tend to participate more in group activities. They interact more with their peers than with those of lower rank. Basically, high status gives people an opportunity to play a more important role in an organization. As a result, lower-status members tend to feel isolated from the mainstream and to show more stress symptoms than higher-ranked members.

In a work organization, status provides a system by which people can relate to each other as they work. Without it, they would tend to be confused and spend much of their time trying to learn how to work together. Though status can be abused, normally it is beneficial because it helps people cooperate with one another.

Status symbols

Status symbols are everywhere.

The status system reaches its ultimate end with *status symbols*. These are the visible, external things that attach to a person or workplace and serve as evidence of social rank. They exist in the office, shop, warehouse, refinery, or wherever work groups congregate. They are most in evidence among different levels of managers, because each successive level usually has the authority to provide itself with surroundings just a little different from those of people lower in the structure.

As shown in Figure 3-6, there are a variety of symbols of status, depending on what employees feel is important. For example, in one office the type of wastebasket is a

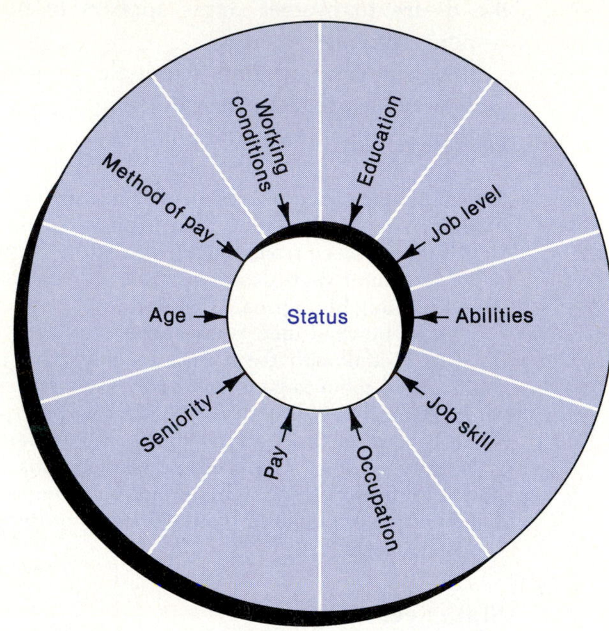

FIGURE 3-6
Major sources of status on the job

mark of distinction. In another, significant symbols are type of desk and telephones. In the executive offices, such items of rank as rugs, bookcases, curtains, and pictures on the wall are important.

Another symbol of much significance is a corner office, because these offices are larger and have windows on two sides. There may even be distinctions between an office with windows and one with no windows. Outside the office, the truck driver who operates the newest or largest truck has a symbol of status.

The clothes people wear at work are also symbols of status. A coat and tie implies higher status than slacks and a sport shirt in most situations. For an airline pilot, the uniform is a symbol of status. The job title, such as senior pilot or captain, also is important.

All this concern for symbols of status may seem amusing, but status symbols are a serious matter. They may endanger job satisfaction because employees who do not have a certain symbol, and think they should, can become preoccupied with that need. When, for example, an employee gives unreasonable attention to status symbols, there is evidence of status anxiety, and this requires management attention.

Many organizations have a policy that persons of equal rank in the same department should receive approximately equal status symbols. There may be some variation between departments, such as production and sales, because the work is different and rank is not directly comparable. In any case, managers need to face the fact that status differences exist and must be managed successfully. Managers have the power to influence and control status relationships somewhat. The organization gives some status, and it can take some away!

Sources of status

Where do we get status?

The sources of status are numerous, but in a typical work situation several sources are easily identified. As shown in Figure 3-7, education and job level are two important sources of higher status. A person's abilities, job skills, and type of work also are major sources of status.

Other sources of status are amount of pay, seniority, and age. Pay gives economic recognition and an opportunity to have more of the amenities of life, such as travel. Seniority and age often earn for their holder certain privileges, such as first choice of vacation dates. Method of pay (hourly versus salary) and working conditions also provide important status distinctions, such as distinguishing blue-collar and white-collar work.

Significance of Status

Status is significant to organizational behavior in several ways. When employees are consumed by the desire for status, it often is the source of employee problems and conflicts that management needs to solve. It influences the kinds of transfers that employees will take, because they don't want a low-status location or job assignment. It helps to determine who will be informal leader of a group, and it definitely serves to motivate those seeking to advance in the organization. Some people are status seekers, wanting a job of high status regardless of other working conditions. These people can be encouraged to qualify themselves for high-status jobs so that they will feel rewarded.

Perhaps surprisingly, those persons who already have high economic status are unlikely to flaunt it. A poll of chief executives of small, medium, and large firms showed that most do not have chauffeurs, private planes, tailor-made suits, bodyguards, or long vacations.[17] Further, their office status does not carry much weight at home, either. They often shop at discount stores, help their spouses with grocery shopping, and do chores around their homes.

- **Furniture, such as a mahogany desk or having a conference table**
- **Interior decorations, such as carpeting, draperies, and artwork**
- **Location of workplace, such as a corner office or window with a view**
- **Facilities at workplace, such as a computer terminal**
- **Quality and newness of equipment used, such as a new vehicle or tools**
- **Type of clothes normally worn, such as a suit**
- **Privileges given, such as a club membership or company automobile**
- **Job title or organizational level, such as vice president**
- **Employees assigned, such as a private secretary**
- **Degree of financial discretion, such as authorizing up to $5000 expenditures**
- **Organizational membership, such as sitting on the Executive Committee**

FIGURE 3-7
Typical symbols of status

Having status in one context clearly does not imply that the same person will have it in another situation. It is not necessarily transferable, but must be earned or acquired in each situation.

ORGANIZATIONAL CULTURE

So far we have suggested that organizational behavior occurs in a complex social system. Employee behavior (*B*), according to social psychologist Kurt Lewin, is a function of the interaction between personal characteristics (*P*) and the environment (*E*) around the person, or $B = f(P,E)$. Part of that environment is the social culture, which provides broad clues as to how a person with a given background will behave. More specifically in the workplace, though, employee actions are affected by the roles assigned to them and the status level accorded to them.

Shared beliefs and values

Inside the organization, however, lies another powerful force for determining individual and group behavior. *Organizational culture,* occasionally called organizational climate, is the set of assumptions, beliefs, values, and norms that is shared among its members. It provides the human environment in which employees perform their jobs.[18] A culture may exist across an entire organization, or it may refer to the environment within a single division, branch, plant, or department. This idea of organizational culture is somewhat intangible, for we cannot see it or touch it, but it is present and pervasive. Like the air in a room, it surrounds and affects everything that happens in an organization. Because it is a dynamic systems concept, culture is also affected by almost everything that occurs within an organization.

Characteristics of cultures

Organizations, like fingerprints and snowflakes, are always unique. Each has its own history, patterns of communication, systems and procedures, statements of philosophy, stories and myths which, in their totality, constitute its culture. Some organizations are fast-paced; others have an easygoing atmosphere. Some are warm and friendly; others are seemingly cold and sterile. Over time, an organization's culture becomes known to both employees and the public. The culture then becomes perpetuated, because an organization tends to attract and retain people who fit its values and beliefs. Just as people may choose to move to a certain geographic region on the basis of its characteristics (such as temperature, humidity, and rainfall), employees also will gravitate toward the organizational culture they prefer as a work environment.

Firms in the computer industry, especially those located in California's Silicon Valley, provide an excellent illustration.[19] Among a variety of reasons for working there, certainly the generally pleasant weather conditions are attractive incentives. But with regard to their cultures, many of the firms have achieved popularity through their "laid-back" atmosphere. Professional employees can work odd hours,

come to the job in very informal dress, exercise their creativity with great freedom, and yet they know that only intense effort can provide the breakthroughs necessary to stay one step ahead of the competition. In a nutshell, the cultures of Silicon Valley firms often suggest that the employees should both "work hard and play hard."

Cultural features

Several other dimensions of cultures are important to note. Their elements are generally consistent with each other (in other words, they fit together like pieces of a puzzle). Also, most members at least accept, if not embrace, the assumptions and values of the culture. Employees seldom talk explicitly about the culture in which they work (although this began to change when the popularity of cultures skyrocketed in the 1980s). Most cultures evolve directly from the examples set by top management, who have a powerful influence on their employees.[20] Finally, cultures can be characterized as relatively "strong" or "weak," depending largely on the degree of their impact on employee behavior.

Research evidence indicates that there is a positive relationship between certain organizational cultures and performance. In a survey of over 43,000 employees in 34 companies, one researcher concluded, "The cultural and behavioral characteristics of organizations have a measurable effect on a company's performance."[21] Just as yeast is the critical ingredient in baking bread, a "culture of productivity" is an essential element in organizational success.

Culture clash

Corporate mergers and hostile takeovers became almost everyday occurrences in the 1980s. Unfortunately, in the rush to acquire firms with complementary product lines or rich resources, some analysts focused too heavily on financial and technical considerations. As a consequence, executives woefully underestimated the task of blending together conflicting cultures. The result of naively assuming that one company's culture can be easily imposed on another often results in *culture clash*—the initial incompatibility of two ways of operating.[22] Examples of major mergers that required integration of cultures include IBM's acquisition of Rolm, Northwest Airline's acquisition of Republic, and General Motors' purchase of Electronic Data Systems.

Measuring culture

It is not easy to systematically measure and compare cultures, but it is important to try. Most early attempts relied on examination of stories, symbols, rituals, and ceremonies to obtain clues. Others have used interviews and open-ended questionnaires in an attempt to assess employee values and beliefs. In other cases, examination of corporate philosophy statements has provided insight into the espoused culture (the beliefs and values that the organization states publicly). Another approach is to survey employees directly and seek their perceptions of the organization's culture.

Two researchers have developed a quantitative instrument that focuses on four dimensions of culture: short-term task support, long-term task innovation, social relationships with a short time frame, and personal freedom over a longer time period.[23] Respondents assess both the current culture and the desired one, with the

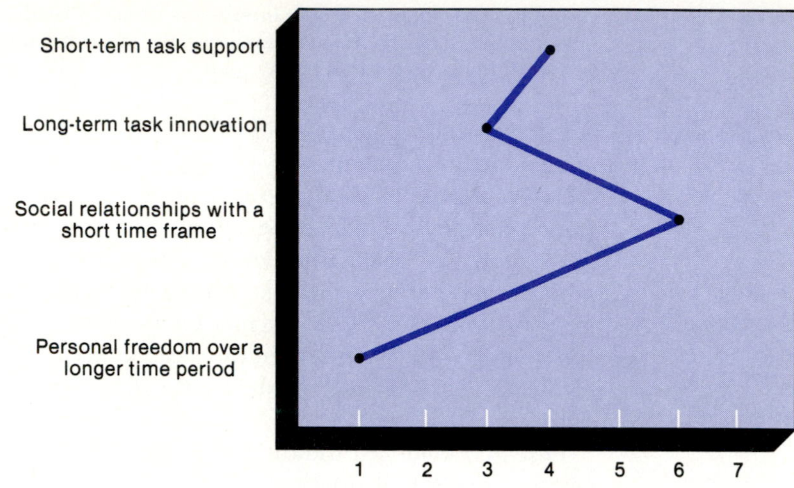

FIGURE 3-8
Illustration of a culture-gap profile
Source: *Adapted from Ralph H. Kilmann and Mary J. Saxton*, Kilmann-Saxton Culture-Gap Survey, *Pittsburgh, Pa.: Organizational Design Consultants, Inc., 1983.*

differences indicating some potential "culture gaps" (see Figure 3-8). When significant gaps appear among a group of employees, the existing norms are then analyzed and discussed for possible changes.

Communicating culture

If organizations are to consciously create and manage their cultures, they must be able to communicate them to employees, especially the newly hired ones. Individuals are generally more willing to adapt themselves to an organizational culture during the early months of their employment when they want to please others, be accepted, and learn about their new work environment. Similarly, organizations are anxious to have the new employees fit in, and therefore an approach that helps make this happen is used by many firms.

Socialization methods

Socialization is the continuous process of transmitting key elements of an organization's culture to its employees.[24] It consists of both formal methods (such as military indoctrination and corporate training) and informal means (like the role modeling provided by mentors) for shaping the attitudes, thoughts, and behavior of employees. Viewed from the organization's perspective, socialization is like placing an organization's fingerprints on people. From the employee's viewpoint, it is the essential process of "learning the ropes" to survive and prosper within the firm.

A reciprocal process occurs in the other direction. Employees can also have an active impact on the nature of the organization's culture and operations.

Individualization

Individualization occurs when employees successfully exert influence on the social system around them at work. The interaction between socialization and individualization is portrayed in Figure 3-9, which shows the types of employees who accept or reject an organization's norms and values, while exerting various degrees of influence.[25] If we assume that the culture of a certain organization invites its employees to challenge, question, and experiment while also not being too disruptive, then the "creative individualist" can infuse new life and ideas for the organization's benefit. The two extremes—rebellion and total conformity—may prove dysfunctional for the organization (and the individual's career!) in the long run.

Multiple dimensions

Organizational cultures have been discussed and researched for several decades. For example, Rensis Likert developed a classic assessment instrument that focused on several features of an organization: leadership, motivation, communication, interaction influence, decision making, goal setting, and control.[26] Based on the respondents' perceptions, he characterized a firm's culture as System 1, 2, 3, or 4, ranging from those that were highly structured and autocratic (1) to those with a more participative and human-oriented culture (4). Consistent with the supportive and collegial models of organizational behavior introduced in Chapter 2, Likert

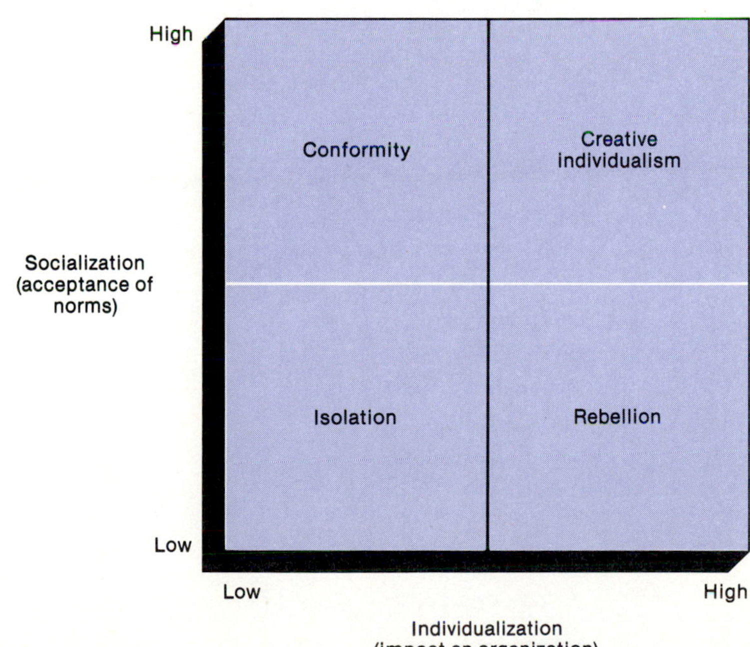

FIGURE 3-9
Four combinations of socialization and individualization

concluded that a higher level of performance and greater job satisfaction would follow from the System 4 culture.

SUMMARY

When people join a work group, they become part of that organization's social system. It is the medium by which they relate to the world of work. The variables in an organizational system operate in a working balance called social equilibrium. Individuals make a psychological contract that defines their personal relationship with the system. When they contribute to the organization's success, we call their behavior functional.

The broad environment that people live in is their social culture, and a major change in it can lead to cultural shock. Important cultural influences include the work ethic and corporate attitudes toward social responsibility.

Role is the pattern of action expected of a person in activities involving others. Related ideas are role perception, mentors, role conflict, and role ambiguity. Status is the social rank of a person in a group, and it leads to status systems and possibly status anxiety. Status symbols are sought as if they were magical herbs, because they often provide external evidence of status for their possessors.

Organizational cultures reflect the assumptions and values that guide a firm. They are intangible, but powerful influences on employee behavior. Participants learn about their organization's culture through the process of socialization, and influence it through individualization.

Terms and concepts for review

Social equilibrium
Functional and dysfunctional effects
Psychological contract
Social culture
Cultural shock
Dual-career couples
The work ethic
Social responsibility
Role
Role conflict
Role ambiguity
Status
Status anxiety
Status symbols
Organizational culture
Socialization
Individualization

Discussion questions

1 What psychological contract do you feel is present in this course? Describe its key features.
2 Discuss a time when you experienced some degree of cultural shock. Per-

haps it was a situation in which you did not know how to behave, or you were surprised by the behavior of others. How did you react? How do you wish you had reacted?

3 A management specialist recently commented about the work ethic, saying, "You can discover if you personally have a work ethic if you think more about the salary you make than about the quality of the product you make (or service provided)." Comment.

4 What does social responsibility mean to you? Does it apply to people as well as institutions? Describe three acts of social responsibility that you have seen, or performed, in the last month.

5 Describe a situation in which you have experienced role conflict or role ambiguity. What caused it? How are the two ideas related, and how are they different?

6 Interview a manager to discover what that person believes to be the five most important status symbols in the work situation.

7 Describe the organizational culture that seems to exist in your class. What are some of the implicit or explicit norms, values, and assumptions?

8 Reflect back on your first few days in college, or in a part-time or summer job. In what ways were you socialized? How did you feel about what was happening to you?

9 Now look at the reciprocal process of individualization. In what ways did you make an impact on the college?

Incidents

LIBERTY CONSTRUCTION COMPANY

Liberty Construction Company is a small company in Colorado. Over half its revenue is derived from the installation of underground water and power lines, so much of its work is seasonal and there is high turnover among its employees.

Michael Federico, a college student, had been employed by Liberty as a backhoe operator for the last three summers. On his return to work for the fourth summer, Federico was assigned the second newest of the company's five backhoes. The owner reasoned that Federico had nine months of work seniority, so according to strict seniority he should have the second backhoe. This action required the present operator of the backhoe, Pedro Alvarez, a regular employee who had been with the company seven months, to be reassigned to an older machine. Alvarez was strongly dissatisfied with this; he felt that as a regular employee he should have retained the newer machine instead of having to give it to a temporary employee. The other employees soon fell into two camps, one supporting Alvarez and one supporting Federico. Job conflicts arose, and each group seemed to delight in causing work problems for the other group. In less than a month Alvarez left the company.

Question

Discuss this case in terms of the social system, equilibrium, the psychological contract, role, status, and status symbols.

Experiential exercise

ROLE PERCEPTIONS OF STUDENTS AND INSTRUCTORS

Consider yourself as the subordinate in this class, with the instructor as your "manager."

1 (Work individually.) In the student-instructor relationship in this class, identify:
   a Your perception of your student roles
   b Your perception of the instructor's roles
   c Your perception of the instructor's perception of your roles as a student (At the same time, the instructor should be identifying his or her perception of the instructor's roles, the instructor's perception of the students' roles, and the instructor's perception of the students' perceptions of his or her roles.)
2 Meeting in small groups of students, combine your ideas into collective statements of perceptions.
3 Report your group's perceptions to the class on all three factors. Request that the instructor share his or her perceptions with the class.
4 Using Figure 3-5 as a guide, explore the areas of agreement and disagreement between the class and the instructor. Identify the implications for possible role conflict and role ambiguity. What action steps could be taken at this time to reduce such problems?

References

1 Edgar H. Schein, *Organizational Culture and Leadership: A Dynamic View*, San Francisco: Jossey-Bass, Inc., Publishers, 1985, p. 2. (Italics in original.)
2 Myron Magnet, "The Decline and Fall of Business Ethics," *Fortune*, Dec. 8, 1986, p. 72.
3 Robert H. Hayes and David A. Garvin, "Managing as if Tomorrow Mattered," *Harvard Business Review*, May–June 1982, pp. 70–79.
4 Herbert George Baker, "The Unwritten Contract: Job Perceptions," *Personnel Journal*, July 1985, pp. 37–41. For a study of the positive effects of psychological contracts, see James D. Portwood and Edwin L. Miller, "Evaluating the Psychological Contract: Its Implications for Employee Job Satisfaction and Work Behavior," in Robert L. Taylor et al. (eds.), *Academy of Management Proceedings*, 1975, Mississippi State, Miss.: Academy of Management, 1976, pp. 109–113.
5 Mark Mendenhall and Gary Oddou, "The Dimensions of Expatriate Acculturation: A Review," *Academy of Management Review*, January 1985, pp. 39–47. Examples of culture shock when managers are transferred to the United States are in Amanda Bennett, "American Culture Is Often a Puzzle for Foreign Managers in the U.S.," *Wall Street Journal*, Feb. 12, 1986, sec. 2, p. 29.
6 Karl Albrecht and Ronald Zemke, *Service America*, Homewood, Ill.: Dow Jones–Irwin, 1985.
7 Alan Trippel, "Spouse Assistance Programs: Relocating Dual-Career Families," *Personnel Journal*, October 1985, pp. 76–77. Also see Richard E. Kopelman, Lyn Rosensweig, and Lauren H. Lally, "Dual-Career Couples: The Organizational Response," *Personnel Administrator*, September 1982, pp. 73–78.
8 Aryeh Kidron, "Work Values and Organizational Commitment," *Academy of Management Journal*, June 1978, pp. 239–247.
9 "Take This Job and Love It," *Arizona Republic*, Sept. 13, 1985, p. G-1 (adapted from a report in the *Journal of the Institute for Socioeconomic Studies*).
10 Daniel Yankelovich, "New Rules in American Life: Searching for Self-Fulfillment in a World Turned Upside Down," *Psychology Today*, April 1981, pp. 35ff.

11 Richard L. Hannah, "The Work Ethic of Coal Miners," *Personnel Journal*, October 1982, pp. 746ff.

12 Timothy S. Mescon and Donn J. Tilson, "Corporate Philanthropy: A Strategic Approach to the Bottom-Line," *California Management Review*, Winter 1987, pp. 49–61. For an attempt to measure corporate social responsibility, see Richard E. Wokutch and Barbara A. Spencer, "Corporate Saints and Sinners: The Effects of Philanthropic and Illegal Activity on Organizational Performance," *California Management Review*, Winter 1987, pp. 62–77.

13 Victoria Berger-Gross and Allen I. Kraut, "'Great Expectations:' A No-Conflict Explanation of Role Conflict," *Journal of Applied Psychology*, May 1984, pp. 261–271. A special case of multiple role perceptions and how to handle them is provided in John W. Newstrom and Melissa S. Leifer, "Triple Perceptions of the Trainer: Strategies for Change," *Training and Development Journal*, November 1982, pp. 90–96.

14 See, for example, Donald W. Myers and Neil J. Humphreys, "The Caveats of Mentorship," *Business Horizons*, July–August 1985, pp. 9–14; John A. Byrne, "Let a Mentor Lead You—But Beware the Pitfalls," *Business Week*, Apr. 20, 1987, p. 95; and the seldom-discussed case of a person who acts as an obstacle to one's career in Tilton L. Willcox, "The Anti-Mentor," in Dennis Ray (ed.), *Southern Management Association Proceedings*, Mississippi State, Miss.: Southern Management Association, 1988, pp. 168–170. To overcome some of the problems identified, peer mentoring is a possibility, as discussed in K. E. Kram and L. A. Isabella, "Mentoring Alternatives: The Role of Peer Relationships in Career Development," *Academy of Management Journal*, January 1985, pp. 110–132.

15 Robert L. Kahn et al., *Organizational Stress: Studies in Role Conflict and Ambiguity*, New York: John Wiley & Sons, Inc., 1964, pp. 56, 99–124; John J. Parkington and Benjamin Schneider, "Some Correlates of Experienced Job Stress: A Boundary Role Study," *Academy of Management Journal*, June 1979, pp. 270–281. The special case of conflict between job and personal role demands is reviewed in Jeffrey H. Greenhaus and Nicholas J. Beutel, "Sources of Conflict between Work and Family Roles," *Academy of Management Review*, January 1985, pp. 76–88.

16 Chester I. Barnard, "Functions and Pathology of Status Systems in Formal Organizations," in William F. Whyte (ed.), *Industry and Society*, New York: McGraw-Hill Book Company, 1946, p. 69.

17 Frank Allen, "Most Bosses Shun Symbols of Status, Help Take Care of Household Tasks," *Wall Street Journal*, Oct. 23, 1981, p. 29.

18 Although many definitions of culture exist, they consistently point to these factors. This definition is consistent with the items suggested in Edgar H. Schein, "Are You Corporate Cultured?" *Personnel Journal*, November 1986, pp. 83–96.

19 An anthropological study of a failed attempt to impose a culture on a Silicon Valley firm is described in Peter C. Reynolds, "Imposing a Corporate Culture," *Psychology Today*, March 1987, pp. 33–38.

20 This position is firmly stated by Noel M. Tichy, "Training as a Lever for Change," *New Management*, Winter 1987, pp. 39–41; and Leonard M. Sayles and Robert V. L. Wright, "The Use of Culture in Strategic Management," *Issues & Observations*, November 1985, pp. 1–9.

21 Daniel R. Denison, "Bringing Corporate Culture to the Bottom Line," *Organizational Dynamics*, Autumn 1984, p. 20. Other arguments for the relationships between culture and productivity are found in Jay B. Barney, "Organizational Culture: Can It Be a Source of Sustained Competitive Advantage?" *Academy of Management Review*, July 1986, pp. 656–665; and Karl E. Weick, "Organizational Culture and High Reliability," *California Management Review*, Winter 1987, pp. 112–127.

22 Examples of culture clash can be found in Beverly Geber, "The Forgotten Factor in Merger Mania," *Training*, February 1987, pp. 28–37; and Mitchell Lee Marks and

Philip Harold Mirvis, "The Merger Syndrome," *Psychology Today*, October 1986, pp. 37–42.

23 Ralph L. Kilmann, "Corporate Culture," *Psychology Today*, April 1985, pp. 62–68; another survey instrument is contained in J. E. Hebden, "Adopting an Organization's Culture: The Socialization of Graduate Trainees," *Organizational Dynamics*, Summer 1986, pp. 54–72.

24 A seven-step socialization process is described by Richard Pascale, "Fitting New Employees into the Company Culture," *Fortune*, May 28, 1984, pp. 28–39; also see Meryl R. Louis, Barry Z. Posner, and Gary N. Powell, "The Availability and Helpfulness of Socialization Practices," *Personnel Psychology*, Winter 1983, pp. 857–866.

25 Edgar H. Schein, "Organizational Socialization and the Profession of Management," *Industrial Management Review*, 1968, vol. 9, pp. 1–15.

26 Rensis Likert, *The Human Organization: Its Management and Value*, New York: McGraw-Hill Book Company, 1967, pp. 3–12.

For additional reading

Deal, Terrence E., and Allan A. Kennedy, *Corporate Cultures: The Rites and Rituals of Corporate Life*, Reading, Mass.: Addison-Wesley Publishing Company, 1982.

Frost, Peter J., et al., *Organizational Culture*, Beverly Hills, Calif.: Sage Publications, 1985.

Kilmann, Ralph H., Mary J. Saxton, Roy Serpa, and Associates, *Gaining Control of the Corporate Culture*, San Francisco: Jossey-Bass Inc., Publishers, 1985.

Kram, Kathy E., *Mentoring at Work: Developmental Relationships in Organizational Life*, Glenview, Ill.: Scott, Foresman and Company, 1985.

Miles, Robert H., *Managing the Corporate Social Environment: A Grounded Theory*, Englewood Cliffs, N.J.: Prentice-Hall, 1987.

Parsons, Talcott, *Social Structure and Personality*, New York: Free Press of Glencoe, 1964.

Raelin, Joseph A., *The Clash of Cultures: Managers and Professionals*, Boston: Harvard Business School Press, 1986.

Ritti, R. Richard, and G. Ray Funkhouser, *The Ropes to Skip and the Ropes to Know: Studies in Organizational Behavior*, 3d ed., Columbus, Ohio: Grid Publishing Company, 1986.

Schein, Edgar H., *Organizational Culture and Leadership: A Dynamic View*, San Francisco: Jossey-Bass Inc., Publishers, 1985.

Sekaran, Uma, *Dual-Career Families: Contemporary Organizational and Counseling Issues*, San Francisco: Jossey-Bass Inc., Publishers, 1986.

Sengoku, Tamotsu, *Willing Workers: The Work Ethics in Japan, England, and the United States*, Westport, Conn.: Quorum Books, 1985.

CHAPTER 4

Managing communications

In a decentralized, customer-driven company, a good leader spends more time communicating than doing anything else.

JAN CARLZON[1]

Simple wandering—listening, empathizing, staying in touch—is an ideal starting point.

THOMAS J. PETERS AND NANCY K. AUSTIN[2]

CHAPTER OBJECTIVES

To understand

The two-way communication process

Barriers to communication

Factors leading to effective communication

Downward and upward communication problems

The roles of performance feedback and listening

Communication networks

Electronic communications

A Hollywood movie company was filming a movie near a small Western town. The script involved some narrow-gauge-railway scenes; and a local resident, regularly a railroad engineer, had been selected as engineer of the narrow-gauge train. He was very proud of his assignment. One evening when both the Hollywood visitors and the engineer were in a local bar, the engineer walked over to the director of the movie company and asked, "John, how did I do with those train scenes today?"

The director, in a good mood, gave his most favorable Hollywood response, "Joe, you are doing one hell of a job."

Joe, not understanding the favorable meaning of this colloquialism, took it as a criticism and was immediately ruffled, replying, "Oh, I don't know about that. You couldn't do any better."

The director, still trying to communicate (but in terms of his own frame of reference), said, "That's what I said, Joe. You are doing one hell of a job."

At this point Joe became angry and an argument broke out, with Joe vowing that he wouldn't be talked to that way in front of friends. Eventually it was necessary to separate the two men to prevent a fight.

Whether one is working for a Hollywood movie company, a manufacturing or service firm, or the federal government, communication is an ever-present activity because it is the means by which people relate to one another. Communication is as necessary to an organization as the bloodstream is to a person. Just as people may develop arteriosclerosis, a hardening of the arteries that impairs their efficiency by restricting the flow of blood and the nutrients it carries, so may an organization develop similar problems with its information arteries. The result is the same—unnecessarily reduced efficiency. And just like in the medical ailment, *preventing* the problem may be easier than trying to find a cure.

The opening quote by the president of the Scandinavian Airlines System (SAS) highlights the importance of managerial communication. Because communication is so significant, we introduce it here before talking about many other topics in organizational behavior.

COMMUNICATION FUNDAMENTALS

Communication is the transfer of information and understanding from one person to another person. It is a way of reaching others with ideas, facts, thoughts, feelings, and values. It is a bridge of meaning among people so that they can share what they feel and know. By using this bridge, a person can safely cross the river of misunderstanding that sometimes separates people.

Two people are required.

A significant point about communication is that it always involves at least two people—a sender and a receiver. One person alone cannot communicate. Only one or more receivers can complete the communication act. This fact is obvious when one thinks of a person lost on an island calling for help when there is no one near enough to hear the call. The relationship is not so obvious to managers who send out bulletins to employees. They tend to think that when their bulletins are sent, they have communicated, but transmission of the message is only a beginning. A manager may send a hundred bulletins, but there is no communication until each bulletin is received, read, and understood. *Communication is what the receiver understands,* not what the sender says.

Understanding is critical for success.

Importance of communication

Organizations cannot exist without communication. If there is no communication, employees cannot know what their coworkers are doing, management cannot receive information inputs, and supervisors cannot give instructions. Coordination of work is impossible, and the organization will collapse for lack of it. Cooperation also becomes impossible, because people cannot communicate their needs and feelings to others. We can say with confidence that *every act of communication influences the organization in some way.*

When communication is effective, it tends to encourage better performance and job satisfaction.[3] People understand their jobs better and feel more involved in them. In some instances they even will make sacrifices of long-established privileges because they see that a sacrifice is necessary.

Management in one firm persuaded production employees to bring their own coffee and have coffee breaks at their machines instead of taking a regular time-lost coffee break in the cafeteria. The company dealt directly and frankly. It presented to employee group meetings a chart of electricity use for the plant showing how power use was less than half of normal for fifteen minutes before and after coffee break, plus the normal production loss during the break. The company made a sound case for the fact that this long period of inactivity and partial activity prevented profitable operation. The power-use charts were convincing, and employees readily accepted the new coffee-break policy.

Open communication

The positive response of those employees supports one of the basic propositions of organizational behavior—that *open communication is generally better than restricted communication.* In effect, if employees know the problems an organization is facing and hear what managers are trying to do, they will usually respond favorably.

It would be easy to focus solely on communication with employees and ignore the needs of managers, but that would be a limited view. Management's role is critical, for managers not only initiate communications but also pass them on to and interpret them for employees. Just as a photograph can be no clearer than the negative from which it is printed, managers cannot transmit a message more clearly than their own understanding of it.

Managers need timely, useful information to make sound decisions. Inadequate or poor data can affect a broad area of performance because the scope of managerial influence is quite wide. Very simply, managerial decisions affect many people and many activities.

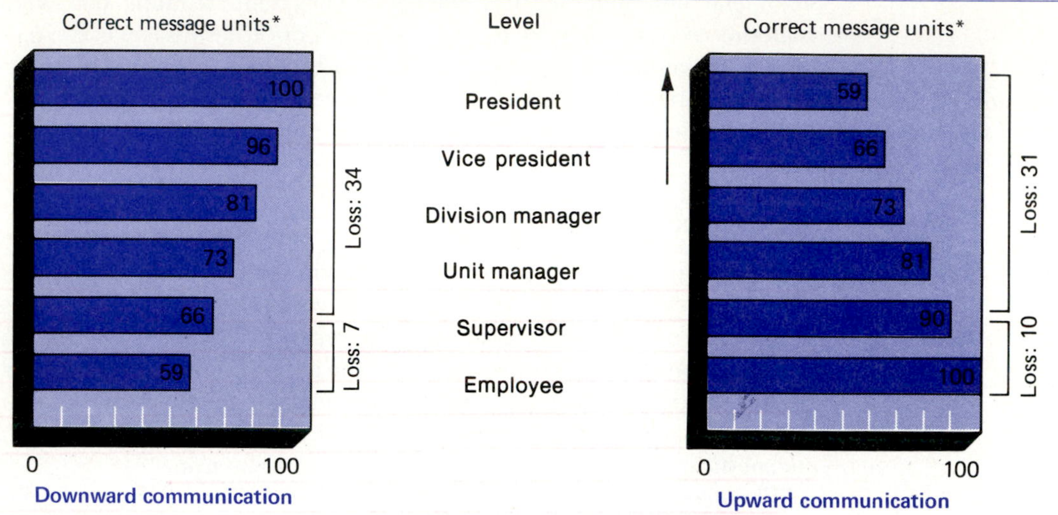

FIGURE 4-1
In a long chain-of-command communication to or from employees, most communication loss tends to be within the management group.

In addition, most of the links in the communication chain, from top to bottom and bottom to top, are in the management group. Figure 4-1 shows how a communication chain from an employee to the president has four management links and only one employee link. Since each link affords an opportunity for loss of information content, the greater proportion of loss tends to be within management when the communication chain is long.[4]

Figure 4-1 shows how most of the communication loss tends to be within management. If we take the six levels shown in the figure and assume a 10 percent loss of information each time a communication is transmitted, then more than three-fourths of an upward or downward message loss is within management. For a downward message, the loss is 34 units out of 100 sent; the message loss upward is 31 units. If management communication does not work well, then employee communication is not likely to work well either.

The two-way communication process

Eight steps in the process

The *two-way communication process* is the method by which a sender reaches a receiver with a message.[5] It requires eight steps whether the two parties talk, use hand signals, or employ some other means of communication. The steps are shown in Figure 4-2.

DEVELOP AN IDEA Step 1 is to *develop an idea* that the sender wishes to transmit. This is the key step, because unless there is a worthwhile message, all the other steps are somewhat useless. This step is represented by the sign, sometimes seen on office or factory walls, that reads, "Be sure brain is engaged before putting mouth in gear."

ENCODE Step 2 is to *encode* the idea into suitable words, charts, or other symbols for transmission. At this point the sender determines the method of transmission so that the words and symbols may be organized in suitable fashion for the type of transmission. For example, back-and-forth conversation usually is not organized the same way as a written memorandum.

TRANSMIT When the message finally is developed, step 3 is to *transmit* it by the method chosen, such as by memo, phone call, or personal visit. Senders also choose certain channels, such as bypassing or not bypassing the superintendent, and they communicate with careful timing. Today may not be the right day to talk to one's manager about that pay raise. Senders also try to keep their communication channel free of barriers, or interference, as shown in Figure 4-2, so that their messages have a chance to reach receivers and hold their attention. In interviewing, for example, freedom from distraction is desirable.

Receiver controls steps 4–8.

RECEIVE Transmission allows another person to *receive* a message, which is step 4. In this step the initiative transfers to receivers, who tune to receive the message. If it is oral, they need to be good listeners, as will be discussed shortly. If the receiver does not function, the message is lost.

DECODE Step 5 is to *decode* the message so that it can be understood. The sender wants the receiver to understand the message exactly as it was sent. For example, if the sender transmits the equivalent of a square and the decoding step produces a circle, then a message has been sent but not much understanding has taken place.

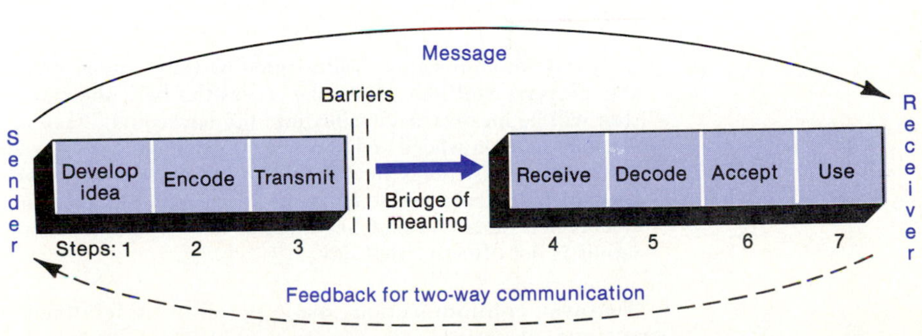

FIGURE 4-2
The communication process

Need for understanding

Understanding can occur only in a receiver's mind. A communicator may make others listen, but there is no way to make them understand. The receiver alone chooses whether to understand or not. Many employers overlook this when giving instructions or explanations. They think that telling someone is sufficient, but the communication cannot proceed until there is understanding. This is known as "getting through" to a person.

The encoding-decoding sequence is somewhat like the activity involved when the old London Bridge was moved to the United States. The bridge could not be moved in one piece, so it had to be disassembled stone by stone, with each stone marked as to its proper location. This was similar to the action of a sender who has an idea and encodes (dismantles) it into a series of words, each marked by location and other means to guide the receiver. In order to move the idea (transmit it), the sender needs to take it apart by putting it into words. The reassembly of the bridge stone by stone in the United States was similar to the action of a receiver who takes words received and mentally reassembles them into whole ideas.

ACCEPT Once the receivers have obtained and decoded a message, they have the opportunity to *accept or reject* it, which is step 6. Senders, of course, would like receivers to accept their communications in the manner intended so that activities can progress as planned. Acceptance, however, is a matter of choice and degree, such that the receiver has considerable control over whether or not to embrace all the message or just parts of it. Some factors affecting the acceptance decision revolve around perceptions of the message's accuracy, the authority of the sender, and the behavioral implications for the receiver.

USE Step 7 in the communication process is for the receiver to *use the information*. The receiver may discard it, perform the task as directed, store the information for the future, or do something else. This is a critical action step, and the receiver is largely in control of what to do.

PROVIDE FEEDBACK When the receiver acknowledges the message and responds to the sender, *feedback* has occurred. Feedback completes the communication loop, because there is a message flow from sender to receiver and back to the sender as shown by the feedback arrow at the bottom of Figure 4-2.

Two-way communication is illustrated by the popular sport of tennis and one of its star players, Steffi Graff. As she serves the ball, she cannot tell herself, "My next shot will be an overhead volley into the backcourt." Her next shot, to be effective, must depend on where and how her opponent returns the serve. Steffi undoubtedly has an overall strategy for the match, but each of her shots must be contingent on how the ball is returned to her— its force, spin, and placement. Unless she carefully selects her shots and matches them to her opponent's game, she will find that her tennis is not effective that day.

Two-way communication, made possible by feedback, has a back-and-forth pattern similar to that observed in watching tennis from courtside. In two-way communication, the speaker sends a message and the receiver's responses come back to the speaker. The result is a developing play-by-play situation in

Senders require feedback.

which the speaker can (and should) adjust the next message to fit the previous responses of the receiver. Senders need feedback—the final step—because it tells them whether the message was received, decoded properly, accepted, and used. When this two-way communication occurs, both parties are more satisfied, frustration is prevented, and work accuracy is much improved.

Potential problems

Two-way communication is not exclusively beneficial. It also can cause difficulties. Two people may strongly disagree about some item but not realize it until they establish two-way communication. When they expose their different viewpoints, they may become even more polarized, but at least two-way communication has helped them understand the nature of their differences.

Possible problem of cognitive dissonance

Another difficulty that may occur is *cognitive dissonance*. This is the internal conflict and anxiety that occurs when people receive information incompatible with their value systems, prior decisions, or other information they may have. Since people do not feel comfortable with dissonance, they try to remove or reduce it. Perhaps they will try to obtain new communication inputs, change their interpretation of the inputs, reverse their decision, or change their values. They may even refuse to believe the dissonant input, or they may rationalize it out of the way.

Senders always need to communicate with care, because communication is a potent form of self-revelation to others. Not only do we disclose something about ourselves when we speak, but others are judging us at the same time.[6] This pressure in two-way communication can cause problems, as this research study found:

Regrettable messages

> **Many people have had the experience of saying something that they wished they had not. Although these "regrettable messages" are often unintended, they usually produce a face-threatening situation for either the sender, receiver, or both.[7] As a result, they typically contribute additional stress to a relationship or even cause it to deteriorate. Regrettable messages include several types, such as outright blunders, personal attacks, stereotyped slurs, sarcastic criticism, or harmful information.**

Communication barriers

Even when the receiver receives the message and makes a genuine effort to decode it, there are a number of interferences that may limit the receiver's understanding. These obstacles act as *barriers to communication*, and they may entirely prevent a communication, filter part of it out, or give it incorrect meaning. Three types of barriers are personal, physical, and semantic.

PERSONAL BARRIERS *Personal barriers* are communication interferences that arise from human emotions, values, and poor listening habits. They are a common occurrence in work situations. We all have experienced how our personal feelings can limit our communications with other people, and these situations happen at work just as they do in private life.

Psychological distance

Personal barriers often involve a *psychological distance*—a feeling of being emotionally separated—between people that is similar to actual physical distance. For example, Marsha talks down to Janet, who resents this attitude, and this resentment separates them.

Our emotions act as filters in nearly all our communications. We see and hear what we are emotionally "tuned" to see and hear, so communication cannot be separated from our personality. We communicate our interpretation of reality instead of reality itself. Someone has said, "No matter what you say a thing is, it isn't," meaning that the sender is merely giving an emotionally filtered perception of it. Under these conditions, when the sender's and receiver's perceptions are reasonably close together, their communication will be more effective.

PHYSICAL BARRIERS *Physical barriers* are communication interferences that occur in the environment in which the communication takes place. A typical physical barrier is a sudden distracting noise that temporarily drowns out a voice message. Other physical barriers include distances between people, walls, or static that interferes with radio messages. People frequently recognize when physical interference occurs and try to compensate for it.

Ecological control

For example, physical barriers can be converted to positive forces through *ecological control*, in which the surroundings are altered by the sender so as to influence the receiver's feelings and behavior. Moderate tidiness, open desk placement, a reasonable amount of status symbols, plants, and wall decorations may all affect a visitor's perceptions. Consider how ecological control operates in this situation:

> **When visitors came to her office, Carmen Valencia used to sit rigidly behind her desk, leaving the other person somewhat distant on the other side of the desk. This arrangement created a psychological distance and clearly established her as the leader and superior in the interaction. Then she rearranged her office so that a visitor sat beside her on the same side of her desk. This suggested more receptiveness and equality of interaction with visitors. It also had the advantage of providing a work area on her desk for mutual examination of work documents. When she wished to establish a more informal relationship, particularly with subordinates, she came around to the front of the desk and sat in a chair near the employee.**

SEMANTIC BARRIERS *Semantics* is the science of meaning, as contrasted with phonetics, the science of sounds. Nearly all communication is symbolic; that is, it is achieved using *symbols* (words, pictures, and actions) that suggest certain meanings. These symbols are merely a map that describes a territory, but they are not the real territory itself; hence they must be decoded and interpreted by the receiver. Before we introduce the three types of symbols, however, an additional form of barrier deserves mention.

Semantic barriers arise from limitations in the symbols with which we communicate. Symbols usually have a variety of meanings, and we have to choose one meaning from many. Sometimes we choose the wrong meaning and misunderstanding occurs. An illustration is the railroad engineer at the beginning of this chapter. He misunderstood what the slang phrase "hell of a job" meant, so he became emotional. In this instance a semantic barrier also led to an emotional barrier, and further communication was blocked.

Fact vs. inference

Whenever we interpret a symbol on the basis of our assumptions, not facts, we are making an *inference.* Inferences are an essential part of most communication. We cannot avoid them by waiting until all communication is factual before accepting it. However, since inferences can give a wrong signal, we need always to be aware of them and to appraise them carefully. When doubts arise, more information can be sought.

Communication symbols

WORDS Words are the main communication symbol used on the job. Many employees spend more than 50 percent of their time in some form of word communication. A major difficulty occurs, however, since nearly every common word has several meanings. Multiple meanings are necessary because we are trying to talk about an infinitely complex world while using only a limited number of words.

The variety of word meanings often is surprising. A standard library dictionary reports 110 different meanings for the popular word "round." Many of the meanings are entirely different, as shown by six examples in Figure 4-3. A study of a larger

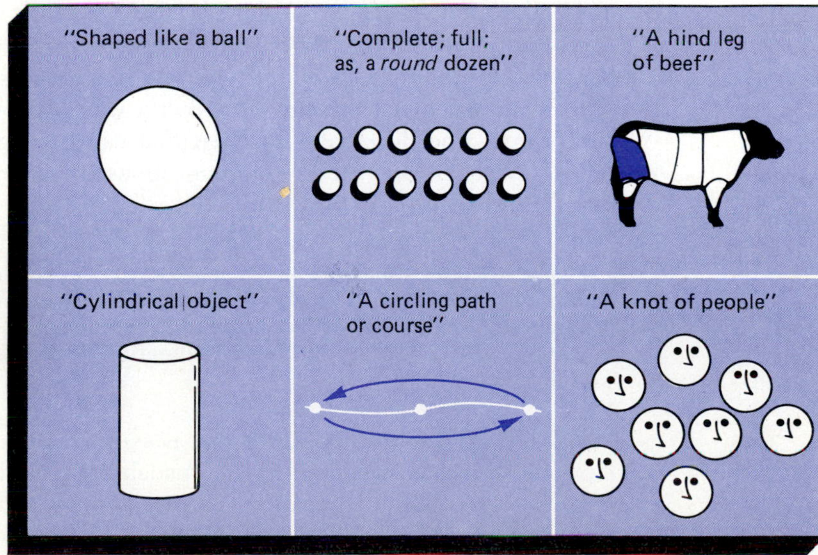
The word "round" has 110 different meanings:
Adjective: 23 Noun: 42 Verb: 16 Preposition: 13 Adverb: 16
Which way did you last use it in conversation?
Did the listener know what you meant?
"Shaped like a ball"
"Complete; full; as, a *round* dozen"
"A hind leg of beef"
"Cylindrical object"
"A circling path or course"
"A knot of people"

FIGURE 4-3
Example of the multiple meanings of a word

Source: Webster's Third New International Dictionary, *Springfield, Mass.: G. & C. Merriam Co., 1976.*

dictionary, the *Oxford Dictionary*, reports an average of twenty-eight separate meanings for each of the 500 most-used words in the English language.[8] No wonder we have trouble communicating with each other!

Context provides meaning.

If words really have no single meaning, how can managers make sense with them in communicating with employees? The answer lies in *context*, which is the environment surrounding the use of a word. For example, using the term "dummy" to describe another in an argument at the office may be derogatory, but its use to refer to the person serving as dummy in a social game of bridge is acceptable. We need to surround key words with the context of other words and symbols until their meanings are narrowed to fairly certain limits and potential confusion is minimized. Consequently, effective communicators are idea-centered rather than just word-centered. They know that *words* do not provide meaning, but *people* do.

Social cues

Context provides meaning to words partially through the cues people receive from their social environment, such as friends and coworkers. *Social cues* are the positive or negative bits of information that influence how people react to a communication. Examples of social cues are job titles, patterns of dress, and the historical use of words in a particular region of the country or ethnic group. Our susceptibility to being influenced by these cues varies, depending on the credibility of the source, our past exposure to the item, the ambiguity of the cue, and individual differences.[9] It is always important for us to be aware of social cues, because use of language with inadequate context creates a semantic smog. Like a real smog, it irritates our senses and interferes with the accuracy of our perceptions.

Readability

Since the meaning of words is difficult to impart even with the use of context, a reasonable assumption is that if these symbols can be simplified, the receiver will understand them more easily. Further, if symbols of the type that receivers *prefer* are used, the receivers will be even more receptive. This is the logic behind the idea of *readability*, which is the process of making writing and speech more understandable. Readability was popularized by Rudolf Flesch and others, who developed formulas that can be applied to magazines, bulletins, speeches, and other communications in order to judge their level of readability.[10]

Figure 4-4 offers some guides for more readable writing according to the Flesch formula. Then it applies these guides to show how the complex writing in the original paragraph can be made more simple in the second one. When you write your next report for a class, check it before submitting it to see if you have successfully practiced the ideas in Figure 4-4.

Much organizational literature that is sent to employees or to customers is more difficult than standard levels of readability. Employee handbooks, annual reports to stockholders, advertisements, and collective-bargaining contracts consistently rate "difficult" and "very difficult," beyond the level of satisfactory reading for typical adults. This has become even worse with the apparent trend

GUIDELINES TO READABLE WRITING

- **Use simple words and phrases, such as "improve" instead of "ameliorate" and "like" instead of "in a manner similar to that of."**
- **Use short and familiar words, such as "darken" instead of "obfuscate."**
- **Use personal pronouns, such as "you" and "them," if the style permits.**
- **Use illustrations, examples, and charts. These techniques are even better when they are tied to the reader's experiences.**
- **Use short sentences and paragraphs. Big words and thick reports may look impressive to people, but the communicator's job is to inform people, not impress them.**
- **Use active verbs, such as "The manager said . . ." rather than "It was said by the manager that. . . ."**
- **Use only necessary words. For example, in the sentence "Bad weather conditions prevented my trip," the word "conditions" is unnecessary. Say, "Bad weather prevented my trip."**

AN EXAMPLE

Original paragraph

There is a remote possibility that in the future there may be somewhat more jobs available. It is estimated that quite a lot of the improvement may be attributed to some of the more important industries and trades which normally become increasingly more active with the onset of warmer weather. In other words, it will be due mainly to the seasonal factors that always cause the overall basis of the rise and fall in the nation's economic activity, and even though there has been no noticeable strengthening of basic conditions, the general business situation is by far considerably better than most of the pessimistic economic forecasters have expected. According to extensive records compiled by the Bureau of Labor Statistics, the unemployment total in April was substantially below the 4½ million mark reached during March and the recent trend of applicants for jobless benefits suggests that the total of national unemployment is possibly now somewhat below 3 million employable persons who are available for work.

164 words
Flesch readability rating: *very difficult*.

Revised paragraph

The job picture looks brighter. Many of our industries increase production at this time of the year. The Bureau of Labor Statistics reports that national unemployment dropped from 4½ million in March to less than 3 million in April.

39 words
Flesch readability rating: *fairly easy to standard*.

FIGURE 4-4
Clear writing: Guidelines and an example
Source: *Adapted from* Readingease: The Key to Understanding, *Employee Relations Staff, General Motors Corporation, n.d.*

toward substituting complex phrases for simple ideas, such as calling a bathroom plunger a "hydroforce blast cup," and the progression from "tax hike" to "revenue enhancement" to "tax base erosion control!" Since the main purpose of communication is to be understood, there is a clear need to consider the needs of receivers and adapt our use of words to their level.

PICTURES A second type of symbol is the picture. Pictures are used to clarify word communication, which is their use in Figure 4-3. Organizations make extensive use of pictures, such as blueprints, progress charts, maps, visual aids in training programs, scale models of products, and similar devices. Pictures can provide powerful visual images, as suggested by the proverb "A picture is worth a thousand words." To be most effective, however, pictures should be combined with well-chosen words and actions to tell a complete story.

One organization, Lake Superior Paper Industries, planned to build a state-of-the-art paper mill. Because of the complexity of the technology involved, the $400 million construction cost, and the serious impact of any delays in the mill's construction, the company decided to build a three-dimensional room-sized model of the entire building and its contents. Company officials claimed that this one "picture," created at a cost of over $1 million, saved them many times that amount by letting designers and construction personnel see precisely where layout problems would occur before costly conflicts actually arose.

Actions have meaning.

ACTION (NONVERBAL COMMUNICATION) A third type of communication symbol is action, also known as *nonverbal communication.* Often people forget that what they do is a means of communication to the extent that it is interpreted by others. For example, a handshake and a smile have meaning. A raise in pay or being late for an appointment also has meaning.

Two significant points about action sometimes are overlooked. One point is that *failure to act* is an important way of communicating. A manager who fails to praise an employee for a job well done or fails to provide promised resources is sending a message to that person. Since we send messages both by action and inaction, we communicate almost all the time at work, *regardless of our intentions.*

Credibility gaps cause problems.

A second point is that action speaks louder than words in the long run. Managers who say one thing but do another will soon find that their employees "listen" mostly to what they do. When there is a difference between what someone says and does, we call that a *communication credibility gap.* The following illustration shows how a large credibility gap can result in a loss of confidence in a person.

Willie Beacon, the zone manager of a sales office, emphasized the idea that he depended upon his employees to help him do a good job because, as he stated it, "You salespeople are the ones in direct contact with the customer, and you get much valuable information and many useful suggestions." In most of his sales meetings he said that he always welcomed employees' ideas and suggestions. But here is how he translated his words into action. In those same sales meetings the schedule was so tight that by the time he finished his pep talk there was no time for anyone to present problems or ask questions, and he would hardly tolerate an interruption during his talk because he claimed this destroyed its "punch."

If a salesperson tried to present a suggestion in Willie's office, Willie usually began with, "Fine, I'm glad you brought in your suggestion." Before long, however, he would direct the conversation to some subject on his mind, or would have to keep an appointment, or would find some other reason for never quite getting to the suggestion. The few suggestions that did get through he rebuffed with, "Yeah, I

thought of that a long time ago, but it won't work." The eventual result was that he received no suggestions. His actions spoke louder than his words. His credibility gap was too large for employees to overcome.

Body language provides meaning.

An important part of nonverbal communication is *body language,* by which people communicate meaning to others with their bodies in interpersonal interaction. Body language is an important supplement to verbal communication in most parts of the world.

The face and the hands are especially important sources of body language in work situations. Examples are eye contact, eye movement, smiles and frowns, touching, and a furrowed brow. In one instance a manager frowned when an employee brought a suggestion, and the employee interpreted the frown as a rejection when in fact it was a headache. In another instance a smile at an inappropriate time was interpreted as a derisive sneer, and an argument erupted. Other types of body language are closeness, hip movements, and breathing rate.

DOWNWARD COMMUNICATION

Communication downward in an organization means that flow is from higher to lower authority. This usually is considered to be from management as a group to first-level employees, but much of it also is within the various levels of management (refer to Figure 4-1). Unfortunately, even with the help of elaborate techniques and skilled staff assistance, management has done a poor job on many occasions. Colorful booklets, expensive multimedia presentations, and elaborately planned employee meetings often fail to achieve employee understanding. The key to better communication lies not just in color, action, and electronic aids, but in more human-oriented managers who are sensitive to human needs, prepare carefully, and anticipate problems.

Prerequisites and problems

Four prerequisites

Part of management's failure has been that it has not prepared for effective communication. It has failed to lay a good foundation, so its communication "house" has been built upon sand. There are four cornerstones that act as prerequisites to a solid approach. First, managers need to *develop a positive communication attitude.* They must convince themselves that communication is an important part of their jobs, as research on managerial responsibilities convincingly shows. Second, managers must continually work to *get informed.* They need to seek out relevant information of interest to employees, share it, and help employees *feel* informed. Third, managers need to consciously *plan for communication,* and do this at the beginning of a course of action. Finally, *developing trust* between senders and receivers is important in all communication. If subordinates do not trust their superiors, they are not as likely to listen or to believe management's messages.

Consider the case of two employees from the same firm who were told by their manager not to discuss pay with each other, because the other one might be unhappy to learn of having a lower salary. Later, at a New Year's eve party, they started talking with each other about their salaries and soon discovered that they were earning exactly the same amount. How much will they trust their manager in the future?

COMMUNICATION OVERLOAD Managers sometimes operate with the philosophy that "more communication is better communication." They give employees enormous amounts of information until employees find that they are overwhelmed with data, but understanding is not improved. What happens is a *communication overload*, in which employees receive more communication inputs than they can process or than they need.[11] The key to better communication is quality, not quantity. It is possible to have better understanding with less total communication if it is of higher quality.

Quality preferable to quantity

Manager Nicolo Fumusa liked to ramble on and on. He thought that more was better. He buried his employees with mountains of information every time he talked with them. After a few experiences of this type, they avoided him. They had a communication overload but were deprived of understanding. One employee commented, "It takes him twenty minutes to say yes and thirty minutes to say no." Another observed philosophically, "You ask him what time it is, and he tells you how the clock works—but he still hasn't told you what time it is."

Nicolo's employees were annoyed and confused by his behavior. They complained to others, and some of them lost interest in their jobs. Management sensed the problem and tried to correct Nicolo, but he did not respond. After about a year, management decided to discharge him. He could not manage because he could not communicate.

ACCEPTANCE OF A COMMUNICATION We pointed out earlier (in the discussion of Figure 4-2) that acceptance of a message by the receiver was critical, or communication would break down. In the final analysis, there are several conditions that encourage acceptance of a communication, as follows:

- Acknowledgement of the legitimacy of the sender to send a message
- Perceived competence of the sender relative to the issue
- Trust in the sender as a leader and person
- Perceived credibility of the message received
- Acceptance of the tasks and goals that the communication is trying to accomplish
- Power of the sender to enforce sanctions on the receiver either directly or indirectly.

If overload can be prevented, and the likelihood of acceptance ensured through the use of these six conditions, then managers can turn their attention toward the satisfaction of four important communication needs of employees.

Communication needs

Employees at lower levels have a number of communication needs. Managers think that they understand these needs, but often their employees do not think so. This fundamental difference in perception tends to exist at each level in organizations, thereby making communication more difficult. It causes downward communicators to be overconfident and probably not to take enough care with their downward messages.

JOB INSTRUCTION One communication need of employees is instructions regarding their work. In a situation like this, managers secure better results if they state their instructions in terms of the objective requirements of the job, so that the instructions do not appear to be a personal wish.

Turnover is reduced by realistic job previews.

The need for objective information is especially important with employees in a new job or organization. Because their high expectations often conflict with reality, they quickly become dissatisfied. To prevent this, firms are using more *realistic job previews*, where job candidates are given a small sample of organizational reality. Just as a medical vaccination stimulates the body to develop natural resistance to a disease, the realistic preview minimizes the employee's unmet expectations by providing both positive and negative information about the potential work environment. When this method is used, turnover of new employees is reduced.[12]

The consequences of inadequate job instruction can be disastrous. A manufacturer of small tools hired a new sales representative, gave him a tour of the plant and a copy of the product catalog, and assigned him to a territory. In a few weeks the representative jubilantly sent in an order for 100,000 units of a multipurpose tool. Only then did the company realize it had neglected to tell him that that product was never promoted to its customers because the tool was priced well below the company's cost of producing it (so as to match a competitor's price). The end result was that the company lost over $10,000 on this one order!

Managers also need to adjust their communications according to the task needs of their receivers. For example, as the uncertainty of a task increases, there is a predictable need for increased information flow in order to maintain a comparable level of performance. Thus an employee performing a standardized, repetitive machine task needs little communication input about the task. On the other hand, an engineer working on a new product may require substantial communication input in order to perform successfully.

Performance is improved by feedback.

PERFORMANCE FEEDBACK Employees also need feedback about their performance. There are many reasons. It helps them know what to do and how well they are meeting their own goals. It shows that others are interested in what they are doing. Assuming that performance is satisfactory, it enhances one's self-image and feeling of competence. Generally, performance feedback leads to both improved performance and improved attitudes.

A review of eighteen studies that examined the effects of feedback on employee job performance provides supporting evidence.[13] In all cases performance increased, ranging from 6 to 125 percent. Where comprehensive measures were used, the median increase in productivity was 16 percent, and that translated into substantial cost savings for the employers.

Guides for giving feedback

Giving feedback is a challenging task for managers. Feedback is more likely to be accepted and cause some improvement when it is properly presented (see Figure 4-5). In general, it should focus on specific job behaviors, rely on objective data rather than perceptions and inferences, be given soon after a critical event, and be checked for understanding by the receiver. Overall, it has the greatest chance of success if it is genuinely desired and if the receiver is allowed to choose a new behavior from alternative recommendations offered.

In spite of the importance of performance feedback, many managers fail to provide enough of it. When asked, managers often report that they give their employees adequate feedback about their performance. However, their employees are likely to say that they are not receiving as much as they would like. Part of the solution may lie in training employees to *ask* for the feedback they want, instead of waiting for it.[14]

Importance of timeliness

NEWS Downward messages should reach employees as news rather than as a stale confirmation of what already has been learned from other sources. Some employers prepare daily recorded telephone messages that employees can receive by dialing a certain number. Messages can be changed during the day as new information becomes available. The systems usually are automatic, operating twenty-four hours daily, so that employees can call from their homes or elsewhere. Some systems are adjusted to allow telephone questions and

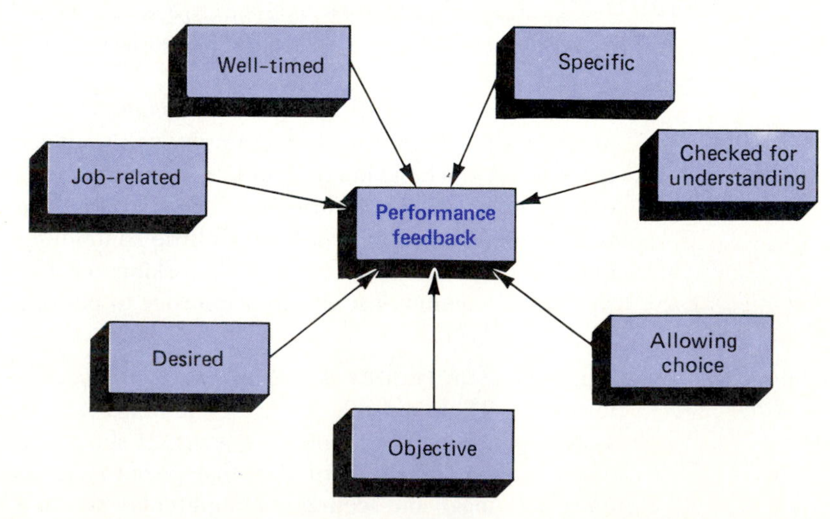

FIGURE 4-5 Guidelines for effective performance feedback

comments from employees. Where an answer is required, it is obtained and put on the system at a later date. In this manner two-way communication is established. Other in-house media include bulletin boards, inserts in pay envelopes, posters, and closed-circuit television.

SOCIAL SUPPORT Another communication need that employees have at work is *social support,* which is the perception that they are cared for, esteemed, and valued. When interpersonal warmth and trust are displayed by managers, there may be positive impacts on psychological and physical health, as well as job satisfaction and performance. It is interesting to note, though, that whether a manager communicates about task assignments, career subjects, personal matters, or performance feedback or responds to questions raised, employees report feeling a greater level of social support.[15] Apparently it is the *presence* of communication, not the topic, that is most important for satisfying this particular need.

UPWARD COMMUNICATION

If the two-way flow of information is broken by poor upward communication, management loses touch with employee needs and lacks sufficient information to make sound decisions. It is, therefore, unable to provide needed task and social support for employees. Management needs to "tune in" to employees in the same way a person with a radio tunes in. This requires initiative, positive action, sensitivity to weak signals, and adaptability to different channels of employee information. It primarily requires an awareness and belief that upward messages are important, as this illustration shows:

> **The need for upward communication is illustrated by the difficult experience of a manufacturing company that grew rapidly over two or three years. Despite work standards, supervisory pressure, and extensive downward communication, employee enthusiasm lagged and productivity declined.**
>
> **Finally, management brought in an interviewing team from the home office. Most complaints were petty ones, but there did seem to be a general feeling among older supervisors and employees that as the company grew, they had become more and more separated from higher management. They felt isolated and unable to discuss their problems with anyone. Gradually, they became alienated from management and tended to spread their alienation to the newer employees who were being hired as the company expanded.**
>
> **As soon as management discovered the basic problem, it was able to take corrective action. However, most of these difficulties could have been prevented if management had developed effective procedures early enough to encourage upward communication.**

Difficulties

Several problems plague upward communication, especially in larger, more complex organizations.[16] The first is *delay,* which is the unnecessarily slow

Delay

movement of information up to higher levels. Managers hesitate to take a problem upward because doing so implies an admission of failure; therefore each level delays the communication while trying to decide how to solve the problem. The second, and closely intertwined, factor is *filtering*. This partial screening out of information occurs because of the natural tendency for an employee to tell a superior only what the employee thinks the superior wants to hear, although there are also legitimate reasons for filtering.

Filtering

Short-circuiting

Sometimes, in an effort to avoid filtering, people *short-circuit* around their superior, which means that they skip one or more steps in the communication hierarchy. On the positive side, this reduces filtering and delays; on the other hand, it upsets those who are bypassed, so employers usually discourage it.

Need for response

Another problem revolves around an employee's legitimate *need for a response*. Since employees initiate upward communication, they are now the senders and they have strong expectations that feedback will occur (and soon!). If management provides a quick response, further upward messages will be encouraged. Conversely, lack of response suppresses future upward communications, as the following example indicates:

Managers of sales branches in one company received a memorandum that encouraged them to make suggestions to improve the firm's customer relations. Shortly after receiving the memo, Esther Helbring, a branch manager, asked the company to review a "fine-print" clause in one of its sales contracts because several customers had objected to it. Immediately after her letter, she received a telephone call from a member of higher management requesting clarification. One year later, she had received no further feedback and the clause had not been amended. She commented to the interviewer, "A response of this kind doesn't encourage further upward communication."

Upward-communication practices

A starting point for building better upward communication is to have a general policy stating what kinds of upward messages are desired. This could include areas where higher management is accountable, controversial topics, matters requiring supervisory advice, or any corporate policy exceptions or changes being recommended. In addition to policy statements, various practices are needed to improve upward communication. Counseling, grievance systems, consultive supervision, suggestion systems, job satisfaction surveys, and other practices are discussed in later chapters. Additional practices discussed at this point are listening, employee meetings, open-door policies, and participation in social groups.

Advantages

LISTENING Hearing is done with the ears, but listening requires use of the mind. Effective listening helps receivers get exactly the idea a sender intended. They then can make better decisions because their information inputs are better. Good listeners also save time because they learn more within a given period of time; and they learn about the person talking, as well as what the person is saying. Good listening is also good social manners; managers, peers, and subordinates think more of us when we listen to them attentively. Finally, our good listening encourages others to respond by listening to what we have to say. It is a form of behavior modeling for them.

Problems

Typical employees spend an average of more than 30 percent of their time listening, so it is an important part of their jobs. Two months later, however, they remember only about 25 percent of what was said. Listening comprehension can be improved by 25 percent or more through various training courses. Participants are taught to avoid daydreaming, focus on the speaker's objective, weigh the evidence, search for examples and clues to meaning, and use idle brain time to review what has already been said. Other suggestions for good listening are given in Figure 4-6.

A large number of organizations offer training programs in listening skills for their employees. One company, for example, sent a phonograph record on listening to all 90,000 employees and enrolled 10,000 of them in more formal classroom or programmed-instruction training courses. To accent the importance of listening, the company even wove it into a major advertising slogan (consistent with the Peters and Austin quote at the beginning of this chapter): "We understand how important it is to listen."[17]

Listening often is a weak link in the chain of two-way communication. Many managers do not actively work at listening well, which is a prerequisite for success.[18] A major reason is that, because the speaker is initiating action on the receiver, listening may threaten a person's self-image. Apparently, most of us would rather speak our own ideas than listen to what someone else says, even if that offers the promise of learning something! In spite of the difficulties of good listening, it is essential for understanding and is a skill that can be learned.

EMPLOYEE MEETINGS One useful practice to build upward communication is meeting with employees. In these meetings, employees are encouraged to talk about job problems, needs, and management practices that both help and interfere with job performance. The meetings attempt to probe in some depth the issues that are on the minds of employees. As a consequence, employee attitudes improve and turnover declines.

AN OPEN-DOOR POLICY An *open-door policy* is a statement that employees are encouraged to come to their supervisor or higher managers with any matter that concerns them. Usually employees are encouraged to see their supervisor first. If their problem is not resolved by the supervisor, then higher management may be approached. The goal is to remove blocks to upward communication. It is a worthy goal, but it is not easy to implement because there often are psychological barriers between managers and employees. Although the manager's door physically is open, psychological and social barriers exist that make employees reluctant to enter.[19] Some employees hesitate to be identified as lacking information or having a problem. Others are afraid they will incur their manager's disfavor.

Barriers may limit its use.

1 *Stop talking!*

You cannot listen if you are talking.
Polonius *(Hamlet):* "Give every man thine ear, but few thy voice."

2 *Put the talker at ease.*

Help a person feel free to talk.
This is often called a permissive environment.

3 *Show a talker that you want to listen.*

Look and act interested. Do not read your mail while someone talks.
Listen to understand rather than to oppose.

4 *Remove distractions.*

Don't doodle, tap, or shuffle papers.
Will it be quieter if you shut the door?

5 *Empathize with talkers.*

Try to help yourself see the other person's point of view.

6 *Be patient.*

Allow plenty of time. Do not interrupt a talker.
Don't start for the door or walk away.

7 *Hold your temper.*

An angry person takes the wrong meaning from words.

8 *Go easy on argument and criticism.*

These put people on the defensive, and they may "clam up" or become angry.
Do not argue. Even if you win, you lose.

9 *Ask questions.*

This encourages a talker and shows that you are listening.
It helps to develop points further.

10 *Stop talking!*

This is first and last, because all other guides depend on it.
You cannot do an effective listening job while you are talking.

□ Nature gave people two ears but only one tongue, which is a gentle hint that they should listen more than they talk.

□ Listening requires two ears, one for meaning and one for feeling.

□ Decision makers who do not listen have less information for making sound decisions.

FIGURE 4-6
Effective listening guides

An even more effective open door is for managers to walk through their own doors and get out among their people. In this way they will learn more than they ever will sitting in their offices.

Social settings for inputs

PARTICIPATION IN SOCIAL GROUPS Informal, casual recreational events furnish superb opportunities for unplanned upward communication. This spontaneous information sharing reveals true conditions better than most formal communications. There are departmental parties, sports events, bowling groups, hobby groups, picnics, and other employer-sponsored activities. Upward communication is not the primary purpose of these events, but it is an important by-product of them.

OTHER FORMS OF COMMUNICATION

Not all communication takes place directly down or up the organizational hierarchy; not all is formally prescribed by the firm; and not all of it takes place either at work or through face-to-face interaction. This concluding section will provide an overview of lateral communication, informal networks, and the impact of some electronic forms of communication.

Lateral communication

Cross-communication

Managers engage in a large amount of *lateral communication*, or *cross-communication*, which is communication across chains of command. It is necessary for job coordination with people in other departments. It also is done because people prefer the informality of lateral communication, rather than going up and down the more official chain of command. Lateral communication often is the dominant pattern within management.

An example is shown in Figure 4-7. It shows the communication patterns of an engineering department in a manufacturing company. The engineers actively communicate with many levels within their own firm both above and below them, but they also interact extensively with many departments outside their own chain of command, as shown on the left side of the chart. This is a realistic portrait of lateral communication, which is necessary in order to bring together the many resources within a firm.

Boundary spanners

Employees who play a major role in lateral communication are referred to as *boundary spanners*. Boundary-spanning individuals have strong communication links within their department, with people in other units, and often with the external community (see the right side of Figure 4-7). These connections with other units allow boundary spanners to gather large amounts of information, which they may filter or transfer to others. This gives them a source of status and potential power.

Networks

Networking

Whereas boundary spanners assume their roles through formal task responsibilities, much lateral communication takes place in less formal ways. A *network* is a group of people who develop and maintain contact to exchange information informally, usually about a shared interest. An employee who becomes active on a network is said to be *networking*. Although networks can

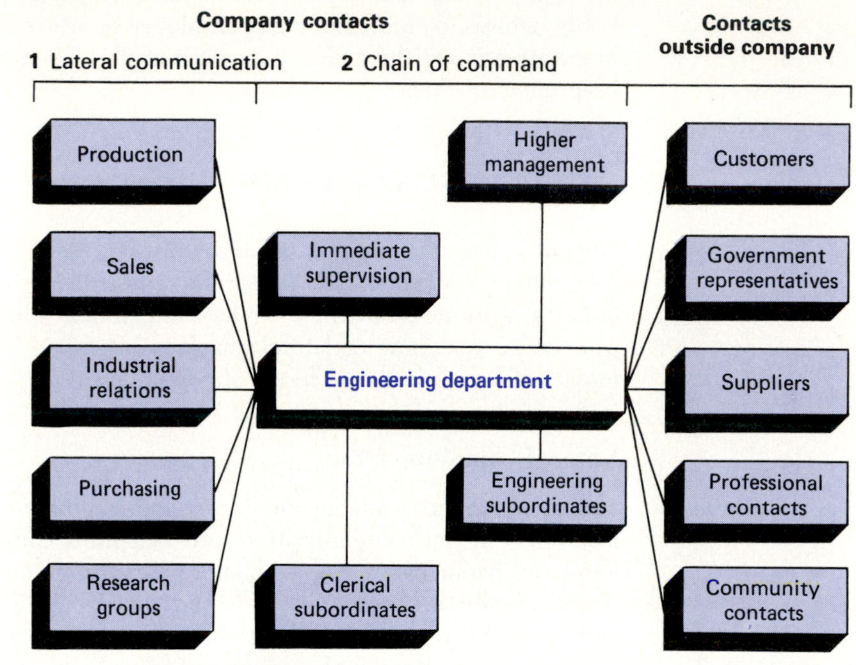

FIGURE 4-7 Communication patterns of an engineering department

be internal as well as external to a company, usually they are built around external interests, such as recreation, social clubs, professional groups, career interests, and trade meetings.[20]

An engineer in the company portrayed in Figure 4-7 may be in a network of research people who keep in touch at professional meetings and occasionally by telephone. She may also be an excellent golfer and be part of a golf network at a local country club. Therefore, she may know personally the top executives of several local corporations, as well as other influential people in the area. Some of her networks may be business-related, some might be career-related, and some will be purely social.

Networks help broaden the interests of employees, keep them more informed about new technical developments, and make them more visible to others. Networks help employees learn who knows what and even who knows those who know. As a result, an alert networker can gain access to influential people and centers of power by drawing upon common backgrounds, bonds of friendship, complementary organizational roles, or community ties. By obtaining job-related information and developing productive working relationships through effective networks, employees gain valuable skills and can perform their jobs better. Suggestions for developing networks are provided in Figure 4-8.

1 Inventory your personal resources, so you know what you have to offer others.

2 Clarify your purpose for establishing or joining a network.

3 Join significant community organizations and *contribute* to them.

4 Initiate contacts with people whenever you can find (or create) a reason.

5 Share news, information, and ideas with others, thereby creating an obligation for them to reciprocate.

6 Seek out responsibilities that will bring you into contact with key people.

7 Demonstrate to other networkers that you can be trusted with confidential information.

8 Identify the key members of your network—those who have the most influence, connections, and willingness to help.

9 Don't hesitate to tap into members of your network for general advice, career contacts, and other useful information.

FIGURE 4-8 Suggestions for developing a personal network

ELECTRONIC MAIL The impact of computers on communication offers both great promise and some problems as well. Two applications of the computer—electronic mail and telecommuting—will be introduced here.

Electronic networks

Electronic mail is a computer-based communication system that allows you to send a message to one or more people almost instantaneously.[21] There it is stored until the recipients turn on their computers and read the message at their convenience, at which time they can respond in the same manner. Some electronic mail systems can send messages in various modes (such as a letter to one correspondent who doesn't have a computer), and others can translate the message into a foreign language. Of particular interest to some firms is *electronic conferencing,* in which a group of people in various locations can each send comments to the initiator of the process, and also to all other participants as well. Each person can thus build on the ideas of the others, and this in itself is a form of networking. The primary advantage of electronic systems is their dramatic speed; the major disadvantage is the loss of face-to-face contact.

TELECOMMUTING A member of a Chicago law firm maintains a permanent residence at a ski resort community in Colorado. An information processing operator works half time at home and half time at a downtown bank. An author in a California beach house, working against a deadline, finishes a manuscript just before 8 A.M. and has a copy on the editor's desk minutes later, about the time she steps into the ocean for a swim. These people are all engaged in *telecommuting,* or the accomplishment of all or part of their work at home through computer links to their offices.

Preliminary evidence on the effects of telecommuting highlight several advantages.[22] Freed from the distractions of the workplace, lost transportation time, and high commuting costs, many employees may be inclined to even contribute a bit more time and effort in exchange for the comfort of working in their homes. At-home programmers working for Control Data, for example, were judged to be 15 to 25 percent more productive than their counterparts at the office.

Optimists predict that there could be 10 million Americans working at home by telecommuting early in the twenty-first century. The reasonableness of that estimate will depend largely on managers' ability to overcome a number of substantial problems that arise from telecommuting. These include the possibility of being overlooked at promotion time, the risk of getting burned out (see Chapter 20) from the convenience of putting in more hours daily, and especially the social isolation that at-home employees may feel.

Telecommuting problems

As a consequence of this isolation, telecommuters may be out of touch with their regular networks, unable to experience intellectual stimulation from their peers, and insulated from most sources of social support. The emotional costs may be unacceptably high unless the employer carefully screens participants, briefs them in advance so they know what to expect, and makes adaptations so they will still have interaction opportunities. Clearly, technological progress in communication is not easily gained without some human costs and organizational effort.

SUMMARY

Organizations need effective communication—downward, upward, and laterally. It is the transfer of information and understanding from one person to another person. The two-way communication process consists of these eight steps: develop an idea, encode, transmit, receive, decode, accept, use, and provide feedback.

To overcome personal, physical, and semantic barriers, managers must pay close attention to communication symbols, such as words, pictures, and nonverbal actions. This requires study and use of semantics—the science of meaning—to encourage understanding.

Managers play a key role in downward and upward communication, sometimes even delaying or filtering the flow of information. They have many tools available to use, such as providing performance feedback and social support, or establishing open-door policies and holding employee meetings. Listening, however, remains one of the most powerful tools. Networks have become popular ways for employees to find out what is going on around them, while the rapid acceptance of computers has made possible electronic mail systems and telecommuting for some employees.

Terms and concepts for review

Communication process
Cognitive dissonance
Ecological control
Semantics
Social cues
Nonverbal communication
Realistic job previews
Performance feedback
Social support
Open-door policy
Boundary spanners
Networks
Electronic mail
Telecommuting

Discussion questions

1 Think of a job that you have had and a situation in which the communication failed or was ineffective. Discuss how the communication process applied in this situation and where (which of the eight steps) the breakdown occurred.
2 Discuss the barriers to communication that exist when you discuss a subject with your instructor in the classroom.
3 Select a situation in which you made a wrong inference, analyze how the misinterpretation was made, and discuss how you might avoid similar misinterpretations in the future. How important is feedback as an aid to avoiding inference problems?
4 Observe your own behavior, and discuss what nonverbal communication habits you typically use. Are there some behaviors that you have that may mislead receivers?
5 How would you communicate the following?
   a A promotion to one of your employees
   b Criticism of one of your employees for work poorly done
   c Instructions for operation of a simple office machine
   d An announcement to shop machinists that sales dropped 15 percent during the last quarter and some employees may need to be laid off
6 Visit an instructor's office, and record your feelings of relative comfort there. What physical elements in the office contributed to your reaction?
7 Examine the "effective listening guides" in Figure 4-6. Which ones do you practice best? Which ones could you improve upon?
8 Think of a part-time or full-time job that you have had.
   a Discuss any communication overload you experienced.
   b Discuss how well management handled downward communication to you.
   c Explain any upward-communication difficulties that you had and what you did to try to overcome them.
9 What networks do you belong to? Explain how you became a part of them, and what they have done for you. What are your future networking plans?
10 Assess electronic mail in the context of this chapter. How does it fit with the eight steps of the communication process? What barriers are most likely to arise when it is used? How can they be overcome, or at least minimized?

Incident

THE EARLY WORK SCHEDULE

Mabel Thomas was employed to work with the food service of Community Hospital. She was married but had no children. The job for which she was employed required that she work two days a week from 5 A.M. to 2 P.M. The other three days she worked the regular day food schedule from 8:30 A.M. to 5:30 P.M. When she was employed, either she failed to hear information about the early work schedule or the employment clerk forgot to tell her. She feels sure that if the early schedule had been mentioned to her, she would have heard it, because under those conditions she would not have taken the job.

During the first two weeks the job required Thomas to work the regular day shift in order to have an instructor show her how to do the job; so Thomas thought she was on the regular day shift. She vaguely remembers that near the end of her first two weeks her supervisor mentioned something to her about beginning her regular schedule, but she did not understand what the supervisor meant and she did not inquire further. The result was that Thomas failed to report to work on the early schedule on the required day. When she did report for work at the regular hour of 8:30 A.M., her supervisor criticized her for lack of responsibility. Thomas said she could not work the early shift for family reasons and resigned.

Question

Analyze the communication blockages in this case. Discuss ideas such as upward and downward communication, listening, feedback, and inference. Then explain how you would handle the employment and probationary work period for Thomas.

Experiential exercise

ONE-WAY COMPARED WITH TWO-WAY COMMUNICATION

The instructor can set up a classroom experiment in which both one-way and two-way communication are tried for performance of some task or communication of a detailed idea not familiar to students. One of the most popular tasks is to have a handout showing rectangles organized in a certain way. Two or more students are selected as receivers, and one or more people are selected as communicators of the layout of the rectangles. The handout is made available to class members and communicators *but not to receivers.* Receivers stand at the front of the room trying to draw on a chalkboard the arrangement described by the communicator. (For each communication it is desirable to have two or more receivers so that their arrangements of the rectangles can be compared.)

For the one-way method, the communicator faces the class and does not look at the figures the receiver is drawing, because that would be a form of feedback. The two-way method may be with the communicator not observing the figures (as by telephone) or with observation of the figures. The figure shown on the next page is a sample arrangement, but instructors should select their own so that it is not available to the class ahead of time.

Following one-way communication, senders and receivers are questioned about their feelings, and the class discusses the advantages and disadvantages of the one-way process. Students should also identify the ways in which managers use one-way communication, and generate some suggestions for making it work better if they need to use that method.

The same procedure is then repeated (with different figures) through the use of two-way communication. This could be simply with verbal exchange, such as through the use of a telephone while not observing the developing figure, or it could be done with conversation while directly watching the emerging figure.

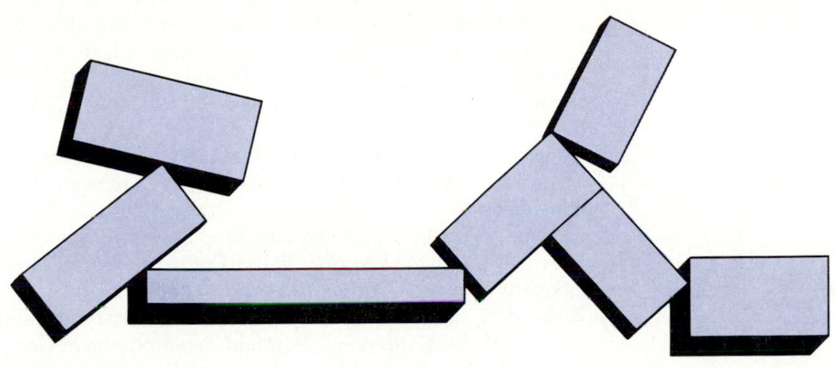

The same analysis by the class should follow this phase, with the relative effectiveness of one-way versus two-way communication then discussed.

References

1 Jan Carlzon, "Moments of Truth," *Success*, May 1987, pp. 53. (The article is adapted from Jan Carlzon, *Moments of Truth*, Hagerstown, Md.: Ballinger Publishing Company, 1987.)

2 Thomas J. Peters and Nancy K. Austin, "Managing by Walking Around," *California Management Review*, Fall 1985, p. 13. (The article is an excerpt from the authors' book, *A Passion for Excellence*, New York: Random House, Inc., 1985.)

3 J. David Pincus, "Communication Satisfaction, Job Satisfaction, and Job Performance," *Human Communication Research*, Spring 1986, pp. 395–419.

4 For a classic research study of message loss within management, see Keith Davis, "Success of Chain-of-Command Oral Communication in a Manufacturing Management Group," *Academy of Management Journal*, December 1968, pp. 379–387.

5 A more complex model of the communication process is in David P. Campbell and Dale Level, "A Black Box Model of Communications," *Journal of Business Communications*, Summer 1985, pp. 37–47.

6 John W. Newstrom and Steven A. Rubenfeld, "Feedback and Disclosure: Avenues for Management Development," *Training and Management Development Methods*, vol. 1, 1987, pp. 2.09–2.16.

7 Mark L. Knapp, Laura Stafford, and John A. Daly, "Regrettable Messages: Things People Wish They Hadn't Said," *Journal of Communication*, Autumn 1986, pp. 40–58.

8 William M. Sattler, "Talking Ourselves into Communication Crises," *Michigan Business Review*, July 1957, p. 30.

9 A study of social cues is Gary J. Blau, "The Effect of Source Competence on Worker Attitudes," *Journal of Applied Communication Research*, Spring 1986, pp. 20–36. Other articles relating social cues to job design are Mary D. Zalesny and Richard V. Farace, "A Field Study of Social Information Processing," *Human Communication Research*, Winter 1986, pp. 268–290; and G. Salancik and J. Pfeffer, "A Social Information Processing Approach to Job Attitudes and Task Design," *Administrative Science Quarterly*, June 1978, pp. 224–253.

10 Rudolf Flesch, *The Art of Readable Writing*, rev. ed., New York: Harper & Row,

Publishers, Inc., 1974. (The earlier edition was published in 1949.) Interest in readability continues to be strong; see, for example, Sherry Sweetnam, "How to Organize Your Thoughts for Better Communication," *Personnel*, March 1986, pp. 38–40; and Mary Ellen Campbell and Robert W. Hollmann, "ABC = Auditing Business Communications," *Business Horizons*, September–October 1985, pp. 60–64.

11 Charles A. O'Reilly III, "Individuals and Information Overload in Organizations: Is More Necessarily Better?" *Academy of Management Journal*, December 1980, pp. 684–696.

12 Interested readers may wish to see, however, James A. Breaugh, "Realistic Job Previews: A Critical Appraisal and Future Research Directions," *Academy of Management Review*, October 1983, pp. 612–619.

13 Richard E. Kopelman, "Improving Productivity through Objective Feedback: A Review of the Evidence," *National Productivity Review*, Winter 1982, pp. 43–55. For examples of specific studies, see P. Christopher Earley, "Trust, Perceived Importance of Praise and Criticism, and Work Performance: An Examination of Feedback in the United States and England," *Journal of Management*, Winter 1986, pp. 457–473; and Paulette A. McCarty, "Effects of Feedback on the Self-Confidence of Men and Women," *Academy of Management Journal*, December 1986, pp. 840–847.

14 The subject of feedback-seeking behavior is reported in Susan J. Ashford and L. L. Cummings, "Proactive Feedback Seeking: The Instrumental Use of the Information Environment," *Journal of Occupational Psychology*, vol. 58, 1985, pp. 67–79; and Susan J. Ashford and L. L. Cummings, "Feedback as an Individual Resource: Personal Strategies of Creating Information," *Organizational Behavior and Human Performance*, vol. 32, 1983, pp. 370–398.

15 Sandra L. Kirmeyer and Thung-Rung Lin, "Social Support: Its Relationship to Observed Communication with Peers and Superiors," *Academy of Management Journal*, March 1987, pp. 138–151; and Larry E. Penley and Brian Hawkins, "Studying Interpersonal Communication in Organizations: A Leadership Application," *Academy of Management Journal*, June 1985, pp. 309–326.

16 A study of upward- and downward-communication effectiveness is reported in Allan D. Frank, "Trends in Communication: Who Talks to Whom?" *Personnel*, December 1985, pp. 41–47.

17 John Louis DiGaetani, "The Sperry Corporation and Listening: An Interview," *Business Horizons*, March–April 1982, pp. 34–39.

18 Listening is important in sales, health care, and many other fields. See Jeremy Main, "How to Sell by Listening," *Fortune*, Feb. 4, 1985; and Edward Krupat, "A Delicate Imbalance," *Psychology Today*, November 1986, pp. 22–26. Suggestions are offered in Cynthia Hamilton and Brian H. Kleiner, "Steps to Better Listening," *Personnel Journal*, February 1987, pp. 20–21.

19 Charles E. Beck and Elizabeth A. Beck, "The Manager's Open Door and the Communication Climate," *Business Horizons*, January–February 1986, pp. 15–19.

20 Two readable reports on networks are Duncan Maxwell Anderson, "The Club," *Success*, May 1987, pp. 54–60 (a report on Yale's Skull and Bones society); and Steve Fishman, "The Art of Networking," *Success*, July–August 1985, pp. 36–43.

21 The process, applications, and software are discussed in Tess Galati, "Electronic Communication: Implications for Training," *Training and Development Journal*, October 1986, pp. 42–46; and Stephen W. Hartman and Joel G. Siegel, "Telecommunications and the Human Resource Professional," *Personnel*, December 1986, pp. 13–17.

22 Carol-Ann Hamilton, "Telecommuting," *Personnel Journal*, April 1987, pp. 90–101; see also Sandra D. Atchison, "These Top Executives Work Where They Play," *Business Week*, Oct. 27, 1986, pp. 132, 134.

For additional reading

Keen, Peter G. W., *Business without Bounds: Telecommunications and Business Strategy*, Hagerstown, Md.: Ballinger Publishing Co., 1986.

Mueller, Robert K., *Corporate Networking: Building Channels for Information and Influence*, New York: Macmillan Company (Free Press), 1986.

Ramsower, R. M., *Telecommuting: The Organizational and Behavioral Effects of Working at Home*, Ann Arbor, Mich.: UMI Research Press, 1985.

Sigband, Norman B., and Arthur H. Bell, *Communication for Management and Business*, Glenview, Ill.: Scott, Foresman and Company, 1986.

Steil, Lyman K., Joanne Summerfield, and George deMare, *Listening: It Can Change Your Life*, New York: John Wiley & Sons, Inc., 1983.

Vervest, Peter, *Electronic Mail and Message Handling*, Westport, Conn.: Quorum Books, 1985.

PART 2

CHAPTER
5

Mainsprings of motivation

Motivation says do this because it's very meaningful for me to do it.

FREDERICK HERZBERG[1]

If you are like a wheelbarrow, going no farther than you are pushed, then do not apply for work here.

Sign at factory employment gate many years ago[2]

CHAPTER OBJECTIVES

To understand

Motivational drives

Primary and secondary needs

Need category systems

Motivational and maintenance factors

Behavior modification

Types of reinforcement schedules

The president of a chain of clothing stores had a problem. The company was about to add ten new stores to its ninety outlets as part of a corporate expansion program, and he had plenty to worry about. Then his key administrative assistant walked in and announced that she hated her job. "What else could she want?" he thought, as he invited her to sit down and talk about her needs and aspirations. "Could it be job security, or better working conditions, or the chance to learn and grow?" he mused. He resolved to listen carefully to her explanation, and search for a way to motivate her.[2]

In many ways, the whole book is about situations like this. The president needs to examine the organizational culture that has been created; he will have a chance to test his listening skills; and he will need to manage the dramatic changes that the organization is experiencing. However, his immediate task is to understand what motivates the administrative assistant, and the next two chapters will help him do that. As the Herzberg quote at the beginning of this chapter suggests, he will need to discover what new tasks would be meaningful *for her*.

A MODEL OF MOTIVATION

Although a few human activities occur without motivation, nearly all conscious behavior is motivated, or caused. It requires no motivation to grow hair, but getting a haircut does. Eventually, anyone will fall asleep without motivation (although parents with young children may doubt this), but going to bed is a conscious act requiring motivation. A manager's job is to identify employees' drives and needs, and channel their behavior toward task performance.

Diagramed very simply, the role of motivation in performance is summarized in the model of motivation in Figure 5-1. Internal needs and drives create tensions that are modified by one's environment. For example, the need for food produces a tension of hunger. The hungry person then examines the surroundings to see which foods (external incentives) are available to satisfy that hunger. Since environment affects one's appetite for particular kinds of food, a South Seas native may want roast fish, while a Colorado rancher prefers broiled steak. Both persons are ready to try to achieve their goal, but they will seek different foods to satisfy their needs. This is an example of both individual differences and cultural influences in action.

E* × *A* = *P

As we saw in the formulas in Chapter 1, performance (*P*) is a product of effort (*E*) and ability (*A*), within a context of the opportunity (such as the right tools and appropriate goals) to perform. When an employee is productive and the organization takes note of it, rewards are distributed, and this results in satisfaction of the employee's original needs and drives. Although there are no simple answers to the motivational question, an important starting point lies in understanding employee needs. Several traditional approaches to classifying drives and needs are presented first, followed by a discussion of a systematic way of modifying employee behavior through the use of rewards that satisfy these needs. Goal setting will also be discussed.

FIGURE 5-1
A model of motivation

MOTIVATIONAL DRIVES

Each person tends to develop certain motivational drives as a product of the cultural environment in which that person lives, and these affect the way people view their jobs and approach their lives. Much of the interest in these patterns of motivation was generated by the research of David C. McClelland of Harvard University.[3] He developed a classification scheme highlighting three of the more dominant drives and pointed out their significance to motivation. His studies revealed that people's motivational drives reflect elements of the culture in which they grow up—their family, school, church, and books. In most nations, one or two of the motivational patterns tend to be strong among the workers because they have grown up with similar backgrounds. In addition to McClelland's discussion of the drives for achievement, affiliation, and power, the competence motive (see Figure 5-2) is an important factor in current attempts to attain high-quality products and services.

Four drives

Achievement motivation

Achievement motivation is a drive some people have to overcome challenges and obstacles in the pursuit of goals. An individual with this drive wishes to develop and grow, and advance up the ladder of success. Accomplishment is important for its own sake, not for the rewards that accompany it.

Characteristics of achievers

A number of characteristics define achievement-oriented employees. They work harder when they perceive that they will receive personal credit for their efforts, when there is only moderate risk of failure, and when they receive specific feedback about their past performance. As managers, they tend to trust

Achievement **A drive to overcome challenges, advance, and grow**

Affiliation **A drive to relate to people effectively**

Competence **A drive to do high-quality work**

Power **A drive to influence people and situations**

FIGURE 5-2
Motivational drives

their subordinates, share and receive ideas openly, set higher goals, and expect that their employees will also be oriented toward achievement.[4]

Red Auerbach, who has been coach, general manager, and president of the perennial world-champion Boston Celtics professional basketball team, had a simple answer when asked how he motivated his players. It revolved around the pride of excellence, the pride of winning, the pride of being part of the greatest team in the world. It was the challenge of seeking, and the joy of wearing, the championship ring as a symbol of their collective achievement.[5]

Affiliation motivation

Comparing achievement and affiliation drives

Affiliation motivation is a drive to relate to people on a social basis. Comparisons of achievement-motivated employees with affiliation-motivated employees will illustrate how the two patterns influence behavior. Achievement-oriented people work harder when their supervisor provides a detailed evaluation of their work behavior. But persons with affiliation motives work better when they are complimented for their favorable attitudes and cooperation. Achievement-motivated people select assistants who are technically capable, with little regard for personal feelings about them; however, those who are affiliation-motivated tend to select friends to surround them. They receive inner satisfactions from being with friends, and they want the job freedom to develop these relationships.

Competence motivation

Competence motivation is a drive to do high-quality work. Competence-motivated employees seek job mastery, develop problem-solving skills, and strive to be innovative. Most important, they profit from their experiences. In general, they tend to perform good work because of the inner satisfaction they feel from doing it and the esteem they gain from others.[6]

Competence-motivated people also expect high-quality work from their associates and may become impatient if those working with them do poor work. In fact, their drive for good work may be so great that they tend to overlook the importance of human relationships on the job or the need to maintain reasonable levels of output.

For example, Joleen is a commercial artist who feels good about herself and receives respect from others when she creates an excellent design. However, she infuriates her supervisor when she misses her deadlines and she antagonizes her coworkers when she fails to socialize with them. Clearly, her competence drive is stronger than her affiliation need.

Power motivation

Power motivation is a drive to influence people and change situations. Power-motivated people wish to create an impact on their organizations and are willing to take risks to do so.[7] Once this power is obtained, it may be used either constructively or destructively.

Institutional vs. personal power

Power-motivated people make excellent managers if their drives are for institutional power instead of personal power. Institutional power is the need to influence others' behavior for the good of the whole organization. In other words, these people seek power through legitimate means, rise to leadership positions through successful performance, and therefore are accepted by others. However, if an employee's drives are toward personal power, that person tends to be an unsuccessful organizational leader.

MANAGERIAL APPLICATION OF THE DRIVES Knowledge of motivational drives helps managers understand the work attitudes of each employee. They can then deal with employees differently according to the strongest motivational drive in each. For example, an achievement-motivated employee can be assigned a job, accompanied by an explanation of its challenges. A competence-motivated employee could be assigned a similar job with emphasis on its requirements for high-quality work. In this way, the supervisor communicates with each employee according to that particular person's needs. As one employee said, "My supervisor talks to me in my language."

HUMAN NEEDS

When a machine malfunctions, people recognize that it needs something. Assume that a machine will not grind a piece of metal to a close enough tolerance. Perhaps it needs oil. Or maybe a nut is loose. First the operator tries to find the trouble. Then the operator asks the supervisor for help. Finally the supervisor calls a maintenance mechanic or an engineer, and so on, until the cause of the problem is found and the machine is put back into working order.

All the people who tried to find the causes of the breakdown did so (or should have done so) in an analytical manner based upon their knowledge of the operations and needs of the machine. It would be wasteful to tighten nuts and oil gears haphazardly in the hope that the trouble could be found. Such action might aggravate the malfunction.

Suppose that the machine operator "malfunctions" by talking back to the supervisor in a way that borders on insubordination. The supervisor may want to reprimand the operator without analyzing the situation, but this is no better than haphazard machine repair. Like the machine, the operator who malfunctions does so because of definite causes that may be related to needs. In order for improvement to occur, the operator requires skilled and professional care just as the machine does. If we treated (maintained) people as well as we do expensive machines, we would have more satisfied and productive workers.

Types of needs

Primary needs

There are various ways to classify needs. A simple one is (1) basic physical needs, called *primary* needs, and (2) social and psychological needs, called *secondary* needs. The physical needs include food, water, sex, sleep, air, and a reasonably comfortable temperature. These needs arise from the basic requirements of life and are important for survival of the human race. They are, therefore, virtually universal among people, but they vary in intensity from one person to another. For example, a child needs much more sleep than an older person.

Needs also are conditioned by social practice. If it is customary to eat three meals a day, then a person tends to become hungry for three, even though two might be adequate. If a coffee hour is introduced in the morning, then that becomes a habit of appetite satisfaction as well as a social need.

Secondary needs

Secondary needs are more vague because they represent needs of the mind and spirit rather than of the physical body. Many of these needs are developed as one matures. Examples are rivalry, self-esteem, sense of duty, self-assertion, giving, belonging, and receiving affection. The secondary needs are the ones that complicate the motivational efforts of managers. Nearly any action that management takes will affect secondary needs; *therefore, management planning should consider the effect of any proposed action on the secondary needs of employees.*

Variations in needs

Secondary needs vary among people much more than primary needs. They even exist as opposites in two different persons. One person has a need for self-assertion and is aggressive with people. A second person, on the other hand, prefers to be submissive and yields to others' aggressions. Needs also change according to time and circumstance.

Analysis of behavior would be simple if a person's actions at a given time were the result of one need and one alone, but this is seldom the case. Needs of all types and intensities influence one another so that a worker's motivation at any single time is a combination of many different forces. Furthermore, some needs are so hidden that an employee's supervisor cannot recognize them. This fact alone makes motivation difficult. For example, dissatisfied workers often say that their dissatisfaction is caused by something easy to identify, such as low wages, but their real problem is something else. Consequently, even when management pays their wage request, they remain dissatisfied.

In summary, secondary needs:

- Are strongly conditioned by experience
- Vary in type and intensity among people
- Are subject to change within any individual
- Work in groups rather than alone
- Are often hidden from conscious recognition
- Are vague feelings instead of specific physical needs

■ Influence behavior (It is said that "we are logical only to the extent that our feelings let us be.")

Whereas the four motivational drives identified earlier were not grouped in any particular pattern, three major classifications of human needs have attempted to do so. At least implicitly, Maslow, Herzberg, and Alderfer each build on the distinction between primary and secondary needs. Also, there are some similarities among the three approaches as well as important differences worth noting. All of them help to create an important basis for the more advanced motivational models to be discussed later.

Maslow's hierarchy of needs

Human needs are not of equal strength, but generally emerge in a certain priority. As the primary needs become reasonably well satisfied, a person places more emphasis on the secondary needs. A need hierarchy by A. H. Maslow that focused on five levels, as shown in Figure 5-3, has received widespread attention and sparked considerable controversy.[8] Need levels 1 (physical) and 2 (security) are typically called *lower-order needs,* and levels 3 (social), 4 (esteem), and 5 (self-actualization) are called *higher-order needs.*

LOWER-ORDER NEEDS The first-level needs involve basic survival. In the typical work situation they rarely dominate because they are reasonably well satisfied. Only an occasional experience, such as two days without sleep or a crumb in one's windpipe, reminds one of the essential nature of basic body needs.

Physical needs

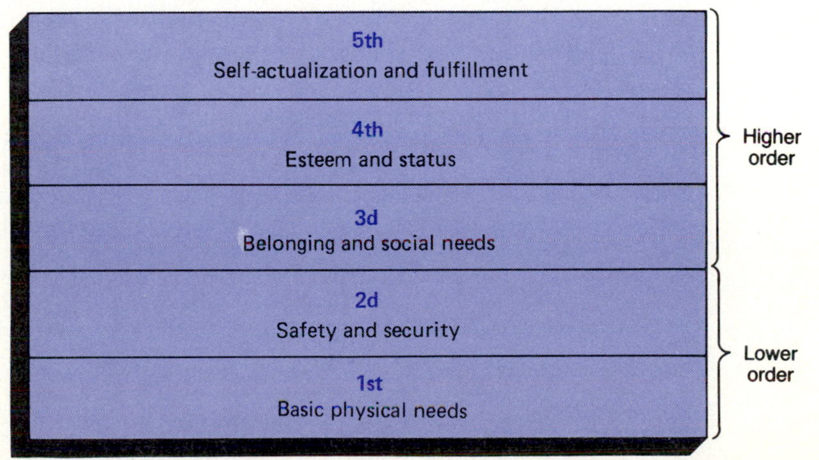

FIGURE 5-3
Hierarchy of human needs according to Maslow

Security needs

People must labor to satisfy their physiological needs, but when these are satisfied to some degree they wish to satisfy other needs. The need level that next tends to dominate is safety and security. It works somewhat as follows. Having met their basic physical needs today, people want some assurance that these needs will be met tomorrow and thereafter. Accordingly they build walls around primitive cities, build granaries for food storage, or establish pension programs. They want bodily safety as well as economic security. Security essentially ensures that primary needs will be met tomorrow and for as long thereafter as possible. In reality, then, second-level needs relate to those at the first level.

Because of individual differences, people seek different amounts of security, but virtually all people have some need for security.[9] People also vary in the ways in which they try to provide their security, as illustrated by the approaches of two sales representatives in a computer office.

One employee tried to obtain his security by spending extra hours writing long reports on the analog control line to ensure that he would be considered so expert in this field that the company could not do without him. The other employee reacted differently, going to school at night to learn about digital theory and application, which was a new product area with the company. She felt that she could best be secure by becoming knowledgeable in the new control equipment. Thus two people reacted differently under the same circumstances and in relation to the same needs.

Social needs

Esteem needs

Self-actualization needs

HIGHER-ORDER NEEDS According to Maslow, there are three levels of higher-order needs. Third-level needs concern love, belonging, and social involvement. Since people spend many of their waking hours at work in a social environment, some of their social needs can (and should) be met there. The needs at the fourth level include those for esteem and status. Employees need to feel that they are worthy, and to believe that others think they are worthy (which gives them status). The fifth-level need is self-actualization, which means becoming all that one is capable of becoming, using one's skills to the fullest, and stretching talents to the maximum.

Will Steger, a rugged outdoorsman, led a party of adventurers on dogsleds to the north pole without being resupplied during the entire thousand-mile journey. It was dangerous due to open strips of water that needed crossing; it was also physically exhausting (the supply-laden sleds initially weighed 1350 pounds each and had to be unloaded and reloaded several times as the group struggled over pressure ridges). The trip was emotionally draining (because of the fear of accidents, the dwindling food, the lack of sleep, the intense cold). When the six members of the party achieved their goal, they were exhilarated, for they knew they had used their individual and group resources to the highest degree possible.

Even after reaching the fifth level, there is room for further progress. The higher-order needs, in particular, can never be fully satisfied, for people will perpetually want more. The highest-paid athletes seek to renegotiate their contracts for more money; the executive seeks new status symbols; and the explorer searches for new and more demanding adventures to pursue. The implication for managers is this: *need satisfaction is a continuous problem for organizations.* It cannot be permanently solved by satisfying a particular need today.

INTERPRETING THE HIERARCHY OF NEEDS Maslow's need-hierarchy model essentially says that people have needs that they wish to satisfy, and gratified needs are not as strongly motivating as unmet needs. That is, *employees are more enthusiastically motivated by what they are seeking than by what they already have.* They may, of course, react protectively to try to keep what they already have, but they move forward with enthusiasm only when they are seeking something else.

Contributions

Interpreted in this way, the Maslow hierarchy of needs has had a powerful impact on contemporary managers, and offers some useful ideas for helping managers think about motivating their employees. As a result of their widespread familiarity with the model, they are more likely to identify employee needs, recognize that they may be different across employees, offer satisfaction for the particular needs, and realize that giving more of the same reward may have a diminishing impact on motivation. These are significant contributions indeed.

Limitations

Despite these benefits, the Maslow model has many limitations, and it has been sharply criticized. As a philosophical framework, it has been difficult to study and has not been fully verified. Research has not supported the presence of all five need levels as unique, nor has the five-step progression from lowest to highest need levels been established. There is, however, some evidence that unless the two lower-order needs (physical and security) are basically satisfied, employees will not be greatly concerned with higher-order needs.[10] The evidence for a more limited number of need levels is consistent with each of the next two models to be discussed.

Herzberg's two-factor model

On the basis of research with engineers and accountants, Frederick Herzberg developed a two-factor model of motivation in the 1950s.[11] He asked his subjects to think of a time when they felt especially good about their jobs and a time when they felt especially bad about their jobs. He also asked them to describe the conditions that led to those feelings. Herzberg found that employees named different types of conditions for good and bad feelings. That is, if a feeling of achievement led to a good feeling, the lack of achievement was rarely given as cause for bad feelings. Instead, some other factor such as company policy was given as a cause of bad feelings.

Herzberg concluded that two separate factors influenced motivation. Prior to that time people assumed that motivation and lack of motivation were merely opposites of one factor on a continuum. Herzberg upset the traditional view by stating that certain job factors primarily dissatisfy employees when the conditions are absent. However, as shown in Figure 5-4, their presence generally brings employees only to a neutral state. The factors are not strongly motivat-

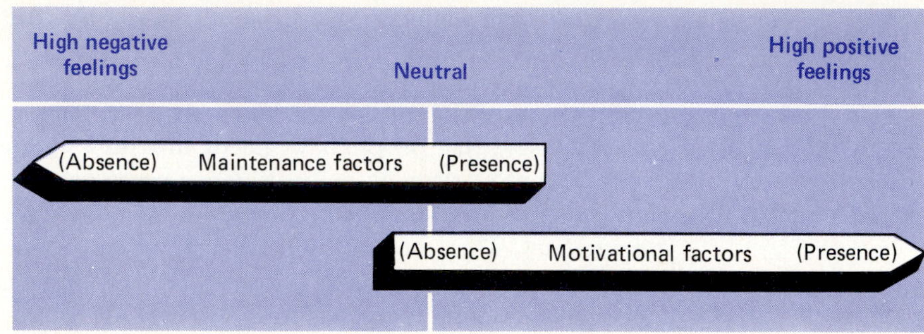

FIGURE 5-4
Maintenance and motivational factors

Maintenance factors

ing. These potent dissatisfiers are called *hygiene factors,* or *maintenance factors,* because they are necessary to maintain a reasonable level of motivation in employees.

Motivational factors

Other job conditions operate primarily to build motivation, but their absence rarely is strongly dissatisfying. These conditions are known as *motivational factors,* motivators, or satisfiers. For many years managers had been wondering why their fancy policies and fringe benefits were not increasing employee motivation. The idea of separate motivational and maintenance factors helped answer their question, because fringe benefits and personnel policies were primarily maintenance factors according to Herzberg.

Job content and context

Figure 5-5 shows the Herzberg factors. Motivational factors such as achievement and responsibility mostly are related directly to the job itself, the employee's performance, and the recognition and growth that are secured from it. Motivators mostly are job-centered; they relate to *job content.*

On the other hand, maintenance factors are mainly related to *job context,* because they are more related to the environment surrounding the job. This difference between job content and job context is a significant one. It shows that employees primarily are motivated strongly by what they do for themselves. When they take responsibility or gain recognition through their own behavior, they are strongly motivated.

Intrinsic and extrinsic motivators

The difference between job content and job context is similar to the difference between intrinsic and extrinsic motivators in psychology. *Intrinsic motivators* are internal rewards that a person feels when performing a job, so there is a direct connection between work and rewards. An employee in this situation is self-motivated. *Extrinsic motivators* are external rewards that occur apart from work, providing no direct satisfaction at the time the work is performed. Examples are retirement plans, health insurance, and vacations.

INTERPRETING THE TWO-FACTOR MODEL As with all motivational theories, the two-factor model has drawn both support and criticism. Prior to Herzberg's research, managers tended to center their attention on extrinsic (maintenance) factors, often with poor results. The distinction between motivators and maintenance items broadened their perspectives by showing the potentially powerful role of intrinsic rewards that evolve from the work itself. (This ties in with a number of other important behavioral developments, such as job enrichment and quality of work life, which are discussed in later chapters.) Nevertheless, managers were also told that they could not neglect to provide a wide range of factors which create at least a neutral working environment.

Contributions

The Herzberg model, like Maslow's, has been widely criticized.[12] It is not universally applicable, as it applies best to managerial, professional, and upper-level white-collar employees. The model sharply reduces the apparent motivational impact of pay, status, and relations with others, since these are identified as maintenance factors. It seems also to be "method-bound," meaning that only Herzberg's approach (asking for self-reports of favorable and unfavorable job experiences) produces the two-factor model. The respondents' egos lead them to produce biased reports, with the result that there is an *appearance* of two factors where in reality there may be only one.

Limitations

Despite these criticisms, the model provides a useful distinction between maintenance items that are necessary but not sufficient and motivational factors that have the potential for improving employee effort. Managers should recognize that the model outlines a general tendency only, as maintenance factors may be motivators to some people who sincerely desire these rewards. Conversely, some motivators may be only maintenance factors to other people. Figure 5-4 shows that there is no absolute distinction; neither factor is wholly one-dimensional in its influence for a specific group of employees. Consequently, a manager must still assess a particular employee's responses to various factors within this general framework.

MAINTENANCE FACTORS	MOTIVATIONAL FACTORS
Dissatisfiers	**Satisfiers**
Hygiene factors	**Motivators**
Job context	**Job content**
Extrinsic factors	**Intrinsic factors**
Examples	*Examples*
Company policy and administration	**Achievement**
Quality of supervision	**Recognition**
Relations with supervisors	**Advancement**
Peer relations	**Work itself**
Relations with subordinates	**Possibility of growth**
Pay	**Responsibility**
Job security	
Working conditions	
Status	

FIGURE 5-5 Herzberg's classification of maintenance and motivational factors

Alderfer's E-R-G model

Existence

Relatedness

Growth

Building upon earlier need models (primarily Maslow's), and seeking to overcome some of their weaknesses, Clayton Alderfer proposed a modified need hierarchy with just three levels.[13] He suggested that employees are initially interested in satisfying their *existence needs*, which combine physiological and security factors. Pay, physical working conditions, job security, and fringe benefits can all address this need. *Relatedness needs* are at the next level, and these involve being understood and accepted by people above, below, and around the employee at work and away from it. *Growth needs* are in the third category, and these involve both the desire for self-esteem and self-actualization.

The impending conversation between the president and administrative assistant described at the beginning of this chapter could be structured around Alderfer's E-R-G model. The president may first wish to identify which level seems to be dominating the assistant's thoughts at this time, and which level or levels seem to be satisfied. For example, a large disparity between their salaries could lead her to be frustrated with her existence needs, despite an objectively healthy economic package. Or her immersion in her work through long hours and heavy travel could have left her relatedness needs unsatisfied. Finally, assuming she has mastered her present job assignments, she may be experiencing the need to develop her capabilities and grow in new areas.

In addition to condensing Maslow's five need levels into three that are more consistent with research, some other differences are apparent. For example, the E-R-G model does not assume as rigorous a progression from level to level. Instead, it accepts the likelihood that all three levels might be active at any time. It also suggests that a person frustrated at either of the two higher levels may return to concentrate on a lower level. Finally, whereas the first two levels are somewhat limited in their requirements for satisfaction, the growth needs not only are unlimited but are actually further awakened each time some satisfaction is attained.

Comparison of the Maslow, Herzberg, and Alderfer models

The similarities among the three models of human needs are quite apparent, as shown in Figure 5-6, but there are important contrasts too. Maslow and Alderfer focus on the internal needs of the employee, while Herzberg differentiates the job conditions (content or context) that could be provided for need satisfaction. Popular interpretations of the Maslow and Herzberg models suggest that in modern societies many workers have already satisfied their lower-order needs, so they are now motivated mainly by higher-order needs and motivators. Alderfer suggests that the failure to satisfy relatedness or growth needs will cause renewed interest in existence needs. Finally, all three models indicate that before a manager tries to administer a reward, it is useful to discover which need a particular employee has at the time. In this way, all need

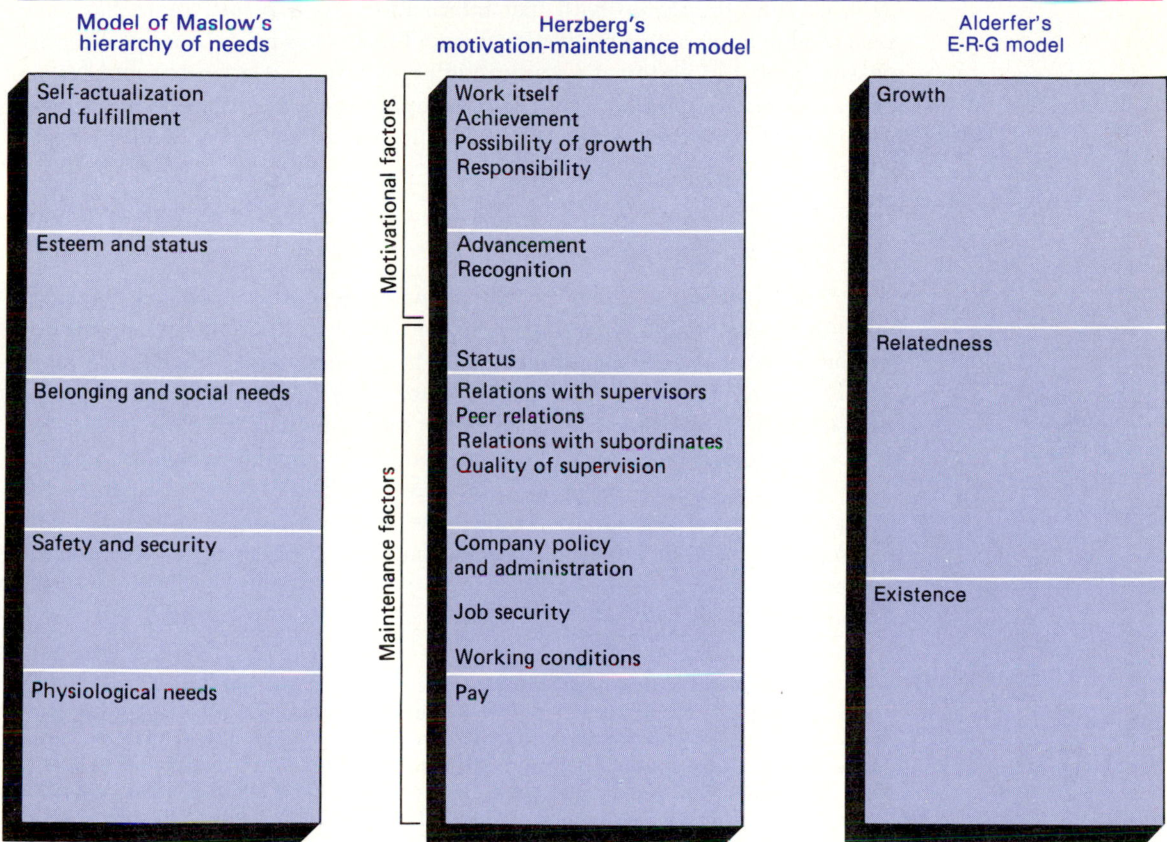

FIGURE 5-6
A comparison of Maslow's, Herzberg's, and Alderfer's models

models provide a foundation for the understanding and application of behavior modification, to be discussed next.

BEHAVIOR MODIFICATION

Cognitive theories

The models of motivation that have been discussed up to this point are known as *cognitive* (or *content*) *theories of motivation* because they are based on thinking and feeling (i.e., cognition). They relate to the person's inner self and how that person's internal state of needs determines behavior.

The major difficulty with cognitive models of motivation is that the needs people have are not subject to observation by managers or precise measurement for monitoring purposes. It is difficult, for example, to measure an employee's esteem needs, or to assess how they change over time. Further, simply knowing about an employee's needs does not directly suggest to managers what they should do with that information. As a result, there has been considerable interest in a motivational model that relies more heavily on careful measurement and systematic application of incentives. *Organizational behavior modification,* or O.B. Mod, is the application in organizations of the principles of behavior modification, which evolved from the work of B. F. Skinner.[14]

O.B. Mod

Law of Effect

O.B. Mod is based on the idea that *behavior depends on its consequences*; therefore, it is possible for managers to control (or at least affect) a number of employee behaviors by manipulating their consequences. O.B. Mod relies heavily on the *Law of Effect,* which states that a person tends to repeat behavior that is accompanied by favorable consequences (reinforcement) and tends *not* to repeat behavior that is accompanied by unfavorable consequences. Two conditions are required for successful application of O.B. Mod—the manager must be able to identify some powerful consequences (as perceived by the employee), and then must be able to administer them in such a way that the employee will see the connection between the behavior to be affected and the consequences.

Some professional sports have developed reward systems that appear to build on these principles. For example, on the Ladies' Professional Golf Association tour, only those players who complete all four rounds of a tournament and have the better total scores collect checks when they are done. Furthermore, the winner's check is nearly double what the second-place finisher receives. The LPGA has identified money as a favorable consequence, and tied its distribution directly to the level of short-term performance by its members. This system presumably encourages the players to participate in numerous tournaments, play all four rounds, and excel.

Focus on consequences

The Law of Effect comes from learning theory, which suggests that we learn best under pleasant surroundings. While cognitive theories argue that *internal* needs lead to behavior, O.B. Mod states that *external* consequences tend to determine behavior. The advantage of O.B. Mod is that it places a greater degree of control (and responsibility) in the hands of the manager. Several firms have used various forms of behavior modification, including Frito-Lay, Weyerhacuser, and B. F. Goodrich.

Alternative consequences

Positive reinforcement

Behavior primarily is encouraged through positive reinforcement. *Positive reinforcement* provides a favorable consequence that encourages repetition of a behavior. An employee, for example, may find that when high-quality work is done, the supervisor gives a reward of recognition. Since the employee likes recognition, behavior is reinforced, and the employee tends to want to do high-quality work again. The reinforcement always should be contingent on the employee's correct behavior.

An example of positive reinforcement is the experience of Emery Air Freight with its containerized shipping operations.[15] The company's practice is to consolidate small packages into large containers in order to reduce handling and shipping costs. The standard is for 90 percent of small packages to be shipped in large containers, but an audit at various locations showed that actual use was about 45 percent. Further study showed that workers were properly trained and reasonably cooperative, but they were not motivated to meet the standard.

To improve performance, management applied a program of positive reinforcement. It trained supervisors to give daily performance feedback, recognition, and other rewards. In the first test office, performance went to 95 percent the first day. As the program was applied in other offices, their performance also went to 90 percent or better, most of them increasing to standard within a single day. The effective results continued for the four years covered in the study. The regular feedback and recognition gave workers consequences that strongly influenced their behavior. In this instance positive reinforcement scored a notable success.

Shaping

Shaping occurs when reinforcements are successively given as one comes closer to the desired behavior. Even though the completely correct behavior does not yet occur, it is encouraged by giving reinforcement for behavior in the desired direction. Shaping is especially useful for teaching complex tasks.

An illustration of shaping is the training procedure used by a supervisor in a retail store. The store was so small that it had no centralized training program for sales clerks, so all sales training was a responsibility of the supervisor. In the beginning a new salesclerk did not know how to deal with customers effectively, so the supervisor explained the proper sales procedure. The supervisor observed the clerk's behavior, and from time to time when the clerk showed improved behavior in some part of the procedure, the supervisor expressed approval and encouraged the employee. This was favorable recognition for the employee, so it helped shape behavior in the correct direction.

Negative reinforcement

Negative reinforcement occurs when behavior is accompanied by removal of an unfavorable consequence; therefore, it is not the same as punishment, which normally adds something unfavorable. Consistent with the Law of Effect, behavior responsible for the removal of something unfavorable is repeated when that unfavorable state is again encountered. An example of negative reinforcement is the experience of a jet aircraft mechanic who learned that if she wore noise suppressors over her ears, she could prevent discomfort from the jet engine noise; this reinforcement encouraged her to wear the proper noise equipment.

Punishment

Punishment occurs when *an unfavorable* consequence accompanies and discourages a certain behavior. Although punishment may be necessary to discourage an undesirable behavior, it has certain limitations. A major one is that punishment only *discourages* an undesirable behavior; it does not directly encourage any kind of desirable behavior.[16] Further, since the punisher is also the person who offers reinforcement at other times, the two roles become confused, which may reduce the punisher's effectiveness when offering future reinforcements. Also, people who are punished may become confused about what specific part of their behavior is being punished, so it is possible that some desirable behaviors may be discouraged.

Extinction

Extinction may occur when there are no significant consequences for a behavior. Learned behavior needs to be reinforced in order to occur in the future. If no reinforcement occurs, the behavior tends to diminish through lack of reinforcement. In one instance an employee made three suggestions to her supervisor over a period of several weeks. The supervisor did not reject the suggestions or accept them or do anything else. The suggestions just disappeared in the bureaucratic maze. Needless to say, the employee's suggestion-making behavior was extinguished by the lack of consequences. In this case the supervisor probably did not intend to cause the extinction, but in other cases extinction is used as a conscious strategy. Then alternative responses that are desired can be reinforced to change behavior.

It would be naive to conclude that supervisors can gain the benefits of extinction by simply ignoring undesirable employee behaviors, however. There are many other sources of need satisfaction inside and outside the workplace, and many of these are beyond the supervisor's control. Managers can generally achieve more favorable results by actively manipulating the favorable or unfavorable consequences of a behavior.

Schedules of reinforcement

Baseline

Before various types of consequences can be applied, managers should monitor employee behavior to learn how often, or how well, it is now being done. The frequency of the behavior creates a *baseline*, or standard, against which improvements can be compared. Then the manager can select a reinforcement schedule, which is the frequency with which the chosen consequence accompanies a desired behavior.

Continuous reinforcement

Reinforcement may be either continuous or partial, as shown in Figure 5-7. *Continuous reinforcement* occurs when a reinforcer accompanies each correct behavior by an employee. In some instances, this level of reinforcement may be desirable to encourage quick learning, but in the typical work situation it usually is not possible to reward an employee for every correct behavior. An example of continuous reinforcement is payment of employees for each acceptable item that they produce.

Partial reinforcement

Partial reinforcement occurs when only some of the correct behaviors are reinforced. Learning is slower with partial reinforcement than with continuous reinforcement. However, a unique feature of partial reinforcement is that learning tends to be retained longer when it is secured under conditions of partial reinforcement.

There are four types of partial-reinforcement schedules: fixed-interval, variable-interval, fixed-ratio, and variable-ratio schedules. These offer a variety of reinforcement approaches.

FIXED INTERVAL A fixed-interval schedule provides a reinforcement after a certain period of time. A typical example is a paycheck that arrives every two weeks. Except in very unusual circumstances, employees can depend on the check arriving on a certain day every two weeks.

REINFORCEMENT SCHEDULE	EXAMPLE
1 *Continuous.* Reinforcement accompanying each correct behavior	A piece rate of 10 cents is paid for each acceptable piece produced.
2 *Partial.* Reinforcement following only some of the correct behaviors	
a *Time intervals*	
□ *Fixed interval.* Reinforcement after a certain period of time	A paycheck arrives every two weeks.
□ *Variable interval.* Reinforcement after a variety of time periods	The safety department makes safety checks of every department four times a year on a random basis.
b *Ratio*	
□ *Fixed ratio.* Reinforcement after a certain number of correct responses	Sales employees are given a bonus after every fifth automobile sold.
□ *Variable ratio.* Reinforcement after a variable number of correct responses	There is a lottery for employees who have not been absent during the week.

FIGURE 5-7
Types of reinforcement schedules

Another example comes from the experience of a major airline.[17] It had five telephone reservation offices with over 1500 employees and it needed to motivate those employees to encourage callers to make actual flight reservations. The company chose a fixed-interval reinforcement along with supervisory improvements. It kept records of the percentage of callers who made flight reservations and then fed back this information daily to each employee. The results were excellent. The ratio of reservations to calls increased from only 1 in 4 to 1 in 2.

VARIABLE INTERVAL Variable-interval schedules give reinforcement after a variety of time periods. Usually the variations are grouped around some target, or average, period of reinforcement. An example is one company's policy of making safety inspections of every department four times a year in order to encourage compliance with safety regulations. The inspections are made on a random basis, so the intervals between them vary.

FIXED RATIO Fixed-ratio schedules occur when there is reinforcement after a certain number of correct responses. An example is payment of sales bonuses after a certain number of large items (such as automobiles) are sold. In one automobile agency, sales personnel are given a bonus after every fifth car sold. This bonus is an encouragement to sell more cars, especially when employees reach a point where they already have sold three or four and need only two or one more to earn the bonus.

VARIABLE RATIO A variable-ratio schedule is a reinforcement after a variable number of correct responses, such as reinforcement after 19, 15, 12, 24, and 17 responses. This type of reinforcement schedule provokes much interest and is preferred by employees for some tasks. It tends to be the most powerful of all the reinforcement schedules. An interesting fact is that slot machines and a number of other gambling devices operate on a variable-ratio schedule, so gamblers experienced the power of this reinforcement schedule before it was isolated and studied by behavioral scientists.

Interpreting behavior modification

Contributions

The major benefit of behavior modification is that it encourages managers to analyze employee behavior, explore why it occurs and how often, and identify specific consequences that will help change it when they are applied systematically. Application of this process often encourages effective supervisors to devote more time to monitoring employee behaviors.[18] Performance feedback and recognition are often parts of this strategy because they tend to be widely desired, and therefore are strong reinforcements. General guidelines for a behavior modification strategy are shown in Figure 5-8. When specific behaviors can be identified and desired reinforcements are properly applied, behavior modification can lead to substantial improvements in specific areas such as absences, tardiness, and error rates.

Collins Food International used behavior modification with clerical employees in its accounting department.[19] One of the items selected for modification was billing error rates. Management measured existing error rates and then met with employees to discuss and set goals for improvement. It also praised employees for reduction of errors, and it reported error results to them regularly. Employees in the accounts payable department responded by reducing error rates from more than 8 percent to less than 0.2 percent.

Behavior modification also worked well in hospital jobs such as admitting patients, keeping medical records, and billing patients. For example, average time used to admit a patient was reduced from 44 to 14 minutes, and clerical costs per admission dropped from $15.05 to $11.73.[20]

Limitations

Behavior modification has been criticized on several grounds, including its philosophy, methods, and practicality. Because of the strong power of desired consequences, behavior modification may effectively force people to change their behavior. In this way it manipulates people and is inconsistent with humanistic assumptions discussed earlier that people want to be autonomous

- □ **Identify exact behavior to be modified.**
- □ **Use positive reinforcement whenever possible.**
- □ **Use punishment only in unusual circumstances and for specific behaviors.**
- □ **Ignore minor undesirable behavior to allow its extinction.**
- □ **Use shaping procedures to develop correct complex behavior.**
- □ **Minimize the time between the correct response and reinforcement.**
- □ **Provide reinforcement frequently.**

FIGURE 5-8
General guidelines for applying behavior modification

and self-actualizing. Some critics also fear that behavior modification gives too much power to the managers, and they raise the question: Who will control the controllers?

Other critics say that behavior modification insults people's intelligence. At the extreme, people could be treated like rats in a training box when in fact they are intelligent, thinking, self-controlled individuals who are capable of making their own choices and perhaps motivating themselves. Another problem is that behavior modification has limited applicability to complex jobs. For example, it is difficult to identify specific behaviors in the jobs of corporate lawyers, flight attendants, or chief executive officers and reinforce them. This challenge may become increasingly difficult as the U.S. economy becomes more and more service-based.

People learn from others.

O.B. Mod has basically overlooked people's cognitive (judgment and choice) skills and only minimally considered the influence of antecedents (i.e., cues) on their behavior. This has led to a more recent adaptation of the process, based on *social learning theory.*[21] Social learning theory suggests that employees gain substantial information about how to perform by observing and imitating those around them. Similarly, they influence others in their environment who are watching them. The importance of social learning theory for motivation is that it reminds managers that employees do not react mechanically to their environment, but carefully observe other people and symbols around them. As a result, much of their behavior is consciously chosen. This leads us to consider the role of goal setting in motivation, which provides important cues to employees about what is important to the organization.

GOAL SETTING

Goals are targets and objectives for future performance. They have been shown by Locke and others to be important both before and after the desired behavior.[22] When involved in goal setting, employees see how their effort will lead to performance, rewards, and personal satisfaction. In this way, goals effectively point workers in acceptable directions. Further, the attainment of goals is rewarding, as it helps to satisfy the achievement drive and needs for esteem and self-actualization. Growth needs are also stimulated, as goal attainment often leads individuals to set even higher goals in the future.

Elements of goal setting

Goal setting, as a motivational tool, is most effective when four elements are present. These are goal acceptance, specificity, challenge, and feedback, as shown in Figure 5-9. Each will be briefly described.

GOAL ACCEPTANCE Just as in the communication process described in an earlier chapter, effective goals need to be not only understood but also *ac-*

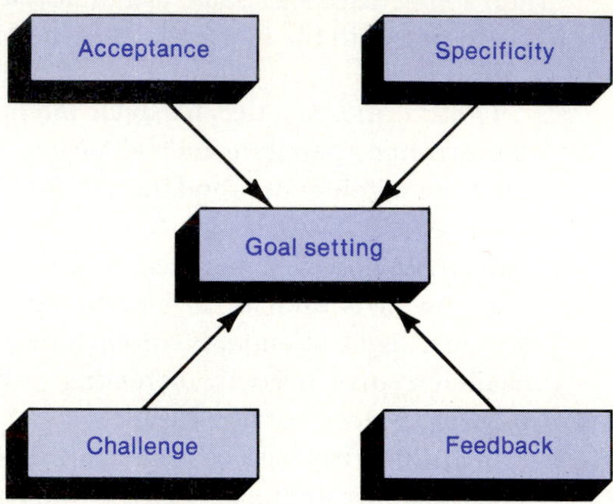

FIGURE 5-9
Elements of effective goal setting

Process creates acceptance.

cepted.[23] As a minimum, supervisors need to explain the purpose behind goals and the necessity for them. Assigning goals to employees, however, may not result in their commitment to them, especially if the goal will be difficult to accomplish. It may be necessary for the manager to involve the employees in the goal-setting process to obtain acceptance. Because of its importance, an entire chapter will be devoted to the participative process later in the book.

SPECIFICITY Goals need to be as specific, clear, and measurable as possible so that employees will know when a goal is reached. It is not very helpful to ask them to improve, to work harder, or "do better," because that kind of goal does not give them a focused target to seek. Specific goals let them know what to reach for, as well as allowing them to measure their own progress.

In one instance goal setting was used with logging-truck drivers to encourage them to carry loads nearer the legal capacity of their trucks.[24] Under instructions to "do your best," the drivers had been carrying about 60 percent of the legal limit. After goals were more specifically set, performance increased to slightly over 90 percent of the legal limit, and this level continued for the next twelve months. Drivers were given no extra rewards other than recognition for their higher production. Nevertheless, they seemed to feel a sense of achievement in meeting their specific goals by loading their trucks to the legal limit, so their performance was better.

CHALLENGE Perhaps surprisingly, most employees work harder when they have difficult goals to accomplish rather than easy ones. Hard goals present a challenge that appeals to the achievement drive within many employees. These goals must, however, still be achievable, given the experience of the individual and the resources available.

The motivational value of a challenge was demonstrated by a motel owner in a small city. Richard Fann was concerned about the time required by housekeepers to change the beds when they cleaned a room. The average time used was about seven minutes, including numerous trips around the bed to strip the sheets and replace the covers. Suggestions made to the housekeepers to reduce their wasted motions were only marginally successful in speeding up the process. Finally, Richard decided to stage a contest, and pit the housekeepers against each other. Not only did the strategy work, but the results overwhelmed him. The winning employee was able to change a bed in less than one minute, and do this by staying on one side! "Why hadn't they done this earlier?" Richard inquired. "Because you didn't challenge us," they responded.

PERFORMANCE FEEDBACK Once employees have participated in setting well-defined and challenging goals, they still need feedback about how well they are performing. Otherwise, they are "working in the dark" and have no way to know how successful they are. A ball team needs to know the score of the game, a marksman needs to see the bullet holes in the target, and the woodchopper needs to see the chips fly and the pile of firewood accumulate. The same can be said for a team on a production line or a worker in an office. Performance feedback tends to encourage better job performance, and self-generated feedback is an especially powerful motivational tool.[25]

SUMMARY

When people join an organization, they bring with them certain drives and needs that affect their on-the-job performance. Sometimes these are immediately apparent, but often they not only are difficult to determine and satisfy but also vary greatly from one person to another. It is useful, though, to understand how needs create tensions which stimulate effort to perform, and this brings the satisfaction of rewards.

Four different approaches to understanding internal drives and needs within employees were examined. Each model makes a contribution to our understanding of motivation, and all the models share some similarities. In general, they encourage managers not only to consider lower-order, maintenance, and extrinsic factors but to use higher-order, motivational, and intrinsic factors as well.

Behavior modification focuses on the external environment by stating that a number of employee behaviors can be affected by manipulating their consequences. Various alternatives for doing this include positive and negative reinforcement, punishment, and extinction. Reinforcement can be applied according to either continuous or partial schedules.

A blending of internal and external approaches is obtained through consideration of social learning theory. Managers are encouraged to use cues, such as goals that are accepted, challenging, and specific, to stimulate desired employee behavior. In this way goal setting, combined with the reinforcement of performance feedback, provides a balanced approach to motivation.

Terms and concepts for review

Drives
Primary and secondary needs
Maslow's hierarchy of needs
Herzberg's two-factor model
Alderfer's E-R-G model
Job content and job context
Intrinsic and extrinsic motivation
Behavior modification
Law of Effect
Positive reinforcement
Shaping
Negative reinforcement
Punishment
Extinction
Social learning theory
Goal setting

Discussion questions

1 Think of someone who, in the past, did an excellent job of motivating you. Describe how this was done. Which of the following approaches did this person use (either explicitly or implicitly)?
   a Lower-order or higher-order needs?
   b Maintenance or motivational factors, and which one(s)?
   c Existence, relatedness, or growth needs?
   d Behavior modification?
   e Goal setting?

2 In your role as a student, do you feel that you are motivated more by Maslow's lower-order or higher-order needs? Explain. Describe how you expect this to change once you graduate.

3 Which one Herzberg factor in the two-factor model is most motivating to you at the present time? Explain. Is this a maintenance or motivational factor?

4 It is relatively easy for a manager to manipulate extrinsic rewards. However, describe some ways in which a manager could affect intrinsic satisfaction of an employee.

5 Indicate the major similarities and differences between the Maslow, Herzberg, and Alderfer models. Then relate the four major drives to these models.

6 Discuss how behavior modification operates to motivate people. Why is it still important to understand people's needs when using this approach?

7 Explain the differences between negative reinforcement and punishment.

8 Discuss the types of reinforcement schedule that various forms of gambling, such as bingo and blackjack, use. Identify two work situations in which the same reinforcement schedule could be applied.

9 Divide the class into two groups (one in favor and one opposed) and debate the proposition "Behavior modification manipulates people."

10 Can you think of any situation in which the *opposite* of the recommended goal characteristics (i.e., assigned, vague, and easy) might work to motivate someone? Explain.

Incident

THE PIANO BUILDER[26]

Waverly Bird builds pianos from scratch. He is a piano consultant to a piano manufacturer. He is on call and works about one week a month, including some travel to solve problems of customers. He also rebuilds about a dozen grand pianos every year for special customers; but, according to Bird, the most satisfying part of his life is his hobby of building pianos from the beginning. "It's the part that keeps a man alive," he says. The challenge of the work is what lures Bird onward. He derives satisfaction from precision and quality, and he comments, "Details make the difference. When you cut a little corner here and a little corner there, you've cut a big hole. A piano is like the human body; all the parts are important."

Bird has a substantial challenge in making a whole piano. His work requires skills in cabinetmaking, metalworking, and engineering, with knowledge of acoustics and a keen ear for music. It requires great precision, because a tiny misalignment would ruin a piano's tune. It also requires versatility, ranging from a keyboard that is balanced to respond to the touch of a finger all the way to the pinblock that must withstand up to 20 tons of pressure. Bird had to make many of his own piano construction tools.

Bird has built forty pianos in his thirty-four-year career. Though construction takes nearly a year, he sells his pianos at the modest price of a commercial piano. He is seeking not money but challenge and satisfaction. He says, "The whole business is a series of closed doors. You learn one thing, and there's another closed door waiting to be opened." Bird says his big dream is to build a grand piano: "It is the one thing I haven't done yet and want to do."

Questions

1 Discuss the nature of Bird's motivation in building pianos. What are his drives and needs? Would a behavior modification program affect his motivation? (Why or why not?) What would be the effect of setting a goal of two pianos per year for him?

2 How could a manufacturer of pianos build the same motivation into its employees as Bird has now?

Experiential exercise

THE NONPARTICIPATING STUDENT

Some professors believe that it is very appropriate for their students to participate actively in class discussions, and they invite them to do so. However, not all class members take advantage of this opportunity. As a consequence of their limited participation, not only are their colleagues deprived of their contributions to the discussion, but the inactive students have missed a chance to develop and demonstrate their thinking and communication skills.

1 Organize yourselves into small groups. Assume that you are a task team acting as consultants to your instructor. You have been asked to develop a motivational program that will be applied to a nonparticipating student in your class to elicit a

substantially greater level of oral contributions (both quantity and quality). Address the following issues, and be ready to present your report to the rest of the class.

2 Identify a means of developing a baseline measure of the student's current behavior. How frequently, and how well, is the student participating in class at this time?

3 Analyze *why* the student is making limited contributions, taking a systems viewpoint. Consider factors both internal and external to the student. Is the performance problem one of limited ability or motivation?

4 Create an *integrated* plan for motivating the student (assuming that is the cause). Specifically, include cues, needs, and consequences in your discussion.

5 Critique your own plan, explaining why it still may not be effective in accomplishing your objectives, despite your best efforts.

References

1 Frederick Herzberg, "Managers or Animal Trainers?" *Management Review*, July 1971, p. 9. The words "for me" are italicized in the original.

2 Adapted from an illustration in Mark B. Roman, "Beyond the Carrot and the Stick," *Success*, October 1986, pp. 39–43.

3 The original work on achievement motivation is David C. McClelland, *The Achieving Society*, New York: Van Nostrand Company, 1961.

4 Tamao Matsui, Akinori Okada, and Takashi Kakuyama, "Influence of Achievement Need on Goal Setting, Performance, and Feedback Effectiveness," *Journal of Applied Psychology*, October 1982, pp. 645–648. Current research is reported in Andre Kukla and Hal Scher, "Varieties of Achievement Motivation," *Psychological Review*, July 1986, pp. 378–380; and Aharon Tziner and Dov Elizur, "Achievement Motive: A Reconceptualization and New Instrument," *Journal of Occupational Behaviour*, July 1985, pp. 209–228.

5 Alan M. Webber, "Red Auerbach on Management," *Harvard Business Review*, March–April 1987, pp. 84–91.

6 The competence motive may be one of the stronger drives that could motivate mid-to-late-career persons. See, for example, Judith Bardwick, *The Plateauing Trap*, New York: AMACOM, 1986.

7 Among its other characteristics, the new generation of corporate employees is described as "craving autonomy and power," See Teresa Carson and John Byrne, "Fast-Track Kids," *Business Week*, Nov. 10, 1986, pp. 90–92.

8 A. H. Maslow, "A Theory of Human Motivation," *Psychological Review*, vol. 50, 1943, pp. 370–396; and A. H. Maslow, *Motivation and Personality*, New York: Harper & Row, Publishers, Inc., 1954. See also A. H. Maslow, *The Farther Reaches of Human Nature*, New York: The Viking Press, Inc., 1971. The need for students of organizational behavior to read the originally published work of classics like these is stressed in W. Dennis Patzig and Barry L. Wisdom, "Some Words of Caution about Having Students Read the Classics," in Dennis Ray (ed.), *Southern Management Association Proceedings*, Mississippi State, Miss.: Southern Management Association, 1986.

9 For discussions of declining job security, and experiments with "guaranteed" employment security, see Robert B. Tucker, "You, Inc.," *Success*, April 1987, pp. 58–59; and Diane Riggan, "Employment Security Revisited in the '80s," *Personnel Administrator*, December 1985, pp. 67–74.

10 For a fuller discussion, see Richard M. Steers and Lyman W. Porter, *Motivation and Work Behavior*, 4th ed., New York: McGraw-Hill Book Co., 1987.

11 Frederick Herzberg, Bernard Mausner, and Barbara Snyderman, *The Motivation to Work*, New York: John Wiley & Sons, Inc., 1959; Frederick Herzberg, *Work and the Nature of Man*, Cleveland, Ohio: World Publishing Company, 1966; and Freder-

ick Herzberg, *The Managerial Choice: To Be Efficient or To Be Human*, rev. ed., Salt Lake City, Utah: Olympus, 1982.

12 Early criticisms were in Martin G. Evans, "Herzberg's Two-Factor Theory of Motivation: Some Problems and a Suggested Test," *Personnel Journal*, January 1970, pp. 32–35; and Valerie M. Bockman, "The Herzberg Controversy," *Personnel Psychology*, Summer 1971, pp. 155–189. The latter article reports the first ten years of research on the model.

13 Clayton P. Alderfer, "An Empirical Test of a New Theory of Human Needs," *Organizational Behavior and Human Performance*, vol. 4, 1969, pp. 142–175.

14 B. F. Skinner, *Science and Human Behavior*, New York: Macmillan Company (Free Press), 1953; and B. F. Skinner, *Contingencies of Reinforcement*, New York: Appleton-Century-Crofts, Inc., 1969. O.B. Mod is discussed in Fred Luthans and Robert Kreitner, *Organizational Behavior Modification and Beyond: An Operant and Social Learning Approach*, Glenview, Ill.: Scott, Foresman and Company, 1985.

15 "At Emery Air Freight: Positive Reinforcement Boosts Performance," *Organizational Dynamics*, Winter 1973, pp. 41–50. A more recent study indicating that O.B. Mod can also affect behaviors outside the organization is Mark J. Martinko, "An O. B. Mod. Analysis of Consumer Behavior," *Journal of Organizational Behavior Management*, Spring–Summer 1986, pp. 19–43.

16 Evidence that workers who observe a coworker being punished increase their own output is in Mel Schnake, "Vicarious Punishment in a Work Setting," *Journal of Applied Psychology*, May 1986, pp. 343–345; for a discussion of punishment's limitations, see Philip M. Podsakoff, William D. Todor, and Richard Skov, "Effects of Leader Contingent and Noncontingent Reward and Punishment Behaviors on Subordinate Performance and Satisfaction," *Academy of Management Journal*, December 1982, pp. 810–821.

17 "Productivity Gains from a Pat on the Back," *Business Week*, Jan. 23, 1978, pp. 56–62.

18 Judith L. Komaki, "Toward Effective Supervision: An Operant Analysis and Comparison of Managers at Work," *Journal of Applied Psychology*, May 1986, pp. 270–279.

19 "Productivity Gains from a Pat on the Back," op. cit., pp. 56–62.

20 Charles A. Snyder and Fred Luthans, "Using OB Mod to Increase Hospital Productivity," *Personnel Administrator*, August 1982, pp. 67–73.

21 Explanations of social learning theory are in Phillip J. Decker, "Social Learning Theory and Leadership," *Journal of Management Development*, vol. 5, no. 3, 1986, pp. 46–58; and Robert Kreitner and Fred Luthans, "A Social Learning Approach to Behavioral Management: Radical Behaviorists 'Mellowing Out,'" *Organizational Dynamics*, Autumn 1984, pp. 47–65.

22 A summary of several goal-setting studies is reported in Gary P. Latham and Edwin A. Locke, "Goal Setting—A Motivational Technique that Works," *Organizational Dynamics*, Autumn 1979, pp. 68–80; a comprehensive update is in Mark E. Tubbs, "Goal Setting: A Meta-Analytic Examination of the Empirical Evidence," *Journal of Applied Psychology*, August 1986, pp. 474–483.

23 For research on goal acceptance, see Miriam Erez and Revital Arad, "Participative Goal-Setting: Social, Motivational, and Cognitive Factors," *Journal of Applied Psychology*, November 1986, pp. 591–597.

24 Gary P. Latham and J. James Baldes, "The Practical Significance of Locke's Theory of Goal Setting," *Journal of Applied Psychology*, February 1975, pp. 122–124.

25 John M. Ivancevich and J. Timothy McMahon, "The Effects of Goal Setting, External Feedback, and Self-Generated Feedback on Outcome Variables: A Field Experiment," *Academy of Management Journal*, June 1982, pp. 359–372.

26 Developed from an article by Liz Roman Gallese, "Stephen Jellen Builds Pianos Not for Money but for Satisfaction," *Wall Street Journal* (Pacific Coast edition), Sept. 6, 1973, pp. 1, 12.

For additional reading

Bandura, Albert, *Social Learning Theory*, Englewood Cliffs, N.J.: Prentice-Hall, 1977.

Blanchard, Kenneth, and Spencer Johnson, *The One Minute Manager*, La Jolla, Calif.: Blanchard-Johnson Publishers, 1981.

Brockner, Joel, *Self-Esteem and Organizational Behavior: Research, Theory, and Practice*, Lexington, Mass.: Lexington Books, 1986.

Cox, Allan, *The Making of the Achiever*, New York: Dodd, Mead and Co., 1985.

Goldratt, Eliyahu M., and Jeff Cox, *The Goal: A Process of Ongoing Improvement* (rev. ed.), Croton-on-Hudson: North River Press, Inc., 1986.

Herzberg, Frederick, Bernard Mausner, and Barbara Snyderman, *The Motivation to Work*, New York: John Wiley & Sons, Inc., 1959.

Lawler, Edward E., *High Involvement Management: Participative Strategies for Improving Organizational Performance*, San Francisco: Jossey-Bass Publishers, Inc., 1986.

Luthans, Fred, and Robert Kreitner, *Organizational Behavior Modification and Beyond: An Operant and Social Learning Theory Approach*, Glenview, Ill.: Scott, Foresman and Company, 1985.

Maslow, A. H., *Motivation and Personality*, New York: Harper & Row, Publishers, Inc., 1954.

McClelland, David, C., *The Achieving Society*, New York: Van Nostrand and Company, 1961.

Pinder, Craig C., *Work Motivation: Theory, Issues, and Applications*, Glenview, Ill.: Scott, Foresman and Company, 1984.

Skinner, B. F., *Science and Human Behavior*, New York: Macmillan Company (Free Press), 1953.

CHAPTER 6

Motivating employees

Psychologists agree that people are motivated to work hard — or not so hard — by an incredibly wide range of factors.

FORD S. WORTHY[1]

People who control the behavior of others do not give them credit for the work they do.

DAVID KIPNIS[2]

CHAPTER OBJECTIVES

To understand

The expectancy model of motivation

How employees perceive their needs

Equity comparisons

The process of attribution

The role of the self-fulfilling prophecy

The relationship among motivational models

Marsha Donner, a skilled advertising specialist, worked on special projects in the advertising office of a large department store chain. On one occasion her manager assigned her Project Symposium, which would require about one-third of her time for the next six months or so. The project required her to work with various business and service organizations in the region served by the department store. Donner felt that she was qualified to handle Project Symposium, and she thought that the project would prove interesting; but she really was not enthusiastic about it. She felt that it would interfere with some of her other duties that were more important.

Donner's supervisor recognized her attitude and on various occasions discussed the project with her, hoping to motivate her. After several discussions he felt that he was making no progress, but one day he remarked to Donner, "Marsha, do you realize that Project Symposium will help you meet most community leaders in this region? You know, your acquaintance with these people will help you with Project Mainstream if we ever decide to go with it." Donner had developed the unique idea of Project Mainstream, and she strongly wanted it to be approved. When she saw that her work with Project Symposium might help her with Project Mainstream, she immediately became motivated on Symposium. She worked hard at it for the next eight months, and both she and her supervisor were pleased with the results.

The situation with Marsha Donner concerns a problem of motivation. Although Donner was cooperative and interested in her work, she really was not motivated until her supervisor explained the connection between her present work and a future challenging project that she wanted. She became motivated when she perceived that her work was connected with something important *to her*. This relationship is the essence of motivation. *Motivated employees are those who see their work as helping them accomplish their important goals.* In this chapter we discuss some contemporary motivational approaches, including the expectancy, equity, attribution, and macromotivation models.

THE EXPECTANCY MODEL

A widely accepted approach to motivation is the *expectancy model,* also known as *expectancy theory,* that was developed by Victor H. Vroom and has been expanded and refined by Porter and Lawler and others.[3] Vroom explains that motivation is a product of three factors: how much one wants a reward (valence), one's estimate of the probability that effort will result in successful performance (expectancy), and one's estimate that performance will result in receiving the reward (instrumentality). This relationship is stated in the following formula:

V × E × I = M

Valence × Expectancy × Instrumentality = Motivation

Valence

Reward preference

Valence refers to the strength of a person's preference for receiving a reward. It is an expression of the amount of one's desire for a goal. For example, if an employee strongly wants a promotion, then promotion has high valence for that employee. Valence for a reward is unique to each employee, is conditioned by experience, and may vary substantially over a period of time as old needs become satisfied and new ones emerge.

It is important to understand the difference between the implications of need-based models of motivation (discussed in Chapter 5) and the idea of valence in the expectancy model. In the first type, broad generalizations are used to predict where a group of employees may have the strongest drives or the greatest unsatisfied needs. In the expectancy model, managers need to gather specific information about *an employee's* preferences among a set of rewards, and continue to monitor changes in these preferences.

Can valence be negative?

Since people may have positive or negative preferences for an outcome, valence may be negative as well as positive. When a person prefers not attaining an outcome compared with attaining it, valence is a negative figure. If a person is indifferent to an outcome, the valence is 0. The total range is from −1 to +1, as shown in Figure 6-1.

Some employees will find intrinsic valence in the work itself, particularly if they have a strong work ethic or competence motivation. They derive satisfaction directly from their work through a sense of completion, of doing a task right, or of creating something. In this instance, outcomes are largely within the employee's own control and less subject to management's reward system.

Expectancy

Effort → performance probability

Expectancy is the strength of belief that work-related effort will result in completion of a task. For example, a person selling magazine subscriptions door to door may know from experience that the volume of sales is directly related to the number of sales calls made. Expectancies are stated as probabilities—the employee's estimate of the degree to which performance will be determined by the amount of effort expended. Since expectancy is the probability of a connec-

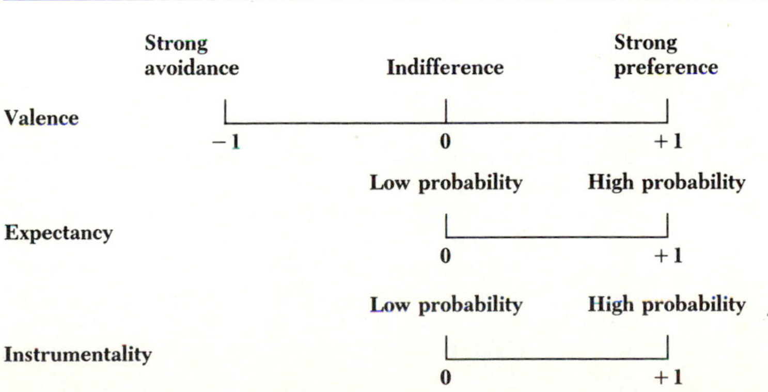

FIGURE 6-1
Range of valence, expectancy, and instrumentality

tion between effort and performance, its value may range from 0 to 1. If an employee sees no chance that effort will lead to the desired performance, the expectancy is 0. At the other extreme, if the employee is highly confident that the task will be completed, the expectancy has a value of 1. Normally, employee estimates of expectancy lie somewhere between these two extremes.

Self-efficacy

One of the forces contributing to effort-performance expectancies is the individual's *self-efficacy*.[4] This is the belief that one has the necessary capabilities to perform a task, fulfill role expectations, or meet a challenging situation successfully. Employees with high levels of self-efficacy are more likely to believe that exerting effort will result in satisfactory performance. This creates a high expectancy assessment.

Imposters

In contrast to high self-efficacy, some employees suffer from the *imposter phenomenon*.[5] Imposters believe that they are not really as capable as they appear to be, and consequently fear that their incompetence will be revealed to others. They are filled with self-doubt, afraid to take risks, and seldom ask for help. Because they believe they lack the necessary competence, they are also likely to doubt that any amount of effort will result in high performance. Impostors, therefore, will predictably have low expectancy assessments for themselves.

Instrumentality

Performance → reward probability

Instrumentality represents the employee's belief that a reward will be received once the task is accomplished. Here the employee makes another subjective judgment about the probability that the organization values the performance and will administer rewards on a contingent basis. The value of instrumentality effectively ranges from 0 to 1.[6] If an employee sees that promotions are based on performance data, instrumentality will be rated high. However, if the basis for such decisions is unclear, a low estimate will be made.

How the model works

The product of valence, expectancy, and instrumentality is *motivation*.[7] It is defined as the strength of the drive toward an action. Here is an example of the expectancy model in operation:

> **Marty Fulmer, age thirty-one, works as a welder in a large factory. Fulmer has very strong desires (high valence) to be in white-collar work instead of his present job, which he no longer enjoys.**
>
> **Fulmer recognizes that good welding will result in high performance appraisals by his supervisor (high expectancy). However, all white-collar jobs in the plant require a college degree, and Fulmer has only a high school diploma. Because of this barrier, Fulmer's instrumentality estimate is low. Being a good welder will not result in promotion to the desired position. Despite his strong desire for something, he sees no viable way to achieve it and, therefore, is not motivated to perform his job better.**

The three factors in the expectancy model may exist in an infinite number of combinations, eight of which are illustrated in Figure 6-2. The multiplicative combination that produces the strongest motivation is high positive valence, high expectancy, and high instrumentality (situation 1 in the figure). If desire for a reward is high but either of the probability estimates are low, then motivation will likely be moderate, at best (situations 2 or 3). If both expectancy and instrumentality are low, then motivation will be weak even if the reward has high valence (situation 4).

A special case occurs when valence is negative (situations 5 to 8). For example, some employees would prefer not to be promoted because of the stress, loss of overtime pay, or additional responsibilities they would bear. Where promotion has a negative valence, the employee will try to avoid earning it. The strength of avoidance behavior depends not only on the negative valence but on the expectancy and instrumentality factors as well.

Through experience, people learn to place a different value on the rewards available to them and also on the varying levels of rewards offered. They also develop expectancy and instrumentality estimates through direct experiences and observations. As a consequence, employees perform a type of cost-benefit analysis for their own behavior at work. If the estimated benefit is worth the cost, then employees are likely to apply more effort.

Employee perceptions are important.

THE ROLE OF PERCEPTION Reaction to rewards is filtered by *perception*, which is an individual's own view of the world. People perceive their environment in an organized framework that they have built out of their own experiences and values. Their own problems, interests, and backgrounds control their perception of each situation. Essentially, each individual is saying, "I behave according to the facts as I see them, not as you see them. *My* needs and wants are paramount, not yours. I act on the basis of my perception of myself and the world in which I live. I react not to an objective world, but to a world seen in terms of my own beliefs and values."

FIGURE 6-2
Some combinations of valence, expectancy, and instrumentality

SITUATION	VALENCE	EXPECTANCY	INSTRUMENTALITY	MOTIVATION
1	**High pos.**	**High**	**High**	**Strong motivation**
2	**High pos.**	**High**	**Low**	**Moderate motivation**
3	**High pos.**	**Low**	**High**	**Moderate motivation**
4	**High pos.**	**Low**	**Low**	**Weak motivation**
5	**High neg.**	**Low**	**Low**	**Weak avoidance**
6	**High neg.**	**High**	**Low**	**Moderate avoidance**
7	**High neg.**	**Low**	**High**	**Moderate avoidance**
8	**High neg.**	**High**	**High**	**Strong avoidance**

Since perceptions are strongly influenced by personal values, managers cannot motivate merely by making rational statements about the intended value of rewards or their likelihood of being received. People insist on acting like human beings rather than rational machines. We must accept them as the emotional beings they are and motivate them in their individual ways. We cannot easily persuade them to adopt the motivational patterns we want them to have. We always motivate people in terms of *their needs,* not ours.

DIFFERENT PERCEPTIONS Since perception is an individual experience, there can be two or more views of the same situation. As shown in the cartoon in Figure 6-3, two people may view the depth of the snow in two different ways. Snow depth is an objective fact that can be measured, but most human situations are complex and not measurable. This fact makes motivation especially difficult unless we try to understand the perceptions of other people. The results of our attempts are sometimes startling, as illustrated here:

One of the authors was surveying employee reactions to a new work schedule that gave workers wide latitude in setting their daily hours. Most responses to a question regarding their new flexibility were highly positive. One woman, however, reported

THE FAMILY CIRCUS®
By Bil Keane
Copyright 1979
The Register and Tribune
Syndicate, Inc
BIL KEANE
"This is nothing. When I was your age we had snow that came all the way up to here on me."

FIGURE 6-3
Two perceptions of the same situation
From The Family Circus *by Bil Keane, Reprinted courtesy of the Register and Tribune Syndicate, Inc.*

that she had *no* flexibility. When asked to explain her curious response, she stated that she had to be home at 3:20 P.M. every day to welcome her children home from school. Consequently, she perceived that the new system offered no flexibility, and indeed it did not—for her.

THE IMPACT OF UNCERTAINTY If we accept the expectancy model, it follows that in order to motivate a person we can pursue two paths. First, we can recognize and attempt to affect the employee's perception of the rewards—the valence and probability of receipt. Second, we can work to strengthen both the actual value of the rewards and the connections between effort and performance as well as performance and rewards.

The connection between effort and ultimate reward is often uncertain. There are so many causes and effects in a situation that rarely can an employee be sure that a desired reward will follow a given action. In addition, there are both primary and secondary outcomes. The *primary outcomes* result directly from an action. Then the *secondary outcomes* follow from the primary ones. For example, as shown in Figure 6-4, an employee secures more training and eventually earns the primary outcome of a promotion and the pay that goes with it. Then secondary outcomes follow. The promotion brings more status and recognition from associates. The higher pay allows the employee and family to purchase more products that they want. The result is a complex and variable series of outcomes from almost any major action.

Primary and secondary outcomes

Another cause of outcome uncertainty is that many outcomes are controlled by others and the employee cannot be sure how they will act. In the case of the employee who is seeking a promotion, both the promotion and the higher pay are given by management, and the higher status is given by one's associates. This second-party relationship often creates great uncertainty.

Since the expectancy model depends on the employee's view of the relationship between effort, performance, and rewards, often a simple, straightforward incentive is more motivating than a complex one. The complex one may involve so much uncertainty that the employee does not sufficiently connect the desired work behavior with a valued reward. The simple incentive, on the other hand, offers a practical course of action that the employee can picture and understand; therefore, it carries higher values for expectancy and instrumentality.

Interpreting the expectancy model

Contributions

The expectancy model is a valuable tool for helping managers think about the mental processes through which motivation occurs. In this model, employees do not simply act because of strong internal drives, unmet needs, or the application of rewards and punishments. Instead, people must be viewed as thinking individuals whose beliefs, perceptions, and probability estimates powerfully influence their behavior. It is a model that values human dignity.

The expectancy approach also encourages managers to design a motivational climate that will stimulate appropriate employee behavior. Managers are en-

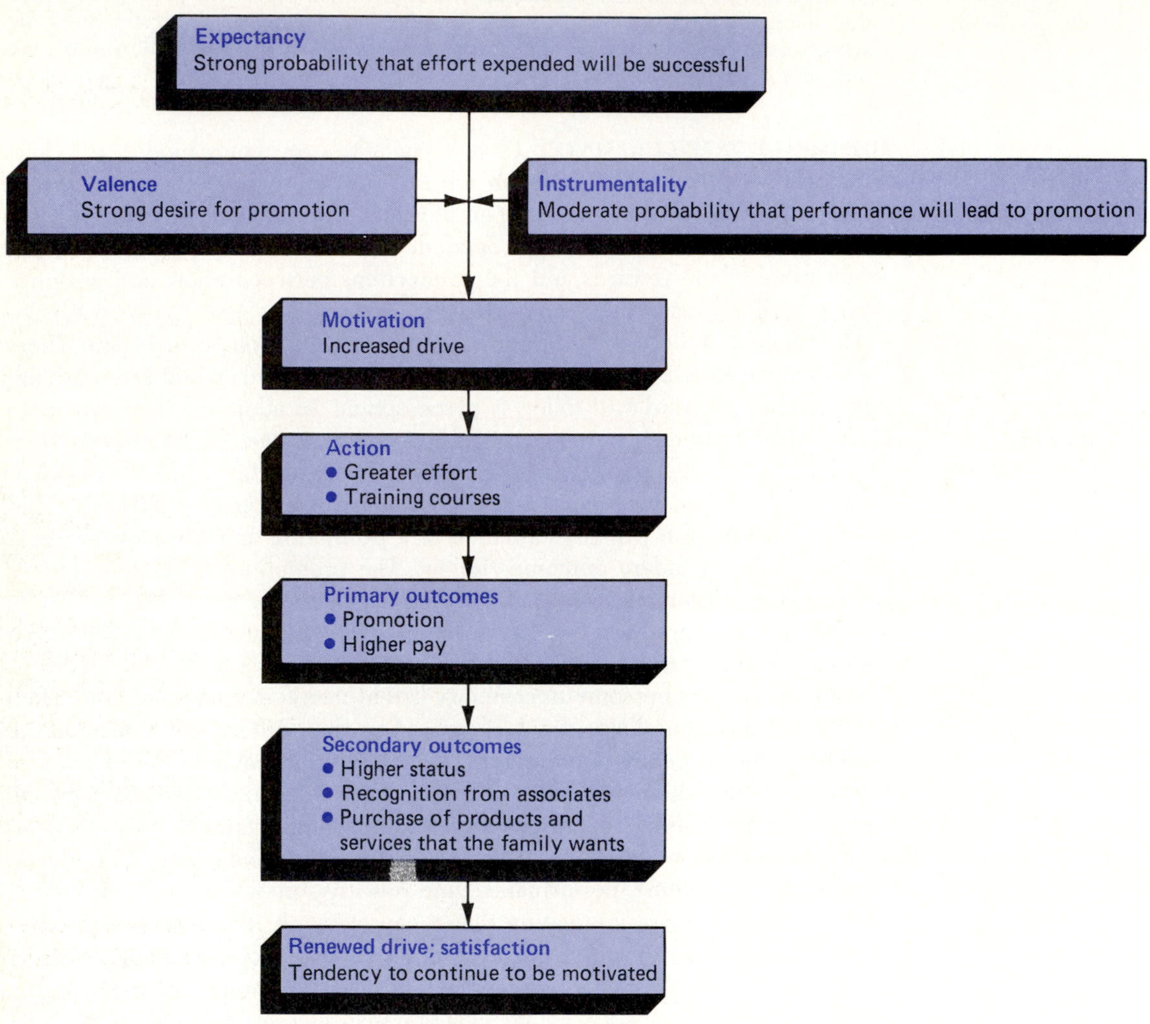

FIGURE 6-4
Operation of the expectancy model

couraged to communicate with employees, asking them three kinds of questions: "What rewards do you value? Do you believe your effort will result in successful performance? How likely is it that you will receive your desired rewards?" Then some difficult tasks may face managers, such as telling employees why some desired rewards are unavailable or explaining to them why other factors may restrict employee performance despite their strong efforts.

Limitations

Despite its general appeal, the expectancy model has some problems. Like any newer model, it needs to be tested to learn how well research evidence supports it. For example, the multiplicative combination of the three elements is still open to question. It is also important to discover what kinds of behavior the model explains and which situations it does not apply to very well.

In addition, reliable measures of valence, expectancy, and instrumentality need to be developed. There is a special need to develop measures that managers can use in actual work settings. When possible, managers need to learn both *what* employees perceive and *why* they hold those valence, expectancy, and instrumentality beliefs.

One research study examined the rewards that salespeople value, and found that a two-step procedure was a useful method for assessing valence.[8] Respondents first ranked the rewards offered from 1 to 12 and then valued them all on thermometer scales (with the best anchored at 100 points). Compared with two other methods, this technique required the least time and was the most acceptable to the respondents. This indicates that useful measures are being created to support the expectancy model.

The model also needs to be made more complete while still remaining practical enough for managers to use. Recent indications are that some additional factors can be added to it to better explain employee behavior. For example, there are often several different rewards available to employees. The valence of each must be assessed and combined with the others to estimate the total motivational force for each employee. As another example of a possible addition, motivated employees must be provided with the *opportunity* to perform (refer back to Figure 5-1).

In addition, other factors may complicate the process of predicting motivation.[9] Some employees may look beyond short-term rewards to future payoffs; others may feel indebted to their employer for past favorable treatment and perform well out of a sense of obligation. Others may lack job alternatives and perform acceptably because of fear of losing their employment. Other employees may simply have very high energy levels or be very talented.

The model raises some fundamental questions: Is it so complex that managers will tend to use only its highlights and not explore its details and implications? Will other managers ignore it altogether? Many managers in operating situations do not have the time or resources to use a complex motivational system on the job. However, as they begin to learn about it, perhaps they can use parts of it.

However, the expectancy model does blend easily with behavior modification. A manager can use the acquired information about employee perceptions of valence to select those rewards which, when applied systematically, will have a predictable effect on employee behavior. The model is also related to a number of other important managerial practices, including management by objectives and goal setting.

COMPARISON MODELS

The previous discussions of motivational models have viewed the employee as an individual, virtually independent of other employees. As pointed out in Chapter 1, however, employees work in a social system in which each is dependent to some degree on the others. Employees interact with each other on tasks and on social occasions. They observe each other, judge one another, and make comparisons. The next two models to be discussed build on this notion of comparison to add new dimensions to our overall understanding of employee motivation. They are the equity and attribution models.

The equity model

Most employees are concerned about more than just having their needs satisfied; they also want their reward system to be fair. This issue of fairness applies to all types of rewards—psychological, social, and economic—and it makes the managerial job of motivation much more complex. J. Stacy Adams's *equity theory* states that employees tend to judge fairness by comparing their relevant inputs and contributions on the job to the rewards they receive, and also comparing this ratio to those of other people (see Figure 6-5).[10] Consistent with the psychological contract discussed in Chapter 3, they analyze the fairness of their own "contract," and then compare their contract with those of other workers, and even with those of others in the community and society. Fairness of rewards may even be judged in comparison to relatively arbitrary criteria like age, as this example shows:

Irene Nickerson is a supervisor in a large public utility. For several years, her friends told her she could consider herself successful when her salary (in thousands

FIGURE 6-5
Key factors in equity assessment

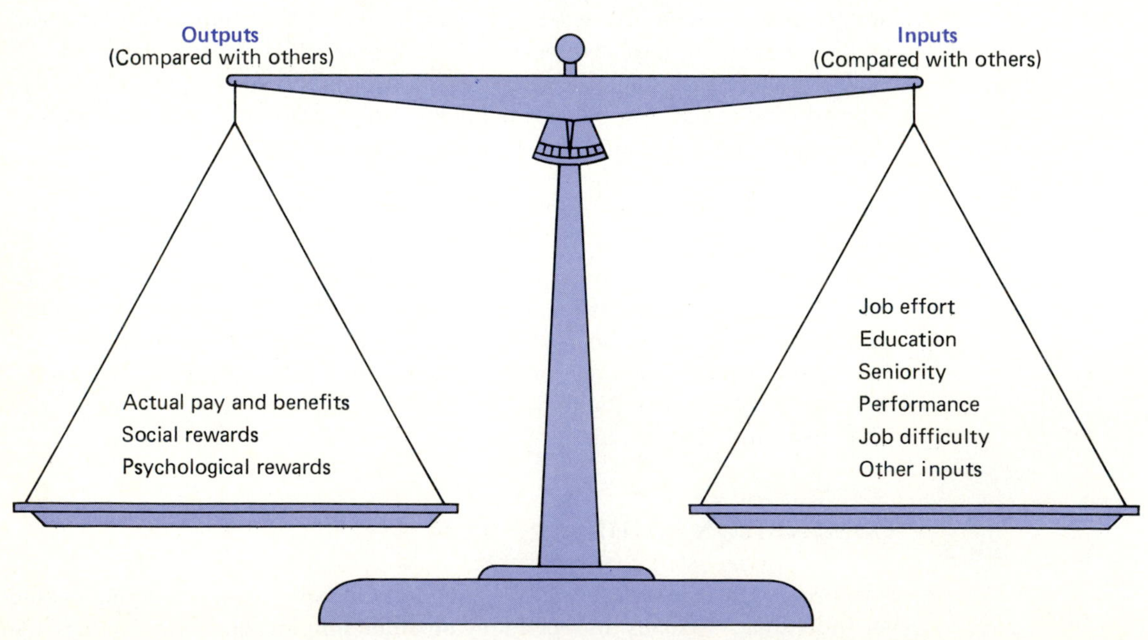

of dollars) surpassed her age. One year, at age thirty-four, she received a substantial salary increase that placed her income at $33,865. She was frustrated, incensed, and demoralized for weeks afterward! For an extra $135, the company could have matched her equity expectations and produced a motivated employee.

Pay was a symbolic scorecard by which Nickerson compared her outputs with her inputs (since she included age with her other inputs of education, experience, and effort). Her reaction is only one of the three combinations that can occur from social comparisons—equity, overreward, and underreward. If employees perceive equity, they will continue to contribute at about the same level. Otherwise they will experience tension that will create the motivation to reduce the inequity. The resulting actions can be either physical or psychological, and internal or external.

If employees feel overrewarded, equity theory predicts that they will feel an imbalance in their relationship with their employer and seek to restore that balance. They might work harder (shown as an internal and physical response in Figure 6-6), they might discount the value of the rewards received (internal and psychological), they could try to convince other employees to ask for more rewards (external and physical), or they might simply choose someone else for comparison purposes (external and psychological).

Workers who feel they have been inadequately rewarded seek to reduce their feelings of inequity through the same types of strategies, but some of their specific actions are now reversed. They might lower the quantity or quality of their productivity, they could inflate the perceived value of the rewards received, or they could bargain for more actual rewards. Again, they could find someone else to compare themselves (more favorably) with, or they might simply quit. In any event, they are reacting to inequity by bringing their inputs into balance with their outputs. This allows managers to predict part of their employees' behavior through understanding when, and under what conditions, workers will experience inequity.

For example, a guest at a resort hotel left her camera at the information counter while she went shopping for the afternoon. The clerk placed the camera under the counter for safekeeping. When the guest returned, the camera was missing. The

TYPE OF INEQUITY REACTION	POSSIBLE OVERREWARD BEHAVIORAL REACTIONS	POSSIBLE UNDERREWARD BEHAVIORAL REACTIONS
Internal, physical	**Work harder**	**Lower productivity**
Internal, psychological	**Discount the reward**	**Inflate value of the reward**
External, physical	**Encourage referent person to obtain more**	**Bargain for more; possibly quit**
External, psychological	**Change the referent person**	**Change the referent person**

FIGURE 6-6
Possible reactions to perceived inequity

clerk called the manager, who eventually gave the guest a $275 credit for the value of the camera. Upon investigation, the manager determined that twenty-seven employees had access to the camera's storage place during the time it was there. He then announced that he would deduct $10 from each of their paychecks to help pay for the camera, although he agreed to return the charge if the thief confessed and paid the $275.

The affected employees were angry and upset. They felt that they were being treated unfairly because they had not taken the camera but were being required to pay for someone else's theft. Most of them resented the fact that their honesty had been questioned. Three employees resigned immediately because of the incident, and two others said they would leave as soon as they could find new jobs. Dissatisfaction and antimanagement attitudes increased, and performance declined noticeably. As stated by one of the employees, "If they are going to give us shabby treatment, then that's what we will give their guests." The employees experienced inequity, and that created a strong (and unfortunately negative) tension within them.

INTERPRETING THE EQUITY MODEL An understanding of equity should remind managers that employees work within several social systems. Studies indicate that employees actually select a number of reference groups both inside and outside the organization.[11] Employees are also inclined to shift the basis for their comparison to the standard that is most favorable to them. Educated people often inflate the value of their education, while employees with longer service favor seniority. Other employees choose somewhat higher (economic) groups as their reference. Many employees have strong egos and high opinions of themselves. Consequently, all of these factors (multiple reference groups, shifting standards, upward orientation, and personal egos) make the task of predicting when inequity will occur somewhat complex.

Equity sensitivity

In general, equity theory has generated extensive research, with many of the results being supportive.[12] In particular, underreward seems to produce motivational tension with predictable consequences, with less consistent results for the overreward condition. This may be reconciled by the idea of *equity sensitivity*, which suggests that individuals have different preferences for equity, with some preferring overreward, some conforming to the traditional equity model, and others preferring to be underrewarded.[13] Identifying which employees fall into each class would help managers predict who would experience inequity and how important it would be in affecting their behavior.

Similar elements—effort (inputs) and rewards (outputs)—can be seen when comparing the equity and expectancy models. In both approaches, perception plays a key role, again suggesting how valuable it is for a manager to gather information *from* employees instead of trying to impose perceptions onto them. The major challenges for a manager using the equity model lie in measuring employee assessments of their inputs and outputs, identifying their choice of references, and evaluating their perceptions of those persons' inputs and outputs.

The attribution model

A recent addition to the motivational literature is attribution theory. *Attribution* is the process by which people interpret the causes of their own and others' behavior. It stems from the work of Fritz Heider and has been expanded and refined by others.[14] Its value lies in the belief that if we can understand how people assign causes to what they see, we will then be better able to predict and affect their future behavior.

Four general attributions

Two basic distinctions underlie the approach, as shown in Figure 6-7. The first is whether people tend to point toward the environment (situation) or personal characteristics as causal factors for their performance. The second requires an assessment as to whether those factors are perceived to be relatively stable or unstable. The combination of those two assessments results in four different potential explanations for an employee's performance on a task—ability, effort, difficulty of the task, or luck.[15]

For example, after each professional football game, the head coach sits down with the assistant coaches and grades each player's performance. After doing so, the coach must also determine whether it was the result of superior or inferior ability, greater or lesser effort, an experienced or inexperienced opponent, or good or bad luck. Since these are subjective assessments, we are interested in what affects the choice of explanations.

One important factor is whether we are evaluating our own behavior or interpreting another's. In general, people tend to overestimate the influence of personal traits when assessing their own successes, and to attribute others' achievements to good luck or easy tasks.[16] The process is reversed for failures,

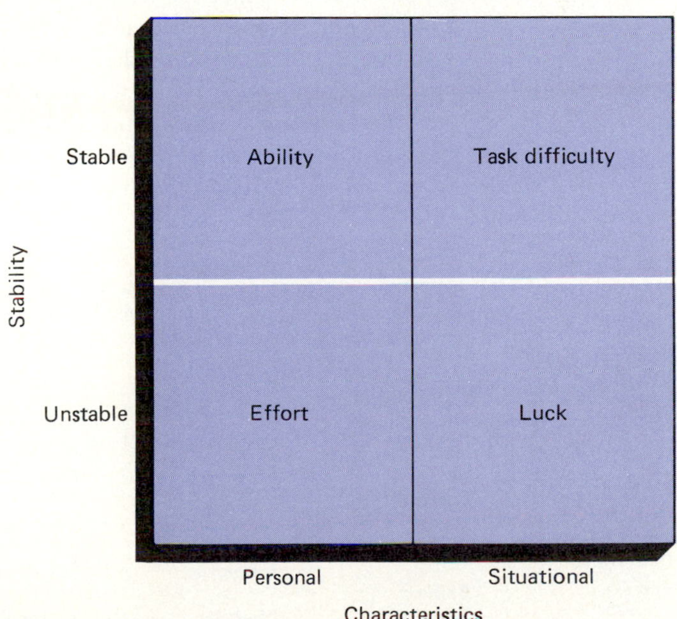

FIGURE 6-7
Situations leading to different attributions

as shown in Figure 6-8. In that case people tend to assign situational causes for their own limited performance, but assume that someone else failed to try hard enough or simply lacked the overall ability to succeed. These attributional tendencies accent the existing role differences between managers and employees.[17]

Consider again the case of Marsha Donner at the beginning of this chapter. At the conclusion of the project, she might appraise her work as successful, see it as consistent with her overall work performance, and conclude that she has exceptional ability (thus reinforcing her competence drive). Her manager may be equally satisfied with the quality of Project Symposium, agree that it reflects her usual level of performance, but conclude that the tasks assigned to her have been too easy (and thus not praise her). What will happen to her future motivation?

Perceptual set

Attributions such as those made by Marsha and her manager illustrate the effects of *perceptual set;* that is, people tend to perceive what they expect to perceive. For this reason perceptual set sometimes causes us to misread a situation and only "see" what we expect to see. Managers, therefore, need to be aware of their own perceptual sets and the effects of these sets on their interaction with others. Similarly, they need to be aware of their employees' perceptual sets in order to understand their workers better.

Self-fulfilling prophecy

The relatively passive idea of perceptual set extends into the behavior of individuals when we witness the power of the *self-fulfilling prophecy,* or the "Pygmalion effect." The self-fulfilling prophecy suggests that a manager's expectations for an employee will cause the manager to treat the employee differently and that the employee will respond in a way that confirms the initial expectations.[18] For example, if a supervisor is told that a new employee is competent, the supervisor is more likely not only to perceive that competence but also to provide opportunities for the employee to demonstrate competence on the job. The supervisor then attributes the task performance to the employee's ability. This shows how important perceptual set and the self-fulfilling prophecy can be in reversing the natural attributional tendencies discussed earlier.[19]

One supervisor's experience shows the roles that perceptual sets and self-fulfilling expectations can play. One of his machinists strongly wanted three days of vacation

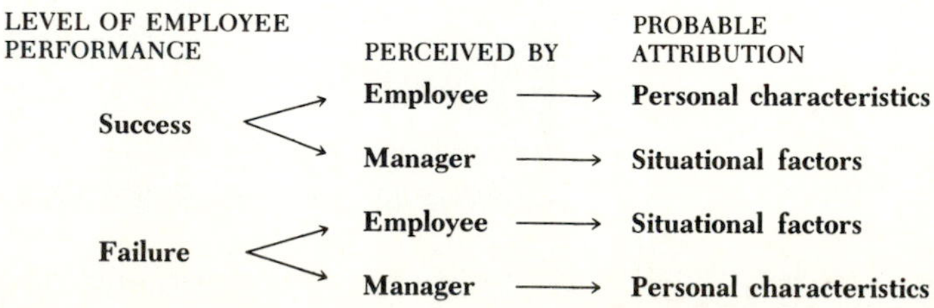

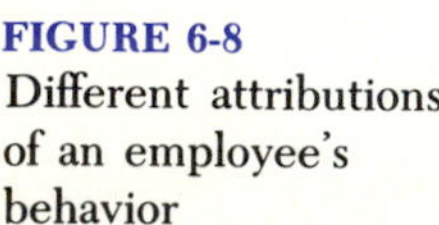
FIGURE 6-8
Different attributions of an employee's behavior

in order to go deer hunting. Since the department was so rushed that it was even working overtime every Saturday, the supervisor would not give him time off.

The machinist also had a record of tardiness. One morning he arrived thirty minutes late. The harassed supervisor, without giving much thought to his words, threatened the employee with three days off without pay if he was tardy again that month.

Guess who was tardy the next morning? You are correct. The machinist perceived the "threat" as an opportunity to go on his desired deer hunt. The supervisor saw no other choice than to give the machinist a disciplinary penalty of three days off without pay. In this way, management policies were applied and the machinist reached his goal of going deer hunting, but the needed work was not done on schedule.

APPLICATIONS OF ATTRIBUTION The attributional model can be easily integrated with our earlier discussion of other motivational approaches. For example, achievement-oriented persons may claim that their accomplishments are the direct result of their high level of effort. Competence-driven employees are more likely to believe that they have a high level of general ability. Although goals are most motivational when they are challenging, employees will examine them closely to determine if they are *too* difficult to attain.

In conjunction with the expectancy model, an employee who fails on a task may feel that the environment prevents success and, therefore, may reduce the level of future effort. Users of behavior modification are cautioned to consider carefully their response to an employee's successful performance. A manager may assume it was due to luck or an easy task and withhold appropriate recognition. The employee, who believes that success was the result of ability or effort, may experience a decline in motivation for the lack of a reward.

Managers might benefit from greater awareness of their own attributional process and how it affects their behavior toward employees.[20] They could also seek to reinforce among subordinates the belief that success is due to the workers' own efforts (effort-performance expectancies) and abilities, while discouraging the employee attribution that failure is due to task difficulty or luck. Simple attributions should be avoided, since employee behavior is also partly determined by the task, social context, and environment, as outlined in Chapter 1.[21]

INTERPRETING MOTIVATIONAL MODELS

Several motivational models have been presented in Chapters 5 and 6. All the models have strengths and weaknesses, advocates and critics. No model is perfect, but all of them add something to our understanding of the motivational process. Other models are being developed, and attempts are being made to integrate existing approaches.[22]

The cognitive models are likely to continue dominating organizational practice for some time, as indicated by the recent attention to the attribution model. They are most consistent with our supportive and holistic view of

Contingent use of motivational models

people. However, behavior modification also has some usefulness, especially in stable situations with minimum complexity, where there appears to be a direct connection between behavior and its consequences. In more complex, dynamic situations, cognitive models will be used more often. In other words, the motivational model used must be adapted to the situation as well as blended with other models.

Micromotivation

Type A motivation

The emphasis of the last two chapters has been on motivation on the job and within the firm. This kind of motivation is called *micromotivation*, or type A motivation. It focuses on motivation within one individual organization. The idea is to change conditions within the firm in order to increase employee productivity, that is, to motivate employees better. However, we cannot ignore the fact that firms employ whole people who live and play away from their work. They bring to the job many attitudes that are conditioned by their environment, and these attitudes influence their job performance.

The macromotivation model

Type B motivation

The area of interest that focuses on environmental conditions outside the firm that influence job performance is basically a *macromotivation* model, or type B motivation.[23] This external environment may have a major influence on performance. For example, does society support work, or does it emphasize leisure as a primary value? Does it perceive factory workers as alienated moneygrubbers or as major contributors to society? Does it increase the tax *rate* as one earns more money from a promotion, thus restricting its use? All these environmental conditions affect the rewards one derives from work.

Consider how macromotivation applies to the expectancy model. Employees usually seek primary outcomes in order to reach secondary outcomes, such as social esteem and the purchase of products and services. These secondary outcomes are frequently controlled by the macromotivational environment, not by the firm. If the tax system penalizes with a higher tax rate the employees who earn a raise in pay, then expectancy for reward from the raise is reduced.

Other models of motivation apply in a similar way. Using the earlier example of the higher tax rate following a raise, the behavior modification model predicts that reinforcement for better performance is reduced. In other instances society may not penalize workers, but it fails to reward them by giving recognition or esteem for their efforts. In that case, there is no reinforcement and the behavior is extinguished.

Since there are two environments (inside and outside the firm) that affect motivation, both need to be improved for high motivation. If job conditions are unrewarding, motivation is likely to be weak no matter how supportive the external environment is. However, the reverse also applies. If environmental conditions do not support better job performance, motivation tends to be weak, even when conditions on the job are favorable. Management cannot alone solve motivation problems. It must have society's support.

SUMMARY

Three additional approaches to motivation presented in this chapter are the expectancy, equity, and attribution models. The expectancy model states that motivation is a product of how much one wants something and the probabilities that effort will lead to task accomplishment and reward. The formula is valence $\times$ expectancy $\times$ instrumentality = motivation. Valence is the strength of a person's preference for an outcome. Expectancy is the strength of belief that one's effort will be successful in accomplishing a task. Instrumentality is the strength of belief that successful performance will be followed by a reward.

The other motivational models specifically relate to the employee's intellectual processes. The equity model has a double comparison in it—a match between an employee's perceived inputs and outcomes, coupled with a comparison to some referent persons' rewards for their input level. The attribution process examines the way people interpret behavior and assign causes to it. Attributions differ, depending on who is making the judgment and whether the behavior was successful or not. Four general attributions are made. Ability and effort are personal factors, while two situational explanations involve the difficulty of the task and luck.

Cognitive models that focus on internal states and mental processes dominate thinking about motivation, but behavior modification, discussed in Chapter 5, also is useful. Most attention has been given to type A motivation (micromotivation), but in order to build a complete motivational environment, increased emphasis must be given to type B motivation (macromotivation).

Terms and concepts for review

The expectancy model
Valence
Expectancy
Instrumentality
Perception
Primary and secondary outcomes
Equity
Attribution
Perceptual set
Self-fulfilling prophecy
Micromotivation (type A)
Macromotivation (type B)

Discussion questions

1 Can the expectancy model be applied to your own personal motivation as a student? Discuss.
2 How would you use the expectancy model in the following situations?

a You want two employees to switch their vacations from the summer to the spring so that job needs will be filled suitably during the summer.

b You believe that one of your employees has excellent potential for promotion and want to encourage her to prepare for it.

c You have a sprained ankle and want a friend to walk to a fast-food restaurant and get you a hamburger.

3 Name two outcomes in your job or classroom that have negative valence for you personally. How would knowledge of these help someone who is trying to motivate you?

4 Apply the equity model to yourself as a student. How do you measure your inputs and outputs? Whom have you chosen as referent individuals? Do you feel equity? If not, how will you attain it?

5 The text suggested that an individual's equity perceptions might be distorted. If so, how would you go about correcting or adjusting them?

6 Think of one success and one failure experience in your life. Did your attribution of the causes on those occasions match the prediction of the attribution model? Explain.

7 Refer back to the four drives presented in Chapter 5. Would an achievement-oriented manager be likely to attribute failure of an employee to different causes than would an affiliation-oriented manager? Discuss.

8 What are the similarities and differences between the expectancy model and behavior modification?

9 What can be done to create a better macromotivational climate by

a A manager?

b An organization?

c Publicly elected officials?

10 Create a set of ten action-oriented guidelines (based on Chapters 5 and 6) that tell managers what they can do to motivate employees.

Incident

JACOB ARNOLD

Jacob Arnold is an engineer in a large design engineering office. Jacob comes from a rural background, and his family had a low income and stern rules. In order to earn his college degree, he had to work, and he paid most of his own expenses.

Jacob is an intelligent and capable worker. His main fault is that he does not want to take risks. He hesitates to make decisions for himself, often bringing petty and routine problems to his supervisor or to other engineers for a decision. Whenever he does a design job, he brings it in rough draft to his supervisor for approval before he finalizes it.

Since Jacob is a capable person, his supervisor wants to motivate him to be more independent in his work. The supervisor believes that this approach will improve Jacob's performance, relieve the supervisor from extra routine, and give Jacob more self-confidence. However, the supervisor is not sure how to go about motivating Jacob to improve his performance.

Question

In the role of supervisor, explain how you would motivate Jacob, using at least three different motivational models. Be as specific as possible.

Experiential exercise

ARE GRADES MOTIVATORS?

1 Each student should individually assess the valence of receiving an A in this course. Assign that A a valence somewhere between −1.0 and +1.0, using gradations of one-tenth (e.g., 0.8, 0.9, 1.0).

2 Now the students should individually assess the probability (between 0.0 and 1.0) that the level of effort they expect to commit to this course will result in high enough performance to merit an A letter grade. This constitutes each student's expectancy score.

3 Then the students should individually assess the probability (between 0.0 and 1.0) that their stellar performance in this course (an A) will substantially improve their overall grade point average. This represents each student's instrumentality score.

4 They should now multiply their *V*, *E*, and *I* scores to produce an overall measure of their likely motivation (on this one task and for this "reward"). This overall score should fall between −1 and +1.

5 Now the class members should share their four scores with each other in a format like that shown here, making particular note of the range of responses for each item.

STUDENT NAME	VALENCE	EXPECTANCY	INSTRUMENTALITY	MOTIVATION
1				
2				
3				
4				
5				
etc.				

6 The students should discuss the possible reasons for the variation within the class in each of the four scores. What are the implications of diverse scores for each of the variables? Assuming that you were the instructor for this course, what could you do to increase the average motivational level of the students?

7 Now poll the class to obtain individual estimates of the total number of hours that each student will devote to this course during this term for those seeking a B letter grade. Identify the person with the lowest, and the individual with the highest, hourly estimates. Now interview both of them with regard to their feelings of equity or inequity. What are the positive and negative implications from experiencing this type of inequity? How could the feelings of inequity be resolved?

References

1 Ford S. Worthy, "You're Probably Working Too Hard," *Fortune*, Apr. 27, 1987, p. 140.

2 David Kipnis, "The View from the Top," *Psychology Today*, December 1984, p. 34.

3 Victor H. Vroom, *Work and Motivation*, New York: John Wiley & Sons, Inc., 1964; Lyman W. Porter and Edward E. Lawler III, *Managerial Attitudes and Performance*, Homewood, Ill.: Dorsey Press and Richard D. Irwin, Inc., 1968.

4 The idea of self-efficacy was introduced by Albert Bandura, "Self-Efficacy: Toward a Unifying Theory of Behavioral Change," *Psychological Review*, vol. 84, 1977, pp. 191–215. The application of self-efficacy to training is proposed in Raymond A. Noe, "Trainees' Attributes and Attitudes: Neglected Influences on Training Effectiveness," *Academy of Management Review*, October 1986, pp. 736–749.

5 Madeline Hirschfeld, "Is There an Imposter in Your Office?" *Management Review*, September 1985, pp. 44–47.

6 The original meaning of instrumentality, as offered by Victor Vroom, reflected the level of *association* between performance and reward, and thus was a correlation that could range between −1 and +1. However, later interpretations and modifications to the expectancy model by other writers have generally limited the effective range of instrumentality to include only positive associations from 0 to +1. For a more thorough discussion, see Craig C. Pinder, "Valence-Instrumentality-Expectancy Theory," in Richard M. Steers and Lyman W. Porter (eds.), *Motivation and Work Behavior*, 4th ed., New York: McGraw-Hill Book Company, 1987, pp. 69–89.

7 Hugh J. Arnold, "A Test of the Predictive Validity of the Multiplicative Hypothesis of Expectancy-Valence Theories of Motivation," *Academy of Management Journal*, March 1981, pp. 128–141.

8 Gilbert A. Churchill and Anthony Pecotich, "Determining the Rewards Salespeople Value: A Comparison of Methods," *Decision Sciences*, July 1981, pp. 456–470.

9 See, for example, Terence R. Mitchell, "Motivation: New Directions for Theory, Research, and Practice," *Academy of Management Review*, January 1982, pp. 80–88.

10 For a detailed review of equity theory, see Richard T. Mowday, "Equity Theory Predictions of Behavior in Organizations," in Richard M. Steers and Lyman W. Porter (eds.), *Motivation and Work Behavior*, 4th ed., New York: McGraw-Hill Book Company, 1987. An early presentation of equity theory is in J. S. Adams, "Inequity in Social Exchange," in L. Berkowitz (ed.), *Advances in Experimental Social Psychology*, vol. 2, New York: Academic Press, 1965, pp. 267–299.

11 Simcha Ronen, "Equity Perception in Multiple Comparisons: A Field Study," *Human Relations*, April 1986, pp. 333–346; and Richard W. Scholl, Elizabeth A. Cooper, and Jack F. McKenna, "Referent Selection in Determining Equity Perceptions: Differential Effects on Behavioral and Attitudinal Outcomes," *Personnel Psychology*, Spring 1987, pp. 113–124.

12 For example, see Joel Brockner et al., "Layoffs, Equity Theory, and Work Performance: Further Evidence of the Impact of Survivor Guilt," *Academy of Management Journal*, June 1986, pp. 373–384.

13 Richard C. Huseman, John D. Hatfield, and Edward W. Miles, "A New Perspective on Equity Theory: The Equity Sensitivity Construct," *Academy of Management Review*, April 1987, pp. 222–234.

14 The attribution process was first presented in Fritz Heider, *The Psychology of Interpersonal Relations*, New York, John Wiley & Sons, Inc., 1958. It was elaborated in H. H. Kelley, "The Processes of Causal Attribution," *American Psychologist*, February 1973, pp. 107–128. It is also related to the self-explanatory processes used to explain "learned helplessness" of individuals; see Robert J. Trotter, "Stop Blaming Yourself," *Psychology Today*, February 1987, pp. 31–39.

15 The same four-cell structure for attributions has been extended to many other domains, such as corporate annual reports and executives' explanations for inferior corporate performance. For an example, see Jeffrey D. Ford, "The Effects of Causal Attributions on Decision Makers' Responses to Performance Downturns," *Academy of Management Review*, October 1985, pp. 770–786.

16 Vandra L. Huber, Philip M. Podsakoff, and William D. Todor, "A Dimensional Analysis of Supervisor and Subordinate Attributions of Success and Failure," *Journal of Occupational Behaviour*, April 1985, pp. 131–142.

17 A model of these conflicting attributions is in Mark J. Martinko and William L. Gardner, "The Leader/Member Attribution Process," *Academy of Management Review*, April 1987, pp. 235–249.

18 The self-fulfilling prophecy was initially presented in Robert K. Merton, "The Self-fulfilling Prophecy," *Antioch Review*, vol. 8, 1948, pp. 193–210. Recent reviews and applications are in Lee Jussim, "Self-Fulfilling Prophecies: A Theoretical and Integrative Review," *Psychological Review*, October 1986, pp. 429–445; and Dov Eden, "OD and Self-Fulfilling Prophecy: Boosting Productivity by Raising Expectations," *Journal of Applied Behavioral Science*, vol. 22, no. 1, 1986, pp. 1–13.

19 An illustration of perceptual set on subsequent supervisory treatment of employees is in Robert Vecchio, "Are You *In* or *Out* with Your Boss?" *Business Horizons*, November–December 1986, pp. 76–78.

20 Related research is reported in James R. Meindl and Sanford B. Ehrlich, "The Romance of Leadership and the Evaluation of Organizational Performance," *Academy of Management Journal*, March 1987, pp. 91–109; and Hugh J. Arnold, "Task Performance, Perceived Competence, and Attributed Causes of Performance as Determinants of Intrinsic Motivation," *Academy of Management Journal*, December 1985, pp. 876–888.

21 Dean Tjosvold, "The Effects of Attribution and Social Context on Superiors' Influence and Interaction with Low Performing Subordinates," *Personnel Psychology*, Summer 1985, pp. 361–376.

22 For example, see Martin G. Evans, "Organizational Behavior: The Central Role of Motivation," *1986 Yearly Review of Management* of the *Journal of Management*, Summer 1986, pp. 203–222.

23 For an example, see George F. Dreher, "The Impact of Extra-Work Variables on Behavior in Work Environments," *Academy of Management Review*, April 1982, pp. 300–304.

For additional reading

Harvey, John H., William Ickes, and Robert F. Kidd (eds.), *New Directions in Attribution Research*, vol. 3, Hillsdale, N.J.: Lawrence Erlbaum, 1981.

Jaques, Elliott, *Equitable Payment*, New York: John Wiley & Sons, Inc., 1961.

Korman, Abraham, *The Psychology of Motivation*, Englewood Cliffs, N.J.: Prentice-Hall, Inc., 1974.

Lawler, Edward E., III, *Motivation in Work Organizations*, Monterey, Calif.: Brooks/Cole Publishing Co., 1973.

Pinder, Craig C., *Work Motivation*, Glenview, Ill.: Scott, Foresman and Company, 1984.

Rosenthal, Robert, *Pygmalion in the Classroom*, New York: Holt, Rinehart and Winston, 1968.

Steers, Richard M., and Lyman W. Porter (eds.), *Motivation and Work Behavior*, 4th ed., New York: McGraw-Hill Book Company, 1987.

Vroom, Victor H., *Work and Motivation*, New York: John Wiley & Sons, Inc., 1964.

Weiner, B. (ed.), *Achievement Motivation and Attribution Theory*, Morristown, N.J.: General Learning Press, 1974.

CHAPTER 7

Appraising and rewarding performance

As we have known for a long time, people in organizations tend to behave as they see others being rewarded.

PETER F. DRUCKER[1]

Our studies indicate that organizations that approach gain sharing strategically and incorporate it as a management philosophy are most likely to be successful.

MICHAEL SCHUSTER[2]

CHAPTER OBJECTIVES

To understand:

Money as an economic and social medium of exchange

The role of money in the motivational models

Behavioral considerations in performance appraisal

Incentive measures that link pay with performance

Uses of profit- and gain-sharing programs

Skill-based pay

Flexible benefits

For twenty-four years Mark McCann worked as a bank teller in a small town. He was the senior person among three tellers, and on rare occasions when both bank officers were away, he was left in charge of the bank. In his community he was a respected citizen. He belonged to a downtown business club and was an elder in his church. Recently he confided to a trusted friend, "I'm looking for another job—just anything to get away from *that bank*." Further questioning revealed that he had been quite satisfied with his job and was still satisfied except for one event. Because of a local labor shortage, one teller's position went unfilled for three months. Finally the bank, in desperation, recruited a young, untrained college man from another city. In order to get him, the bank paid him a monthly salary $25 higher than Mark received. Mark suddenly felt bypassed and forgotten. His whole world had come tumbling down the day he learned of the new teller's rate. He felt that his community social standing had collapsed and that his self-image was destroyed. The employee he was *training* was earning $25 more!

This case illustrates how economic rewards are important to employees and how pay relationships carry immense social value. Management has not always recognized their social importance to workers. In the nineteenth and early twentieth centuries employees were supposed to want primarily money; therefore, money was believed to produce direct motivation—the more money offered, the more motivation. Roethlisberger and his followers successfully buried this idea by showing that economic rewards operated through the attitudes of workers in the social system to produce an *indirect* incentive.

In this chapter we discuss the complex relationship between economic reward systems and organizational behavior. More details about these systems will be found in books about compensation and human resource management; only their significant behavioral aspects are examined here. The focus of this chapter is on money as a means of rewarding employees, motivational models applied to pay, cost-reward comparisons, and behavioral considerations in performance appraisal. Then we discuss incentive pay, where each worker's pay varies in relation to employee or organizational performance. Finally, we show how incentives are combined with other parts of wage administration to build a complete reward system that encourages motivation.

MONEY AS A MEANS OF REWARDING EMPLOYEES

Money has social value.

It is evident that money is important to employees for a number of reasons. Certainly money is valuable because of the goods and services that it will purchase. This is its economic value as a medium of exchange for allocation of economic resources; however, money also is a *social medium of exchange*. All of us have seen its importance as a status symbol for those who have it and can thus save it, spend it conspicuously, or give it generously. Money has status value when it is being received and when it is being spent. It represents to employees what their employer thinks of them. It is also an indication of one employee's relative status compared with that of other employees. It has about as many values as it has possessors. Here is an example of how people respond differently to it:

> **A manager gave two field sales representatives the same increase in pay because each had done a good job. One sales representative was highly pleased with this recognition. She felt she was respected and rewarded because the raise placed her in a higher income bracket. The other sales representative was angered because he knew the raise amounted to the minimum standard available; so he considered it an insult rather than an adequate reward for the outstanding job he felt he was doing. He felt that he was not properly recognized, and he saw this small raise as a serious blow to his own esteem and self-respect. This same raise also affected the security of the two employees in a different manner. The first employee now felt she had obtained more security, but the second employee felt that his security was in jeopardy.**

Application of the motivational models

DRIVES A useful way to think about money as a reward is to apply it to some of the motivational models presented in Chapters 5 and 6. For example, golfers keep score (a record of their total swings) to assess their performance; achievement-oriented employees maintain a symbolic scorecard in their minds by monitoring their total pay and comparing it with others'. It is a measure of their accomplishments. Money also relates to other drives, since it can be used to buy our way into expensive clubs (affiliation) and give us the capacity (power) to influence others, such as through our political contributions.

Money satisfies many needs and drives.

NEEDS In the Herzberg model, pay is primarily viewed as a hygiene factor, although it may have at least short-term motivational value as well. In the other need-based models, pay is most easily seen in its capacity to satisfy the lower-order needs (like Maslow's physiological and security needs, or Alderfer's existence needs). However, we can easily see how it relates to other levels as well, like Mark McCann's esteem needs in the opening example for this chapter.

ATTRIBUTION Pay also relates to the attribution model, if we assume that most employees want more money than they are now receiving. When evaluating their own successful performance, they tend to attribute it to ability or skill, which are legitimate bases for receiving additional rewards. When explaining unsuccessful results, they attribute those to overly difficult tasks or bad luck. These are both factors that are beyond their control and presumably would not be punished by the employer's withholding rewards.

EXPECTANCY MODEL As you will recall, expectancy theory states that valence × expectancy × instrumentality = motivation. This means that if money is to act as a strong motivator, then an employee must want more of it (valence), believe that effort will be successful (expectancy), and trust that the monetary reward will follow better performance (instrumentality).

Valence of money is not easily influenced by management. It is contingent upon an employee's personal values, experiences, and needs as well as the macromotivational environment. For example, if an employee has an independent income, a small increase in pay may have little valence. The same conclusion applies to an employee who cherishes other values and only desires a subsistence income. Similarly, the direct value of money to people in an affluent society tends to decline, since money tends to satisfy lower-order needs more directly than higher-order needs. However, since money has many social meanings to people, employees may seek it for its social value even when its economic value has low valence. This means that *most employees do respond to money as a reward.*

Money has social value.

With regard to instrumentality, many employees are not sure that additional performance will lead to additional pay. They see some employees deliver minimum performance, yet receive almost the same pay increases as high performers. They often see promotions based more on seniority or personal relationships than on performance. Instrumentality is an area where management has much opportunity for positive action, because it can change substantially the connection between increased performance and reward.

Two desired instrumentality conditions

The two desired conditions for instrumentality (which is closely related to contingent rewards under behavior modification) are shown in Figure 7-1 as situations 1 and 4. In each case employees can see that there is a direct connection between performance and reward. The undesirable states are situations 2 and 3, where rewards are withheld from high performers or given to low performers. When these conditions are allowed to occur, many employees will at least be confused about how to perform, and may even be highly dissatisfied with the reward system.

Consider the case of four employees (each of whom was treated differently by the employer) and the possible thoughts running through their minds. Shannon received a substantial pay increase for her outstanding performance ("I think I'll try even harder in the future, since good work is obviously noticed.") Chet's productivity record mirrored Shannon's, but he received only a token salary increase ("If that's all my effort is worth to them, I'm going to really cut back next year.") Travis did not have a good performance record, but because the organization enjoyed a successful year, he was still given a healthy raise ("This is a great place to work, as I can slide by and still do all right.") Pam had an equally poor record, so her supervisor withheld any increase from her ("I guess if I want to get ahead, I need to perform better in the future.") In each case, the reward received (when compared to performance) sends a strong signal regarding future instrumentality.

FIGURE 7-1
Desirable and undesirable instrumentality conditions

SITUATION	LEVEL OF PERFORMANCE	LEVEL OF ECONOMIC REWARD	INSTRUMENTALITY CONDITION
1	**High**	**High**	**Desirable**
2	**High**	**Low**	**Undesirable**
3	**Low**	**High**	**Undesirable**
4	**Low**	**Low**	**Desirable**

Additional considerations in the use of money

EXTRINSIC AND INTRINSIC REWARDS Money is essentially an extrinsic reward rather than an intrinsic one, so it is easily administered in behavior modification programs. However, it also has all the limitations of extrinsic benefits. No matter how closely management attaches pay to performance, pay is still something that originates outside the job and is only useful away from the job. Therefore, it tends to be less immediately satisfying than intrinsic job rewards. For example, the personal satisfaction of a job well done is a powerful motivator for many people. Economic rewards, by contrast, cannot provide all the needed rewards for a psychologically healthy person.

Difficult to integrate

An important task for management is how to integrate extrinsic and intrinsic rewards successfully. One problem is that employees differ in the amount of intrinsic and extrinsic rewards that they want, and jobs and organizational conditions also differ. Another problem occurs when employers begin paying employees for work they previously found satisfying, since some evidence indicates that payment of an extrinsic reward decreases the intrinsic satisfaction received.[3] In addition, it is difficult for managers to administer intrinsic rewards on a systematic basis. These conditions suggest that what is needed is a contingency approach to rewards that considers needs of workers, type of job, organizational environment, and different rewards. Special benefits, such as recognition or status, are sometimes especially valuable to employees because they have more psychological and social meaning.[4]

Some companies, like AT&T, have set up unique opportunities for employees to create and run "independent" businesses within the larger corporate structure.[5] The managers act as entrepreneurs, and are encouraged to take risks in establishing new small businesses that are jointly funded by the parent company and the managers. If successful, the managers then share in the extra financial rewards that are generated, while also enjoying the experience of achievement and the status it brings. Though less extreme, other companies like 3M encourage employees to spend up to 15 percent of their time and some corporate resources on their own pet projects. The potential intrinsic satisfaction from these programs is truly immense.

EQUITY It is evident that many complex issues determine how employees will respond to economic rewards. There is no simple answer for employers in their attempt to create equitable systems. The employee's solution to this complex problem is a rough type of *cost-reward comparison*, similar to the break-even analysis that is used in financial assessments. The employee identifies and compares personal costs and rewards to determine the point at which they are approximately equal, as shown in Figure 7-2.[6] Employees consider all the costs of higher performance, such as more effort. Then they compare these costs with probable rewards, both intrinsic and extrinsic. Both costs and rewards always are valued *from the individual's point of view*. Management can provide the rewards, but the individual employee determines their value.

Cost-reward comparisons

The break-even point of costs and rewards is the point at which costs and rewards are equal for a certain level of performance, as shown by point *B* on the

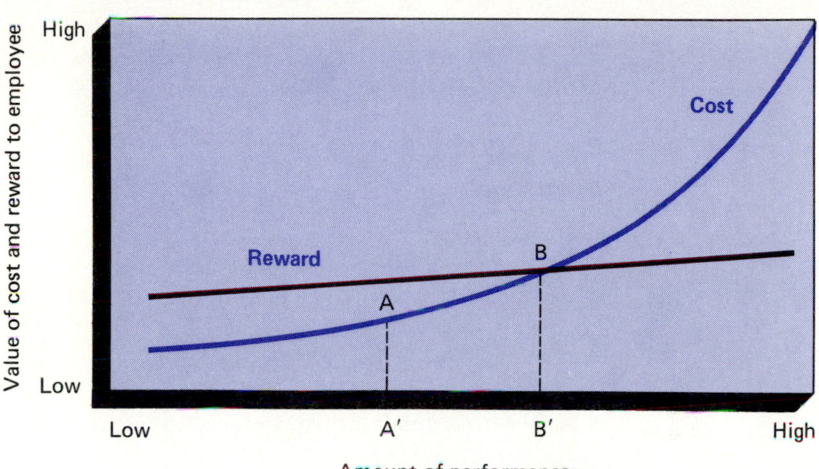

FIGURE 7-2
Cost of performance in relation to reward for an employee. Employee's performance will tend to be in the area of *A′ B′*.

chart. Employee performance tends to be near the break-even point but below it, because typically the employee does not try to be so precise as to maximize the cost-reward relationship. Rather, the employee tries for a satisfactory relationship in which rewards are relatively favorable in relation to costs. Performance tends to be somewhere along the line *A′B′*.

In Figure 7-2 employee costs are shown rising more steeply near the highest level of performance to represent the additional difficulty that maximum effort and concentration require. Each employee's line will have a different shape, representing individual values. The reward line is shown as a straight line, such as that provided by a piece-rate system, but in most instances it rises only in steps after a certain amount of performance improvement occurs. If management can make the reward line rise more steeply by means of larger rewards, then the break-even point will be at a higher level of performance.

Many salespeople work on some form of commission plan that provides them with periodic bonuses.[7] In many cases, the bonuses become larger as the salesperson reaches higher levels of performance, under the assumption that this will stretch the employee to excel. However, this principle is sometimes ignored, as it was by a distributor interviewed by one of the authors. He actually *reduced* the level of bonuses provided as his salespeople reached new plateaus of sales during the month. His explanation? "I don't want my employees getting rich off of me," he said.

COMPLIANCE WITH THE LAW In addition to the need to understand the effects of the various motivational models, compensation management is also complicated by the need to comply with a wide range of federal and state laws. The most significant one, adopted in some states, demands that reward systems be designed so that persons in comparable jobs receive equal pay.[8] Although this program, called *comparable worth*, is a desirable objective to strive for, the law has proven to be difficult for many firms to implement because of the subjec-

Comparable worth

tivity involved in comparing jobs. It has been especially difficult for managers of smaller firms, who may lack expertise in evaluating jobs. A variety of other laws affecting organizational behavior, such as those that apply to equal employment opportunity, will be discussed in Chapter 18.

ORGANIZATIONAL BEHAVIOR AND PERFORMANCE APPRAISAL

Reasons for employee appraisal

Performance appraisal plays a key role in reward systems. It is the process of evaluating the performance of employees. As shown in Figure 7-3, appraisal is necessary in order to (1) allocate resources in a dynamic environment, (2) reward employees, (3) give employees feedback about their work, (4) maintain fair relationships within groups, (5) coach and develop employees, and (6) comply with regulations. Appraisal systems, therefore, are necessary for proper management and for employee development.

The first recorded appraisal system in industry was Robert Owen's use of character books and blocks in his New Lanark cotton mills in Scotland around 1800. The character books recorded each worker's daily reports. The character blocks were colored differently on each side to represent an evaluation of the worker ranging from bad to good, and they were displayed at each employee's workplace. Owen was quite impressed by the way the blocks improved worker behavior.[9]

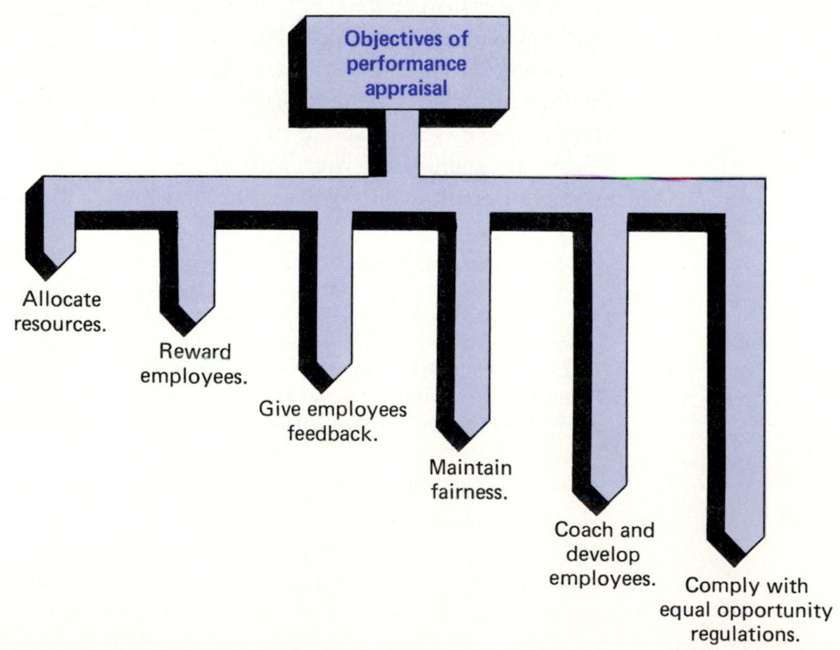

FIGURE 7-3
Objectives of performance appraisal

The performance appraisal system—

- □ **Is an organizational necessity**
- □ **Is based on well-defined, objective criteria**
- □ **Is based on careful job analysis**
- □ **Uses only job-related criteria**
- □ **Is supported by adequate studies of its reliability and validity**
- □ **Is applied by trained, qualified raters**
- □ **Is applied objectively throughout the organization**
- □ **Can be shown to be nondiscriminatory as defined by law**

FIGURE 7-4
Necessary criteria to ensure equal employment opportunity in performance appraisal

The social environment surrounding organizations has changed considerably since Owen developed his system. Federal and state laws have added to the complexity and difficulty of appraisal plans. For example, as shown in Figure 7-4, criteria for compliance with equal employment laws are stringent. Management needs to design and operate its appraisal systems carefully in order to comply with these laws.

Appraisal philosophy

A generation ago, appraisal programs tended to emphasize employee traits, deficiencies, and abilities, but modern appraisal philosophy emphasizes present performance and future goals. Modern philosophy also stresses employee participation in mutually setting goals with the supervisor. Thus the hallmarks of modern appraisal philosophy are (1) performance orientation, (2) focus on goals or objectives, and (3) mutual goal setting between supervisor and employee.[10]

Mutual goal setting

The underlying philosophy behind mutual setting of goals is that people will work harder for goals or objectives that they have participated in setting. The assumption is that people want to satisfy some of their needs through work and that they will do so if management will provide them with a supportive environment. Among their desires are to perform a worthwhile task, share in a group effort, share in setting their objectives, share in the rewards of their efforts, and continue personal growth. Mutual setting of objectives helps accomplish these needs. For example, employees who participate in goal setting for performance appraisal also show significantly better performance. As the saying goes, "If you know where you want to go, you are more likely to get there."

The appraisal interview

Most organizational appraisal systems require supervisors to assess employees on various aspects of their work performance. Regardless of the system used, the assessment is then communicated to the employee in an *appraisal inter-*

view. This is a session in which supervisors provide feedback to their employees on past performance and discuss any problems that have arisen. Then they set objectives for the next time period, and inform employees about their future salaries.

Appraisal problems

The need to perform these multiple functions in the appraisal interview makes it difficult for many managers. In addition, there are several behavioral problems inherent in the process.[11] It can be *confrontational*, because each party is trying to convince the other that one view is more accurate. (These views are distorted by attributional tendencies, as we discussed in Chapter 5.) It is typically *emotional*, since the manager's role calls for a critical perspective, while the employee's desire to "save face" easily leads to defensiveness. It is *judgmental*, because the manager must evaluate the employee's behavior and results, and this places the employee in a clearly subordinate position. Further, performance appraisals are *complex* tasks for managers, requiring job understanding, careful observation of performance, and sensitivity to the needs of employees. Managers are also called upon to handle the issues that spontaneously arise within the discussion itself.

Managers sometimes fail to conduct effective appraisal interviews because they lack vital skills. Perhaps they failed to gather data systematically. Maybe they weren't specific on the expected performance improvements in the previous appraisal. They could be reluctant to address difficult topics, or they could fail to involve the employee in the assessment process and discussion. Some managers may have grown cynical about the probability that attitudinal or behavioral changes will occur. A few may see appraisals as a meaningless game and even intentionally distort the ratings and feedback given. All of these factors can place powerful limits on the usefulness of the appraisal interview, unless it is conducted properly.

Ingredients for success

A review of the research[12] shows that appraisals are most likely to be successful when the appraiser:

- Is knowledgeable about the employee's job
- Has gathered evidence frequently about performance
- Seeks and uses inputs from other observers in the organization
- Sharply limits the amount of criticism (to perhaps two major items)
- Provides support, acceptance, and praise for tasks well done
- Allows participation in the discussion.

Self-appraisal

The last point has been extended even further in recent approaches to the performance appraisal interview. Some organizations in both the private and public sectors include *self-appraisal* as a formal part of the process.[13] Although poor performers tend to attribute their problems to situational factors, and many people rate themselves too leniently, these limitations are offset by the fact that employees are quite candid when asked to identify and compare their strengths and their weaknesses. In addition, self-assessments are much less threatening than those received from others, and therefore provide a more fertile soil for growth and change.

MANAGERIAL EFFECTS Conducting performance appraisals also has substantial impact on the appraiser. On the positive side, a formal appraisal system encourages managers to do more analytical and constructive thinking about their employees. The requirement of a face-to-face interview encourages managers to be more specific about identifying each employee's abilities, interests, and motivation. Managers often perceive that each employee is truly different and must be treated that way. For example, greater participation may be more appropriate when an employee is knowledgeable, has a strong independence need, and has demonstrated acceptable performance in the past.

Realistically, however, managers sometimes avoid giving appraisals because they don't want to disrupt an existing smooth relationship with an employee by providing negative feedback. It is particularly difficult to deal with low-performing employees, who may require more frequent monitoring and reviews. In other cases, managers simply don't see any organizational rewards coming to them from the appraisal process.[14] Where there is no extrinsic or intrinsic incentive to perform the task, managers may neglect it entirely, as in this example:

Gordy, an employee in a utility, reported that for many years his supervisor would simply hand him a folded slip of paper with his next year's salary written on it. This was the sum total of his "performance appraisal"! Only recently did the utility become concerned about effective organizational behavior practices and begin training and rewarding its managers for appraising employees. Now Gordy enjoys the benefits of open discussion of his performance and mutual goal setting.

Even when appraisal interviews are capably conducted by managers, it is doubtful whether they will produce long-term performance changes by themselves. The appraisal acts only as a source of feedback and a psychic reward, and economic incentives are still needed to obtain employee motivation. Various approaches will be described next, along with an assessment of their advantages and disadvantages.

ECONOMIC INCENTIVE SYSTEMS

Pay varies with performance

An *economic incentive system* of some type could be applied to almost any job. The basic idea of them all is to vary an employee's pay in proportion to some criterion of individual, group, or organizational performance. These criteria could include employee production, company profit, units shipped, or the ratio of labor cost to sales prices. Payment may be immediate or may be delayed, as in a profit-sharing plan.

Our discussion of economic incentives focuses on their behavioral implications. We do not attempt to discuss all types of incentives or all details about them. The ones selected for presentation are wage incentives, which are a widely used individual incentive, and profit sharing and gain sharing, which are popular group incentives. Finally, we show how incentives are combined with other parts of wage administration to make a complete pay program.

Although most of our discussion is on long-run incentive programs, it should be recognized that temporary incentives also have a role to play in compensation. Sometimes they provide just the right amount of added motivation to cause a desired increase in performance. Here is an example:

> **A manufacturer of specialized business equipment experienced a substantial decline in sales for one of its models. The decline was so severe that it had scheduled a one-month closing of this model's production line during the Christmas season. At the sales manager's suggestion, the company offered to give its salespeople a new $10 bill for each item of this model sold during the month of December. The offer was made in the context of an extra Christmas bonus opportunity. The response was so great that the production line was kept operating, and some salespeople earned over $4000 in bonus money paid in $10 bills. A $4000 bonus amounted to 10 to 20 percent of a typical salesperson's annual income.**

Incentives linking pay with performance

There are several broad types of incentives that link pay with performance.[15] Major ones are shown in Figure 7-5. Perhaps the most popular measure is for the amount of output to determine pay, as illustrated by a sales commission or a *piece rate*. It provides a simple, direct connection between performance and reward. Those workers who produce more are rewarded more. Often pay is determined by a combination quantity-quality measure in order to ensure that a high quality of product or service is maintained. For example, a piece rate usually is paid only for those pieces that meet quality standards.

Piece rate

In other instances an incentive bonus is given only to those employees who reach established goals. For example, a bonus might be given for selling fifteen automobiles during a month, but there would be no bonus for selling only fourteen. Rewards also may be given on the basis of profit success, as in a profit-sharing plan. Another measure is to link pay with cost efficiency. An example is gain sharing, discussed later in this chapter. Regardless of the type of incentive

INCENTIVE MEASURE	EXAMPLE
Amount of output	**Piece rate: sales commission**
Quality of output	**Piece rate only for pieces meeting the standard; commission only for sales that are without bad debts**
Success in reaching goals	**Bonus for selling fifteen automobiles (but not fourteen)**
Amount of profit	**Profit sharing**
Cost efficiency	**Gain sharing**
Employee skills	**Skill-based pay**

FIGURE 7-5 Major incentive measures to link pay with performance

that is used, its objective is to link a portion of a worker's pay to some measure of employee or organizational performance.

Improved motivation

POTENTIAL ADVANTAGES Incentives provide several potential employee advantages. A major advantage is that they increase employee beliefs (instrumentality) that reward will follow high performance. If we assume that money has valence to an employee, then motivation should increase.

Incentives also appear favorable from the point of view of equity theory. Those who perform better are rewarded more. This kind of input-output balance is perceived by many people to be equitable. Further, if more pay is a valued reward, then incentive systems are favorable from the point of view of behavior modification. They provide a desirable consequence (pay) that should reinforce behavior. Rewards, such as sales commissions, often are rather immediate and frequent, which is consistent with the philosophy of behavior modification.

Another advantage from the employee's point of view is that incentives are comparatively objective. They can be computed from the number of pieces, dollars, or similar objective criteria. Compared with a supervisor's subjective performance ratings, the objective approach tends to have higher acceptance by employees.

POTENTIAL DIFFICULTIES With so many favorable conditions supporting incentives, it seems that workers would welcome almost any incentive because of the rewards it could bring. However, there are difficulties that tend to offset some of the potential advantages. Potential equity is offset by other developments that are perceived as inequities. In behavior modification terms, there are unfavorable consequences that exist alongside the favorable consequences of more pay, so they tend to reduce the potential advantages of incentive pay. When workers make their cost-reward analysis, they find that costs have risen along with rewards. The result may be that the break-even point has changed very little, if at all. The extra problems caused by the incentive may offset much of the economic gain expected. For example, new employees may have difficulty learning the system; other employees with declining energy may experience a decrease in total pay; and some unions may resist the incentive idea. The key thought is that *incentive systems produce both positive and negative employee consequences.* Both must be evaluated in determining the desirability of an incentive system. Economic consequences are likely to be positive, but the direction of psychological and social consequences is less certain.

Evaluate pros and cons.

USE OF WAGE INCENTIVES

More pay for more production

Basically, *wage incentives* provide more pay for more production. The main reason for use of wage incentives is clear: they nearly always increase productivity while decreasing unit labor costs. Workers under normal conditions without wage incentives have the capacity to produce more, and wage incentives are one way to release that potential. The increased productivity often is substantial.

Lincoln Electric Company pioneered the development of individual wage incentives over fifty years ago.[16] Workers seem to enjoy the incentive system. Despite the pressure to be productive, employee turnover is only 6 percent a year, which is one-sixth the rate for comparable firms. Another example is Nucor, a builder and operator of steel-producing minimills. It pays weekly bonuses, based on a measure of acceptable production. Groups typically receive a bonus more than 100 percent above base pay. Turnover rates, after the start-up period, are so small that the company doesn't even bother measuring them.

Criteria for incentive systems

In order to be successful, a wage incentive needs to be simple enough for employees to have a strong belief that reward will follow performance. If the plan is so complex that workers have difficulty relating performance to reward, then higher motivation is less likely to develop. The objectives, eligibility requirements, performance criteria, and payment system all need to be established and understood by the participants.[17]

When incentive systems operate successfully, they are evaluated favorably by participants, probably because they provide psychological as well as economic rewards. Employees receive satisfaction from a job well done, which fulfills their achievement drive. Their self-image may improve because of greater feelings of competence. They may even feel they are making a contribution to society by helping in its attempt to regain a productivity leadership position among nations. Some incentives may encourage cooperation between workers because of the need for employees to work together to earn incentive awards.

One of the authors visited a small assembly plant in rural Illinois. After other workers performed a variety of preliminary tasks, two-person crews on an incentive system installed a variety of hardware—hinges, braces, locks, decorative trim, and handles—on large pieces of furniture. The work speed of the crew that was observed seemed almost unbelievable, as the workers literally flew around their workstation. Their productive interaction was almost like a ballet—it was perfectly choreographed and wordlessly performed. They always seemed to know not only their individual assignment but what their partner would be doing, with only an occasional nod of the head needed as a signal between them. They had been given a fair piece rate, they had the necessary skills and tools, and they both wanted to earn higher pay. As a result they worked furiously for a couple of hours at a time, took breaks whenever they needed them, and still earned more incentive pay than any other team in the factory.

Difficulties with wage incentives

Production wage incentives furnish an example of the kinds of difficulties that may develop with many incentive plans, despite their potential benefits. Management's job is to try to prevent or reduce the problems while increasing benefits, so that the incentive plan works more effectively.

Disruption of social systems

The basic human difficulty with wage incentives of this type is that disruptions in the social system may lead to feelings of inequity and dissatisfaction. At times these disruptions are severe enough to make incentive workers less satisfied with their pay than workers who are paid an hourly wage, even though the incentive workers are earning more.

For any wage incentive plan to be successful, it needs to be coordinated carefully with the whole operating system. If there are long periods when employees must wait for work to arrive at their workplace, then the incentive loses its punch. If the incentive is likely to replace workers, then management needs to plan for their use elsewhere so that employee security is not threatened. If work methods are erratic, then they must be standardized so that a fair rate of reward can be established. This is a complex process leading to many difficulties.

Rate setting

1 Wage incentives normally require establishment of performance standards. *Rate setting* is the process of determining the standard output for each job, which becomes the fair day's work for the operator. Rate setters are often resented not only because subjective judgment is involved but also because they are believed to be a cause of change and more difficult standards.

2 Wage incentives may make the supervisor's job more complex. Supervisors must be familiar with the system, so that they can explain it to employees. Paperwork increases, resulting in greater chance of error and more employee dissatisfaction. Relationships are compounded, and supervisors are required to resolve different expectations from higher management, rate setters, workers, and unions.

Loose rates

3 A thorny problem with production wage incentives is *loose rates.* A rate is loose when employees are able to reach standard output with less-than-normal effort. When management adjusts the rate to a higher standard, employees predictably experience a feeling of inequity.

4 Wage incentives may cause disharmony between incentive workers and hourly workers. When the two groups perform work in a sequence, hourly workers may feel discriminated against because they earn less. If the incentive workers increase output, hourly workers further along the process must work faster to prevent a bottleneck. The incentive workers earn more for their increased output, but the hourly workers do not.

Hourly workers who precede incentive workers in the production process can on occasion "take it easy" and produce less with no cut in pay. But the incentive worker's income is cut when less work is available. The same problem occurs if an hourly worker is absent and reduces the flow of material to incentive workers. Conflicts of this type are so difficult to resolve that it is best for management not to mix the two groups in any closely integrated production sequence.

Output restriction

5 Another difficulty with wage incentives is that they may result in *output restriction,* by which workers limit their production and thus defeat the purpose of the incentive. This phenomenon is caused by several factors—

group insecurities that the production standard will be raised, resistance to change by the informal social organization, and the fact that people are not comfortable working always at full capacity.

Although restriction of work tends to be more evident in factory incentive plans, it also exists in sales work. This is illustrated by the following situation involving salespeople on commission.

Industrial equipment salespeople in one company received a substantial salary plus a commission of 1 percent on sales until a total commission of $20,000 was earned. Any commission thereafter was at 0.25 percent. Each salesperson had an annual quota, but annual sales often varied as much as 100 percent because of the nature of the product. Some salespeople worked only until their quota was earned and then held back, because (1) they were afraid their quota might be raised the next year and they did not want the strain of trying to make a difficult quota or (2) they objected to the commission reduction from 1 to 0.25 percent which occurred at about the same time their quota was reached. Others sold a little more than their quota, because they "wanted to look good on the record" regardless of commission rate; but then they held back because they feared the company would split their territory if sales became too high. Other salespeople tried to sell all they could all the time, regardless of incentive factors.

PROFIT SHARING

Mutual interest is emphasized.

Profit sharing is a system that distributes to employees some portion of the profits of business, either immediately following the fiscal year or deferred until a later date. It was first tried in industry at the beginning of the industrial revolution, but did not become popular until after World War II. The growth of profit sharing has been encouraged by federal tax laws that allow employee income taxes to be deferred on funds in profit-sharing pension plans.

Basic pay rates, performance pay increases, and most incentive systems recognize individual differences, while profit sharing recognizes mutual interests. Employees become interested in the economic success of their employer when they see that their own rewards are affected by it. Greater institutional teamwork tends to develop.

Young organizations working on the fringes of science have found that profit sharing especially is useful to give them the vigor to forge ahead of competitors. If they are successful, the rewards are great, and this possibility builds strong motivation and mutual interest among their employees.

For example, the president of a young computer company in Massachusetts became concerned about the lack of cooperation that developed as his company grew larger. He commented, "Different departments were becoming like little kingdoms. People were becoming more concerned over their own little department, its growth and problems, than they were about the company."[18]

In order to encourage more cooperation, the president made an unusual and substantial offer to his employees. He said that if they would double sales and earnings during the following year, he would give all of them a free one-week trip to London or Disney World. They met their goal satisfactorily, so he shut down the

plant and gave them their free one-week trip. Employees traveled as a group, and each received full pay, most trip expenses, and $100 spending money. Family members or guests could accompany an employee at cost.

Employees liked the award, so the following year the president offered a trip to Rome for another doubling of sales and earnings. Employees again met their goal.

In general, profit sharing tends to work better for fast-growing, profitable organizations in which there are opportunities for substantial employee rewards. It is less likely to be useful in stable and declining organizations with low profit margins and intense competition. Profit sharing also is more applicable to managers and high-level professional people, because their decisions are more likely to have a significant effect on their firm's profits. Operating workers, on the other hand, have more difficulty connecting their isolated actions with their firm's profitability, so profit sharing has less appeal to them.

Some difficulties with profit sharing

Even in those situations where profit sharing seems appropriate, some general disadvantages are relevant:

Indirect relationship

1 Profits are not directly related to an employee's effort on the job. Poor market conditions may nullify an employee's hard work.

Delay

2 The lengthy time interval that employees must wait for their reward diminishes its impact.

Lack of predictability

3 Since profits are somewhat unpredictable, total worker income may vary from year to year. Some workers may prefer the security of a more stable wage or salary.

The social aspects of profit sharing are just as significant as its economic and tax aspects, if not more so. For profit sharing to develop a genuine community of interest, workers need to understand how it works and feel a sense of fairness in its provisions. If they do not, they may resent it, as in the following situation:

Marvin Schmidt, an idealistic owner of a small retail store, employed twenty-five people. He had worked hard to pyramid his meager investment into a prosperous store in the short period of seven years. Much of his success resulted from loyal, cooperative employees who had worked for him several years. He recognized their contributions and wanted to give them extra rewards, but he always had been short of capital.

Finally he had a very prosperous year, so he decided to begin a cash profit-sharing plan to be given as a bonus at Christmas. The generous bonus amounted to 30 percent of each person's pay for the year. It was announced and given as a surprise with the weekly paycheck immediately preceding Christmas. Not one employee thanked him, and most of his employees were cool and uncooperative thereafter. He eventually learned that they felt if he could give that large a bonus, he must have been unjustly exploiting them for years, even though they admitted they had been receiving more than the prevailing wage.

The union view

Just as workers sometimes dislike profit sharing, many unions and their leaders are suspicious of it. Union opposition arises basically because unions have very little control of the factors influencing profit, with the exception of labor costs. They also fear that it will undermine union loyalty, collective bargaining, and organizing campaigns. Profit sharing varies wage earnings from company to company, a fact that may conflict with union goals to establish uniform nationwide rates for their members. There is, however, nothing in profit sharing contrary to union objectives for advancing workers' welfare. Many profit-sharing companies have unions representing their workers, and practical-minded local unions do not oppose it as long as it works.

GAIN-SHARING PLANS

Another useful group incentive is gain sharing (or production sharing). A *gain-sharing* plan is a program that establishes a historical base period of organizational performance, measures improvements, and shares the gains with employees on some formula basis. Examples of the performance factors measured include inventory levels, labor hours per unit of product, usage of materials and supplies, and quality of finished goods.[19] The idea is to pinpoint areas that are controllable by employees and then give them an incentive for identifying and implementing ideas that will result in cost savings.

Scanlon plan

An example of gain-sharing plans is the *Scanlon plan.* It was developed by Joseph N. Scanlon at a small steel company in 1938, and it has been used in a number of other organizations. It is an incentive plan that pays employees for improvements in labor costs that are better than standard. It allocates to labor a standard labor cost based on experience and analysis, such as 42 percent of the total product cost or the total sales value of production. If the employees work more efficiently to reduce that percentage cost, the value of the savings is shared with workers regardless of a firm's profit or loss. The share usually is in proportion to actual earnings of each employee during the period. Figure 7-6 summarizes how the Scanlon plan bonus is calculated.

FIGURE 7-6
Summary of calculations for monthly gain-sharing (Scanlon plan) bonus

MONTHLY BONUS CALCULATION

Net sales for month	**$11,500,000**
Inventory increase	**300,000**
Sales value of production	**$11,800,000**
Standard payroll costs (42 percent of sales value)	**$ 4,956,000**
Less actual payroll	**4,031,000**
Gain-sharing bonus	**$ 925,000**
Bonus as percentage of payroll (to be distributed to each participant in proportion to earnings)	**18.66%**

Gain-sharing plans utilize several fundamental ideas from organizational behavior, and are much more than pay systems. They encourage employee suggestions, provide an incentive for coordination and teamwork, and promote improved communication. Union-management relations often improve, since the union gains status because it takes responsibility for the benefits gained. Attitudes toward technological change improve because workers are aware that greater efficiency leads to larger bonuses. Gain sharing especially broadens the understanding of employees as they see a larger picture of the system through their participation, rather than confining their outlook to the narrow specialty of their job.

Contingency factors

The success of gain sharing is contingent upon a number of key factors, such as moderately small size of the unit, sufficient operating history to allow creation of standards, existence of controllable cost areas, and a relatively stable business.[20] In addition, management must be receptive toward employee participation, the organization must be willing to share the benefits of production increases with employees, and the union should be favorable to such a cooperative effort. Managers need to be receptive to ideas and tolerant of criticism from employees.

A gain-sharing program replaced a piece-rate system at Peabody Barnes, a small (250 employees, $30 million annual sales) producer of industrial pumps and hydraulic equipment.[21] After careful design and implementation, a two-year follow-up study revealed a 24 percent improvement in direct labor efficiency, coupled with 58 percent decreases in both scrap costs and warranty costs. Annual savings estimated at $500,000 resulted from 676 suggestions. Employee acceptance of the plan was indicated by a 95 percent vote to continue it, despite the fact that bonuses were earned in only one-third of the potential bonus periods.

SKILL-BASED PAY

Rewarded for skill and knowledge

In contrast to salaries (which pay someone to hold a job) and wage incentives (which pay for the level of performance), *skill-based pay* (also called knowledge-based pay) rewards individual employees for what they know how to do.[22] They start working at a flat hourly pay rate, and receive increases for either developing skill within their primary job or learning how to perform other jobs within their work unit. Some companies provide increases for each new job learned; others require employees to acquire blocks of new skills. Some skill-based pay systems have supervisors evaluate the knowledge and skill of new employees; others allow work teams to assess the progress of each trainee.

Advantages and disadvantages

Although skill-based pay systems are quite new, they have several potential strengths.[23] They provide strong motivation for employees to develop their work-related skills, they reinforce an employee's sense of self-esteem, and they provide the organization with a highly flexible work force that can fill in when someone is absent. Since workers rotate among jobs to learn them, boredom should be reduced. Pay satisfaction should be relatively high, for two reasons. First, the employee's hourly rate received (for having multiple skills) is often higher than the rate that would be paid for the task being performed, since only in a perfect system would all employees be constantly using their highest skills. As a result, some employees may even feel temporarily overpaid. Second, workers should perceive the system as equitable both in the sense of their costs and rewards being matched and in the knowledge that all employees with the same skills earn the same pay.

Direct and indirect costs

Two direct costs, as well as indirect ones, accrue to the employer. Since most employees will voluntarily learn higher-level jobs, the average hourly pay rate will be greater than normal. This should be more than offset by productivity increases, however. In addition, a substantial investment in employee training must be made, especially in the time spent coaching by supervisors and peers. Not all employees like skill-based pay because it places pressure on them to move up the skill ladder. The subsequent dissatisfaction may lead to a variety of consequences, including employee turnover.

Skill-based pay, like other incentive programs, works best when the organizational culture of the firm is generally supportive and trusting. The system should be understood by employees, they must have realistic expectations about their prospects for higher pay levels, and it must be possible for them to learn new skills and have them promptly evaluated. Under these conditions, the program is consistent with the other incentives discussed in this chapter, since it links employee pay with (the potential for) increased performance.

A COMPLETE PROGRAM

Rating jobs, employees, and the organization

Many types of pay are required for a complete economic reward system. Job analysis and wage surveys *rate jobs,* comparing one job with another according to levels of responsibility. Performance appraisal and incentives *rate employees* in their performance and give them more reward. Profit sharing *rates the organization* in terms of its general economic performance and rewards employees as partners in it. Together these three systems are the incentive foundation of a complete pay program, as roughly diagramed in the pay pyramid in Figure 7-7. Each can contribute something to the employee's economic reward.

Relating pay to objectives and skill-based pay

The three systems are complementary because each reflects a different set of factors in the total situation. Base pay and skill-based pay motivate employees to progress to jobs of higher skills and responsibility. Performance pay is an

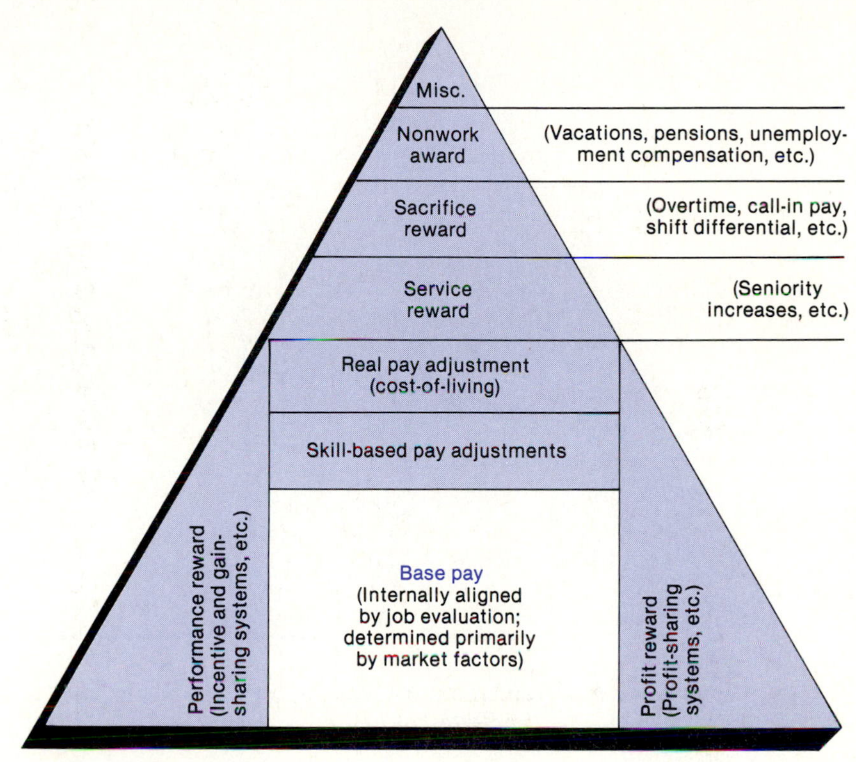

FIGURE 7-7
The pay pyramid: The makeup of a complete pay program (read from bottom)

incentive to improve performance on one's job. Profit sharing motivates toward teamwork to improve an organization's performance.

Other payments, primarily nonincentive in nature, are added to the incentive foundation. Seniority pay adjustments are made to reward workers for extended service and to encourage them to remain with their employer, as is humorously shown in Figure 7-8. If an employer asks workers to sacrifice by working overtime, working on their day off, or working at undesirable hours, the workers may be paid extra for this inconvenience. Other payments are given for periods when an employee does not work, such as vacations, holidays, jury service, and layoffs subject to guaranteed pay.

The additions to the incentive foundation of the pay pyramid have little direct incentive value because they do not increase according to improved job performance. Some of these additions may result in indirect incentive through better attitudes. Other additions, such as seniority pay, actually may decrease worker incentive. It is clear that not one but many factors enter into computation of a worker's paycheck. Some of these factors are related less to incentive than they are to such broad objectives as security, equity, and social justice. An

FIGURE 7-8
Seniority sometimes imprisons an employee in a poor work situation.
Source: The Register and Tribune Syndicate. Used with permission.

effective program of economic rewards is a balance of most of these factors. In this way a variety of employee needs are served.

Flexible benefits

Cafeteria programs

The particular combination of economic rewards that an employer uses is contingent on the needs of employees, type of work, and organizational environment. In order to serve employee needs in a better way, some organizations provide *flexible benefit programs*, also called *cafeteria benefit programs*, because they allow employees to select their individual combination of benefits as they would select food in a cafeteria. Each employee receives a certain total economic allowance for a job, and then—within a range of choices available—the employee selects a preferred combination of individually priced economic rewards that use the allowed total.[24]

For example, a young employee with several dependents may choose to divert some benefit money from the retirement plan into larger amounts of life insurance and expanded medical and dental coverage. A single person nearing retirement may reduce life insurance while accenting contributions to the pension plan and specialized items, such as optical care and financial counseling. The capacity of these cafeteria programs to meet individual needs was demonstrated at American Can Company. There, a survey showed that 89 percent of the eligible employees enjoy being able to adjust their package of benefits each year.[25] Since not everyone actually makes changes every year, employee satisfaction apparently stems from the perceived opportunity to do so.

SUMMARY

Economic rewards provide social as well as economic value. They play a key role within several motivational models, blending with expectancy, equity, behavior modification, and need-based approaches. Employees perform a rough cost-reward comparison and work somewhat near but below the break-even point.

Performance appraisal provides a systematic basis for assessment of employee contributions and distribution of economic rewards. Modern appraisal philosophy focuses on performance, objectives, and goal setting. Nevertheless, the appraisal interview can be difficult for both manager and employee.

Incentive systems provide different amounts of pay in relation to some measure of performance. They tend to increase employee expectations that rewards will follow performance, although the delay may range from a week to a year. Incentives often stimulate greater productivity, but also tend to produce some offsetting negative consequences. Wage incentives reward greater output by individuals or groups, while profit sharing emphasizes mutual interest with the employer to build a successful organization. Gain sharing emphasizes improvement in various indices of organizational performance, while skill-based pay rewards employees for acquiring greater levels or types of skills.

Since employees have different needs to be served, many types of pay are required for a complete economic reward system. In some organizations, flexible benefit programs allow employees to select individual combinations of economic rewards.

Terms and concepts for review

Money as a social medium of exchange
Motivational models applied to pay
Cost-reward comparisons
Performance appraisal
Economic incentive systems
Piece rate
Wage incentives
Rate setting
Loose rates
Output restriction
Profit sharing
Gain sharing
Scanlon plan
Skill-based pay
Complete pay program
Flexible benefit program

Discussion questions

1 Explain how money can be both an economic and a social medium of exchange. As a student, how do you use money as a social medium of exchange?

2 Think of a job that you formerly had or now have.

a Discuss specifically how the expectancy model applied (applies) to your pay.

b Discuss how you felt (feel) about the equity of your pay and why you felt (feel) that way.

c Develop and explain a cost-reward comparison chart for your pay and effort.

3 Explain some of the behavioral benefits of modern performance appraisal systems compared with more traditional appraisal programs.

4 What are the major measures used to link pay with production? Which ones, if any, were used in the last job you had? Discuss the effectiveness of the measure or measures used.

5 Discuss some of the advantages and difficulties linked with incentive rewards.

6 Would you use profit sharing, gain sharing, skill-based pay, or wage incentives in any of the following jobs? Discuss your choice in each instance.

a Employees in a small, fast-growing computer company

b Teacher in a public school

c Clerks processing insurance claims in an insurance office

d Automobile repair mechanic in a small repair shop

e Farm worker picking peaches

f Production worker in a shoe factory making men's shoes

7 Form into small groups, each led by a member who has worked for a sales commission. Discuss how the commission related to both equity theory and expectancy theory, and report highlights of your discussion to your entire classroom group.

8 Have you ever participated in restriction of output (*a*) in a job and/or (*b*) in an academic course? Discuss why you did it and what its consequences were.

9 "Skill-based pay is a waste of company money, because we are paying for potential performance instead of actual performance." Discuss this statement.

10 During your first ten years after leaving college, would you want a flexible benefit program in your employment? Discuss why or why not.

Incident

THE NEW PERFORMANCE-RATING PROGRAM

Miles Johnson is supervisor of a district sales office in a town of about half a million persons. Several months ago Johnson studied various articles and pamphlets about performance appraisal in order to determine if he could improve the approach that he used with his salespeople. On the basis of his reading, he did develop a new system that has been in effect for six months. Recently he made the following statement about his new plan:

> *The new plan definitely has increased morale and productivity of my employees. Formerly I ranked my people strictly on dollar volume. The highest producer was number one, and so on down the line. The ranking was posted on the bulletin board so*

that each salesperson knew the ranking of all other salespeople. The purpose was to increase competition, and it did accomplish this goal, but it did not tell the whole story about their performance. For example, the top producer in sales was also the worst in delinquent accounts receivable. Some of the lower producers in sales were better in sales discount expense than some of their higher-producing colleagues. I now have a performance appraisal that recognizes a person's rank in each of ten important categories of the total job, and this new approach has given my organization a tremendous boost. My people now work for achievement of the whole job, rather than for the one measure of sales volume.

Questions

1 Has Johnson improved his performance appraisal program? Explain how in terms of expectancy theory, equity theory, and other models.
2 Can you recommend further improvements for Johnson? If so, explain them.

Experiential exercise

PERFORMANCE APPRAISAL/REWARD PHILOSOPHY

1 Read the following set of statements about people and indicate your degree of agreement or disagreement on the rating scales.

		STRONGLY AGREE				STRONGLY DISAGREE
A	Most people don't want equity; they want to earn *more* than their peers.	1	2	3	4	5
B	Skill-based pay won't work well because employees will learn the minimum necessary to earn a higher rate and then forget what they learned.	1	2	3	4	5
C	Most employees are too comfortable with the status quo to want to devote effort to learning new skills.	1	2	3	4	5
D	Most employees neither understand what profits are nor appreciate their importance; therefore profit-sharing systems are doomed to fail.	1	2	3	4	5
E	If allowed to make their own decisions in a flexible benefit system, many employees, without guidance, would make short-term choices that they would later regret.	1	2	3	4	5
F	The division between management and labor is so great that both gain-sharing and profit-sharing systems are likely to fail.	1	2	3	4	5
G	Since people do not want to hear about their weaknesses and failures, performance appraisal interviews will not change employee behavior.	1	2	3	4	5
H	The idea that employees assess the costs and rewards associated with any major behavior is ridiculous; they simply decide whether or not they feel like doing something and then do it.	1	2	3	4	5

2 Meet in small discussion groups, tabulate the responses to each question (frequency distribution and mean), and explore reasons for any significant disagreements within your group's ratings.
3 In your group, develop alternative statements for any items you do not support (ratings of 3, 4, or 5) at present. Explain how your new statements reflect your knowledge of human behavior gained through reading the early chapters of this book.

References

1 Peter F. Drucker, "How to Make People Decisions," *Harvard Business Review*, July–August 1985, p. 26.
2 Michael Schuster, "Gain Sharing: Do It Right the First Time," *Sloan Management Review*, Winter 1987, p. 18.
3 This was originally proposed by Edward L. Deci, "Effects of Externally Mediated Rewards on Intrinsic Motivation," *Journal of Personality and Social Psychology*, vol. 18, 1971, pp. 105–115. Recent field-research support for his proposal appears in Paul C. Jordan, "Effects of an Extrinsic Reward on Intrinsic Motivation: A Field Experiment," *Academy of Management Journal*, June 1986, pp. 405–412.
4 Numerous examples of corporate recognition systems appear in Bob Martin and Margaret Magnus, "A Case for Rewarding Recognition," *Personnel Journal*, December 1986, pp. 65–76. Also see Rosabeth Moss Kanter, "Holiday Gifts: Celebrating Employee Achievements," *Management Review*, December 1986, pp. 19–21.
5 Rosabeth Moss Kanter, "The Attack on Pay," *Harvard Business Review*, March–April 1987, pp. 60–67. The 3M example is drawn from A. Arthur Geis, "Making Merit Pay Work," *Personnel*, January 1987, pp. 52–60.
6 A related discussion is Philip C. Grant, "Explaining Motivation Phenomena with the Effort-Net Return Model," *Nevada Review of Business & Economics*, Spring 1982, pp. 29–32.
7 James S. Overstreet, "The Case for Merit Bonuses," *Business Horizons*, May–June 1985, pp. 53–58.
8 Examples of firms that have made progress toward this objective are provided by Aaron Bernstein, "Comparable Worth: It's Already Happening," *Business Week*, Apr. 28, 1986, pp. 52, 56.
9 Robert Owen, *The Life of Robert Owen*, New York: Alfred A. Knopf, Inc., 1920, pp. 111–112 (from the original published in 1857).
10 Summaries of the research appear in David E. Smith, "Training Programs for Performance Appraisal: A Review," *Academy of Management Review*, January 1986, pp. 22–40; and Clive Fletcher, "The Effects of Performance Review in Appraisal: Evidence and Implications," *Journal of Management Development*, vol. 5, no. 3, 1986, pp. 3–12.
11 Berkeley Rice, "Performance Review: The Job Nobody Likes," *Psychology Today*, September 1985, pp. 30–36. The four problems are drawn from Robert E. Lefton, "Performance Appraisals: Why They Go Wrong and How to Do Them Right," *National Productivity Review*, Winter 1985–86, pp. 54–63.
12 See, for example, Peter W. Dorfman, Walter G. Stephan, and John Loveland, "Performance Appraisal Behaviors: Supervisor Perceptions and Subordinate Reactions," *Personnel Psychology*, Autumn 1986, pp. 579–597; Paulette A. McCarty, "Effects of Feedback on the Self-Confidence of Men and Women," *Academy of Management Journal*, December 1986, pp. 840–847; and Ted Cocheu, "Performance Appraisal: A Case in Points," *Personnel Journal*, September 1986, pp. 48–55.
13 Brent S. Steel, "Participative Performance Appraisal in Washington: An Assessment

of Post-Implementation Receptivity," *Public Personnel Management*, Summer 1985, pp. 153–171.

14 Nancy K. Napier and Gary P. Latham, "Outcome Expectancies of People Who Conduct Performance Appraisals," *Personnel Psychology*, Winter 1986, pp. 827–837. One response to managers who don't give performance appraisals is for employees to initiate the process; see Susan J. Ashford, "Feedback-Seeking in Individual Adaptation: A Resource Perspective," *Academy of Management Journal*, September 1986, pp. 465–487.

15 The pay-performance linkage is discussed in Carla O'Dell and Jerry McAdams, "The Revolution in Employee Rewards," *Management Review*, March 1987, pp. 29–33; Rosabeth Moss Kanter, "Pay and Hierarchy," *Management Review*, June 1986, pp. 11–12; and E. James Brennan, "The Myth and the Reality of Pay for Performance," *Personnel Journal*, March 1985, pp. 73–75.

16 Data on Lincoln Electric stems from William Baldwin, "This Is the Answer," *Forbes*, July 5, 1982, pp. 50ff; the Nucor system is described in the interview, "Nucor's Ken Iverson on Productivity and Pay," *Personnel Administrator*, October 1986, pp. 46ff.

17 Daniel C. Rowland and Bob Greene, "Incentive Pay: Productivity's Own Reward," *Personnel Journal*, March 1987, pp. 49–57.

18 Stephen Solomon, "How a Whole Company Earned Itself a Roman Holiday," *Fortune*, Jan. 15, 1979, pp. 80–83.

19 Warren C. Hauck and Timothy L. Ross, "Sweden's Experiments in Productivity Gainsharing: A Second Look," *Personnel*, January 1987, pp. 61–67.

20 Michael Schuster, "Gain Sharing: Do It Right the First Time," *Sloan Management Review*, Winter 1987, pp. 17–25; Edward E. Lawler, III, "Gainsharing Research: Findings and Future Directions," Working Paper T 85-1 (67). University of Southern California: Center for Effective Organizations (see especially Table 3, p. 7).

21 Timothy L. Ross, Larry Hatcher, and Ruth Ann Ross, "The Multiple Benefits of Gainsharing," *Personnel Journal*, October 1986, pp. 14ff.

22 General introductions are provided in Henry Tosi and Lisa Tosi, "What Managers Need to Know about Knowledge-Based Pay," *Organizational Dynamics*, Winter 1986, pp. 52–64; and Dale Feuer, "Paying for Knowledge," *Training*, May 1987, pp. 57–66.

23 Balanced presentations of advantages and disadvantages appear in both Edward E. Lawler, III, and Gerald E. Ledford, Jr., "Skill-Based Pay: A Concept That's Catching On," *Management Review*, February 1987, pp. 47–51; and Rosabeth Moss Kanter, "From Status to Contribution: Some Organizational Implications of the Changing Basis for Pay," *Personnel*, January 1987, pp. 12–37.

24 *Flexible Benefits: Will They Work for You?* Chicago: Commerce Clearing House, Inc., 1984.

25 John A. Haslinger, "Cafeteria Plans: From Bread-and-Butter to Caviar," *Management Focus*, November–December 1984, pp. 22–25.

For additional reading

Belcher, David W., and Thomas J. Atchison, *Compensation Administration*, 2d ed., Englewood Cliffs, N.J.: Prentice-Hall, Inc., 1987.

Bernardin, H. John, and Richard W. Beatty, *Performance Appraisal: Assessing Human Behavior at Work*, Boston: Kent Publishing Company, 1984.

Doyle, Robert J., *Gainsharing and Productivity*, New York: AMACOM, 1983.

Lawler, E. E., III, *Pay and Organizational Effectiveness: A Psychological View*, New York: McGraw-Hill Book Company, 1971.

Leisieur, F. G. (ed.), *The Scanlon Plan*, Cambridge, Mass.: M.I.T. Press, 1958.
Maier, N. R. F., *The Appraisal Interview*, New York: John Wiley & Sons, Inc., 1958.
Moore, Brian E., and Timothy L. Ross, *Productivity Gainsharing*, Englewood Cliffs, N.J.: Prentice-Hall, Inc., 1983.
Rausch, Erwin, and Michael H. Frisch, *Win-Win Performance Management/Appraisal*, Somerset, N.J.: John Wiley & Sons, Inc., 1985.
Wallace, Marc J., and Charles H. Fay, *Compensation Theory and Practice*, Boston: Kent Publishing Company, 1983.

CHAPTER

8

Employee attitudes and their effects

The issue is how to manage an organization so that employees can be both happy and productive—a situation where workers and managers are both satisfied with the outcomes.

BARRY M. STAW[1]

[Managers and executives] sorely need to know how to build a culture and environment that fosters long-term loyalty in the workforce.

GORDON F. SHEA[2]

CHAPTER OBJECTIVES

To understand

The nature of job satisfaction

The relationship between performance and satisfaction

Job involvement and organizational commitment

Some positive and negative effects of employee attitudes

Characteristics of a satisfied employee

Benefits of studying employee attitudes

Design and use of surveys

Negative employee attitudes are a likely cause of deteriorating conditions in an organization. When attitudes decline, they may result in wildcat strikes, work slowdowns, absences, and employee turnover. They may also be a part of grievances, low performance, poor product quality, employee theft, and disciplinary problems. The organizational costs associated with poor employee attitudes may be astronomical, as shown in this illustration:

> **General Motors Corporation reports that its rate of casual absenteeism—failure of employees to report to work as scheduled—is 5 percent.[3] This translates into 25,000 employees absent each day, and 50 million hours lost each year. The total annual cost to the company is a staggering $1 billion.**

Favorable attitudes, on the other hand, are desired by management because they tend to be connected with the positive outcomes that managers want. Employee satisfaction, along with high productivity, is a hallmark of well-managed organizations, as the opening quote suggests. Favorable attitudes are the product of effective behavioral management, the continuing process of building a supportive human climate in an organization. This chapter focuses on the attitudes of employees toward their jobs, ways to obtain information about those attitudes, and how to use this information effectively.

THE NATURE OF EMPLOYEE ATTITUDES

Attitudes affect perceptions.

Attitudes are the feelings and beliefs that largely determine how employees will perceive their environment. Attitudes are a mental set that affects how a person will view something else, much as a window provides a framework for our view into or out of a building. The window allows us to see some things, but the size and shape of the frame prevents us from observing other elements. In addition, the color of the glass may affect the accuracy of our perception, just as the "color" of our attitudes has an impact on how we view and judge our surroundings at work. As managers of organizational behavior, we are vitally interested in the nature of the attitudes of our employees toward their work, the organization, and their careers.

Job satisfaction

Feelings, thoughts, and intentions

NATURE *Job satisfaction* is a set of favorable or unfavorable feelings with which employees view their work. There is an important difference between these job-related feelings and two other elements of employee attitudes. Job satisfaction is a *feeling* of relative pleasure or pain ("I enjoy having a variety of tasks to do") that differs from objective *thoughts* ("My work is complex") and behavioral *intentions* ("I plan to quit this job in three months"). Together, the three parts of attitudes help managers understand the reactions of employees to their jobs and predict the effect of those reactions on future behavior.

Job satisfaction typically refers to the attitudes of a single employee. For example, an administrator might conclude, "Antonio Ortega seems very pleased with his recent promotion." Job satisfaction also may refer to the general level of attitudes within a group, as in "The job satisfaction of the tool and die department is at an all-time high." In addition, the term *morale* refers to group attitudes, which are important to assess since individuals often take their social cues from their work associates and adapt their own attitudes to be consistent with those of the group.

Job satisfaction can be viewed as an overall attitude, or it can apply to the parts of an individual's job. For example, although Antonio Ortega's general job satisfaction may be high and he likes his promotion, he may be dissatisfied with his vacation schedule. Job satisfaction studies, therefore, often focus on the parts that are believed to be important, since these predispose an employee to behave in certain ways. The studies may also divide their attention between the elements that are directly related to job content (the nature of the job) and those that are part of the job context (the supervisor, coworkers, and organization).

Content and context

Job satisfaction, like any attitude, is generally acquired over a period of time as an employee gains more and more information about the workplace. Nevertheless, job satisfaction is dynamic, for it can decline even more quickly than it developed. Managers cannot establish the conditions leading to high satisfaction now and then neglect it, for employee needs may change suddenly. Managers need to pay attention to employee attitudes week after week, month after month, year after year.

Job satisfaction is one part of life satisfaction. The nature of one's environment off the job influences one's feelings on the job. Similarly, since a job is an important part of life, job satisfaction influences one's general life satisfaction. The result is that there is a *spillover effect* that occurs in both directions between job and life satisfaction. Consequently, managers may need to monitor not only the job and immediate work environment but also their employees' attitudes toward other parts of life, as shown in Figure 8-1.

Spillover effect

The behavior of Nancy Rickson, a secretary in a small office, was difficult for her supervisor to understand. She had recently received a promotion and a raise, but still seemed increasingly unhappy, distracted, and careless in her work habits. Numerous conversations that probed her job-related attitudes provided no clues as to the source of dissatisfaction.

One day, the supervisor happened to ask about one of her children, whose pictures were on her desk. Almost immediately, she poured out a series of heart-wrenching tales including her two divorces, the delinquency of her children, the lack of support from her parents, and her failure to master an attempted recreational pursuit (tennis). These problems, and having no one to share them with, were affecting her job attitudes and performance. As the complete picture emerged, the supervisor began to be aware of the intimate connection between Nancy's life satisfaction and job satisfaction.

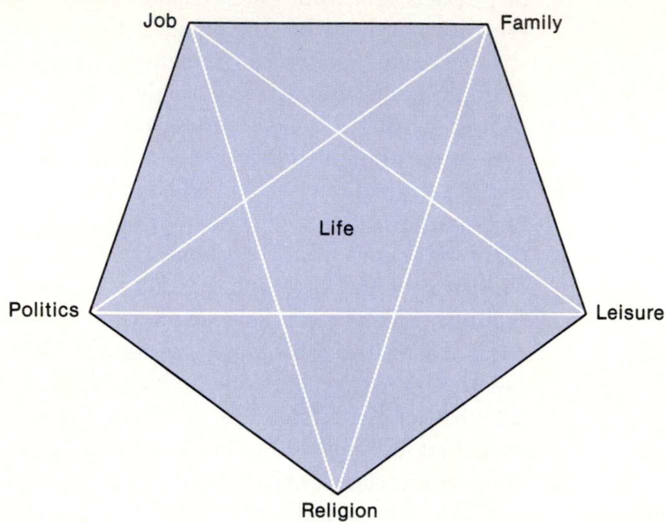

FIGURE 8-1
Some related elements of life satisfaction

IMPORTANCE Should managers study the job satisfaction of their employees and seek to improve it where appropriate? Aside from a desire to apply the "golden rule" or build a better organization or society, the answer revolves around four critical questions to be addressed below:

- Is there room for improvement?
- Who is relatively more dissatisfied?
- What contributes to employee satisfaction?
- What are the effects of negative employee attitudes?

LEVEL OF JOB SATISFACTION Long-term nationwide studies indicate that general job satisfaction has been relatively high and stable in the United States. Although worker expectations have both increased and changed in their focus over time, the quality of management practices also has improved. As a result, more than 80 percent of those in the work force usually report that they are reasonably satisfied with their jobs.[4] Managers should not be complacent, however, for this also suggests that millions of workers are unhappy, and many other millions (like Antonio Ortega) are probably dissatisfied with some specific aspect of their jobs. In addition, many of the "satisfied" workers may have simply resigned themselves to their work situations, with the result that they are neither satisfied nor dissatisfied.

Most workers are satisfied.

The *level* of job satisfaction across groups is not constant, but it is related to a number of variables. This allows managers to predict which groups are more likely to exhibit the problem behaviors associated with dissatisfaction. The key variables revolve around age, occupational level, and organizational size.

Who is satisfied?

As workers grow older, they tend to be slightly more satisfied with their jobs. Apparently they lower their expectations to more realistic levels and adjust themselves better to their work situations. Predictably, too, people with higher-level occupations tend to be more satisfied with their jobs. As we might expect, they are usually better paid, have better working conditions, and hold jobs that make fuller use of their abilities. Finally, there is some evidence to suggest that levels of job satisfaction are higher in smaller organizational units (such as a branch plant). This is because larger organizations tend to overwhelm people, disrupt supportive processes, and limit the amounts of personal closeness, friendship, and small-group teamwork that are important to the satisfaction of many people.

Possible managerial actions

SOURCES OF SATISFACTION If management desires to increase the potential for employee satisfaction, there are many routes to pursue. For example, as we discussed in the preceding chapter, many employees respond well to monetary incentives, especially if they are tied closely to individual performance. Satisfaction is also a product of employee perceptions of the overall level, as well as the equity, of pay. The goal-setting model of motivation indicates that employees will feel satisfaction when they can achieve difficult goals, so challenging jobs are desirable.

Many people also dislike ambiguity, so clear role expectations with specific task assignments can help overcome their concern. People are also hungry for information on how they are doing, which suggests that frequent feedback would be useful. Employees often feel most comfortable with a considerate supervisor—one who will show concern for their feelings, and also provide opportunities for them to participate in decision making. Chapters 9 and 10 are devoted to these topics. In summary, job satisfaction is a critical factor in organizational behavior. It needs to be understood, monitored, and dealt with so as to avoid some of the potential by-products of dissatisfaction that may haunt organizations.

Job involvement and organizational commitment

Job involvement

In addition to job satisfaction, two other employee attitudes are important to many employers. *Job involvement* is the degree to which employees immerse themselves in their jobs, invest time and energy in them, and view work as a central part of their overall lives.[5] Holding meaningful jobs and performing them well are important inputs to their own self-images, which helps to explain the traumatic effects of job loss on their esteem needs. Job-involved employees are likely to believe in the work ethic, have high growth needs, and enjoy participation in decision making. As a result, they seldom will be tardy or absent, are willing to work long hours, and will attempt to be high performers.

Organizational commitment

Organizational commitment is the degree to which an employee identifies with the organization and wants to continue actively participating in it.[6] Like a strong magnetic force attracting one metallic object to another, it is a measure of the employee's willingness to remain with a firm in the future. It often reflects the employee's belief in the mission and goals of the firm, willingness to expend effort in their accomplishment, and intentions to continue working there. Broader in scope than just loyalty,[7] it is usually stronger among longer-term employees, those who have experienced personal success in the organization, and those working within a committed employee group. Organizationally committed employees will usually have good attendance records, willing adherence to company policies, and lower turnover rates.

Because job satisfaction has received much attention from both researchers and managers, we will take a careful look at some of the effects of job satisfaction and dissatisfaction. However, a comprehensive approach to organizational behavior suggests that a manager should consider ways in which the work environment can help produce all three key employee attitudes—job satisfaction, job involvement, and organizational commitment.

EFFECTS OF EMPLOYEE ATTITUDES

When employees are dissatisfied with their jobs, and the feelings are both strong and persistent, we need to understand what impact this may have on their subsequent behaviors. Specifically, we are concerned about whether a dissatisfied employee is more likely to be tardy or absent, lessen the productivity level, steal from the organization, or quit. A large number of studies have addressed these questions, and the basic nature of the results are reported here.

EMPLOYEE PERFORMANCE Some managers cling to an old myth—that high satisfaction always leads to high employee performance—but this assumption is not correct.[8] Satisfied workers actually may be high, average, or even low producers, and they will tend to continue the level of performance that previously brought them satisfaction (according to the behavior modification model). The satisfaction-performance relationship is more complex than the simple path of "satisfaction leads to performance."

A complex relationship

Professional athletes often experience the effects of becoming overly satisfied with their performances. Prior successes periodically lead them to become complacent and play carelessly, with their team suffering a subsequent defeat. Some of the roles of a coach are to keep the players *dissatisfied* with their own contributions, instill a renewed desire to win, and motivate the players to perform even better. In this case, *dissatisfaction* may lead to better performance!

A more accurate portrait of the relationship is that high performance contributes to high job satisfaction, as shown in Figure 8-2.[9] The sequence is that better performance typically leads to higher economic, sociological, and psychological rewards. If these rewards are seen as fair and equitable, then improved satisfaction develops because employees feel that they are receiving rewards in proportion to their performance. On the other hand, if rewards are

Importance of equitable rewards

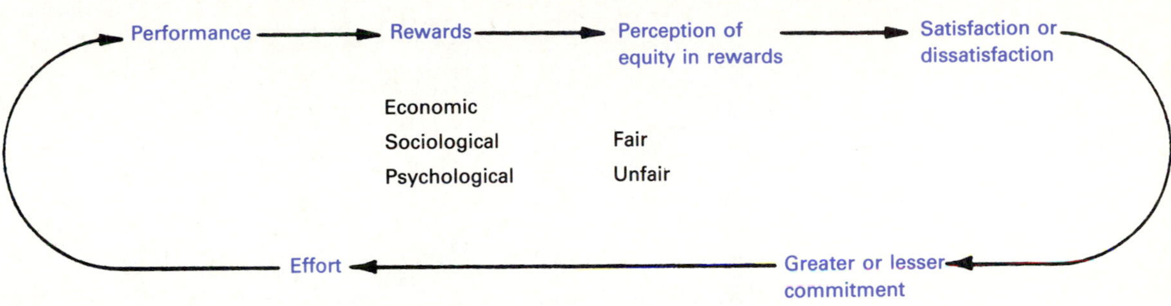

FIGURE 8-2
The performance-satisfaction-effort loop

seen as inadequate for one's level of performance, dissatisfaction tends to arise. In either case, one's level of satisfaction leads to either greater or lesser commitment, which then affects effort and eventually performance again. The result is a continuously operating *performance-satisfaction-effort loop*. The implication for management is to devote its efforts to aiding employee performance, which will likely produce satisfaction as a by-product.

Who tends to leave?

TURNOVER As might be expected, higher job satisfaction is associated with lower employee *turnover*, which is the proportion of employees leaving an organization. More satisfied employees are less likely to think about quitting, search for a new job, or announce their intention to quit, and thus are more likely to stay with their employer longer.[10] Similarly, as shown in Figure 8-3, those employees who have lower satisfaction usually have higher rates of turnover. They may lack self-fulfillment, receive little recognition on the job, or experience continual conflicts with a supervisor or peer, or they may have reached a personal plateau in their career. As a result they are more likely to seek greener pastures elsewhere and leave their employers, while their more satisfied associates remain.

An unusual problem related to turnover has occurred in several organizations that were forced to lay off large numbers of their employees when their business declined sharply. For example, Amax, Inc., cut its work force in half in just four years, and the employees remaining (the "survivors") experienced guilt, anger, anxiety, and relief.[11] If the entire layoff procedure is not handled well, the morale and trust of the remaining employees may drop sharply. This could result in the resignation of the very employees that the company wishes to retain.

Employee turnover can have several negative consequences, especially if the turnover rate is high. Often it is difficult to replace the departed employees, and the direct and indirect costs to the organization of replacing workers are expensive. The remaining employees may be demoralized from the loss of valued coworkers, and both work and social patterns may be disrupted until replacements are found. Also, the organization's reputation in the community

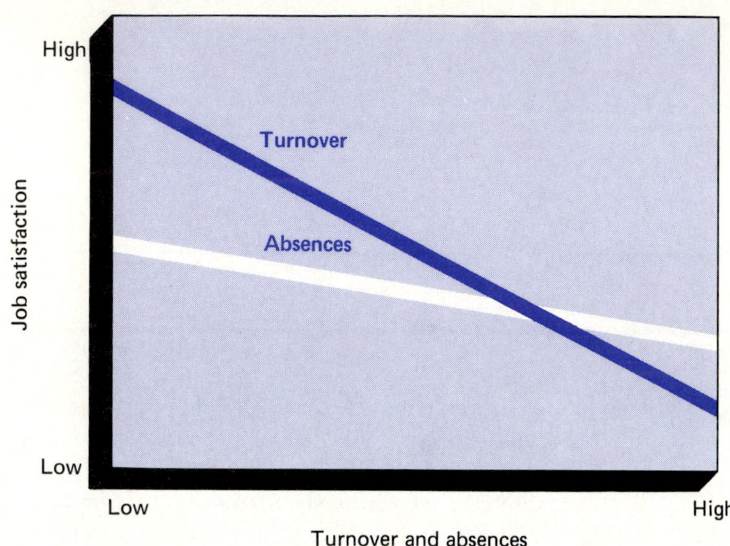

FIGURE 8-3
Relationship of job satisfaction to turnover and absences

may suffer. However, some *benefits* may arise from turnover, such as more opportunities for internal promotion and the infusion of expertise from newly hired employees. In other words, turnover may have functional effects, as the following illustration shows:

Some turnover is functional.

> **Merrill Lynch used a matrix similar to Figure 8-4 to initiate a program which lowered its broker turnover rate from 8 percent above the industry average to 11 percent below the average.[12] The firm developed a compensation program focused on retaining the more desirable employees while also recognizing that some turnover is not only acceptable but desirable (see cells *b* and *d*). By doing this, the firm reduced the number of brokers that otherwise would have become a costly statistic (cell *c* of the matrix). The message for managers is to look beyond the frequency of turnover and examine instead the functionality of each departure—are the right persons staying?**

Absenteeism reasons

ABSENCES Figure 8-3 also shows that those employees who have less job satisfaction tend to be absent more often. The connection is not always sharp, for a couple of reasons. First, some absences are caused by legitimate medical reasons and therefore a satisfied employee may have a valid absence. Second, dissatisfied employees do not necessarily plan to be absent, but they seem to find it easier to respond to the opportunities to do so. These voluntary (attitudinal) absences often occur with high frequency among a certain cluster of employees, and usually occur on Mondays or Fridays. Whereas involuntary (medically related) absenteeism can often be reduced through the use of more thorough preemployment physical exams and work-history record checks, different approaches are needed for absences caused by poor attitudes.[13]

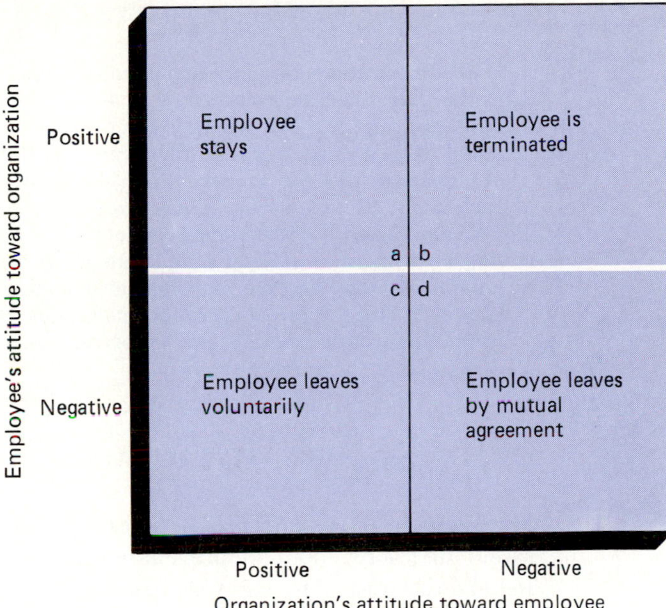

FIGURE 8-4
Four products of employee-organization attitudes

The Delco Remy Division of General Motors developed a four-pronged absence control program.[14] The division removed the financial incentives that previously rewarded casual absences, applied a strict disciplinary procedure, educated employees on the costs of absenteeism, and distributed the savings from reduced absenteeism to the work group. The controllable absenteeism rate fell from 4.5 percent to 2.1 percent, a decrease of over 50 percent.

Tardiness

Another way in which employees may exhibit their dissatisfaction with job conditions is through *tardiness*. A tardy employee is one who arrives at work late. Tardiness is a type of short-period absenteeism ranging from a few minutes to several hours for each event, and it is another way in which employees withdraw from active involvement in the organization. It may impede the timely completion of work and disrupt productive relationships with coworkers. Although there may be legitimate reasons for an occasional tardy arrival, a pattern of tardiness is often a symptom of negative attitudes requiring managerial attention.

THEFT Although there are many causes of employee theft, some employees may steal because they are frustrated by the impersonal treatment that they receive from their organization. In their own minds, employees may justify this extraordinary behavior as a way of gaining revenge for what they consider ill treatment at the hands of a supervisor. In contrast to the situation with absenteeism and tardiness, tighter organizational controls and threats of punishment do not always solve theft problems, since they are directed at the symptoms and not at the underlying causes such as severe dissatisfaction.[15]

One of the authors once toured a pizza manufacturing plant. Toward the completion of the tour, the guide was asked what the major human problems were. Without hesitation, she replied, "Theft." "You mean the employees steal the pizzas?" she was asked. "Oh, no," she replied, "they aren't worth that much. But we do lose hundreds of pepperoni sticks each year." Then she showed us a cart of the sticks. They were each about 40 inches long, 3 inches in diameter, and weighed perhaps 20 pounds. "We don't know how the employees get them out the door," she said, "but we assume they steal them as indirect compensation for the relatively low wages they receive (minimum wage) and the monotonous (assembly-line) jobs they perform." Looking back at Figure 8-2, we can see that a perception of inequity produced dissatisfaction, which apparently caused some employees to lower their commitment enough to rationalize stealing from the firm.

STUDYING JOB SATISFACTION

Management needs information on employee job satisfaction in order to make sound decisions, both in preventing and solving employee problems. This section discusses the types of benefits that management can gain and the conditions under which a study of job satisfaction will be most likely to succeed. Some of the more popular methods are explained, and guidelines for their use are given.

Job satisfaction surveys

A typical method used is a job satisfaction survey, also known as a morale, opinion, attitude, climate, or quality-of-work-life survey. A *job satisfaction survey* is a procedure by which employees report their feelings toward their jobs and work environment. Individual responses are then combined and analyzed.

Benefits of job satisfaction study

Job satisfaction surveys can produce positive, neutral, or negative results. If properly planned and administered, they will usually produce a number of important benefits, such as the following.[16]

GENERAL JOB SATISFACTION One benefit of surveys is that they give management an indication of general levels of satisfaction in a company. Surveys also indicate specific areas of satisfaction or dissatisfaction (as with employee services) and particular groups of employees (as in the tool department or among those over the age of forty). In other words, a survey tells how employees feel about their jobs, what parts of their jobs these feelings are focused on, which departments are particularly affected, and whose feelings are involved (for example, supervisors, employees, or staff specialists). The survey is a powerful diagnostic instrument for assessing employee problems.

In one company, for example, major changes were made in human resources policies, and the company wanted to check on employee reaction to the changes. Another company had recently doubled its work force, and it wished to determine how well new employees were being integrated into the firm. After a survey a utility discovered that employees were quite satisfied with their benefits but wanted better pay.[17] The president used the information to guide contract negotiations with the union, to the satisfaction of both parties.

COMMUNICATION Another benefit is the valuable communication brought by a job satisfaction survey. Communication flows in all directions as people plan the survey, take it, and discuss its results. Upward communication is especially fruitful when employees are encouraged to comment about what is on their minds instead of merely answering questions about topics important to management.

IMPROVED ATTITUDES One benefit, often unexpected, is improved attitudes. For some, the survey is a safety valve, an emotional release, a chance to get things off their chests. For others, the survey is a tangible expression of management's interest in employee welfare, which gives employees a reason to feel better toward management.

Aaron Goldberg had strong feelings about how management could improve its ways of working with people. He felt that some changes were needed. For more than a year he had been waiting for the right opportunity to express his viewpoints, but the opportunity never seemed to develop. His ideas were bottled up within him, and he was beginning to feel agitated. At about this time management distributed a job satisfaction survey that included generous space for employee comments. Aaron filled out the comments pages and then felt much better because finally he had a chance to give management his ideas.

TRAINING NEEDS Job satisfaction surveys are a useful way to determine certain training needs. Usually employees are given an opportunity to report how well they feel their supervisor performs certain parts of the job, such as delegating work and giving adequate job instructions. Since employees experience these supervisory acts, their perceptions may provide useful data about the training needs of their supervisors.

UNION BENEFITS Surveys may also bring benefits to unions. As explained by one union officer, both management and union often argue about what the employees want, but neither really knows. The job satisfaction survey is one way to find out. Unions rarely oppose surveys, and occasionally they give them support when they know that the union will receive the data.

PLANNING AND MONITORING CHANGES Alert managers are aware of the need to assess employee reactions to major changes in policies and programs. Advance surveys are useful for identifying problems that may arise, comparing the response to several alternatives, and encouraging managers to modify their original plans. Follow-up surveys allow management to evaluate the actual response to a change and study its success or failure.

For example, numerous firms have explored the move of their operations from northern locations to the "sun belt." Others have tested the possibility of moving corporate headquarters from large metropolitan areas to suburban or rural settings. A number of organizations have solicited information from employees on the interior design and layout of new work spaces, and other firms have wanted to know what employees thought about proposed personal computer systems or the merits of new work schedules. In many of these decisions, survey input from employees helped identify employee reactions and gain useful ideas for modifying the proposals.

Ideal survey conditions

Desired prerequisites

Surveys are most likely to produce some of the benefits reviewed above when the following conditions are met:

- Top management actively supports the survey.
- Employees are fully involved in planning the survey.
- A clear objective exists for conducting the survey.
- The study is designed and administered consistent with standards for sound research.
- Management is capable and willing to take follow-up action.
- Both the results and action plans are communicated to employees.

Use of existing job satisfaction information

Daily contacts

Before they conduct formal job satisfaction surveys, managers might examine two other methods for learning about current employee feelings—daily contacts and existing data. These approaches recognize that formal job satisfaction surveys are similar to an annual accounting audit in the sense that both are merely periodic activities; yet there is a day-by-day need to monitor job satisfaction just as there is a regular need to keep up with the financial accounts.

Existing data

Management stays in touch with the level of employee satisfaction primarily through face-to-face contact and communication. This is a practical and timely method of determining the job satisfaction level of individuals, but there are also a number of other satisfaction indicators already available in an organization. As shown in Figure 8-5, examples include absences, grievances, and exit interviews. This information is usually collected separately for other purposes, but it readily can be assembled into a monthly report that gives management insights into the general level of satisfaction among employees.

Some of the items in Figure 8-5 are behavioral indicators of job satisfaction, such as turnover, absenteeism, and tardiness, while others, such as medical

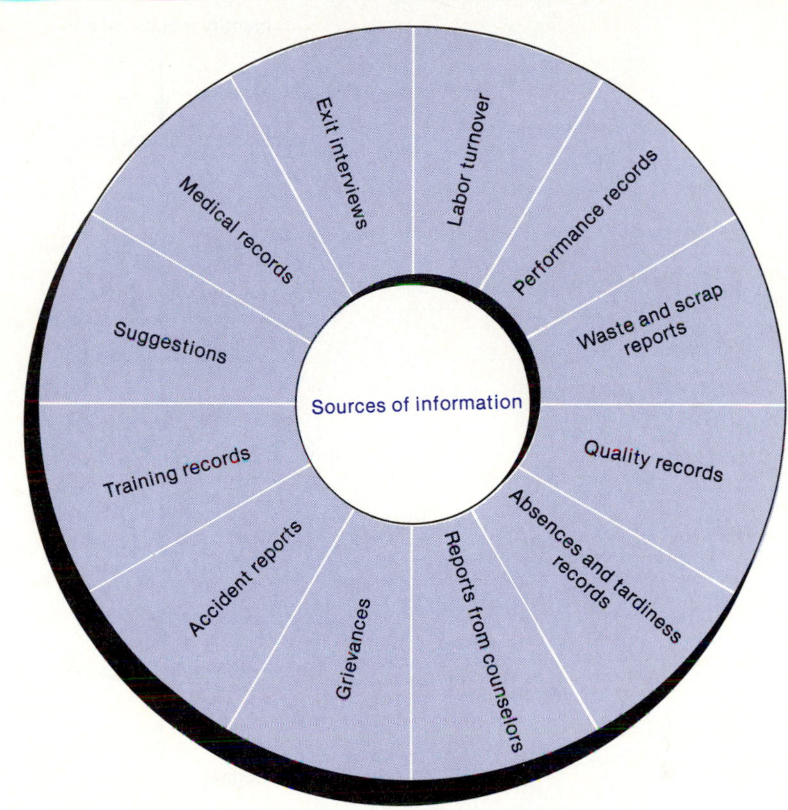

FIGURE 8-5
Examples of job satisfaction-related information frequently available in organizations

and training records, provide only indirect clues that something may be wrong. Carefully interpreted, they form a substantial body of knowledge about worker satisfaction in an organization. Their chief advantages are that in most cases they are already available, many of them provide quantifiable data, and they are a good measure of trends over a period of time.

SURVEY DESIGN

Steps in the process

A systematic approach to conducting surveys is shown in Figure 8-6. In general, managers need to identify a purpose for the attitude assessment, obtain top management and union support, and then develop the measurement instrument. Intermediate steps consist of administering the survey, followed by tabulation and analysis of the results. Conclusions should be fed back to the participants soon afterward, and action plans need to be developed and activated. Since the reasons for monitoring employee attitudes have already been

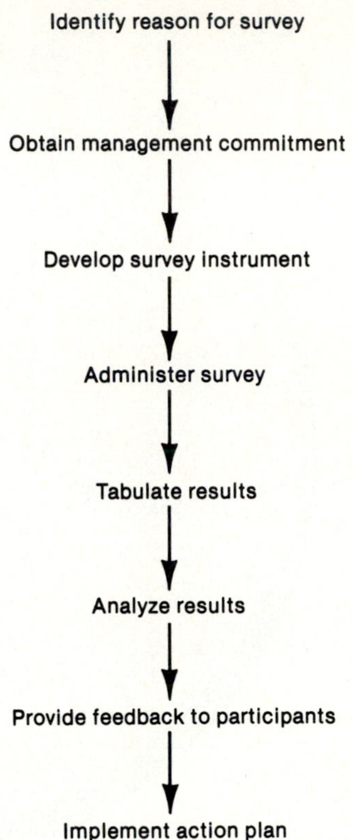

FIGURE 8-6
Major steps in the conduct of surveys

suggested, this section will focus on the types of survey instruments that can be designed. It will conclude with an examination of related factors for their successful use.

Types of survey questions

Studies of job satisfaction typically gather data either by survey questionnaires or by interviews. Whichever method is used, careful attention should be paid to the form of question asked and the nature of the response allowed. *Objective surveys* present both questions and a choice of answers in such a way that employees simply select and mark the answers that best represent their own feelings. *Descriptive surveys* present questions on a variety of topics but let employees answer in their own words. The typical survey form uses both objective and descriptive approaches.

Providing structured responses

OBJECTIVE SURVEYS There are various kinds of objective surveys, but a hallmark of each is the high degree of structure in the response categories.[18] One popular type (for example, the Index of Organizational Reactions) uses multiple-choice questions. Here respondents read all the answers to each question and then mark the response that comes closest to their own feelings. Other surveys use questions with "true or false" or "agree or disagree" answers. The frequently used Job Descriptive Index provides respondents with a set of statements (e.g., "My work is routine") and asks them to indicate whether the term describes their work situation by checking either "Yes," "No," or "?" ("I can't decide") responses. Somewhat more flexible are the surveys that present a statement and request employees to respond by checking a numerical scale to indicate their degree of agreement or disagreement, as shown here:

My feeling of security in my job (circle one number):

How much is there now? (min.) 1 2 3 4 5 (max.)

Because of concern over the meaning that employees may attach to only numbers in a response scale, instruments like the Minnesota Satisfaction Questionnaire provide brief descriptions for each number on the scale—for example, 1 = not satisfied, 2 = slightly satisfied, 3 = satisfied, 4 = very satisfied, and 5 = extremely satisfied. These aid employees in selecting their responses and help management interpret the data.

The chief advantage of objective surveys is that they are easy to administer and to analyze statistically. Much of the tabulation and analysis can be performed by computers, which minimizes clerical time, costs, and errors when large numbers of employees are surveyed. The chief defect of objective surveys is that management or a survey consultant writes all the structured responses available to employees, none of which may be viewed as an accurate expression of their real feelings. In other words, the objective approach really does not give employees a full opportunity to express themselves.

Seeking personal feelings

DESCRIPTIVE SURVEYS In contrast to objective surveys, descriptive surveys seek responses from employees in their own words. This unstructured approach permits employees to express their feelings, thoughts, and intentions fully. These more personal comments usually make a strong impression on management, especially if large numbers of employees agree and state their feelings in powerful language. For example, managers may not be too impressed if they discover that thirty-nine employees think the sick-leave plan is poor, but how would they react to thirty-nine comments similar to the following: "Our sick-leave plan stinks! You don't let us carry over unused leave more than two years, so I have no protection for serious illness that causes me to be absent more than a month." Now management may be more inclined to listen, and respond.

Figure 8-7 shows two types of descriptive surveys. The directed question focuses employee attention on a specific part of the job and asks questions about it. This approach permits depth analysis of satisfaction with a specific job condition. On the other hand, the undirected question asks for general comments about the job. In this way management learns about the topics that currently are troubling employees and seem important to them.

Directed question

What do you think of the company's pension program? ______________________

____

____

Undirected question

What are the three things you like most about your job?

1 ______________________

2 ______________________

3 ______________________

FIGURE 8-7
Types of descriptive survey questions on job satisfaction

A survey that uses personal interviews to gather data is by its nature more descriptive than objective. A suitable interview usually takes from one to two hours for each interviewee; hence it is both time-consuming and expensive. In order to ensure that the same material is covered in a consistent manner with each employee, each interviewer is carefully trained and follows a standardized interviewer's guide that tells what material to cover and how to phrase questions.

Critical issues

Job satisfaction survey procedures are more complicated than they appear to be at first glance. It seems simple enough to go to employees, get their responses, and then interpret them, but experience shows that careless errors in survey design can seriously limit the usefulness of a survey. Reliability and validity are two elements that serve as the backbone of any effective study. *Reliability* is the capacity of a survey instrument to produce consistent results, regardless of who administers it. If an instrument is reliable, we can be confident that any difference found between two groups is real, and not the product of ambiguous questions or widely varying administrative procedures.

Reliability

Validity

In addition to reliability, studies of job satisfaction need to be *valid*, or measure what they claim to measure. The difference between reliability and validity becomes clear when we attempt to use a wooden yardstick to measure metric distances. In this case, the yardstick is consistently accurate at what it does (it is reliable), but it is invalid since it measures the wrong thing. Obviously, we need to seek to improve *both* the reliability and validity of our measures of job satisfaction. This task is easier with objective surveys but much more difficult with the qualitative nature of descriptive surveys.

Many critical issues arise in the process of question construction and survey administration.[19] As shown in Figure 8-8, particular attention needs to be given to sample selection, maintenance of anonymity for employees, the use of norms

- Should participation be voluntary or mandated?
- Should a sample be used, or the total population?
- Should responses be signed or anonymous?
- Should norms be used for comparison, or not?
- Should the forms be returned to the supervisor or to an independent consulting firm?
- Should the survey be designed and conducted by internal staff or by external consultants?
- Should a deadline be stated for return of the surveys, or should no date be set?
- Should a standardized instrument be used, or should one be created for this situation?
- How should feedback be given to employees?

FIGURE 8-8
Some issues in survey design and administration

Socially desirable responses

in interpreting data, the voluntary participation of employees, and other factors. Response rates can be raised by requiring that surveys be returned in a short period of time. The tendency of employees to respond in a socially desirable fashion (for example, overestimating the importance of a challenging job) can be controlled.[20] Norms from comparable organizations can be useful to interpret response patterns. Although no attempt is made here to cover the many details and pitfalls in survey procedures, the following description of one organization's survey provides an overview:

> Management decided it needed more information about employee attitudes and called a consultant, who developed—with management's assistance—a set of objectives and written policies for the survey. These were approved by an executive committee with the company president in attendance. At this time they selected the questionnaire method and decided to survey all managers and workers. Then the consultant, the personnel director, and a personnel specialist planned the details. In addition, the president appointed a committee of seven middle managers to help draft questions for the survey. The consultant guided the committee and served as chairperson. The committee also approved an official announcement of the survey (six weeks before it was given) and aided in informal publicity for the event.
>
> The consultant made the survey on three consecutive days. Somewhat different questionnaires were used for office, managerial, and production employees. Each questionnaire took about forty-five minutes to complete, so a new group of employees was surveyed every hour in a large conference room. The personnel director introduced the consultant and left the room, after which the consultant explained the survey and administered it. Employees placed responses in a locked ballot box.
>
> After the survey was completed, the consultant quickly prepared a full report for management and a condensed report for employees. The consultant also advised the executive committee as it planned its program of action on the survey.

USING SURVEY INFORMATION

Once job satisfaction information has been collected and tabulated, the big question remaining is: What does all this mean in terms of my organization and my employees? Although gathering this information is chiefly a matter of technique, analysis and use of the resulting data requires skilled management judgment. It is the final important step in a job satisfaction survey. When appropriate action is taken, results can be excellent.

In one survey at a General Electric Company branch, more than half the employees reported that they were unhappy with two areas: (1) the information they received and (2) opportunities for promotion.[21]

As a result of the survey, management began to hold regular monthly meetings with employees, brought in qualified people to answer difficult questions, and started a newsletter. Management gave special emphasis to information about opportunities for advancement.

When a survey was made a year later, the number of employees who felt they lacked information had dropped to zero! Even though opportunities for promotion were limited, employees who were unhappy about them dropped to 20 percent. Management explained that at least employees understood the situation, and "that made the difference."

Survey feedback

The first step in using job satisfaction information is to communicate it to all managers so that they can understand it and prepare to use it. This is known as *survey feedback.* Managers will be the ones to make any changes suggested by the data, so they want to see the evidence in order to make their own judgments. The recommendations of job satisfaction specialists are helpful, but managers must make the final decisions.

Managers require evidence.

COMPARATIVE DATA In larger organizations, comparisons among departments are an effective way to encourage managers to sit up and take note of satisfaction data. Just as a lagging baseball team makes every effort to pass other teams in its league, managers whose departments do not show high job satisfaction will be spurred to improve their employees' attitudes by the time the next study is made. Comparisons of this type must be handled with skill so that the lower performers will not feel intimidated.

Survey data spur competition.

If there is a chance of hurt feelings or personality clashes, it is wise to designate each department with a letter such as *A* or *B*. Departmental managers are told privately which letter represents their own department. They then can compare their score with other departmental scores, but they cannot identify which score belongs to which department. Scores, however, must not be overemphasized in a way that makes "score-happy" managers. The real goal is to encourage desirable behavioral changes in managers, and a single score can only partially represent the complexity of the total situation. The score is not a goal but a tool for making comparisons.

There are a number of useful comparisons besides departmental ones, as shown in Figure 8-9.

For example, comparisons according to age groups may reveal a trend toward more satisfaction for older employees, as mentioned earlier in this chapter. However, if the survey reports that younger workers are more satisfied, it suggests that condi-

FIGURE 8-9
Types of variables often studied with job satisfaction information

- **Departments, divisions, branches**
- **Age**
- **Seniority**
- **Marital status**
- **Formal education**
- **Company training received**
- **Sex**
- **Work shift**
- **Building where work is performed**
- **General type of work done, such as professional, clerical, and production**
- **Trends over time**

tions for older employees are atypical and perhaps unsatisfactory. In this instance, management needs to investigate and, if appropriate, take corrective action.

If earlier surveys have been made, trends over time can be plotted. More elaborate statistical comparisons and correlations can be made if the evidence looks promising. For example, do those who say their supervisor is a good manager say also that they have more pride in their organization as a place in which to work? Ultimately, all the questions and job satisfaction categories can be compared with each other in a search for meaningful relationships.

The managers' interests in job satisfaction statistics are heightened by asking them to predict their subordinates' attitudes toward various items and then to compare their predictions with actual survey results. Wherever their prediction misses its mark, they are forced to ask themselves why they misjudged this condition. Even if a prediction is accurate, it may still encourage soul-searching. Consider the case of a department head who predicted his employees would report dissatisfaction with grievance handling. They did report dissatisfaction, which forced him to ask: "If I knew about this condition before the survey—and apparently I did—why didn't I do something about it?"

EMPLOYEE COMMENTS As mentioned earlier, employee comments are very useful. This information often makes a greater impression on management than scores, statistics, and charts do. In terms of communication, this gets through to them because it is more personal.

Some comments are about very minor conditions, but these conditions do annoy someone and are therefore worthy of management's sincere attention. It is a mistake to correct only the big problems shown in a survey while ignoring many minor conditions that will add up to big problems.

In a marketing department survey, the comments of several field sales representatives showed negative attitudes toward the sales paperwork required of them. Although the subject appeared to be minor, management redesigned the paperwork so that it was reduced by about 30 percent. The bottom-line results were more sales calls each week and 8 percent higher unit sales with the same sales force. This change helped the salespeople earn more commissions and helped management reduce its costs, so both parties benefited.

Administrative follow-up

COMMITTEE WORK One way to get managers to introduce change in their departments following a survey is to set up working committees whose responsibility is to review the survey data and develop plans for corrective action.

In one company, for example, the president appointed a special executive committee to follow up a survey and recommend changes. Then the general manager appointed supervisory committees in each department to discuss how the survey applied to local departmental problems. The supervisory committees worked out their own solutions on departmental matters, but if their proposed action affected other departments, it had to be forwarded to the executive committee for approval.

Committees recommend action.

The personnel director chaired each committee, which usually met monthly. At each meeting, a separate part of the survey was discussed in some depth. Meetings continued for more than a year, ensuring an extended follow-up of the information uncovered by the survey. This long-run approach kept executives thinking about the survey and gave it time to soak in.

The long-run approach to using job satisfaction information is important. Too many employers make the mistake of giving a survey immense publicity and interest for a few weeks and then forgetting about it until another survey is run. They shoot the works, giving their surveys all the fanfare of a Mardi Gras—but when Mardi Gras has passed, they return to their old way of living.

Feedback and action are required.

FEEDBACK TO EMPLOYEES When corrective action is taken as the result of a survey, details of what was done should be shared with employees as soon as possible. Only in this way will the people who participated feel that management listened to them and took action on the basis of their ideas. This also assures employees that their ideas really were wanted—and are wanted still. In fact, good publicity to managers and employees is essential from start to finish in a job satisfaction study in order to explain what the study intends to accomplish, to report the information gathered, and to announce what corrective action has been taken.

One thing is sure: if a job satisfaction survey is made, management should be prepared to take action on the results. Employees feel that if they cooperate in stating their feelings, management should try to make some of the improvements they suggest. A sure way to close off future expressions of employee opinion is to fail to take action on opinions already given. It should be remembered that management asked employees for their ideas, so employees are justified in feeling that action will be taken on at least some of them.

Surveys of manager satisfaction

Surveys of manager satisfaction are just as important as surveys of employee satisfaction. Managers have human needs, just like other people. If they are dissatisfied, their unhappiness can spread throughout a whole department because of their broad management influence. Their feelings also may filter into their communities through both their families and their many public contacts outside the company. Job satisfaction surveys should also be distributed to managers to diagnose deficiencies in their satisfaction and to take corrective action.

SUMMARY

Employee attitudes are important to monitor, understand, and manage. They develop as the consequences of the feelings of equity or inequity in the reward system (as discussed in Chapter 7), as well as from supervisory treatment (which will be addressed in Chapter 9). Managers are particularly concerned with three types of attitudes—job satisfaction, job involvement, and organizational commitment.

Job dissatisfaction may lead to increased absenteeism, turnover, and other undesirable behaviors, so employers want to develop satisfaction among their employees. The vast majority of workers in the United States report that they are satisfied with their jobs, although they may be dissatisfied with specific parts of them. Older employees and higher occupational levels especially tend to have higher satisfaction.

Higher job involvement leads to dedicated, productive workers. High performance and equitable rewards encourage high satisfaction through a performance-satisfaction-effort loop. Higher job satisfaction usually is associated with lower turnover and fewer absences. Committed employees are also more likely to embrace company values and beliefs (its culture).

We can obtain useful attitudinal information by using questionnaires and interviews, as well as by examining existing human resource data. Information is communicated to managers through survey feedback that uses summary data, makes relevant comparisons, and supports the conclusions with actual employee comments. Follow-up is accomplished by committees to assure employees that appropriate action is taken after a survey. Ultimately, information on employee attitudes is useful only if it influences managers to improve their performance.

Terms and concepts for review

Attitudes
Job satisfaction
Performance-satisfaction-effort loop
Job involvement
Organizational commitment
Turnover
Objective survey
Descriptive survey
Reliability
Validity
Survey feedback

Discussion questions

1 Explain, in your own words, why you feel that employee attitudes are important. Do you think that today's managers overemphasize or underemphasize attitudes?
2 Assume that a survey of the twenty employees in your department found that 90 percent of them were basically satisfied with their jobs. What are the implications for you as a manager?
3 "A happy employee is a productive employee." Discuss this statement.
4 Think of a job you have held. List the areas of your job in which you were most satisfied and those that satisfied you least. Note in each case the degree to which management had some control over the item mentioned. What could the managers have done to improve your satisfaction?
5 Assume that job satisfaction, job involvement, and organizational commitment are independent of each other—any one may be present without the others. Describe a situation in which an employee might be committed but not satisfied or involved. Tell what you would do with such an employee.
6 Prepare a series of directed and undirected questions, and interview three friends to determine their areas of satisfaction and dissatisfaction. Discuss the results.
7 Select an industry (e.g., financial institutions or hospitals), and contact three organizations within it to learn of their absenteeism and turnover rates. What have they done to reduce them?
8 Construct a short questionnaire using objective questions, and survey the members of a small work team about their job satisfaction. Tabulate and analyze your results, including a list of recommendations for change.
9 Prepare a plan for using the data from a job satisfaction survey in an insurance office to provide feedback to managers and employees.
10 Contact a local fast-food restaurant, and ask the manager to estimate the proportion of turnover that can be attributed to effective employees leaving of their own choice. What suggestions could you make to reduce this problem?

Incident

BARRY NILAND

Barry Niland, supervisor of a small sales department, noticed that one of his industrial sales representatives, Henry Hunter, had a problem. Among other signs, Hunter's sales had declined in the last six months, although most other sales representatives regularly were exceeding their quotas. Niland decided to try to boost his sales representative's performance by reminding him of the many opportunities for satisfaction in a sales job.

Niland explained his actions as follows:

I pointed out that in his customer's eyes he alone is the company. He has the opportunity to help his customer. He has the opportunity to show his ability and knowledge to many types of people. He has the opportunity through his own efforts to help many types of people. He has the opportunity to support the people who make our products, to reward the stockholders, and to control his financial return through his own know-how. He has the opportunity of testing his creative ideas, with immediate feedback about their value. He has the opportunity to meet constantly changing conditions, so there is no boredom in his job. There is no quicker way to achieve personal satisfaction than sales work.

Questions

1 Comment on Niland's approach in dealing with his sales representative.
2 Suggest approaches for increasing Hunter's:
 a Job satisfaction
 b Job performance
 c Job involvement
 d Organizational commitment

Experiential exercise

ATTITUDES IN THE CLASSROOM

The discussion of attitudes that was presented in this chapter can also be related to the college classroom.

1 Working individually, class members should rate, on a scale from 1 to 10 (1 = low, 10 = high) their:
 a Overall satisfaction with the course
 b Feeling of involvement in the educational process
 c Commitment to the college
2 The instructor should predict the average ratings of the class on each of the three items.
3 Share the ratings obtained in step 1, and compute averages for each.
4 Working in small groups of four or five persons, discuss the reasons for the overall level of job satisfaction, involvement, and commitment in the class. Assess the accuracy of the instructor's predictions. Develop a realistic action plan for improving the level of each of the three dimensions.
5 Discuss the probable reliability and validity of the data gathered in steps 1 and 2 above. Suggest ways in which you could gather evidence of the data's reliability and validity.

References

1 Barry M. Staw, "Organizational Psychology and the Pursuit of the Happy/Productive Worker," *California Management Review*, Summer 1986, p. 40.
2 Gordon F. Shea, *Company Loyalty: Earning It, Keeping It*, New York: AMACOM, 1987, p. 15.
3 Clarence R. Deitsch and David A. Dilts, "Getting Absent Workers Back on the Job:

The Case of General Motors," *Business Horizons*, September–October 1981, pp. 52–58.

4 One article places the proportion at more than 70 percent; see Donald L. Kanter and Philip H. Mirvis, "Managing Jaundiced Workers," *New Management*, Spring 1986, pp. 50–54.

5 Gary J. Blau, "Job Involvement and Organizational Commitment as Interactive Predictors of Tardiness and Absenteeism," *Journal of Management*, Winter 1986, pp. 577–584; Gary J. Blau and Kimberly B. Boal, "Conceptualizing How Job Involvement and Organizational Commitment Affect Turnover and Absenteeism," *Academy of Management Review*, April 1987, pp. 288–300.

6 Research is reported in Jon L. Pierce and Randall B. Dunham, "Organizational Commitment: Pre-employment Propensity and Initial Work Experiences," *Journal of Management*, Spring 1987, pp. 163–178; and James P. Curry et al., "On the Causal Ordering of Job Satisfaction and Organizational Commitment," *Academy of Management Journal*, December 1986, pp. 847–858. An illustration of a "commitment gap" at the FBI is reported in Donald C. Witham and John D. Glover, "Recapturing Commitment," *Training and Development Journal*, April 1987, pp. 42–45.

7 The literature written for practitioners tends to use the term "loyalty" as a substitute for organizational commitment. See Shea, op. cit.; Bruce Nussbaum et al., "The End of Corporate Loyalty," *Business Week*, Aug. 4, 1986, pp. 42–49; and Walter Kiechel, III, "Resurrecting Corporate Loyalty," *Fortune*, Dec. 9, 1985, pp. 207, 210–211.

8 For example, Bill Marriott, chairman of the corporation that bears his name, said, "My father knew if he had happy employees, he would have happy customers, and then that would result in a good bottom line." See Mike Sheridan, "J. W. Marriott, Jr.," in Delta Airlines' *Sky*, March 1987, p. 48.

9 For a classic description of this relationship, see Edward E. Lawler III and Lyman W. Porter, "The Effect of Performance on Job Satisfaction," *Industrial Relations*, October 1967, pp. 20–28.

10 Brendan D. Bannister and Rodger W. Griffeth, "Applying a Causal Analytic Framework to the Mobley, Horner, and Hollingsworth (1978) Turnover Model: A Useful Reexamination," *Journal of Management*, Fall 1986, pp. 433–443. Ways to address turnover problems are in Richard T. Mowday, "Strategies for Adapting to High Rates of Employee Turnover," *Human Resource Management*, Winter 1984, pp. 365–380.

11 Larry Reibstein, "Survivors of Layoffs Receive Help to Lift Morale and Reinstall Trust," *Wall Street Journal*, Dec. 5, 1985, sec. 2, p. 33.

12 Allen C. Bluedorn, "Managing Turnover Strategically," *Business Horizons*, March–April 1982, pp. 6–12. The model is tested in John R. Hollenbeck and Charles R. Williams, "Turnover Functionality versus Turnover Frequency: A Note on Work Attitudes and Organizational Effectiveness," *Journal of Applied Psychology*, November 1986, pp. 606–611; and extended in David C. Martin and Kathryn M. Bartol, "Managing Turnover Strategically," *Personnel Administrator*, November 1985, pp. 63–73.

13 Absence control emphasizing prevention is in Frank E. Kuzmits, "What to Do about Long-Term Absenteeism," *Personnel Administrator*, October 1986, pp. 93–100; and a balanced approach is reviewed in Gary Johns, "The Great Escape," *Psychology Today*, October 1987, pp. 30–33.

14 David A. Dilts and Clarence R. Deitsch, "Absentee Workers Back on the Job: The Case of GM," *Business Horizons*, March–April 1986, pp. 46–51.

15 A preventive approach is to screen new employees. See Ed Bean, "More Firms Use 'Attitude Tests' to Keep Thieves Off the Payroll," *Wall Street Journal*, Feb. 27, 1987, sec. 3, p. 33.

16 See, for example, Maryellen Lo Bosco, "Employee Attitude Surveys," *Personnel,* April 1986, pp. 64–68; and D. Kim McKinnon, "Reaping the Real Rewards of Employee Surveys," *Training,* November 1985, pp. 49–52.

17 Martin Wright, "Helping Employees Speak Out about Their Jobs and the Workplace," *Personnel,* September 1986, pp. 56–60.

18 The Index of Organizational Reactions is described in F. J. Smith and L. W. Porter, "What do Executives Really Think about Their Organizations?" *Organizational Dynamics,* Autumn 1977, pp. 68–80. The Job Descriptive Index is reported in P. C. Smith, L. M. Kendall, and C. L. Hulin, *The Measurement of Satisfaction in Work and Retirement,* Chicago: Rand McNally & Company, 1969. The scale shown in the color example on page 189 is adapted from Lyman W. Porter, "A Study of Perceived Need Satisfactions in Bottom and Middle Management," *Journal of Applied Psychology,* January 1961, pp. 1–10. The Minnesota Satisfaction Questionnaire is presented in D. J. Weiss, R. V. Dawis, G. W. England, and L. H. Lofquist, *Manual for the Minnesota Satisfaction Questionnaire, Minnesota Studies in Vocational Rehabilitation: XXII,* University of Minnesota Industrial Relations Center, Work Adjustment Project, 1967.

19 Guidelines are offered in David R. York, "Attitude Surveying," *Personnel Journal,* May 1985, pp. 70–73; and Patricia Smith et al., "Guidelines for Clean Data: Detection of Common Mistakes," *Journal of Applied Psychology,* August 1986, pp. 457–460.

20 Wilfred J. Zerbe and Delroy L. Paulhus, "Socially Desirable Responding in Organizational Behavior: A Reconception," *Academy of Management Review,* April 1987, pp. 250–264.

21 "A Productive Way to Vent Employee Gripes," *Business Week,* Oct. 16, 1978, pp. 168–171.

For additional reading

Cascio, Wayne F., *Costing Human Resources: The Financial Impact of Behavior in Organizations,* 2d ed., Boston: PWS-Kent Publishing Company, 1987.

Dilts, David A., Clarence R. Deitsch, and Robert J. Paul, *Getting Absent Workers Back on the Job: An Analytical Approach,* Westport, Conn.: Quorum Books, 1985.

Gardner, James E., *Stabilizing the Workforce: A Complete Guide to Controlling Turnover,* Westport, Conn.: Quorum Books, 1986.

Goodman, P. S., and R. S. Atkin (eds.), *Absenteeism: New Approaches to Understanding, Measuring, and Managing Employee Absence,* San Francisco: Jossey-Bass Inc., Publishers, 1984.

Hershey, Robert, *Organizational Morale,* Kings Point, N.Y.: Kings Point Press, 1985.

Herzberg, F., B. Mausner, R. O. Peterson, and R. Capwell, *Job Attitudes: Review of Research and Opinions,* Pittsburgh, Pa.: Pittsburgh Psychological Services, 1957.

Hollinger, Richard C., and John P. Clark, *Theft by Employees,* Lexington, Mass.: Lexington Books, 1983.

Mowday, Richard T., Lyman W. Porter, and Richard M. Steers, *Employee-Organization Linkages: The Psychology of Commitment, Absenteeism, and Turnover,* Orlando, Fla.: Academic Press (HBJ Publishers), 1982.

Organ, Dennis W., *Organizational Citizenship Behavior,* Lexington, Mass.: Lexington Books, 1988.

Price, James I., *The Study of Turnover,* Ames, Iowa: Iowa State University Press, 1977.

Schappi, John V., *Improving Job Attendance,* Washington, D.C.: BNA Books, 1988.

Shea, Gordon F., *Company Loyalty: Earning It, Keeping It,* New York: AMACOM, 1987.

PART

Leadership and organizational change

CHAPTER

9

Leadership and supervision

Excellent leaders are not pussycats.

NANCY K. AUSTIN[1]

Participative, supportive, relationship-oriented ... managerial behavior may all be subjectively preferred by subordinates without objectively enhancing worker performance.

HARVEY HORNSTEIN ET AL.[2]

CHAPTER OBJECTIVES

To understand

The nature of leadership

The path-goal model of leadership

Power and politics in organizations

Distinctions between Theory X and Theory Y

Different leadership styles

Contingency approaches to leadership

Views of the supervisor's leadership role

eadership is the process of encouraging and helping others to work enthusiastically toward objectives. It is the human factor that helps a group identify where it is going and then motivates it toward its goals. Without leadership, an organization would be only a confusion of people and machines, just as an orchestra without a conductor would be only musicians and instruments. The orchestra and all other organizations require leadership to develop their precious assets to their fullest.

The leadership process is similar in effect to that of the secret chemical that turns the insect pupa into a butterfly with all the beauty that was the pupa's potential. *Leadership, then, transforms potential into reality.* This role is often seen in giant firms, as when Lee Iacocca led the Chrysler Corporation from the brink of bankruptcy. It is equally important in tiny firms, like the Microsoft Corporation, which Bill Gates started and guided to national prominence as a developer of microcomputer software. In all cases, leadership is the ultimate act that identifies, develops, and uses the potential that is in an organization and its people.

In this chapter we discuss the nature of leadership—the behaviors, roles, assumptions, and skills that combine to form different leadership styles. A contingency approach is presented to encourage managers to examine the fit between the situation and the style to be used. We conclude with a special section on supervision, since supervisors often face a unique set of problems and pressures that are somewhat different from those of higher managers.

THE NATURE OF LEADERSHIP

Leadership is an important part of management but not all of it. Managers are required to plan and organize, for example, but the primary role of a leader is to influence others to seek defined objectives enthusiastically. This means that strong leaders may be weak managers if their poor planning causes their group to move in wrong directions. Though they can get their group going, they just cannot get it going in directions that best serve organizational objectives.

Other combinations also are possible. A person can be a weak leader and still be a relatively effective manager, especially if one happens to be managing people who clearly understand their jobs and have strong drives to work. This set of circumstances is less likely, and therefore we expect excellent managers to have reasonably high leadership ability. Fortunately, this ability can be acquired through management training and work experience.

Leadership behavior

People have been concerned about the nature of leadership since the beginning of history. Early research tried to identify the traits that differed between leaders and nonleaders, or between successful and unsuccessful leaders.[3] Some studies focused on personality factors, like intelligence, ambition, and aggressiveness; others examined physical characteristics like height, build, and attractiveness. In general, though, no consistent set of traits that are stable across groups and tasks has emerged despite continued attempts.

Personality types

An example of a currently popular instrument that classifies managers as one of sixteen different personality types is the Myers-Briggs Type Indicator. This controversial test, based on the work of psychologist Carl Jung, labels managers as extroverts or introverts, thinkers or feelers, sensers or intuitors, and judges or perceivers. Although the approach has been criticized, many companies like Compass Computer, Transamerica Corporation, and the Charlotte Observer (newspaper) have used the test as a basis for building teams and improving communications.[4]

Three leadership skills

Much of the recent emphasis has shifted away from traits and toward identifying leadership *behaviors*. In this view, successful leadership depends on appropriate behaviors, skills, and actions, not personal traits. This is highly significant, since behaviors can be learned and changed, while traits are relatively fixed. The three different types of skills leaders use are technical, human, and conceptual. Although these skills are interrelated in practice, they can be considered separately.

Technical skill refers to a person's knowledge and ability in any type of process or technique. Examples are the skills learned by accountants, engineers, word processing operators, and toolmakers. This skill is the distinguishing feature of job performance at the operating level, but as employees are promoted to leadership responsibilities, their technical skills become proportionately less important, as shown in Figure 9-1. They increasingly depend

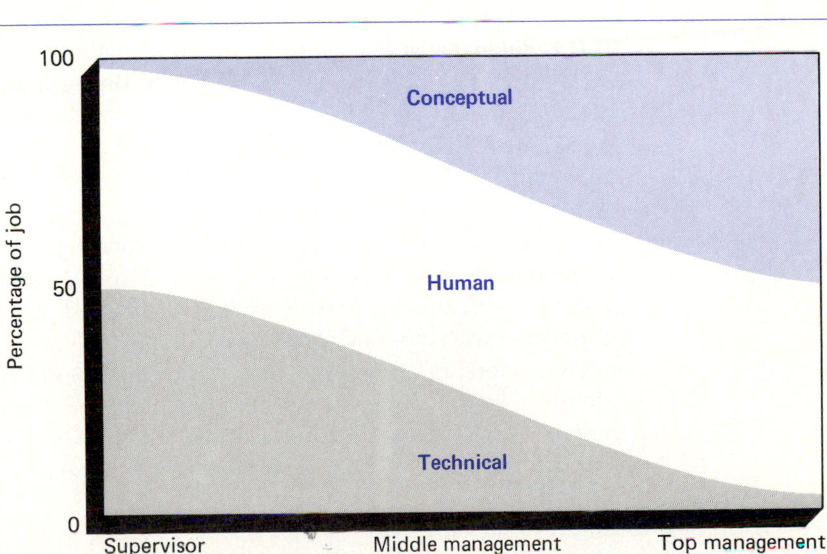

FIGURE 9-1
Variations in use of leadership skills at different organizational levels

on the technical skills of their subordinates and in many cases have never practiced some of the technical skills that they supervise.

Human skill is the ability to work effectively with people and to build teamwork. No leader at any organizational level escapes the requirement for effective human skill. It is a major part of leadership behavior and is discussed throughout this book.

Conceptual skill is the ability to think in terms of models, frameworks, and broad relationships, such as long-range plans. It becomes increasingly important in higher managerial jobs. Conceptual skill deals with ideas, while human skill concerns people and technical skill involves things.

Analysis of leadership skills helps to explain why outstanding department heads sometimes make poor vice presidents. They may not be using the proper mixture of skills required for the higher-level job, particularly additional conceptual skill.

Situational aspects

Three elements to consider

Successful leadership requires behavior that unites and stimulates followers toward defined objectives in specific situations. All three elements—leader, followers, and situation—are variables that affect each other in determining appropriate leadership behavior.

The interdependence of leader, follower, and situation is illustrated by a hard-boiled superintendent, Gregg Hicks, who still is managing the way he was twenty years ago. He thinks that leadership resides in himself alone, untouched by outside influences. He fails to realize that as his people and environment change, he needs to change his leadership. Though his style of leadership was acceptable twenty years ago, it is not acceptable today.

It is evident that leadership is situational. In one situation, action A may be the best cluster of leadership acts, but in the next situation, action B will be best. To try to have all an organization's leaders fit a standard pattern will suppress creative differences and be inefficient as well, because many square pegs will be trying to fit into round holes. Leadership is part of a complex system, so there is no simple way to answer "What makes a leader?"[5]

Sometimes leaders must resist the temptation to be visible in a situation. Even though good leadership involves a set of behaviors, it should not be confused with mere activity when it is not needed. Aggressiveness and constant interaction with others will not guarantee good leadership. At times the appropriate leadership action is to stay in the background keeping pressures off the group, to keep quiet so that others may talk, to be calm in times of uproar, to hesitate, and to delay decisions. At other times a leader must be more directive and controlling, as indicated in the opening quotation for this chapter.

Leaders as followers

With few exceptions, leaders in organizations are also *followers*. They nearly always report to someone else. Even the president reports to a board of directors. Leaders must be able to wear both hats gracefully, to be able to relate both upward and downward. They need validation from higher authority just as much as they need support from followers. In formal organizations of several levels, ability to follow is one of the first requirements for good leadership. It is the key that unlocks the door to leadership opportunities and keeps the leader in balance with the rest of the organization.

Followership skills

A vice president of Saga Corporation suggests that most people fail in jobs because they lack followership skills. These are behaviors that help a person to be an effective subordinate and may include avoiding competition with the leader, acting as a loyal devil's advocate, and constructively confronting the leader's ideas, values, and behavior.[6]

What must a leader do to obtain these behaviors from employees? The next section will present a model of leadership behavior that revolves around goals and a support system for accomplishing them.

PATH-GOAL MODEL OF LEADERSHIP

Robert House and others have further developed a path-goal view of leadership initially presented by Martin G. Evans which is derived from the expectancy model of motivation (see Chapter 6).[7] The *path-goal model of leadership* states that the leader's job is to use structure, support, and rewards to create a work environment that helps employees reach the organization's goals. The two major roles involved are to create a goal orientation and to improve the path toward the goals so that they will be attained.

Figure 9-2 shows the path-goal process. Leaders identify employee needs, provide appropriate goals, and then connect goal accomplishment to rewards by clarifying expectancy and instrumentality relationships. Barriers to performance are removed, and guidance is provided to the employee. The result of the process is job satisfaction, acceptance of the leader, and greater motivation.

Goal setting

Goal setting plays a central role in the path-goal process. It is the establishment of targets and objectives for successful performance, both long run and short run. It provides a measure of how well individuals and groups are meeting performance standards.

People are goal-directed.

The basic premise underlying goal setting is that *human behavior is goal-directed,* as we discussed in Chapter 5. Group members need to feel that they have a worthwhile goal that can be reached with the resources and leadership available. Without goals, different members may go in different directions. This difficulty will continue as long as there is no common understanding of the goals involved.

The MBO process

MANAGEMENT BY OBJECTIVES A popular approach that revolves around goal setting is *management by objectives* (MBO). Generally, MBO is a system in

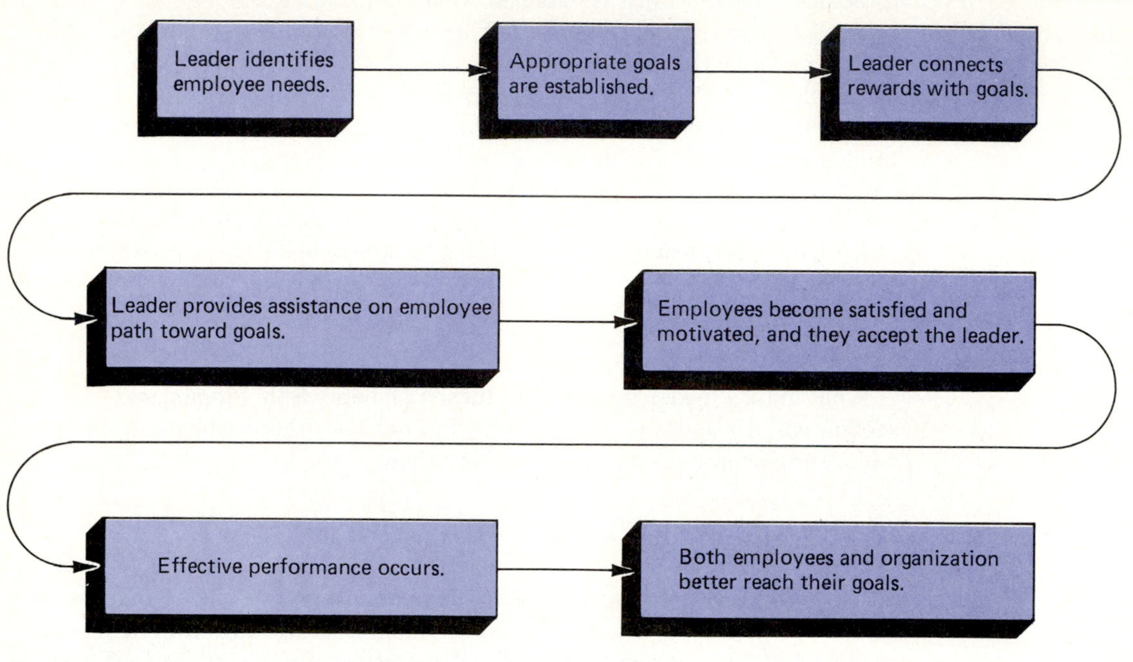

FIGURE 9-2
The path-goal leadership process

which managers and subordinates mutually agree on the employee's routine, project-oriented, and personal objectives for the next year and on the criteria that will be used to measure accomplishment of the objectives.[8] The major steps in this circular, self-renewing process are shown in Figure 9-3. The highlights include an emphasis on mutual goal setting, relatively autonomous action planning, and periodic reviews of progress. The freedom given to employees in an MBO system provides opportunities for the satisfaction of their growth needs. Goals with the greatest motivational value are those which are accepted, specific, and challenging and which provide opportunities for performance feedback.

Top managers require vision.

VISION A special type of goal setting is the creation and communication of a vision for an organization. A *vision* is a long-range image or idea of what can and should be accomplished; properly explained to others, it serves to stimulate their commitment and enthusiasm.[9] A vision may also integrate the shared beliefs and values that serve as a basis for the creation and change of an organization's culture. Vision is a particularly key element in the leadership roles of top managers. They are responsible for assessing their environments, projecting future conditions, and developing master strategies for achieving their visions. When an executive's vision is properly explained to other managers and employees, it becomes the basis for developing their own goals and objectives.

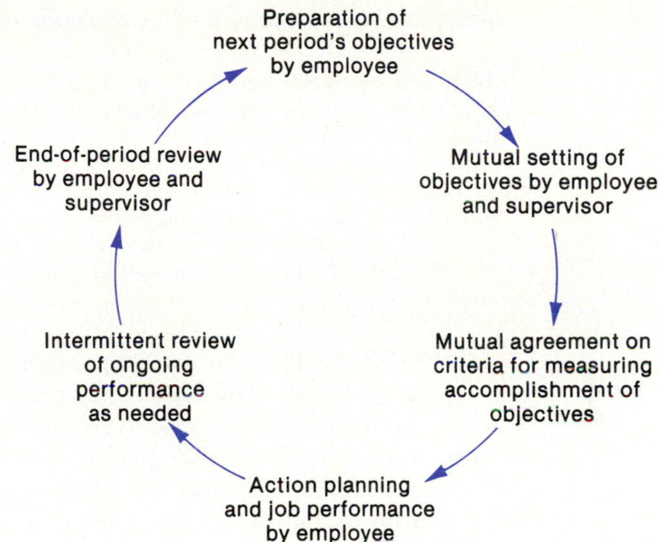

FIGURE 9-3
Circular process of management by objectives

The value, and the complexity, of instilling a vision is illustrated by the experience of a new university president. He was chosen to lead the institution when the interview team was impressed with his master plan for transforming the university from a position of mediocrity to one of focused excellence. Despite generally positive reaction to his *general* vision for the university, however, acceptance of his specific proposals (and receipt of new funding) dragged out over several years. Progress toward implementing the new vision was slowed by the need to obtain support from legislators, regents, faculty, students, and alumni. Success in selling one's vision requires building and using skills in political power, like those we'll discuss in the path improvement section that follows.

Path improvement

The steps surrounding goal setting represent only half of the path-goal leadership process. Leaders also need to consider some contingency factors (such as employee personality characteristics and nature of the task) before deciding how to go about smoothing the path toward a goal. A discussion of path-oriented ideas, including support and role modeling, follows.

Employees need support.

TASK AND PSYCHOLOGICAL SUPPORT Leaders provide both task and psychological support for their employees. They provide task support when they help assemble the resources, budgets, power, and other elements that are essential to get the job done. Equally important, they can remove environmental constraints that sometimes inhibit employee performance, exhibit upward influence, and provide recognition contingent upon effective effort and performance. But psychological support is also needed.[10] Leaders must stimulate people to want to do the job. The combination of task and psychological support in a leader is described by a telephone company employee as follows:[11]

> *There is a supervisor here in the Western Area who is the epitome of a leader. The reason? He cares. He cares about people [psychological support] and about getting the job done right [task support]. His enthusiasm is real, not forced, and it's quite contagious. His employees want to work for him and learn from him.*
>
> *It all stems from two basic reasons: he knows what he's talking about and he treats subordinates like they are rational human beings with the ability to do the job. And he expects them to do it. He gives them the recognition that their work is important. Therefore, people get the feeling that they are working with him to get the entire job done.*

Leaders are role models.

ROLE MODELING It is said that "supervisors tend to supervise as they themselves are supervised." The same thought applies to leaders. They serve as *role models*, or examples, for their followers, who tend to act in about the same way that the leaders do.[12] For example, if a leader is considerate and supportive with followers, their responses are likely to be similar. If a leader follows an opposite pattern, however, employees also may turn opposite.

> **In a state tax office, a manager named Rebecca Lapp blamed either followers or superiors whenever a problem developed. She also delayed work until deadlines approached, which led to rushed work and pressure on the group. She was impatient with others. Gradually, over time, her employees developed similar behavior, so performance in the office was poor. Rebecca was not an effective role model.**

Power and politics

All leaders deal with power and politics.[13] *Power* is the ability to influence other people and events. It is the leader's stock-in-trade, the way that leaders extend their influence to others. It is somewhat different from authority, because authority is delegated by higher management. Power, on the other hand, is earned and gained by leaders on the basis of their personalities, activities, and the situations in which they operate.

Politics relates to the ways that leaders gain and use power. It is necessary to help a leader keep "on top of a situation" and control events toward desired objectives. Politics concerns balances of power, saving face, "horse trading," "mending fences," ingenious compromises, trade-offs, and a variety of other activities. It has been a classic human activity since the beginning of civilization, so it is not unique to modern organizations. But modern organizations are a fertile place for politics to thrive. Observers say that leaders who are otherwise capable but who lack basic political skills will have trouble rising to the top in modern organizations. Clearly, political skills are essential for leaders, both for their personal success and for smoothing the path to employee performance.

Types of power

Four sources of power

Power develops in a number of ways. Following are four major types of organizational power and their sources.

PERSONAL POWER *Personal power*—also called referent power, charismatic power, and power of personality—comes from each leader individually. It is the ability of leaders to develop followers from the strength of their own personalities. They have a personal magnetism, an air of confidence, and a belief in objectives that attracts and holds followers. People follow because they want to do so; their emotions tell them to do so. The leader senses the needs of people and promises success in reaching them. Well-known historical examples are Joan of Arc in France, Mahatma Gandhi in India, and Franklin D. Roosevelt in the United States.

LEGITIMATE POWER *Legitimate power*, also known as position power and official power, comes from higher authority. It arises from the culture of society by which power is delegated legitimately from higher established authorities to others. It gives leaders the power to control resources and to reward and punish others. People accept this power because they believe it is desirable and necessary to maintain order and discourage anarchy in a society. There is social pressure from peers and friends who accept it and expect others to accept it.

EXPERT POWER *Expert power*, also known as the authority of knowledge, comes from specialized learning. It is power that arises from a person's knowledge of and information about a complex situation. It depends on education, training, and experience, so it is an important type of power in our modern technological society. For example, if your spouse were having an attack of some type in a hospital emergency room, you would be likely to give your attention to the physician who comes in to provide treatment rather than to the helper who is delivering fresh laundry supplies. The reason is that you expect the physician to be a capable expert in the situation.

POLITICAL POWER *Political power* comes from the support of a group. It arises from a leader's ability to work with people and social systems to gain their allegiance and support. It develops in all organizations.

The types of power are developed from different sources, but they are interrelated in practice. When one power base is removed from supervisors, employees may perceive that other bases of influence will decline as well. Studies also indicate that the use of a power base must fit its organizational context for it to be effective. Political power thrives when the organizational and technical environment is uncertain, and it will now be presented in greater detail.

Tactics used to gain political power

There are a number of tactics that leaders can use to gain political power; several examples are given in Figure 9-4. Two of the most popular ones are social exchanges and alliances of various types. Social exchange implies, "If you'll do something for me, I'll do something for you." It relies on the powerful

Norm of reciprocity

norm of reciprocity in society, where two people in a continuing relationship

TACTIC USED	EXAMPLE
Social Exchange	**In a trade-off the chief engineer helps the factory manager get a new machine approved if the manager will support an engineering project.**
Alliances	**The information system manager and the financial vice president join together to work for a new computer system.**
Identification with higher authority	**The president's personal assistant makes minor decisions for her.**
Control of information	**The research and development manager controls new product information needed by the marketing manager.**
Selective service	**The purchasing manager selectively gives faster service to more cooperative associates.**
Power and status symbols	**The new controller arranges to double the size of the office, decorate lavishly, and employ a personal assistant.**
Power plays	**Manager A arranges with the vice president to transfer part of manager B's department to A.**
Networks	**A young manager joins a racquetball club.**

FIGURE 9-4
Examples of tactics used to gain political power

feel a strong obligation to repay their social "debts" to each other. When these trade-offs are successfully arranged, both parties get something they want. Continuing exchanges over a period of time usually lead to an alliance in which two or more persons join in a longer-term power group to get benefits that they mutually desire.[14]

Another popular path toward political power is to become identified with a higher authority and/or a powerful figure in an organization. Then, as the saying goes, some of the power "rubs off" on you. Often this identification gains you special privileges, and in many cases you become recognized as a representative or spokesperson for the more powerful figure. Others may share problems with you, hoping that you will help them gain access to the higher figure. An example of identification is the president's personal assistant who represents the president in many contacts with others.

In one company the president's personal assistant, Howard Janus, became widely accepted as the president's representative throughout the company. He issued instructions to other managers in the name of the president, so other managers accepted them as orders. He represented the president on special assignments. He controlled access to the president, and he partly controlled the flow of information both to and from the president. He handled power effectively and gradually became a major influence in the corporation. When the president retired, the assistant became a major executive and was accepted by other managers.

Another popular way to acquire political power is to give service selectively to your supporters. For example, a purchasing manager gives faster service and "bends the rules" to help friends who support the purchasing function. Another tactic is to acquire power and status symbols that imply that you are an important person in the firm, although this can backfire if you do not have power equal to your symbols.

Some managers use the more aggressive tactic of power plays to grab power from others. This approach is risky because others may retaliate in ways that weaken the power-grabbing manager's power.

A common tactic for increasing power is to join or form interest groups that have a common objective. These networks operate on the basis of friendships and personal contacts, and may provide a meeting place for influential people. A young manager who joins the chamber of commerce or a racquetball club is opening the door to new contacts that may be useful.

As illustrated by the following example, power and politics are a basic part of leadership success in an organization.

Management in a state office was considering whether to move a certain activity from one department to another. Finally the director of the entire operation decided to hold a staff meeting of all senior managers to decide where the disputed activity should be located. Prior to the meeting the manager of the department that wanted the activity prepared an elaborate and convincing report that fully supported moving the activity to her department. Meanwhile the manager of the department that might lose the activity was visiting all committee members to mend fences, make trades, and support her department's point of view.

When the committee met two weeks later, most of its members already had decided in favor of the manager who used the political approach. The convincing logic of the written report was ignored, and the committee voted to retain the activity in its present location. Political skills won the dispute.

To relate political power with the path-goal model, a leader works collaboratively with employees to help them see and obtain objectives that support the overall vision of the organization. The leader states role expectations (goals) for the employees, uses political power to obtain needed resources, and receives some level of productivity in response. The actual productivity level may vary with the quality of the *exchange* relationship established, depending on the amount of trust, interaction, support, and rewards provided.[15] Employees can also exert political influence on their supervisor in attempts to gain additional support.

LEADERSHIP STYLE

The total pattern of leaders' actions, as perceived by their employees, is called *leadership style*. It represents their philosophy, skills, and attitudes in practice. The styles that are discussed differ on the basis of motivation, power, or orientation toward tasks and people. Although they are typically used in combination or even applied differently to various employees, they are discussed separately to highlight the contrasts among them. The impact of assumptions on leadership style is presented first.

Theory X and Theory Y

In 1957, Douglas McGregor presented a convincing argument that most management actions flow directly from whatever theory of human behavior managers hold.[16] The idea is that *management philosophy controls practice.* Management's personnel practices, decision making, operating practices, and even organizational design flow from assumptions about human behavior. The assumptions may be implicit rather than explicit, but they can be inferred from observing the kinds of actions that managers take.

Theory X assumptions

Theory X is a traditional set of assumptions about people. As shown in Figure 9-5, it assumes that most people dislike work and will try to avoid it if possible. They engage in various work restrictions, have little ambition, and will avoid responsibility if at all possible. They are relatively self-centered, indifferent to organizational needs, and resistant to change. The common rewards given by organizations are not enough to overcome their dislike for work, so the only way that management can secure high employee performance is to coerce, control, and threaten them. Though managers may deny that they have this view of people, their actions strongly suggest that Theory X is their typical assumption about employees.

Theory Y assumptions

Theory Y implies a more human and supportive approach to managing people. It assumes that people are not inherently lazy. Any appearance they have of being that way is the result of their experiences with organizations; but if management will provide the proper environment to release their potential, work will become as natural to them as play or rest. They will exercise self-direction and self-control in the service of objectives to which they are committed. Management's role is to provide an environment in which the potential of people can be released at work.

THEORY X	THEORY Y
□ **The typical person dislikes work and will avoid it if possible.**	□ **Work is as natural as play or rest.**
□ **The typical person lacks responsibility, has little ambition, and seeks security above all.**	□ **People are not inherently lazy. They have become that way as a result of experience.**
□ **Most people must be coerced, controlled, and threatened with punishment to get them to work.**	□ **People will exercise self-direction and self-control in the service of objectives to which they are committed.**
	□ **People have potential. Under proper conditions they learn to accept and seek responsibility. They have imagination, ingenuity, and creativity that can be applied to work.**
With these assumptions the managerial role is to coerce and control employees.	**With these assumptions the managerial role is to develop the potential in employees and help them release that potential toward common objectives.**

FIGURE 9-5
McGregor's Theory X and Theory Y, alternative assumptions about employees

McGregor's argument was that management has been ignoring the facts about people. It had been following an outmoded set of assumptions about people because it adhered to Theory X when the facts are that most people are closer to the Theory Y set of assumptions. There are important differences among people, so a few may come closer to Theory X, but nearly all employees have some Theory Y potential for growth. Therefore, McGregor argued, management needed to change to a whole new theory of working with people: Theory Y. The relationship between alternative assumptions about human behavior and leadership styles can be seen throughout the following paragraphs.

Types of leadership style

Many different classifications of leadership styles have been proposed and found to be useful. The simplest of these are based on a single dimension, while others focus on two or more ways to distinguish among styles. Although there are often similarities among the approaches, we will differentiate styles on the basis of a leader's use of rewards, power, or primary emphasis on consideration versus structure.

Rewards or penalties?

POSITIVE AND NEGATIVE LEADERS There are differences in the ways leaders approach people to motivate them. If the approach emphasizes rewards—economic or otherwise—the leader uses *positive leadership*. Better employee education, greater demands for independence, and other factors have made satisfactory employee motivation more dependent on positive leadership.

If emphasis is placed on penalties, the leader is applying *negative leadership*. This approach can get acceptable performance in many situations, but it has high human costs. Negative leaders act domineering and superior with people. To get work done, they hold over their personnel such penalties as loss of job, reprimand in the presence of others, and a few days off without pay. They display authority in the false belief that it frightens everyone into productivity. They are bosses more than leaders.

A continuum of leadership styles exists, ranging from strongly positive to strongly negative. Almost any manager uses both styles somewhere on the continuum every day, but the dominant style sets a tone within the group. Style is related to one's model of organizational behavior. The autocratic model tends to produce a negative style; the custodial model is somewhat positive; and the supportive and collegial models are clearly positive. Positive leadership generally achieves higher job satisfaction and performance.

Styles and the use of power

AUTOCRATIC, PARTICIPATIVE, AND FREE-REIN LEADERS The way in which a leader uses power also establishes a type of style. Each style—autocratic, participative, and free-rein—has its benefits and limitations. A leader uses all three styles over a period of time, but one style tends to be the dominant one. An illustration is a factory supervisor who is normally autocratic, but she is

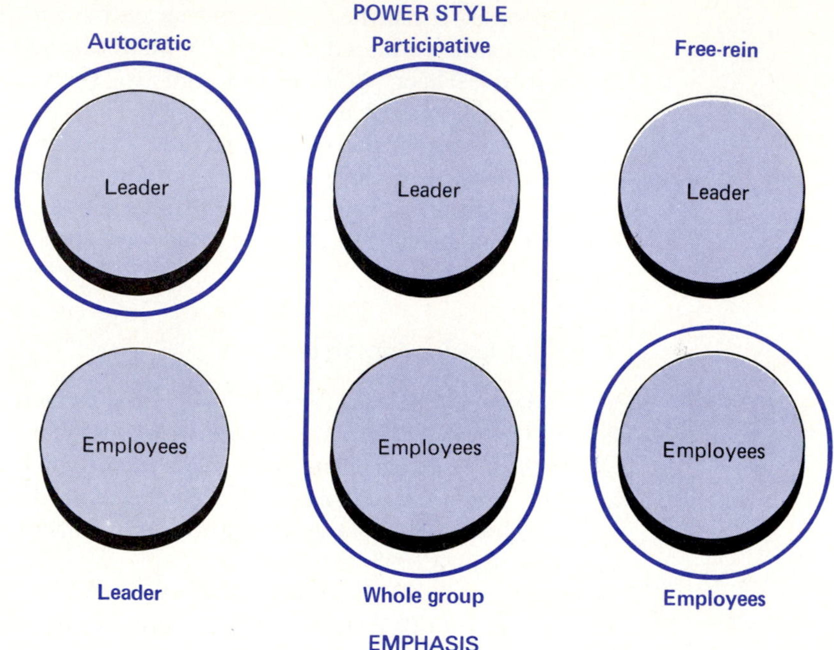

FIGURE 9-6
Different emphasis (shown by colored lines) results from different leadership styles in use of power.

participative in determining vacation schedules, and she is free-rein in selecting a department representative for the safety committee.

Autocratic leaders centralize power and decision making in themselves, as shown in Figure 9-6. They structure the complete work situation for their employees, who are expected to do what they are told. The leaders take full authority and assume full responsibility. Autocratic leadership typically is negative, based on threats and punishment; but it can be positive, as demonstrated by the *benevolent autocrat* who chooses to give some rewards to employees.

Some advantages of autocratic leadership are that it is often satisfying for the leader, permits quick decisions, allows the use of less competent subordinates, and provides security and structure for employees. The main disadvantage is that most employees dislike it, especially if it is extreme to the point of creating fear and frustration.

Participative leaders decentralize authority. Participative decisions are not unilateral, as with the autocrat, because they arise from consultation with followers and participation by them. The leader and group are acting as a social unit, as illustrated in Figure 9-6. Employees are informed about conditions affecting their jobs and encouraged to express their ideas and make suggestions. The general trend is toward wider use of participative practices because they are consistent with the supportive and collegial models of organizational behavior.[17] Because of its importance, participative management is discussed in the next chapter.

Free-rein leaders avoid power and responsibility. They depend largely upon the group to establish its own goals and work out its own problems. Group members train themselves and provide their own motivation. The leader plays only a minor role. Free-rein leadership ignores the leader's contribution approximately in the same way that autocratic leadership ignores the group. It tends to permit different units of an organization to proceed at cross-purposes, and it can degenerate into chaos. For these reasons normally it is not used as a dominant style but is useful in those situations where a leader can leave a choice entirely to the group.

LEADER USE OF CONSIDERATION AND STRUCTURE Two different leadership styles with employees are *consideration* and *structure*, also known as employee orientation and task orientation. There is consistent evidence that leaders secure somewhat higher performance and job satisfaction if high consideration is their dominant leadership style. Considerate leaders are concerned about the human needs of their employees. They try to build teamwork, provide psychological support, and help employees with their problems. Structured, task-oriented leaders, on the other hand, believe that they get results by keeping people constantly busy and urging them to produce.

Employee and task orientations

The difference between the two orientations is illustrated by the reply of Paul Blumberg, a mine superintendent in a Western mining town. A clerk brought him the following news about one of his truck drivers: "John Jones just ran the truck off the road into Mile Deep Canyon." The superintendent's task-oriented reply was, "Get another truck out there right away and get that ore to the mill." (We wonder what happened to Jones.)

Consideration and structure appear to be somewhat independent of each other, so they should not necessarily be viewed as opposite ends of a continuum. A manager who becomes more considerate does not necessarily become less structured. A manager may have both orientations in varying degrees. If consideration exists alone, production may be bypassed for superficial popularity and contentment; so it appears that *the most successful managers are those who combine relatively high consideration and structure, giving somewhat more emphasis to consideration.*[18]

Early research on consideration and structure was done at the University of Michigan and Ohio State University. In several types of environment, such as truck manufacturing, railroad construction, and insurance offices, the strongly considerate leader achieved somewhat higher job satisfaction and productivity. Subsequent studies confirm this general tendency and report desirable side effects, such as lower grievance rates, lower turnover, and reduced stress within the group.[19] Conversely, turnover, stress, and other problems are likely to occur if a manager is unable to demonstrate consideration.

CONTINGENCY APPROACHES TO LEADERSHIP STYLE

The positive, participative, considerate leadership style is not always the best style to use. At times there are exceptions, and the prime need for leaders is to identify when to use a different style. A number of models have been developed that explain these exceptions, and they are called *contingency approaches.* These models state that the most appropriate style of leadership depends on an analysis of the nature of the situation facing the leader. Key factors in the situation need to be identified first. When combined with research evidence, these will indicate which style should be more effective. Two contingency models of this nature will be briefly examined.

Fiedler's contingency model

An early, but often controversial, contingency model of leadership was developed by Fred Fiedler and his associates.[20] This model builds upon the previous distinction between task and employee orientation, and suggests that the most appropriate leadership style depends on whether the overall situation is favorable, unfavorable, or in an intermediate stage of favorability to the leader. As the situation varies, leadership requirements also vary.

Three situational variables

Fiedler shows that a leader's effectiveness is determined by the interaction of employee orientation with three additional variables that relate to the followers, the task, and the organization. They are leader-member relations, task structure, and leader position power. *Leader-member relations* are determined by the manner in which the leader is accepted by the group. If, for example, there is group friction with the leader, rejection of the leader, and reluctant compliance with orders, then leader-member relations are low. *Task structure* reflects the degree to which one specific way is required to do the job. *Leader position power* describes the organizational power that goes with the position the leader occupies. Examples are power to hire and fire, status symbols, and power to give pay raises and promotions.

The relationship among these variables is shown in Figure 9-7. High and low employee orientations are shown on the vertical scale. Various combinations of the other three variables are shown on the horizontal scale, arranged from leader-favorable conditions to leader-unfavorable conditions. Each dot on the chart represents the data from a specific research project. The chart clearly shows that the considerate, employee-oriented manager is most successful in situations that have intermediate favorableness to the leader (the middle of the chart). At the chart's extremes, which represent conditions either quite favorable or quite unfavorable to the leader, the structured, task-oriented leader seems to be more effective.

For example, the members of an automobile assembly-line crew have a structured task and a supervisor with strong position power. If leader-member relations are positive, the situation is favorable for task-oriented leaders who can use their

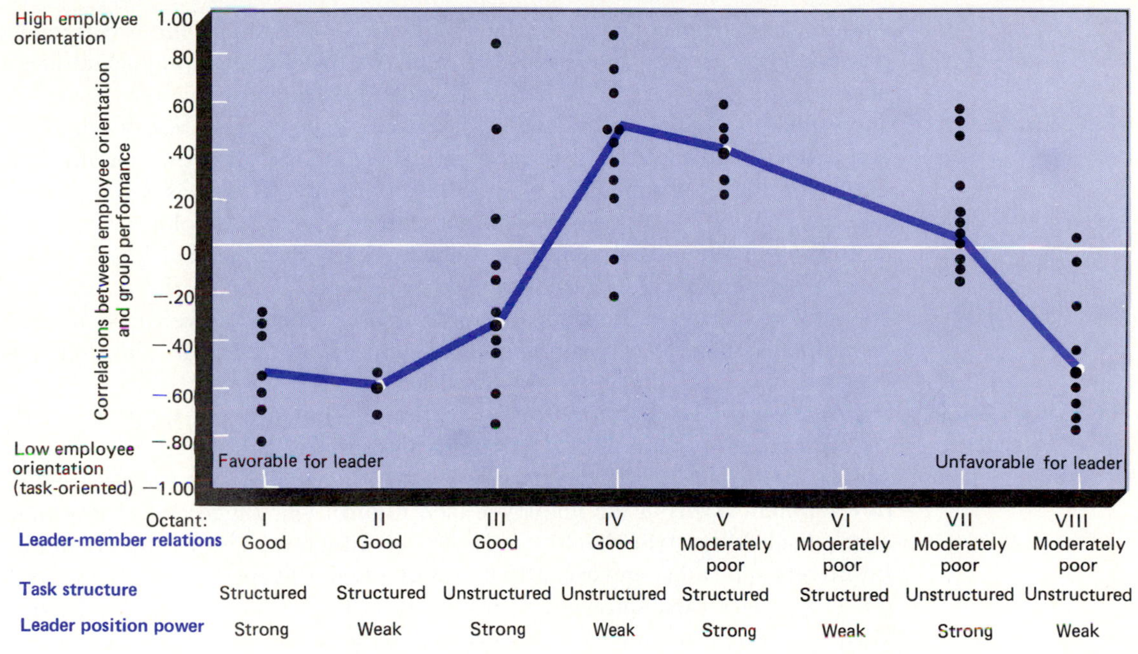

FIGURE 9-7

Research showing how the contingency model of leadership applies

Adapted from A Theory of Leadership Effectiveness, *by Fred E. Fiedler, p. 146. Copyright © 1967 by McGraw-Hill Book Company. Used with permission of McGraw-Hill Book Company.*

strengths. Similarly, a structured leader is more effective in a position of weak power, low task structure, and poor leader-member relations. However, in intermediate conditions of favorableness, the considerate leader is often the most effective; and these situations are the most common ones in work groups.

The conclusions of the Fiedler model may be explained in the following manner. In highly unstructured situations the leader's structure and control are seen as removing undesirable ambiguity and the anxiety that results from it, so a structured approach may be preferred. In situations where the task is highly routine and the leader has good relations with the employees, they may perceive a task orientation as supportive to their job performance (clearing the path). The remaining broad middle ground requires better leader-member relations to be established, so a more considerate, employee-oriented leader is effective.

Despite criticism, Fiedler's contingency model has made a major contribution to discussions on leadership style. For example, managers are encouraged to:

- Examine their situation—the people, task, and organization
- Be flexible in the use of various skills within an overall style
- Consider modifying elements of their jobs to obtain a better match with their preferred style

Hersey and Blanchard's situational leadership model

Development level

Another contingency approach, the situational leadership (or life-cycle) model developed by Hersey and Blanchard, suggests that the most important factor affecting the selection of a leader's style is the development (maturity) level of a subordinate.[21] *Development level* is the task-specific combination of employee competence and motivation to perform. Managers assess it by examining an employee's level of job knowledge, skill, and ability, as well as willingness to take responsibility and capacity to act independently. Employees typically (according to Theory Y assumptions) become better developed on a task as they receive appropriate guidance, gain job experience, and see the rewards for cooperative behavior. Both the *competence* to perform a given task and the *commitment* to do so can vary among employees, and therefore development levels demand different responses from leaders.

Four styles match four levels.

Hersey and Blanchard use a combination of guidance and supportive (also called task and relationship) orientations to create four major styles—telling, selling, participating, and delegating. These are matched with the progressive development levels of the employee (see Figure 9-8), suggesting that a manager's leadership style should vary with the situation. The model is simple, intuitively appealing, and accents an important contingency factor (the *individual* employee's capabilities on a specific task) that is sometimes overlooked. However, it ignores several other critical elements that determine leadership style, and it does not yet have a widely accepted research base. Despite these limitations, it has achieved considerable popularity and also awakened many managers to the idea of contingency approaches to leadership style.

Two employees named Cindi and Marv were hired by the same firm to perform similar jobs. Although they had comparable educational backgrounds, Cindi had several more years of relevant work experience than Marv did. Applying the situational leadership model, their supervisor identified Marv as being moderately low in development ("willing, but not yet fully able to perform"), while Cindi was assessed as having a moderately high development level ("fully able, but lacking some confidence to perform"). Following this analysis, the supervisor decided to treat them differently during their first months on the job, by "selling" with Marv and "participating" with Cindi. Approximately two years later, the supervisor was able to use different styles with each, now "participating" with Marv and "delegating" with Cindi, since each had gained skills and self-confidence.

FIGURE 9-8
Situational leadership recommendations for leadership style to be used with each developmental stage

DEVELOPMENTAL STAGE	RECOMMENDED STYLE
1 (Low ability; low willingness)	Telling (directive; low support)
2 (Low ability; high willingness)	Selling (directive; supportive)
3 (High ability; low willingness)	Participating (supportive; low direction)
4 (High ability; high willingness)	Delegating (low direction; low support)

FIGURE 9-9
Some potential substitutes for leadership

Adapted from Jon P. Howell and Peter Dorfman, "Substitutes for Leadership: Test of a Construct," Academy of Management Journal. *December 1981, pp. 714–728.*

SOURCE	NATURE
Task	**1 Intrinsic satisfaction**
	2 Feedback from the task itself
	3 Routine, predictable tasks
Organization	**1 Cohesive work groups**
	2 Explicit plans, goals, and procedures
	3 Decentralized decision making
Employees	**1 Professional orientation**
	2 Ability, experience, training, and knowledge
	3 Capacity for self-management

Substitutes for leadership

A totally different approach to leadership that still has a contingency flavor has been proposed by Kerr and others.[22] Previous leadership models have suggested that a formal leader is necessary to provide task direction, structure, and rewards, plus the consideration and social support that employees require. Unfortunately, these leadership roles may create an unhealthy dependency on the leaders which stifles subordinate growth and autonomy. In particular, when the leader is not immediately available, work may slow or stop altogether if key roles are not played.

Role of substitutes

However, there appears to be a set of factors that act as *substitutes for leadership*, by making leadership roles unnecessary through replacing them, or even preventing leaders from having any substantial effect on employees. These factors are found in the task, organization, and employees, as shown in Figure 9-9. Many of these serve to decrease the need for a leader's task orientation. This helps to explain why the supervisor's consideration behavior and overall supportiveness are essential roles. Research studies indicate, however, that these substitutes differ between professional and nonprofessional groups of employees. With professionals, some factors may serve to substitute for the support role of managers.[23]

SELF-LEADERSHIP A unique substitute for leadership is the idea of *self-leadership.*[24] This process has two thrusts—leading oneself to perform naturally motivating tasks, as well as managing oneself to do work that is required but not naturally rewarding. Self-leadership may involve employees' observing their own behavior, setting their own goals, cueing themselves to perform, rehearsing effective behaviors, and administering rewards and punishments to themselves. Although self-leadership may not be possible for all employees, it may work well with those whom Hersey and Blanchard identify at the fourth level of development (Figure 9-8).

The supervisor's unique leadership role

Supervisors are leaders who occupy positions at the lowest management level in organizations. They supervise *nonmanagement employees*, while higher managers primarily supervise *other managers* below them. This means that supervisors, not managers, are the point of direct contact with most employees.

Five views

Supervisors need to be leaders just as other managers do. However, the unique organizational positions of supervisors complicates their leadership job and merits further discussion. There are five rather different views of the supervisor's job, as discussed below: key person, supervisor in the middle, marginal supervisor, another worker, and behavioral specialist.

KEY PERSON IN MANAGEMENT The traditional management view of supervisors is that they are key persons in management. They make decisions, control work, interpret policy, and generally are the key people in the process of accomplishing work. They represent management to the workers, and they also represent workers to management. Higher management knows its workers primarily through supervisors. They are an essential element because they are strategically located on the chains of authority and communication; they can block anything going upward or downward. A supervisor is like the hub of a wheel, around which everything revolves.

SUPERVISOR IN THE MIDDLE According to the in-the-middle viewpoint, supervisors are pressed between opposing social forces of management and workers. Management has one set of expectations for supervisors. It wants them to prevent waste, keep employees disciplined, control production, and otherwise carry out its plans. It demands loyalty and maximum effort. Its expectations are largely technical or production-centered.

The pressures brought by workers, on the other hand, are largely matters of feeling. They want their supervisor "to be a good supervisor," to keep them out of trouble, to interpret their fears and wants to management, and to be loyal to them. In short, management expects one set of responses from the supervisor and workers expect another. The supervisor is caught between opposing forces, knowing that the expectations of both cannot always be met. The result is that many supervisors find themselves in ambiguous situations in which, because of different expectations from different groups, they are not sure of the right course of action. In-the-middle supervisors become frustrated because they are victims of the situation, not supervisors of it.

THE MARGINAL SUPERVISOR The marginal supervisor is left out of, or is at the margin of, the principal activities and influences that affect the department. Unaccepted by management, ignored by the staff, and not one of the workers, the supervisor is truly the one who walks alone. Top management has stockholders, other managers, and staff specialists supporting it. Workers have their union, their shop stewards, and their informal groups. But who supports the supervisor?

Though the picture of marginal supervisors is bleak indeed, they sometimes are found in organizations. The fact that supervisors manage operating employees instead of other managers places them in a position to feel marginal in the beginning. In addition, various staff specialists make decisions and issue instructions that supervisors merely transmit, if they see them at all. Further, the supervisory role in labor relations is mostly a passive one. Others above the supervisors conduct labor negotiations, and any labor decisions the supervisors make are subject to review through the grievance procedure. They feel obligated to act like managers, yet they do not receive the reward of full participation in management. They are marginal persons.

ANOTHER WORKER A fourth view of supervisors is that they remain employees in all but title. First, they often lack authority. The center of decision making is elsewhere, so that supervisors are only expediters who carry out decisions. They perform operating work. They run errands, communicate, and make records. Second, supervisors feel they are not a part of the management group. They lack management status, and their thought patterns are much closer to those of workers than to those of higher management. This means that supervisors often tend to interpret management policies and actions in a way different from that intended by management.

A BEHAVIORAL SPECIALIST Management in some situations looks upon the supervisor as primarily a behavioral specialist. According to this view, supervisors are specialists, just like most of the staff people with whom they interact. They look after the human side of operations, and the staff handle its technical side. Supervisors are not marginal, because they are definitely a part of activities. Neither are they key persons; instead, they are among the many specialists who deal with operating problems. Their specialty is human behavior. This viewpoint tends to be found in centralized, repetitive manufacturing, as on an assembly line.

Is the view of the supervisor as a behavioral specialist valid? It is partly, but only partly. As shown in Figure 9-1 earlier in this chapter, human skills are a significant part of every leader's job, but other skills also are needed. Together, these skills form a balanced package. No capable supervisor is just a specialist in one skill, such as human behavior.

What is the supervisor's leadership role?

Different parts of the supervisory job may fit all five of the viewpoints just mentioned. Supervisors are partly marginal persons, just another worker, and so on. There also are major differences among jobs such as assembly-line supervisor and supervisor of clerks in an insurance office. But there are basic similarities that permit description of the supervisor's job in general terms.

Perhaps foremost, supervisors are management people.[25] They direct the work of others. Since supervisors are management's point of contact with workers and vice versa, they certainly are key people in management; but they also receive pressures from both sides (similar to the in-the-middle concept), and they need to be behavioral specialists in dealing with their people. These

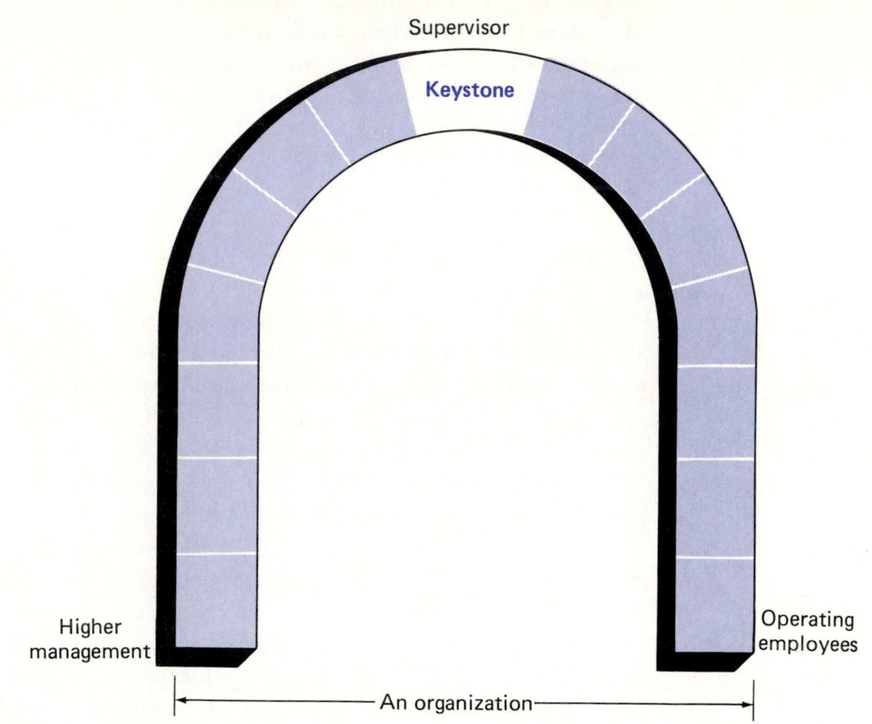

FIGURE 9-10
The supervisor's keystone role in the organizational arch

The supervisor is a keystone.

three ideas can be reconciled by considering the supervisor as the *keystone*, not in management, but in the structure of the organization. As shown in Figure 9-10, the supervisor is like the keystone in an arch, the element that connects both sides and makes it possible for each to perform its function effectively. The sides are effectively joined only by using the keystone. It takes the pressures of both sides and uses them to strengthen, not weaken, the overall arch and to make success possible for the organization.

To the extent that supervisors feel marginal, they are out of the arch and unable to serve in their keystone function. To the extent that they are like other workers, they are not in the keystone locations. The marginal-supervisor and another-worker concepts have no place in the keystone model of the supervisor's leadership role.

SUMMARY

Leadership is the process of encouraging and helping others to work enthusiastically toward objectives. It is determined primarily by one's role behavior, not by one's personal traits. Leaders' roles combine technical, human, and conceptual skills, which leaders apply in different degrees at various organizational levels. Their behavior as followers is also important to the organization.

The path-goal model of leadership accents two major roles. One is goal setting, which is a powerful motivational approach discussed earlier. Management by objectives is a system that clarifies goals and gives employees some freedom in determining how to go about accomplishing them. Vision also provides a broad image of where the organization can and should be going. In their second major role, leaders engage in path support by helping employees accomplish tasks, and here power and politics become important tools.

Leaders apply different leadership styles, ranging from free-rein to autocratic. Although a positive, participative, considerate leader tends to be more effective in many situations, the contingency approaches suggest that a variety of styles can be successful. The leader must first analyze the situation and discover the key factors in the task, employees, or organization that suggest which style might be best.

Supervisors have somewhat different leadership roles because they are the point of direct contact with most employees. When an organization is compared to an arch, the supervisor is the keystone uniting higher management with employees.

Terms and concepts for review

Leadership
Technical, human, and conceptual skills
Path-goal leadership
Goal setting
Management by objectives
Vision
Task and psychological support
Role modeling
Types of power
Politics
Theory X and Theory Y
Fiedler's contingency model
Hersey and Blanchard's situational model
Substitutes for leadership
Self-leadership
Keystone role of supervisors

Discussion questions

1 Think of the best leader you have ever worked with on a job, in sports, or in any other activity, and then the worst leader. Discuss the contrasting styles and skills used by the two. How did you respond to each? What could they have done differently?
2 Explain why conceptual leadership skills become more important, and technical skills less important, at higher organizational levels.
3 A manager once told a subordinate, "To be a good leader, you must first become a good follower." Discuss this statement.
4 Think back to situations in which you were a leader. What leadership style did you use? Using hindsight, what would you have done differently?

5 Discuss the relationship between the path-goal model and management by objectives and vision.
6 Think of an organization in which you participated, and discuss the power and politics in it. What types of power were used? How did people react? What types of political tactics were apparent? Were they successful?
7 Explain how Theory X and Theory Y relate to leadership styles, especially the contingency approaches. Comment on the statement "Management philosophy controls practice."
8 How does the idea of self-leadership relate to Theory X and Theory Y? Explain.
9 Is the path-goal model a contingency approach, too? Indicate why, or why not.
10 The chapter indicated that substitutes for leadership may be different for professionals and nonprofessionals. How might the use of substitutes (as replacements for, or barriers to, leadership) vary from top to bottom of an organization?

Incident

THE WORK ASSIGNMENT

Effie Pardini supervised eleven accounting clerks in the budget and planning department of a large computer manufacturer. None of the clerks had accounting degrees, but all were skilled in handling records and figures. They primarily prepared budgetary plans and analyses for operating departments. Data inputs were secured from the departments and from company records. Pardini assigned projects to the clerks on the basis of their interests and skills. Some projects were more desirable than others because of prestige, challenge, the contacts required, or other factors; so there were occasional conflicts over which clerk was to receive a desirable project. One clerk who seemed especially sensitive and regularly complained about this issue was Sonia Prosser.

On one occasion Pardini received a desirable project and assigned it to a clerk by the name of Joe Madden. Prosser was particularly distressed because she felt she should have had the assignment. She was so distressed that she retaliated by gathering up her present assignment and putting it away in her desk. Then she took a book from her desk and started reading it. Since all the clerks were together in the same office, most of them observed her actions. She announced to one in a voice loud enough to be heard by others, "Nobody around here ever gives me a good assignment."

Pardini overheard Prosser's comment and looked up from her desk, noting what was happening. Pardini was angered, but she sat at her desk for five minutes wondering what to do. Meanwhile Prosser continued reading her book.

Questions

1 What leadership issues are raised by this incident?

2 Discuss what action Pardini should take. Consider politics and power, the path-goal model of leadership, and contingency approaches to leadership before making your decision.

Experiential exercise

WESTGATE COMMUNITY HOSPITAL

Manuel Martinez was the administrator of Westgate Community Hospital. The controller, Sam Westin, reported to him and directed the financial affairs of the hospital. Westin's general attitude was to be a tight-fisted guardian of the dollar. He was rigid in attitude, not wanting to approve any action that was a departure from routine or a variance from policy. Martinez was the type who desired to take action, regardless of the restrictions of past practice or policy. The differing attitudes of the two men had led to conflicts in the past, and on two occasions Martinez had warned, "If you can't follow my orders, Sam, I am going to have to fire you." Westin held his ground and usually won his arguments, contending that his approach was proper accounting practice and, therefore, not subject to challenge by Martinez.

One afternoon Martinez approached Westin and commented, "Sam, here's a merit wage increase that I just put through for Clara Nesbit. She's the best floor supervisor we have, and she deserves an increase. She threatened to leave unless we raised her. I promised this on her next paycheck, so be sure to put it through at once."

Westin looked at the merit increase form and commented, "Manuel, you know I can't put this through. It is contrary to policy. She is already making the top rate allowed for her classification."

MARTINEZ That doesn't make any difference. Put it through. I'm the administrator of this hospital, and when I say 'do it,' then put it through.

WESTIN I can't do it. It's against policy.

MARTINEZ I'm the boss here, and I say do it.

WESTIN I'm not going to violate policy.

Martinez pointed his finger at Westin and talked so loudly that it attracted the attention of the others in the office: "Who's the boss here, Sam?"

WESTIN You are.

MARTINEZ (heatedly) Then put through this raise.

WESTIN No.

A shouting match developed that diverted the attention of the whole office. Finally Martinez said, "Sam, I have had enough. You are fired."

WESTIN You can't fire me for that.

MARTINEZ I just did it. You are through.

Martinez did not retract his action. Westin was removed from the payroll and left the hospital that afternoon.

Assignment

Divide the class into pairs of individuals. One person in each pair should assume the role of Martinez, and the other the role of Westin. Role-play the interaction over the wage increase again, but this time Martinez should consider using other leadership behaviors that would have a more productive outcome. Discuss the results in class.

References

1 Nancy K. Austin, "Leaders Are Not Pussycats," *Success*, October 1986, p. 10.

2 Harvey A. Hornstein et al., "Responding to Contingent Leadership Behavior," *Organizational Dynamics*, Spring 1987, p. 64.

3 For summaries of early research, see Cecil E. Goode, "Significant Research on Leadership," *Personnel*, March 1951, pp. 342–350; and Ralph Stogdill, "Personal Factors Associated with Leadership: A Survey of the Literature," *The Journal of Psychology*, January 1948, pp. 35–71. A recent study supporting traits is by Larry Peppers and John Ryan, "Discrepancies between Actual and Aspired Self: A Comparison of Leaders and Nonleaders," *Group and Organization Studies*, September 1986, pp. 220–228; other support for traits is in Robert G. Lord, Christy L. De Vader, and George M. Alliger, "A Meta-Analysis of the Relation between Personality Traits and Leadership Perceptions: An Application of Validity Generalization Procedures," *Journal of Applied Psychology*, August 1986, pp. 402–410.

4 Thomas Moore, "Personality Tests Are Back," *Fortune*, Mar. 30, 1987, pp. 74–82.

5 For a discussion of the nine complex roles that leaders play, see John W. Gardner, "The Tasks of Leadership," *New Management*, Spring 1987, pp. 8–14.

6 Robert W. Johnston, "Leader-Follower Behavior in 3-D, Part 2," *Personnel*, September–October 1981, pp. 50–60. A review of research on followership is in Trudy Heller and Jon Van Til, "Leadership and Followership: Some Summary Propositions," *Journal of Applied Behavioral Science*, vol. 18, no. 3, 1982, pp. 405–414.

7 Robert J. House, "A Path Goal Theory of Leadership Effectiveness," *Administrative Science Quarterly*, September 1971, pp. 321–328. For the original explanation, see M. G. Evans, The Effects of Supervisory Behavior upon Worker Perceptions of Their Path-Goal Relationships, unpublished doctoral dissertation, New Haven, Conn.: Yale University, 1968. Considerable support for the model is provided in Julie Indvik, "Path-Goal Theory of Leadership: A Meta-Analysis," in John A. Pearce II and Richard B. Robinson (eds.), *Academy of Management Best Papers Proceedings 1986*, Chicago: Academy of Management, 46th annual meeting, Aug. 13–16, 1986, pp. 189–192.

8 The origin of MBO can be traced to Peter F. Drucker, *The Practice of Management*, New York: Harper & Row, Publishers, Inc., 1954. Current overviews are provided in Bob Richards, "Three Classes of Objectives and Plans Make MBO More Effective," *Personnel Journal*, December 1986, pp. 28–30; and Heinz Weihrich, *Management Excellence: Productivity through MBO*, New York: McGraw-Hill Book Company, 1985.

9 Discussions of vision are in Marshall Sashkin, "True Vision in Leadership," *Training and Development Journal*, May 1986, pp. 58–61; Robert Terry, "The Leading Edge," *Minnesota*, January–February 1987, pp. 17–22; and Walter Kiechel III, "Wanted: Corporate Leaders," *Fortune*, May 30, 1983, pp. 135ff; as well as several of the books listed at the end of this chapter.

10 See, for example, Sandra L. Kirmeyer and Thung-Rung Lin, "Social Support: Its Relationship to Observed Communication with Peers and Superiors," *Academy of*

Management Journal, March 1987, pp. 138–151; and Robert Eisenberger et al., "Perceived Organizational Support," *Journal of Applied Psychology,* August 1986, pp. 500–507.

11 "Mgr. Forum," *Mgr.* (American Telephone and Telegraph Company, Long Lines Division), no. 4, 1976, p. 2.

12 The potential value of role modeling is presented in Charles D. Orth, Harry E. Wilkinson, and Robert C. Benfari, "The Manager's Role as Coach and Mentor," *Organizational Dynamics,* Spring 1987, pp. 66–74.

13 Sample discussions are in Nancy C. Roberts, "Organizational Power Styles: Collective and Competitive Power under Varying Organizational Conditions," *Journal of Applied Behavioral Science,* vol. 22, no. 4, 1986, pp. 443–458; and Don R. Beeman and Thomas W. Sharkey, "The Use and Abuse of Corporate Politics," *Business Horizons,* March–April 1987, pp. 26–30.

14 Reciprocity and trust underlie the "shoelace theory" of leadership in which managers build complementary relationships; see Louis B. Barnes and Mark P. Kriger, "The Hidden Side of Organizational Leadership," *Sloan Management Review,* Fall 1986, pp. 15–25.

15 Examples of research and critique on the "leader-member exchange model" are in Terri A. Scandura, George B. Graen, and Michael A. Novak, "When Managers Decide Not to Decide Autocratically: An Investigation of Leader-Member Exchange and Decision Influence," *Journal of Applied Psychology,* November 1986, pp. 579–584; and Richard M. Dienesch and Robert C. Liden, "Leader-Member Exchange Model of Leadership: A Critique and Further Development," *Academy of Management Review,* July 1986, pp. 618–634.

16 Theory X and Theory Y were first published in Douglas McGregor, "The Human Side of Enterprise," in *Proceedings of the Fifth Anniversary Convocation of the School of Industrial Management,* Cambridge, Mass.: Massachusetts Institute of Technology, Apr. 9, 1957.

17 Data supporting a democratic approach is in Terry A. Beehr and Nina Gupta, "Organizational Management Styles, Employee Supervisory Status, and Employee Responses," *Human Relations,* January 1987, pp. 45–58; a general argument for the motivational effects is William L. Ginnodo, "Consultative Management: A Fresh Look at Employee Motivation," *National Productivity Review,* Winter 1985, pp. 78–80.

18 Gregory H. Dobbins and Stephen J. Zaccaro, "The Effects of Group Cohesion and Leader Behavior on Subordinate Satisfaction," *Group and Organization Studies,* September 1986, pp. 203–219; and Chester A. Schriesheim, "The Great High Consideration–High Initiating Structure Leadership Myth: Evidence on its Generalizability," *The Journal of Social Psychology,* April 1982, pp. 221–228.

19 Examples of early reports from each university are Daniel Katz et al., *Productivity, Supervision and Morale in an Office Situation,* Ann Arbor, Mich.: University of Michigan Press, 1950; and E. A. Fleishman, *"Leadership Climate" and Supervisory Behavior,* Columbus, Ohio: Personnel Research Board, Ohio State University Press, 1951.

20 Fred E. Fiedler, *A Theory of Leadership Effectiveness,* New York: McGraw-Hill Book Company, 1967; and Fred E. Fiedler and Martin M. Chemers, *Leadership and Effective Management,* Glenview, Ill.: Scott, Foresman and Company, 1974. For a critique, see Arthur G. Jago and James W. Ragan, "The Trouble with Leader Match Is That It Doesn't Match Fiedler's Contingency Model," *Journal of Applied Psychology,* November 1986, pp. 555–559.

21 Paul Hersey and Kenneth H. Blanchard, *Management of Organizational Behavior,* 5th ed., Englewood Cliffs, N.J.: Prentice-Hall, Inc., 1988. A slightly modified approach is in Kenneth H. Blanchard et al., *Leadership and the One Minute Manager,* New York: Wm. Morrow & Company, 1985.

22 Steven Kerr and J. M. Jermier, "Substitutes for Leadership: Their Meaning and Measurement," *Organizational Behavior and Human Performance*, December 1978, pp. 375–403.

23 Jon P. Howell and Peter W. Dorfman, "Leadership and Substitutes for Leadership among Professional and Nonprofessional Workers," *Journal of Applied Behavioral Science*, vol. 22, no. 1, 1986, pp. 29–46.

24 A. Bandura, *Social Learning Theory*, Englewood Cliffs, N.J.: Prentice-Hall, Inc., 1978; Charles C. Manz, "Self-Leadership: Toward an Expanded Theory of Self-Influence Processes in Organizations," *Academy of Management Review*, July 1986, pp. 585–600; and Charles C. Manz, Kevin W. Mossholder, and Fred Luthans, "An Integrated Perspective of Self-Control in Organizations," *Administration and Society*, May 1987, pp. 3–24.

25 The changing role of the middle manager—the position to which supervisors will likely be promoted—is discussed in Joel C. Polakoff, "Will Middle Managers Work in the 'Factory of the Future'?" *Management Review*, January 1987, pp. 50–51; and Steven Kerr, Kenneth D. Hill, and Laurie Broedling, "The First-Line Supervisor: Phasing Out or Here To Stay?" *Academy of Management Review*, January 1986, pp. 103–117.

For additional reading

Bennis, Warren, and Burt Nanus, *Leaders: Strategies for Taking Charge*, New York: Harper & Row, Publishers, Inc., 1985.

Block, Peter, *The Empowered Manager*, San Francisco: Jossey-Bass Inc., Publishers, 1986.

Burns, James McGregor, *Leadership*, New York: Harper & Row, Publishers, Inc., 1976.

Cialdini, Robert B., *Influence: How and Why People Agree to Things*, New York: Wm. Morrow & Company, 1984.

Fiedler, Fred E., *A Theory of Leadership Effectiveness*, New York: McGraw-Hill Book Company, 1967.

Kotter, John P., *The Leadership Factor*, New York: Free Press (Macmillan Company), 1988.

Kouzes, James M., and Barry Z. Posner, *The Leadership Challenge*, San Francisco: Jossey-Bass Inc., Publishers, 1987.

Leavitt, Harold, *Corporate Pathfinders: Building Vision and Values into Organizations*, Homewood, Ill.: Dow Jones–Irwin, 1986.

Levinson, Harry, and Stuart Rosenthal, *CEO: Corporate Leadership in Action*, New York: Basic Books, Inc. (Harper & Row, Publishers, Inc.), 1986.

Manz, C., and H. Sims, Jr., *Superleadership*, Englewood Cliffs, N.J.: Prentice-Hall, Inc., 1988.

McGregor, Douglas, *The Human Side of Enterprise*, New York: McGraw-Hill Book Company, 1960.

Tichy, Noel M., and Mary Anne Devanna, *The Transformational Leader*, New York: John Wiley & Sons, Inc., 1986.

CHAPTER

10 The nature and use of participation

Nothing creates more self-respect among employees than being included in the process of making decisions.

JUDITH M. BARDWICK[1]

The problem with participative management is that it works.

RAYMOND E. MILES[2]

CHAPTER OBJECTIVES

To understand

The idea of participation

The participative process

Prerequisites for participation

Benefits of participation

Types of participative programs

Limitations of participation

s discussed in the preceding chapter, a participative style is often important for effective leadership. Participation has excellent potential for building teamwork, but it is a difficult practice and can fail if poorly applied. When participation is effectively applied, two of its best results are acceptance of change and a commitment to goals that encourages better performance.

Observe in the experience of one company how participation improved safety. A large aircraft manufacturer employed from 5000 to 20,000 shop workers during a ten-year period. It used a safety committee system in which each department was represented on the committee by one of its workers. During these ten years not one person had a disabling injury while serving as safety committee member. When people became safety committee members, they ceased having disabling injuries! This record occurred despite the fact that there were hundreds of members during the decade, and sometimes "accident-prone" workers were appointed committee members in order to make them safety-conscious. The facts of this situation show a significant difference between committee members and nonmembers. Part of this difference surely came from the fact that the committee members were responsible, participating people with regard to safety.

THE NATURE OF EMPLOYEE PARTICIPATION

What is participation?

Participative managers consult with their employees, bringing them in on problems and decisions so that they work together as a team. The managers are not autocrats, but neither are they free-rein managers who abandon their management responsibilities. Participative managers still retain ultimate responsibility for the operation of their units, but they have learned to share operating responsibility with those who perform the work. The result is that employees feel a sense of involvement in group goals. As shown in Figure 2-4, the "employee psychological result" of supportive management is "participation." It follows that *participation is mental and emotional involvement of persons in group situations that encourage them to contribute to group goals and share responsibility for them.* There are three important ideas in this definition—involvement, contribution, and responsibility.

Elements in participation

MENTAL AND EMOTIONAL INVOLVEMENT First, and probably foremost, participation means mental and emotional involvement rather than mere muscular activity.[3] A person's *self* is involved, rather than just one's skill. This involvement is psychological rather than physical. A person who participates is *ego-involved* instead of merely *task-involved.* Some managers mistake task involvement for true participation. They go through the motions of participation, but nothing more. They hold meetings, ask opinions, and so on, but all the time it is perfectly clear to employees that their manager is an autocratic boss who wants no ideas. This is *busywork*, not participation. Employees fail to become ego-involved.

Ego involvement

The difference between ego-involved participation and task-involved activity is shown by a description of a part of a day for a worker named Joseph Carter. He wakens to the music of his clock-radio, interrupted occasionally by an announcer he does not know, cannot see, and cannot talk back to. After eating alone, since his family does not awake so early in the morning, his next personal interaction is with a bus driver whom he does not know and who works for some abstract transportation system that Carter does not understand and in which he has no control.

At the company he shows his badge to a guard, though he does not know the guard's name and does not really care when he asks, "How are you feeling this morning?" In fact, he is irked because the guard keeps asking to see his badge, though surely after three years the guard must know he is an employee. Going into the shop, he has to stop by the personnel office to sign an insurance paper which he cannot understand and which is thrust at him by an employee who acts as if she were selling soap in a grocery store. Finally, he enters his work area to be greeted by a supervisor whose name he does know, but that is about all, because the supervisor is only in the department temporarily for training and is to be sent somewhere else soon by "somebody upstairs." And so it goes throughout the day.

Though Joseph Carter has been furiously active all day, most of this was routine, impersonal activity that was imposed on him. How much was he ego-involved in his activity? How much did he participate?

MOTIVATION TO CONTRIBUTE A second important idea in participation is that it motivates people to contribute. They are given an opportunity to release their own resources of initiative and creativity toward the objectives of the organization, just as Theory Y predicts. In this way participation differs from "consent." The practice of consent uses only the creativity of the manager who brings ideas to the group for the members' consent. The consenters do not contribute; they merely approve. Participation is more than getting consent for something that has already been decided. Its great value is that it taps the creativity of all employees.

Employees use their creativity.

Participation especially improves motivation by helping employees understand and clarify their paths toward goals. According to the path-goal model of leadership, the improved understanding of path-goal relationships produces a higher responsibility for goal attainment. The result is improved motivation.

For example, one of Xerox Corporation's manufacturing plants in New York was losing money.[4] Top management concluded that the only alternative was to subcontract the production of some components. In an attempt to save 180 employees from being laid off, an employee team was formed to gather proposals for cost

savings. After six months of intense effort and analysis, the team proposed a wide-ranging series of changes that projected an annual savings of $3.7 million. The recommendations were accepted by management and the union, avoiding the layoffs and making the plant profitable again. The team members, with the help of many other interested employees, had a strong motivation to contribute, and they succeeded.

ACCEPTANCE OF RESPONSIBILITY A third idea in participation is that it encourages people to accept responsibility in their group's activities. It is a social process by which people become self-involved in an organization and want to see it work successfully. When they talk about their organization, they begin to say "we," not "they." When they see a job problem, it is "ours," not "theirs." Participation helps them become responsible employee-citizens rather than nonresponsible, machinelike performers.

Responsibility builds teamwork.

As individuals begin to accept responsibility for group activities, they see in it a way to do what *they* want to do, that is, to get a job done for which they feel responsible. This idea of getting the group to want teamwork is a key step in developing it into a successful work unit. When people *want* to do something, they will find a way. Under these conditions employees see managers as supportive contributors to the team. Employees are ready to work actively with managers rather than reactively against them.

Why is participation popular?

Managers have for years recognized various benefits of participation, but these benefits were first experimentally demonstrated in classic studies in industry by Roethlisberger, Bavelas, Coch and French, and others.[5] Conducted by skillful social scientists under controlled conditions, these experiments were useful in drawing attention to the potential value of participation. Their collective results suggested the general proposition that, *especially in the introduction of changes, participation tends to improve performance and job satisfaction.* Later research in organizations basically supported this proposition, as suggested by the authors of a comprehensive review: "Participation has an effect on both satisfaction and productivity, and its effect on satisfaction is somewhat stronger than its effect on productivity."[6]

Research conclusions

In addition to the keen interest shown by American businesses in any managerial practice that promises to increase productivity,[7] there are other reasons for the popular use of participative practices. The educational level of the work force has increased substantially in recent years. In addition to greater skill development, educated employees have acquired a greater *desire* for influencing work-related decisions and an *expectation* that they will be allowed to participate in them.[8] An equally strong argument has been made that participation is an *ethical imperative* for managers.[9] This view rests on the conclusion that highly nonparticipative jobs cause both psychological and physical harm to employees in the long run. As a result of this knowledge, managers

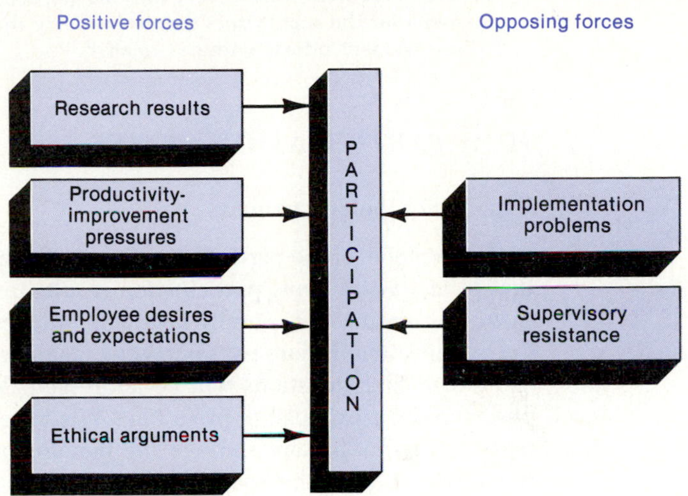

FIGURE 10-1
Opposing forces affecting the use of participation

are urged to create participative conditions that will allow employees to experience greater autonomy in their work.

Problems with participation

The four major forces toward increased practice of participation are shown in Figure 10-1. They are partially offset by other factors pushing in the opposite direction, such as occasional failure experiences and resistance from supervisors.

Implementation problems

Participation in organizations generally has been successful, although there have been problems and even failures. One insurance company, for example, found that employee decision making became too independent. Sometimes two employees were calling on the same customer. Other employees were seeking only easy accounts, leaving the hard ones for someone else. Eventually the company had to restore some controls. Even though failures of this type may be the result of improper implementation, they often receive undue publicity that prevents other managers from using participation.

Supervisory resistance

A serious pressure slowing the use of participation stems from the resistance of first-line supervisors. They may hold Theory X beliefs, fear losing their current status, or honestly question the organization's capacity to change. Many have not been trained in team-management skills, and now feel uncomfortable in their new roles as coaches and facilitators.

One study explored the attitudes of supervisors in eight plants toward employee involvement programs.[10] In general, they reported that they believed the programs were good for the company (72 percent agreement) and good for the employees (60

percent agreement). However, only 31 percent perceived that participation was beneficial for the supervisors themselves. Are the other 69 percent likely to support the involvement efforts enthusiastically?

HOW PARTICIPATION WORKS

The participative process

A simple model of the participative process is shown in Figure 10-2. It indicates that *in many situations* participation results in mental and emotional involvement that produces generally favorable outcomes for both the employees and the organization. Before we review the major types of participative programs in use today, four questions will be addressed. What happens to a supervisor's power under participative programs? What are the prerequisites to successful participation? What are some of the benefits of participation? What factors in the situation affect the success of participative programs?

The impact on supervisory power

Leader-member exchange

Participation is a sharing process among managers and employees. It is built upon the *leader-member exchange* concept—the idea that leaders and their followers exchange information, resources, and role expectations that determine the quality of their interpersonal relationship. Because of time limitations, some relationships will be warm, supportive, and trusting but others will not. Research suggests that when a supervisor perceives that an employee has high ability and that a high-quality exchange relationship exists, the supervisor will allow a greater degree of influence in decisions.[11]

When managers first consider allowing employees greater influence in making decisions, they often ask, "If by means of participation I share authority with my employees, don't I lose some of it?" This is a normal worry, but it is not a justifiable one because participative managers still retain final authority. All

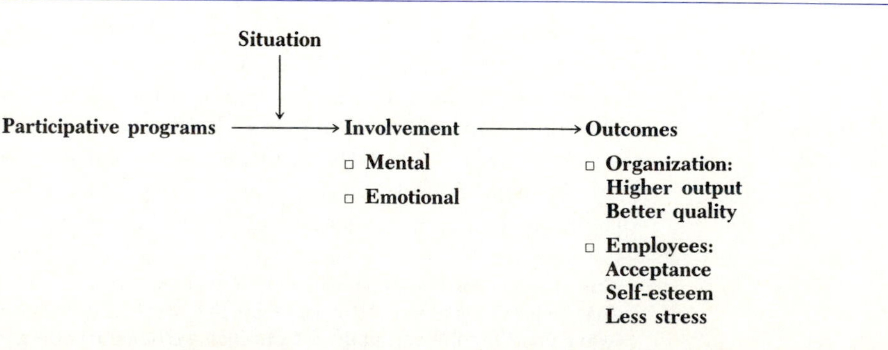

FIGURE 10-2
The participative process

AUTOCRATIC VIEW	PARTICIPATIVE VIEW
Power—	**Power—**
□ Is a fixed amount	**□ Is a variable amount**
□ Comes from the authority structure	**□ Comes from people through both official and unofficial channels**
□ Is applied by management	**□ Is applied by shared ideas and activities in a group**
□ Flows downward	**□ Flows in all directions**

FIGURE 10-3
Two views of power and influence

they do is share the use of authority so that employees will become more involved in the organization. Managers engage in a two-way social exchange with workers, in contrast to imposing ideas from above. They give employees some power, and receive employee creativity in return.

TWO VIEWS OF POWER Strange as it may seem, participation actually may increase the power of both managers and their employees. It is evident that employees gain more power with participation, but what about managers? The autocratic view of management is that power is a fixed quantity, so someone must lose what another gains.

Participation expands influence

However, as shown in Figure 10-3, the participative view is that power in a social system can be increased without taking it from someone else. The process works like this. Managerial power depends partly on conditions such as employee trust in management, feeling of teamwork, and sense of responsibility. Participation improves these conditions. Since employees feel more cooperative and responsible, they are likely to be more responsive to managerial attempts to influence them. In a sense, what occurs is that managers make social transactions with their work groups that improve goodwill and responsibility. These conditions are similar to a savings deposit that managers can draw upon later (perhaps with interest!) when they need to apply their power.

Here is an example that shows how a manager may increase power by sharing it. The manager of a computer operation having over fifty employees felt that some changes were needed. In the beginning she tried the usual autocratic approach, aided by a consultant. Desired changes were proposed, but the employees would not accept them. Finally, the effort was abandoned.

The manager continued to think that changes were necessary, so a year later she decided to try again, using more participatory approaches. She discussed the need with her supervisors and several key employees. Then she set up committees to work on designated parts of a "self-examination study." The groups worked hard, and in a few months they submitted a capable report that recommended a number of important changes. In this instance the members felt a sense of pride and ownership in the report. It was theirs. They had created it. The result was that they made a genuine effort to implement it. With the full support of the whole group, they made substantial changes. Participation had increased the manager's power and influence.

1 Adequate time to participate
2 Potential benefits greater than costs
3 Relevance to employee interests
4 Adequate employee abilities to deal with the subject
5 Mutual ability to communicate
6 No feeling of threat to either party
7 Within the area of job freedom

FIGURE 10-4 Prerequisites for participation

Prerequisites for participation

The success of participation is directly related to how well certain prerequisite conditions are met, as shown in Figure 10-4. Some of these conditions occur in the participants; some exist in their environment. They show that participation works better in some situations than in others—and in certain situations it works not at all. Major prerequisites are as follows:[12]

1 There must be time to participate before action is required. Participation is hardly appropriate in emergency situations.

2 The potential benefits of participation should be greater than its costs. For example, employees cannot spend so much time participating that they ignore their work.

3 The subject of participation must be relevant and interesting to the employees; otherwise employees will look upon it merely as busywork.

4 The participants should have the ability, such as intelligence and technical knowledge, to participate. It is hardly advisable, for example, to ask janitors in a pharmaceutical laboratory to participate in deciding which of five chemical formulas deserve research priority; but they might participate in helping resolve other problems related to their work.

5 The participants must be able mutually to communicate—to talk each other's language—in order to be able to exchange ideas.

6 Neither party should feel that its position is threatened by participation. If workers think their status will be adversely affected, they will not participate. If managers feel that their authority is threatened, they will refuse participation or will be defensive.

Area of job freedom

7 Participation for deciding a course of action in an organization can take place only within the group's area of job freedom. Some degree of restriction is required on parts of an organization in order to maintain unity for the whole. Each separate subunit cannot make decisions that violate policy, collective-bargaining agreements, legal requirements, and similar restraints. Likewise

there are restraints due to the physical environment (a flood closing the plant is an extreme example) and due to one's own limitations (such as not understanding electronics). The *area of job freedom* for any department is its area of discretion after all restraints have been applied. In no organization is there complete freedom, even for the top executive.

Within the area of job freedom, participation exists along a continuum, as shown in Figure 10-5. Within a period of time a manager will practice participation at many points along the continuum. That is, a manager may seek the group's ideas before deciding vacation schedules, but the same manager decides overtime schedules independently. Similarly, a manager may find it necessary to limit the participation used with one employee while consulting freely with another. Since a consistent approach provides employees with a predictable environment, each manager gradually becomes identified with some general style of participation as a usual practice. The popular terms designated for amounts of participation along the continuum are representative of a broad area on the continuum instead of a certain point. Several of these terms are defined later in this chapter.

FIGURE 10-5
Participation exists along a continuum.
Adapted from Robert Tannenbaum and Warren H. Schmidt, "How to Choose a Leadership Pattern." Harvard Business Review, *March–April 1958, p. 96.*

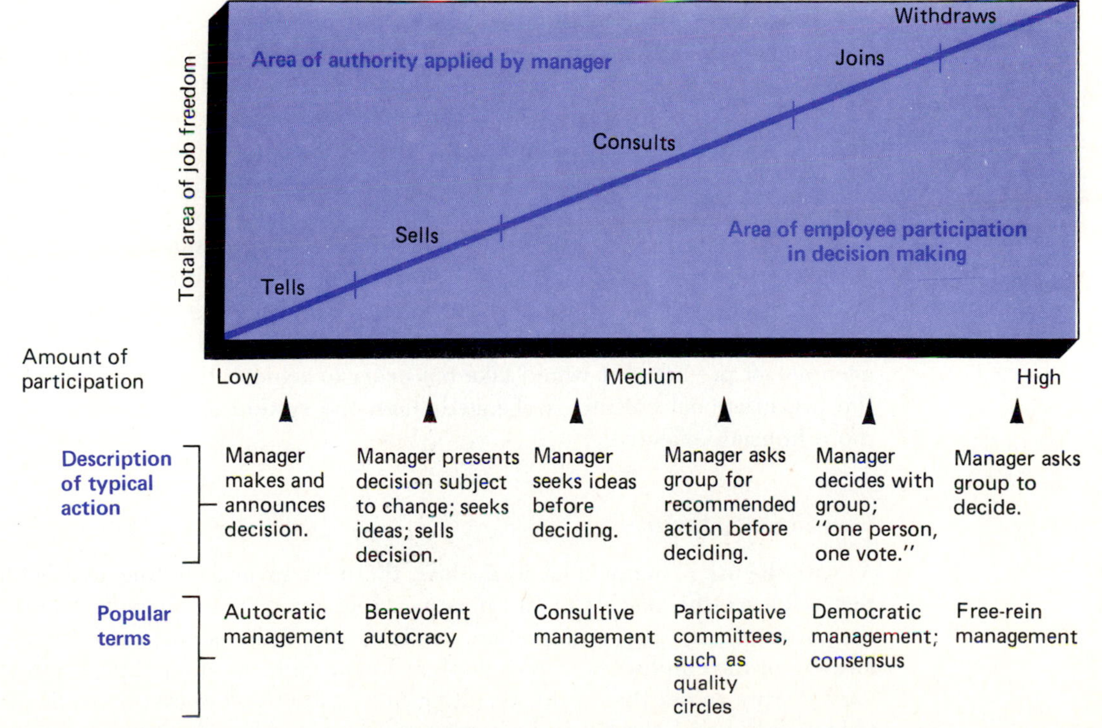

Benefits of participation

In various types of organizations under many different operating conditions, participation has contributed to a variety of benefits. Some of these are direct and others are less tangible. Participation typically brings higher output and a better quality of output. In certain types of operations the quality improvement alone is worth the time invested in participation. Employees often make suggestions for both quality and quantity improvements. Although not all the ideas are useful, there are enough valuable ones to produce genuine long-run improvements.

In one firm, for example, computer operations were running $100,000 over budget, and management sought ways to reduce this drain on resources. In the beginning, management discussed the problem in several meetings, but the managers could not agree on any major cost-saving changes. Then management sought the advice of a consultant. Although the consultant recommended some changes, they produced minor savings.

Finally one manager suggested that management should ask employees for ideas. Some managers doubted that this approach would help, but after discussion they decided to bring employees in the computer department into full participation on the program. Within thirty days the employees suggested cost-saving ideas that eventually provided about double the savings needed.

Participation tends to improve motivation because employees feel more accepted and involved in the situation. Their self-esteem, job satisfaction, and cooperation with management also may improve. The results often are reduced conflict and stress, more commitment to goals, and better acceptance of change.[13] Employees also may reduce turnover and absences, because they feel that they have a better place to work and that they are being more successful in their jobs. Finally, the act of participation by itself establishes better communication as people mutually discuss work problems.

Benefits may emerge slowly.

The results clearly show that participation has broad systems effects that favorably influence a variety of organizational outputs. The benefits may not appear immediately, however. When one company adopted participative management, it predicted it would take *ten years* to achieve the full effect. Once the organizational culture is changed, then the system as a whole becomes more humanly effective.

Contingency factors

As with the use of many behavioral ideas, there are several contingency factors that influence the success of participative programs.[14] These may be found in the environment, the organization, its leadership, the nature of tasks performed, or the employees. For example, national cultures and political systems vary sharply across the world, resulting in a restrictive environment for participation in a dictatorship and a more supportive one in a democracy. Organizational practices also need to be adapted to the pace of change in their environments, which can range from stable to turbulent.

We have previously discussed (Chapter 9) the impact of Theory X or Theory Y beliefs on a manager's selection of a leadership style. There is also evidence that top executives' beliefs and values, as reflected in the organization's culture, have a strong impact on the use of participation by lower managers. Task characteristics need to be examined before choosing a participative program; intrinsically satisfying tasks may diminish the need for greater participation, while routine tasks may suggest that participation could produce fruitful results. There are also a variety of tasks in which employees can be involved, including goal setting, decision making, problem solving, and planning major organizational changes.

DIFFERENT EMPLOYEE NEEDS FOR PARTICIPATION Some employees desire more participation than others. As indicated earlier, educated and higher-level workers often seek more participation, because they feel more prepared to make useful contributions. When they are not allowed to contribute, they tend to have lower performance, less satisfaction, lower self-esteem, and more stress. However, some other employees desire only a minimum of participation and are not upset if they are not actively involved.

Compare desired and actual participation.

The difference between one's desired and actual participation gives a measure of the potential effectiveness of participation, assuming the employee has the ability to contribute. When employees want more participation than they have, they are "participatively deprived" and there is *underparticipation*. In the opposite situation, when they have more participation than they want, they are "participatively saturated" and there is *overparticipation*.

Where there is either underparticipation or overparticipation, people are less satisfied than those who participate in a degree that closely matches their needs. This relationship is shown in Figure 10-6. As participation comes closer to matching either high or low needs, satisfaction with the organization goes up. Conversely, as a mismatch increases, these positive feelings decline. Participation is not something that should be applied equally to everyone. Rather, it should match each person's needs (if the other contingency factors allow it).

A consultant was asked to assess employee attitudes within a department in one company. One question asked of the employees focused on the frequency with which they were allowed to participate in decision making. The contrast in responses was striking. For example, one employee replied "All the time—about three or four times a week." Another responded by saying "Almost never—only three or four times a week."

It is apparent from this example that employee *perceptions* of the situation are highly important. The evidence suggests that participation will be more successful where employees feel they have a valid contribution to make, it will be valued by the organization, and they will be rewarded for it. It is also imperative that they believe that management is truly interested in their ideas and will use them, so their time and energy will not be wasted. Overall, it is clear that several contingency factors play a key role in determining the effectiveness of any participative program.

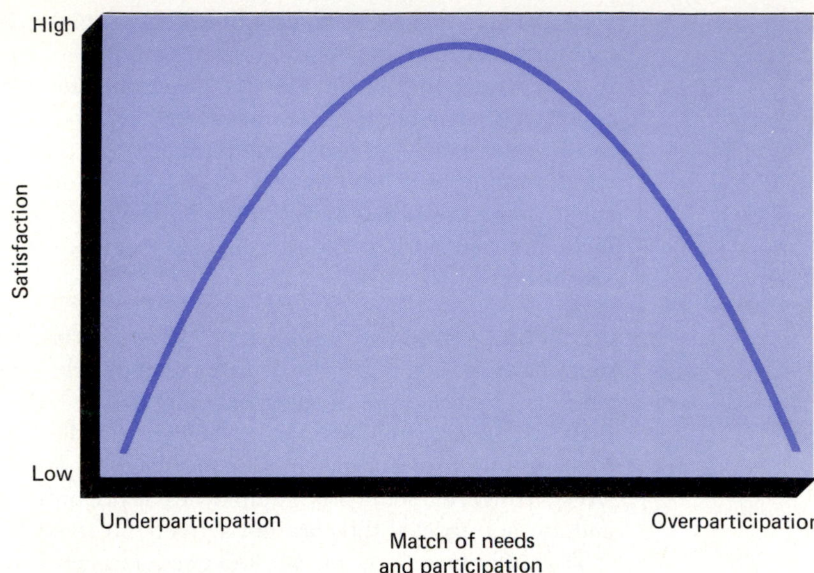

FIGURE 10-6
The relation of satisfaction to the match of need and actual participation

PROGRAMS FOR PARTICIPATION

We can further understand how participation works if we examine selected programs to develop it, as shown in Figure 10-7. These programs usually are clusters of similar practices that focus on specific approaches to participation. One or more can be used within a single company; often an organization gives its managers the freedom to choose which program to use in their own areas. When a company uses a sufficient number of programs to develop a widespread sense of involvement among its employees, it is said to practice *participative management*.

Consultive management

Consultive management is the kind of participation that managers can often practice even though the people above them do not apply it. *Consultive management*, as the name implies, means that managers consult with their employees in order to encourage them to think about issues and contribute their own ideas before decisions are made. Managers do not consult on every issue, but they do create a pattern of consultation.

Vroom model

A useful model of consultive management that clearly takes a contingency approach was developed by V. H. Vroom and others.[15] They recognized that problem-solving situations differ, and so they developed a structured approach for managers to examine the nature of those differences. In this model, manag-

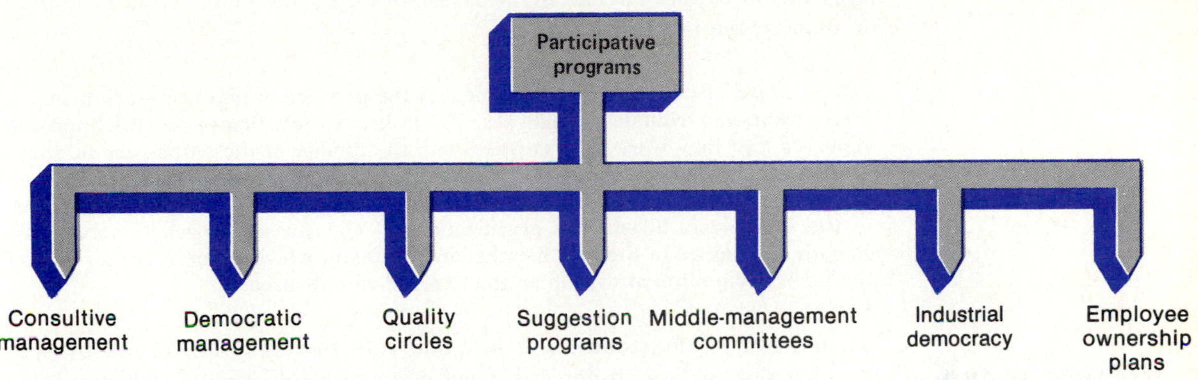

FIGURE 10-7
Selected types of participative programs

Quality and acceptance.

ers assess a current problem according to the perceived importance of *decision quality and employee acceptance*. Decision-quality dimensions include cost considerations, availability of information, and whether or not the problem is structured. *Employee-acceptance* dimensions include the need for their commitment, their prior approval, the congruence of their goals with the organization's, and the likelihood of conflict among the employees. Other items to consider are the level of subordinate information, time constraints, geographical dispersion of subordinates, the leader's motivation to conserve time, and the leader's motivation to develop subordinates. By following this structured analysis, several unique kinds of problems are identified and classified. Guidelines are then offered to help managers select one of five approaches to use in each situation.

The usefulness of Vroom's model rests on two key assumptions. First, it assumes that managers can accurately classify problems according to the criteria offered. Second, it assumes that managers are able and willing to adapt their leadership style to fit the conditions they face. If these assumptions are valid, the model holds considerable promise for helping managers choose the appropriate degree of consultation.

Democratic management

Democratic management goes further than consultive management and more consistently allows a number of major decisions to be made by employee groups, as shown at the right side of Figure 10-5. The main process by which democratic management occurs is group discussion, which makes full use of group ideas and group influence. In its extreme form it operates according to consensus and reflects many of the Theory Z ideas adapted from successful Japanese firms. Democratic management applies well in voluntary social organizations, where the lack of time pressure and a natural community of interests make it easier to achieve consensus on some issues. It has traditionally been more difficult to apply in hierarchical, task-oriented situations, where competition over scarce resources is likely.

One example of democratic management is the practice of allowing work teams to hire, orient, and train new employees.[16] A study of twenty firms using this approach reported that they were very satisfied with the quality of the employees selected, while legal risks were minimized through careful training in using job-based criteria. The increased cost of having multiple sets of hiring teams was offset by low turnover of the individuals hired. The organizations in the survey especially valued the smooth acceptance of the new member by the team, which occurred as a result of the team's commitment to helping the new individual succeed.

Self-managing teams

Hiring new team members is just one role that may be played by self-managing teams. Sometimes called autonomous work groups, *self-managing teams* are groups that are given a large degree of decision-making autonomy and expected to control their own behavior and results.[17] Typically, team members possess several relevant skills and make joint decisions about work schedules and the assignment of tasks. Team performance is monitored, and compensation may be based on its overall effectiveness. Under this democratic approach, the more useful leadership behaviors involve encouraging individuals and the team as a whole to engage in self-observation, self-evaluation, and self-reinforcement.

Quality circles

For many years, both union and nonunion firms have organized groups of workers and their managers into committees to consider and solve job problems. These groups may be called work committees, labor-management committees, work-improvement task forces, or involvement teams. They have broad usefulness for improving productivity and communications because most of the employees can be involved. A currently popular use of committees for this purpose is called a quality circle.

Quality circles are voluntary groups that receive training in statistical techniques and problem-solving skills and then meet to produce ideas for improving productivity and working conditions. They meet regularly—often on company time—and generate solutions for management to evaluate and implement. Quality circles have expanded rapidly as an involvement technique in the United States and Europe after achieving widespread success in Japan.

Effects of quality circles

One research study compared the attitudes and performance of six quality circles in a manufacturing firm with a matched group of noninvolved workers.[18] Quality-circle participation favorably influenced employee attitudes toward decision making, group communication, and a feeling of accomplishing something worthwhile. Productivity rose by 23 percent, versus a 2 percent increase in the control group. Absenteeism declined steadily in the quality-circle group to a level 27 percent below where it began, while it showed erratic movement in the comparison group.

Not all quality circles are as successful as the one reported here, and many have a relatively short life.[19] However, the approach does help employees feel that they have some influence on their organization even if not all of their recommendations are accepted by higher management.[20] Quality circles provide opportunities for personal growth, achievement, and recognition. Further, employees are committed to the solutions they generate, because they "own" them.

Guidelines

To be successful, quality circles should follow these guidelines:

- Use them for measurable, short-term problems.
- Obtain continuous support from top management.
- Apply the group's skills to problems within the circle's work area.
- Train supervisors in facilitation skills.
- View quality circles as one starting point for other more participative approaches to be used in the future.

Suggestion programs

Suggestion programs are formal plans to encourage individual employees to recommend work improvements. In most companies the employee whose suggestion results in a cost saving may receive a monetary award in proportion to the first year's saving, so the award can be a substantial sum of money. Pitney Bowes, for example, awards its suggestors from $25 up to a maximum of $50,000, payable over two years.[21] About 25 percent of suggestions are accepted in most organizations, but the rate varies from firm to firm.

Limitations

Although many suggestion programs provide useful ideas, they are a limited form of participation that accents individual initiative rather than group problem solving. They often require major administrative efforts to keep them working, and the programs can be hurt by slow response to the submissions. The written form of communication lacks the motivation that might arise from face-to-face discussion of problems. Perhaps most significantly, some supervisors have difficulty looking constructively upon the suggestions, and instead view them as criticisms of their own ability and practices.

Middle-management committees

Multiple management

Middle-management committees are group mechanisms to improve participation of managers below top organizational levels. They also are known as *multiple management,* a term used by McCormick and Company, a tea and spice company that developed the practice in the 1930s.[22]

Multiple management has been used successfully around the world in hundreds of companies, both unionized and nonunionized. Its central core is a junior board of directors that is given the opportunity to study any problem and to recommend courses of action. Employer information is made freely available to the board, and its meetings are unrestrained by the presence of senior executives. Members make their own bylaws and rotate their membership. The program encourages careful study of ideas before they are presented to management; therefore top management rarely vetoes a recommendation.

Multiple management has many benefits, especially for the sometimes overlooked middle managers. It is an excellent way to develop executive skills among middle managers and train them for top management. It encourages their growth and helps them develop a spirit of cooperation as they work together. It also taps their reserve of creativity, so new ideas are brought to management. The process itself encourages them to study policy issues carefully, take responsibility for their decisions, and broaden their experience. The result is a program that helps meet their desire to participate and does so in a way that benefits managers, workers, owners, and customers alike. As with any program, there have been occasional failures.

Industrial democracy

Industrial democracy is government-mandated worker participation at various levels of the organization with regard to decisions that affect workers. Occasionally the term also is applied to voluntary programs rather than mandated ones. At lower levels it is applied through *works councils;* at the top level it is called *codetermination* and typically means that workers or their representatives have rights to seats on the boards of directors of firms.[23] It was established in West Germany in the 1940s, when steel firms were required to organize boards with one-third worker representation. Since that time the practice has spread gradually to other nations in Western Europe, although the form used varies among them. The idea has not gained strong support from labor in the United States.

Codetermination

The basic philosophy of industrial democracy is to institutionalize worker participation in management in order to encourage cooperation rather than the traditional attitude of labor against management. This process also should build both worker and management understanding of each other's problems. Offsetting disadvantages include weakened ability of management to manage, excessive paperwork and meeting time, slower decision making, bypassing of middle management, and occasional unauthorized release or misuse of confidential information. In some situations labor-management conflict has increased rather than decreased. In many cases worker apathy is a problem; labor representatives are more interested in workplace issues than policy decisions.

Employee ownership plans

Employees have often been urged to "buy the product you make"; today, that slogan has occasionally been replaced with "buy the company you work for."

Employee ownership of a firm emerges when employees provide the capital to purchase control of an existing operation. The stimulus often comes from threatened closings of marginally profitable plants, where workers see little hope of other employment in a devastated local economy. Employee ownership has been tried in diverse industries such as plywood, meat packing, steel, and furniture manufacturing. On the surface, these plans appear to offer the highest degree of participative decision making, as employees take control. Better management, heightened morale, and improved productivity have all been predicted to follow.

The National Center for Employee Ownership surveyed 3000 participants in 37 employee-owned companies.[24] Stock ownership generally increased employee interest in the company's financial success and encouraged workers to remain with the company longer. However, it did not increase their perception of influence in decision making, they did not feel like they were treated more equally by their managers, and they did not report working harder on the job. It appears that the potential financial rewards, coupled with a greater understanding of organizational problems and practices, are the biggest benefits from employee ownership.

Does ownership imply involvement?

The use of employee ownership plans continues to expand, with as many as 10 million employees covered in the United States alone. Although some large firms like Eastern Airlines, the Hallmark greeting card company, and W. L. Gore have some form of employee ownership or stock trusts, the financial benefits may be more apparent to employees in smaller firms. Job security also has been gained for thousands of workers who were in danger of losing their jobs. However, employee ownership plans do not necessarily result in greater day-to-day control or direct involvement by employees in key decisions. Some firms have even found that the compensation gaps between workers and management have widened, and labor-management relations have sometimes deteriorated from previous levels. Clearly, employee ownership has costs as well as benefits as a participative tool.[25]

IMPORTANT CONSIDERATIONS IN PARTICIPATION

Labor-union attitudes toward participation

Some union leaders feel that if they participate in helping management decide courses of action, the union's ability to challenge those actions is weakened. These union leaders prefer to remain aloof, having freedom to express disagreement with management and to challenge it at any time. The opposite point of view, held by other leaders, is that participation gives them an opportunity to get on the inside and to express their viewpoints *before* action is taken, which is superior to disagreement and protest *after* a decision is made. In practice most union viewpoints are somewhere between these two extremes; some types of participation are considered acceptable, but others are not.

Limitations of participation

For several pages we have been commenting favorably on participation, so it is now appropriate to put the brakes on enthusiasm and toss a few brickbats. Participation does have its costs as well as gains. All the prerequisites discussed earlier are limitations to some extent, but there are others.

Technology and organizations today are so complex that specialized work roles are required, making it difficult for people to participate successfully if they are very far beyond their specialties. This means that lower-level workers can participate successfully in operating matters, but they usually have difficulty in policy matters.

Difficulties especially arise when workers make proposals in areas where they are not competent. Then, when their idea is rejected, they refuse to support whatever course of action was adopted and become alienated. A related problem is that some workers *expect* to be consulted on every issue, even those to which they cannot contribute. When they are not consulted, they become resentful and uncooperative.

Rigid expectations may result.

Another issue is an employee's right *not* to participate. There is no evidence that participation is desired by everybody. We have said only that participation is a useful means of building better relations in a group, and we also have said that people are all different. There is evidence that many individuals do not want to be bothered with participation. Shall we, regardless, push them into it merely because we think it is good for them?

Authority is threatened.

A further problem is that supervisors have difficulty adjusting to participation. It tends to threaten their traditional authority. Unless higher management makes changes to give supervisors new responsibilities that use their surplus capacity, they may become dissatisfied. For example, one study of twelve companies that had increased worker participation found that supervisors were the most dissatisfied and frustrated people in the company.

Another difficulty with participation—as was the case with scientific management—is that practitioners become lost in the procedures of participation while overlooking its philosophy. The substance of participation does not automatically flow from its procedures; there is no such mechanistic connection. Procedures do not automatically lead to participation; rather, when they are used at the right time and in the right way, they make it possible for participation to develop in the minds of employees.

A serious issue with participation is that it can be used to manipulate employees. This manipulation is not necessarily by management. It may be by the union or by undercover cliques led by members skilled in group dynamics—the social engineers of consent. Too often groups are used to impose conformity on individualistic members. It is no wonder, then, that some employees prefer the open tyranny of an autocratic boss to the sometimes hidden tyranny of a group.

Concluding thoughts

In spite of its numerous limitations, participation generally has achieved substantial success.[26] It is not the answer to all organizational problems, but experience does show its general usefulness. The demand of employees to participate is not a passing fancy. It appears to be rooted deeply in the culture of free people around the world, and it is probably a basic drive in human beings. They want some control over things that affect them. Because of its significance, participation is the kind of practice to which organizational leaders need to devote long-range efforts. It affords a means of building some of the human values needed at work. It has been so successful in practice that it has become widely accepted in more advanced nations.

SUMMARY

Participation is an important contributor to organizational effectiveness. Participation is mental and emotional involvement of persons in group situations that encourage them to contribute to group goals and share responsibility for them. For employees, it is the psychological result of supportive management.

Participation is a sharing process that may increase the power of both employees and the supervisor, because power is an expandable resource. When participation's prerequisites are met, it can provide a variety of benefits for both employees and employers. Some employees desire more participation than others, so it is most effective when it reasonably matches their needs. If there is underparticipation or overparticipation, both satisfaction and performance may decline.

There are a number of participative programs that are effective. All have their benefits as well as their limitations. A program that is desirable for some employees is not necessarily good for all of them. Labor unions typically support management's participative efforts, but they are more hesitant about becoming officially involved in these efforts.

Terms and concepts for review

Participation
Leader-member exchange
Prerequisites for participation
Area of job freedom
Overparticipation and underparticipation
Consultive management
Democratic management
Self-managing teams
Quality circles
Suggestion programs

Multiple management
Industrial democracy
Codetermination
Employee ownership plans
Limitations of participation

Discussion questions

1 Think of your last full-time or part-time job. Discuss the amount of participation that was there. Was it more or less than you needed? What was the effect on you?

2 Ask several persons outside the class what is meant by "participation." Explain why their answers might differ.

3 How is it possible for participation to increase the power and influence of both manager and employee?

4 Discuss the prerequisites for effective participation. Do they help explain why some managers are relatively autocratic?

5 Most employees desire more participation. Managers were employees at one time. Why, then, don't these managers provide more opportunities for participation?

6 What benefits can participation provide? Compare the various programs on the basis of benefits.

7 Have you ever worked in a firm with a suggestion program? Did you or your friends use it? Discuss.

8 Appraise the comment, "Managers get enough participation. They are on the 'inside' and make all the decisions, so they certainly do not need any participative aids such as multiple management."

9 What was the area of job freedom in your last job? Was it adequate for your needs? What groups or institutions restricted this freedom? Based on your experiences and reading, do you think government controls are bringing a net increase or decrease in job freedoms? Discuss.

10 Think of a time when you were a member of a student group assigned to complete some project. Was the group a self-managed team? Explain. Did anyone in the group help you to observe, evaluate, and reinforce appropriate behaviors?

Experiential exercise

USING THE VROOM MODEL

1 Through brief class discussion, identify a problem on campus or in the local community that is currently creating considerable interest. Indicate who is in charge of solving the problem (such as a mayor or university president) and which people are most directly affected.

2 Divide the class in half, with one half assuming the role of mayor (or president) and the other being assigned the role of community group (or students). These two types of groups may be further divided to create face-to-face discussion groups.

3 Working as a group (from the perspective of the role you have been assigned), assess the importance of each of the major dimensions from Vroom's model on the form provided below. (Place an *X* in the appropriate column.)

DIMENSION	ASSESSMENT (LOW) 1	2	3	4	5 (HIGH)
1 Importance of cost considerations					
2 Availability of information					
3 Degree of problem structure					
4 Need for group's commitment					
5 Degree to which prior approval has already been obtained					
6 Congruence of individual and organizational goals					
7 Likelihood of conflict among group members over preferred solution					
8 Level of information available in the group					
9 Constraints on time available					
10 Geographical dispersion of group members					
11 Leader's motivation to conserve time					
12 Leader's motivation to develop group members					

4 What do the results of this assessment tell you about which leadership approach to use in this case? Which dimensions push a manager toward the autocratic approach, and which toward the consensus group method of decision making? What other information would you like to have?

5 Discuss the usefulness of analyzing several dimensions of the problem situation, as you did here, before choosing a decision-making approach. What is the likelihood that managers would apply this approach to major problems that they face? What would prevent them from doing so, and what would encourage them to do so?

Incident

JOE ADAMS

Joe Adams is supervisor in the final assembly department of an automobile body plant. Work in this department is not dependable, with temporary layoffs or short weeks occurring three or four times a year. The work is physically difficult, but the skill required is minimal; so most employees are high school graduates only. Some do not even have a high school education. About one-third of the work force comes from ethnic and racial minority groups. The work procedure and pace of work are tightly controlled by industrial engineers and other staff groups.

Adams attended a one-day conference of his Supervisors' Association recently and learned the many potential benefits of participation. In his own words, "This conference sold me on participation," so now he wishes to establish it in his assembly department. Management feels that conditions on an assembly line are not suitable for participation. Further, it believes that the majority of workers employed have an autocratic role expectation of supervision. In addition, management has said that the production schedule will not allow time off for participation during the workday. This means that if Adams wants to hold any meetings about participation, he will have to do so after work and on the workers' own time. Adams feels sure that his employees will not wish to remain after work on their own time, and he is not even sure that they would do so if he paid them overtime.

Questions

1 Recommend a course of action for Adams.
2 Would any ideas from the following be helpful in this case: McGregor, Herzberg, McClelland, Fiedler, models of organizational behavior, prerequisites for participation, area of job freedom, and programs for participation?

References

1 Judith M. Bardwick, "How Executives Can Help 'Plateaued' Employees," *Management Review*, January 1987, p. 45.
2 Raymond E. Miles, in Bill Saporito, "The Revolt Against 'Working Smarter,'" *Fortune*, July 21, 1986, p. 58.
3 The actual degree of involvement in various participative programs varies substantially from passive to active, as noted by Peter R. Richardson, "Courting Greater Employee Involvement through Participative Management," *Sloan Management Review*, Winter 1985, pp. 33–43.
4 Peter Lazes, "Employee Involvement Activities: Saving Jobs and Money Too," *New Management*, Winter 1986, pp. 58–60.
5 F. J. Roethlisberger and W. J. Dickson, *Management and the Worker*, Cambridge, Mass.: Harvard University Press, 1939; Norman R. F. Maier, *Psychology in Industry*, Boston: Houghton Mifflin Company, 1946, pp. 264–266; Lester Coch and John R. P. French, Jr., "Overcoming Resistance to Change," *Human Relations*, vol. 1, no. 4, 1948, pp. 512–532.
6 Katherine I. Miller and Peter R. Monge, "Participation, Satisfaction, and Productivity: A Meta-Analytic Review," *Academy of Management Journal*, December 1986, pp. 727–753.
7 John W. Newstrom and Jon L. Pierce, "Popular Business Books: Implications for Management Development," paper presented at the 47th annual Academy of Management conference, New Orleans, La., Aug. 9–12, 1987.
8 Edward E. Lawler III, "Education, Management Style, and Organizational Effectiveness," *Personnel Psychology*, Spring 1985, pp. 1–26.
9 Marshall Sashkin, "Participative Management Remains an Ethical Imperative," *Organizational Dynamics*, Spring 1986, pp. 62–75.

10 Janice A. Klein, "Why Supervisors Resist Employee Involvement," *Harvard Business Review,* September–October 1984, pp. 87–95. Related arguments are Rosabeth Moss Kanter, "The New Workforce Meets the Changing Workplace: Strains, Dilemmas, and Contradictions in Attempts to Implement Participative and Entrepreneurial Management," *Human Resource Management,* Winter 1986, pp. 515–537; and Bob Crosby, "Employee Involvement: Why It Fails, What It Takes to Succeed," *Personnel Administrator,* February 1986, pp. 95ff.

11 Terri A. Scandura, George B. Graen, and Michael A. Novak, "When Managers Decide Not to Decide Autocratically: An Investigation of Leader-Member Exchange and Decision Influence," in John A. Pearce II and Richard B. Robinson (eds.), *Academy of Management Best Papers Proceedings 1986,* Chicago: Academy of Management, 46th annual meeting, Aug. 13–16, 1986. This exchange perspective is supported by the conclusion that subordinates associate participation with the quantity and quality of communication they experience with their superior; see Teresa M. Harrison, "Communication and Participative Decision Making: An Exploratory Study," *Personnel Psychology,* Spring 1985, pp. 93–116.

12 See Robert Tannenbaum, Irving R. Weschler, and Fred Massarik, *Leadership and Organization: A Behavioral Science Approach,* New York: McGraw-Hill Book Company, 1961, pp. 88–100.

13 Susan E. Jackson, "Participation in Decision Making as a Strategy for Reducing Job-Related Strain," *Journal of Applied Psychology,* February 1983, pp. 3–19.

14 Examples of contingency factors are found in Vijay Govindarajan, "Impact of Participation in the Budgetary Process on Managerial Attitudes and Performance: Universalistic and Contingency Perspectives," *Decision Sciences,* Fall 1986, pp. 496–516; and Edwin A. Locke, David M. Schweiger, and Gary P. Latham, "Participation in Decision Making: When Should It Be Used?" *Organizational Dynamics,* Winter 1986, pp. 65–79.

15 V. H. Vroom and P. W. Yetton, *Leadership and Decision Making,* Pittsburgh, Pa.: University of Pittsburgh Press, 1973, contains both an individual (consultive) model and a similar one for group decision making. Recent research is reported in Victor H. Vroom and Arthur G. Jago, *The New Leadership: Managing Participation in Organizations,* Englewood Cliffs, N.J.: Prentice-Hall, Inc., 1988.

16 James Kochanski, "Hiring in Self-Regulating Work Teams," *National Productivity Review,* Spring 1987, pp. 153–159. For an even more dramatic approach, see John W. Newstrom, Mark Lengnick-Hall, and Steven Rubenfeld, "How Employees Can Choose Their Own Bosses," *Personnel Journal,* December 1987, pp. 121–126.

17 Charles C. Manz and Henry P. Sims, Jr., "Leading Workers to Lead Themselves: The External Leadership of Self-Managing Work Teams," *Administrative Science Quarterly,* March 1987, pp. 106–128; for a cross-cultural example of self-management, see Warner P. Woodworth, "Managing from Below," *Journal of Management,* Fall 1986, pp. 391–402.

18 Mitchell Lee Marks et al., "Employee Participation in a Quality Circle Program: Impact on Quality of Work Life, Productivity, and Absenteeism," *Journal of Applied Psychology,* February 1986, pp. 61–69.

19 See, for example, Edward E. Lawler III and Susan A. Mohrman, "Quality Circles: After the Honeymoon," *Organizational Dynamics,* Spring 1987, pp. 42–54; and Mitchell Lee Marks, "The Question of Quality Circles," *Psychology Today,* March 1986, pp. 36–46.

20 The impact on perceived influence is reported in Keith Bradley and Stephen Hill, "Quality Circles and Managerial Interests," *Industrial Relations,* Winter 1987, pp. 68–82; and Anat Rafaeli, "Quality Circles and Employee Attitudes," *Personnel Psychology,* Autumn 1985, pp. 603–615. A high correlation of employee self-esteem and circle performance is reported in Joel Brockner and Ted Hess, "Self Esteem and Task Performance in Quality Circles," *Academy of Management Journal,* September 1986, pp. 617–623.

21 Phil Farish, "HRM Update," *Personnel Administrator*, February 1984, p. 29; also see George G. Rich, "Revamped Suggestion System Saves MDAC Millions of Dollars Annually," *Personnel Journal*, January 1987, pp. 31–34.

22 Charles P. McCormick, *Multiple Management*, New York: Harper & Row, Publishers, Inc., 1938; this is updated in "Five Decades of Participative Management," *Training and Development Journal*, July 1983, pp. 10–11.

23 See, for example, Klaus Bartolke et al., "Workers' Participation and the Distribution of Control as Perceived by Members of Ten German Companies," *Administrative Science Quarterly*, September 1982, pp. 380–397.

24 Katherine J. Klein, "Employee Ownership," *New Management*, Spring 1986, pp. 55–61; and Corey Rosen, Katherine J. Klein, and Karen M. Young, "When Employees Share the Profits," *Psychology Today*, January 1986, pp. 30–36.

25 Alternative views of employee ownership are found in J. Lawrence French, "Employee Perspectives on Stock Ownership: Financial Investment or Mechanism of Control?" *Academy of Management Review*, July 1987, pp. 427–435; and J. L. Pierce and C. Furo, "Employee Ownership and Managerial Implications: Design Features, Process, and Effects," paper presented to Small Business Institute Directors' Association conference, San Francisco, Calif., Feb. 11–14, 1988.

26 John L. Cotton, David A. Vollrath, Kirk L. Froggatt, Mark L. Lengnick-Hall, and Kenneth R. Jennings, "Employee Participation: Diverse Forms and Different Outcomes," *Academy of Management Review*, January 1988, pp. 8–22.

For additional reading

Crocker, Olga L., Cyril Charney, and Johnny Sik Leung Chiu, *Quality Circles: A Guide to Participation and Productivity*, New York: New American Library, 1986.

Crosby, Philip B., *Quality without Tears: The Art of Hassle-Free Management*, New York: McGraw-Hill Book Company, 1984.

Lawler, Edward E., III, *High-Involvement Management: Participative Strategies for Improving Organizational Performance*, San Francisco: Jossey-Bass Inc., Publishers, 1986.

Powers, David R., and Mary F. Powers, *Making Participatory Management Work*, San Francisco: Jossey-Bass Inc., Publishers, 1983.

Quarrey, Michael, Joseph Blasi, and Coren Rosen, *Taking Stock: Employee Ownership at Work*, Cambridge, Mass.: Ballinger Publishing Co., 1986.

Rosen, Corey M., Katherine J. Klein, and Karen M. Young, *Employee Ownership in America: The Equity Solution*, Lexington, Mass.: Lexington Books, 1986.

Rubinstein, Sidney P., *Participative Systems at Work: Creating Quality and Employment Security*, New York: Human Sciences Press, Inc., 1987.

Stern, Robert N., and Sharon McCarthy (eds.), *International Yearbook of Organizational Democracy*, vol. 3, *The Organizational Process of Democracy*, New York: John Wiley & Sons, Inc., 1986.

Vroom, Victor H., and Arthur G. Jago, *The New Leadership: Managing Participation in Organizations*, Englewood Cliffs, N.J.: Prentice-Hall, Inc., 1988.

Vroom, V. H., and P. W. Yetton, *Leadership and Decision Making*, Pittsburgh, Pa.: University of Pittsburgh Press, 1973.

Woodworth, Warner, Christopher Meek, and William Foote Whyte, *Industrial Democracy: Strategies for Community Revitalization*, Beverly Hills, Calif.: Sage Publications, 1986.

CHAPTER 11

Interpersonal and group dynamics

Cooperation takes advantage of all the skills represented in a group as well as the mysterious process by which that group becomes more than the sum of its parts.

ALFIE KOHN[1]

Group memberships can be traumatic and alienating, or rewarding.

SETH ALLCORN[2]

CHAPTER OBJECTIVES

To understand

Conflict situations and approaches

Assertive behavior

Transactional analysis

Group dynamics

Differences between task and social leaders

Weaknesses of meetings

Brainstorming, nominal, and Delphi techniques

Nature of teamwork

"Oh, no! Not another committee meeting," the executive groaned. "It's only Wednesday morning, and I've been to five meetings already this week. When am I going to get my work done?" Meetings, conferences, and committees have on various occasions been described as a waste of executive time, a source of confusion, and an excuse for indecision. Managers sometimes comment, "A committee of one is the best committee" and "The only thing that comes out of a meeting at my company is people." In spite of all this condemnation, committees and other group activities have continued to flourish. Instead of becoming extinct, they are an important part of organizational behavior. The modern executive seldom gets through a day without attending a meeting of some type, and executives occasionally complain of fatigue and anxiety from too many unproductive meetings.

Meetings are necessary but they do introduce more complexity and more chances of problems when improperly used. Some committees are used not to reach decisions but to put them off and not to develop employees but to hide incompetence. On occasion, emotional issues overshadow the decision to be made, and interpersonal relations require delicate handling.

This chapter discusses the benefits that can occur when people relate to each other in face-to-face interaction or group situations. Managers can demonstrate greater interpersonal competence in these situations through appropriate use of conflict management tactics, assertiveness, and transactional analysis. An understanding of group dynamics, and alternative roles and structures to be used, is also important.

INTERPERSONAL DYNAMICS

The nature of conflict

Conflict arises from disagreement over the goals to attain or the methods used to accomplish them. In organizations, conflict among different interests is inevitable, and sometimes the amount of conflict is substantial. One survey reported that managers spend an estimated 20 percent of their time dealing with conflict.[3]

Sources of conflict

Interpersonal conflict arises from a variety of sources, such as:[4]

- Organizational change
- Personality clashes
- Different sets of values
- Threats to status
- Contrasting perceptions and points of view

Some conflict is a response to actions taken by the employer. Several of the sources, however, are a direct reflection of the Law of Individual Differences that was presented in Chapter 1.

Effects of conflict

Conflict is often seen by participants as destructive, but this is a limited view. In fact, one observer notes that "by adeptly avoiding conflict with coworkers, some executives eventually wreak organizational havoc."[5] Conflict is not all bad, but rather may result in either productive or nonproductive outcomes. A more positive view, then, is to see conflict as nearly inevitable and search for ways in which it can result in constructive outcomes.

Advantages

One of the benefits produced by conflict is that people are stimulated to search for improved approaches that lead to better results. It energizes them to be more creative and to experiment with new ideas. Another benefit is that once-hidden problems are brought to the surface, where they may be confronted and solved. Just as fermentation is necessary in the production of fine wines, a certain amount of ferment can create a deeper understanding among the parties involved in a conflict. And once the conflict is resolved, the individuals may be more committed to the outcome through their involvement in solving it.

Disadvantages

There are also possible disadvantages, especially if the conflict lasts a long period of time or becomes too intense. At the interpersonal level, cooperation and teamwork may deteriorate. Distrust may grow among people who need to coordinate their efforts. For individuals, some may feel defeated, while the self-image of others will decline. Predictably, the motivation level of some employees will be reduced. It is important, then, for managers to be aware of the potential for interpersonal and intergroup conflicts, to anticipate their likely outcomes, and to use appropriate conflict resolution strategies. Each of these will now be introduced.

Two types of conflict

INTERPERSONAL CONFLICT Interpersonal conflicts are a serious problem to many people because they deeply affect a person's emotions. There is a need to protect one's self-image and self-esteem from damage by others. When these self-concepts are threatened, serious upset occurs and relationships deteriorate. Sometimes the temperaments of two persons are incompatible and their personalities clash. In other instances, conflicts develop from failures of communication or differences in perception.

An office employee was upset by a conflict with another employee in a different department. It seemed to the first employee that there was no way to resolve the conflict. However, when a counselor explained the different organizational roles of the two employees as seen from the whole organization's point of view, the first employee's perceptions changed and the conflict vanished.

INTERGROUP CONFLICT Intergroup conflicts between different departments also cause problems. On a minor scale these are something like the wars between juvenile gangs. Each group sets out to undermine the other, gain power, and improve its image. Conflicts arise from such causes as different viewpoints, group loyalties, and competition for resources. Resources are limited in any organization. Most groups feel that they need more than they can secure, so the seeds of intergroup conflict exist wherever there are limited resources. For example, the production department may want new and more efficient machinery, while the sales department wants to expand its sales force, but there are only enough resources to supply the needs of one group.

Outcomes and approaches

Four outcomes

CONFLICT OUTCOMES Conflict may produce four distinct outcomes, depending on the approaches taken by the people involved.[6] Figure 11-1 illustrates the different outcomes. The first situation is termed "lose-lose," in which a conflict deteriorates to the point that both parties are worse off than they were before. An extreme example is the case of an executive who fires the only person who knows the secret formula for the organization's most successful product. The second quadrant is "lose-win," a situation in which one person (individual A) is defeated while the other one (B) is victorious. In quadrant three ("win-lose") the situation is reversed, with individual B losing to individual A. The fourth outcome is "win-win," in which both persons perceive that they are in a better

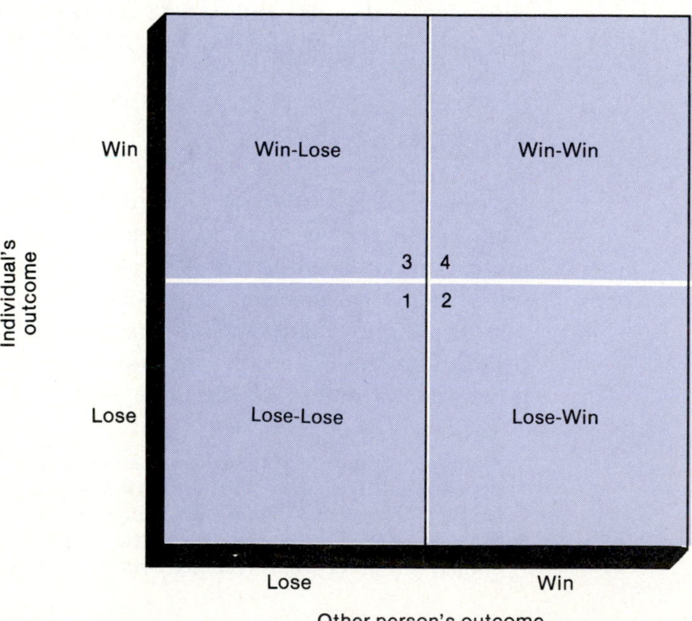

FIGURE 11-1
Four possible outcomes of conflict

position than they were before the conflict began. This is the ideal outcome to try to achieve.

Intentions affect strategies.

PARTICIPANT INTENTIONS Conflict outcomes are a product of the participants' *intentions*, as well as their *strategies*. For example, Jason may actually *seek* a lose-win outcome in a conflict with Becky because of the perceived benefits of being defeated on a particular issue. He may fear the consequences of retribution from too many earlier victories over Becky, or he may try to lose in hopes that Becky will reciprocate on another issue in the future. At the other extreme, Marcia may hope for a win-lose outcome in her conflict with Jessica. This intended effect is often caused by a "fixed-pie" (or zero-sum) viewpoint, in which Marcia believes that she can succeed only at the expense of Jessica.

Four strategies

RESOLUTION STRATEGIES Intentions help participants select their strategies. Once they have been chosen and implemented, the strategies have a substantial impact on the outcomes reached (actual winning or losing). This is shown in Figure 11-2. The simplest strategies focus on either cooperation or competition, but a widely used approach suggests that there are at least four clearly different strategies.[7] These are:

- Avoiding—physical or mental withdrawal from the conflict
- Smoothing—accommodating the other party's interests
- Forcing—using power tactics to achieve a win
- Confronting—facing the conflict directly, and working it through to a mutually satisfactory resolution.

Although any of the four strategies may be effective for its intended purpose of winning or losing, the confronting approach has many behavioral benefits. Both parties will see the recent conflict as productive, since both received gains. Also important is their perception that the process was a supportive one, in which problem solving and collaboration helped integrate the positions of both parties. As a result, research shows that participants find the confronting approach to be the most satisfying.[8] Many labor-management groups have been

FIGURE 11-2 Probable relationships between conflict resolution strategies and outcomes

RESOLUTION STRATEGY	PROBABLE OUTCOME
Avoidance	**Lose-lose**
Smoothing	**Lose-win**
Forcing	**Win-lose**
Confronting	**Win-win**

formed with the objective of seeking new ways to confront each other in constructive ways.

Assertive behavior

Confronting conflict is not easy for some people. When faced with the need to negotiate with others, some managers may feel inferior or be in awe of the other person's power. Under these conditions they are likely to suppress their feelings (part of the avoidance strategy) or strike out in unintended anger. Neither response is truly productive.

Assertiveness

A constructive alternative is to practice assertive behaviors. *Assertiveness* is the process of expressing feelings, asking for legitimate favors, and giving and receiving honest feedback.[9] An assertive individual is not afraid to request that another person change an offensive behavior, and also feels comfortable refusing unreasonable requests from someone else. Assertiveness training involves teaching people to develop effective ways of dealing with a variety of anxiety-producing situations.

Assertive people are direct, honest, and expressive. They feel confident, gain self-respect, and make others feel valued. By contrast, aggressive people may humiliate others, and unassertive people elicit either pity or scorn from others. Both alternatives to assertiveness typically are less effective for achieving a desired goal.

Stages in assertiveness

Being assertive in a situation involves five stages, as shown in Figure 11-3. When confronted with an intolerable situation, assertive people describe it, express their feelings, and empathize with the other's position. Then they offer alternatives, and indicate the consequences that will follow. Not all five steps may be necessary in all situations. As a minimum, it is important to describe the present situation and make recommendations for change. Use of the other steps would depend on the significance of the problem and the relationship between the people involved. Assertiveness training programs generally pre-

STAGE	EXAMPLE
1 Describe the behavior.	**"When you do this. . . ."**
↓	
2 Express your feelings.	**"I feel. . . ."**
↓	
3 Empathize.	**"I understand why you. . . ."**
↓	
4 Negotiate a change.	**"I want you to. . . ."**
↓	
5 Indicate consequences.	**"If you do (don't), I will. . . ."**

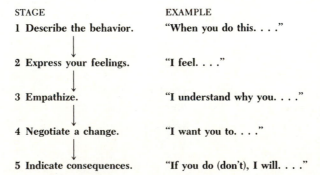

FIGURE 11-3
Stages in assertive behavior

sent the steps available to use, provide a role model to observe, and encourage trainees to practice assertive behavior.

One organization that tried assertiveness training on a pilot basis and later implemented it throughout the organization is Barclay's Bank International.[10] Begun as a device to give women employees the confidence and skills to compete effectively with men, the program soon was expanded to include many male employees who were not assertive. Follow-up studies showed the program to be successful in changing employee behaviors toward greater assertiveness.

Assertive behavior generally is most effective when it integrates a number of verbal and nonverbal components. Eye contact is a means of expressing sincerity, while an erect body posture and direct body positioning may increase the impact of a message. Appropriate gestures may be used, congruent facial expressions are essential, and a strong but modulated voice tone and volume will be convincing. Perhaps most important is the spontaneous and forceful expression of an honest reaction, such as "Tony, I get angry when you always turn in your report a day late!"

Transactional analysis

When people interact in assertive or nonassertive ways, there is a social transaction in which one person responds to another. The study of these social transactions between people is called *transactional analysis* (TA). Transactional analysis was developed by Eric Berne for psychotherapy in the 1950s. Its application to ordinary interactions soon was apparent and was popularized by Berne's book *Games People Play* (1964) and by Harris, Jongeward, and others.[11] The objective of TA is to provide better understanding of how people relate to each other, so that they may develop improved communication and human relationships.

Three ego states

EGO STATES According to Berne, people interact with each other from one of three psychological positions, known as *ego states*. These ego states are called Parent, Adult, and Child, and a person can operate from any one of the three. People whose *Parent ego state* is in control may be protective, controlling, nurturing, critical, or instructive. They may dogmatically refer to policies and standards with such comments as "You know the rule, Angelo. Now follow it."

The *Adult ego state* will appear as rational, calculating, factual, and unemotional behavior. It tries to upgrade decisions by seeking facts, processing data, estimating probabilities, and holding factual discussions.

The *Child ego state* reflects the emotions developed in response to childhood experiences. It may be spontaneous, dependent, creative, or rebellious. Like an actual child, the Child ego state desires approval from others and prefers immediate rewards. It can be identified by its emotional tone, as when an employee comments to the supervisor, "You're always picking on me!"

Several comments about ego states are in order. First, conversations often are a mixture of reactions from Parent, Adult, and Child. Second, each ego state has both positive and negative features—it can add to or subtract from a person's feeling of satisfaction. Third, we can detect the ego state that is in control by carefully observing not only the words used but also a person's tone, posture, gestures, and facial expression.

Complementary

TYPES OF TRANSACTIONS Transactions may be complementary or noncomplementary. They are *complementary* when the ego states of the sender and receiver in the opening transaction are simply reversed in the response. When the pattern between ego states is charted, the lines are parallel. This relationship is shown in Figure 11-4, in which the supervisor speaks to an employee as Parent to Child and the employee responds as Child to Parent. For example, the supervisor says, "Janet, I want you to stop what you're doing and hurry to the supply room to pick up a box they have for me." The employee responds, "I don't want to go, because I'm busy; but I will, since you are the boss."

If a supervisor initiates a transaction in a Parent-to-Child pattern, the employee tends to respond from a Child state. Unfortunately, *a superior-subordinate relationship tends to lead to Parent-Child transactions,* especially

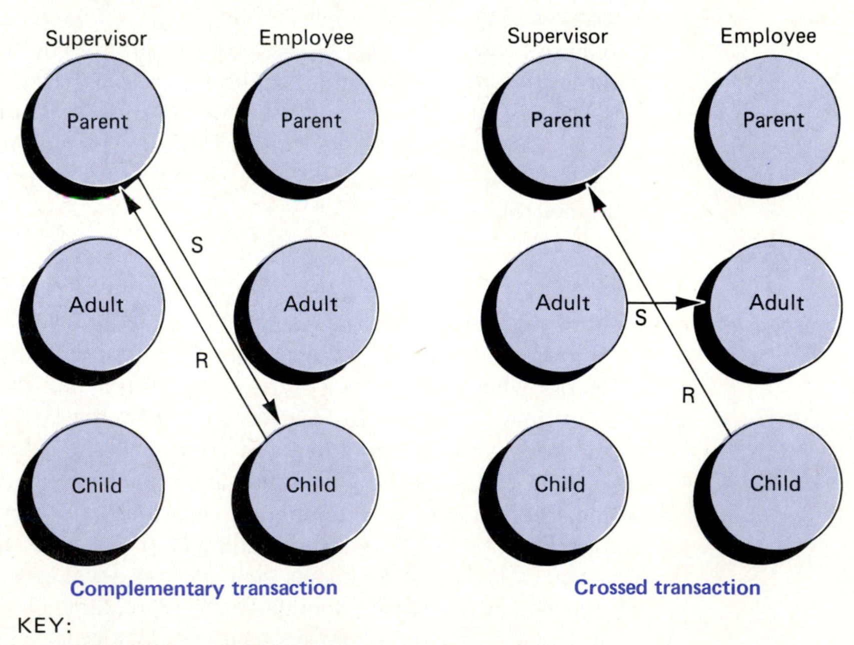

FIGURE 11-4
Complementary and crossed transactions in transactional analysis

when instructions are given or appraisals are conducted. If the supervisor's behavior is dominated by this pattern, it may lead to reduced interpersonal and group effectiveness.

Crossed

Noncomplementary transactions, or *crossed transactions,* occur when the stimulus and response lines are not parallel, as also shown in Figure 11-4. In this instance the supervisor tries to deal with the employee on an Adult-to-Adult basis, but the employee responds on a Child-to-Parent basis. For example, the supervisor asks, "George, how do you think we ought to handle that late delivery on the IC order?" The employee then responds not from an Adult state but with the following Child-to-Parent comment: "That's not my problem. You are paid to make the decisions here." The important point is that when crossed transactions occur, communication tends to be blocked and a satisfactory transaction is not accomplished. Conflict often follows soon afterward.

In general, the transaction that is likely to be most effective at work is that of Adult to Adult. This kind of transaction encourages problem solving, treats people as reasonable equals, and reduces the probability of emotional conflicts between people. However, other complementary transactions can operate with acceptable success. For example, if the supervisor wants to play the Parent role and the employee wants the role of Child, they may develop a working relationship that is reasonably effective. In this situation, however, the employee fails to grow, mature, and learn how to contribute ideas. The conclusion is that, although other complementary transactions do work, the one with best results and least chance of problems at work is the Adult-to-Adult transaction.

LIFE POSITIONS Each person tends to exhibit one of four life positions. Very early in childhood a person develops a dominant way of relating to people. That philosophy tends to remain with the person for a lifetime unless major experiences occur to change it; hence it is called a *life position.* Although one life position tends to dominate a person's transactions, other positions may be exhibited from time to time in specific transactions. That is, a life position dominates, but it is not the only position ever taken.

Viewing yourself and others

Life positions stem from a combination of two viewpoints, as shown in Figure 11-5. First, how do people view themselves? Second, how do they view other people in general? Either a positive response (OK) or a negative response (not OK) results in four possible life positions, which are:

- I'm not OK—you're OK.
- I'm not OK—you're not OK.
- I'm OK—you're not OK.
- I'm OK—you're OK.

The desirable position and the one that involves the greatest likelihood of Adult-to-Adult transactions is "I'm OK—you're OK." It shows healthy acceptance of self and others. The other three life positions are less psychologically

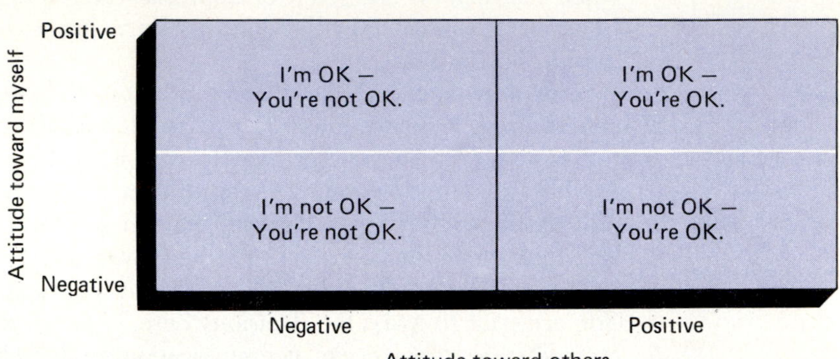

FIGURE 11-5
Four life positions

mature and less effective. The important point is that, regardless of one's present life position, the "I'm OK—you're OK" position can be learned. Therein lies society's hope for improved interpersonal transactions.

One study assessed the use of humor in management as it relates to both ego states and life positions.[12] Some interesting patterns emerged from an assessment of thirty-six different functions played by humor in superior-subordinate relations. Most (harmless) humor at work was seen as stemming from the playful Child ego state (announcing, for example, "It's playtime!") The Parent state also uses humor, but more often to ridicule, express disapproval, or maintain social distance. There is limited use of humor from the Adult, but it can be used to create social cohesion, break down pretenses, or even introduce change nondisruptively.

The use of humor varies sharply across life positions, with the least use by an "I'm not OK—you're not OK" person. The most positive uses are by the "I'm OK—you're OK" individual, who is likely to use humor to facilitate self-disclosure, create spontaneity, or relieve tension. This study illustrates just one of the many applications of TA in work situations.

STROKING People seek stroking in their interaction with others.[13] *Stroking* is defined as any act of recognition for another. It applies to all types of recognition, such as physical, verbal, and eye contact between people. In most jobs the primary method of stroking is verbal, such as "Pedro, you had an excellent sales record last month." Examples of physical strokes are a pat on the back and a firm handshake.

Types of strokes

Strokes may be either positive, negative, or mixed. Positive strokes feel good when they are received and contribute to a person's sense of being OK. Negative strokes hurt physically or emotionally and make us feel less OK about ourselves. An example of a mixed stroke is the supervisor's comment, "Oscar, that's a good advertising layout, considering the small amount of experience you have in this field." In this instance the supervisor is communicating in a judgmental Parent-to-Child pattern, and perhaps the negative stroke about lack of experience is included to show superiority or in retaliation for an earlier negative stroke given by the employee.

The supervisor normally secures a better result by avoiding the punishing Parent-to-Child approach and initiating an Adult-to-Adult communication. Using this approach with a tardy employee, the supervisor might say, "Good morning, Maria. Did you have some problem this morning?" The discussion might then develop into an Adult problem-solving conversation (I'm OK—you're OK) that will reduce the probability of future tardiness.

There also is a difference between conditional and unconditional strokes. *Conditional strokes* are offered to employees if they perform correctly or avoid problems. A sales manager may promise "I will give you a raise if you sell three more insurance policies." *Unconditional strokes* are presented without any connection to behavior. Although they may make a person feel good (for example, "You're a good employee"), they may be confusing to employees because they do not indicate how more strokes may be earned. Supervisors will get better results if they give more strokes in a behavior modification framework, where the reward is contingent upon the desired activity.

Employee hunger for strokes, and the occasional reluctance of supervisors to use them, is demonstrated in this conversation. Melissa, a stockbroker, had just made a presentation to a group of prospective customers. Later, she excitedly asked her manager how she had done. "You did a nice job," he began (and Melissa's eyes lit up in pleasure). "Not a great job, but a nice job." Although she didn't show her disappointment, we can guess that her spirits were considerably dampened by his qualified remark.

TA AND LEADERSHIP When managers transact primarily from a single ego state, they limit their choice of leadership styles. For example, the person with a dominant Parent ego state will tend toward a more autocratic style. If the Child state is dominant, the free-rein style may be used extensively. However, a supervisor who feels "I'm OK—you're OK" and has a well-developed Adult state is more likely to collect data prior to making a choice of style. The style chosen by the Adult state generally will allow ample freedom for employees to participate in the decision process.

TA AND CONFLICT RESOLUTION There are several natural connections between TA and the approaches to resolving conflict that were discussed earlier in this chapter. The Parent ego state may lead to the use of a forcing strategy, while the Child state may smooth over conflicts, or try to avoid them. The "I'm OK—you're OK" person is more likely to seek a win-win outcome, applying the Adult ego state and a confrontational strategy. Other probable connections are shown in Figure 11-6. Once more, the relationship among a number of behavioral ideas and actions is apparent.

BENEFITS OF TA Organizations that have used TA report that it has been moderately successful. Training in TA can give employees fresh insights into

FIGURE 11-6 Probable relationships of life positions with conflict resolution strategies and assertiveness

LIFE POSITION	RESOLUTION STRATEGY	PROBABLE BEHAVIOR
I'm not OK—you're not OK.	**Avoidance**	**Nonassertiveness**
I'm not OK—you're OK.	**Smoothing**	**Nonassertiveness**
I'm OK—you're not OK.	**Forcing**	**Aggressiveness**
I'm OK—you're OK.	**Confronting**	**Assertiveness**

their own personalities, and it also can help them understand why others sometimes respond as they do. A major benefit is improved interpersonal communication. Employees can sense when crossed communication occurs and then can take steps to restore complementary communication, preferably in the Adult-to-Adult pattern. The result is a general improvement in interpersonal transactions. TA especially is useful in sales and other areas where success depends on customer relations.

One company gave its managers a week-long course that combined three days of transactional analysis with two days of motivation theory. The motivation theory helped the managers make better use of the TA training. A year following the training, resignation rates of employees were compared for departments supervised by managers who had the training and those who did not. The rate in departments of trained managers had dropped to 3 percent monthly, but in other departments the rate was four times as high. This was a significant difference and appeared to result from the training, since other conditions were relatively equal.

Assertiveness training and transactional analysis in combination can be powerful tools for increasing one's interpersonal effectiveness. They both share the goal of helping employees to feel "OK" about themselves and others. Both also endorse the use of more Adult-based problem solving. The result is that they help improve communication and interpersonal cooperation. Although they can be practiced by individuals, these tools will be most effective when they are widely used throughout the organization and supported by top management.[14] Together, they form an important foundation for the more complex challenges that confront people who work in small groups and committees.

GROUP DYNAMICS

Small groups have existed since the time of the first human family. In recent years, however, people have started to study scientifically the processes by which small groups work. Some of the questions they have addressed are: What is the role of "leader" in a small group? Does the role vary with different objectives? Does a group have different kinds of leaders operating concurrently? In what ways and under what conditions are group decisions better than individual ones? These questions still remain partly unanswered, but progress is being made.

What is group dynamics?

The social process by which people interact face-to-face in small groups is called *group dynamics*. The word "dynamics" comes from the Greek word meaning "force"; hence "group dynamics" refers to the study of forces operating within a group. Two important historical landmarks in our understanding of small groups are the research of Elton Mayo and his associates in the 1920s and 1930s and the experiments in the 1930s of Kurt Lewin, the founder of the group dynamics movement. As discussed in earlier chapters, Mayo showed that workers tend to establish informal groups that affect job satisfaction and effectiveness. Lewin showed that different kinds of leadership produced different responses in groups.

Groups have properties of their own that are different from the properties of the individuals who make up the group. This is similar to the physical situation in which a molecule of salt (sodium chloride) has different properties from the sodium and chlorine elements that form a "group" to make it. The special properties of groups are illustrated by a simple lesson in mathematics. Let us say, "One plus one equals three." In the world of mathematics that is a logical error, and a rather elementary one at that. But in the world of group dynamics it is entirely rational to say, "One and one equals three." In a group there is no such thing as only two people, for no two people can be conceived without their *relationship*, and that makes three.

There are two principal types of group interaction. One exists when people are discussing ideas or solving problems. This is generally called a *meeting*. The other exists when people perform tasks together, and this is called a *team*. Meetings will be discussed here, and a discussion of teams will be included in the chapter on organizational development.

MEETINGS

Meetings are convened for many purposes, such as to share information, seek advice, make decisions, negotiate, coordinate, and stimulate creative thinking.

Committees

A *committee* is a specific type of group meeting in which members in their group role have been delegated authority with regard to the problem at hand. The group's authority usually is expressed in terms of one vote for each member. This means that if a supervisor and a worker serve as members of the same committee, both usually have equal committee roles. The worker may even have greater actual influence on the committee's outcome due to differences in expertise, interest, or experience. Committees often create special human problems because people are unable to make adjustments from their normal work roles and relationships.

One challenge for members is the fact that committees and other groups often pass through a series of developmental stages as their members work together.[15] These stages are not rigidly followed, but represent a broad pattern that may be observed in many settings. The identifiable stages are the result of a variety of issues that the committee faces, such as "Who should be included?" and "How should the group be structured?" In addition, members want to know what rules to follow and what each person will contribute. Four typical stages in a group's life can be described as:

Group life stages

1 Members' getting to know each other, and becoming oriented toward the group's task

2 Development of conflict over issues of status, control, and appropriate group direction

3 Emergence of group norms to guide behavior, and development of cooperative feelings

4 Integration of functional roles, and completion of various tasks

Awareness of these stages can be helpful to group members, who can better understand what is happening to themselves and help each other work through the issues involved. Groups are always different, of course, and consequently not all groups will experience all of the stages.

Identifying and responding to these stages can be challenging for a leader. However, a useful way to approach the management of committees is to apply the systems idea discussed in Chapter 1. As shown in Figure 11-7, effective committees require consideration of their inputs (size, composition, and agenda), the group process (leadership roles and alternative structures), and outcomes (quality of the decision and the group's support for it). Following those discussions, the problems inherent in groups will be reviewed.

Systems view

Factors to consider

SIZE The size of a meeting tends to affect the way that it works. If membership rises above seven, communication tends to become centralized because mem-

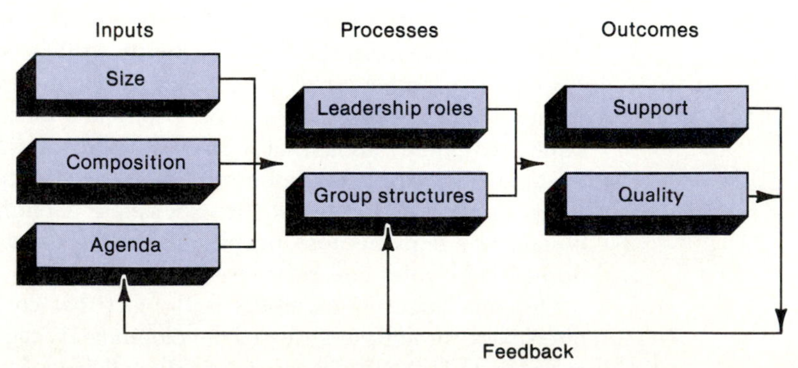

FIGURE 11-7
Systems view of effective committees

bers do not have adequate opportunity to communicate directly with one another. If it is necessary to have a larger committee to represent all relevant points of view, special effort and extra time are required to ensure good communication. A meeting of five people seems to be preferred for typical situations. A smaller meeting sometimes has difficulty functioning because conflicts of power develop.

COMPOSITION Leaders of committees, problem-solving groups, and task forces often have the opportunity to select the members. When doing so, they need to consider various factors, such as the committee's objective, the members' interest level and time available to serve, and the past history of working relationships among the potential members.

One study examined the personal characteristics sought in appointees to seven types of committees.[16] In general, the top-level administrators preferred persons who had a high stake (interest) in the outcome and were respected by their peers. Desire for persons who were knowledgeable, cooperative, and either advocated or opposed the official's position varied considerably, depending upon the type of committee to be created.

Surface and hidden

AGENDAS Meetings work simultaneously at two different levels. One level is the official task of the group, known as the *surface agenda.* The other level involves members' private emotions and motives, which they have brought with them but keep hidden under the conference table. These are the *hidden agendas* of the meeting. Frequently when a group reaches a crisis in its surface agenda, these hidden agendas come to life to complicate the situation. Conversely, sometimes a group seems to be making no progress and then suddenly everything is settled. What may have happened is that a hidden agenda finally was solved (even though members did not know they were working on it), making it easy to settle the surface agenda. An example is that of the staff specialist who is searching for a way to retaliate against a supervisor, and the specialist is blind to everything else until the hidden agenda can be resolved satisfactorily.

Task roles

LEADERSHIP ROLES Groups tend to require not one but two types of leadership roles: that of the *task leader* and that of the *social leader.*[17] Figure 11-8 provides illustrations of the nature of each role. The task leader's job in a meeting is to help the group accomplish its objectives and stay on target. The idea is to provide necessary structure by stating the problem, giving and seeking relevant facts, periodically summarizing the progress, and checking for agreement.

Social roles

Difficulties sometimes arise because the task leader may irritate people and injure the unity of the group. It is the social leader's role to restore and maintain group relationships by recognizing contributions, reconciling disagreements, and playing a supportive role to help the group develop. An especially challenging task is to blend the ideas of a deviant member with the

Task roles

- Define a problem or goal for the group.
- Request facts, ideas, or opinions from members.
- Provide facts, ideas, or opinions.
- Clarify a confused situation; give examples; provide structure.
- Summarize the discussion.
- Determine whether agreement has been reached.

Social roles

- Support the contributions of others; encourage them by recognition.
- Sense the mood of the group and help members become aware of it.
- Reduce the tension and reconcile disagreements.
- Modify your position; admit an error.
- Facilitate participation of all members.
- Evaluate the group's effectiveness.

FIGURE 11-8
Task and social leadership roles

thoughts of other participants. Although one person can fill both the task and social roles, often they are separate. When they are separate, it is important for the task leader to recognize the social leader and try to form a coalition of the two leaders for improved effectiveness.

An example of moderate group activity is the committee meeting in Figure 11-9. In this committee all members except Fleming communicated with the leader. Seven of the ten members communicated with members other than the leader, but they tended to talk only to members near them, probably because of the committee's large size and layout. Johnson, Smith, and Fleming participated the least; all the other members participated actively. The chart shows clearly that the leader's principal means of creating discussion was to ask questions.

Structured approaches

The committee meetings discussed above generally involve open discussion of a problem or issue. Other methods have been developed that work for specific objectives or provide greater control over the process. Three important alternative structures are brainstorming, nominal groups, and Delphi decision making.

Defer judgment.

BRAINSTORMING *Brainstorming* is a popular method of encouraging creative thinking.[18] Its main advantage is *deferred judgment,* by which all ideas—even unusual and impractical ones—are encouraged without criticism or evaluation. Ideas are recorded as fast as they can be suggested; then they are evaluated for usefulness at a later time. The purpose of deferred judgment is to encourage

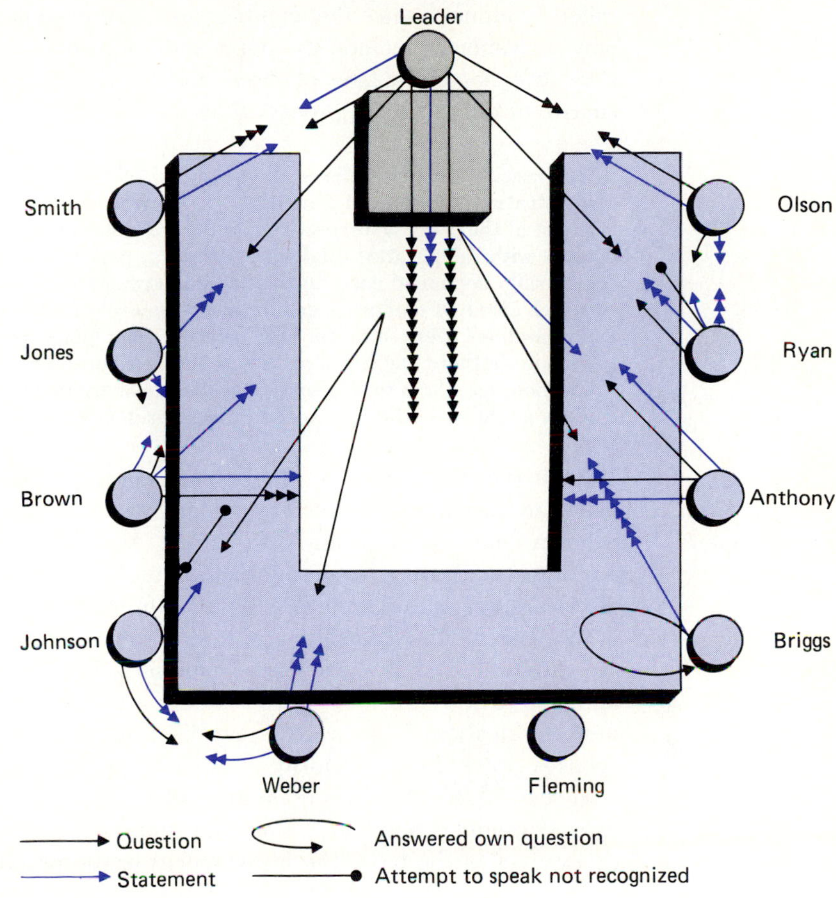

FIGURE 11-9
Participation diagram of a meeting
From Conference Leadership, *U.S. Department of the Air Force, pp. 9–11, n.d.*

people to propose bold, unique ideas without worrying about what others think of them; this approach typically produces more ideas than the conventional approach of thinking and judging concurrently. Brainstorming sessions last from ten minutes to one hour and require no preparation other than general knowledge of the subject.

Other advantages of brainstorming are enthusiasm, broader participation, greater task orientation, building upon ideas exchanged, and the feeling that the final product is a team solution.

Work independently; combine ideas.

NOMINAL GROUPS *Nominal groups* are another means that may be used for decision making. Here individuals are presented with a problem, and they each develop solutions independently. Then their ideas are shared with others in a structured format and their suggestions are discussed for clarification. Finally, group members choose the best alternatives by secret ballot. The process is called "nominal," since the members are, on the whole, part of a group in name only. Advantages include the opportunity for equal participation by all members, the nondominance of discussion by any one member, and the tight control of time that the process allows.

One research study explored the quality of solutions that were offered to a marketing strategy problem in a nominal group procedure.[19] Ideas generated at various stages of the process were scored on the basis of quality and creativity. Although the ideas with the greatest quality (practicality, pervasiveness, and long-range impact) generally appeared early in the nominal group discussion, the most creative ideas (which also had moderate quality) were generated late in the session. Two possible explanations were offered. The process may place pressure on participants to contribute their fair share as they see others continuing to provide suggestions. In addition, members may be encouraged to take greater risks to share nonconforming ideas as they see the structured process protect other members.

Survey the experts.

DELPHI DECISION MAKING In *Delphi* decision groups, a series of questionnaires are distributed to the respondents, who do not need to meet face-to-face. All communication typically is in writing. Members are selected because they are experts or have relevant information to share. They are asked to share their assessment of a problem or predict a future state of affairs (e.g., corporate sales in the year 2000). Explanations of their conclusions also can be shared. Replies are gathered from all participants, summarized, and fed back to the members for their review. Then they are asked to make another decision based on the new information. The process may be repeated several times until the responses converge satisfactorily.[20]

Success of the Delphi process depends on adequate time, participant expertise, communication skill, and the motivation of members to immerse themselves in the task. The major merits of the process are:

- Elimination of interpersonal problems
- Efficient use of experts' time
- Adequate time for reflection and analysis
- Diversity and quantity of ideas generated
- Accuracy of predictions and forecasts made

Potential outcomes

Acceptance

SUPPORT FOR DECISIONS Probably the most important by-product of meetings is that people who participate in making a decision feel more strongly motivated to accept it and carry it out. In many instances this is more than a by-product—it is the primary purpose of the meeting. Meetings undoubtedly are one of the best means available to commit people to carry out a course of action. A person who has helped make a decision is more interested in seeing it work.

Furthermore, if several group members are involved in carrying out a decision, group discussion helps each understand the part others will play, so that they can coordinate their efforts.

Group decisions also carry more weight with those who are not group members. Associates, subordinates, and even superiors are more likely to accept group decisions. They feel that decisions of this type are more free from individual prejudice because they are based on a combination of many viewpoints. Further, the combined social pressure of the entire group stands behind the decision.

Problem solving

QUALITY OF DECISIONS In addition to supporting decisions, groups often are effective problem-solving tools. In comparison with an individual, groups typically have greater information available to them, a variety of experiences to draw upon, and the capacity to examine suggestions and reject the incorrect ones. As a result, groups can frequently produce more and better-quality solutions to some problems than individuals can.

Another issue

CONSENSUS Is unanimous agreement a necessary prerequisite to effective group decisions? Without total consensus, group members may be expected to carry out decisions they did not support. Divided votes also may set up disagreements that carry beyond the meeting. On the other hand, a requirement of unanimity has its disadvantages.[21] It may become the paramount goal, causing people to suppress their opposition or to tell the group they agree when honestly they do not. It is frustrating to all members to have to keep discussing a subject long after their minds are made up, simply because they are hoping to convince honest dissenters. This is a waste of time and an embarrassment to the dissenters. It can delay worthwhile projects unnecessarily.

Is consensus necessary?

Unless the decision is of utmost personal importance to the dissenter, agreement of most of the members should be sufficient for consensus. Though an isolated minority needs to be heard and respected, so does the majority. Organizations must get on with their work rather than stopping to engage in endless debates in an effort to reach total agreement. Most employers, therefore, do not expect or require unanimity for committee decisions. In practice, consensus is often interpreted to mean that all members feel they have had an opportunity to state their views, and believe that they can support the decision reached despite their reservations.

Weaknesses of groups

A distinguished executive was sitting at home one evening in 1927 as his wife was reading the newspaper account of Lindbergh's historic solo flight from New York to Paris. "Isn't it wonderful," she exclaimed, "and he did it all alone." Her husband's classic reply after a hard day at the office was, "Well, it would have been even more wonderful if he had done it with a committee!"

Because the group approach has weaknesses as well as strengths, some people have developed the attitude "You go to the meeting and I'll tend the store," meaning that meetings are unproductive labor and someone has to keep production humming. Some meetings are unproductive, but a single case does not prove the generality. Meetings are an essential and productive part of work organizations. Part of our trouble is that we expect too much of them, and when they do not meet our expectations, we criticize. But we will get nowhere criticizing a tennis court because it is a poor football field.

Properly conducted meetings can contribute to organizational progress by providing participation, integrating interests, improving decision making, committing and motivating members to carry out a course of action, encouraging creative thinking, broadening perspectives, and changing attitudes. The fundamental decision that must be made with groups, therefore, is not whether to have them but how to make the best use of them. To use them, one must know their weaknesses, which fall into five major categories: slowness and expensiveness, the leveling effect, polarization, escalating commitment, and divided responsibility.

SLOWNESS AND EXPENSIVENESS As one manager observed: "Committees keep minutes and waste hours!" Meetings of all types are a slow and costly way to get things done. On occasion, delay is desirable. There is more time for thinking, for objective review of an idea, and for the suggestion of alternatives. But when quick, decisive action is necessary, an individual approach is more effective. A manager, for example, does not call a committee meeting to decide whether to tell the fire department that the building is on fire!

THE LEVELING EFFECT One of the most convincing criticisms of meetings is that they often lead to conformity and compromise. This tendency of a group to bring individual thinking in line with the average quality of the group's thinking is called the *leveling effect*, or "groupthink."[22] A person begins to think less individually about a problem and adapts to the desires of other members. The result can be that the ideas of the most dominant person, rather than the better ideas, are accepted.

Groupthink

Leveling is not wholly undesirable, however. It serves to temper unreasonable ideas and to curb the autocrat. But it is a group tendency that needs to be held in check by training both committee members and leaders in appropriate decision-making skills. The groupthink process can also be reduced by appointing a "devil's advocate" for each meeting, whose role is to challenge ideas, question facts and logic, and provide constructive criticism.

POLARIZATION In contrast to the leveling effect, an alternative behavior that sometimes appears is group *polarization*. Here, individuals bring to the group their predispositions toward the topic, and group discussion only serves to clarify and sharpen their attitudes. As a result, the group's decision may be even more extreme (either risky or conservative) than the merits of the case would predict or support.

ESCALATING COMMITMENT Closely related to the problem of groupthink is the idea that group members may persevere in advocating a course of action despite rational evidence that it will result in failure. In fact, they may even allocate additional resources to the project, thereby *escalating their commitment.*[23] Examples abound of automakers continuing to make certain types of cars despite powerful consumer trends away from those types, pharmaceutical companies investing millions in the development of drugs that are not likely to receive federal approval, and communities that spend heavily on tourist attractions in the face of evidence that they can never recoup their investments.

Why escalation occurs

There are many reasons why decision makers do this. Sometimes they may unconsciously fall prey to selective perception, and bias the choice of information used to support their arguments. The competence motive also affects their decisions, since their desire to protect their self-esteem prevents them from admitting failure until the evidence is overwhelming. Having previously argued for an alternative in public makes it more difficult to reverse oneself (for fear of "losing face"). In many cultures, there is strong admiration for leaders who are risk takers and persist in the face of adversity. All of these forces suggest that members of groups need to be especially alert to the escalation phenomenon in themselves and others, and be willing to admit and accept their losses in some situations.

DIVIDED RESPONSIBILITY Management literature always has recognized that divided responsibility is a problem whenever group decisions are made. It often is said that "actions which are several bodies' responsibility are nobody's responsibility." Group decisions undoubtedly do dilute and thin out responsibility. They also give individual members a chance to shirk responsibility, using justifications such as "Why should I bother with this problem? I didn't support it in the meeting."

Many of the disadvantages of group meetings can be overcome readily. The preceding discussion suggested that the proper group structures must be selected, that group size is an important factor, and that various leadership roles must be played. Figure 11-10 presents a set of additional guidelines.

Emerging directions

Contingency models

Two themes hold major promise for further advancing our knowledge about groups in organizations. One is the preliminary development of *contingency models.* Though not fully developed and researched at this time, a number of models are emerging that are designed to help managers know when to take different actions.[24] Some of these approaches prescribe the amount of freedom to allow the group for decision-making purposes. Other models assess some of the desired outputs discussed earlier (such as acceptance and quality) and use that analysis to indicate whether nominal, Delphi, or regular group processes are most appropriate. When further refined, these models will help managers choose the method most effective for each situation.

- **Distribute the agenda and background material in advance.**
- **Clarify the objective.**
- **Compose the group appropriately.**
- **Encourage the expression of minority viewpoints.**
- **Separate idea generation from evaluation.**
- **Make assumptions explicit.**
- **Legitimize questioning attitudes.**
- **Control irrelevant discussions.**
- **Test the level of support for a decision.**
- **Evaluate the group's effectiveness.**
- **End on a positive note and assign responsibilities.**

FIGURE 11-10
Guidelines for effective groups

Support systems

Another promising development is the *group decision support system.* These support systems use computers, decision models, and technological advances to remove communication barriers, structure the decision process, and generally direct the group's discussion.[25] An example is the electronic boardroom, featuring instant display of members' ideas on a large screen, computerized vote solicitation and display of results, and electronic transfer of messages among individual participants. The potential gains in quality of decisions are substantial from the integration of communication, computer, and decision technologies. What is not yet known are the effects on members' satisfaction, the participants' sense of involvement, or the balance of task and social roles that will be needed. Nevertheless, group decision support systems are an exciting development that holds substantial promise for the future.

SUMMARY

Interpersonal and intergroup conflict often arise when there is disagreement regarding goals or the methods to attain them. Several methods exist for handling conflict, and they vary in their potential effectiveness. Assertive behavior is also a useful response in situations where a person's needs have been disregarded.

Transactional analysis is the study of social transactions between people. One useful approach is the classification of Parent, Adult, and Child ego states. An Adult-to-Adult complementary transaction especially is desirable at work. Crossed transactions tend to cut off communication and produce conflicts. Stroking is sought in social transactions, because it contributes to the satisfaction of recognition needs.

Group dynamics is the process by which people interact face-to-face in small groups. Groups have properties different from those of their members, just as molecules are different from the atoms composing them. Meetings are a widely used form of group activity, and they can create quality decisions that are supported by the participants. Three other forms of group structures are brainstorming, nominal groups, and the Delphi technique. Weaknesses of groups include the time and cost involved in reaching a decision, the leveling effect, polarization, escalating commitment, and divided responsibility. Future developments may occur in the areas of contingency models and group decision support systems.

Terms and concepts for review

Conflict
Confronting
Assertiveness
Transactional analysis
Parent, Adult, and Child ego states
Life positions
Stroking
Group dynamics
Task and social leader roles
Surface and hidden agendas
Brainstorming
Nominal and Delphi groups
Groupthink
Escalating commitment
Group decision support systems

Discussion questions

1 Discuss the relationship between Theory X and Theory Y, conflict resolution strategies, and life positions.
2 Explain the relationship between assertiveness and the supportive approach to human behavior.
3 Consider this issue: "Resolved, that all employees should be trained to become more assertive." Prepare to present both the pros and cons in a class debate.
4 Review the elements of transactional analysis. Would TA be useful for training employees in the service department of an electric utility to deal more effectively with customers who make complaints about their service? Explain.
5 Review the typical stages in a group's life. Think of a time when you were a member of a committee. Were those stages all represented? Did they appear in a different order? Did some of them emerge more than once? Explain.
6 Distinguish between the roles of task leader and social leader. Why is it difficult for one person to fulfill both responsibilities? Describe how two people, one playing each role, might work together to lead a budget committee meeting.
7 Identify five things you will do to create an effective committee the next time you are a leader (or member) of one.

8 Prepare a matrix, with "Strengths" listed on one side (for example, "generates many alternative solutions"), and the three forms of group structure across the top. Indicate, by checking the blanks, which strengths each form seems to have. (Note that you are basically preparing your own contingency model.)
9 What does consensus mean to you? Has it changed since reading this chapter? What other interpretations do you think the term has for other people?
10 The chapter mentioned five major weaknesses in groups. Prepare a counterargument that describes some of the benefits of using groups.

THE ANGRY AIRLINE PASSENGER

Margie James was night supervisor for an airline in Denver. Her office was immediately behind the ticket counter, and occasionally she was called upon to deal with passengers who had unusual problems that employees could not solve. One evening about 11 P.M. she was asked to deal with an angry passenger who approached her with the comment, "You incompetent employees have lost my bag again, and your **** baggage attendant isn't helping me at all. I want some service. Is everybody incompetent around here? I have an important speech in that bag that I have to deliver at 9 o'clock in the morning, and if I don't get it, I'll sue this airline for sure."

Question

How should James respond to the passenger? Would transactional analysis help her? Would assertiveness training help?

THE OBSTINATE COMMITTEE

William James is chairperson of a seven-person committee that is considering a controversial wage incentive plan for production workers in his company. Among its members are representatives of management and employees. Discussion frequently becomes emotional. When this occurs, James sometimes tells jokes to try to relax the committee and keep it in a problem-solving mood, but he has not had much success. On other occasions he tries to get the group away from emotionalism by autocratically demanding that members stay on the subject, but this approach also has failed. When he is autocratic, usually the group becomes angry with him in addition to being emotional concerning the subject under discussion.

James has read that participation helps meetings; consequently, when emotions get heated, he often tries to get more people to participate. This approach seems merely to intensify emotionalism.

Question

Appraise the events reported in this case and offer James some guidance to improve results.

Experiential exercise

CHOOSING YOUR LEADER

1 Divide the class into groups of five to seven people. For the first ten minutes, have members introduce themselves by sharing not only their names but also other significant information (for example, major accomplishments or future aspirations).

2 Now ask each group member to take out a piece of paper and write the name of the person who the member thinks would make the best leader of the small group. Then ask the members to collectively brainstorm, while recording the items on a sheet of paper, all the factors they used to select a leader (e.g., what characteristics were important to them?). Have them give all the slips to one person, who should tabulate the votes for leader. Have the new leader facilitate a discussion of the characteristics used to select him or her. Ask the groups to briefly discuss the validity of the selection process.

3 Now direct the groups to reflect on the discussion experience. Have them identify who the task and social leaders were, what the hidden agendas were, and who played the most assertive roles. What ego states dominated? How would they change their behavior if they were to do the exercise again?

References

1 Alfie Kohn, "How to Succeed without Even Vying," *Psychology Today*, September 1986, p. 28.

2 Seth Allcorn, "What Makes Groups Tick," *Personnel*, September 1985, p. 52.

3 Kenneth W. Thomas and Warren H. Schmidt, "A Survey of Managerial Interests with Respect to Conflict," *Academy of Management Journal*, June 1976, pp. 315–318. A measurement instrument is described in Boris Kabanoff, "Predictive Validity of the MODE Conflict Instrument," *Journal of Applied Psychology*, February 1987, pp. 160–163.

4 Other sources, such as large unit size, financial measures of success, and contrasting areas of functional expertise, are discussed in Gordon Cliff, "Managing Organizational Conflict," *Management Review*, May 1987, pp. 51–53.

5 Chris Argyris, "Skilled Incompetence," *Harvard Business Review*, September–October 1986, pp. 74–79.

6 For research on conflict, see Victor D. Wall, Jr., and Linda L. Nolan, "Small Group Conflict," *Small Group Behavior*, May 1987, pp. 188–211; and Richard A. Cosier and Thomas L. Ruble, "Research on Conflict-Handling Behavior: An Experimental Approach," *Academy of Management Journal*, December 1981, pp. 816–831.

7 Robert R. Blake and Jane S. Mouton, *Managing Intergroup Conflict in Industry*, Houston: Gulf Publishing Co., 1964. Note that both these authors and others often include an intermediate strategy, called *compromising*.

8 Wall and Nolan, op. cit.; sources of information on methods for avoiding common mistakes are in Max H. Bazerman. "Why Negotiations Go Wrong," *Psychology Today*, June 1986, pp. 54–58; seven contingency dimensions for diagnosing conflict situations are discussed in Leonard Greenhalgh, "Managing Conflict," *Sloan Management Review*, Summer 1986, pp. 45–51.

9 For a current assessment, see Walter Kiechel III, "Getting Aggressiveness Right," *Fortune*, May 27, 1985, pp. 179–180. Examples of early books were H. Fensterheim and J. Baer, *Don't Say Yes When You Want to Say No*, New York: David McKay Company, Inc., 1975; and L. Z. Bloom, K. Coburn, and J. Pearlman, *The New Assertive Woman*, New York: Delacorte Press, Dell Publishing Co., Inc., 1975.

10 Nancy Paul, "Assertiveness without Tears: A Training Programme for Executive Equality," *Personnel Management*, April 1979, pp. 37–40.

11 Eric Berne, *Transactional Analysis in Psychotherapy*, New York: Grove Press, Inc., 1961; Eric Berne, *Games People Play*, New York: Grove Press, Inc., 1964; Thomas A. Harris, *I'm OK—You're OK: A Practical Guide to Transactional Analysis*, New York: Harper & Row Publishers, Inc., 1969; Dorothy Jongeward, *Everybody Wins: Transactional Analysis Applied to Organizations*, Reading, Mass.: Addison-Wesley Publishing Company, 1973.

12 William P. Galle, Jr., "Transactional Analysis as a Tool for Humor Applications in Management," in James O. Smith and Carl W. Gooding (eds.), *1985 American Institute for Decision Sciences Proceedings*, vol. 2, Las Vegas, Nov. 11–13, 1985, pp. 193–195.

13 See, for example, David J. Cherrington and B. Jackson Wixom, Jr., "Recognition Is Still a Top Motivator," *Personnel Administrator*, May 1983, pp. 87–91.

14 The importance of management support and other actions to encourage behavioral change is discussed in John W. Newstrom, "Leveraging Management Development through Transfer of Training Strategies," *Journal of Management Development*, vol. 5, no. 5, 1986, pp. 33–45.

15 The four stages were originally identified by B. W. Tuckman, "Developmental Sequence in Small Groups," *Psychological Bulletin*, vol. 63, 1965, pp. 384–399. They are often called forming, storming, norming, and performing. Examples of current research and applications on group stages are in Donald K. Carew, Eunice Parisi-Carew, and Kenneth H. Blanchard, "Group Development and Situational Leadership: A Model for Managing Groups," *Training and Development Journal*, June 1986, pp. 46–50; and Bart C. Kuypers et al., "Developmental Patterns in Self-Analytic Groups," *Human Relations*, September 1986, pp. 793–815.

16 Mary Lippitt Nichols, "An Exploratory Study of Committee Composition as an Administrative Problem-Solving Tool," *Decision Sciences*, April 1981, pp. 338–351.

17 Task and social roles were originally presented by R. F. Bales, *Interaction Process Analysis*, Cambridge, Mass.: Addison-Wesley Publishing Company, 1950; research on assessment instruments is in Myron W. Lustig, "Bale's Interpersonal Rating Forms: Reliability and Dimensionality," *Small Group Behavior*, February 1987, pp. 99–107.

18 Brainstorming was developed by Alex F. Osborn and is described in his book *Applied Imagination*, New York: Charles Scribner's Sons, 1953. See also Stephen R. Grossman, "Brainstorming Updated," *Training and Development Journal*, February 1984, pp. 84–87; and Tony Proctor, "'Brain:' The Computer Program that Brainstorms," *Simulation and Games*, December 1986, pp. 485–491.

19 Gene E. Burton, "The 'Clustering Effect': An Idea-Generation Phenomenon during Nominal Grouping," *Small Group Behavior*, May 1987, pp. 224–238. Other research is reported in D. M. Hegedus and R. V. Rasmussen, "Task Effectiveness and Interaction Process of a Modified Nominal Group Technique in Solving an Evaluation Problem," *Journal of Management*, Winter 1986, pp. 545–560; and Stuart L. Hart, "Toward Quality Criteria for Collective Judgments," *Organization Behavior and Human Decision Processes*, October 1985, pp. 209–229.

20 Recommendations ranging from two to five iterations of the Delphi process have been made. One study found that results stabilized after four rounds; see Robert C. Erffmeyer and others, "The Delphi Technique: An Empirical Evaluation of the Optimal Number of Rounds," *Group & Organization Studies*, March–June 1986, pp. 120–128.

21 See, for example, Anne Gero, "Conflict Avoidance in Consensual Decision Processes," *Small Group Behavior*, November 1985, pp. 487–499. A study of the reasons why members may inappropriately reach consensus is reported in John F. Viega, "Propensity to Give Up Control in a Decision Making Group: An Explanation and a Measure," in John A. Pearce II and Richard B. Robinson (eds.), *Academy of Management Best Papers Proceedings 1986*, Chicago: Academy of Management, 46th annual meeting, Aug. 13–16, 1986.

22 See Cheryl Posner-Weber, "Update on Groupthink," *Small Group Behavior*, February 1987, pp. 118–125; and Gregory Moorhead and John Montanari, "An Empirical Investigation of the Groupthink Phenomenon," *Human Relations*, May 1986, pp. 399–410.

23 Barry M. Staw and Jerry Ross, "Knowing When to Pull the Plug," *Harvard Business Review*, March–April 1987, pp. 68–74. A detailed case study is in Jerry Ross and Barry M. Staw, "Expo 86: An Escalation Prototype," *Administrative Science Quarterly*, June 1986, pp. 274–297; a readable summary is Barry M. Staw and Jerry Ross, "Good Money after Bad," *Psychology Today*, February 1988, pp. 30–33. Alternative interpretations are provided by Glen Whyte, "Escalating Commitment to a Course of Action: A Reinterpretation," *Academy of Management Review*, April 1986, pp. 311–321; and Michael G. Bowen, "The Escalation Phenomenon Reconsidered: Decision Dilemmas or Decision Errors?" *Academy of Management Review*, January 1987, pp. 52–66.

24 Two examples of contingency models are Victor H. Vroom and Arthur G. Jago, *The New Leadership*, Englewood Cliffs, N.J.: Prentice-Hall, Inc., 1988; and Stephen A. Stumpf, Dale E. Zand, and Richard D. Freedman, "Designing Groups for Judgmental Decisions," *Academy of Management Review*, October 1979, pp. 589–600.

25 Gerardine DeSanctis and R. Brent Gallupe, "A Foundation for the Study of Group Decision Support Systems," *Management Science*, May 1987, pp. 589–609.

For additional reading

Back, Ken, and Kate Back, *Assertiveness at Work: A Practical Guide to Handling Awkward Situations*, New York: McGraw-Hill Book Company, 1982.

Blake, Robert R., and Jane Srygley Mouton, *Solving Costly Organizational Conflicts: Achieving Intergroup Trust, Cooperation, and Teamwork*, San Francisco: Jossey-Bass Inc., Publishers, 1984.

Delbecq, Andre L., Andrew H. Van de Ven, and David H. Gustafson, *Group Techniques for Program Planning*, Glenview, Ill.: Scott, Foresman and Company, 1975.

Fox, William M., *Effective Group Problem Solving: How to Broaden Participation, Improve Decision Making, and Increase Commitment to Action*, San Francisco: Jossey-Bass Inc., Publishers, 1987.

Fraser, Niall M., and Keith W. Hipel, *Conflict Analysis: Models and Resolutions*, New York: Elsevier Science Publishing Co., Inc., 1984.

Goodman, Paul S., and Associates, *Designing Effective Work Groups*, San Francisco: Jossey-Bass Inc., Publishers, 1986.

Jandt, Fred E., with Paul Gillette, *Win-Win Negotiating: Turning Conflict Into Agreement*, New York: John Wiley & Sons, Inc., 1985.

Lax, David A., and James K. Sibenius, *The Manager as Negotiator: Bargaining for Cooperation and Competitive Gain*, New York: Macmillan Company (Free Press) 1986.

Napier, Rodney W., and Matti K. Gershenfeld, *Groups: Theory and Experience* (3d ed.), Boston: Houghton Mifflin Company, 1985.

Smith, Kenwyn K., and David N. Berg, *Paradoxes of Group Life*, San Francisco: Jossey-Bass Inc., Publishers, 1987.

Stulberg, Joseph B., *Taking Charge/Managing Conflict*, Lexington, Mass.: Lexington Books, 1987.

Tjosvold, Dean, *Managing Work Relationships: Cooperation, Conflict, and Power*, Lexington, Mass.: Lexington Books, 1986.

CHAPTER

12

Managing change

For the forseeable future, organizations must learn to cherish change and to take advantage of constant tumult as much as they have resisted change in the past.

TOM PETERS[1]

He that complies against his will,
Is of his own opinion still.

SAMUEL BUTLER[2]

CHAPTER OBJECTIVES

To understand

The nature of change

Costs and benefits of change

Psychic costs of change

Resistance to change

Basic frameworks for interpreting change

The learning curve for change

Practices to build support for change

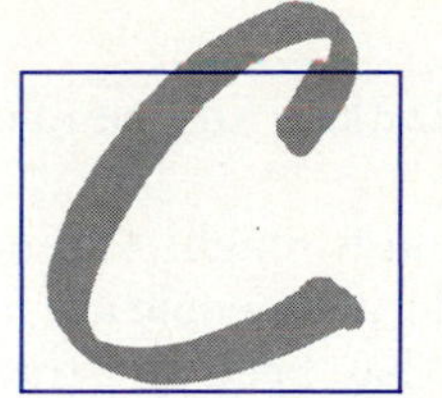

hange is everywhere, and is constantly present. It is all around people—in the seasons, in their social environment, and in their own biological processes. Beginning with the first few moments of life, a person learns to meet change by being adaptive. A person's very first breath depends on ability to adapt from one environment to another one that is dramatically different. Each hour of the day offers people new experiences and challenges throughout their lives. The same is true for organizations, as pointed out by Tom Peters in the opening quote for this chapter.

Human beings are certainly familiar with change, and often prove themselves quite adaptive to it. Why, then, do they often resist change in their *work* environment? This question has troubled managers since the beginning of the industrial revolution. The faster pace of change required by the electronic age, the shift to a service economy, and global competition has made the solution to this question even more important. Even when managers use their most logical arguments and persuasive skills to support a change, they frequently discover that employees remain unconvinced of the need for it. This chapter will examine the nature of change, reasons for resistance to it, and ways to introduce it more successfully.

WORK CHANGE

The nature of work change

Work change is any alteration that occurs in the work environment. Its effect can be illustrated by an experiment using an air-filled balloon. When a finger (which represents external change) is pressed against a point on the balloon (which represents the organization), the contour of the balloon visibly changes (it becomes indented) at the point of contact. Here an obvious pressure, representing change, has produced an obvious deviation at the point of pressure. What is not so obvious, however, is that the entire balloon (the *rest* of the organization) has also been affected and has stretched slightly. As shown by this comparison, a safe generalization is that *the whole organization tends to be affected by change in any part of it.*

Effects are widespread.

The molecules of air in the balloon represent a firm's employees. It is apparent that those at the spot of pressure must make drastic adjustments. Though the change did not make direct contact with the employees (molecules), it has affected them indirectly. Though none is fired (i.e., leaves the balloon), the employees are displaced and must adjust to a new location in the balloon. This comparison illustrates an additional generalization: *change is a human as well as a technical problem.*

Human and technical problem

The comparison using a balloon may be carried further. Repeated pressure at a certain point may weaken the balloon until it breaks. So it is with an organization. Changes may lead to pressures and conflicts that eventually cause a breakdown somewhere in the organization. An example is an employee who becomes dissatisfied and resigns.

Admittedly, the foregoing comparison is rough. An employing institution is not a balloon; a person is not a molecule; and people are not as free and flexible as air molecules in a balloon. What has been illustrated is a condition of molecular equilibrium. Organizations, too, tend to achieve an equilibrium in their social structure. This means that people develop an established set of relations with their environment. They learn how to deal with each other, how to perform their jobs, and what to expect next. Equilibrium exists; employees are adjusted. When change comes along, it requires them to make new adjustments as the organization seeks a new equilibrium. When employees are unable to make adequate adjustments, the organization is in a state of unbalance, or disequilibrium. *Management's general human objective regarding change is to restore and maintain the group equilibrium and personal adjustment that change upsets.*

Fortunately, many of the organizational changes that occur on a daily basis are somewhat minor. They may affect only a few people, be incremental in nature, and be relatively predictable. For example, as new procedures evolve or new members are added to a work group, existing employees generally do not need to change all dimensions of their jobs or acquire totally new behaviors. Here a new equilibrium may be readily reached.

A wide variety of forces, however, may bring about more dramatic changes that touch the entire core of an organization.[3] Many of these have become much more common, as the economy, competition, and pace of technological change have become more volatile. Examples include the dramatic breakup of AT&T, hostile takeovers of firms, leveraged buyouts and subsequent organizational restructuring, and natural disasters like oil spills and gas leaks. Crises like these, whether positive or negative, demand that managers help guide employees through the emotional shock that accompanies them back to a new equilibrium.

Responses to change

Work change is further complicated by the fact that it does not produce a direct adjustment as in the case of air molecules. Instead, it operates through each employee's attitudes to produce a response that is conditioned by feelings toward the change. This relationship was illustrated in a series of classic experiments by Roethlisberger and his associates. In one instance lighting was improved regularly according to the theory that better lighting would lead to greater productivity. As was expected, productivity did increase. Then lighting was decreased to illustrate the reverse effect—reduced productivity. Instead, productivity increased further! Lighting was again decreased. The result was still greater productivity! Finally, lighting was decreased to 0.06 of a footcandle, which is approximately equivalent to moonlight. According to Roethlisberger, "Not until this point was reached was there any appreciable decline in the output rate."[4]

Roethlisberger's experiments

THE "X" CHART: A MODEL OF HOW ATTITUDES AFFECT RESPONSE TO CHANGE Obviously, better lighting was not by itself causing greater output. There was no direct connection between the change and the response. Some other intervening variable, later diagnosed as employee attitudes, had crept in to upset the expected pattern. Roethlisberger later illustrated the new pattern by means of a model of response to change known as the *"X" chart*. It is shown in Figure 12-1. Each change is interpreted by individuals according to their attitudes. *The way that people feel about a change then determines how they will respond to it.* These feelings are not the result of chance; they are caused. One cause is personal history, which refers to people's biological processes, their backgrounds, and all their social experiences away from work. This is what they bring to the workplace. A second cause is the work environment itself. It reflects the fact that workers are members of a group and are influenced by its codes, patterns, and norms.

Feelings are nonlogical.

Feelings are not a matter of logic. They are neither logical nor illogical but entirely apart from logic. They are *nonlogical*. Feelings and logic belong in two separate categories, just as inches and pounds do. For that reason, logic alone is an ineffective means of trying to modify feelings because it does not get at them directly. Feelings are not much better refuted by logic than this book's length in inches or centimeters is refuted by its weight in pounds or kilograms!

HAWTHORNE EFFECT One cause of favorable feelings in the groups studied by Roethlisberger was the interest shown by the researchers in employee problems. This phenomenon later was called the *Hawthorne effect*, named after the factory where the research took place. The Hawthorne effect means that the mere observation of a group tends to change it. When people are observed, they act differently. These changes usually are unintended and not recognized. They contaminate the research design, but normally they cannot be prevented.

Observation affects behavior.

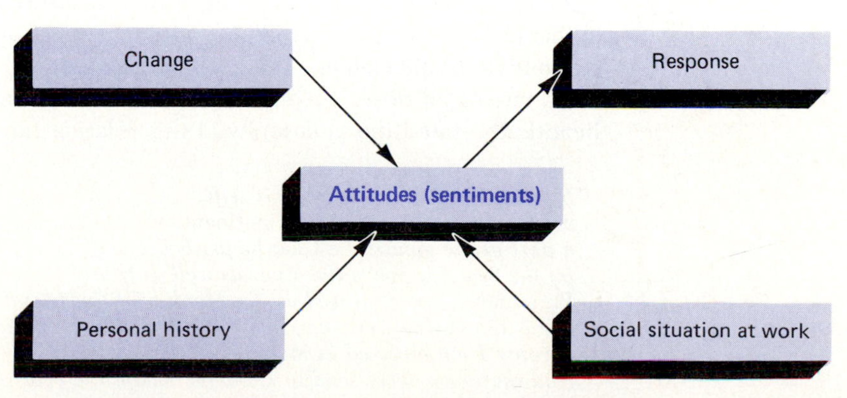

FIGURE 12-1
Roethlisberger's original "X" chart
From F. J. Roethlisberger, Management and Morale, *Cambridge, Mass.: Harvard University Press, 1941, p. 21. Used with permission.*

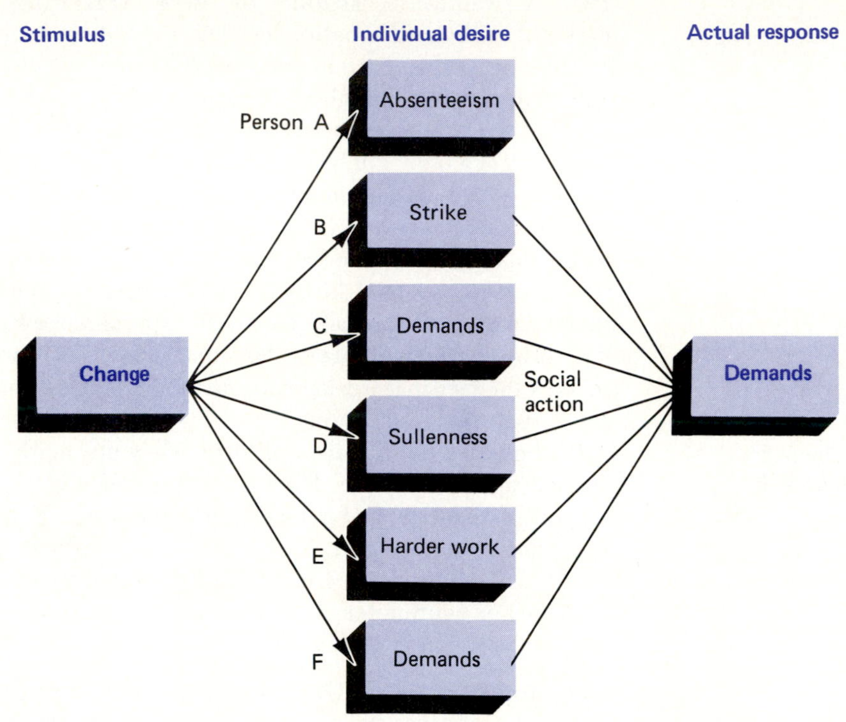

FIGURE 12-2
Unified social response to change

GROUP RESPONSE TO CHANGE Though people individually interpret change, they often show their attachment to the group by joining with it in some uniform response to the change, as shown in Figure 12-2. This response makes possible such seemingly illogical actions as walkouts when obviously only a few people actually want to walk out. Other employees who are unhappy seize upon the walkout as a chance to show their dissatisfaction and to confirm their affiliation with the group by joining with it in social action. Basically, the group responds with the feeling, "We're all in this together. Whatever happens to one of us affects all of us." John Donne, the seventeenth-century English poet, beautifully stated the philosophy of this relationship as follows:

> *No man is an* Iland, *intire of it selfe;*
> *every man is a peece of the* Continent,
> *a part of the maine; if a* Clod *be washed away*
> *by the Sea, Europe is the lesse, as well as if a*
> Promontorie *were, as well as if a* Mannor *of thy friends*
> *or of* thine owne *were; any man's death diminishes me,*
> *because I am involved in* Mankinde:
> *And therefore never send to know for whom the bell tolls;*
> *It tolls for thee.*[5]

HOMEOSTASIS In trying to maintain equilibrium, a group develops responses to return to its perceived best way of life whenever any change occurs. Each pressure, therefore, encourages a counterpressure within the group. The net result is a self-correcting mechanism by which energies are called up to restore balance whenever change threatens. This self-correcting characteristic of organizations is called *homeostasis;* that is, people act to establish a steady state of need fulfillment and to protect themselves from disturbance of that balance.[6]

Costs and benefits

All changes are likely to have some costs. For example, a new work procedure may require the inconvenience of learning new practices. It temporarily may disrupt work and reduce motivation. There also may be the cost of new equipment or relocation of old equipment. These costs are not merely economic; they also are psychological and social. They usually must be paid in order to gain the benefits of proposed changes.

Because of the costs associated with change, proposals for change are not always desirable. They require careful analysis to determine usefulness. Each change requires a detailed cost-benefit analysis. Unless changes can provide benefits above costs, there is no reason for the changes. It is illogical to emphasize benefits while ignoring costs. The organizational goal always is benefits greater than costs.

In determining benefits and costs, all types of each must be considered. It is useless to examine only economic benefits and costs, because even if there is a net economic benefit, the social or psychological costs may be too large. Although it is not very practical to reduce psychological and social costs to numbers, they must nevertheless be included in the decision-making process. Almost any change, for example, involves some psychological loss because of the strain that it imposes on people as they try to adjust. Psychological costs also are called *psychic costs* because they affect a person's inner self (psyche).

Psychic costs

Approaches have now been developed that relate employee attitudes to behavioral measures of interest to the organization (such as absenteeism and turnover). These are then converted into actual costs per employee per month. Through this "behavior costing" method of attaching dollar values to employee attitudes, managers can predict the financial impact on the organization of improvements or declines in employee attitudes.[7]

For example, a program to improve the attitudes among a bank's 160 tellers was estimated to save nearly $30,000 of direct costs. These predicted benefits were then compared with the estimated costs of the change to determine the net effect of the proposal. By the same reasoning, the psychic costs to the organization of another proposed change that would temporarily *lower* employee attitudes could be easily estimated. Hopefully, this information would lead the organization to explore how it might minimize such costs.

Experience shows that people react in different ways to change. Some will perceive only the benefits, while others see only what it costs them. Others will react fearfully at first, even though all the effects are actually positive for them. Part of these conflicting reactions reflects reality, since frequently there is no clear-cut 100 percent benefit for all. Rather, there are a series of separate costs and benefits that must be considered on an individual basis. The supportive and collegial models of organizational behavior imply that management will consider each individual case and try to help each person gain as much from change as possible.

Psychic costs and health

Stress

In some cases the psychic costs of change can be so severe that they affect the psychological and even the physical health of employees. Each person has a tolerance level for change. When that level is exceeded, responses related to stress develop, and they can undermine health. In some instances there is sustained change over a period of time, producing cumulative stress that finally builds to overload a person's system. In other instances there is a single major change of such significance that it overloads a person's ability to cope with the situation.

An example occurred in the merger of two major airlines.[8] Although the new company emerged financially and competitively stronger, many employees initially saw only the negative effects on themselves. Job loss, job changes, a sharp change in cultures, and the impending integration of two seniority systems shocked many employees. Some employees were frightened for their job security. Others were unhappy about relocating their families, or became emotionally torn by the union struggles. A number of employees resisted the change, and stories of intentional errors in baggage handling and delayed departures and arrivals tarnished the company's image for months afterward. In general, the psychological costs of the merger were substantial.

Psychic costs of promotion

An important type of change is promotion. Employees often seek changes of this kind for growth and more recognition. Even though these types of moves are desired by an employee, they nevertheless have substantial psychic costs. Employees are required to learn new skills and make new friendships. They move to a different role and often to a different work group. Their status also may change. All of these actions involve psychic costs because they require employees to cope with new situations.

Since millions of employees are promoted every year in the United States, the costs can be substantial.

For example, one large company calculated that it had a promotion every ten working minutes. In another firm, as shown in Figure 12-3, the promotion of a higher manager set off a chain reaction that led to the promotion of ten other people at lower levels. The subsequent moves ranged from the New York office (administration) to the Central Territory to the Southern Territory to the Dallas Division.

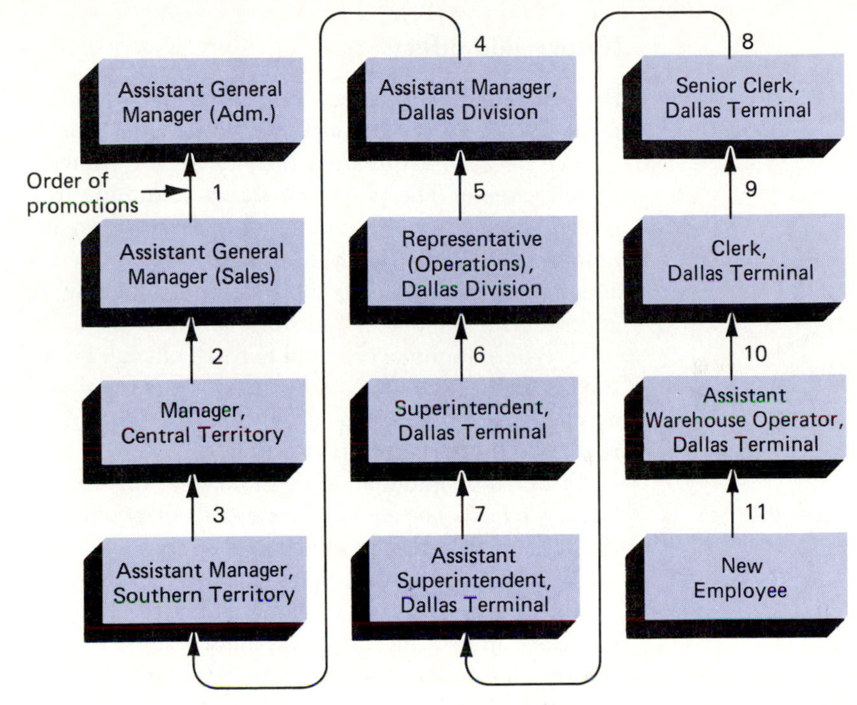

FIGURE 12-3
Chain of eleven promotions resulting from promotion of a higher-level manager

Psychic costs of employee relocation

Family costs

As Figure 12-3 shows, some of the promotions required moves to other locations. These changes tend to have high psychic costs because they require more adjustments. They also may involve the employee's family, so coping becomes more difficult. If there are children, they may not want to move from their friends and familiar surroundings. The spouse may have a job and not want to leave it. Companies that require employees to relocate have found that they need to give careful attention to human needs in order to reduce the psychic costs involved. Services such as counseling, two-way communication, and financial assistance may be required.

For example, one study reported that the typical major U.S. corporation spent about \$35,000 per person while transferring nearly 200 employees per year.[9] Consequently, the total direct cost of transfers averaged about \$7 million per year for each of those companies. The indirect costs of relocation are also substantial. Many employees incur thousands of dollars of unreimbursed costs. Of this group, 77 percent said that they would not transfer again if it would prove financially troublesome. For employees, these financial costs only add to the burden of the psychological adjustment required by relocation, such as uncertainty over how long they will stay, or fear that they will be "forgotten" in a field location.

RESISTANCE TO CHANGE

Nature and effects

Why resistance occurs

Resistance to change consists of any employee behaviors designed to discredit, delay, or prevent the implementation of a work change. Employees resist change because it threatens their needs for security, social interaction, status, or self-esteem. The perceived threat stemming from a change may be real or imagined, intended or unintended, large or small. Regardless of its nature, employees will try to protect themselves from the effects of change. Their actions may range from complaints, foot-dragging, and passive resistance up to absenteeism, sabotage, and work slowdowns.[10]

All types of employees tend to resist change because of the psychic costs that accompany it. Managers as well as workers resist it. Change can be resisted just as stubbornly in a white-collar worker as in a blue-collar worker. It does not respect either type of dress or job.

Although people tend to resist change, this tendency is offset by their desire for new experience and for the rewards that come with change. Certainly not all changes are resisted, as some are actively sought by employees. Other changes are so trivial and routine that resistance, if any, is too weak to be evident. One lesson for management is that a change is likely to be either a success or a problem, depending on how skillfully it is managed to minimize resistance. Another lesson, according to the president of Honeywell, is that "change comes very slowly and exacts a high cost in planning and resources."[11]

Chain-reaction effect

Insecurity and change are conditions that illustrate how a *chain-reaction effect* may develop in organizational behavior. A chain-reaction effect is a situation in which a change (or other condition) that directly affects only one person or a few persons may lead to a reaction from many people, even hundreds or thousands, because of their mutual interest in it. This is quite similar to a nuclear chain reaction.

For example, in one plant a routine dispute arose over the transfer of one employee. Several other workers felt insecure about their transfer rights and supported the employee. Soon the whole department walked out, and shortly the entire factory of 4000 people was temporarily closed—all because of one person's transfer.

The fact that a group is intelligent does not necessarily mean that it will better understand and accept change. Often the opposite is true, because the group uses its extra intelligence to rationalize more reasons to resist change. Intelligence can be used either for or against change, depending on how the change is introduced.

For example, Fred Landini supervised a group of unskilled laborers in a grocery warehouse. Higher management planned to install certain mechanized materials-handling equipment to reduce costs. Reasoning that his employees were poorly educated and had little knowledge of productivity and cost-cutting ideas, Fred worked hard to sell them on the change and to involve them in it. The new system

was installed with full employee cooperation. As he put it, "The change went through without a hitch."

Some years later Fred had the job of installing a quality-control system among a group of technical people. He reasoned that these employees were educated and understood the company's problems, so they could see reasons for the new program. They would not need the special selling effort that he had applied earlier to his warehouse laborers. This mistake in judgment cost him his job, because his employees resisted the change until it was defeated and Fred was discharged. Though his employees had the intellectual potential to see the reasons for the change, they chose not to do so.

Three types of resistance

Resistance to change is of three different types, as shown in Figure 12-4. These types work in combination to produce each employee's total attitude toward a change. The three types may be expressed by three different uses of the word "logical," as follows:

- *Logical.* Based on rational reasoning and science
- Psycho*logical.* Based on emotions, sentiments, and attitudes
- Socio*logical.* Based on group interest and values

Logical, rational objections

- □ **Time required to adjust**
- □ **Extra effort to relearn**
- □ **Possibility of less desirable conditions, such as skill downgrading**
- □ **Economic costs of change**
- □ **Questioned technical feasibility of change**

Psychological, emotional attitudes

- □ **Fear of the unknown**
- □ **Low tolerance of change**
- □ **Dislike of management or other change agent**
- □ **Lack of trust in others**
- □ **Need for security; desire for status quo**

Sociological factors; group interests

- □ **Political coalitions**
- □ **Opposing group values**
- □ **Parochial, narrow outlook**
- □ **Vested interests**
- □ **Desire to retain existing friendships**

FIGURE 12-4
Types of employee resistance to change

Logical Logical resistance arises from the time and effort required to adjust to change, including new job duties that must be learned. These are true costs borne by the employees. Even though a change may be favorable for employees in the long run, these short-run costs must first be paid.

Psychological Psychological resistance is "logical" in terms of attitudes and feelings of individual employees about change. They may fear the unknown, mistrust management's leadership, or feel that their security is threatened. Even though management may believe there is no justification for these feelings, they are real to employees and must be recognized.

Sociological Sociological resistance is "logical" in terms of group interests and values. Social values are powerful forces in the environment, so they must be carefully considered. There are political coalitions, opposing labor union values, and even different community values. On a small-group level there are work friendships that may be disrupted by changes. Employees will ask questions such as: Is the change consistent with group values? Does it maintain group teamwork? Since employees have these kinds of questions on their minds, administrators need to try to make these conditions as favorable as possible if they intend to deal successfully with sociological resistance.

Clearly all three types of resistance must be anticipated and treated effectively if employees are to accept change cooperatively. If administrators work with only the technical, logical dimension of change, they have failed in their human responsibilities. It can be seen that psychological resistance and sociological resistance are not illogical or irrational; rather, they are logical according to different sets of values. They are based on the beat of a different drummer.

In a typical operating situation, full support cannot be gained for every change that is made. Some moderate support, weak support, and even opposition can be expected. People are different and will not give identical support to each change. What management seeks is a climate in which people have a positive feeling toward most changes and feel secure enough to tolerate other changes. If management cannot win support, it may need to use authority. However, it must recognize that authority can be used only sparingly. If authority is overused, it eventually will become worthless.

Possible benefits of resistance

Resistance is not all bad. It can bring some benefits. Resistance may encourage management to reexamine its change proposals so that it can be more sure they are appropriate. In this way employees operate as a check and balance to ensure that management properly plans and implements change. If reasonable employee resistance causes management to screen its proposed changes more carefully, then employees have discouraged careless management decisions.

Resistance also can help identify specific problem areas where a change is likely to cause difficulties, so that management can take corrective action before serious problems develop. At the same time, management may be encouraged to do a better job of communicating the change, an approach that in the long run should lead to better acceptance. Resistance also gives management information about the intensity of employee emotions on an issue, provides emotional release for pent-up employee feelings, and may encourage employees to think and talk more about a change so that they understand it better.

IMPLEMENTING CHANGE SUCCESSFULLY

Change agent

Since management initiates much change, it primarily is responsible for implementing change successfully. Management often is called a *change agent* because its role is to initiate change and help make it work. Though management initiates change, employees typically control its final success. They are the ones who actually make most changes operate. For these reasons, employee support becomes a major goal in the change process.

Management is not always the source of organizational changes. Many changes originate in the external environment. Government passes laws, and the organization must comply with them. Developments in technology require a multitude of changes. Then there are customers, labor unions, communities, and others who originate changes. For example, customers may want new products that require new machinery, new production methods, and new job skills throughout an organization. The amount of change that is required of a firm depends on the environment in which it operates. Stable environments mean less change. Dynamic environments require more change.

Occasionally dynamic environments can lead to fast-moving changes that leave an employee almost bewildered. For example, how would you like to walk into your office one morning and find that the whole office of fifty people had disappeared, leaving a bare room? That is what happened to Mary Manusco. Mary said she was startled and bewildered, and suddenly felt left out of everything. Mary had been on vacation for two weeks and made the discovery when she returned to work Monday morning.

Mary's office was in a separate building at a factory that had a number of buildings spread over 40 acres. She later learned that some quick changes were necessary to prepare her building for new activities. Her office group had been moved to another building during her absence. Nevertheless, the way the move was handled raised questions for Mary. She asked: Why didn't they tell me? They knew where I was, so they could have telephoned me. Why didn't they write me so that I would have the letter at home when I returned? Why didn't a friend call me at home the night before? Why didn't my supervisor try to contact me? Does anybody care?

A three-step change process

It is not always easy to manage change successfully, as illustrated by management's failure to contact Mary Manusco. Not only do managers sometimes overlook important details, but they may fail to develop a master strategy for planned change. An overall plan might address behavioral issues, such as the employees' difficulty of "letting go" of old methods, and the uncertainties inherent in change that cause workers to be fearful.

Some organizations also recognize the need to develop people's capacity to learn from the experience of change. This process is called *double-loop learning.*[12] Its name is derived from the fact that the way a change is handled should not only reflect current information gathered (the first loop) but also *prepare* the participants to manage future changes even more effectively (the second loop). This is in sharp contrast to *single-loop learning,* in which employees are simply expected to adapt to changes that have been imposed on them. The double-loop process not only makes the current change more successful; it also increases the chances that employees will be more ready for the next change to be introduced.

Behavioral awareness in managing change is aided by viewing change as involving three steps, as follows:[13]

- Unfreezing
- Changing
- Refreezing

Unfreezing means that old ideas and practices need to be cast aside so that new ones can be learned. Often this step of getting rid of old practices is just as difficult as learning the new ones. It is an easy step to overlook while concentrating on the proposed change itself, but this is what often leads to resistance to change. Just as a farmer must clear a field before planting new seeds, so must a manager help employees clear their minds of old roles and old purposes.[14] Only then will they be able to embrace new ideas.

Changing is the step in which the new ideas and practices are learned so that an employee can think and perform in new ways. It can be a time of confusion, disorientation, and despair mixed with hope and discovery. *Refreezing* means that what has been learned is integrated into actual practice. In addition to being intellectually accepted, the new practices become incorporated into the employee's routine behavior. Merely knowing a new procedure is not enough to ensure its use. As a farmer once said when confronted with suggestions for improvement, "I'm not farming half as good as I already know how." Successful *practice,* then, must be the ultimate goal of the refreezing step.

Reaching a new equilibrium

An organization at any given time is a dynamic balance of forces supporting and restraining any practice. The system is in a state of relative equilibrium (see the left side of Figure 12-5), so current practices will continue in a steady way until change is introduced. Like a spacecraft hurtling on its course through space, people and organizations may have substantial inertia that sustains current behavior and inhibits change. The speed of the craft is determined not only by

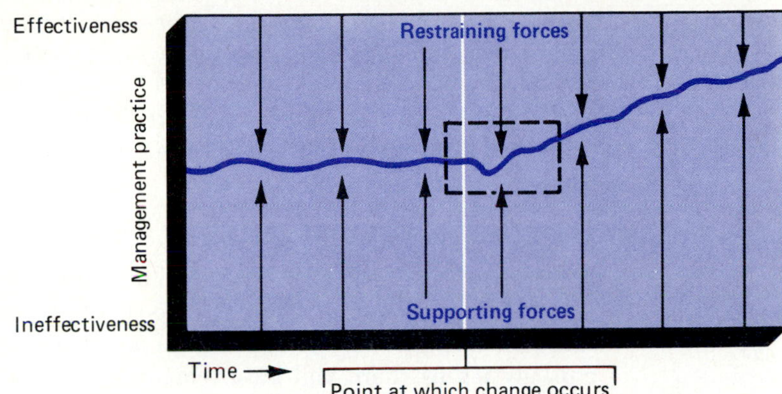

FIGURE 12-5
A model of the change process. (See Figure 12-7 for an expansion of the dashed area.)

the force propelling it forward but also by the resistance it encounters in space. There are similar balancing forces in organizations.

For example, in a factory operation, there are pressures both for and against higher output. Management typically wants the higher output. Industrial engineers conduct studies to try to improve it. Supervisors push for it. Some workers, on the other hand, may feel that they are already working hard enough. More effort would cause feelings of inequity, so they do not want additional strain and tension. They do not want to feel more tired when they go home. They enjoy their rest breaks. The result is that they act as a restraining force, so the current amount of output will tend to continue until some type of change is introduced.

Change supporting and restraining forces

Change is introduced within a group by a variety of methods, as shown in Figure 12-6. Supporting forces may be added or strengthened, while restraining forces may be weakened, removed, or converted to supporting ones. At least one of these approaches must be used to change the equilibrium, with greater success likely when more than one is adopted. The idea is to help

FIGURE 12-6
General approaches for changing an equilibrium

1. **Adding new supporting forces**
2. **Removing restraining forces**
3. **Increasing the strength of a supporting force**
4. **Decreasing the strength of a restraining force**
5. **Converting a restraining force into a supporting force**

change be accepted and integrated into new practices. For example, making people responsible for the quality of the product they produce has been used as a supporting force for higher-quality work. Another supporting force involves programs to increase the employees' pride in their work. In the other direction, restraining forces on quality can be reduced by better maintenance of machines, so that better work can be done on them.

The organizational learning curve for change

Learning curve for change

Figure 12-5 shows a small drop in the line of effectiveness after change occurs. This part is expanded in Figure 12-7 to show a typical *organizational learning curve for change.*[15] It is the period of adaptation that follows change, and it typically means there will be a temporary decline in effectiveness before a group reaches a new equilibrium. Employees need time to understand and adapt in order to accept change. During this period they are trying to integrate the change, and they are likely to be less effective than they formerly were. They have to get rid of old habits (unfreeze) and apply the new ones (refreeze). There are many problems to be worked out. Procedures are upset, and communication patterns are disrupted. Conflicts develop about the change, and cooperation declines. Problems arise, and time must be taken to resolve them. The result is that, as the statement goes, "Things are likely to get worse before they get better."

During the transition period when people are adjusting to a change, they are likely to become discouraged because of the problems that develop. At this time the change is especially subject to criticism, attack, and even failure, because it appears not to be working. Only after the passage of time, when teamwork and efficiency are restored, is the change likely to produce the favorable results intended.[16]

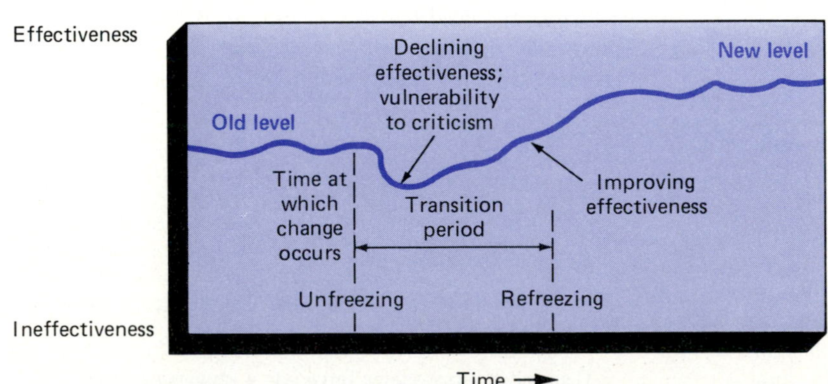

FIGURE 12-7
A typical organizational learning curve for change

Building support for change

Assuming that management is following the model of the change process in Figure 12-5, then forces of support need to be built before, during, and after a change. Selected activities to build support are described below.

USE OF GROUP FORCES Effective change focuses on the group along with individuals. Usually more than one person is involved, but more important is the fact that the group is an instrument for bringing strong pressure on its members to change. One's behavior is firmly grounded in the groups to which one belongs, so changes in group forces will encourage changes in individual behavior. The idea is to help the group join with management to encourage desired change.

The power of a group to stimulate change in its members depends partly upon the strength of their attachment to it. The more attractive the group is to each member, the greater its influence on that person can be. Influence is further increased if members with top prestige in the group support a change.

Change should not disrupt the group's social system more than is necessary. Any change that threatens the group will tend to meet with resistance.

LEADERSHIP FOR CHANGE Capable leadership reinforces a climate of psychological support for change.[17] The leader presents change on the basis of the impersonal requirements of the situation, rather than on personal grounds. Leaders are asking for trouble when they introduce change with a comment such as "I have always felt you should not be able to leave the department during rest periods, and beginning tomorrow it will not be permitted." The natural responses are "It's not the supervisor's business where we go" and "Let's get together and figure out a way to beat the supervisor." Surely there must be some better reasons for the change, and if so, they should be given. If not, maybe the intended change needs to be abandoned. Ordinary requests for change should be in accord with the objectives and rules of the organization. Only a strong personal leader can use personal reasons for change without arousing resistance.

Expectations are important.

Change is more likely to be successful if the leaders introducing it have high expectations of success. In other words, expectations of change may be as important as the technology of change, as suggested earlier in this chapter by the "X" chart, which showed the importance of attitudes toward change. For example, a manufacturer of clothing patterns had four almost identical plants. When a job enrichment and rotation program was introduced, managers in two of the plants were given inputs predicting that the program would increase productivity. Managers of the other two plants were told that the program would improve employee relations but not productivity.

During the next twelve months productivity did increase significantly in the two plants where the managers were expecting it. In the two plants where the managers were not expecting it, it did not increase. The result showed that high leader expectations were the key factor in making the change successful.[18]

PARTICIPATION A fundamental way to build support for change is through participation, which was discussed in an earlier chapter. It encourages employees to discuss, to communicate, to make suggestions, and to become interested in change. Participation encourages commitment rather than mere compliance with change. Commitment implies motivation to support a change and to work to assure that it operates effectively.[19]

As shown in Figure 12-8, a general model of participation and change indicates that as participation increases, resistance to change tends to decrease. Resistance declines because employees have less cause to resist. Their needs are being considered, so they feel secure in a changing situation.

Employees need to participate in a change *before* it occurs, not after. When they can be involved from the beginning, they feel protected from surprises and feel that their ideas are wanted. On the other hand, employees are likely to feel that involvement after a change is nothing more than a selling device and manipulation by management.

SHARED REWARDS Another way to build employee support for change is to be sure that there are enough rewards for employees in the change situation. It is only natural for employees to ask, "What's in this for me?" If they see that a change brings them losses and no gains, they can hardly be enthusiastic about it.

Economic and psychic rewards

Rewards say to employees, "We care. We want you as well as us to benefit from this change." Rewards also give employees a sense of progress with a change. Both economic and psychic rewards are useful. Employees appreciate a pay increase or promotion, but they also appreciate emotional support, training in new skills, and recognition from management.

It is desirable for a change to pay off as directly and as soon as possible. From an employee's point of view, what's good in general is not necessarily good for

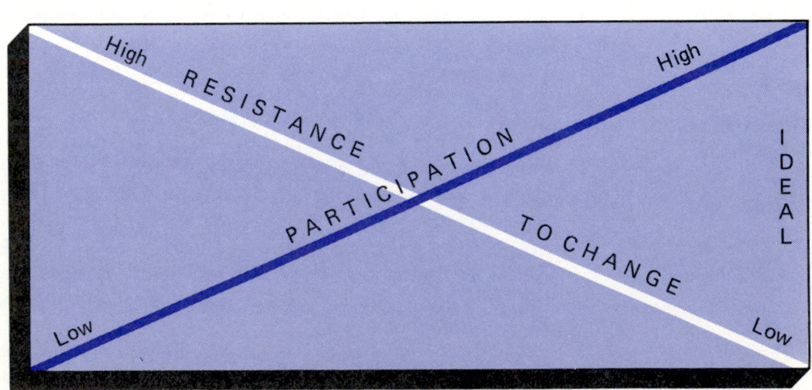

FIGURE 12-8
A model of participation and resistance to change

the employee, and what's good for the long run may not be good for the short run.

EMPLOYEE SECURITY Along with shared rewards, existing employee benefits need to be protected. Security during a change is essential. Many employers guarantee workers protection from reduced earnings when new machines and methods are introduced. Others offer retraining and delay installation of labor-saving machinery until normal labor turnover can absorb displaced workers. Seniority rights, opportunities for advancement, and other benefits are safeguarded when a change is made. Grievance systems give employees a feeling of security that benefits will be protected and differences about them fairly resolved. All these practices help employees feel secure in the presence of change.

COMMUNICATION Communication is essential to improve support for change. Even though a change will affect only one or two in a work group of ten persons, all of them need to know about the change in order to feel secure and to maintain group cooperation. Management often does not realize that activities that help get change accepted, such as communication, usually are disrupted by change. In other words, communication may be weakest at the time it is needed most, so special effort is required to maintain it in times of change.

One retail business learned the hard way about the importance of maintaining communication during a change. Central management decided to change from manual to computer credit records in two branch offices. This was a technical decision in which the credit clerks did not participate. In the Oakhurst Branch the plan was to transfer and lay off twenty-three employees and retain five. In the Bay City Branch twenty-five were to be transferred or laid off and seven retained. In both branches most employees had an opportunity to transfer to other work, but major retraining was required in some cases. All employees who were remaining in the credit records activity would require substantial retraining.

The manager of the Oakhurst Branch informed all her employees about the impending change, even those employees in other departments who were not affected by it. As the change progressed, she continued to inform her employees and discuss operating details with them. The Bay City manager took a contrasting approach. She decided not to tell her employees about the change until the week of the changeover because she did not want to upset them. She made elaborate precautions to keep information about the change tightly confined within the management group. When employees officially learned of the change, they were visibly upset.

Three months after the changeover management made an inspection of its success. In the Oakhurst Branch the change was progressing smoothly and most displaced employees had been transferred and retrained. In contrast, the Bay City Branch was in turmoil. Many displaced employees were so shocked or disillusioned that they had resigned. The employees who remained in the credit activity were having difficulty adjusting, and billings were late. Cooperation had declined. Job satisfaction was low. The situation definitely had caused depreciation of the organization's human resources.

Dissatisfaction stimulates change.

STIMULATING EMPLOYEE READINESS Closely related to communication is the idea of helping employees become aware of the need for a change. This approach builds on the premise that *change is more likely to be accepted if the people affected by it recognize a need for it before it occurs.* This awareness may happen naturally, as when a crisis occurs, or it can be induced by management through sharing operating information with employees. One of the more powerful ways, however, occurs when workers discover for themselves that a situation requires improvement. Then they will truly be ready, as this incident shows:

> **The personnel director of a major bank aided the self-discovery process by hiring a consultant to conduct an assessment of the department's innovativeness.[20] The provocative conclusions shocked the staff into awareness that changes were needed. According to the director, the results of the report "seemed to crystallize new perspectives about the potential of the department." Task forces were created, and their recommendations implemented. Desired new behaviors emerged—risk taking, self-reliance, and decentralized decision making. All of this occurred because the employees suddenly became aware that a problem existed, and they personally experienced the need for some changes.**

WORKING WITH UNIONS Management in the performance of its function is primarily an initiator of change. The union, on the other hand, serves more as a restraint on management and a protector of security for its members. It frequently is cast in the role of resisting change. These differences between management and unions tend to cause union-management conflict about change, but there are many exceptions. Unions sometimes support management in encouraging workers to accept change. Most unions, as a matter of policy, favor improvement through technological change and will approve a change that is carefully planned to protect member interests. Union approval does not ensure that there will be no opposition, because insecure workers sometimes resist changes even when their union pressures them not to do so.

Guidelines for change

WORKING WITH THE TOTAL SYSTEM Resistance to change can be reduced by helping employees recognize the need for each change, participate in it, and gain from it.[21] In summary, five management guidelines for responsible change are:

1 Make only necessary and useful change. Avoid unnecessary change.

2 Change by evolution, not revolution (that is, gradually, not dramatically).

3 Recognize the possible effects of change, and introduce it with adequate attention to human needs.

4 Share the benefits of change with employees.

5 Diagnose the problems remaining after a change occurs, and treat them.

Change, when improperly handled, manifests itself in slowdowns and showdowns.

For example, Robert Barrows, an engineer, failed to consider the total system when he introduced changes in an operating department. He needed to make some routine studies of machine downtime in a factory. Without explaining what his purpose was, he set up machine records to be kept by each machine operator reporting the length, time of day, and cause of all machine downtime. The supervisor was told to require his employees to keep these records for thirty days. Both the supervisor and the employees stalled and complained and finally kept such inadequate records that they were not usable. Robert concluded that the department was full of obstructionists who did not have the organization's interests at heart.

Closer examination revealed some human aspects of this routine technical requirement. Keeping records was more work for the employees, and some of them were not oriented toward paperwork. The machine work required them to have dirty hands, but they felt obligated to try to keep the downtime records clean. They also felt that the records pried into their activities, because some downtime was for personal reasons. They saw no direct benefit from the study, and some of them feared it would bring changes that would reduce their incentive earnings.

The supervisor likewise saw no direct benefit coming to him or his department from the study. He feared unknown changes in his department; and he disliked the chore of enforcing the record system, especially since his employees resented it. The result was that the supervisor and employees complained to Robert and to one another. Soon everyone was obstructing rather than cooperating, and Robert was wondering why there was so much commotion about "this little piece of paperwork." He was sure that a company with so many obstructionists would never be efficient. However—and here is a key point—one of the reasons the company had so many obstructionists was that it had technical people like Robert who did not understand and work with the total social system. People like Robert were the cause of the problem, rather than the victims of it.

SUMMARY

The work environment is filled with change that upsets the social system and requires employees to adjust. The "X" chart shows that they respond with their emotions as well as rational reasoning. Resistance to change can be logical, psychological, and sociological.

Change has costs as well as benefits, and both must be considered to determine net benefits. Employees tend to resist change because of its costs, including psychic costs. Management reduces resistance by influencing the supporting and restraining forces for change. It applies a change procedure of unfreezing, changing, and refreezing activities. Since there is an organizational learning curve for change, time is required for the potential benefits of change to occur.

Selected activities to support change were discussed. Another major activity for change is organizational development. It is discussed in the next chapter.

Terms and concepts for review

Work change

Roethlisberger's "X" chart

Hawthorne effect

Homeostasis

Psychic costs
Resistance to change
Chain-reaction effect
Types of resistance to change
Change agent
Unfreezing and refreezing
Organizational learning curve for change

Discussion questions

1 Think of an organizational change that you have experienced. Was there resistance to the change? Discuss. What could have been done to prevent or diminish it?

2 Considering the change mentioned in question 1, outline both the costs and benefits of it under the three headings of "logical," "psychological," and "sociological." Discuss. Were the benefits greater than the costs for (*a*) the employees and (*b*) the employer?

3 Continuing the analysis of this change, how did management alter the restraining and supporting forces for it? Discuss.

4 Considering that change even further, was there an organizational learning curve for it? Discuss its length, shape, and some of the problems that developed.

5 Think of an organizational change that you have resisted at some time. Why did you resist? How did you resist it? What could the organization have done to reduce your resistance?

6 Roethlisberger's "X" chart implies that attitude changes must precede behavioral responses, but some people believe that it is easier to change an employee's behavior first, and then let the attitude change follow. Discuss the merits and probabilities of both approaches to change. Give examples of each.

7 Resistance to change is often viewed negatively. Discuss some possible benefits of resistance to change in an organization.

8 Select some change that you have experienced, and discuss the difficulties you had in unfreezing your earlier patterns of thought and behavior. How did it finally occur?

9 List a variety of methods for helping employees unfreeze their attitudes and behaviors. Why aren't these used more often?

10 Nine methods for supporting change were introduced. Identify a possible risk associated with each of them. In other words, how might they backfire?

Incident

THE NEW SALES PROCEDURES

The Marin Company had more than 100 field sales representatives who sold a line of complex industrial products. Sales of these products required close work with buyers to determine their product needs; so nearly all sales representatives were college graduates in engineering and science. Other product lines of Marin Company, such as consumer products, were sold by a separate sales group.

Recently the firm established a new companywide control and report system using a larger computer. This system has doubled the amount of time the industrial sales representatives spend filling out forms and supplying information that can be fed into the computer. They estimate that they now spend as much as two hours daily processing records, and they have complained that they now have inadequate time for sales effort. A field sales manager commented, "Morale has declined as a result of these new controls and reports. Sales is a rewarding, gratifying profession that is based on individual effort. Sales representatives are happy when they are making sales, since this directly affects their income and self-recognition. The more time they spend with reports, the less time they have to make sales. As a result they can see their income and recognition declining, and thus they find themselves resisting changes."

Questions

1 Comment on the sales manager's analysis.

2 What alternative approaches to this situation do you recommend? Give reasons.

Experiential exercise

THE INDUSTRIAL ENGINEERING CHANGE

An industrial engineer was assigned to an electronics assembly department to make some methods improvements. In one assembly operation he soon recognized that a new fixture might reduce labor costs by about 30 percent. He discussed the situation with the group leader and then the supervisor. The group leader was indifferent, but the supervisor was interested and offered additional suggestions.

Feeling that he had the supervisor's approval, the industrial engineer had the fixture made. With the permission of the supervisor, he assigned a woman assembler to try the fixture. She was cooperative and enthusiastic and on the first day exceeded the expected improvement of 30 percent. When the group leader was shown the results at the end of the day, he claimed that this was one of the fastest workers in the department and that her results could not be generalized for the whole department.

The next day the industrial engineer asked the supervisor for another operator to help prove the fixture. At this point the supervisor noted that the fixture did not include her ideas fully. The industrial engineer explained that he had misunderstood but that he would include the other suggestions in the next fixture built. The supervisor, however, continued to be negative about the fixture.

When the industrial engineer attempted to instruct the second woman the way he had instructed the first one, her reaction was negative. In fact, when he stopped instructing her, it seemed that the woman deliberately stalled as she used the fixture. She also made some negative comments about the fixture and asked the industrial engineer if he felt he deserved his paycheck for this kind of effort. At the end of the day this woman's production was 10 percent below normal production by the old method.

Questions

1 Form small discussion groups, and analyze the causes of the problem.
2 Review the nine management activities for supporting change that are mentioned late in this chapter. Rank these from 1 (highest) to 9 (lowest) in terms of their potential usefulness to the industrial engineer. Compare your rankings with those of the other groups, and discuss any differences.
3 Select two people, and have them role-play a meeting of the industrial engineer and the supervisor.

References

1 Tom Peters, "There Are No Excellent Companies," *Fortune*, Apr. 27, 1987, p. 352.
2 Samuel Butler, *Hudibras, III*, first published in 1678.
3 Amir Levy, "Second-Order Planned Change: Definition and Conceptualization," *Organizational Dynamics*, Summer 1986, pp. 4–20.
4 F. J. Roethlisberger, *Management and Morale*, Cambridge, Mass.: Harvard University Press, 1941, p. 10. See also F. J. Roethlisberger and William J. Dickson, *Management and the Worker*, Cambridge, Mass.: Harvard University Press, 1939. An update is Ronald G. Greenwood et al., "Hawthorne a Half Century Later: Relay Assembly Participants Remember," *Journal of Management*, Fall–Winter 1983, pp. 217–231.
5 John Donne (1572–1631), *The Complete Poetry and Selected Prose of John Donne and the Complete Poetry of William Blake*, New York: Random House, Inc., 1941, p. 332. Italics in original.
6 In contrast to the positive effects of homeostasis, some firms develop "organizational defensive routines" that not only protect the organization from threat but also prevent it from learning how to remove the causes of that threat. See Chris Argyris, "Reinforcing Organizational Defensive Routines: An Unintended Human Resources Activity," *Human Resource Management*, Winter 1986, pp. 541–555.
7 Wayne F. Cascio, "The Financial Impact of Employee Attitudes," in *Costing Human Resources: The Financial Impact of Behavior in Organizations*, 2d ed., Boston: PWS-Kent Publishing Company, 1987, chap. 5, pp. 101–118.
8 Ellen Foley, "Republic, Northwest Workers Worried," *Minneapolis Star and Tribune*, Sept. 28, 1986, pp. 1ff.
9 Betsy D. Gelb and Michael R. Hyman, "Reducing Reluctance to Transfer," *Business Horizons*, March–April 1987, pp. 39–43.
10 C. A. Carnall, "Toward a Theory for the Evaluation of Organizational Change," *Human Relations*, August 1986, pp. 745–766.
11 James J. Renier, "Turnaround of Information Systems at Honeywell," *The Academy of Management Executive*, February 1987, p. 50.
12 Chris Argyris, "The Executive Mind and Double-Loop Learning," *Organizational Dynamics*, Autumn 1982, pp. 4–22.
13 The three steps have also been described as a three-part psychological process in William Bridges, "Managing Organizational Transitions," *Organizational Dynamics*, Summer 1986, pp. 24–33.
14 Some examples are in Harlan Cleveland, "Inventing the Future," *New Management*, Fall 1986, pp. 55–56.

15 A discussion of the productivity gains that should follow experience with a procedure is in George S. Odiorne, "Measuring the Unmeasurable: Setting Standards for Management Performance," *Business Horizons*, July–August 1987, pp. 69–75.

16 A process model of organizational change containing initiation, adoption, adaptation, and persistence phases is presented in Gerald E. Ledford, Jr., "The Persistence of Organizational Change: Variance Theory and Process Theory Models," Western Academy of Management, 1985.

17 Examples of the role of leaders as agents of change are in James F. Bolt, "The Future Is Already Here," *New Management*, Winter 1987, pp. 27–29; and Edmund F. Metz, "Managing Change toward a Leading-Edge Information Culture," *Organizational Dynamics*, Autumn 1986, pp. 28–40.

18 Albert S. King, "Expectation Effects in Organizational Change," *Administrative Science Quarterly*, June 1974, pp. 221–230; and Dov Eden and Gad Ravid, "Pygmalion versus Self-Expectancy: Effects of Infrastructure and Self-Expectancy on Trainee Performance," *Organizational Behavior and Human Performance*, December 1982, pp. 351–364.

19 The difficulty of establishing a participative management style in a Honeywell operation is discussed in Richard J. Boyle, "Wrestling with Jellyfish," *Harvard Business Review*, January–February 1984, pp. 74–83.

20 William Shea, "The Dilemmas of a Changemaker," *New Management*, Spring 1986, pp. 6–14.

21 Tools for change are summarized in Michael Beer, "Revitalizing Organizations: Change Process and Emergent Model," *Academy of Management Executive*, February 1987, pp. 51–55; a contingency model for selecting from among tools is John P. Kotter and Leonard A. Schlesinger, "Choosing Strategies for Change," *Harvard Business Review*, March–April 1979, pp. 106–114.

For additional reading

Argyris, Chris, *Strategy, Change and Defensive Routines*, Cambridge, Mass.: Ballinger Publishing Co., 1985.

Guest, Robert H., Paul Hersey, and Kenneth H. Blanchard, *Organizational Change through Effective Leadership*, Englewood Cliffs, N.J.: Prentice-Hall, Inc., 1977.

Huse, Edgar F., and Thomas G. Cummings, *Organization Development and Change*, 3d ed., St. Paul, Minn.: West Publishing Company, 1985.

Kanter, Rosabeth Moss, *The Change Masters*, New York: Simon and Schuster, 1983.

Kirkpatrick, Donald L., *How to Manage Change Effectively*, San Francisco: Jossey-Bass Inc., Publishers, 1985.

Lippitt, Gordon L., Petter Langseth, and Jack Mossop, *Implementing Organizational Change*, San Francisco: Jossey-Bass Publishers, Inc., 1985.

Odiorne, George S., *The Change Resisters: How They Can Prevent Progress and What Management Can Do about Them*, Englewood Cliffs, N.J., Prentice-Hall, Inc., 1981.

Roethlisberger, F. J., and William J. Dickson, *Management and the Worker*, Cambridge, Mass.: Harvard University Press, 1939.

Sims, Henry P., Jr., Dennis A. Gioia, and associates, *The Thinking Organization: Dynamics of Organizational Social Cognition*, San Francisco: Jossey-Bass Publishers, Inc., 1986.

Walton, Richard E., *Innovating to Compete: Lessons for Diffusing and Managing Change in the Workplace*, San Francisco: Jossey-Bass Publishers, Inc., 1987.

CHAPTER 13

Organization development

An OD intervention is effective in boosting productivity in direct proportion to the expectations it arouses for improved performance.

DOV EDEN[1]

For developing and refining a supervisor's skills in conducting difficult discussions with employees, behavior modeling is second to none.

KENNETH E. HULTMAN[2]

CHAPTER OBJECTIVES

To understand

The meaning of OD

What its characteristics are

The process by which it operates

Experiential learning methods

Frameworks of some OD programs

Teamwork and team building

In the early 1980s, the world's largest company—American Telephone and Telegraph (AT&T)—successfully met two immense changes from its environment (the government). Within the span of two years, the Federal Communications Commission allowed AT&T to provide some deregulated products and services, and an agreement was reached with the Justice Department whereby AT&T agreed to divest itself of its operating telephone companies. The massive transition represented one of the most complex and significant planned changes in a U.S. firm in this century. Yet the evidence indicates that top management at AT&T was able to balance its concern for strategic issues with strong efforts to maintain the human organization.

This illustration shows that AT&T executives faced a challenging task of preparing the organization to meet a new situation. Although changes in the environment have a powerful effect on what organizations can do, many firms also have chosen to engage in self-examination as a basis for making themselves more adaptive before they are forced to do so. This chapter broadens the themes from Chapter 12 by focusing on planned change efforts that can help transform individuals, groups, and organizations. The meaning of organization development and how it works is discussed. Possible benefits and problems, as well as the different types of programs, are presented.

UNDERSTANDING ORGANIZATION DEVELOPMENT

In the 1950s and 1960s a new, integrated type of training originated known as *organization development* (OD). Organization development is an intervention strategy that uses group processes to focus on the whole culture of an organization in order to bring about planned change. It seeks to change beliefs, attitudes, values, structures, and practices so that the organization can better adapt to technology and live with the fast pace of change.[3]

OD arose in response to needs. Conventional training methods often had limited success for building better organizational behavior, so a new approach was needed. The National Training Laboratories and Esso Standard Oil Company began working on the problem, and eventually OD evolved from their efforts.[4]

Why was OD necessary?

There were two main causes that made OD necessary. First, the reward structure on the job did not adequately reinforce conventional training, so it often failed to carry over to the job. Too many well-designed training programs failed because the job environment provided inadequate support. Under these conditions the reasonable next step is to try to change the entire organization so that it will support the training. This is exactly what OD tries to do.

A second cause is the fast pace of change itself, which requires organizations to be extremely flexible in order to survive and prosper.[5] OD attempts to develop the whole organization so that it can respond to change more uniformly

OD's general objective

and capably. It tries to encourage open communication by increasing the amount and accuracy of information through better group dynamics and problem confrontation. In short, its general objective is to change all parts of the organization in order to make it more humanly responsive, more effective, and more capable of self-renewal.

Characteristics of OD

A number of characteristics are implied in the definition of OD. Many of these are consistent with the dominant themes of organizational behavior presented earlier in this book. The characteristics are discussed in the following paragraphs and summarized in Figure 13-1. Although OD differs substantially from traditional training programs, it is also apparent that OD has begun to have an impact on the way those programs are designed and presented.

SYSTEMS ORIENTATION Change is so abundant in modern society that organizations need all their parts working together in order to solve the problems—and opportunities—that are brought by change. OD is a comprehensive program that is concerned with interactions of various parts of the organization as they affect each other. It is concerned with working relationships as well as personal ones. It is concerned with structure and process as well as attitudes. The basic issue to which it is directed is: How do all of these parts work

FIGURE 13-1
Characteristics of organization development

together to be effective? Emphasis is on how the parts relate, not on the parts themselves.

What does OD value?

HUMANISTIC VALUES OD programs typically are based on *humanistic values*, which are positive beliefs about the potential and desire for growth among employees. To be effective and self-renewing, an organization needs employees who want to expand their skills and can increase their contributions. The best climate for this to happen is one that creates opportunities for growth by stressing collaboration, open communications, interpersonal trust, shared power, and constructive confrontation. They all provide a value base for OD efforts and help ensure that the new organization will be responsive to human needs.

USE OF A CHANGE AGENT OD programs generally use one or more *change agents*, whose role is to stimulate, facilitate, and coordinate change. The change agent usually acts as a catalyst, sparking change within the system while remaining somewhat independent of it. Although change agents may be either external or internal, they are usually consultants from outside the company. Advantages of using external change agents are that they are more objective and have diverse experiences. They are also able to operate independently without ties to the hierarchy and politics of the firm.[6]

To offset their limited familiarity with the organization, external change agents usually are paired with an internal coordinator from the human resources department. These two then work with line management. The result is a three-way relationship that draws on the strengths of each for balance, much like a three-legged milking stool provides the dairy farmer with needed support. Sometimes, especially in large firms, the organization has its own in-house OD specialist. This person replaces the external consultant and works directly with the firm's managers to facilitate improvement efforts.

Problems of change agents

Change agents have difficult roles. They may not always be welcome in the units to which they are assigned. This is because some employees resist change for many reasons, such as fear for their job security. Roles as facilitators are not easily understood, especially if employees expect change agents to act as expert problem solvers. Finally, like the physician who seldom learns whether or not the prescribed treatment cured a patient's ailment, the external change agent may not be there to see the long-term effects of the changes made. Any of these forces can cause change agents to become frustrated with their roles.

Action research

PROBLEM SOLVING OD emphasizes the process of problem solving. It trains participants to identify and solve problems rather than to discuss them theoretically, as in a classroom. These problems are real ones that the participants face at work, so they are stimulating and interesting. This focus on improving problem-solving skills by discussing data-based system problems is called *action research*. In other words, employees are "learning how to learn" from their experiences, so they can solve new problems in the future.

FEEDBACK OD relies heavily on feedback to participants so that they have useful data on which to base decisions. Feedback encourages them to understand how they are seen by others and take self-correcting action.

An example is a feedback exercise in one OD program. Participants are separated into two groups representing two different departments in the organization. Both groups are asked to develop answers to the following questions:

- **What characteristics best describe our group?**
- **What characteristics best describe the other group?**
- **How will the other group describe us?**

After the separate groups have prepared their answers, they assemble and present their answers to the other group. They give concrete feedback about impressions each group has of the other, and there usually are major misunderstandings. In this presentation no arguments are allowed. Questions are accepted only to clarify what the other group is saying.

The groups again are separated to discuss two other questions:

- **How did these misunderstandings occur?**
- **What can we do to correct them?**

With this new feedback, the groups meet to develop specific plans of action for solving their misunderstandings. In each instance feedback about themselves is the basis for their next activities.

CONTINGENCY ORIENTATION OD usually is said to be situational and *contingency-oriented.* Unlike many other training approaches that emphasize only one right way to deal with a problem, OD is flexible and pragmatic, adapting actions to fit particular needs. Although an occasional OD change agent may try to impose a single best way on the group, usually there is open discussion of several better alternatives rather than a single best way.

EXPERIENTIAL LEARNING *Experiential learning* means that participants learn by experiencing in the training environment the kinds of human problems they face on the job. Then they can discuss and analyze their own immediate experience and learn from it. This approach tends to produce more changed behavior than the traditional lecture and discussion, in which people talk about abstract ideas. Theory is necessary and desirable, but the ultimate test is how it applies in a real situation. OD helps to provide some of the answers. Participant experiences help solidify, or refreeze, new learning.

Real problems experienced by participants

INTERVENTIONS AT MANY LEVELS The general goal of OD is to build more effective organizations—ones that will continue to learn, adapt, and improve. OD accomplishes this by recognizing that problems may occur at the individual, interpersonal, group, intergroup, or total organization level. An overall OD strategy is then developed with one or more *interventions,* which are structured activities designed to help individuals or groups improve their work effectiveness. These interventions are often classified by their emphasis on individuals (such as career planning) or groups (such as team building). Another

OD interventions

way to view interventions is whether they focus on *what* people are doing (clarifying and changing their job tasks) or on *how* they do it (the interpersonal process that occurs). Because OD programs often target work teams as the most potent area for achieving improvements, team building will be discussed at length later in this chapter.

In summary, the OD process applies behavioral science knowledge and strategies to improve an organization. It is a long-range, continuing effort that tries to build cooperative work relationships through the use of a change agent. It seeks to integrate into an effective unit the four elements of people, structure, technology, and environment that were discussed in Chapter 1.

An example of an OD intervention in a public-sector organization occurred at the Utah Department of Public Safety.[7] Using an action research approach, 750 employees completed a diagnostic survey focused on 19 areas of organizational and management effectiveness. Then they received feedback on the results, and helped develop action plans where deficiencies were noted.

In a follow-up study two years later, most of the supervisors reported that communications had improved, teams were more cohesive, and participative management was used more frequently. Employees were receiving more feedback on their performance, and had a greater sense of ownership and responsibility for work outcomes. In units where the OD approach was less successful, the barriers were related to a lack of management support, resource constraints, and low support from peers.

The OD process

OD is a complex process. It may take a year or more to design and implement, and the process may continue indefinitely. OD tries to move the organization from where it is now (requiring diagnosis) to where it should be (by action interventions). Even then the process continues, as it is desirable to evaluate the outcomes and maintain the momentum. Although there are many different approaches to OD, a typical complete program includes most of the following steps. They are summarized in Figure 13-2.

Phases in OD

1 *Initial diagnosis.* The consultant meets with top management to determine the nature of the firm's problems, to develop the OD approaches most likely to be successful, and to ensure the full support of top management. During this step the consultant may seek inputs by means of interviews with various persons in the organization.

2 *Data collection.* Surveys may be made to determine organizational climate and behavioral problems. The consultant usually meets with groups away from work to develop information from questions such as these:

- What kinds of conditions contribute most to your job effectiveness?
- What kinds of conditions interfere with your job effectiveness?
- What would you most like to change in the way this organization operates?

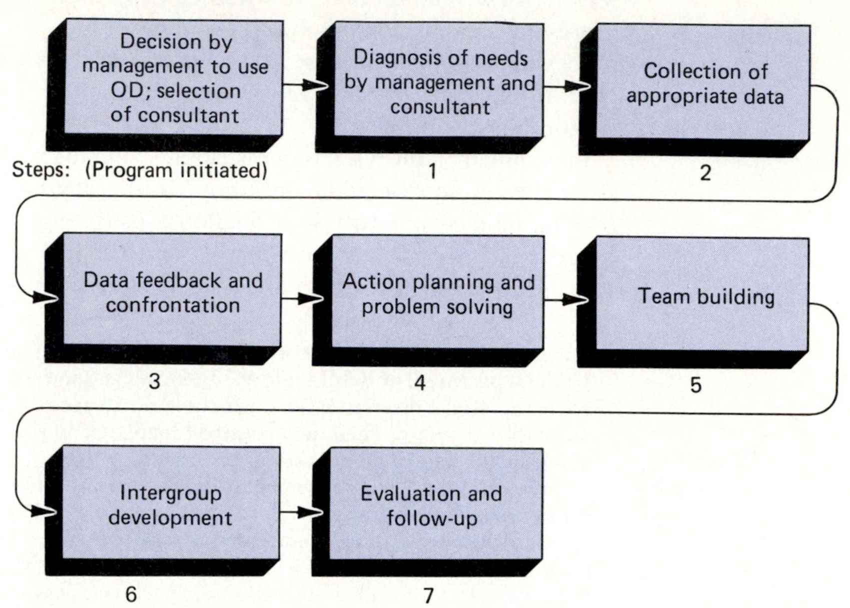

FIGURE 13-2
Steps in the OD process

3 *Data feedback and confrontation.* Work groups are assigned to review the data collected, to mediate among themselves areas of disagreement, and to establish priorities for change.

4 *Action planning and problem solving.* Groups use the data to develop specific recommendations for change. Discussion focuses on actual problems in their organization. Plans are specific, including who is responsible and when the action should be completed.

5 *Team building.* During the entire period of group meetings the consultant encourages the groups to examine how they work together. The consultant helps them see the value of open communication and trust as prerequisites for improved group functioning. Team building may be encouraged further by having individual managers and their subordinates work together as a team in OD sessions.

6 *Intergroup development.* After development of small-group teams, there may be development among larger groups comprising several teams.

7 *Evaluation and follow-up.* The consultant helps the organization evaluate the results of its OD efforts and develop additional programs in areas where additional results are needed.

For example, in one organization, the consultant asked managers to provide tapes of committee meetings that they chaired subsequent to the program. The consultant

analyzed these tapes and used them to discuss with managers how well each was applying what was learned in the OD program.

The steps in OD are part of a whole process, so all of them need to be applied if a firm expects to gain the full benefits of OD. A firm that applies only two or three steps, such as diagnosis and team building, is likely to be disappointed with the results. However, the whole process can produce quite favorable results.

Mobil Oil has implemented numerous OD programs, and it reports these results:

- **Improved supervisor-employee communications**
- **Streamlined paperwork requirements**
- **More systematic problem analysis and problem solving**
- **Better interdepartmental relationships**

The company concluded that the most critical step in OD is the first one—obtaining permission, active support, and total involvement from top management.[8]

TRAINING METHODS USED

The OD process shown in Figure 13-2 does not preclude the use of conventional training methods, which are useful for some purposes. Coaching, lecture and discussion, films, and the case method are appropriate tools for providing an understanding of behavior or developing analytical skills. Many employees also need this type of training.

Laboratory training

Laboratory training has impact.

OD programs rely heavily on experiential learning, and the approach emphasized is *laboratory training*. It provides situations in which the trainees themselves experience through their own interactions some of the conditions they are talking about. In this way they more or less experiment on themselves. This kind of training tends to have a greater impact on them than conventional training methods and encourages transfer of the new skills to the job. The following laboratory methods will be discussed: role playing, simulation, behavior modeling, gaming, and encounter groups.

ROLE PLAYING *Role playing* is a laboratory method that can be used rather easily as a supplement to conventional training methods as well as in OD. It is spontaneous acting of a realistic situation involving two or more people under classroom conditions. Dialogue spontaneously grows out of the situation as it is developed by the trainees assigned to it. Other trainees in the group serve as observers and critics. Role playing is often considered a substitute for experience. In a sense it is more than experience because it permits techniques of observation, discussion, and emphasis that are not customarily a part of experience.

Since people assume roles every day, they are somewhat experienced in the art, and with a certain amount of imagination they can project themselves into roles other than their own. This idea is not new, because dramatics is as old as recorded history. In role playing trainees can broaden their experience by trying different approaches, while in actual situations they often have only one chance. People may, in two hours in a role-playing group, observe as many different approaches to a problem as they would in two years of normal experience. By evaluating these different ways of handling the same situation, they are able to see the strengths and weaknesses of each approach. Here is a sample introduction to a role-playing exercise:

> **"Suppose that you and another student decided to save money by sharing the text for this course. Everything worked fine until the night before the first test, when you both claim to have a desperate need to use the book for at least three hours of studying. It is now 8:30 P.M."**
>
> **At this point you might be asked to meet with another role player to act out your approach to the problem. When the role playing is finished, the trainer would likely ask for a report of the various outcomes from different pairs and then discuss examples of how the problem was solved and the behavioral ideas that were demonstrated.**

Weaknesses of role playing

Role playing also has weaknesses that partly offset its strengths. It is time-consuming and expensive. It requires experienced trainers because it can easily turn sour without effective direction and subsequent discussion. The trainees may resent it as a childish approach to serious problems unless it is introduced carefully. Some trainees are embarrassed and hesitant to take part. Conversely, other trainees may place more emphasis on acting and showing off than on the problem involved.

SIMULATIONS While role playing exercises are often relatively brief, *simulations* may last for hours or even days. Simulations are comprehensive experiential approaches that create many dimensions of work life in organizations.[9] This may include the physical setting, the organizational hierarchy and roles, and even the production tasks. Simulations are a large step toward re-creating reality, and they provide a more natural setting for observing behavior. Communication patterns, decision-making styles, and conflict resolution approaches provide rich data for assessment and feedback to the participants. Upon completion of the simulation, consultants can lead the group in analyzing what took place. Some issues are:

- What occurred, and why?
- Who talked to whom, and who was excluded?
- How did participants feel about their behavior in the simulation?
- What could they have done better?
- What did they learn that will help them in the future?

One difficulty with simulations is their cost, for they can be expensive to design and operate. Unless the facilitators are carefully trained, there is also a risk that participants will be criticized unless they made the "right" decisions. As with any laboratory method, not all participants are willing to experiment with new behaviors. Unless this happens, the potential learning for both themselves and their colleagues may be limited.

BEHAVIOR MODELING One effective form of laboratory training that builds upon the social learning processes of observation and imitation is *behavior modeling*. It is a method for teaching skills to handle commonly encountered behavioral problems.[10] For example, the method is used to help supervisors learn to motivate a poor performer, how to deal with a tardy employee, and how to give recognition to an outstanding performer. Behavior modeling relies on demonstration, explanation, practice, and feedback.

Here is how a typical program works. After a brief introduction, the trainees see a videotape of one or more successful ways to solve a work problem. A tape or film using professional actors may be used, but typically people in the company do the acting for the sake of greater realism. Trainees discuss why the solution was effective, and then they practice similar solutions in increasingly harder situations.

As trainees leave the class, they are asked to try the new approach before the next class. When they return for the next class, they discuss and even demonstrate their experiences with the new approach. Then a new tape with a different problem is shown and the training cycle is repeated.

Traditional training vs. modeling

As shown in Figure 13-3, the training model used for behavior modeling is entirely different from the traditional training model. For example, traditional lecture-and-discussion methods are used to teach new behavioral frameworks which are supposed to help change attitudes. In turn, the changed attitudes should lead to changed behavior and better results. The assumption is that attitude changes must precede behavioral changes.

FIGURE 13-3
Training models for traditional training and behavior modeling

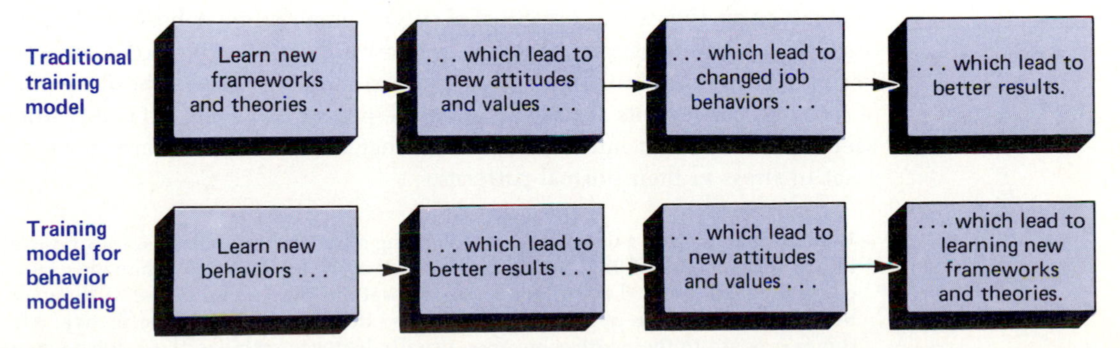
Traditional training model
Learn new frameworks and theories . . .
. . . which lead to new attitudes and values . . .
. . . which lead to changed job behaviors . . .
. . . which lead to better results.
Training model for behavior modeling
Learn new behaviors . . .
. . . which lead to better results . . .
. . . which lead to new attitudes and values . . .
. . . which lead to learning new frameworks and theories.

By way of contrast, behavior modeling teaches the behavior first. As the new behavior is observed, trainees see that it produces superior results. After the principles underlying the new behavior are explained, the trainees practice and receive feedback and reinforcement. With this preparation, they return to their jobs with the confidence to experiment. When the behavioral skills work on the job, the trainees fully accept the value of the approach and enthusiastically return for more training in new skills. In this case, behavior change occurs before a change in attitude.

Behavior modeling programs have proved to be successful in changing supervisory behaviors, although it is somewhat costly. Because it is practical and easy to understand, the participants usually like the approach. Behavior modeling has been used most frequently for training supervisors in areas such as handling employee complaints, conducting meetings, and coaching.[11]

Seventeen first-level supervisors in a wood products plant received behavior modeling training on topics such as handling absenteeism, safety violations, and inadequate performers.[12] Results showed that the employees in the plant perceived that their supervisors became more active listeners, engaged in more participative problem solving, and used positive reinforcement more extensively. Turnover and absenteeism rates declined significantly, and three measures of performance improved. Further, the behavior changes were sustained over the six-month follow-up period.

Definition

GAMING *Organizational gaming* essentially is a group exercise in sequential decision making under simulated organizational conditions. Although there are many variations, usually a number of participants work in small groups, each group in competition with the others. Groups make decisions within a system model that has been created for them and is at least partly unknown to them. Decisions then are processed through a computer according to the model, thus providing feedback that will guide subsequent decisions. Usually, time is compressed; that is, a quarter-year of operations may be covered in an afternoon training session.

A game can show how leadership evolves, what kinds of communication are effective, the disastrous market results of internal group conflict, human factors influencing decisions, and the effect of success upon group cohesion. Different organizational systems can be tried to see how each affects the people involved. Perhaps more realistically than other training methods, games show the effect of stress on participants as they undergo the pressure of time and competition. Members become so intensely involved that they let their guard down and react to stress in their normal patterns.

When managers play a decision game following other OD experiences, they typically fail to apply many of the behavioral ideas they have learned. When this fact is pointed out to them, they often overcompensate in the second phase of the game, becoming so conscious of interpersonal factors that they are again ineffective. After this is brought to their attention, they usually begin to stabilize their behavior and apply some of their newly learned ideas in the latter stages of the game.

ENCOUNTER GROUPS *Encounter groups* involve unstructured small-group interaction under stress in a situation that requires people to become sensitive to one another's feelings in order to develop reasonable group activity. The method was developed by the National Training Laboratories, a private group, to fill a need for better human relations. The training groups themselves often are called "T-groups." There are a number of variations, such as human potential training and sensitivity training.[13]

What happens in an encounter group?

Encounter groups are not role playing, because participants are acting their own true roles. They are themselves; however, their environment is so artificial that their ordinary social patterns prove to be no longer workable. For example, perhaps the group consultant provides virtually no leadership or has the group participate in structured exercises in order to break down social barriers and create an informal atmosphere. In this environment, the participants are encouraged to examine their own self-concepts and to become more receptive to what others say and feel. In addition, they begin to perceive how a group interacts, recognize how culture affects it, and develop skills in working with others. In summary, therefore, encounter groups seek to improve understanding of self, others, group process, culture, and general behavioral skills.

As an illustration of how encounter groups work, here are some of the events that developed in one unstructured group. Prior to the meeting, members were told to dress informally. When they arrived at the meeting room, they found no chairs, only pillows on the floor for them to sit on during their discussions. The consultant or "resource person," Mark Thomas, briefly told the group the basic purpose of the program and then backed off, providing virtually no leadership. In the leaderless vacuum, the members started arguing among themselves about what they should do and how they should do it. Rather quickly, differences developed between members with an autocratic, directive approach and those who were more open and permissive. From time to time the consultant raised questions about these difficulties. His purpose was to help the members understand how groups work and how to be more effective in them.

In the second session, the consultant handed out pieces of paper with names of songs on them. Each member was asked to hum the tune and form a subgroup by finding all the other members who were humming the same tune. This informal approach helped break down social barriers and get members further away from their official roles in their organizations.

Following are examples of problems that arose in the training group. One member was upset because his ideas were ignored by others. Another member took the initiative, became authoritarian, and inspired group resentment. Another's superior attitude was uncovered as defensiveness about her weaknesses. In all this turmoil the consultant tried to remain somewhat detached, keep some stability, create learning situations, and introduce ideas.

All encounter groups are not as unstructured as the one just described. In many groups the consultant plays a more active role, such as making surveys, giving feedback, and making assignments. However, it is evident that encounter groups can be challenging and even frustrating experiences for members. Advocates of encounter groups believe that these kinds of experiences are necessary for members to become involved personally and learn more about how groups work. The emphasis in this kind of training is predominantly on group process (that is, how groups work) and on learning from the group experience (experiential learning).

Criticisms

There have been a number of criticisms of encounter groups, especially when they treat people in harsh ways. Most criticisms are related to the following points.

- Some hard-hitting sessions are emotionally traumatic for participants, who are required to lay bare their emotions. Consequently, consultants must keep sessions in control so that they do not become overly stressful to sensitive participants.
- It is said that some sessions are an invasion of privacy when they require excessive exposure of one's inner emotions. Further, in most instances the exposure is not necessary for appropriate learning.
- Others claim that highly unstructured situations allow the consultants to force their own social viewpoints on groups. For example, the consultant may convince the group that consensus is necessary for its success when, in fact, consensus is not required.
- Other critics question whether encounter group training produces on-the-job improvements. Although it is difficult to prove results from this kind of training, often there is some improvement.

Most of the criticisms have been caused by poorly trained or overenthusiastic consultants, so problems can be overcome by well-trained professionals. They keep the training goals in mind and avoid unnecessary stress. Therefore, less stressful forms of encounter groups often are used in OD programs.

Examples of OD programs

The ideal OD program is one that is tailored to the needs of a single organization. In this way the consultant or change agent can develop mutually with top management a program to meet specific organizational needs. However, many OD consultants have built their programs around some type of basic framework for their ideas. Following are two programs of this type that are used extensively. Both are well accepted and have produced favorable results.

Six phases in grid OD

THE MANAGERIAL GRID Robert R. Blake and Jane S. Mouton developed the *managerial grid.*[14] The full program consists of six phases, although not every organization may proceed through all of them. Phase 1 is the presentation of a framework called the managerial grid, as shown in Figure 13-4. The grid is based on the management style dimensions of concern for people and concern for production, which essentially represent the dimensions of consideration and structure discussed in an earlier chapter. The grid clarifies how the two dimensions are related and establishes a uniform language and framework for

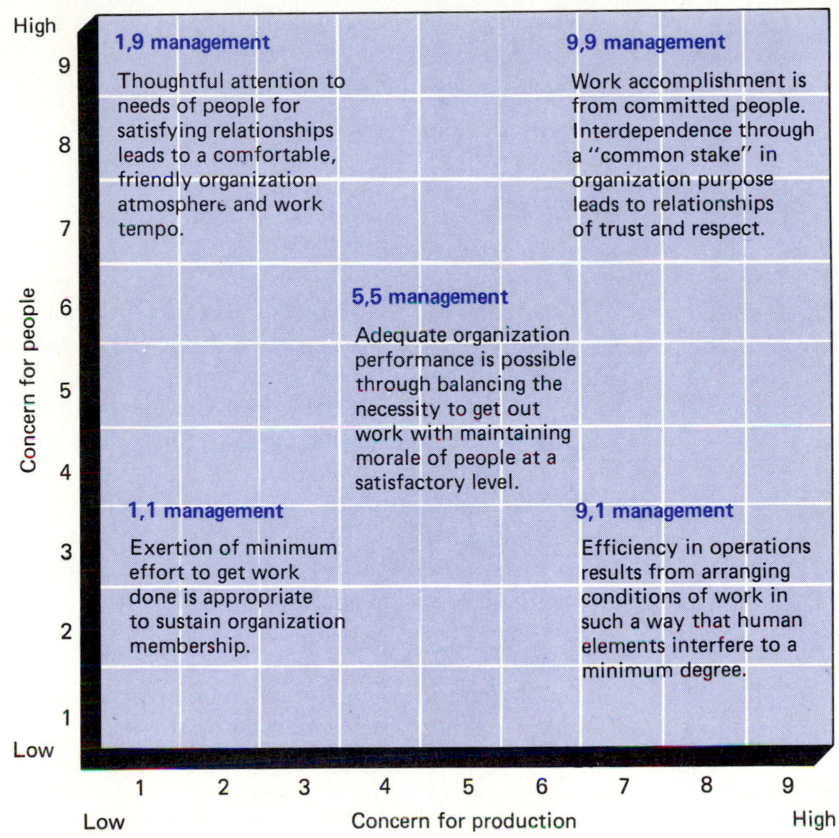
High
9
8
7
6
5
4
3
2
1
Low
Concern for people
1,9 management
Thoughtful attention to needs of people for satisfying relationships leads to a comfortable, friendly organization atmosphere and work tempo.
9,9 management
Work accomplishment is from committed people. Interdependence through a "common stake" in organization purpose leads to relationships of trust and respect.
5,5 management
Adequate organization performance is possible through balancing the necessity to get out work with maintaining morale of people at a satisfactory level.
1,1 management
Exertion of minimum effort to get work done is appropriate to sustain organization membership.
9,1 management
Efficiency in operations results from arranging conditions of work in such a way that human elements interfere to a minimum degree.
1 2 3 4 5 6 7 8 9
Low
Concern for production
High

FIGURE 13-4
The managerial grid
Source: *Robert R. Blake and Jane S. Mouton, "Managerial Facades,"* Advanced Management Journal, *July 1966, p. 31, copyright. Used with permission.*

communication about behavioral issues. The "1,9 managers" are high in concern for people but so low in concern for production that output is low. They are "country-club managers." The "9,1 managers" are overly concerned with production. They tend to be authoritarian bosses.

A more desirable balance of the two dimensions is from "5,5" to "9,9." Using the grid, the entire managerial job can be discussed, such as the "backup style" of managers. The backup style is the one managers tend to use when their normal style does not get results. It tends to be more autocratic and concerned with production.

Phase 2 of the program is concerned with team development, using the grid as a framework for discussion. Focus is upon a single team and the manager to whom it directly reports. Phase 3 is concerned with intergroup development to reduce conflict among groups. This phase tries to reduce win-lose power struggles among groups by showing how cooperation can lead to benefits for all parties. Phase 4 develops an ideal organizational model, phase 5 seeks to apply the model, and phase 6 provides evaluation of the program.

SYSTEMS 1 THROUGH 4 An OD framework using four systems of management was developed by Rensis Likert.[15] The systems are as follows:

- *System 1:* Exploitative-authoritative
- *System 2:* Benevolent-authoritative
- *System 3:* Consultative
- *System 4:* Participative

As shown in Figure 13-5, System 1 is the most autocratic and System 4 is the most participative. The object of the OD program is to move an organization as far as possible toward the participative system, which is considered the best one. The OD consultant in the Likert program administers a written climate survey to find out about the system now used in the organization. The consultant also surveys participants to determine their view of the ideal system that the organization should have.

The difference between the present system and the desired system represents a potential area of improvement for the OD program to seek. The complete System 4 remains an ultimate goal, but a firm should move toward it gradually. The Likert approach also is known as a survey feedback method because of its heavy use of feedback based on surveys.

Causal, intervening, and end-result variables

In order to analyze the present system and move toward a better one, the Likert program uses a model of an organization with three types of variables. They are causal, intervening, and end-result variables, as shown in Figure 13-6. The *causal variables* are the significant ones, because they affect both intervening and end-result variables. Causal variables are the ones that management should try to change; they include organizational structure, controls, policies, and leadership behavior. The *intervening variables* are those that

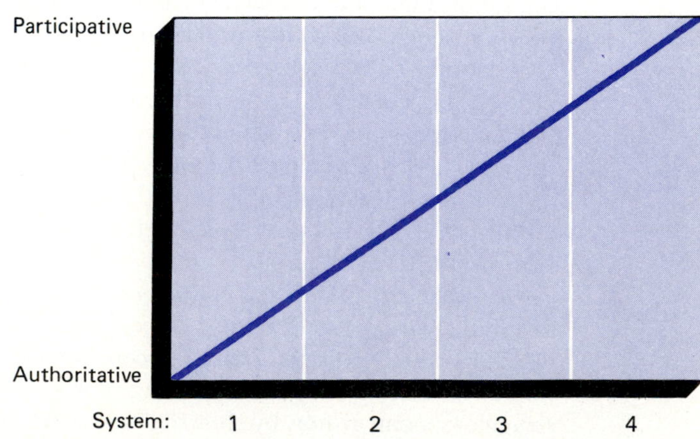

FIGURE 13-5
Systems 1 through 4 in relation to participation

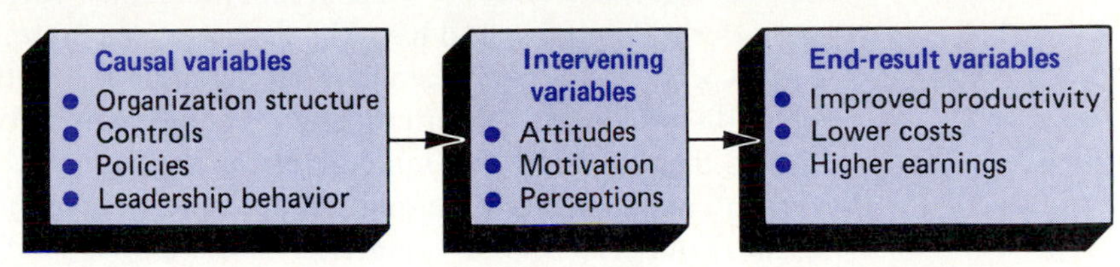

FIGURE 13-6
The Likert model of an organization

subsequently are affected by the causal variables. They include employee attitudes, motivation, and perceptions. Finally, the *end-result variables* represent the objectives sought by management. They usually include improved productivity, lower costs, and higher earnings. They represent the reason that the OD program was initiated.

One problem with the managerial grid and Systems 1 through 4 programs is that they both suggest that there is a preferred organizational style (such as 9,9 and System 4). This is inconsistent with the contingency approach to organizational behavior, which suggests that proper analysis is needed to identify which alternative best fits each problem. The grid and Systems 1 through 4 programs are useful, however, for emphasizing the diagnostic and participative action-planning stages of OD.

TEAMWORK

Task team

Individual employees perform operating tasks, but the vast majority of them work in small groups where their efforts must fit together like the pieces of a picture puzzle. When their work is interdependent, they act as a *task team* and seek to develop a cooperative state called teamwork. A task team is a cooperative small group in regular contact that is engaged in coordinated action. When the members know their objectives, contribute responsibly and enthusiastically to the task, and support each other, they are exhibiting *teamwork*. At least four ingredients contribute to the development of teamwork: a supportive environment, skills matched to role requirements, superordinate goals, and team rewards.

Ingredients of effective teams

SUPPORTIVE ENVIRONMENT Teamwork is most likely to develop when management builds a supportive environment for it. Supportive measures help the group take the necessary first steps toward teamwork. These steps contribute to further cooperation, trust, and compatibility, so supervisors need to develop an organizational culture that builds these conditions.

SKILLS AND ROLE CLARITY Team members must each be reasonably qualified to perform their jobs, and have the desire to cooperate.[16] Beyond this, they can only work together as a team after all the members of the group know the roles of all the others with whom they will be interacting. When this understanding exists, members can act immediately as a team based on the requirements of that situation, without waiting for someone to give an order. In other words, team members respond voluntarily to the demands of the job and take appropriate actions to accomplish team goals.

An example is a hospital surgical team whose members all respond to a crisis during an operation. Their mutual recognition of the emergency alerts them to the need for simultaneous action and coordinated response. Each knows what the others can do, and trusts them to perform capably. The result is a highly efficient level of cooperation characteristic of a team.

All members must contribute.

If one member of a surgical team fails to perform in the right way at the right time, a person's life may be endangered. In more ordinary work situations, a life may not be in danger but product quality or customer service may suffer by the failure of just one member. All the members are needed for effective teamwork, and this is illustrated with the example of the typewriter key in Figure 13-7. Just one malfunctioning key destroys the typewriter's effectiveness.

SUPERORDINATE GOALS A major responsibility of managers is to try to keep the team members oriented toward their overall task. Sometimes, unfortunately, an organization's policies, record-keeping requirements, and reward systems may fragment individual efforts and discourage teamwork. A district supervisor for a petroleum company tells the following story of the effect on sales representatives of below-quota reports:

As in many businesses, each month we are expected to make our sales quota. Sales representatives are expected to make quotas in their individual territories in the same way that the Eastern district as a whole is expected to make its quota. Many times in the past the district has failed to make its quota in certain products—for instance, motor oil. It is a known practice for some of the sales representatives in the field to delay a delivery in their territories until the next month if they already have their quotas made.

TEAMWORK

My supervisxr txld me that teamwxrk depends xn the perfxrmance xf every single persxn xn the team. I ignxred that idea until my supervisxr shxwed me hxw the xffice typewriter perfxrms when just xne single key is xut xf xrder. All the xther keys xn xur typewriter wxrk just fine except xne, but that xne destrxys the effectiveness xf the typewriter. Nxw I knxw that even thxugh I am xnly xne persxn, I am needed if the team is tx wxrk as a successful team shxuld.

FIGURE 13-7
An illustration of teamwork

The outlook of the sales representatives is not whether the district makes its quota, but their concern is their own. Any sales representative who is below quota in a product for a month must report the reason for this reduction. A sales representative who makes a large sale of several hundred gallons of motor oil to a customer knows that the next month or two that customer may not buy any oil, causing the representative to be below quota that month and to have to file a report.

This supervisor might consider the creation of a *superordinate goal,* which is a higher goal that integrates the efforts of two or more persons. Superordinate goals can *only* be attained if all parties carry their weight. They serve to focus attention, unify efforts, and stimulate more cohesive teams. For example, in a hospital meeting the leader said, "We are all here to help the patient. Can we think of today's problem in those terms?" When the superordinate goal was recognized, several minor internal conflicts were resolved.

TEAM REWARDS Another element that can stimulate teamwork is the presence of team rewards.[17] These may be financial, or they may be in the form of recognition. They are most powerful if they are valued by the team members and administered contingent on the group's task performance. Innovative team rewards for responsible behavior may include the authority to select new members of the group, make recommendations regarding a new supervisor, or propose discipline for team members.[18]

Potential team problems

Effective teams in action are a pleasure to observe. Members are committed to the firm's success, they share common values regarding product safety and customer satisfaction, and they share the responsibility for completing a project.

Being complex and dynamic, teamwork is sensitive to all aspects of organizational environment. Like the mighty oak, teamwork grows slowly, but on occasion it declines quickly, like that same oak crashing to the forest floor. For example, too many changes and personnel transfers interfere with group relationships and prevent the growth of teamwork.

An international company built a new plant in a community of about 1/2 million people where it already had three operating plants doing related work. The new plant was staffed for the most part by new hires, and within a short time excellent teamwork and productivity developed.

In about three years there was a moderate layoff affecting all four plants. Since layoff was according to seniority among the four plants and since employees in the new plant had least seniority, people from the other plants forced new-plant employees into layoff. As a result, most teams in the newest plant received three to five transferees from other plants (about 25 to 50 percent of the team). Though these transfers-in were more experienced and had good records, teamwork was disrupted and deteriorated quickly. Visits to first aid tripled, accidents increased slightly, and production declined 30 to 50 percent. Nearly one year of effort and emotional strain was required to get the plant back on its feet. (We wonder if management considered these potential costs when it decided on the layoffs.)

Other potential problems also exist. The departure from classical lines of authority may be difficult for some employees to handle responsibly. The extensive participation in decision making consumes large amounts of time. Experimentation with team activities may lead to charges of partiality from other employees. Also, the combination of individual efforts may not result in improved overall performance. For example, when employees think their contributions to a group cannot be measured, they may lessen their output. Reasons for this *social loafing* include a perception of unfair division of labor, a belief that coworkers are lazy, or a feeling of being lost in the crowd and therefore unable to receive adequate individual recognition.

Social loafing

Since an improperly managed team can result in numerous problems, an effective manager needs to apply a contingency framework to determine whether or not to use a team approach. It is wise to analyze the nature of the task, the qualifications and desires of the participants, and the time and cost constraints. Many managers have found managing teams to be a whole new set of challenges after years of one-on-one supervision.

Team building

Team members must work together to be effective, but also cooperation is needed among all the teams that make up the whole organization. OD attempts to integrate all these groups into one collaborative group. To do this, OD efforts often rely heavily on *team building* for both individual teams and large groups.[19] Team building encourages team members to examine how they work together, identify their problems, and develop more effective ways of cooperating. The goal is to make the team more effective. High-performance teams accomplish their tasks, learn how to solve problems, and enjoy satisfying interpersonal relationships with each other.[20]

The team-building process follows the same overall OD pattern shown previously in Figure 13-2. A change agent may assist the members in diagnosing a problem. Data are collected and then fed back for analysis and the creation of action plans. While working on the task, the attention of group members is often directed equally toward the group's process so that they will learn to monitor their own effectiveness. The result can be a skilled team with high morale and self-confidence.

A unique form of team building involves one of several varieties of "wilderness experiences."[21] In these courses, managers participate in week-long adventures such as mountain climbing, white-water rafting and kayaking, or outdoor obstacle courses. The physical challenge to survive is substantial, and many participants believe the experience prepares them for psychological survival in the corporate world.

Some programs have participants cross over raging rivers on wire cables, scale 13-foot-high walls, sleep on narrow mountain ledges, and cross (imaginary) snake pits on narrow boards and cinder blocks. Creativity and risk taking are encouraged, as are communication skills. Trust is essential, and groups recognize the importance of problem-solving skills. Team members learn to balance each others' strengths and weaknesses, and strong bonds of caring often emerge among members. A range of

organizations from small (Fel-Pro, Inc.) to large (Martin Marietta and Xerox) have used wilderness experience laboratories with satisfactory results.

Benefits and limitations of OD

OD is a useful organizational intervention. Its chief advantage is that it tries to deal with change in a whole organization or a major unit of it. In this manner it accomplishes more widely dispersed improvement. Other benefits include improved motivation, productivity, quality of work, job satisfaction, teamwork, and resolution of conflict. There also are reduced negative factors such as absences and turnover.[22] The benefits and limitations are summarized in Figure 13-8.

After an OD program in one organization, there were statistically significant improvements in trust, supportive environment, commitment to objectives, and other conditions of organizational climate. With regard to supervisory behavior, there was improvement in listening, handling of conflict, relations with others, willingness to change, and other activities. With regard to performance, there were changes in quality level and profit that were attributed to the OD program. Clearly the effect of the program was widespread in the organization.[23]

As with any complex program, OD has problems and limitations. It is time-consuming and expensive. Some benefits have a delayed payoff period, and an organization may not be able to wait that long for potential benefits. Even when a professionally capable consultant is used, it may fall flat. There are questions of invasion of privacy and psychological harm in some of its methods. There are charges that participants are sometimes coerced toward group attitudes and conformity. There are other charges that excessive emphasis is given to behavioral processes rather than to job performance. Group processes seem to be given priority over needs of the organization.

BENEFITS	LIMITATIONS
□ **Change throughout organization**	□ **Major time requirements**
□ **Greater motivation**	□ **Substantial expense**
□ **Increased productivity**	□ **Delayed payoff period**
□ **Better quality of work**	□ **Possible failure**
□ **Higher job satisfaction**	□ **Possible invasion of privacy**
□ **Improved teamwork**	□ **Possible psychological harm**
□ **Better resolution of conflict**	□ **Potential conformity**
□ **Commitment to objectives**	□ **Emphasis on group processes rather than performance**
□ **Increased willingness to change**	□ **Possible conceptual ambiguity**
□ **Reduced absences**	□ **Difficulty in evaluation**
□ **Lower turnover**	

FIGURE 13-8 Benefits and limitations of organization development

In spite of its problems and limitations, OD generally seems to be a useful and successful practice. It has contributed to improved results. It is most likely to succeed when it starts at the top of an organization, is based on extensive analysis, and is supported by the firm's reward system.

SUMMARY

Organization development is an intervention strategy that uses group processes to focus on the whole culture of an organization in order to bring about planned change. It emphasizes the whole organization as an operating system. The process covers such steps as diagnosis, data collection, feedback and confrontation, action planning, team building, intergroup development, and follow-up.

Organization development makes heavy use of laboratory training approaches, such as role playing, simulation, behavior modeling, gaming, and encounter groups. Typical programs are the managerial grid and Systems 1 through 4. Many OD efforts focus heavily on improved teamwork through the process of team building.

Although OD has limitations, it is an excellent practice for introducing change and self-renewal in organizations. It differs from traditional training methods by its focus on the entire system and its advocacy of humanistic values. OD programs typically use a change agent to assist with action research and feedback, and apply a variety of experiential learning methods within a contingency framework.

Terms and concepts for review

Organization development (OD)
Humanistic values
Change agents
Action research
Experiential learning
Interventions
Steps in the OD process
Laboratory training
Role playing
Simulations
Behavior modeling
Organizational gaming
Encounter groups
The managerial grid
Systems 1 through 4
Superordinate goals
Team building

Discussion questions

1 A manager suggested that "traditional training helps employees learn something, but OD helps them learn how to learn something." Discuss this distinction.
2 Summarize the different phases by which an OD program develops. How

does this differ from conducting attitude surveys, as presented in Chapter 8?

3 Explain how the reward structure on the job may not reinforce teamwork. Form groups of three to five people and discuss what actions management could take to improve reinforcement of teamwork on the job. Then report your results to your classroom group.

4 All adults have had experiential learning, whether it was in a classroom or not. Select a situation in which you had experiential learning, describe it, and then describe how it affected you. Why were you affected the way you were?

5 Explain how experiential learning differs from classroom lecture-and-discussion learning. Form groups of three to five students and discuss the strengths and weaknesses of both types of learning. Then report your results.

6 How do role playing, simulation, behavior modeling, organizational gaming, and encounter groups differ as training methods? Do they have similarities also?

7 Discuss both the strengths and weaknesses of encounter groups for training.

8 Discuss how behavior modeling is different from typical lecture-and-discussion training. Since they are so different, why might both still be used?

9 Review the managerial grid and Systems 1 to 4. From the information given, which OD characteristics are reflected in each program?

10 After reviewing Figure 13-8, identify three major benefits and three major limitations of OD. Do you think that the benefits outweigh the costs? Report your choices to the class, giving reasons for your selection.

GROUPS IN CONFLICT

One division of a firm consisted of four departments, with the supervisor of each reporting to the division general manager (GM). The four departments ranged considerably in size, from two employees in the smallest (A) to fourteen in the largest (D). The other two departments (B and C) each had eight employees.

Intense interdepartmental rivalry frequently arose over the allocation of resources. This problem was compounded by the favoritism that the GM allegedly showed toward units A and B and his reliance on majority-rule decision making at staff meetings. This, complained the supervisors of C and D, often resulted in the leaders of A and B forming a coalition with the GM to make a decision, even though they only represented ten of the thirty-two employees. In response, units C and D were charged with empire building, power plays, and a narrow view of the mission of the division.

Question

You are an OD consultant, called in by the GM to help resolve the problem. Outline the approach you would recommend taking.

Experiential exercise

THE ENCOUNTER GROUP

Assume that you have been given the opportunity to participate in an encounter group. Rate your willingness to join the group on a five-point scale (5 = very interested; 3 = neutral; 1 = strongly opposed). Have all class members share their responses, and count the numbers of 1s, 2s, 3s, 4s, and 5s. Now form mixed groups of advocates and opponents to participation in encounter groups, and discuss why you have those feelings. How would you convince people to attend when they are opposed to it? How would you defend your right not to attend when all others in your work group intend to participate?

References

1 Dov Eden, "OD and Self-Fulfilling Prophecy: Boosting Productivity by Raising Expectations," *The Journal of Applied Behavioral Science*, vol. 22, no. 1, 1986, p. 5.

2 Kenneth E. Hultman, "Behavior Modeling for Results," *Training and Development Journal*, December 1986, p. 60.

3 The basic concepts of OD are discussed in Wendell L. French and Cecil H. Bell, Jr., *Organization Development: Behavioral Science Interventions for Organization Improvement*, 3d ed., Englewood Cliffs, N.J.: Prentice-Hall, Inc., 1984.

4 Wendell L. French, "The Emergence and Early History of Organization Development: With Reference to Influences on and Interaction among Some of the Key Actors," *Group and Organization Studies*, September 1982, pp. 261–278.

5 Some of these changes, and how organizations have responded to them, are explained in John Naisbitt, *Megatrends: Ten New Directions Transforming Our Lives*, New York: Warner Books, 1982.

6 The need for change agents to have political sensitivity is addressed in Anthony T. Cobb, "Political Diagnosis: Applications in Organizational Development," *Academy of Management Review*, July 1986, pp. 482–496.

7 Debra D. Burrington, "Organization Development in the Utah Department of Public Safety," *Public Personnel Management*, Summer 1987, pp. 115–125.

8 A. M. Barrat, "Organizational Improvement in Mobil Oil," *Journal of Management Development*, vol. 1, no. 2, 1982, pp. 3–9.

9 See, for example, "Teaching Engineers How to Manage," *Management Review*, March 1987, pp. 10–12. A popular simulation exercise is "Looking Glass, Inc.," created by the Center for Creative Leadership, Greensboro, North Carolina.

10 Kenneth E. Hultman, "Behavior Modeling for Results," *Training and Development Journal*, December 1986, pp. 60–63; and Phillip J. Decker, "Social Learning Theory and Leadership," *Journal of Management Development*, vol. 5, no. 3, 1986, pp. 46–58.

11 A review of research is in Steven J. Mayer and James S. Russell, "Behavior Modeling Training in Organizations: Concerns and Conclusions," *Journal of Management*, Spring 1987, pp. 21–40; other research is in Charles C. Manz and Henry P. Sims, "Beyond Imitation: Complex Behavioral and Affective Linkages Resulting from Exposure to Leadership Training Models," *Journal of Applied Psychology*, November 1986, pp. 571–578.

12 Jerry I. Porras et al., "Modeling-Based Organizational Development: A Longitudinal Assessment," *Journal of Applied Behavioral Science*, vol. 18, no. 4, 1982, pp. 433–446.

13 For an overview of encounter groups, see Peter B. Smith, "The T-Group Approach," in Cary L. Cooper (ed.), *Improving Interpersonal Relations*, Englewood Cliffs, N.J.: Prentice-Hall, Inc., 1982, pp. 90–107.

14 The original program is described in Robert R. Blake and Jane S. Mouton, *The Managerial Grid*, Houston, Tex.: Gulf Publishing Company, 1964. A related OD program, in which four styles in a grid are judged as effective or ineffective, produces eight managerial style options; see William J. Reddin, *Managerial Effectiveness*, New York: McGraw-Hill Book Company, 1970.

15 Rensis Likert, *The Human Organization: Its Management and Value*, New York: McGraw-Hill Book Company, 1967; and Rensis Likert, *New Patterns of Management*, New York: McGraw-Hill Book Company, 1961.

16 An argument for the ingredients of ability, organizational support, and member effort is in John R. Schermerhorn, Jr., "Team Development for High Performance Management," *Training and Development Journal*, November 1986, pp. 38–41. The element of task interdependence as a prerequisite to effective groups is in Gregory P. Shea and Richard A. Guzzo, "Group Effectiveness: What Really Matters?" *Sloan Management Review*, Spring 1987, pp. 25–31.

17 A strong argument for honoring entrepreneurial teams instead of individuals is in Robert B. Reich, "Entrepreneurship Reconsidered: The Team as Hero," *Harvard Business Review*, May–June 1987, pp. 77–83.

18 Donald F. Barkman, "Team Discipline: Put Performance on the Line," *Personnel Journal*, March 1987, pp. 58–63; and John W. Newstrom, Mark Lengnick-Hall, and Steven Rubenfeld, "How Employees Can Choose Their Own Bosses," *Personnel Journal*, December 1987, pp. 121–126.

19 An illustration of team building in a start-up manufacturing operation is Patricia Galagan, "Work Teams That Work," *Training and Development Journal*, November 1986, pp. 33–35.

20 Discussions of the effects of team building are in Paul F. Buller, "The Team Building–Task Performance Relation: Some Conceptual and Methodological Refinements," *Group and Organization Studies*, September 1986, pp. 147–168; and Paul F. Buller and Cecil H. Bell, Jr., "Effects of Team Building and Goal Setting on Productivity: A Field Experiment," *Academy of Management Journal*, June 1986, pp. 305–328.

21 Examples are in Margery A. Neely and Emily B. Kling, "Effects of Leadership Training during Wilderness Camping," *Small Group Behavior*, May 1987, pp. 280–286; and Marilyn Wellemeyer, "Away from It All on a Granite Mountain," *Fortune*, Apr. 13, 1987, pp. 119–120. A critique is in John W. Newstrom, "'Mod' Management Development: Does It Deliver What It Promises?" *Journal of Management Development*, vol. 4, no. 1, 1985, pp. 3–11.

22 A study of the results of OD through the perceptions of OD practitioners is in Jerry I. Porras and Susan J. Hoffer, "Common Behavior Changes in Successful Organization Development Efforts," *The Journal of Applied Behavioral Science*, vol. 22, no. 4, 1986, pp. 477–494.

23 John R. Kimberly and Warren R. Nielsen, "Organizational Development and Change in Organizational Performance," *Administrative Science Quarterly*, June 1975, pp. 191–206.

For additional reading

Blake, Robert, Jane Mouton, and Robert Allen, *Spectacular Teamwork: What It Is, How to Recognize It, How to Bring It About*, Somerset, N.J.: John Wiley & Sons, Inc., 1987.

Golembiewski, Robert T., *Humanizing Public Organizations*, Mt. Airy, Md.: Lomond Publications, Inc., 1985.

Guest, R. H., *Work Teams and Team Building*, Elmsford, N.Y.: Pergamon Press, 1986.

Hardie, K. R., and R. G. Harrison, *Organization Development: An Annotated Bibliography for the Practitioner*, Greensboro, N.C.: Center for Creative Leadership, 1987.

Huse, Edgar F., and Thomas G. Cummings, *Organization Development and Change*, 3d ed., St. Paul, Minn.: West Publishing Company, 1985.

Kolb, David A., *Experiential Learning: Experience as the Source of Learning and Development*, Englewood Cliffs, N.J.: Prentice-Hall, Inc., 1984.

Margerison, Charles, and Dick McCann, *How to Lead a Winning Team*, Bradford, England: MCB University Press Limited, 1984.

PART 4

Organizational environment

CHAPTER 14

Structure, technology, and people

The essence of modern organization is to make individual strengths and knowledge productive and to make individual weaknesses irrelevant.

PETER F. DRUCKER[1]

The greatest barrier to success will be outmoded views of what an "organization" must look like and how it must be managed.

RAYMOND E. MILES AND CHARLES C. SNOW[2]

CHAPTER OBJECTIVES

To understand

Classical organization theory

Contingency organizational design

Matrix organization

Sociotechnical systems

Organizational effects of technology

Impact of work systems on people

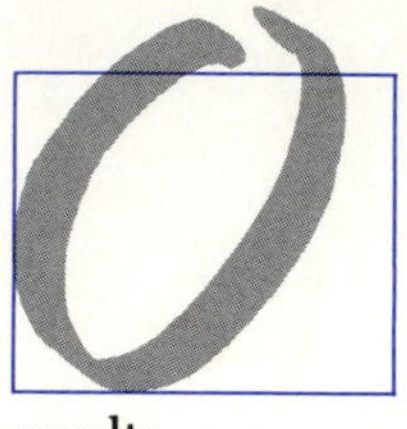

rganizations are the grand strategies created to bring order out of chaos when people work together. Organization creates predictable relationships among people, technology, jobs, and resources. Wherever people join in a common effort, organization must be employed to get productive results.

The necessity for organization—and the havoc of disorganization—are illustrated by disorganizing a short sentence: "riirggnagesnotztlsuse." In this form it is nonsense. Now let us reorganize it substantially: "organizinggetsresults." In this condition it is workable, but difficult. By the slight change of converting to a capital "O" and adding two spaces, it reads: "Organizing gets results." Yes, the organizing of people and things is essential for coordinated work.

Sociotechnical systems

In this chapter we discuss classical organization theory and contingency organizational design as they relate to organizational behavior. Then we examine the relationship of technology to people at work, which is known as *sociotechnical systems*.[3] The following chapter focuses on informal organization as a response to structure and technology, and Chapter 16 explores the current approaches to creating a high quality of work life.

CLASSICAL ORGANIZATION THEORY

Most organizations depend upon classical organization for building their structures because it deals with essential elements in an institution, such as division of labor, delegation, authority, specialization, and interdependence of parts. Modern developments are amending classical theory, but its essential elements remain and must be understood in order to work with people in organizations. Organizational structure is significant because it is a primary vehicle for translating the organization's strategy into productive action. It also partly determines the power of people in organizations, and affects their perceptions of their roles. In addition, it can have a strong impact on job satisfaction.

The organizing process may be viewed in two ways. It may be considered as a process of *construction* in which a great number of small work units are built into jobs, departments, divisions, and finally a whole institution. Or an organization may be viewed as a process of *analysis* by which a particular area of work is subdivided into divisions, departments, and finally jobs assigned to particular people. This latter approach is more appropriate when organizing a work group because one starts with the total amount of work to be done. Viewed in this way, organizing is achieved by means of division of work and delegation.

Division of work

The manner by which work is divided can be illustrated by considering that a small triangle represents the work that a department must do. There are sixteen people, including the department head, available to do the work. The department head organizes the work by dividing it into levels and functions and then assigning people and resources to the jobs that result. Division into levels, represented in Figure 14-1, is called the *scalar process* because it provides a scale, or grading, of duties according to levels of authority and responsibility. The scalar process is nearly universal and exists wherever there are two people in a supervisor-subordinate relationship.

Scalar process

Concurrently with division into levels, the work must be divided into different kinds of duties. This is *functionalization.* To use an illustration, the difference between an office supervisor and a machine shop supervisor is functional. Scalar and functional divisions are superimposed on each other to form a framework such as that shown in Figure 14-1. By a simple two-way division of duties, all the work to be done (as represented by the area of the triangle) is now assigned. Assuming that organizing is done perfectly, there are no unassigned areas, no overlaps of assignments, and no confusion about responsibilities.

Functionalization

Delegation

The relationships and duties determined by division of work are communicated and assigned to people by means of *delegation,* which is defined as the assignment of duties, authority, and responsibility to others. Each person who accepts the assignment then becomes a manager's "delegate" and is responsible for the assignment. If there is no acceptance, delegation has merely been attempted. Delegation permits managers to extend their influence beyond the limits of their own personal time, energy, and knowledge.

Some managers, however, delegate more often than others do. One study of claims adjusters and their supervisors in an insurance company indicated that several factors apparently contributed to a higher degree of delegation.[4] Among them were

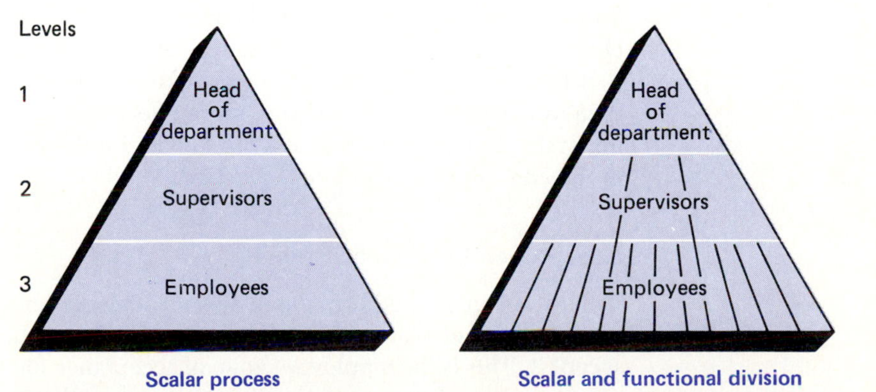

FIGURE 14-1
Division of labor by the scalar process and functionalization

supervisory perceptions of subordinates as capable and trustworthy and the presence of a heavy work load on the supervisor. Delegation of authority is also more likely when supervisors believe that employees hold the necessary background information to make a wise decision, and when the outcome of an employee's decision would create only minimal risk for the organization.

A cause of managerial failure

Poor delegation is a primary cause of managerial failure. Some managers feel that delegation is giving away something, so they cannot psychologically bring themselves to do it for fear it will weaken them. Others are such perfectionists that they have no confidence in letting others do the work for which they are responsible. However, all need to realize that *delegation is the act that initiates management*. If there is no delegation to others, there is no one to be managed. As a matter of fact, more delegation often is the effective remedy for a problem.

In one company, an executive was worried by the fact that Marge Lindberg, a purchasing specialist, could make costly mistakes if she were given more authority. Closer examination revealed that the costliest error she could make would involve only $100,000, but that it cost $142,000 annually in executive time, forms to fill out, and other precautions to ensure against her error. There were further possible losses as a result of delayed purchasing decisions. Was the possible loss from independent decision making great enough to require the certain costs and delays of the checkup procedure? Finally, the executive decided to delegate more authority to Marge.

Linking pins

When the scalar process, functionalization, and delegation are performed correctly, the result is an intricate web of relationships that links people together into a working organization. Each level has functional teams that are linked to the next level through the scalar process. This is known as the *linking pin concept*, as shown in Figure 14-2. Each manager serves as a linking pin connecting that manager's group with the remainder of the organization. If all linking pin connections are effective, then the organization can operate as an integrated whole. On the other hand, if there is a weakness anywhere in the chain of linking pins, the organization tends to be less effective.

Managers are links between groups.

When managers see themselves as linking pins uniting the whole team rather than as bosses, they can function more effectively. Similarly, when employees understand a manager's role as a linking pin for the whole team, they can relate to it better and become more effective.

Acceptance theory of authority

Delegation gives authority to a lower manager; however, the power of a manager to use that authority depends on the willingness of employees to accept it. This is the employee "zone of acceptance for authority" and results in an *acceptance theory of authority*. Although authority gives people power to act officially within the scope of their delegation, this power becomes somewhat

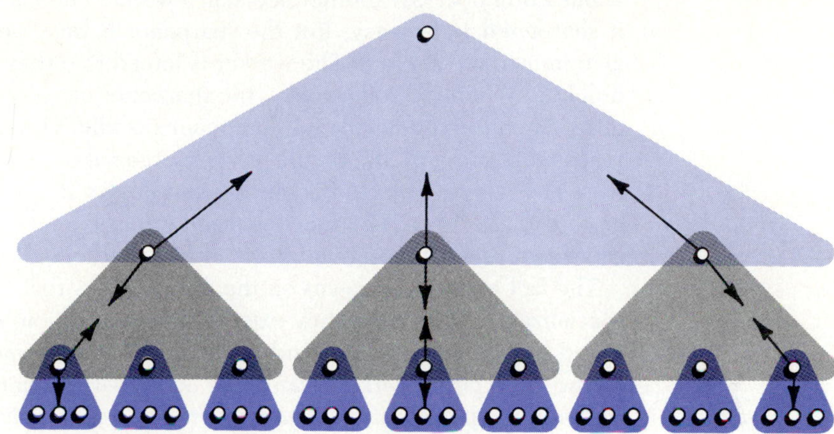
(The arrows indicate the linking pin function)

FIGURE 14-2
Likert's linking pin concept
From New Patterns of Management *by Rensis Likert, p. 113. Copyright © 1961 by McGraw-Hill Book Company. Used with permission of McGraw-Hill Book Company.*

meaningless unless those affected accept it and respond to it. In most cases when delegation is made, a subordinate is left free to choose a response within a certain range of behavior. But even when an employee is told to perform one certain act, the employee still has the choice of doing it or not doing it and taking the consequences. It is, therefore, the subordinate who controls the response to authority. Managers cannot afford to overlook this human fact when they use authority.

Specialization

Functionalization leads to specialization. A farm situation illustrates how this occurs. If fifty workers are hoeing corn, each doing the same work, the only division of labor is that the work has been broken into human units for each person to perform. If the work is reorganized and forty-nine workers hoe while the fiftieth sharpens the hoes and keeps the water jug filled, division of labor *of a different kind* has taken place. This is functionalization. In the course of time, the fiftieth worker will become more adept at sharpening hoes than the forty-nine are, and they will be more productive at hoeing than the sharpener is. This is because each is *specializing* as a natural result of functionalization.

Benefits of specialization

Specialization brings great benefits to a work group. Modern industrial society could not exist without it, because it permits people to develop unique skills and knowledge that will produce more of society's wants. It is one of the really fundamental ideas of civilization.

Like other benefits to society, specialization brings disadvantages that must be weighed against all its benefits. Let us return to our fifty fieldworkers to illustrate some of these disadvantages. The one worker who is sharpening hoes may not sharpen them to please one of the forty-nine, who always complains about a dull hoe. On another occasion a worker chips a hoe on a rock and wants it sharpened right away, but the sharpener is busy getting water and cannot give immediate service. The worker is forced to either wait or continue with a dull hoe. When the soil is rocky, the sharpener has too much to do, and hoes go dull. When the soil is soft, the sharpener sits idle. One day when the sharpener is absent because of illness, the workers argue about who will sharpen hoes that day. The worker selected is clumsy and delays the work. And so the trouble goes, day after day. The functionalized group is more complex and difficult to coordinate than the original group of fifty workers all doing the same work.

The fact eventually dawns on the fifty workers that the productivity gains of specialization (assuming they exist in this illustration) can be achieved only if sound human relationships and coordination can be maintained. This problem of the fifty farm workers can now be translated into a general statement applying to specialization: *The benefits of specialization are largely economic and technical, but its disadvantages are primarily human.* This means that more specialization usually leads to more human problems also. For example, conflicts between groups tend to develop, and some employees become bored with their specialized jobs. However, specialization is a key part of advanced social systems. Whatever problems it causes must be weighed against its vast benefits. The world needs the skills of physicians, teachers, counselors, and the thousands of other occupations that specialization provides.

Human costs of specialization

The span of management

A basic idea of classical organization is the *span of management* (or span of control), which refers to the number of people a manager directly manages. Many factors determine the number of employees that one person can manage effectively. Some of these are capacity and skill of the manager, complexity of the work supervised, capacity and skill of the employees managed, stability of operations, contacts with other chains of command, contacts outside the organization, and geographic distance of subordinates.

Tall and flat structures

A small span in an organization causes a *tall structure* and a large span causes a *flat structure*, as shown in Figure 14-3. Each structure has its advantages and limitations. In the tall structure, closer coordination and control are permitted because each manager works with fewer people, so there tends to be less role conflict and ambiguity. However, communication lines are longer, providing more opportunities for misinterpretation and editing.

Effects of flat structures

The flat structure has a shorter, simpler communication chain. In this structure managers have so many people to supervise that they cannot spend much time with any one member of their group. This can be frustrating for employees who value direct contact with their supervisor. It also can lead to errors by new employees who require training and closer supervision. The pressure for lowering costs during the past decade has led many firms to reduce the number of managers, effectively increasing the span of management for those remain-

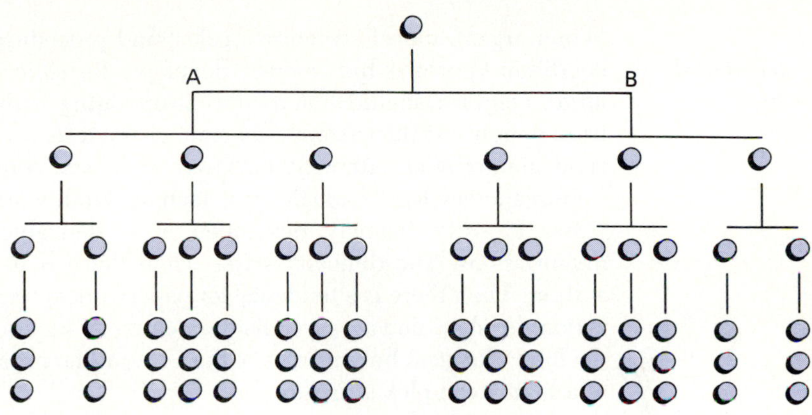

Tall organization
(Maximum span of management: 3. Four levels of management.)

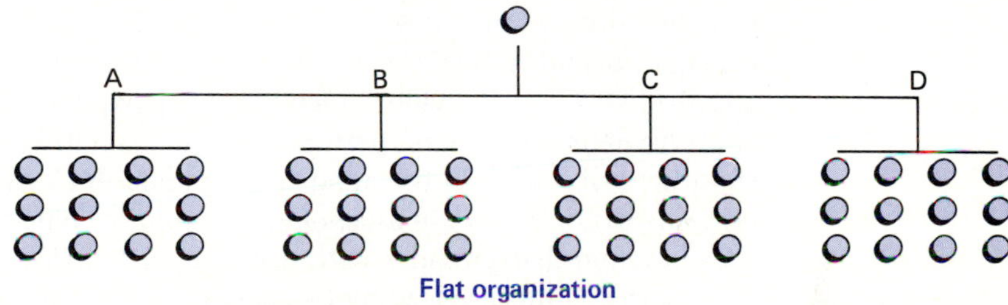

Flat organization
(Maximum span of management: 12. Two levels of management.)

FIGURE 14-3
Tall and flat organizational structures caused by different spans of management for forty-eight employees

ing.[5] However, the span grew so wide in one firm that managers often waited for two hours outside the president's office to get a brief chance to confer over decisions to be made!

The 3M Company uses a unique method to uncover problems with its spans of management.[6] Based on general norms for its managers' spans, the firm examines the number of levels of management in a unit, the ratio of managers to workers, and the proportion of time that each supervisor actually spends managing. The system helps to identify the overstretched and understretched managers. Then a consultant helps the group create a new structure that will more efficiently contribute to achievement of its goals.

Employees in a tall organization tend to feel removed from the managers in power. Further, since their manager is free to spend considerable time supervising them, they tend to desire more operating freedom. Since a flat structure is more free of frequent supervision, employees tend to prefer it. They like the autonomy they have, and feel less stress from their job environment.

Bureaucracy

Characteristics of bureaucracy

When organizational structures, rules, and procedures are rigidly followed, a condition known as bureaucracy develops. *Bureaucracy* is characterized by a large, complex administrative system operating with impersonal detachment from people. At the extreme, its main characteristics are high specialization, a rigid hierarchy of authority, elaborate rules and controls, and impersonality.

Bureaucracy has its advantages, such as stability and unified focus on objectives. It was originally developed as a desirable way to manage large organizations. The difficulty arises when there is too rigid adherence to the system. Then there is a tendency for paperwork systems to expand, managerial action to slow down, psychological costs to increase, and effectiveness to decline. The giant bureaucracy of the U.S. military system provides an example of a highly complex structure.[7]

Interpreting classical organization theory

Classical organization theory has its strengths as well as its weaknesses. For example, organizational structure can support people as well as suppress them. Classical structure provides much task support, such as specialized assistance, appropriate resources to perform the job, security, and fairly dependable conditions of work. On the other hand, although classical structure is strong in task support, *it is weak in psychological support*. What is needed is an organizational system that provides both task support and psychological support.

Decline in use of structure

New viewpoints are leading to a decline in the use of structure and authority in modern organizations. The modern approach is to be more flexible with organizational systems, changing them according to a contingency relationship with their environment. One reason is changing social values, but it also is evident that horizontal relations between chains of command are more important for effectiveness than was formerly realized. Supervisory influence with peers, service people, and other chains of command is becoming more significant. The pace and complexity of work today make horizontal communication more necessary.

CONTINGENCY ORGANIZATIONAL DESIGN

As discussed in the preceding paragraph, the trend is toward more *contingency organizational design*. This recognizes that different organizational structures and processes are required for effectiveness in alternative situations. Some major forces affecting the choice of structure are the organization's strategy, its technology, its size, and even the preferences of its top managers.[8] Environments differ also, and what is an appropriate organizational design in one environment may not be appropriate in another. Since environments change over time (sometimes rapidly), there is a special need for organizational designs to be *flexible* so that they can be changed to keep a best fit with the changing environment.

The contingency point of view requires a fundamental change in philosophy from the traditional view that there are preferred ways of organizing that could remain relatively fixed over time. The next section will highlight these differences by contrasting two extreme organizational patterns. Two major research studies that identify different technologies and alternative environments will be summarized. Then a flexible approach to organizing—the matrix structure—will be reviewed.

Mechanistic and organic patterns of organizing

Mechanistic characteristics

Some of the earliest research on contingency design was by Burns and Stalker in Britain.[9] They distinguished between *mechanistic* and *organic* organizations. The mechanistic form fits the traditional hierarchical way of organizing. People are specialized into many activities that are supervised by layers of supervision. Each higher level has more power and influence until the top is reached, where central direction of the whole organization takes place. Work is carefully scheduled, tasks are certain, roles are defined strictly, and most formal communication flows along the lines of hierarchy. The whole structure is organized like a well-designed machine.

Organic characteristics

Organic organizations are more flexible and open. Tasks and roles are less rigidly defined, allowing people to adjust them to situational requirements. Communication is more multidirectional. It consists more of information and advice rather than instructions and decisions. Authority and influence flow more directly from the person who has the ability to handle the problem at hand. Decision making is more decentralized, being shared by several levels and different functions. The organization also is more open to its environment.

Burns and Stalker showed that mechanistic forms are more effective than organic forms in certain situations. If tasks are stable and well defined, changing very little from month to month and year to year, a mechanistic form tends to be superior. If changes in the technology, market, and other parts of the environment are minimal, then a mechanistic structure seems to be more effective. Worker attitudes also are a contingency factor. If workers prefer more routine tasks and direction from others, then a mechanistic form better meets their needs. If they are threatened by ambiguity and insecurity, then a mechanistic approach is better.

Organic forms are more effective in other situations, and these situations tend to be more typical in modern society. Organic forms work better if the environment is dynamic, requiring frequent changes within the organization. They also work better when the tasks are not well enough defined to become routine. If employees seek autonomy, openness, variety, change, and opportunities to try new approaches, then an organic form is better.

The contingency approach to organizing may even be applied within the same organization, where various departments may be organized differently to meet their needs. The research department may have an organic structure, and the production department may require a mechanistic structure.

Types of production technology

Research by Woodward with 100 firms in Britain shows that the most effective form of organization tends to vary with types of production technology.[10] Woodward classified firms into three types of technology, listed in increasing order of complexity:

- *Unit and small-batch production.* Produces one or a small number of a product, such as a locomotive, usually on the basis of an order
- *Mass and large-batch production.* Produces a large number of a product in an assembly-type operation
- *Process production.* Produces in a continuous flow, such as an oil refinery or a nylon plant

Technology—a contingency factor

Woodward found that the most successful firms in each class of technology tended to group around a certain type of structure, while the less successful firms varied from the structure. As shown in Figure 14-4*a*, the mass-production firms were more successful with mechanistic structures, while unit and process firms were more successful with organic structures. In essence, *the most appropriate type of organization was contingent on the firm's type of technology.* In relation to the amount of structure the relationship was curvilinear, with high structure required for the middle level of technology (mass production) and low structure required for either extreme of technology.

Span of management and technology

Woodward's research also showed a curvilinear relationship between the supervisor's span of management and technology (see Figure 14-4*b*). In three types of production technology the average span of management varied as follows:

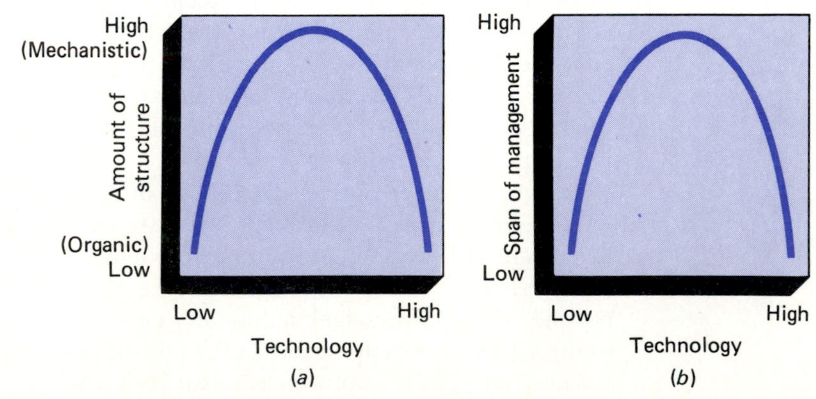

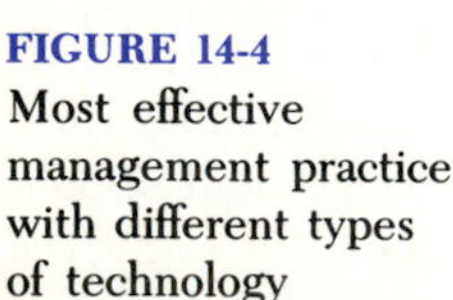
FIGURE 14-4
Most effective management practice with different types of technology

- **Unit or small-batch production** **23 people**
- **Mass production and assembly line** **49 people**
- **Process and continuous production** **13 people**

The differences are substantial. The mass-production technology used a span more than three times as large as process production. These data further support the contingency approach to organizing.

Stable and changing environments

Lawrence and Lorsch in the United States studied industrial organizations, grouping them by amount of market and technological change.[11] Their work expanded and supported Burns and Stalker. They found that organizations in the more changing environments required increasing differentiation in their structure. That is, they required many different sections, departments, occupational roles, and specialized patterns of thinking. These different parts enabled the firms to gain a variety of inputs that would allow them to react effectively to their uncertain environments. *Because of differentiation, greater efforts toward integration were required.* There was much coordination at lower levels, horizontal communication, interdisciplinary teams, and emphasis on flexibility. This system was similar to Burns and Stalker's concept of the organic organization. The firms with organic systems tended to function more successfully in changing environments.

Differentiation and integration

Firms in more stable, certain environments required less differentiation. Standard rules and procedures provided sufficient integration in their stable environment, so they tended to be more hierarchical and centralized. The open systems and horizontal communication that were needed in the changing firms were not so necessary in the stable firms. Consequently, firms with mechanistic systems tended to be more successful in stable environments.

Matrix organization

Another development to meet changing organizational needs is *matrix organization.* It is an overlay of one type of organization on another so that there are two chains of command directing individual employees. It is used especially for large, specialized projects that temporarily require large numbers of technical people with different skills.

A simple example of matrix organization is an annual United Way fund drive for contributions to community charities. It could be handled through the traditional hierarchy, but often it is assigned to a temporary hierarchy of employees as a part-time duty. They carry the assignment to completion and are then disbanded.

The effect of matrix structure is to separate some of the organization's activities into projects that then compete for allocations of people and resources. The traditional hierarchy provides the regular work group for an employee, but project groups are established temporarily for up to several

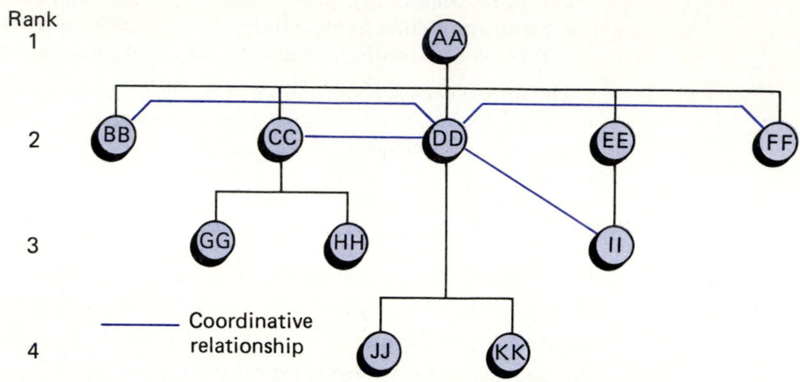

Matrix organization structure for Project Roger

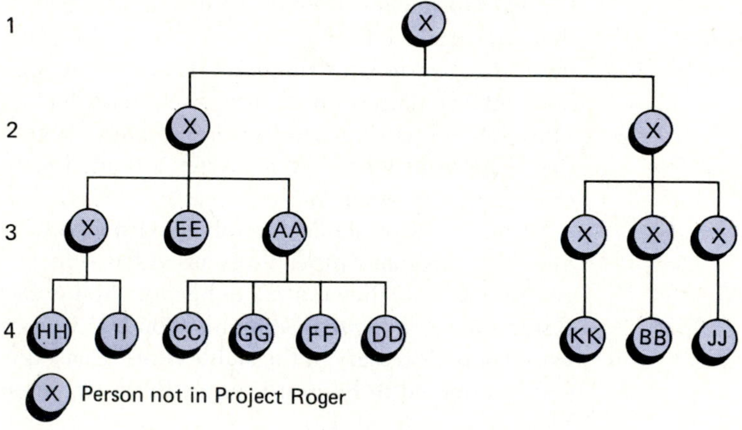

Permanent organizational assignment of employees in Project Roger

FIGURE 14-5
A comparison of the matrix structure and the permanent organizational assignment for employees in Project Roger

years. Employees are assigned to a project for its limited life or as long as their specialty is needed on the project. As one assignment is completed, employees move back to permanent assignments in traditional departments, or they are assigned to other projects. In fact, an employee can be assigned part time to two or more projects at the same time.

Figure 14-5 portrays relationships of employees in Project Roger, a project in an electronics firm. It shows how ranks, peer relations, and supervisor-subordinate relationships vary between the permanent organizational structure and the matrix structure. With regard to rank, employee DD is permanently attached to the fourth level, but she has a key second-level rank in the matrix structure. With regard to peer relations, GG and HH work in separate departments in the permanent organization, but they work together in the matrix organization. Concerning supervisor-

subordinate relationships, GG works for AA in the regular structure, but in the matrix structure he works for CC, who is his peer in the regular structure. In essence, matrix structure overlays one or more project structures simultaneously on the permanent organization.

THE PROJECT MANAGER In matrix organization a project manager is established to direct all work toward completion of a major project, such as development of a new computer system. The project manager especially needs to have role adaptability to interact with people both within and without the structure. Project managers occupy *boundary roles* that require an ability to interact with a variety of groups in order to keep their project successful. Each group has its own special language, values, and style of relationships, so project managers need to be sensitive and flexible in order to secure project needs from other groups. Project managers often have relatively weak authority, so their mission is best accomplished by communication, developing challenging assignments, negotiation, and contributing through their own expertise.

Boundary roles

EFFECTS OF MATRIX ORGANIZATION Matrix organization represents a dramatic change from simple organization structures, and its impact can vary from highly positive to negative. When first implemented, matrix structure can be confusing to its members. It requires multiple roles for people, and sometimes they get frustrated in these ambiguous roles. Insecurities may arise over what will happen to them when the project is completed. The authority of the functional (line) manager who "loses" some staff temporarily may be diminished, while the problems of maintaining coordination and control increase. In addition, a condition called "projectitis" may arise, in which the commitment to the project team is so strong that unhealthy competition and rivalries appear. Some problems of the matrix form can be seen in the following illustration:

The engineering division of an aircraft manufacturing firm was organized functionally, with separate groups for design, drafting, and testing.[12] A reorganization created a matrix structure, with project managers responsible for integrating the work on each of the development projects in progress. Measures of attitudes and behaviors were administered at various times, and compared with a control group of employees in another location.

The most substantial effects occurred in the drafting group, where the physical relocation and work-group restructuring were greatest. Although the quantity of communications increased, the quality declined. Role ambiguity increased, and both coordination and job satisfaction decreased. Surprisingly, employees did not report significant levels of role conflict.

In spite of its complexity, matrix organization is used for a number of reasons. It focuses resources on a single project, permitting better planning and control to meet budgets and deadlines. Especially on repetitive projects, the members gain valuable experience and the team develops a strong identity. The structure is more open and flexible than a traditional hierarchy, so it can better handle the changes that occur in complex projects. Its distribution of authority and status also is more in agreement with democratic norms of technical employees. For example, more emphasis is given to authority of knowledge that a specialist can contribute to a project and less emphasis is given to rank in the permanent hierarchy. The matrix organization may improve motivation because people can focus more directly on completion of one project than they can in the traditional organization. It also improves communication by encouraging direct contact and reducing the inhibitions that result from formal rank.

CONTINGENCY FACTORS Although matrix organization has limited application, where it does apply it is psychologically more advanced than traditional work hierarchies. Its use is contingent upon conditions such as the following:[13]

- Special projects, particularly major ones
- Need for diverse occupational skills, particularly higher-level ones
- Conditions of change during project operation
- Complex issues of coordination, problem solving, and scheduling
- High needs for authority of knowledge and expertise compared with existing functional authority

TECHNOLOGICAL CHANGE

Features of technology

Four general features

In addition to the recent evolution of new forms of organization, technology is adding another powerful force in the work environment.[14] Technology has certain general features, such as specialization, integration, discontinuity, and change.

As technology increases, specialization also tends to increase. As work gets broken into smaller parts, integration is required to put them back together again to make a whole product, a whole organization, and a whole society. This integration is much more difficult in a high-technology society than in a low-technology one, because high technology tends to make a system more complex and make its parts more interdependent.

The flow of technology is not a continuous stream but rather a series of bursts of new developments. As a consequence, the price that technology requires for the progress it brings is that people must adapt to unexpected changes. The technological revolution produces, perhaps with a time lag, an associated social revolution. Technology is moving so fast that it is creating social problems long before society is able to develop solutions. At the workplace new forms of organization, new ways of supervision, new reward structures, and a host of other changes are being required in order to absorb technology. For adjustment to technology what is needed is more mobility—economic as well as social, occupational as well as geographic, managerial as well as employee.

Technology and occupations

More white-collar jobs

As technology changes, jobs also change. Technology tends to require more professional, scientific, and other white-collar workers to keep the system operating. In most advanced installations the ratio of white-collar to blue-collar employees has increased. Since people by nature are not efficient machines, it seems appropriate to replace routine jobs with automated systems that can do the job faster and better, thus releasing people to do more advanced work, which usually is white-collar work. Technology generally upgrades the skill and intellectual requirements of the total work force.

How do robots compare with people?

ROBOTICS One product of technological change and the computer revolution is *robotics*, or the design and use of programmable mechanical devices to move parts and perform a variety of tasks. Industrial robots (or "steel-collar" workers) are expensive to create and still in their infancy with regard to their vision, sense of touch, and so forth. Compared with humans, however, they can work longer hours, work more shifts, survive in harsh environments, and apply great strength.

The total number of industrial robots in use is relatively small (about 100,000). Although the number of robots introduced into the workplace will grow over the next few decades, the actual number of workers displaced will not be large. This is especially true since many firms have created retraining programs that help displaced workers learn new skills and remain with their employer. A number of retrained workers are actually relieved from the drudgery of repetitive tasks by robots, and can move on to more challenging jobs.

In addition to knowing the expected impact of introducing robots, managers need to be concerned about the perceptions of employees. These are important to monitor both before and after robots begin performing their new roles. The available research evidence on employee perceptions and reactions is mixed, as these studies show.

One investigation divided employees into those with low-skill and high-skill jobs.[15] Predictably, low-skill workers reacted negatively to the introduction of robots, fearing a threat to their job security. High-skill workers were more positive, viewing robots as providing opportunities for expanding their skills. In another survey of robotics users, only 2 percent reported that negative employee reactions followed the introduction of robots, while 59 percent reported that their employees had positive reactions.[16]

Employee responses to the use of robots on the job can be expected to vary greatly, depending on a number of factors. Certainly if an individual is laid off as a direct result, that employee will likely be unhappy. If employees are transferred to other jobs within the firm, their reactions will largely be a product of their perceptions of their new jobs—are they better or worse than they were before? An understanding of employee perceptions of their former jobs would also be helpful, since they may have had an easy, slow-paced set of tasks in a clean environment or high-pressure, rapidly paced job requirements in a disagreeable work setting.

Managers need to help employees understand and accept the presence of robots by communicating clearly about the organization's intentions. In addition to paying attention to what jobs the displaced workers are coming from and going to, managers also need to be alert to the *process* by which robots are introduced. Discussions need to be held, and apprehensions listened to and accepted. Plans should be shared with the union so that it will not be caught by surprise. Employee involvement in planning and implementing the move to robots is also a useful process for reducing resistance to change.

Technology and education

More education necessary

The modern need for higher skills means that a premium is put upon education in the labor market. More education and training become necessary in order to avoid a surplus of underdeveloped people and a shortage of highly developed people.

MULTIPROFESSIONAL EMPLOYEES The need for an educated work force with high-level skills has increased the demand for *multiprofessional employees.* These are people trained in two or more professions or intellectual disciplines, such as engineering and law or accounting and science. Since these people are competent in more than one discipline, they are able to perform some of the integrative work required by modern work systems. The demand is especially high for multiprofessional managers who are qualified in some technical specialty in addition to management so that they can more easily manage technical work.

An example of a multiprofessional employee is Paula. After receiving her degree in computer science, she worked for a government agency for several years. Returning to college, she chose to pursue a master's degree in business administration rather than specializing further in computers. As a result, she obtained a supervisory position and directed the work of several other programmers.

A KNOWLEDGE SOCIETY The steady advancement of technology has led to the development of a knowledge society in the United States. A *knowledge society* is one in which the use of knowledge and information dominates work and employs the largest proportion of the labor force.[17] The distinguishing feature of a knowledge society is that it emphasizes intellectual work more than manual work—the mind more than the hands. Examples of knowledge jobs are those of news editors, accountants, computer programmers, and teachers. Even the surgeon, who must use a delicate manual skill, is primarily working from a knowledge or intellectual base.

More intellectual work

Intellectual work requires a different quality of motivation than manual work. Normally a person can be persuaded by the use of authority to dig a ditch. The threat of penalty usually is enough to get results. However, it takes more sophisticated motivation to lead a person to do research or write creative advertising copy. Intellectual work requires internal motivation and a more positive motivational environment. If employers of knowledge workers fail to provide this type of environment, their employees will work less effectively.

Technology and labor

Luddites and technophobia

In eighteenth-century England, a band of workers known as Luddites challenged the industrial revolution by roaming the countryside, smashing machinery and burning factories along the way. They believed that machinery threatened jobs. Employees in the twentieth century have faced technology with more maturity but nevertheless with considerable anxiety. Some workers, like the Luddites, view technology with a *technophobia,* that is, an emotional fear of all technology regardless of its consequences.

Workers who think that technology will abolish the exact jobs they now have probably are correct. With technology moving as fast as it is, few jobs will remain static during an employee's working life. Technology does not destroy jobs for all time, but it does create different jobs that workers often are not prepared to fill.[18] Therefore, it produces employee insecurity, stress, anxiety, and possible layoff, which management needs to handle most carefully in introducing technology.

RETRAINING New technology may force a firm to lay off employees who have satisfactory work records but outdated skills. A social alternative is to create *retraining* programs for them, where selected employees are provided opportunities to learn new skills, followed by guaranteed jobs within the company. Even when management is able to offer complete job and wage security, workers still make sacrifices of their time and energy for retraining. Certainly they expect to make some sacrifices to advance productivity for their society, but this situation also obligates management to be sensitive to employee needs so that the changeover will be as smooth as possible.

The transitions associated with retraining are not always easy. A laid-off steelworker from West Virginia named Frank LaRosa later became a computer programmer, but the financial and psychological costs were great.[19] Frank had to borrow several thousand dollars for his training, accept a one-third cut in pay, work under constant deadlines, accept management's values, and live without the satisfaction of making a basic product like steel. Despite these pressures, he is happy to have "a job with a future."

THE UNION VIEW In spite of employee difficulties with technology, many union leaders have recognized that it is essential for long-run employee gains and have voiced their support. For example, when the head of one union was asked whether technology destroys jobs, he responded, "The real issue is whether the *lack* of technological change destroys even more jobs."[20] In practice, some union leaders have opposed it as being too sudden, too broad in coverage, or inappropriate to the circumstances. They also have bargained heavily for retraining rights, severance pay, and other benefits that soften dislocations caused by technology. Approaches differ among unions because technology affects their members differently and because unions have different philosophies.

WORK SYSTEMS AND PEOPLE

Structure and procedures

There are two basic ways in which work is organized. The first relates to the flow of authority and is known as *organizational structure* or merely organization, as discussed earlier. The second relates to the flow of work itself from one operation to another and is known as *procedure*. Other names are "method," "system," and "work flow." People usually recognize the human side of organizational structure because of the superior-subordinate relationship that it establishes, but more often than not they ignore or overlook the human side of work flow. They see work flow as an *engineering* factor that is separate from *human* factors. In the usual case, however, work flow has many behavioral effects because it sets people in interaction as they perform their work.

Initiation of action

One important point about a work system is that it determines who will "initiate" an activity and who will "receive" it. At each step in the flow of work one person sends material to the next person who will work on it. Along the way, staff experts give instructions. This process of sending work and/or instructions to another is an *initiation of action* on another person. Receivers of an initiation often feel psychologically inferior, because they may receive it from someone who "just shouldn't be pushing them around." In one plant, for example, operator B was a fast worker and caused work to pile up at the next work station, controlled by operator C. Considerable resentment was shown by C, who thought B made C look like a laggard.

Problems caused by initiation

Initiations that tend to be trouble spots are summarized in Figure 14-6. When initiation comes from someone with distinctly less skill, or someone of lower status, human problems can become serious. These problems tend to be compounded if the relationship involves pressure on the receiver, as in the following example from an early study of restaurants.[21]

Large restaurants sometimes used teenagers as runners to communicate the needs of the serving pantry to the kitchen. This placed the runner in the position of "telling" the cooks to prepare and send particular types of food. The result was that teenagers initiated action on high-status cooks. In essence, they were telling cooks what to do. This relationship often was a trouble spot in the restaurants studied. Cooks resented the control exercised on them by teenagers of inferior restaurant status. Practical solutions included (1) using a mechanical voice system that eliminated face-to-face contact and (2) changing the initiator to someone of higher status.

FIGURE 14-6
Types of initiation of action that may cause human problems

- Initiation from a fast worker to a slow one
- Initiation from an inexperienced worker to one with more experience
- Initiation from a low-seniority worker to one with high seniority
- Initiation from an unskilled worker to a skilled one
- Initiation from a young person to an older one
- Initiation from a worker with low authority to one with higher authority
- Initiation from a worker with lesser status to one with higher status
- Initiation that puts pressures on another worker
- Initiation that affects sensitive areas of a worker's job

Further problems tend to arise when an initiation affects "sensitive" areas such as how much work employees do (as in time study) and their rates of pay (as in job evaluation). In general we can conclude that initiations of action that place job or personal pressures on a receiver tend to be trouble spots.

System design for better teamwork

Another point about procedure is that it requires people to work together as a team. Teamwork can be engineered out of a work situation by means of layouts and job assignments that separate people so that it is impractical for them to work together, even though the work flow requires teamwork. In one instance two interdependent employees were unnecessarily on separate shifts, which prevented them from coordinating their work. In another instance, one operator fed parts to two separate lines that were in competition, and each line regularly claimed that the operator favored the other.

An early illustration of teamwork engineered out of a job was A. K. Rice's study of a textile mill in India.[22]

The mill was reengineered according to basic industrial engineering procedures. Each job had carefully assigned work loads based on engineering study. In one room there were 224 looms operated and maintained by twelve occupational groups. Each weaver tended twenty-four or thirty-two looms, each battery filler served forty to fifty looms, and each smash hand served an average of seventy-five looms. The other nine occupations were service and maintenance, and each worker had either 112 or 224 looms.

Teamwork initially prevented

Although the mill appeared to be superbly engineered, it failed to reach satisfactory output. Research disclosed that close teamwork of all twelve occupations was required to maintain production, yet work organization prevented this teamwork. Each battery filler served all looms of one weaver and part of the looms of a second weaver, which meant a weaver and battery filler were not a team unit, even though the nature of the process required it. In effect, a weaver tending twenty-four looms and using a battery filler serving forty looms worked with three-fifths of a battery filler, while another weaver shared two-fifths of the filler. The situation was even more confused with smash hands who tended seventy-five looms.

Eventually work was reorganized so that a certain group of workers had responsibility for a definite number of machines. Workers then were able to set up interaction and teamwork that caused production to soar.

Sociotechnical approach needed

A sociotechnical approach was required to integrate the technology, structure, and human factors into a productive system. When one element is changed, a mismatch is likely to emerge. Management needs to stay in close touch with the workers to understand their needs and avoid making costly mistakes.

Communication patterns

It is well known that plant layout and work flow have much to do with the opportunities that people have to talk with one another. In an insurance office, for example, the layout of desks was such that people who needed to talk to coordinate their work were separated by a broad aisle. Employees met the problem by loudly calling across the aisle, but this eventually had to be stopped because of the disturbance. The result was poor communication. In another company, sewing machines were located so that talking was discouraged, but management soon discovered that another layout that permitted talking led to higher productivity. Apparently, talking relieved the monotony of routine work.

Managers often overlook the fact that layout also can affect off-duty interaction of employees. Some years ago a new factory was built that was a model of engineering efficiency. Although the lunchroom was spotless and efficiently designed, it was located in the basement directly beneath stamping and light forging presses! Vibration was so terrific it stopped conversation. The floor and ceiling shook; the dishes rattled; there was no sound-deadening tile on the ceiling. The space beneath the presses apparently was not needed for other functions; so the cafeteria received it, but employee communication and relaxation were thereby excluded at mealtime. Lunch hours in the plant were staggered into four periods, which meant that the presses operated during the time most employees ate. When the cafeteria location was questioned, management's answer was, "The cafeteria is for eating only, and anyway the noise shouldn't bother anyone."

The potential effects of office layout on communication patterns raise several important issues. One dilemma in office design is whether to provide enclosed work cubicles for each employee, or create a more open, landscaped work area with lower (or no) partitions between work spaces. A basic issue revolves around the desire of some employees for privacy and personal space while they work. Many employees feel a need to establish their own *territory*—a space they can call their own, within which they can control what happens. Cubicles provide an opportunity for them to have their own territory, design and modify their work layout, and even decorate to their own satisfaction.

Alternatively, the organization may want a layout that encourages easy interaction and exchange of ideas among employees engaged in related tasks.

Some firms have accomplished this by creating offices designed as activity settings that include both home-base areas for privacy and bullpen areas for group interaction.[23] These settings have proven especially effective for providing employees with a way to "escape" from their computer terminals for short periods of time. Other organizations have created *neighborhoods,* which are centers of related individual offices to encourage the formation of social groups. This builds on the idea that proximity, or closeness, creates greater opportunities for interaction. The social groups that form contribute substantially toward satisfying employee needs for belonging.

Red tape

Another difficulty with procedure is *red tape.* It is procedure that appears to be unnecessary to those who are following it. It delays and harasses people everywhere. The term originated from the real red tape used to tie government documents, many of which have long been challenged as unnecessary by those who prepare them.

Causes of red tape

Red tape often becomes excessive. One cause is normal resistance to change. A procedure tends to become a habit, and people resist changing it. Another cause is that red tape often is determined by a higher authority who does not understand work problems. In these cases, people do not know why they are performing a procedure; consequently they cannot know whether it is useless or not, and they do not dare to expose their "ignorance" by questioning a procedure that their boss may be able to prove essential beyond a shadow of a doubt. People do not like to get caught not knowing something about their work.

Another reason for excessive red tape is that most procedures cross lines of authority, jumping from one chain of command to another. Under these conditions, no one employee feels a personal responsibility to change the procedure. An additional reason is that the people who created the procedures are often supervisors who do not have to follow them; so they tend to forget about them, letting them go on and on—and on.

The human problem with red tape is that it frustrates and irritates people and encourages worry and carelessness while they make their way through it. They do not like to do work that they think is useless. It challenges their human dignity and undermines their feeling that their work is worthwhile and necessary. In this way the apparently nonhuman activity called "procedure" can have a very definite effect on human behavior. Departments that are active in procedure creation, such as industrial engineering and accounting, need to give appropriate weight to the human dimensions of their procedures, because procedures that upset human relationships can do more harm than good. One sure way to raise the blood pressure of any group is to harness it with red tape.

An example of procedural rigidity occurred in a government agency. Around midmorning, it began to snow heavily in one community. As required by procedure, the

office supervisor called the district headquarters and requested permission to close the office. The response was "No, it's not snowing here [200 miles away]." Two hours later, the district headquarters called the office supervisor with this message, "You can close your office now; it's snowing here."

Alienation

Alienation may result from poor design of sociotechnical systems. Since work systems usually are planned by someone other than the operators, often the operators do not understand why the system operates the way it does. In addition, division of labor lets each operator perform only a small portion of the total work to be done, so jobs begin to lose their social significance and appear meaningless. Workers no longer see where they fit in the scheme of things; no longer do they see the value of their efforts. When these feelings become substantial, an employee may develop *alienation*, which is a feeling of powerlessness, lack of meaning, loneliness, disorientation, and lack of attachment to the job, work group, or organization. When workers are performing an insignificant task, frustrated by red tape, isolated from communication with others, prevented from engaging in teamwork, and controlled by initiations of action from others, then alienation is bound to develop.

Causes of alienation

There is evidence that alienation tends to be low in high-technology process industries as compared with mechanized assembly-line operations. Using Woodward's classification, unit and process production tend to have low alienation, while mass production has high alienation.[24] The relationship is curvilinear, as shown in Figure 14-7. This relationship suggests that much of modern industry that is now in the

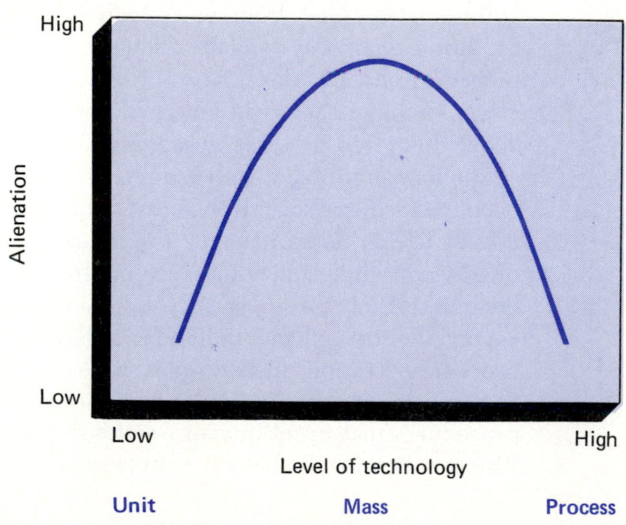

FIGURE 14-7
Relationship of alienation and level of technology

mass-production stage will move toward less alienating conditions as technology advances. In this manner, advancing technology will be favorable to workers.

The relationship of alienation to technology is only a general one. In some instances mass production may be welcomed by employees because it reduces their physical labor, improves working conditions, and provides them with new equipment. In other instances even professional workers may find satisfaction in formal work patterns.

The relationship between organizational formalization (standard practices, job descriptions, and policies) and alienation was explored in a study of both professional and nonprofessional employees.[25] Somewhat surprisingly, higher formalization actually seemed to *reduce* alienation among the employees. Apparently, increased rules and procedures decreased role ambiguity and increased the employee's level of organizational commitment. The researchers concluded that the structured flow of work procedures may, under some conditions, decrease the likelihood of alienation.

When alienation threatens to become serious, management needs to take corrective action, but it should act carefully, since alienation has many causes.

Effects of work systems

The evidence is clear that work systems have a substantial effect on human behavior. They do this by:

1 Determining who initiates action on whom, and some of the conditions in which the initiation occurs

2 Influencing the degree to which the employees performing interdependent activities can work together as a team

3 Affecting the communication patterns of employees

4 Creating possibilities for unnecessary procedures, generally called red tape

5 Providing tasks that seem insignificant and weak in power, thereby contributing to alienation

The general conclusion is that *relationships among workers in a system can be just as important as relationships of the work in that system.* In the design of any system it is folly to spend all one's time planning work relationships but ignoring worker relationships.

SUMMARY

Classical organizational structure is established by functional and scalar division of work, and it is communicated to participants by means of delegation.

Organization brings immense technical advantages, but there often are human costs. An example is specialization. Essentially, classical structure is strong in task support but weak in psychological support. Highly structured organizations are known as bureaucracies.

Organizational structure tends to exist in a contingency relationship with other variables, but certain general tendencies are evident. Generally, mechanistic organization is more appropriate for stable, mass-production environments in which employees desire security. Organic organization is more appropriate in dynamic environments with unit or continuous production and flexible employees. Matrix organization is a useful way to adapt to dynamic environments, especially when large technical projects are involved.

Technology is a powerful economic and social tool that can bring substantial benefits to society. Its effects are variable, but it tends to require higher worker skills, more white-collar work, and more multiprofessional employees. The result is a knowledge society. Labor unions generally accept technology as beneficial to society as a whole, but they want security provisions and retraining programs to protect individuals dislocated by it.

The flow of work especially affects people in organizations. It determines who initiates action on whom, influences the degree to which employees can work together as a team, affects communication patterns, creates possibilities of red tape, and may cause alienation. The conclusion is that the relationships of workers in a system can be just as important as the relationships of the work in that system.

Terms and concepts for review

Sociotechnical systems
Classical organization theory
Linking pin concept
Acceptance theory of authority
Contingency organizational design
Mechanistic and organic organizations
Matrix organization
Boundary roles
Robotics
Multiprofessional employees
Knowledge society
Technophobia
Initiation of action
Employee territories
Neighborhoods of offices
Red tape
Alienation

Discussion questions

1 Discuss how the linking pin concept is seen as a way of building a unified team within a whole organization.

2 Distinguish between a tall and a flat organizational structure. What advantages and disadvantages do each bring? Relate them to the span of management.

3 Discuss differences between mechanistic and organic patterns of organization. With what situations is each appropriate?
4 Explain how matrix organization works. What are its strengths and weaknesses? What situations are more appropriate for its use?
5 Assume that you lose your job due to technological change five years from now. Describe your probable feelings. How would your feelings differ if the same thing happened again just five years before you reached retirement age? Discuss.
6 Suppose you have an office with three secretaries who divide their time evenly between typing, filing, and staffing the receptionist desk. What are some of the ways that you could organize their work, and what would be the probable effects of each way?
   a If one of them typically is rude and unpleasant with other people, would that make a difference? Explain.
   b If one of them clearly is the best typist but typing is the least desirable job, would that make a difference? Explain.
   c Suppose one of them has a 50 percent hearing loss that cannot be corrected. Would that make a difference?
7 Think of a job about which you have some personal knowledge. How is the flow of work to and from the job organized? What are the probable effects of this work system?
8 Did you experience any red tape in your registration for college? Discuss.
9 What are some of the job-caused origins of employee alienation? Discuss some of the ways in which effective organizational behavior can reduce these causes.
10 Discuss how a knowledge society may affect jobs:
   a In the next decade
   b In the next twenty-five years

Incident

THE CENTRAL MOTOR POOL

A sales company established a central motor pool for its sales representatives, after years of allowing each representative to have an automobile. The pool was established to achieve significant cost savings, because sales representatives spent about one-third of their time in the office and only two-thirds of their time visiting customers.

On the basis of this information and your knowledge of human behavior, what would you predict regarding:

1 Sales representatives' feelings about not having their own cars
2 Competition over who would get which car to use
3 Care with which they handled the cars
4 Amount of time spent traveling under the new system

Because of difficulties with the pool, management finally decided that all sales representatives traveling over 1000 miles a month could have their own automobile. Then most of them started traveling that much even though there was no apparent need for many of them to do so.

Questions

1 Analyze and discuss the sociotechnical relationships in this situation.
2 Determine the sales behavior desired of the representatives, and offer an automobile arrangement to obtain it.

Experiential exercise

MECHANISTIC AND ORGANIC STRUCTURES

1 Indicate your general *preference* for working in one of these two organizational structures by circling the appropriate response:

Mechanistic 1 2 3 4 5 6 7 8 9 10 **Organic**

2 Indicate your perception of the form of organization that is used in this class by circling the appropriate response for each item:

A Task-role definition

Rigid 1 2 3 4 5 6 7 8 9 10 **Flexible**

B Communication

Vertical 1 2 3 4 5 6 7 8 9 10 **Multidirectional**

C Decision making

Centralized 1 2 3 4 5 6 7 8 9 10 **Decentralized**

D Sensitivity to the environment

Closed 1 2 3 4 5 6 7 8 9 10 **Open**

3 Meet in groups of four to six persons. Share your data from parts 1 and 2. Discuss the reasons for your responses, and analyze the factors that probably encouraged your instructor to choose the type of structure that now exists.

References

1 Peter F. Drucker, "A New Discipline," *Success*, January–February 1987, p. 18. (The article was adapted from Drucker's book, *The Frontiers of Management*, New York: Truman Talley Books, E. P. Dutton, 1986.)
2 Raymond E. Miles and Charles C. Snow, "Network Organizations: New Concepts for New Forms," *California Management Review*, Spring 1986, p. 72.
3 See, for example, Joyce M. Ranney, "Bringing Sociotechnical Systems from the Factory to the Office," *National Productivity Review*, Spring 1986, pp. 124–133.
4 Carrie R. Leana, "Predictors and Consequences of Delegation," *Academy of Management Journal*, December 1986, pp. 754–774.
5 John O. Whitney, "Organizing for a Turnaround," *Management Review*, December 1986, pp. 50–53.

6 Gregory S. Whitney, "Organizational Analysis: Its Application to Performance Improvement," *National Productivity Review*, Spring 1987, pp. 168–176.

7 Alan Ned Sabrosky, James Clay Thompson, and Karen A. McPherson, "Organized Anarchies: Military Bureaucracy in the 1980s," *Journal of Applied Behavioral Science*, vol. 18, no. 2 1982, pp. 137–153.

8 See, for example, Danny Miller and Cornelia Droge, "Psychological and Traditional Determinants of Structure," *Administrative Science Quarterly*, December 1986, pp. 539–560.

9 T. Burns and G. M. Stalker, *The Management of Innovation*, London: Tavistock Publications, 1961.

10 Joan Woodward, *Industrial Organization: Theory and Practice*, London: Oxford University Press, 1965, especially chap. 12 and p. 69.

11 Paul R. Lawrence and Jay W. Lorsch, *Organization and Environment: Managing Differentiation and Integration*, Boston: Harvard Graduate School of Business Administration, 1967; and Jay W. Lorsch and John J. Morse, *Organizations and Their Members: A Contingency Approach*, New York: Harper & Row, Publishers, Inc., 1974. The effect of structure on managerial perceptions of the environment is explored in Masoud Yasai-Ardekani, "Structural Adaptations to Environments," *Academy of Management Review*, January 1986, pp. 9–21.

12 William F. Joyce, "Matrix Organization: A Social Experiment," *Academy of Management Journal*, September 1986, pp. 536–561.

13 See, for additional discussion, Robert K. Kazanjian and Robert Drazin, "Implementing Internal Diversification: Contingency Factors for Organization Design Choices," *Academy of Management Review*, April 1987, pp. 342–354; and Robert Drazin and Andrew H. Van de Ven, "Alternative Forms of Fit in Contingency Theory," *Administrative Science Quarterly*, December 1985, pp. 514–539.

14 For examples of technological developments and their impacts, see "Technology in the Workplace," a special report (section 4) in *Wall Street Journal*, Nov. 10, 1986, pp. 1D–44D.

15 Georgia T. Chao and Steve W. J. Kozlowski, "Employee Perceptions on the Implementation of Robotic Manufacturing Technology," *Journal of Applied Psychology*, February 1986, pp. 70–76; also see Terry Feulner and Brian H. Kleiner, "When Robots Are the Answer," *Personnel Journal*, February 1986, pp. 44–47.

16 Charles J. Hollon and George N. Rogol, "How Robotization Affects People," *Business Horizons*, May–June 1985, pp. 74–80.

17 For an early discussion of the implications of this type of technology, see Peter F. Drucker, *The Age of Discontinuity*, New York: Harper & Row, Publishers, Inc., 1969; see also Keith Davis, "Some Fundamental Trends Affecting Management in the Future," in Lewis Benton (ed.), *Management for the Future*, New York: McGraw-Hill Book Company, 1978, pp. 63–76.

18 An example of the effects of technological change in the banking industry is Paul Adler, "New Technologies, New Skills," *California Management Review*, Fall 1986, pp. 9–28.

19 Carol Hymowitz, "Culture Shock Affects Steelworker Who Switched to White-Collar Job," *Wall Street Journal*, June 1983, p. 31. Also see Michael A. Pollock, "Business Is Dragging Its Feet on Retraining," *Business Week*, Sept. 29, 1986, pp. 72–73.

20 W. J. Kelty, Secretary of the Australian Council of Trade Unions, quoted in "Unions Must Adapt, Labor Leader Says," *Resource* (American Society for Personnel Administration), October 1986, p. 7.

21 This example is from a classic study by William F. Whyte, *Human Relations in the Restaurant Industry*, New York: McGraw-Hill Book Company, 1948, pp. 49–63.

22 A. K. Rice, "Productivity and Social Organization in an Indian Weaving Shed," *Human Relations*, vol. 6, no. 4, 1953, pp. 297–329.

23 Philip J. Stone and Robert Luchetti, "Your Office Is Where You Are," *Harvard Business Review*, March–April 1985, pp. 102–117; and Clark Malcolm, "Paradox in the Office: Fitting the Work Place for People," *National Productivity Review*, Spring 1986, pp. 142–149.

24 Robert Dewar and James Werbel, "Universalistic and Contingency Predictions of Employee Satisfaction and Conflict," *Administrative Science Quarterly*, September 1979, pp. 426–448. For a contrary opinion not supporting alienation of mass-production workers, see William H. Form, "Technology and Social Behavior of Workers in Four Countries: A Sociotechnical Perspective," *American Sociological Review*, December 1972, pp. 727–738.

25 Philip M. Podsakoff, Larry J. Williams, and William D. Todor, "Effects of Organizational Formalization on Alienation among Professionals and Nonprofessionals," *Academy of Management Journal*, December 1986, pp. 820–831.

For additional reading

Benveniste, Guy, *Professionalizing the Organization: Reducing Bureaucracy to Enhance Effectiveness*, San Francisco: Jossey-Bass Inc., Publishers, 1987.

Cleveland, Harlan, *The Knowledge Executive: Leadership in an Information Society*, New York: E. P. Dutton/Truman Talley Books, 1985.

Diebold, John, *Managing Information: The Challenge and the Opportunity*, New York: AMACOM, 1984.

Green, Mark, and John F. Berry, *The Challenge of Hidden Profits: Reducing Corporate Bureaucracy and Waste*, New York: W. Morrow & Company, 1985.

Love, John F., *McDonald's: Behind the Arches*, New York: Bantam Books, 1986.

Mintzberg, Henry, *The Structuring of Organizations*, Englewood Cliffs, N.J.: Prentice-Hall, Inc., 1979.

Morgan, Gareth, *Images of Organization*, Newbury Park, Calif.: Sage Publications, 1986.

O'Neill, Gerard K., *The Technology Edge: Opportunities for America in World Competition*, New York: Simon & Schuster, Inc., 1983.

Raymond, H. Alan, *Management in the Third Wave*, Glenview, Ill.: Scott, Foresman and Company, 1985.

Webster, Frank, and Kevin Robins, *Information Technology: A Luddite Analysis*, Norwood, N.J.: Ablex, 1986.

CHAPTER 15

Informal organizations

Cliques of technicians had formed, some of which, Mafia-like, made the real decisions about what would be done.

WILLIAM H. PEACE[1]

Trying to squelch a rumor is like trying to unring a bell.

ANONYMOUS

CHAPTER OBJECTIVES

To understand

The nature of informal organization

Benefits and problems with informal systems

How informal organizations may be charted

Organizational grapevines and their causes

Accuracy and patterns of grapevines

Rumor and its control

When Bill Smith graduated from engineering school and joined the laboratory of a large manufacturing company, he was assigned the task of supervising four laboratory technicians who checked production samples. In some ways he did supervise them. In other ways he was restricted by the group itself, which was quite frustrating to Bill. He soon found that each technician protected the others so that it was difficult to fix responsibility for sloppy work. The group appeared to restrict its work in such a way that about the same number of tests were made every day regardless of his urging to speed up the work. Although Bill was the designated supervisor, he observed that many times his technicians, instead of coming to him, took problems to an older technician across the aisle in another section.

Bill also observed that three of his technicians often had lunch together in the cafeteria, but the fourth technician usually ate with friends in an adjoining laboratory. Bill usually ate with other laboratory supervisors, and he learned much about company events during these lunches. He soon began to realize that these situations were evidence of an informal organization and that he had to work with it as well as with the formal organization.

Beneath the cloak of formal relationships in every organization there is a more complex system of social relationships consisting of many informal organizations. They are related to the socialization of employees, which was discussed in an earlier chapter.[2] Although there are many different informal groups, not one, we refer to them collectively as the informal organization. It is a powerful influence on productivity and job satisfaction. Both the formal and the informal systems are necessary for group activity, just as two blades are essential for a pair of scissors. This chapter presents a general overview of informal organizations at work, including their communication system, popularly called the grapevine.

THE NATURE OF INFORMAL ORGANIZATION

Informal organization compared with the formal

Definition of informal organization

Widespread interest in informal organization developed as a result of the Western Electric studies in the 1930s, which concluded that it was an important part of the total work situation. These studies showed that *informal organization* is a network of personal and social relations not established or required by the formal organization but arising spontaneously as people associate with one another. The emphasis within informal organization is on people and their relationships, while formal organization emphasizes official positions in terms of authority and responsibility. Informal power, therefore, attaches to a *person,* while formal authority attaches to a *position* and a person has it only when occupying that position. Informal power is personal, but formal authority is institutional. These differences are summarized in Figure 15-1.

FIGURE 15-1
Differences between formal and informal organizations

FORMAL ORGANIZATION	BASIS OF COMPARISON	INFORMAL ORGANIZATION
Official	**General nature**	**Unofficial**
Authority & responsibility	**Major concepts**	**Power and politics**
Position	**Primary focus**	**Person**
Delegated by management	**Source of leader power**	**Given by group**
Rules	**Guidelines for behavior**	**Norms**
Rewards and penalties	**Sources of control**	**Sanctions**

Informal power

Power in informal organization is given by group members, rather than delegated by managers; therefore, it does not follow the official chain of command. It is more likely to come from peers than from superiors in the formal hierarchy; and it may cut across organizational lines into other departments. It is usually more unstable than formal authority, since it is subject to the sentiments of people. Because of its subjective nature, informal organization cannot be controlled by management in the way that formal organization is.

A manager typically holds some informal (personal) power along with formal (positional) power, but usually a manager does not have more informal power than anyone else in the group. This means that the manager and the informal leader usually are two different persons in work groups.

As a result of differences between formal and informal sources of power, formal organizations may grow to immense size, but informal organizations (at least the closely knit ones) tend to remain smaller in order to keep within the limits of personal relationships. The result is that a large organization tends to have hundreds of informal organizations operating throughout it. Some of them are wholly within the institution; others are partially external to it. Because of their naturally small size and instability, informal organizations are not a suitable substitute for the large formal aggregates of people and resources that are needed for modern institutions.

Secondary role

Workers usually recognize the different roles played by formal and informal organizations, including the more secondary role normally played by the informal. One study of workers reported that, although workers and managers saw the informal organization as influential and beneficial, they viewed the formal organization as more influential and beneficial.[3]

How does the informal organization emerge?

The contingency organization model discussed in Chapter 14 produces a structure that is designed by management to be consistent with its environment, technology, and strategy. This structure, with its rules, procedures, and job descriptions, creates a set of prescriptions for employees to follow. Individuals and groups are *expected* to behave in certain ways. If they perform their tasks as prescribed, the organization is efficient. This may not happen as much as managers would like, however, for the following reason.

The informal organization emerges from within the formal structure as predictably as flowers growing in the spring. The result is different from what managers may have expected in at least three ways.[4] First, employees *act* differently than required. They may work faster or slower than predicted, or they may gradually modify a work procedure based on their experience and insight. Second, employees often *interact* with different people, or with different frequencies, than their jobs require. Georgia may seek advice from Melissa instead of Todd, and Candy may spend more time helping John than Steve. Third, workers may embrace a different set of *attitudes, beliefs, and sentiments* than the organization expects of them. Instead of all being loyal, committed, and enthusiastic about their work, some employees may become disenchanted, while others are openly alienated. The lesson for managers is painfully obvious—they must be aware of the informal activities, interactions, and sentiments of employees in addition to the required ones.

Member status and informal leaders

Among the members of the marketing department in one firm there were remarkable, but somewhat typical, differences. Their ages ranged from 30 to 72; their seniority in the organization varied from newly hired to 39 years; and the highest-paid member earned about 80 percent more than the lowest-paid individual. Some of the group had grown up in the local area, while others had moved across the United States to accept their jobs. Also, their offices differed in many dimensions such as size, availability of natural lighting, and proximity to noise.

Members of work groups like this have identifiable characteristics that distinguish them from each other and give rise to status differences. As seen in the example, some of the ways in which they differ are age, seniority, earnings, birthplace, and nature of their workplace. Other factors, such as technical competence, freedom to move around the work area, and personality are also recognizable. Each of these elements can provide *status* to its holder, largely based on what the group members value. The causes of informal status are nearly numberless.

The employee with the largest amount of status in the informal organization usually becomes its *informal leader*. This person emerges from within the group, often acquiring considerable informal power. Informal leaders may help socialize new members into the organization, and they may be called upon by the group to perform the more complex tasks. A young neurosurgeon, for example, related how the group's senior partner would often stop by the operating room during a particularly delicate operation to assist briefly in the removal of a brain tumor, and then quietly move on when help was no longer needed.

In return for their services, informal leaders usually enjoy certain rewards and privileges. Perhaps the informal leader is permitted by coworkers to choose a vacation time first, or the leader might be spared from a messy cleanup chore. A predictable reward is the high esteem in which the informal leader is held, and this is significant enough to balance the responsibilities the person shoulders.

Informal groups overlap to the extent that one person may be a member of several different groups, which means that there is not just one leader but several of varying importance. The group may look to one employee on matters pertaining to wages and to another to lead recreational plans. In this way several people in a department may be informal leaders of some type. There might be an experienced person who is looked upon as the expert on job problems, a listener who serves as counselor, and a communicator who is depended upon to convey key problems to the managers.[5]

One primary leader

Although several persons in a group may be informal leaders of various types, there is usually one primary leader who has more influence than others. Each manager needs to learn who the key informal leader is in any group and to work with that leader to encourage behavior that furthers rather than hinders organizational objectives. When an informal leader is working against an employer, the leader's widespread influence can undermine motivation and job satisfaction.

The informal organization is a desirable source of potential formal leaders, but it should be remembered that an informal leader does not always make the best formal manager. History is filled with examples of successful informal leaders who became arrogant bosses once they received formal authority. Some informal leaders fail as formal ones because they fear official responsibility—something they do not have as informal leaders. They often criticize management for lacking initiative or for not daring to be different, but when they take a management job, they become even more conservative because they are afraid to make a mistake. Other informal leaders fail because their area of official management authority is broader and more complex than the tiny area in which they had informal power. The fact that Joe is the leader in departmental social activities does not mean that he will be successful as the departmental manager.

The difficult transition from informal to formal leader may be partially explained by the results of a research study of emergent leaders in small groups.[6] By using members' ratings of each other on the degree to which they were goal-directed, gave directions, summarized, and appeared self-assured after their first task, the researcher was able to predict eight out of nine emergent leaders. However, it was also discovered that the informal leaders typically rated quite highly as "quarrelsome," but not as being "sensible." It appears that candidates for informal leadership require many of the same skills as formal leaders, but their other characteristics may later impair their effectiveness as formal leaders.

FIGURE 15-2
Potential benefits and problems associated with informal organizations

BENEFITS	PROBLEMS
□ Makes a more effective total system.	□ Develops undesirable rumor.
□ Lightens work load on management.	□ Encourages negative attitudes.
□ Helps get the work done.	□ Resists change.
□ Tends to encourage cooperation.	□ Leads to interpersonal and intergroup conflicts.
□ Fills in gaps in a manager's abilities.	□ Rejects and harasses some employees.
□ Gives satisfaction and stability to work groups.	□ Weakens motivation and satisfaction.
□ Improves communication.	□ Operates outside of management's control.
□ Provides a safety valve for employee emotions.	□ Supports conformity.
□ Encourages managers to plan and act more carefully.	□ Develops role conflicts.

Benefits of informal organizations

Better total system

Although informal systems may lead to several problems, they also bring a number of benefits to both employers and employees, as shown in Figure 15-2. Most important is that they blend with formal systems to make an effective total system.[7] Formal plans and policies cannot meet every problem in a dynamic situation because they are preestablished and partly inflexible. Some requirements can be met better by informal relations, which can be flexible and spontaneous.

Lighter work load for management

Another benefit of informal organization is to lighten the work load on management. When managers know that the informal organization is working with them, they feel less compelled to check on the workers to be sure everything is shipshape. Managers are encouraged to delegate and decentralize because they are confident that employees will be cooperative. In general, informal group support of a manager probably leads to better cooperation and productivity. It helps get the work done.

Informal organization also may act to fill in gaps in a manager's abilities. If a manager is weak in planning, an employee informally may help with planning. In this way, planning is accomplished in spite of the manager's weakness.

Work-group satisfaction

A significant benefit of informal organization is that it gives satisfaction and stability to work groups. It is the means by which workers feel a sense of belonging and security. It gives workers a feeling that they have something worth remaining with, so satisfaction is increased and turnover reduced.

In a large office, for example, an employee named Rose McVail may feel like only a payroll number, but her informal group gives her personal attachment and status. With the members of her group she is somebody, even though in the formal structure she is only one of a thousand clerks. She may not look forward to posting

750 accounts daily, but the informal group can give more meaning to her day. When she can think of meeting her friends, sharing their interests, and eating with them, her day takes on a new dimension that makes easier any difficulty or tedious routine in her work. Of course, these conditions can apply in reverse: the group may not accept her, thereby making her work more disagreeable and driving her to a transfer, absenteeism, or a resignation.

An additional benefit is that informal organization can be a useful channel of employee communication. It provides the means for people to keep in touch, to learn more about their work, and to understand what is happening in their environment.

A safety valve for emotions

Another benefit, often overlooked, is that the informal organization is a safety valve for employee frustrations and other emotional problems. Employees may relieve emotional pressures by discussing them with someone else in an open and friendly way, and one's associates in the informal group provide this type of environment.

Consider the case of Max Schultz, who became frustrated and angry with his supervisor, Frieda Schneider. He felt like striking her, but in a civilized organization that was not appropriate behavior. He wanted to tell her what he thought of her, using uncomplimentary words, but he might have been disciplined for that. His next alternative was to have lunch with a close friend, and to share with his friend exactly how he felt. Having vented his feelings, he was able to return to work and interact with Schneider in a more relaxed way.

A benefit of informal organization that is seldom recognized is that its presence encourages managers to plan and act more carefully than they would otherwise. Managers who understand its power know that it is a check and balance on their unlimited use of authority. They introduce changes into their groups only after careful planning because they know that informal groups can undermine even a worthwhile project. They want their projects to succeed because they will have to answer to formal authority if they fail.

Cohesiveness

The benefits of informal organization are more likely to appear if the group is *cohesive* and its members have favorable attitudes toward the firm.[8] Cohesiveness is indicated by how strongly the employees stick together, rely on each other, and desire to remain members. Productivity among members of cohesive groups is often quite uniform, and turnover low.

Problems associated with informal organizations

Many of the benefits of informal systems can be reversed to show potential problems that may develop. In other words, informal systems can help and harm an activity at the same time. For example, while useful information is being spread by one part of the system, another part may be communicating a malicious rumor. An informal system also can change its mood in a positive or negative way. A work group, for example, may welcome and nurture a new employee or reject the employee, causing an unhappy employee and a resignation.[9] Both positive and negative effects exist side by side in most informal systems.

Resistance to change

One major problem with informal organizations is resistance to change. There is a tendency for a group to become overly protective of its way of life and to stand like a rock in the face of change. What has been good is believed to be good enough for the future. If, for example, job A has always had more status than job B, it must continue to have more status and more pay, even though conditions have changed to make job A less difficult. If restriction of productivity was necessary in the past with an autocratic management, it is necessary now, even though management is participative. Although informal organizations are bound by no chart on the wall, they are bound by convention, custom, and culture.

Conformity

A related problem is that the informal organization can be a significant cause of employee conformity. The informal side of organizations is so much a part of the everyday life of workers that they hardly realize it is there, so they usually are unaware of the powerful pressures it applies to persuade them to conform to its way of life. The closer they are attached to it, the stronger its influence is.

Norms

Conformity is encouraged by *norms*, which are informal group requirements for the behavior of members.[10] These norms may be strong or weak, depending on the importance of the behavior to the group. Groups rigidly expect their members to follow strong norms, while individuals may choose to accept or reject weak ones. Research studies show that groups have norms for both their task responsibilities and personal relationships at work.[11] They also generate norms for their superior and subordinates, as well as their peers.

The group whose norms a person accepts is a *reference group*. Employees may have more than one reference group, such as the engineering manager who identifies with the engineering profession and its standards, plus one or more management groups. A reference group often uses rewards and penalties, called *sanctions*, to persuade its members to conform to its norms. The combination of informal norms with their related sanctions consistently guides opinion and applies power to reduce any behavior that tends to vary from group norms. Nonconformers may be pressured and harassed until they capitulate or leave.

Sanctions

Examples of harassment are interference with work (such as hiding one of the offender's tools), ridicule, interference outside of work (such as letting the air out of the offender's automobile tires), and isolation from the group. In Britain it is said that a person isolated from the group is "being sent to Coventry."[12] In these instances the group refuses to talk with the offender for days or even weeks, and group members may even refuse to use any tool or machine the offender has used. Actions of this type can drive a worker from a job.

Role conflict

Another problem that may develop is role conflict. Workers want to meet the requirements of both their group and their employer, but frequently these requirements are in conflict. What is good for the employees is not always good for the organization. Coffee breaks may be desirable, but if employees spend an extra fifteen minutes socializing in the morning and afternoon, productivity may be reduced to the disadvantage of both the employer and consumers. Much of this role conflict can be avoided by carefully cultivating mutual interests with informal groups. The more the interests of formal and informal groups can be integrated, the more productivity and satisfaction can be expected. However, there always will be some differences between formal and informal organizations. This is not an area where perfect harmony exists.

A major difficulty with any informal organization is that it is not subject to management's direct control. The "authority" that it depends on is the social system rather than management. All that management can do is influence it here and there.

Personal and group conflicts

Informal organizations also develop interpersonal and intergroup conflicts that can be damaging to their organization. When employees give more of their thoughts and energies to opposing each other, they are likely to give less to their employer. Conflicts and self-interests can become so strong in informal organizations that they reduce both motivation and satisfaction. The result is less productivity, which harms both the employer and employees. No one gains.

Charting the informal organization

Sociogram

One way to gain a better understanding of an informal system is to prepare a chart of it. A diagram of the feelings of group members toward each other is called a *sociogram*. This study and measurement of feelings of group members toward one another was pioneered by J. L. Moreno in the 1930s and is called *sociometry*. Moreno classified feelings as attraction, repulsion, and indifference. To learn these feelings in a work group, he asked members to rank their choices of people with whom they would like to work or not to work. The person receiving the most positive votes is the star, or sociometric leader. If the ranking focused on *task* relationships, the person selected may be the informal leader who can motivate the group to action. Alternatively, if the ranking probed the group's *interpersonal* feelings, the star may simply be the person liked the most. This employee may not have the skills to lead the group toward its work goals, but may be essential to building an atmosphere of cooperation and trust.

Grapevine charts

Another charting approach is to diagram the actual informal interactions of people, such as with whom an individual spends the most time and with whom one communicates informally. Charts of these relationships are called *informal organization charts*, or *grapevine charts*.[13] These charts may be superimposed on the formal organization chart in order to show variations between the two. This type of chart is illustrated by Figure 15-3. Superimposed on the formal chart are lines showing the patterns of communication that developed from an event known to the managers in positions 27 and 234. Most of these communications were outside formal chains of command, illustrating how the informal system is not bound by the official organizational structure. Discussion of informal communication continues in the next section.

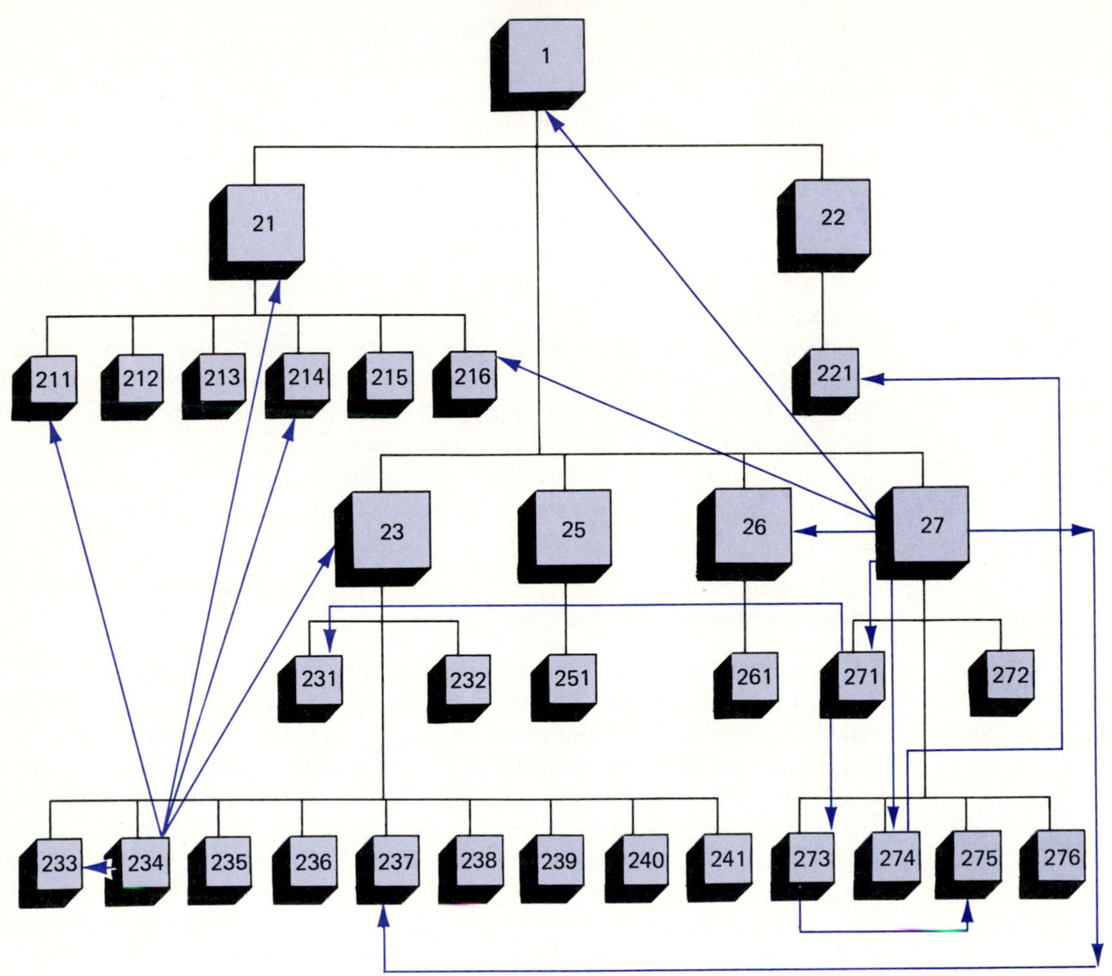

FIGURE 15-3
Patterns of communication about an event known to managers in positions 27 and 234 in a manufacturing company

INFORMAL COMMUNICATION

The *grapevine* is the communication system of informal organization. It coexists with management's formal communication system. The term "grapevine" arose during the War Between the States. Intelligence telegraph lines were strung loosely from tree to tree in the manner of a grapevine, and wild grapevines grew over the lines in some areas. Since messages from the lines often were incorrect or confusing, any rumor was said to be from the grapevine. Today the term applies to all informal communication, including company information that is communicated informally between employees and people in the community.

Although grapevine information tends to be sent orally, it may be written. Handwritten or typed notes sometimes are used, but in the modern electronic office these messages typically are flashed on computer screens, creating the new era of the *electronic grapevine*.[14] This system can speed the transmission of more units of information within a very short time. It won't replace the face-to-face grapevine, however, for two reasons. For one, not every employee has access to a network of personal computers at work. The other reason is that many workers enjoy the more personal social interaction gained through the traditional grapevine.

Electronic grapevine

Figure 15-4 is a copy of a grapevine communication sent by teletypewriter between company branches in two cities. During a period of months two employees had developed an active interest in operations in each other's branch. Though they never heard each other's voice, they frequently "talked" by teletype when the leased system was not in use. Observe that they were talking about their employer, and some of what they learned undoubtedly was passed along on the local grapevine.

Since the grapevine arises from social interaction, it is as fickle, dynamic, and varied as people are. It is the expression of their natural motivation to communicate. It is the exercise of their freedom of speech and is a natural, normal activity. In fact, only employees who are totally disinterested in their work do not engage in shoptalk about it.

Employee interest in associates is illustrated by the experience of one company. The wife of a plant supervisor had a baby at 11 P.M., and a plant survey the next day at 2 P.M. showed that 46 percent of the management personnel knew of it through the grapevine.[15]

In a sense, the grapevine is a human birthright, because whenever people congregate into groups, the grapevine is sure to develop. It may use smoke signals, jungle tom-toms, taps on the prison wall, ordinary conversation, or some other method, but it will always be there. Organizations cannot "fire" the grapevine because they did not hire it. It is simply there.

How accurate is the grapevine?

Both accuracy and inaccuracy

If we count the units of information in Figure 15-4 and then verify which are true and which are false, we will find that most of them are true. This is the way research on grapevine accuracy is done, and it shows that in normal work situations well over three-fourths of grapevine information is accurate.[16] People tend to think the grapevine is less accurate than it is because its errors are more dramatic and consequently more impressed on memory than its day-by-day routine accuracy. Moreover, one inaccurate part may make a whole story inaccurate.

On one grapevine, for example, a story about a welder marrying the general manager's daughter was true with regard to his getting married, the date, the

IS JOE* THERE GA[1]

YES

PUT HIM ON TELEX PLS[2] GA

THIS JOE

THIS SUE AND I AM A LITTLE CURIOUS ABOUT UR[3] TELEX YESTERDAY COAST CLEAR NOW SO WHAT DO THEY ASK YOU GA

THE FIRST STUPID QUESTION WAS THEY WANTED TO KNOW WHAT HAPPENED TO CERTAIN ITEMS THAT WERE ON THE INVENTORY ONE MONTH AND NOT ON THE NEXT MONTH I TOLD THEM IT WAS ONLY LOGICAL TO ASSUME THEY WERE SOLD SO THEY ASKED TO WHOM TOLD THEM TO LOOK IT UP ON THEIR COPIES OF THE DR'S[4] GA

UR ANSWER WAS PRETTY GOOD UR RIGHT THINGS LIKE THAT COME UP ALL THE TIME BUT UNFORTUNATELY I HAVE TO FIGURE OUT MOSTLY FROM HERE WHAT ELSE JOE GA

THEY SAID MY INVENTORY WAS SHORT 25 TONS AND WANTED TO KNOW WHY I ASKED THEM FOR THE FIGURES THEY USED AND I CHECKED IT OUT ONLY TO FIND THEY CANT EVEN COPY THE RIGHT FIGURES DOWN GA

WELL SOMETIMES I GUESS THEY MAKE BOBOS[5] LIKE THAT BUT UR LUCKY ONLY BEING OFF 25 TONS WE WERE OFF 400 TONS AND IT TOOK ME AWHILE TO FIND IT WHAT ELSE

THIS IS PROBABLY THE FUNNIEST I PAY THE LOCAL PAPER HERE EVERY MONTH FOR ADVERTISING AND WHEN OUR STATEMENTS COME HERE FROM CHICAGO THEY NEVER HAVE ANYTHING CHARGED TO ADVERTISING WHICH AMOUNTS TO A FEW THOUSAND A YEAR I ASKED ABOUT IT AND THEY WERE SURPRISED I GUESS THEY DONT LOOK AT THE COPIES OF THE CHECKS THAT I MAKE OUT GA

WELL THEY SURE LOOK AT OURS BECAUSE THEY CONSTANTLY ASK US WHY AND TO WHOM AND WHAT FOR WE PAID THIS AND THAT THE ONLY ONE WHO KNOWS ABOUT CHECK COPIES IS MAX SMITH AND I THINK HE KEEPS GOOD TRACK OF IT BUT U[6] ARE RIGHT THAT IS FUNNY OH GOOD GA

ANYWAY I REMEMBER GEORGE TELLING ME ABOUT UR PROBLEM AND I JUST WANTED TO LET U KNOW U WERE NOT THE ONLY ONES THAT KEEP IN DAILY COMMUNICATION WITH CHICAGO GA

I THINK IT WAS VERY NICE OF U AND AS FAR AS I CAN SEE I HAVE IT WORSE THAN U SO MY COMPLIMENTS TO YOU AND THANKS AGAIN FOR UR CONCERN GA

THATS ABOUT ALL FROM HERE GA

OK JOE BIBI[7]

Key: *All names are disguised.
[1]Go ahead.
[2]Please.
[3]"Your" or "you are," depending on the sentence.
[4]Delivery receipts.
[5]Errors; "boo-boos."
[6]You.
[7]Bye bye.

FIGURE 15-4
Actual transcript of a teletypewriter grapevine over a company private wire between two warehouse clerks in separate cities

location, and other details. The one wrong detail in this 90 percent accurate story was that the woman was not the general manager's daughter but happened to have the same last name. This one wrong point made the whole communication wrong in general meaning even though it was 90 percent accurate in detail.

Not the whole truth

It also is true that grapevine information usually is incomplete, so it may be seriously misinterpreted even though the details it does carry are accurate. That is, even though the grapevine tends to carry the truth, it rarely carries the whole truth. These cumulative inadequacies of the grapevine mean that in total it tends to produce more misunderstanding than its small percentage of wrong information suggests.

The grapevine pattern

Managers occasionally get the impression that the grapevine operates like a long chain in which A tells B, who tells C, who then tells D, and so on, until twenty persons later, Y gets the information—very late and very incorrect. Sometimes the grapevine may operate this way, but it generally follows a different pattern, as shown in Figure 15-5. Employee A tells three or four others (such as B, J, and F). Only one or two of these receivers will pass the information forward, and they usually will tell more than one person. Then as the information becomes older and the proportion of those knowing it gets larger, it gradually dies out because not all those who receive it repeat it. This

FIGURE 15-5
Types of grapevine chains

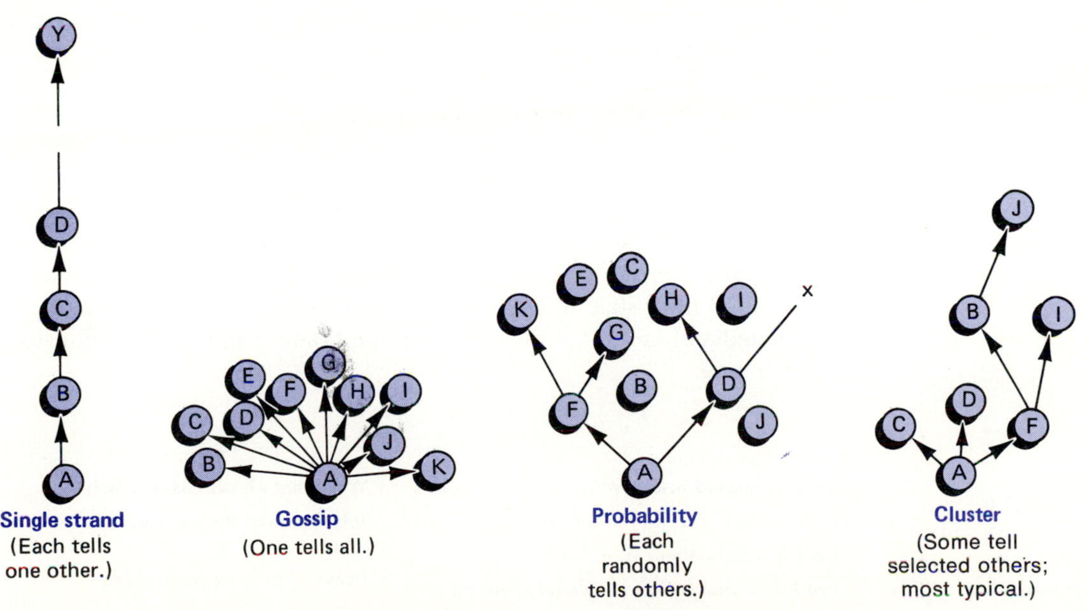

Cluster chain

network is a *cluster chain*, because each link in the chain tends to inform a cluster of other people instead of only one person. Other types of chains also are shown in the figure, but they are used less.

If we accept the idea that this cluster chain is predominant, it is reasonable to conclude that only a few people are active communicators on the grapevine for any specific unit of information. If, for example, eighty-seven clerks in an office know that Mabel was married secretly on Saturday, probably the word was spread to these eighty-seven by only ten or fifteen clerks. The remainder received the information, but did not spread it. These people who keep the grapevine active are called *liaison individuals*.

Liaison individuals

For example, in one company when a quality-control problem occurred, 68 percent of the executives knew about it, but only 20 percent of them spread the information. In another case, when a manager planned to resign, 81 percent of the executives knew about it, but only 11 percent passed the news on to others.

Grapevine causes

The grapevine is more a product of the situation than it is of the person. This means that *given the proper situation and motivation, any of us tends to become active on the grapevine*. Some of the situations that encourage people to be active are listed in Figure 15-6.

One cause is that any group tends to be more active on the grapevine during periods of excitement and insecurity. Examples are a layoff, an unfriendly takeover attempt, or the installation of a new computer in the office. At times like this, the grapevine is humming with activity, which means that managers need to watch it with extra care and "feed" it true information to keep it from getting out of hand.

People also are active on the grapevine when their friends and work associates are involved. This means that if Mary is to be promoted or Jack fired, employees need to know the full story as soon as possible. If they are not informed, they will fill in the gaps with their own conclusions; that is, people fill in missing signals according to their own perceptions.

Friendships lead to grapevines.

People also are most active on the grapevine when they have news, as distinguished from stale information. The greatest spread of information happens immediately after it is known; so it is important to get out the right story in the beginning.

FIGURE 15-6
Typical causes of grapevine communication

- **Excitement and insecurity**
- **Involvement of friends and associates**
- **Recent information**
- **Procedure that brings people into contact**
- **Work that allows conversation**
- **Job that provides information desired by others**
- **Personality of communicator**

The grapevine exists largely by word of mouth and by observation; so procedures that regularly bring people into contact will encourage them to be active on the grapevine.

For example, in one company the chief link between two offices was the manager's secretary, who stopped by the other office right after lunch every day to pick up reports. In another office the link was an accounting clerk who every morning telephoned 300 yards across the company property to secure some cost data. In a similar manner employees having nearby desks are likely to communicate more than two employees in separate buildings.

Jobs affect grapevine activity.

The foregoing examples show that the type of job possessed by an employee has an important influence on that person's role on the grapevine. Some jobs give employees more opportunity to communicate than others, and some jobs provide employees with more news that might be worth communicating. The result is that certain employees are more active on the grapevine, not because of personality but because of their jobs in the organization. Their jobs give them a strong basis for being key people on the grapevine network. For example, one study showed that secretaries to managers were four times more likely to be key grapevine communicators, compared with other employees.[17]

Personalities affect grapevines.

Although type of job is an important grapevine influence, some employees are more active for personality reasons. Perhaps they like to talk about people, have a strong interest in what is happening in their organization, or have special communication abilities. However, there does not appear to be any sex difference in grapevine activity. Both women and men are equally active on the grapevine.

Features of the grapevine

The grapevine gives managers much feedback about employees and their jobs. It also helps interpret management to the workers. It especially helps translate management's formal orders into employee language, in this way helping to make up for management failures in communication.

In several instances the grapevine carries information that the formal system does not wish to carry and purposely leaves unsaid. For example, a supervisor who is in a bad mood because of personal or job problems usually cannot announce this fact officially to employees. The better approach is to "put it on the grapevine" so that employees are forewarned informally not to make requests that can be delayed. How often it is said, "Don't talk to the manager about a raise today."

Grapevines are fast.

Another grapevine feature is its fast pace. Being flexible and personal, it spreads information faster than most management communication systems. With the rapidity of a burning powder train, the grapevine filters out of the woodwork, past the manager's office, through the locker rooms, and along the corridors. Its speed makes it quite difficult for management to stop undesirable rumors or to release significant news in time to prevent rumor formation.

One company, when it signed its labor contract at 11 P.M., had to keep its publication staff busy all night in order to have a suitable bulletin ready for supervisors and employees when they came to work the next morning. This was the only way that it could match the grapevine's speed.

One study showed the speed of the grapevine in government. The study covered Canadian government engineers who had been transferred, and 32 percent reported that they first heard of their transfer on the grapevine.[18]

Grapevines are influential.

Another grapevine feature is its unusual ability to penetrate even the tightest company security screen because of its capacity to cut across organizational lines and deal directly with the people who know. The grapevine is well known as a source of confidential information.

All evidence shows that the grapevine is influential, both favorably and unfavorably. The grapevine accomplishes so much positively and so much negatively that it is difficult to determine whether its net effects are positive or negative. Undoubtedly its effects vary among work groups and organizations. Research with managers and white-collar employees reported that 53 percent of them viewed the grapevine as a negative factor in the organization. Only 27 percent viewed it as a positive factor, and 20 percent considered it as neutral.[19]

Management response to grapevines

Influencing grapevines

Regardless of the grapevine's net effects, it cannot be done away with, so the organization needs to adjust to it. Managers are coming to realize that they need to learn who its leaders are, how it operates, and what information it carries. Though they used to ignore it, they now listen to it and study it. Many managers also try to influence the grapevine in various ways. Their objective is to reduce negative effects and increase positive effects. They try to reduce anxiety, conflict, and misunderstanding so that the grapevine will have less cause to spread negative information.

A positive approach taken by some managers is to leak useful information to the grapevine so that it will have more accurate information.[20] Some managers are even observant enough to identify the networks that their employees belong to (as discussed in Chapter 4). By knowing their employees' internal and external contacts, they can use the grapevine to the company's advantage by sharing selected information with key people. Those managers who still prefer to ignore the grapevine, letting it go its separate way, overlook the important role it plays in organizations.

Rumor

Definition of rumor

The major problem with the grapevine—and the one that gives the grapevine its poor reputation—is rumor. The word "rumor" sometimes is used as a synonym for the whole grapevine, but technically there is an important difference between the two terms. *Rumor* is grapevine information that is communicated without secure standards of evidence being present. It is the unverified and untrue part of the grapevine. It could by chance be correct, but generally it is incorrect; so it is presumed to be undesirable. It has been a problem since the beginning of human history, as illustrated by Figure 15-7, an operatic aria of the early 1800s about rumor.

Interest and ambiguity lead to rumor.

Rumor is primarily a result of both interest and ambiguity in a situation.[21] If a subject is unimportant or has no interest to a person, then that person has no cause to pass along a rumor about it. For example, the authors of this book have never rumored about the coconut output on the island of Martinique for the preceding year. Similarly, if there is no ambiguity in a situation, a person has no cause for rumor because the correct facts are known. This means that both interest and ambiguity normally must be present both to begin and to maintain a rumor.

An example of these two factors in action occurred in the financial community. The rumor flew around the country that "the roof caved in on Bank X." The origin of the

"Don Basilio's Slander Aria" from *The Barber of Seville*

English translation by Boris Goldovsky

Start a rumor, a mere invention,
Any story you'd care to mention.
Start it circulating lightly,
Oh so gently, oh so slightly.
Very soon it gets around all by itself.

Did you hear it? Most appalling. . . . Just imagine! Quite enthralling. . . .
Once it's born each idle rumor just keeps growing like a tumor,
No one knows where it has started, but he's anxious to repeat, to impart it.
And with every repetition it receives a fresh addition.
Is it fact or is it fiction? No one knows and no one cares.

There is no one to deny it; no one bothers to defy it,
Soon it blossoms like a flower, and begins to gain in power.
Now the tempest from the distance nearer grows with more insistence,
Rumbling louder, ever louder, till the storm is at its worst.

Like a sudden flash of lightning, now the skies are rent asunder,
With an awful roar of thunder, and the rumor grows and fattens
Without reason, without rhyme.

There's no formal accusation, just a whispered intimation.
But the people are convinced that he's committed every crime.
He can give no explanation for his ruined reputation,
But the world has been aroused and will convict him every time.

FIGURE 15-7
An operatic aria of the early 1800's about rumor

rumor, of course, was an ambiguous situation with different meanings. There were water leaks in the ceiling of the bank's building and this, coupled with the interest of both employees and financial analysts, was translated into a rumor of financial problems at the bank. Once the ambiguity was clarified, the rumor disappeared.

Details are lost.

Since rumor largely depends on the interest and ambiguity that each person has, it tends to change as it passes from person to person. Its general theme usually can be maintained, but not its details. It is subject to *filtering* by which it is reduced to a few basic details that can be remembered and passed on to others. Generally people choose details in the rumor to fit their own interests and view of the world.

People also add new details, often making the story worse, in order to include their own strong feelings and reasoning; this is *elaborating*.

For example, Marlo Green, a factory worker, heard a rumor that an employee in another department had been injured. When she passed the rumor to someone else, she elaborated by saying that the injury probably was caused by the supervisor's poor machine maintenance. Apparently she made this elaboration because she did not like the supervisor, so she felt that if someone was injured, it must have been the supervisor's fault.

Control of rumor

Since rumor generally is incorrect, a major outbreak of it can be a devastating epidemic that sweeps through an organization as fast as a summer storm—and usually with as much damage. Rumor should be dealt with firmly and consistently, but how and what to attack must be known. It is a serious mistake to strike at the whole grapevine merely because it happens to be the agent that carries rumor; that approach would be as unwise as throwing away a typewriter because of a few misspelled words. Several ways to control rumor are summarized in Figure 15-8 and discussed in the following paragraphs.

Use preventive approach

REDUCTION OF CAUSES The best way to control rumor is to get at its causes, rather than trying to stop it after it already has started. Getting at causes is a wise use of the preventive approach, instead of a tardy corrective approach. When people feel reasonably secure, understand the things that matter to

- **Remove its causes in order to prevent it.**
- **Apply efforts primarily to serious rumors.**
- **Refute rumor with facts.**
- **Deal with rumor as soon as possible.**
- **Emphasize face-to-face supply of facts, confirmed in writing if necessary.**
- **Provide facts from reliable sources.**
- **Refrain from repeating rumor while refuting it.**
- **Encourage assistance of informal and union leaders if they are cooperative.**
- **Listen to all rumor in order to understand what it may mean.**

FIGURE 15-8
Guides for control of rumor

them, and feel part of the team, there are few rumors, because there is very little ambiguity in the situation. But when people are emotionally upset or inadequately informed about their environment, they are likely to be rumormongers. This is a normal defensive reaction by which they attempt to make their situation more meaningful and secure.

In spite of all that can be done, rumors do start. Then what? In general, not all rumors should be fought, for that would be a needless waste of organizational time. Most rumors are relatively harmless and soon die out. On the other hand, some rumors tend to be harmful. For example, when a rumor of a layoff developed in a factory, the amount of products coming off the end of the assembly line decreased a few percentage points. People appeared to be working just as hard, but the flow of products declined. In situations such as this, the rumor may be serious enough to require management action to try to stop it.

USE OF FACTS The best way to stop or weaken rumor is to release the facts. Ambiguity is reduced, so there is less reason for rumor, and the truth tends to prevail. Serious rumors should be attacked as early as possible because once the general theme of a rumor is known and accepted, employees distort future happenings to conform to the rumor. Thus, if employees accept the rumor that there are plans to move the firm's offices to a new building, every minor change thereafter will be interpreted as a confirmation of that rumor (even, for example, when an electrician comes to repair an electric outlet). If the rumor were dead, this same change could be made without any employee upset at all.

Face-to-face supply of facts is helpful.

Usually, a face-to-face supply of facts is the most effective way, because it helps answer the ambiguities in each individual's mind and is preferred by people when they are uncertain and under stress. However, the facts should be given directly without first mentioning the rumor, because when a rumor is repeated at this time, some people will hear it instead of the refutation. They then assume you have confirmed the rumor! Here is an example of a suitable approach:

> **In one company John Reston cut two fingers of his left hand at his machine one morning. He was sent to the medical office for first aid, and he returned to his job in about thirty minutes with his fingers bandaged. Meanwhile, word had spread through the shop that John had cut his fingers. The farther from John's department the story traveled, the more gruesome were his injuries, until finally the story had him losing his left hand. Alert supervisors soon observed the effect of this rumor on morale and investigated the facts. Management then announced over the public address system that the most serious injury treated that morning was two cut fingers of a machine operator who received treatment and returned to his job in Department 37. No mention was made of the rumor, but this announcement brought the rumor under control.**

Use reliable sources.

The communication of facts is more effective if it comes from a source that employees think is in a position to know the true facts. The source also should be a person who has a dependable communication record. In addition, informal leaders can help management stop a rumor if the facts are shared with them as soon as possible. Though face-to-face refutation is the most effective, management may wish to reinforce the facts by confirming them in writing.

Union leaders can be helpful.

USE OF THE UNION Managers sometimes ask union leaders to help combat rumor. Although the union does not control the grapevine any more than management does, it has some influence. Since rumors are worst when management and labor are in conflict, any reduction of conflict should reduce rumors. Marked improvement frequently occurs in a department when management gains the union's cooperation in combating rumor, especially when the union leaders are powerful informal leaders.

Rumors carry useful messages.

LISTENING TO RUMOR Regardless of the importance of a rumor, it should be listened to carefully because, even though untrue, it usually carries a message about employee feelings. Each manager needs to ask, "Why did that rumor originate? What does it mean?" In this way a manager gains insight into where ambiguities are and what the interests of employees are. It may seem unrealistic to listen to rumors that are untrue, but listening can be useful.

For example, a labor relations director during a strike listened carefully to what the workers said management was going to do. The director, Mark Peerless, knew that these employee statements were rumors because management had not yet decided what to do. Nevertheless, he listened, because these rumors gave him insight into worker attitudes toward management and what kind of settlement they might agree to make.

Influencing informal organizations

Guidelines for action

Management did not establish informal organizations, and it cannot abolish them. Nor would it want to do so. But management can learn to live with them and have some measure of influence on them. Management guidelines for action are:

1 Accept and understand informal organization.

2 Consider possible effects on informal systems when taking any kind of action.

3 Integrate as far as possible the interests of informal groups with those of the formal organization.

4 Keep formal activities from unnecessarily threatening informal organizations.

Formal and informal combinations

The most desirable combination of formal and informal organizations appears to be a predominant formal system to maintain unity toward objectives, along with a well-developed informal system to maintain group cohesiveness and teamwork. In other words, the informal organization needs to be strong enough to be supportive, but not strong enough to dominate.

SUMMARY

Informal social systems exist in all organizations because they arise naturally from the interaction of people. Informal organizations have major benefits, but they also lead to problems that management cannot easily ignore.

Informal communication, called the grapevine, develops in the form of a cluster chain. Its accuracy in normal situations tends to be above 75 percent, but there may be inaccurate key details, and the whole story rarely is communicated. The grapevine is fast and influential. Employees tend to depend on it for information, even though they often view it as a negative factor. Rumor is grapevine information communicated without secure standards of evidence. It occurs when there is ambiguity and interest in the information.

Management can have some influence on the grapevine, and its basic objective is to integrate interests of the formal and informal systems so that they can work together better.

Terms and concepts for review

Informal organization
Informal leader
Cohesiveness
Norms
Reference group
Sanctions
Sociogram
Grapevine
Electronic grapevine
Cluster chain
Liaison individuals
Rumor
Filtering
Elaborating

Discussion questions

1. Think of a part-time or full-time job that you now hold or formerly held. Identify three different informal organizations that are (were) affecting your job or work group. Explain how they differ from the formal organization.
2. Still thinking of the job in question 1, discuss how the informal leaders probably rose to their positions and how they operate. What amount of informal cooperation with management exists (existed)?
3. Have you ever been in a situation where informal group norms put you in role conflict with formal organization standards? Discuss.
4. Discuss some of the benefits and problems that informal organizations may bring to:
   - **a** A work group
   - **b** An employer
5. Think of a small group that you belonged to recently. Assess the level of its cohesiveness on a scale from 1 (low) to 10 (high). What factors contributed to, or prevented, its cohesiveness?

6 Thinking of that same small group, in what ways were the members' actions, interactions, and sentiments different in practice from what they were supposed to be when the group was formed? Explain.
7 Discuss the accuracy of the grapevine, including various reasons for its inaccuracy.
8 Select a grapevine story that you heard, and discuss how it was communicated to you and how accurate it was.
9 Did you communicate the story in question 8 to others? Discuss why or why not. Then discuss the general reasons people are active on the grapevine.
10 Discuss how causes for rumor may be reduced and how rumor may be weakened or stopped after it has started.

Incidents

EXCELSIOR DEPARTMENT STORE

The Excelsior Department Store had a large department that employed six salesclerks. Most of these clerks were loyal and faithful employees who had worked in the department store more than ten years. They formed a closely knit social group.

The store embarked on an expansion program requiring four new clerks to be hired in the department within six months. These newcomers soon learned that the old-timers took the desirable times for coffee breaks, leaving the most undesirable periods for newcomers. The old-time clerks also received priority from the old-time cashier, which required the newcomers to wait in line at the cash register until the old-timers had their sales recorded. A number of customers complained to store management about this practice.

In addition, the old-timers frequently instructed newcomers to straighten merchandise in the stockroom and to clean displays on the sales floor, although this work was just as much a responsibility of the old-timers. The result was that old-timers had more time to make sales and newcomers had less time. Since commissions were paid on sales, the newcomers complained to the department manager about this practice.

Questions

1 How is the informal organization involved in this case? Discuss.
2 As manager of the department, what would you do about each of the practices? Discuss.

PEERLESS MINING COMPANY

Ben Greenbaum, a maintenance employee of Peerless Mining Company, asked for a six-month leave of absence for personal reasons. The request was granted because it was in accord with company and union policy. A few weeks later Fred Bart, the industrial relations manager of Peerless, heard by the grapevine that Ben actually had taken his leave to work on a construction project in another part of the state. The report was that Ben needed some extra money, and he had taken this job in order to earn contract construction wages as a carpenter, because these wages were approximately twice those earned on his regular maintenance job.

The act of taking leave for personal reasons, with the hidden purpose of working for another employer during the leave period, was contrary to the labor contract, and the penalty for this could be dismissal. After investigation to determine that the grapevine information probably was correct, Fred prepared a "notice of hearing concerning dismissal action" to be mailed to Ben at his local address where his wife and children remained. The letter of notice was dictated by Fred on Thursday morning.

Thursday night Ben called Fred at his home, saying that he had heard that the notice was being prepared and that he felt there was a misunderstanding. He said that he thought his action was acceptable under the contract, but if it was not acceptable, he wanted to return immediately, because he did not want to give up his permanent job. When Fred pressed him to learn how he knew about the pending dismissal notice, Ben said that his wife had called him that evening. He said that his wife had reported that another wife at a local grocery store had told her about the pending dismissal notice.

Questions

1 Is there any evidence in this case that both management and employees use the grapevine for their benefit? Discuss.
2 Assume grapevine facts are as follows: Fred's secretary told a fringe benefit clerk about the dismissal notice, and the clerk, not realizing the information might be confidential, told someone else. If you were Fred, would you try to suppress grapevine leaks of this type? Discuss.
3 After Ben's telephone call, what action should Fred take?

Experiential exercise

THE GRAPEVINE STORY

The best way to understand the filtering and elaboration that occur in the grapevine is to experience how they work. Select four people who will be communicators and receivers for a grapevine story. The instructor will select for communication a news story with ten to twenty-five units of information similar to the sample story at the end of this exercise. The plan is that the four people selected will try to pass their message sequentially from one to the other. There should be no tricks and each should try to communicate as accurately as possible. The rules are that each can tell the story only once, it must be told orally, and there can be no notes.

The procedure is that three people will leave the room and the instructor will read the story once to the remaining person. Then a second person is called in, and the first tells the story as well as possible to the second. The sequence is repeated for the third and the fourth. The fourth then repeats the story to the entire class; the instructor reads the accurate story so that all can hear it; and the class members discuss their experiences.

Following is a sample story:

John Edward Dobson, familiarly known as "Cowboy," was thrown for a loss Tuesday as a jury in Judge Walter Stein's county court at law convicted him of burglary of a store that sold western clothes. Dobson was given one year in the county corral. This was the maximum he could have received for his offense.

References

1 William H. Peace, "I Thought I Knew What Good Management Was," *Harvard Business Review,* March–April 1986, p. 61.

2 For a discussion of various socialization approaches, see Gareth R. Jones, "Socialization Tactics, Self-Efficacy, and Newcomers' Adjustments to Organizations," *Academy of Management Journal,* June 1986, pp. 262–279. On a more formal level of socialization, see Richard Pascale, "Fitting New Employees in to the Corporate Culture," *Fortune,* May 28, 1984, pp. 28ff.

3 William E. Reif, Robert M. Monczka, and John W. Newstrom, "Perceptions of the Formal and Informal Organization: Objective Measurement through the Semantic Differential Technique," *Academy of Management Journal,* September 1973, pp. 389–403.

4 The idea that the informal organization's activities, interactions, and sentiments emerge from the formal organization is drawn from George C. Homans, *The Human Group,* New York: Harcourt, Brace, Jovanovich, 1950.

5 A number of other informal roles are discussed in Fred Luthans, *Organizational Behavior,* 4th ed., New York: McGraw-Hill Book Company, 1985.

6 Beatrice Shultz, "Communicative Correlates of Perceived Leaders in the Small Group," *Small Group Behavior,* February 1986, pp. 51–65.

7 Nancy Foy, "Networkers of the World Unite!" *Personnel Management,* March 1983, p. 27.

8 Stuart Drescher, Gary Burlingame, and Addie Fuhriman, "Cohesion: An Odyssey in Empirical Understanding," *Small Group Behavior,* February 1985, pp. 3–30. For discussion of a reliable instrument to measure cohesion, see Nancy J. Evans and Paul A. Jarvis, "The Group Attitude Scale: A Measure of Attraction to Group," *Small Group Behavior,* May 1986, pp. 203–216.

9 Four types of work-group reaction (acceptance, avoidance, confrontation, and nurturance) are discussed by James W. Fairfield-Sonn, "Work Group Reactions to New Members: Tool or Trap in Making Selection Decisions?" *Public Personnel Management,* Winter 1984, pp. 485–493.

10 Daniel Feldman, "The Development and Enforcement of Group Norms," *Academy of Management Review,* January 1984, pp. 47–53.

11 Monika Henderson and Michael Argyle, "The Informal Rules of Working Relationships," *Journal of Occupational Behaviour,* vol. 7, 1986, pp. 259–275.

12 The term "sent to Coventry" is derived from the citizens of Coventry, England, who so disliked soldiers that people seen talking to one were isolated from their social community, so those few who felt like talking to soldiers did not dare do so. Hence a soldier sent to Coventry was isolated from community interaction.

13 For a field study and charts, see Donald F. Schwartz and Eugene Jacobson, "Organizational Communication Network Analysis: The Liaison Communication Role," *Organizational Behavior and Human Performance,* vol. 18, February 1977, pp. 158–174. For survey methods for securing grapevine data, see Keith Davis, "Methods for Studying Informal Communication," *Journal of Communication,* Winter 1978, pp. 112–116.

14 Daniel Goleman, "The Electronic Rorschach," *Psychology Today*, February 1983, pp. 36–43.

15 Keith Davis, "Management Communication and the Grapevine," *Harvard Business Review*, September–October 1953, p. 44.

16 Our own research discloses an accuracy of 80 to 99 percent for noncontroversial company information. Accuracy probably is lower for personal or highly emotional information.

17 Keith Davis, "Grapevine Communication among Lower and Middle Managers," *Personnel Journal*, April 1969, pp. 269–272.

18 Ronald J. Burke, "Quality of Organizational Life: The Effects of Personnel Job Transfers," in Vance F. Mitchell et al. (eds.), *Proceedings of the Academy of Management*, Vancouver, Canada: University of British Columbia, 1973, p. 242.

19 John W. Newstrom, Robert E. Monczka, and William E. Reif, "Perceptions of the Grapevine: Its Value and Influence," *Journal of Business Communication*, Spring 1974, pp. 12–20.

20 See, for example, Walter Kiechel III, "In Praise of Office Gossip," *Fortune*, Aug. 19, 1985, pp. 254–256.

21 Gordon W. Allport and Leo Postman, *The Psychology of Rumor*, New York: Holt, Rinehart and Winston, 1947, p. 33; and Allan D. Frank, *Communicating on the Job*, Glenview, Ill.: Scott, Foresman and Company, 1982, pp. 148–149. Anxiety is also included as a factor by Fredrick Koenig, *Rumor in the Marketplace: The Social Psychology of Commercial Hearsay*, Dover, Mass.: Auburn House Press, 1985, pp. 31–32.

22 "Leaks and Rumors," *Wall Street Journal*, June 6, 1984, p. 33.

For additional reading

Allport, Gordon W., and Leo Postman, *The Psychology of Rumor*, New York: Holt, Rinehart and Winston, 1947.

Frank, Allan D., *Communicating on the Job*, Glenview, Ill.: Scott, Foresman and Company, 1982.

Homans, George, *The Human Group*, New York: Harcourt, Brace, Jovanovich, 1950.

Koenig, Fredrick, *Rumor in the Marketplace: The Social Psychology of Commercial Hearsay*, Dover, Mass.: Auburn House Press, 1985.

Ritti, R. Richard, and G. Ray Funkhouser, *The Ropes to Skip and the Ropes to Know: Studies in Organizational Behavior*, 3d ed., Columbus, Ohio: Grid Publishing Company, 1986.

Roethlisberger, F. J., and W. J. Dickson, *Management and the Worker*, Cambridge, Mass.: Harvard University Press, 1939.

Szilagyi, Andrew D., Jr., and Marc J. Wallace, *Organizational Behavior and Performance*, Glenview, Ill.: Scott, Foresman and Company, 1987, especially chap. 8.

CHAPTER 16

Quality of work life and sociotechnical systems

When organizations have addressed the issue of quality of working life, they have always achieved great productivity breakthroughs.

JEROME M. ROSOW[1]

QWL programs and new sociotechnical systems in greenfield sites have better results than redesigns of existing systems.

DANIEL A. ONDRACK AND MARTIN G. EVANS[2]

CHAPTER OBJECTIVES

To understand

Quality of work life

Job enrichment

Core dimensions of jobs

Natural work modules and teams

Benefits and limitations of job enrichment

The impact of social cues

Enriched sociotechnical work systems

An ambitious, innovative program to improve the quality of work life in a General Foods pet-food plant has been operating successfully for two decades. The plant was built to use work teams of seven to fourteen members. Careful attention was given even to items such as plant design to reduce traditional status symbols found in most plants. There was an open parking lot and a common entrance for plant and office people, and decor in the offices and locker rooms was similar. Distinctions between technical specialists and workers were reduced because most specialized support activities were assigned to each operating team. Examples of support activities performed by each team are maintenance, quality control, custodial work, and personnel activities such as helping select new employees for one's team. Teams were given high autonomy over almost all activities for which they had capability. The role of supervisor changed to provide less direct supervision and more general management duties. Other innovations included:

- **A single job classification for all operators, with pay increases geared to mastering additional jobs in the team and in the plant**
- **Decision-making information for operators of the type that formerly only managers received**
- **Enlarged jobs with most routine work mechanized**
- **Team control of task redistribution when members are absent**
- **Team counseling of members who fail to meet team standards**

Results were favorable compared with other plants using traditional systems. Quality problems were reduced 90 percent, and absenteeism and turnover were less. Productivity increased, but this resulted partly from the technology of the new plant.

General Foods is one of many organizations that recognized the high human costs of traditional work designs. Despite their benefits to society, changing times have made these human costs less acceptable. Therefore, organizations gradually began experimenting with work designs that provide effective human results along with high efficiency. This chapter presents approaches to more humanized jobs and work environments, including job enrichment and enriched sociotechnical work systems. The purpose is to develop a better quality of work life for employees and higher productivity for the employer.

UNDERSTANDING QUALITY OF WORK LIFE

What is QWL?

Quality of work life (QWL) refers to the favorableness or unfavorableness of a job environment for people.[3] The basic purpose is to develop work environments that are excellent for people as well as for the economic health of the organization. The elements in a typical QWL program include many items discussed earlier in this book—open communications, equitable reward systems, a concern for employee job security, and participation in job design. Many QWL efforts focus on job enrichment, which is a major topic in this chapter. In addition to programs for improving the sociotechnical work system, QWL programs usually emphasize employee skill development, the reduction of occupational stress, and the development of more cooperative labor-management relations.[4]

QWL is a large step forward from the traditional job design of scientific management, which focused mostly on specialization and efficiency for the performance of narrow tasks. As it evolved, it used full division of labor, rigid hierarchy, and standardization of labor to reach its objective of efficiency. The idea was to lower costs by using unskilled, repetitive labor that could be trained easily to do a small part of the job. Job performance was controlled by a large hierarchy that strictly enforced the one best way of work as defined by technical people.

Since classical design gave inadequate attention to quality of work life, many difficulties developed. There was excessive division of labor and overdependence on rules, procedures, and hierarchy. Specialized workers became socially isolated from their coworkers because their highly specialized work weakened their community of interest in the whole product. Many workers were so deskilled that they lost pride in their work. The result was higher turnover and absenteeism. Quality declined, and workers became alienated. Conflict arose as workers tried to improve their conditions.

Management's response to this situation was to tighten controls, to increase supervision, and to organize more rigidly. These actions were intended to improve the situation, but they only made it worse, because they further dehumanized the work. Management made a common error by treating the symptoms rather than the causes of the problems. The real cause was that in many instances the job itself simply was not satisfying. The odd condition developed for some employees that the more they worked, the *less* they were satisfied. Hence, the desire to work declined.

A factor contributing to the problem was that the workers themselves were changing. They became more educated, more affluent (partly because of the effectiveness of classical job design), and more independent. They began reaching for higher-order needs, something more than merely earning their bread. Perhaps classical design was best for a poor, uneducated, often illiterate work force that lacked skills, but it was less appropriate for the new work force. Design of jobs and organizations had failed to keep up with widespread changes in worker aspirations and attitudes. Employers now had two reasons for redesigning jobs and organizations for a better QWL:

Reasons for QWL improvement

1 Classical design originally gave inadequate attention to human needs.

2 The needs and aspirations of workers themselves were changing.

Options available to management

Several options for solving these problems were available to management.

1 Leave the job as it is, and employ only workers who like the rigid environment and routine specialization of classical design. Not all workers object to this form of work. Some may even relish it because of the security and task support that it provides.

2 Leave the job as it is, but pay workers more so that they will accept the situation better. Since classical design usually produces economic gain, management can afford to share the gain with workers.

3 Mechanize and automate routine jobs so that the labor that is unhappy with the job is no longer needed. Let industrial robots do the routine work.

4 Redesign jobs to have the attributes desired by people, and redesign organizations to have the environment desired by people. This approach seeks to improve QWL.

Although all four options have usefulness in certain situations, the one that has captured the interest of people is option number 4. There is a need to give workers more of a challenge, more of a whole task, more opportunity to use advanced skills, more opportunity for growth, and more chance to contribute their ideas. The classical design of jobs was to construct them according to the technological imperative, that is, to design them according to the needs of technology and give little attention to other criteria. The new approach is to provide a careful balance of the human imperative and the technological imperative. *Work environments, and the jobs within them, are required to fit people as well as technology.* This is a new set of values and a new way of thinking that focuses on QWL.

Humanized work

Why should we humanize work?

QWL produces a more humanized work environment. It attempts to serve the higher-order needs of workers as well as their more basic needs. It seeks to employ the higher skills of workers and to provide an environment that encourages them to improve their skills. The idea is that workers are human resources that are to be developed rather than simply used. Further, the work should not have excessively negative conditions. It should not put workers under undue stress. It should not damage or degrade their humanness. It should not be threatening or unduly dangerous. Finally, it should contribute to, or at least leave unimpaired, workers' abilities to perform in other life roles, such as citizen, spouse, and parent. That is, work should contribute to general social advancement.

The basic assumption of humanized work is that work is most advantageous when it provides a "best fit" among workers, jobs, technology, and the environment. Accordingly, the best design will be different to fit different arrangements of these variables. Since a job design is required to fit the current situation, it is not a one-time thing to be established and retained indefinitely. Rather, there needs to be a regular readjustment among the factors just mentioned in order to maintain the best fit.

The fact that organizations usually pursue multiple approaches to improving their QWL was demonstrated in a survey of 125 firms in the northeastern United States.[5] Although 10 percent of them had no QWL program, about half of them had three or

more programs in various stages of planning and implementation. Average company satisfaction was quite high with all twelve programs studied, and the average likelihood of continuing the programs ranged from 85 to 100 percent.

JOB ENRICHMENT

Job enrichment vs. job enlargement

The modern interest in quality of work life developed through an emphasis on job enrichment. The term was coined by Frederick Herzberg based on his research with motivators and maintenance factors. Strictly speaking, *job enrichment* means that additional motivators are added to a job to make it more rewarding, although the term has come to apply to almost any effort to humanize jobs. Job enrichment is an expansion of an earlier concept of *job enlargement,* which sought to give workers a wider variety of duties in order to reduce monotony. The difference between the two ideas is illustrated in Figure 16-1. Here we see that job enrichment focuses on satisfying higher-order needs, while job enlargement concentrates on adding additional tasks to the worker's job for greater variety. The two approaches can even be blended together, by both expanding the number of tasks and adding more motivators for a two-pronged attempt to improve QWL.

Benefits of job enrichment

Job enrichment brings many benefits.[6] Its general result is a role enrichment that encourages growth and self-actualization. The job is built in such a way that intrinsic motivation is encouraged. Because motivation is increased, performance should improve, thus providing both a more human and a more produc-

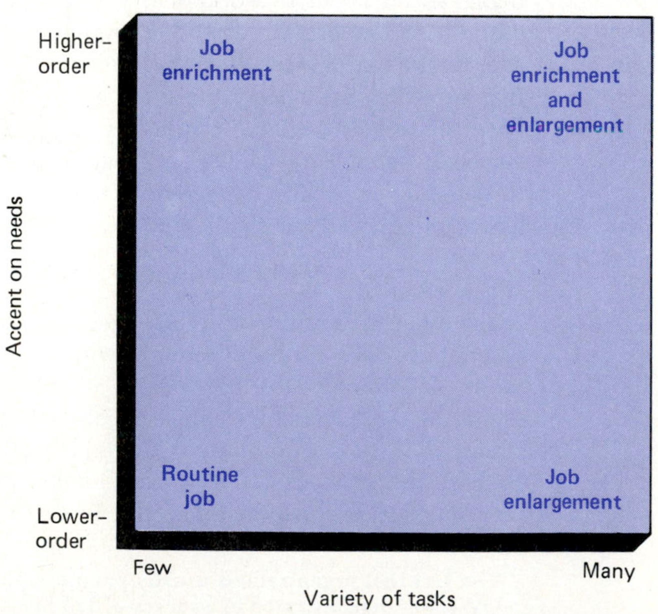

FIGURE 16-1
Difference between job enrichment and job enlargement

tive job. Negative effects also tend to be reduced, such as turnover, absence, grievances, and idle time. In this manner both the worker and society benefit. The worker performs better, has more job satisfaction, and is more self-actualized, thus being able to participate in all life roles more effectively. Society benefits from the more effectively functioning person as well as better job performance. Following is an example of both quality and quantity improvements with job enrichment.

Unusually high results were obtained with job enrichment in the assembly of electric hot plates in a manufacturing firm. Originally the employees worked on an assembly line, each worker performing a small part of the total assembly. Productivity met the established expectations. Management decided on job enrichment, not because there was a problem but because the task seemed appropriate for enrichment. In the enriched procedure, each worker completed a whole hot plate, being personally responsible for it. The workers rapidly developed improved interest in their work. Controllable rejects dropped from 23 to 1 percent, and absenteeism fell from 8 to 1 percent. As shown in Figure 16-2, productivity improved as much as 84 percent

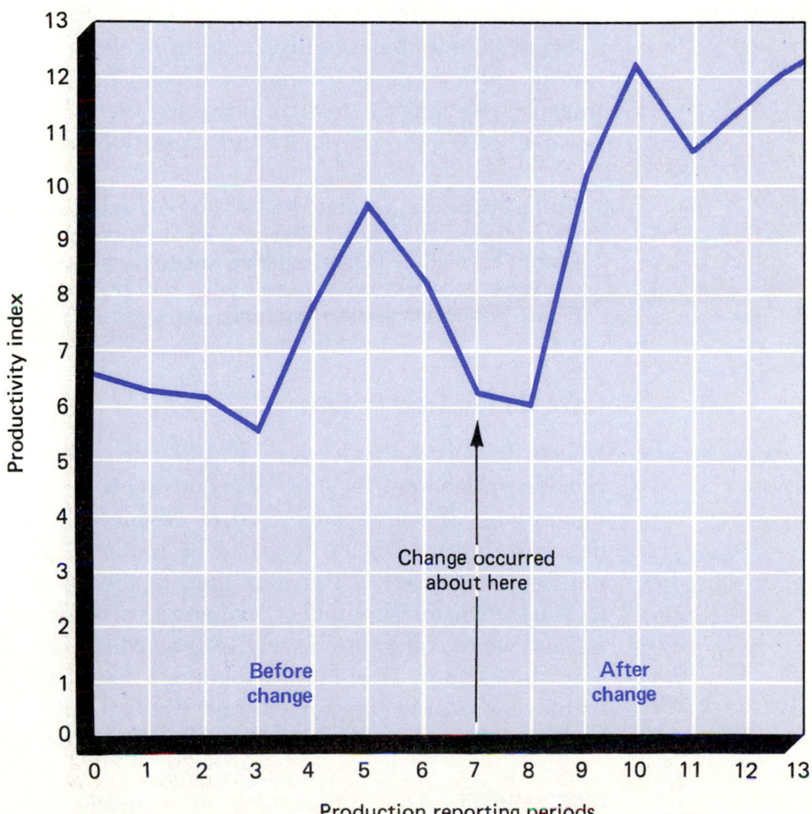

FIGURE 16-2
Productivity increases from job enrichment in hot-plate assembly work
Source: *Edgar F. Huse and Michael Beer, "Eclectic Approach to Organizational Development,"* Harvard Business Review, *September–October 1971, p. 106, copyright © 1971. Reprinted with permission.*

within six months. Since no other changes were made in the department, most of these results appeared to stem from job enrichment.

Applying job enrichment

Viewed in terms of Herzberg's motivational factors, job enrichment occurs when the work itself is more challenging, when achievement is encouraged, when there is opportunity for growth, and when responsibility, feedback, and recognition are provided. However, *employees are the final judges of what enriches their jobs.* All that management can do is gather information about what tends to enrich jobs, try these changes in the job system, and then determine whether employees feel that enrichment has occurred.

In trying to build motivational factors, management also gives attention to maintenance factors. It attempts to keep maintenance factors constant or higher as the motivational factors are increased. If maintenance factors are allowed to decline during an enrichment program, then employees may be less responsive to the enrichment program because they are distracted by inadequate maintenance. The need for a systems approach to job enrichment is satisfied by the practice of *gainsharing,* in which employees receive a substantial portion of the cost savings produced when their jobs are improved.

Gainsharing satisfies maintenance needs.

Since job enrichment must occur from each employee's personal viewpoint, *not all employees will choose enriched jobs if they have an option.* A contingency relationship exists in terms of different job needs, and some employees may prefer the simplicity and security of more routine jobs.

In one instance a manufacturer set up production in two different ways.[7] Employees were allowed to choose between work on a standard assembly line and at a bench where they individually assembled the entire product. In the beginning few employees chose to work the enriched jobs, but gradually about half the workers chose them. The more routine assembly operation seemed to fit the needs of the other half.

Core dimensions of jobs

Five core dimensions

Hackman and Oldham have identified five core dimensions that especially provide enrichment for jobs.[8] It is desirable for a job to have all five of these dimensions. If one is perceived to be missing, workers are psychologically deprived and motivation tends to be reduced. The core dimensions tend to improve motivation, satisfaction, and quality of work and to reduce turnover and absenteeism. Their effect on quantity of work is less dependable.[9] Managerial and white-collar jobs, as well as blue-collar jobs, often are deficient in some core dimensions. Admittedly there are large individual differences in how employees react to core dimensions, but the typical employee finds them to be basic for internal motivation. The dimensions are shown in Figure 16-3.

TASK VARIETY One core dimension is *variety in the job.* Variety allows employees to perform different operations that often require different skills. It is illustrated by the following anecdote:

Core dimensions **are those that especially enrich jobs.**

- **If any are missing, workers are psychologically deprived.**

Core dimensions are:

- ***Task variety.*** **Different operations to perform**
- ***Task identity.*** **Performing a complete piece of the work**
- ***Task significance.*** **Work that appears to be important**
- ***Autonomy.*** **Some control by employees over their own tasks**
- ***Feedback.*** **Information about performance**

FIGURE 16-3
Core dimensions of jobs

A tourist in Mexico stopped at a woodcarver's shop to inquire about the price of a chair that was hand-carved. The woodcarver replied, "Fifty pesos."

The tourist said that she liked the chair and wanted three more exactly like it. Hoping to receive a quantity discount, she asked, "How much for four chairs?"

The woodcarver replied, "Two hundred fifty pesos for four chairs."

Shocked that the price per unit for four chairs was more than for one chair, the tourist asked why. The woodcarver replied, "But, señorita, it is very boring to carve four chairs that are exactly alike."

Jobs that are high in variety are seen by employees as more challenging because of the range of skills involved. These jobs also relieve monotony that develops from any repetitive activity. If the work is physical, different muscles are used, so that one muscular area is not so overworked and tired at the end of the day. Variety gives employees a greater sense of competence, because they can perform different kinds of work in different ways.

TASK IDENTITY A second core job dimension is *task identity,* which allows employees to perform a complete piece of the work. Many job enrichment efforts have been focused on this dimension, because in the past the scientific management movement led to overspecialized, routine jobs. Individual employees worked on such a small part of the whole that they were unable to identify any product with their efforts. They could not feel any sense of completion or responsibility for the whole product. When tasks are broadened to produce a whole product or an identifiable part of it, then task identity has been established. This kind of whole job occurred in assembly of the hot plates mentioned earlier in this chapter. Other examples are a radio factory where each worker assembles a pocket radio and an office where a single employee prepares a major report rather than a part of it.

A crane operator working on high-rise construction projects in Washington is known as "Johnny Crane."[10] He works up to 16-hour days in a tiny cage 210 feet above the construction site, moving materials and equipment. What is the main source of his satisfaction? He replies, "I can drive around Washington and point to the buildings I've built." This is an example of a job that apparently does not need to be enriched any further on the task identity dimension. Although Johnny Crane technically does

not construct entire buildings, he clearly identifies with the whole task and feels a sense of completion when the job is finished.

TASK SIGNIFICANCE A third core dimension is *task significance*. It refers to the amount of impact, as perceived by the worker, that the work has on other people. The impact can be on others in the organization, as when the worker performs a key step in the work process, or it may be on those outside the firm, as when the worker helps to make a lifesaving medical instrument. The key point is that workers believe they are doing something important in their organization and/or society. The story has been told about workers who were instructed to dig holes in various parts of a storage yard. Then the supervisor looked at the holes and told the workers to fill them and dig more holes in other places. Finally the workers revolted, because they saw no usefulness in their work. Only then did the supervisor tell them that they were digging the holes to try to locate a water pipe.

Even routine factory work can have task significance. St. Regis Paper Company had customer complaints about seams tearing and bottoms dropping out of about 6 percent of grocery bags made in three plants.[11] Management attempted to solve the problem by adding more inspectors and making production changes, but these efforts were not successful.

Finally management decided to work with the bag-machine operators to show them the significance of their work. One step was to circulate customer complaint letters so that the operators could see how serious the problem was. Management also arranged to have the signature of each operator imprinted on the bottom of the bags as follows: "Another quality product by St. Regis. Personally inspected by . . . employee's name)."

Employees responded by reducing defective bags from 6 to ½ percent. They were proud of their work and its direct significance to customers. Employees even started taking their nameplates with them during rest breaks because they wanted to be responsible personally for bags that had their signature.

AUTONOMY A fourth core dimension is *autonomy*. It is the job characteristic that gives employees some discretion and control over job-related decisions, and it appears to be fundamental in building a sense of responsibility in workers. Although they are willing to work within the broad constraints of an organization, they also insist on a degree of freedom. You may remember that in the discussion of Maslow's need hierarchy in Chapter 5, autonomy was mentioned as a possible additional step on the need scale since it is so important to many people. The popular practice of management by objectives (MBO) is one way of establishing more autonomy because it provides a greater role for workers in setting their own goals and pursuing plans to achieve them.

FEEDBACK A fifth core dimension is feedback. *Feedback* refers to information that tells workers how well they are performing. It comes from the job itself, management, and other employees. The idea of feedback is a simple one, but it is of much significance to people at work. Since they are investing a substantial part of their lives in their work, they want to know how well they are doing.

Further, they need to know rather often because they recognize that performance does vary, and the only way they can make adjustments is to know how they are performing now.

Monthly output reports often are inadequate because the time lag is too great. (For example, one manager equated monthly reports with trying to drive a car by looking in the rear-view mirror. By the time you find out where you have been, it's often too late.) Weekly and daily reports are better, and hourly and continuous reporting may be even better if the work process allows this type of feedback. For example, operators attending cigarette-making machines have automatic inspection that provides continuous feedback to panels on the machines, so that operators know at all times if the work is progressing satisfactorily. The same is also true for bottlers at bottling machines. Note in these illustrations that workers receive complete job feedback, both positive and negative. If they receive only negative feedback, it may not be motivating.

The motivating potential of jobs

Job Diagnostic Survey

An instrument used to determine the relative presence of the five core dimensions in jobs is the *Job Diagnostic Survey.*[12] Before job enrichment is begun, an employer studies jobs to assess how high they are on task variety, task identity, task significance, autonomy, and feedback. Scales are created for each dimension, and then each job is rated according to where it fits on each scale. For example, on a scale of 1 through 10, variety may be given a rating of 6 and autonomy a lower rating of 4. Employees are usually involved in this assessment process, since it is their perceptions that are most important.

Motivating potential score

After the data are collected, an overall index that measures the *motivating potential score* (MPS) of a job may be computed. The MPS indicates the degree to which the job is perceived to be Meaningful, (M, or average of variety, identity, and significance), foster Responsibility (R, or autonomy), and provide Knowledge of Results (KR, or feedback). The formula is:

$$MPS = M \times R \times KR$$

Jobs that have been enriched to create a high MPS increase the probability of high motivation, provided that employees:

Conditions for job enrichment

- Have adequate job knowledge and skills
- Desire to learn, grow, and develop
- Are satisfied with their work environment

Profile chart

A useful way to compare jobs (or perceptions of them by managers and employees) is to place their scores on a *profile chart,* which graphically displays the data. Figure 16-4 shows that job A has moderate autonomy but is high in the other four dimensions. In general, job B has less enrichment than job A. Once the profile of a job is determined, then the job can be studied in detail to

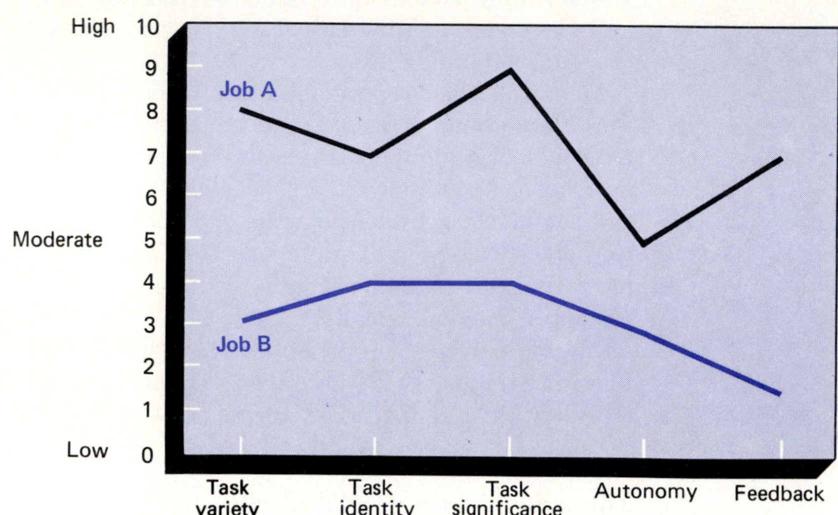

FIGURE 16-4
Profile chart of core dimensions for two jobs

determine how the weak dimensions may be improved. Not all jobs can be made outstanding on all dimensions, but most jobs can have some enrichment. When they are enriched, the payoff can be great, as seen in this example:

> **Most job enrichment attempts have been conducted in manufacturing operations, but many have also been attempted in banks, insurance companies, and other service organizations. Salespersons in a large department store provided the subjects for a field experiment in job redesign for enrichment purposes.[13] After providing their perceptions of their current jobs as measured by a set of scales that produce a motivating potential score, they implemented a series of job changes designed to increase the variety, identity, significance, autonomy, and feedback gained from their jobs.**
>
> **The salespersons' MPS scores increased significantly (from 25.6 to 41.5) following the experiment, indicating that they believed their jobs had become enriched. Dysfunctional behaviors such as misuse of idle time and absence from the workstation decreased, while functional behaviors (selling and stocking) increased moderately. Several measures of employee satisfaction also improved.**

The impact of social cues

Not all attempts to enrich jobs have been as successful as the experiment that was just described. In some cases employees do not report significant changes in their perceptions of the job characteristics after job enrichment despite objective evidence that the job changed. This has been the source of considerable frustration for both job design specialists and managers.

Sources of social cues

An explanation for the lack of predicted changes from enrichment seems to lie in the presence of *social cues*. In addition to the possibility that employees will not perceive the degree of changes that management introduces, there is evidence to suggest that employees are quite receptive to information received from their social surroundings.[14] These social cues may come from coworkers, leaders, other organizational members, customers, and family members. Social cues may serve either to support or to counteract the direction of objective task characteristics, as shown in Figure 16-5.

An integrated approach to job design suggests that managers must focus on managing the social context of job changes, as well as the job enrichment process itself.[15] They must discover which groups are important sources of social cues, perhaps using group discussions to reinforce an employee's initial tendencies to assess job changes positively. Managers can also create expectations (in the minds of employees and coworkers) that the enriched jobs will be more satisfying. The recognition and use of social cues in job design, called *social information processing*, once again provides support for the QWL theme that both human and technical factors must be considered for a change to be successful.

Limitations of job enrichment

Job enrichment has a number of limitations, as shown in Figure 16-6. It is more appropriate for some situations than for others, and in certain situations it may not be appropriate at all.[16] Some workers do not want increased responsibility, and other workers do not adapt to the group interaction that is sometimes required. In other words, enrichment is contingent on attitudes of employees and their capability to handle enriched tasks. It can be argued that employees should accept job enrichment because it is "good," but it is more consistent

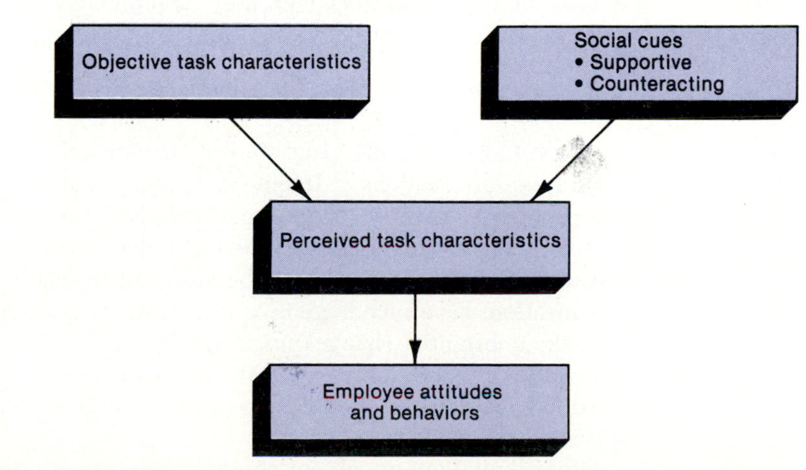

FIGURE 16-5
Social cues affect employee reactions to tasks.

- Some workers may not want enriched jobs:
  - —If they are unable to tolerate increased responsibility
  - —If they dislike more complex duties
  - —If they are uncomfortable with group work
  - —If they dislike relearning
  - —If they prefer security and stability
  - —If they are comfortable with supervisory authority
  - —If skills are not adaptable
  - —If they prefer to quit their jobs
- Expensive equipment may not be adaptable.
- The program may unbalance the production system.
- Supervisory or staff roles may be reduced.
- Enriched jobs may increase pay dissatisfaction.
- Costs may increase:
  - —Start-up costs such as training
  - —Long-run costs such as more equipment
- Unions may oppose some enrichment efforts.

FIGURE 16-6
Some limitations of job enrichment and QWL programs

with human values to recognize and respect individual differences of employees.

Those planning job enrichment and QWL programs need to ask such questions as the following about employee needs and attitudes:

- Can the employee tolerate responsibility?
- How strong are employee growth and achievement needs?
- What is the employee's attitude toward working with groups?
- Can the employee work with more complexity?
- How strong are the employee's drives for security and stability?
- Will the employees view the job changes as significant?

Enrichment may not apply.

CONTINGENCY FACTORS In a similar manner, job enrichment does not apply to all types of situations.[17] It appears to apply more easily to higher-level jobs, compared with lower-level ones, particularly if the lower-level jobs are dictated by the technological process. If the technology is stable and highly automated, the costs of job enrichment may be too great in relation to the rewards. Some organizations have such huge investments in equipment that they cannot afford to make substantial changes until the equipment is replaced. When difficult technological conditions are combined with negative employee attitudes toward job enrichment, then it becomes inappropriate until the environment for it can be changed.

Other limitations on job enrichment apply when it must be coordinated with other jobs, departments, or branches. For example, anticipated gains can be diminished because of effects on surrounding work systems. A projected enrichment in one organization assigned quality control to workers producing the product. Several highly paid quality-assurance people were put out of jobs, and the enrichment was delayed while their problems were resolved. In other organizations job enrichment for operating employees reduced the supervisory role, so the programs were not successful until the supervisors' jobs also were enriched.

PAY RELATIONSHIPS Job enrichment also may upset pay relationships. Management typically assumes that the intrinsic rewards of the enriched job are sufficient. Employees, however, may become unhappy because they think they are not paid in proportion to their increased duties. They want more money, but a pay increase adds to costs and may upset comparative pay relationships.

In a branch operation a supervisor enriched the jobs of salesclerks by allocating more responsibility to them. The clerks requested more pay, and the supervisor recommended it. The home office rejected the pay increase, thereby effectively rejecting the enrichment program. The home office was fearful that salesclerks in other branches would want similar pay, even if their jobs were not enriched. Either higher costs would occur or lower morale would develop when raises were not given. The other alternative, enriching clerks' jobs in all branches, was not practical at the time.

OTHER COSTS There are other costs in addition to pay. Equipment and floor space may need to be redesigned. In some instances more space and tools will be needed so that teams can work independently. Even work-in-process inventory may have to be increased so that individual workers or teams can have enough supplies. In addition, there are substantial training costs in order to prepare employees for their new patterns of work. There also are likely to be temporary quality and output problems during the period of change because existing teamwork among employees is disrupted. Some employees even resign. Although these costs may be acceptable in relation to benefits, they need to be considered carefully.

UNION ATTITUDES An additional contingency factor is union attitudes. Job enrichment may upset existing job classifications, thereby causing union resistance. In some instances enrichment may create jurisdictional disputes between the territories of two unions. Likely places for this problem are maintenance work and construction work. Distinctions between jobs may be so narrow and rules so rigid that unions will not tolerate some changes. However, there is evidence that a majority of union members want to become involved with QWL efforts.[18]

Desirability, contingency, and cost-benefit

CONCLUSIONS The limitations and difficulties with job enrichment lead to three conclusions, as summarized in Figure 16-7. First, job enrichment and QWL programs generally are desirable for both human and performance

FIGURE 16-7
Conclusions about job enrichment and QWL programs

1 **In a general way, job enrichment and QWL programs are desirable for both human and performance needs. They help employees, and they help the firm.**

2 **There is a contingency relationship. QWL improvements achieve better results in some situations than in others.**

3 **QWL programs bring costs as well as benefits. Both must be considered to determine net benefits and the desirability of a change.**

needs. They help both employees and the firm. Second, there is a contingency relationship. QWL improvements work better in some situations than others. They are not the best for every situation. A third conclusion is that QWL programs bring costs as well as benefits. Both must be evaluated to determine the desirability of a change. The key issue is how favorable the net benefits are.

With the many contingencies that exist in job enrichment, the best strategy is to study the need for it carefully and then to try it in the most appropriate places first. As success is achieved, there can be a gradual move toward more applications. The organization that suddenly becomes sold on job enrichment and then takes a blanket approach to it is likely to generate more problems than it can handle.

ENRICHED SOCIOTECHNICAL WORK SYSTEMS

Natural work teams

Natural work modules and teams

The next step above enriched jobs is to focus on work teams. When jobs have been designed so that a person performs a complete cycle of work to make a whole product or a subunit of it, then that person is performing a *natural work module*. The work flows naturally from start to finish and gives an individual a sense of task identity and significance. In a similar manner several employees may be arranged into a *natural work team* that performs an entire unit of work. In this way employees whose task requires them to work together are better able to learn each other's needs and to develop teamwork. Natural work teams even allow those who are performing routine work to develop a greater feeling of task significance, because they are attached to a larger team that performs a major task. It is surprising how our desire to develop specialization often leads to separation of people who are needed to make natural work teams.

Consider the experience of a telephone company with its service-order department.[19] Originally the service representatives and typists who prepared service orders were in separate areas of the office, and each took orders in rotation as they were received. Then different teams of representatives were assigned their own geographical region, and a few typists were moved to be with them, working only on their service orders. The employees now became a natural work team that could

cooperate in performing a whole task. The result was that orders typed on time increased from 27 percent to between 90 and 100 percent, and service-order accuracy exceeded the expected standard.

Employment enrichment

The next step above enriched jobs and natural work teams is *enriched sociotechnical work systems* in which a whole organization or a major portion of it is built into a balanced human-technical system. The objective is to develop complete *employment enrichment,* as shown in Figure 16-8. This requires changes of a major magnitude, particularly in manufacturing that has been designed along specialized lines. The entire production process may require reengineering in order to integrate human needs, and layouts may require changes to permit teamwork. The fundamental objective is to design a whole work system that serves needs of people as well as production requirements.

Flexible work schedules

Employees control their schedules.

Flexible working time, also known as "flexitime," or "flextime," is an example of employment enrichment. It gives workers more autonomy but in a manner different from job enrichment. With flextime employees gain some latitude for the control of their work environment—a factor beyond the design of the job itself—to fit their own lifestyles or to meet unusual needs, such as a visit to a physician. The idea is that, regardless of starting and stopping times, employees will work their full number of hours each day. Employees always work within the restraints of the installation's business hours, and if a job requires teamwork, all employees on a team must flex their work together.

An office provides an example. The office is open from 7 A.M. to 7 P.M., and employees may work their eight hours anytime during that period. One employee is an early riser and prefers to arrive at work at 7 A.M., leaving at 3:30 P.M. in order to shop or engage in sports. Another employee is a late riser and prefers to come to work at 10 A.M., leaving at 6:30 P.M. Another employee arranges her work period to fit a commuter train schedule. Still another employee prefers to take two hours for lunch and occasional shopping. Each employee sets a schedule to fit personal needs.

LEVEL	ACTION
System	**Enriched sociotechnical work systems**
	↑
Group	**Natural work teams**
	↑
Employee	**Natural work modules and Enriched job content**

FIGURE 16-8
The complete employment enrichment process

A certain percentage of workers must be at the office for certain core hours in order to meet the public, but otherwise their schedule is relatively free.

An advantage to the employer is that tardiness is eliminated, since the employee works a full number of hours regardless of arrival time. Since employees are able to schedule outside activities such as appointments during their working day, they tend to have fewer one-day absences for these purposes. Perhaps the main benefit is that greater autonomy leads to greater job satisfaction, and sometimes productivity improves as well.[20]

Sociotechnical experiments

A number of innovative experiments in QWL and enriched sociotechnical systems were developed in the 1970s at Volvo in Sweden and at General Motors in the United States. Another, at General Foods in Topeka, was described in the opening illustration for this chapter. Follow-up information on these provides insight into what has been learned from each. More recent experiments, such as those at Digital Equipment, continue to emerge. The diversity of approaches will be apparent in these summaries.

Volvo

Teams replace assembly lines.

Volvo built a new car assembly plant in Kalmar, Sweden, in the early 1970s in which it attempted to incorporate technical, managerial, and social innovations that better served the needs of employees.[21] The design cost about 10 percent more than a comparable conventional plant, but Volvo took the risk because it hoped to secure increased satisfaction and productivity as well as reduced turnover and absenteeism. The factory was designed to assemble 60,000 automobiles annually, using teams of fifteen to twenty-five workers for each major task. One team, for example, assembles electrical systems, while another assembles brakes. Each team has its own work area, and each is given substantial autonomy. The team is completely in charge of allocation of work among members and of setting the rhythm of its work.

There is no assembly line. Teams obtain a car from a buffer zone when they want one, moving it to their workplace on a trolley. When work is completed, the car is placed in the next buffer zone, a procedure that allows each team to work at its own pace as long as it can meet production requirements. Teams handle their own material procurement and manage their own inventory. The situation is much different from that of a traditional assembly line.

Volvo continued its efforts to increase efficiency and improve QWL through other experiments at its engine, bus assembly, cab, and truck plants throughout Sweden. Independent evaluations of Volvo's success at Kalmar showed that both assembly and office workers' costs were the lowest in the company. Employees report that their jobs are better than those on a traditional assembly line, but still report a greater desire for initiative and personal growth on the job.

General Motors: Tarrytown

Union-management relations in the auto industry have traditionally been adversarial. At the urging of the United Auto Workers, a National Committee on Quality of Work Life was created in 1973.[22] The Tarrytown assembly plant of General Motors was chosen as the pilot site because of a desire to solve the more difficult problems first. Tarrytown ranked seventeenth in quality (of eighteen plants); it had one of the highest grievance rates and experienced more strikes, and its absenteeism rate averaged 12 percent.

A steering committee was formed, a QWL philosophy statement was created and distributed, and actions were taken to build trust and respect between management and workers. A training program was initiated to provide employees with skills in problem solving, cost analysis, team building, and communications. Remarkably, all but 10 of the 3600 employees volunteered to participate.

Climate is a prerequisite.

The QWL program was comprehensive, was introduced slowly, and had a dual base of support from both management and the union. A profitable plant emerged: it rose to number one in quality and efficiency, absenteeism dropped to 3 percent, and grievances declined by 97 percent. Clearly, employees perceived a new environment in which their suggestions were sought and implemented, and the workers were valued for their skills and ideas.

General Motors: Fremont

A long history of labor-management conflict, poor quality, and extremely high absenteeism characterized the General Motors auto assembly plant in Fremont, California.[23] Then Toyota and GM created a joint venture that has since received international recognition for its quality, productivity, and labor climate. New United Motor Manufacturing, Inc. (NUMMI), now operates with virtually the same unionized labor force, but an entirely new sociotechnical system.

The labor contract was reduced from over 400 pages to 15, a collaborative problem-solving system was established, and a strong job security provision was provided. As a result, absenteeism was reduced, eighty-two job classifications were reduced to four, and employees work as teams. The number of grievances filed is almost negligible.

The reasons for this success appear to lie in the NUMMI philosophy, which has several elements. Employees are urged to search constantly for improvements, develop their full potential, and do their best to create a superior quality product. Team performance and mutual trust are emphasized. Every employee is expected to think and act like a manager. In return, NUMMI will attempt to provide its employees with a stable livelihood that has minimal risks of layoffs.

The emphasis at NUMMI is on creating a quality of work life that builds on pride of the employees in themselves, their group, and their work. Teamwork is heavily emphasized, as is full communication. Problems are solved through consensus approaches. Employees are urged to recognize and respect each other's rights. The impact of Toyota is especially clear in the insistence that there be harmony among the culture, structure, and operating systems.

Digital Equipment: Enfield

Unlike NUMMI, which ran the risk of inheriting previous labor-management problems, Digital Equipment Corporation's Enfield, Connecticut, plant is a greenfield site—it started shipping products in 1983.[24] The Enfield plant is small, with just 200 employees making printed-circuit-board modules for computer storage systems. The organizational hierarchy has just three levels, with employees reporting to group managers, who report to the plant manager.

There are two essential features of Enfield's sociotechnical approach— participative team management and job enrichment. Operating teams of twelve to eighteen members are encouraged to be self-managing, and each employee is trained to have multiple skills and perform a wide range of tasks on the total product. Skill-based pay is used to reward employees for acquiring new skills and knowledge. Regular group meetings are held for goal setting, problem solving, and communication. Teams of workers have the capacity to set their own work hours under a flextime system.

The results at Enfield are substantial. Compared with traditional facilities, the Enfield plant reduced the standard module-building time by 40 percent, using half the employees and half the space usually required. Overhead is also 40 percent less than normal, and scrap costs were reduced by 50 percent.

Results of sociotechnical experiments

Not all attempts to create a better QWL have been successful. One of the earliest, at Non-Linear Systems, was discarded when the firm's product leadership declined and productivity failed to keep pace with that of competitors.[25] Despite numerous behavioral innovations, the participative system proved too cumbersome to respond to quickly needed changes, and the firm was forced to return to a more traditional work system to survive.

The design and implementation of complex organizational systems for better QWL is far more difficult than many casual observers realize. Some employees object when other team members earn more after learning additional tasks. Some employees prefer to work on traditional tasks and avoid the extra group work and added responsibility. Both team leaders and entire work teams occasionally become autocratic, exerting excessive peer pressure for conformity to group norms. Role confusion also can occur.

There are substantial costs as well as benefits, and the payoffs may not come immediately. Sometimes the programs are oversold to the employees and the public, so it is important to examine carefully what does and does not work. Many years of additional experiments will be required before effective practices can be identified and applied with a high probability of success.[26]

SUMMARY

Quality of work life (QWL) refers to the favorableness or unfavorableness of the job environment for people. Since people and the environment have changed, increased attention needs to be given to improving the QWL. Jobs are required to fit people as well as technology.

Job enrichment applies to any efforts to humanize jobs, particularly the addition of motivators to jobs. Core dimensions of jobs that especially provide enrichment are task variety, task identity, task significance, autonomy, and feedback. It is helpful if natural work modules and natural work teams can be built. In spite of its desirability, job enrichment is a contingency relationship, being more applicable in some situations than others. Its effectiveness is affected by the social cues that employees receive.

Enriched sociotechnical work systems provide a balanced human-technical system that seeks complete employment enrichment. Major experiments with these systems have been made by many firms, such as Volvo, General Motors, and Digital Equipment. There are costs as well as benefits, but results generally are favorable.

Terms and concepts for review

Quality of work life (QWL)
Job enrichment
Job enlargement
Gainsharing
Core dimensions of jobs
Job Diagnostic Survey
Motivating potential score
Social cues
Profile charts of core dimensions
Natural work modules
Natural work teams
Flexible working time (flextime)
Enriched sociotechnical work systems

Discussion questions

1 Do employees differ in their view of what a good QWL is for them? Discuss. If they differ, discuss specific steps that an employer can take to provide a better QWL for all employees.
2 Form discussion groups of four to five people, and develop a list of the top six QWL items that your group wants in a job. Present your group report, along with your reasons, to other class members. Then discuss similarities and differences among groups.
3 Think of the job you now have or a job that you formerly had. Discuss both the favorable and unfavorable QWL characteristics that it had.
4 This chapter discussed gainsharing to increase the effectiveness of job enrichment. How does this relate to earlier discussions of motivational and maintenance factors, lower- and higher-order needs, and extrinsic-intrinsic rewards?

5 A survey of supervisor Herman Kahn's department shows that employees uniformly feel that the core dimension of feedback is low. Kahn refutes this conclusion by commenting: "That's not true. I give the group lots of feedback. They will confirm that I tell them every time they don't make production for the week and every time they violate a rule. I share all problems that arise with my employees." Discuss.
6 Select two jobs in a firm, and then prepare a profile chart of their core dimensions. Discuss your results.
7 Discuss some of the limitations of job enrichment and QWL programs.
8 Select from outside sources a major QWL program other than the ones presented in this chapter, and discuss it in class.
9 Has the United States made any progress in building better QWL in the last twenty years? Perform outside reading and interviews, and discuss this subject in class.

Incident

VALLEY ELECTRONICS

Valley Electronics produces a line of electronic equipment, including a miniature tape recorder that can be held in one's hand. In the final assembly of the tape recorder, fourteen employees work on an assembly line, using parts from parts bins. Each employee performs a different operation and then passes the assembly to the next person. The last two steps on the line are inspection and boxing. Inspection includes an operational test of each recorder. If a recorder fails inspection, it is placed at a bench where another employee reworks it. If the stack of recorders at the bench grows too large for the benchworker to handle, one of the regular assemblers is assigned overtime benchwork to reduce the backlog.

A recent job satisfaction survey showed that the assembly employees are reasonably satisfied. They have a friendly group, and the assembly design encourages conversation because there are seven employees on each side of the line facing each other. Turnover and absenteeism are considered normal by management. The employees are organized by a national labor union, but none of them appears to be active in the union. There are four racial minority members and several ethnic minorities in the group.

Questions

1 How favorable is the QWL for the assembly group? Discuss.
2 Do you recommend any changes in the assembly jobs? Discuss, including what specific changes you would make and what they are intended to accomplish.

Experiential exercise

THE ENRICHED STUDENT

1 Consider your academic "job" as a student. Rate it on each of the five core dimensions according to how much of each is presently in it (1 = low amount; 10 = high amount).

JOB DIMENSION	YOUR RATING	GROUP AVERAGE
Task variety	_____	_____
Task identity	_____	_____
Task significance	_____	_____
Autonomy	_____	_____
Feedback	_____	_____

2 Form into small groups of four to six persons, share your scores, and compute an average group score for each dimension. Then compute a motivating potential score for your group by using the MPS formula given in the text. What does this tell you?

3 Discuss five important steps that university administrators and professors could take to enrich your job if they had the data you generated.

References

1 Jerome M. Rosow, in Karen E. Debats (ed.), "The Continuing Personnel Challenge," *Personnel Journal*, May 1982, p. 344.

2 Daniel A. Ondrack and Martin G. Evans, "Job Enrichment and Job Satisfaction in Greenfield and Redesign QWL Sites," *Group and Organization Studies*, March 1987, p. 19. A greenfield site for a quality of work life program is a location where an organization constructs a totally new operation, and therefore it has no prior job designs or systems in place.

3 A discussion of various definitions of QWL is in David A. Nadler and Edward E. Lawler III, "Quality of Work Life: Perspectives and Directions," *Organizational Dynamics*, Winter 1983, pp. 20–30.

4 George Burstein, "Enhancing the Quality of Work Life," *Business Forum* (California State University, Los Angeles), Winter 1987, pp. 23–27.

5 Gerald D. Klein, "Employee-Centered Productivity and QWL Programs: Findings from an Area Study," *National Productivity Review*, Autumn 1986, pp. 348–362.

6 One survey of fifty-eight companies that had used job enrichment reported that the five areas of most frequent improvement were higher productivity, better job satisfaction, improved quality of work, less turnover, and less absenteeism. See Antoine Alber, "Job Enrichment for Profit," *Human Resource Management*, Spring 1979, pp. 15–25.

7 Edward E. Lawler III, "For a More Effective Organization—Match the Job to the Man," *Organizational Dynamics*, Summer 1974, pp. 19–29.

8 J. Richard Hackman, Greg R. Oldham, R. Janson, and K. Purdy, "A New Strategy for Job Enrichment," *California Management Review*, Summer 1975, pp. 57–71.

9 Ricky W. Griffin, Ann Welsh, and Gregory Moorhead, "Perceived Task Characteristics and Employee Performance: A Literature Review," *Academy of Management Review*, October 1981, pp. 655–664. A critical review is in Jiing-Lih Farh and W. E. Scott, Jr., "The Experimental Effects of 'Autonomy' on Performance and Self-Reports of Satisfaction," *Organizational Behavior and Human Performance*, April 1983, pp. 203–222.

10 George J. Church, "The Work Ethic Lives!" *Time*, Sept. 7, 1987, pp. 40–42.

11 "The Signature of Quality," *Management in Practice* (American Management Associations), March–April 1977, pp. 2–3.

12 Readers interested in details of the Job Diagnostic Survey, which measures MPS, should read J. Richard Hackman and Greg R. Oldham, "Development of the Job Diagnostic Survey," *Journal of Applied Psychology*, April 1975, pp. 159–170.

13 Fred Luthans et al., "The Impact of a Job Redesign Intervention on Salespersons' Observed Performance Behaviors: A Field Experiment," *Group and Organization Studies*, March 1987, pp. 55–72.

14 Social cues in job design were first discussed in G. R. Salancik and J. Pfeffer, "A Social Information Processing Approach to Job Attitudes and Task Design," *Administrative Science Quarterly*, vol. 23, 1978, pp. 224–253. Sources of social cues are reported in Joe G. Thomas, "Sources of Social Information: A Longitudinal Analysis," *Human Relations*, September 1986, pp. 855–870.

15 Ricky W. Griffin et al., "Objective and Social Factors as Determinants of Task Perceptions and Responses: An Integrated Perspective and Empirical Investigation," *Academy of Management Journal*, September 1987, pp. 501–523; Thomas S. Bateman, Ricky W. Griffin, and David Rubenstein, "Social Information Processing and Group-Induced Shifts in Responses to Task Design," *Group and Organization Studies*, March 1987, pp. 88–108.

16 The need to balance internal and external factors is presented in Randall B. Dunham, Jon L. Pierce, and John W. Newstrom, "Job Context and Job Content: A Conceptual Perspective," *Journal of Management*, Fall–Winter 1983, pp. 187–202; mixed results from a literature review are in Richard E. Kopelman, "Job Redesign and Productivity: A Review of the Evidence," *National Productivity Review*, Summer 1985, pp. 237–255.

17 Four different job design approaches for different situations are described in Michael A. Campion and Paul W. Thayer, "Job Design: Approaches, Outcomes, and Trade-offs," *Organizational Dynamics*, Winter 1987, pp. 66–79.

18 James W. Thacker and Mitchell W. Fields, "Union Involvement in Quality-of-Worklife Efforts: A Longitudinal Investigation," *Personnel Psychology*, Spring 1987, pp. 97–111.

19 Robert N. Ford, "Job Enrichment Lessons from AT&T," *Harvard Business Review*, January–February 1973, pp. 96–106; an update is Robert F. Craver, "AT&T's QWL Experiment: A Practical Case Study," *Management Review*, June 1983, pp. 12–16.

20 A comprehensive review of the flexible work schedule options, and their effects, is in Jon L. Pierce, John W. Newstrom, Randall B. Dunham, and Alison Barber, *Alternative Work Schedules*, Newton, Mass.: Allyn and Bacon, 1989.

21 Pehr G. Gyllenhammar, *People at Work*, Reading, Mass.: Addison-Wesley Publishing Company, 1977; and Pehr G. Gyllenhammar, "How Volvo Adapts Work to People," *Harvard Business Review*, July–August 1977, p. 102–113. Recent results are reported in Berth Jonsson and Alden G. Lank, "Volvo: A Report on the Workshop on Production Technology and Quality of Working Life," *Human Resource Management*, Winter 1985, pp. 455–465.

22 Robert Guest, "Quality of Work Life—Learning from Tarrytown," *Harvard Business Review*, July–August, 1979, pp. 76–87.

23 Robert R. Rehder and Marta Medaris Smith, "Kaizen and the Art of Labor Relations," *Personnel Journal*, December 1986, pp. 83–93.

24 Barcy H. Proctor, "A Sociotechnical Work-Design System at Digital Enfield: Utilizing Untapped Resources," *National Productivity Review*, Summer 1986, pp. 262–270. For another example of QWL program success in small organizations, see Peter F. Sorensen, Jr., Thomas C. Head, and Dick Stotz, "Quality of Work Life and the Small Organization: A Four-Year Case Study," *Group and Organization Studies*, September 1985, pp. 320–339.

25 A discussion of this early failure is presented in Erwin L. Malone, "The Non-Linear System Experiment in Participative Management," *The Journal of Business*, January 1975, pp. 52–64.

26 For discussions of the future of sociotechnical systems, see Albert Cherns, "Principles of Sociotechnical Design Revisited," *Human Relations*, March 1987, pp. 53–62; and William Barko and William Pasmore (eds.), "Sociotechnical Systems: Innovations in Designing High-Performing Systems," *The Journal of Applied Behavioral Science*, vol. 22, no. 3, 1986, especially Thomas G. Cummings, "A Concluding Note: Future Directions of Sociotechnical Theory and Research," pp. 355–360.

For additional reading

Connor, Patrick E., and Linda K. Lake, *Managing Organizational Change*, New York: Praeger Publishers, Inc., 1988.

Davis, Louis E., and James C. Taylor (eds.), *Design of Jobs*, 2d ed., Santa Monica, Calif.: Goodyear Publishing Company, 1979.

Griffin, Ricky W., *Task Design: An Integrative Approach*, Glenview, Ill.: Scott, Foresman and Company, 1982.

Hackman, J. Richard, and Greg R. Oldham, *Work Redesign*, Reading, Mass.: Addison-Wesley Publishing Company, 1980.

Pierce, Jon L., John W. Newstrom, Randall B. Dunham, and Alison Barber, *Alternative Work Schedules*, Newton, Mass.: Allyn and Bacon, 1989.

Steele, Fritz, *Making and Managing High-Quality Workplaces*, Scranton, Penn.: Harper & Row Publishers, Inc. (Teachers College Press), 1986.

PART

5

Social environment

CHAPTER 17

The individual in the organization

The critical issue of breached privacy hinges then on the business necessity and employee's expectation of privacy.

SUZANNE H. COOK[1]

CHAPTER OBJECTIVES

To understand

Conformity

A model of legitimacy of organizational influence

How rights to privacy are interpreted

Dealing with substance abuse in organizations

Different approaches to discipline

Mutual individual-organization responsibilities

Whistle-blowing as a prosocial organizational behavior

When you read fiction and social commentary, you often find a common symbolic thread. It is that organizations are systems that suppress their victim, the *individual*. Individuals live in conformity, stripped of their self-esteem and in an artificial environment. There is no challenge and no chance for psychological fulfillment. There is only security in return for saying "Yes," smiling, and wearing a neat business suit. Individuals are too numb from all this to rebel, but they *should* rebel. In turn, the organization stands socially and morally condemned.

Throughout history there has been this view of people and organizations in perpetual conflict, but now we realize that they can live in some degree of mutual interest and harmony. Individuals use organizations as instruments to achieve their goals just as much as organizations use people to reach objectives. There is a mutual social transaction in which each benefits the other.

In this chapter we discuss some of the relationships of individuals to organizations, including conformity, rights of privacy, the individual and drug abuse, discipline, and individual-organization responsibilities.

ISSUES ABOUT CONFORMITY

The basic thesis of conformity

What is conformity?

Conformity is a dependence on the norms of others without independent thinking. The basic thesis of individual conformity to the organization was stated by Whyte and Argyris in separate books in the 1950s. In *The Organization Man*, Whyte wrote about individuals who were so involved in corporate life that they became psychologically dependent on it. They tended to conform to corporate values and actions without seriously questioning them.[2]

Argyris's *Personality and Organization* was concerned especially with psychological issues such as self-actualization. Argyris believed that people wanted to be treated as mature persons, but the large corporation expected them to conform to rules and practices in an unquestioning, immature way. This lack of agreement between expectations and reality led to conflict and frustration. The basic philosophy in Argyris's own words is as follows:[3]

> *An analysis of the basic properties of relatively mature human beings and formal organization leads to the conclusion that there is an inherent incongruency between the self-actualization of the two. This basic incongruency creates a situation of conflict, frustration, and failure for the participants.*

One possible product of this incongruency is that employees may become passive in their attempt to adapt to a restrictive work environment. Later, if the organization changes to allow greater employee autonomy and self-actualization, they remain passive, alienated, and incapable of reacting positively to the

Learned helplessness

new opportunity. This is called *learned helplessness*—a condition where employees continue to act in a dependent manner even after organizational changes make greater independence possible.[4] This represents one of the risks involved in stressing conformity in organizations.

Neither Whyte nor Argyris argued that people should return to a primitive civilization to live without organizations. The conflict that exists is seen solely as a challenge that requires better resolution for better results.

To what does one conform?

There are several different ways in which a person may be said to conform to an organization. First, there is a type of conformity by which one "conforms" to the requirements of technology. That is, when the pot boils, take it off the fire; or when the batch in the furnace is ready, take it out. Some "conformity" in industry is actually a response to the technology; but this is a distortion of the term, because such situations do not involve the norms of others. Furthermore, this "conformity" is the same in or out of an organization.

Looking at the more usual conformity to group norms, there are three major groups to which one conforms. One of these is the organization itself. Another is the informal work group, and the last is the external community. It is evident that the last two represent conformity expressed *inside* the organization but not conformity to the organization. The organization does not impose these last two norms; they are simply there because the organization operates in a social system rather than a vacuum. Excluding the two groups just mentioned, what is the extent and legitimacy of the organization's influence?

Areas of legitimate organizational influence

Every organization develops certain policies and requirements for performance. If the organization and an individual define the boundaries of legitimate influence differently, then organizational conflict is likely to develop. It can be sufficient to interfere with effectiveness. For example, if employees believe that it is legitimate for management to control the personal telephone calls they make at work, they may dislike management interference with their freedom on this matter, but they are unlikely to develop serious conflict with management about it. However, if employees believe that personal calls are their own private right, then this issue may become a focus of conflict with management.

Agreement avoids conflict.

This same type of reasoning applies to other issues. As long as there is agreement on the legitimacy of influence among the parties, they should be satisfied with the power balance in their relationship.

Limited research shows that there is reasonable agreement among the population concerning legitimate areas of organizational influence on employees.[5] Studies have covered labor leaders, business managers, Air Force managers, university students in three areas of the nation, and men compared with women. There is general agreement on areas of legitimacy among all groups, with high rank-order correlations for fifty-five survey items ranging from .88 to .98. Managers give somewhat

more support to legitimacy than labor leaders, with students ranking in the middle; however, the important point is the substantial agreement among all groups.

Areas of agreement and disagreement

Following are examples of areas of agreement and disagreement. There is general approval of organizational influence on job conduct, such as the tidiness of one's office and one's working hours. There also is agreement that organizational influence should be low on personal activities off the job, such as the church one attends, where charge accounts are maintained, and where one goes on vacation.

On the other hand, there is some disagreement between managers and others in a few areas, primarily those concerned with off-the-job conduct that could affect company reputation. Examples are degree of participation in various community affairs and personal use of company products. Obviously, if you work at a plant that assembles automobiles and you drive a competitor's automobile to work, your employer will be concerned about your lack of support of company products and the effect of your actions on product image.

A model of legitimacy of organizational influence

The model's variables

The model of legitimacy of organizational influence that has been developed from research is shown in Figure 17-1. The two key variables in the model are conduct on the job or off of it and conduct that is job-related or not job-related. As shown in the model, there is agreement on high legitimacy when conduct is on the job and job-related. Legitimacy tends to become less accepted as an act's connection with the job becomes more hazy. If the act is on the job but not job-related, such as playing cards during lunch hours, questions arise about legitimacy. Generally only moderate legitimacy is supported, depending on the situation.

For example, management might accept a situation in which employees were playing cards but not gambling in a dining area in the manufacturing department during lunch. On the other hand, assume the card players are bank tellers playing poker with money at their desks in the public areas of a bank during lunch. Surely in this case both managers and others will agree that management has high legitimacy to forbid this conduct because of its possible effects on customers, even though the game is not being played on company time.

Off-the-job conduct

We can begin a discussion of off-the-job conduct with the general statement that the power of a business to regulate employee conduct off the job is very limited. Certainly when the conduct is not job-related, there is little reason for the employer to become involved. On the other hand, some activities off the job may affect the employer, so questions of organizational influence arise. The basic relationship is as follows: *The more job-related one's conduct is when off the job, the more support there is for organizational influence on the employee.*

Job-related conduct

FIGURE 17-1
Model of legitimacy of organizational influence on employees

TYPE OF CONDUCT	Job-related	Not job-related
On-the-job	**High legitimacy**	**Moderate legitimacy**
Off-the-job	**Moderate legitimacy**	**Low legitimacy**

Interpretations become difficult in some borderline situations. For example, what kinds of controls should be applied to off-job conduct of an employee living on company property at an oil pumping site and on twenty-four-hour call? Even when an employee has departed company property and is not on call, the boundaries of employer interest are still not fixed. Consider the angry employee who waited until the supervisor stepped outside the company gate and then struck the supervisor several times in the presence of other employees. In cases of this type, arbitrators consistently uphold company disciplinary action because the action is job-related. In the United States at least, the organization's jurisdictional line is clearly functional, related to the total job system and not the property line.

In recent years, a number of issues potentially involving job-related behaviors have received extensive attention. These issues include substance abuse, genetic screening of prospective employees for health risks, and assessments of the ethical values of job applicants. Controversy arises out of concern for the accuracy of the measures used, as well as from conflicting views over the legitimacy of assessing such factors. These disagreements have served to focus attention on employee rights of privacy, which will be discussed next.

RIGHTS OF PRIVACY

Rights of privacy primarily refer to organizational invasion of a person's private life and unauthorized release of confidential information about a person in a way that would cause emotional harm or suffering.[6] Business activities that may involve rights of privacy are listed in Figure 17-2, and several of these are discussed in the following paragraphs.

FIGURE 17-2
Business activities that may involve employee rights of privacy

- **Lie detectors**
- **Personality tests**
- **Encounter groups**
- **Medical examinations**
- **Treatment of alcoholism**
- **Treatment of drug abuse**
- **Surveillance devices**
- **Computer data banks**
- **Confidential records**
- **Genetic screening**

Employees, customers, and others believe that their religious, political, and social beliefs are personal and should not be subject to snooping or analysis, although there are exceptions—such as being employed by a church or a political party. The same view applies to personal acts, conversations, and locations such as company lavatories and private homes. Exceptions are permitted grudgingly only when job involvement is clearly proved, and burden of proof is on the employer. For example, it may be appropriate to know that a bank teller is deeply in debt as a result of betting on horse races, or that an applicant for a national credit card twice has been convicted for stealing and using credit cards.

Conditions defining invasion of privacy

One research study surveyed over 2000 employees to determine when they perceived that their privacy had been invaded.[7] Four conditions led to perceptions of invasion: personality (versus performance) information was used, no permission was obtained before disclosure, there were unfavorable consequences, and the disclosure was external (rather than inside the company). Clearly, these situations should be minimized to avoid employee reactions.

Policy guidelines relating to privacy

Because of the importance of employee privacy, most large employers have developed policy guidelines to protect it. These guidelines also help establish uniform practices and make it easier to handle any unusual situations that may develop. Following are some of the policy guidelines on privacy that organizations are using:[8]

- *Relevance* Only necessary, useful information should be recorded and retained. Obsolete information should be removed periodically.
- *Notice* There should be no personal data system that is unknown to an employee.
- *Fiduciary duty* The keeper of the information is responsible for its security.
- *Confidentiality* Information should be released only to those who have a need to know, and release outside the organization normally should occur only with the employee's permission.
- *Due process* The employee should be able to examine records and challenge them if they appear incorrect.
- *Protection of the psyche* The employee's inner self should not be invaded or exposed except with prior consent and for compelling reasons.

Surveillance devices

Protection of the psyche, for example, means that, except for compelling reasons, there should be no surveillance of private places such as locker rooms or secret surveillance unknown to the employee, as with secret listening

Some surveillance acceptable

devices. Surveillance that is known to employees and has a compelling job reason usually is not considered to be an undue infringement on privacy. Banks, for example, have hidden cameras that make photographs during robberies. These photographs include employees, but this hardly infringes on their privacy provided that use of the photographs is confined to the original purpose.

An example of regular surveillance is provided by a fast-food chain that installed moving-picture cameras in a number of its stores. The camera photographed the cash register whenever it was open. Employees knew that it was there to control theft, although it also could photograph robberies. The camera worked effectively, providing an unexpected increase of about 10 percent in receipts.

The polygraph

Science has determined that conscience usually causes physiological changes when a person tells a significant lie. The *polygraph* (lie detector) is an instrument that was developed on the basis of this information. It is used extensively in business, primarily to control the multibillion-dollar problem of employee theft and to deal with other matters involving honesty among employees. Two issues have occasionally arisen when the polygraph is used, and these concern its validity and invasion of privacy. The validity of the polygraph, although high, needs further improvement to minimize the risk of falsely identifying innocent individuals.[9] In regard to the second issue, some people believe that the use of the polygraph tends to invade their privacy. Consequently, about half of the states and the United States government now regulate its use.

If these two issues could be constructively addressed, the use of the polygraph might actually help to protect some employee interests. For example, dishonest employees may take property of other employees, cast suspicion on them in case of theft, or place them in compromising situations that threaten their jobs; and polygraph use can discourage these types of behaviors. In some situations it may even help employees develop a more effective working environment.

The nature of the polygraph examination allows it to be given only with a person's consent, so the examinee has a choice of refusing the test. However, refusal may lead to suspicions that will reduce a person's chances of getting and keeping a job. Employees especially object to having to prove themselves innocent, that is, take a test routinely even when no theft has been discovered or no evidence points to them as thieves. They object less to a specific test about a specific known theft of major proportions. In this situation they may welcome a test to take the pressure of suspicion off them.

Psychological stress evaluator

Another type of lie detector is the *psychological stress evaluator*. It analyzes changes in voice patterns to determine whether a lie is being told. It requires no hookup to a machine, as a polygraph does. As with the polygraph, the test taker's own conscience provides the evidence by showing stress when a significant lie is told.

Treatment of alcoholism

Alcoholism presents major medical and job problems, so employers need to develop responsible policies and programs to deal with it without endangering rights of privacy. It is estimated that between 5 and 10 percent of employees are alcoholics and that they cost employers more than $10 billion annually in absenteeism, poor work, lost productivity, and related costs. Absence rates for alcoholic employees are two to four times those of other employees.

Alcoholics are found in all types of industries, occupations, and job levels. Sometimes the job environment may contribute to an employee's alcoholism, but the employee's personal habits and problems are also major contributors. In some instances employees are well on the road to alcoholism before they are hired.

REASONS FOR COMPANY PROGRAMS Regardless of the causes of alcoholism, an increasing number of firms are recognizing that they have a role to play in helping alcoholics control or break their habit.[10] One reason is that the firm and employee already have a working relationship on which they can build. A second is that any success with the employee will save both a valuable person for the company and a valuable citizen for society. A third reason is that the job appears to be the best environment for supporting recovery because a job helps an alcoholic retain a self-image as a useful person in society.

How should companies treat alcoholics?

SUCCESSFUL PROGRAMS Successful employer programs treat alcoholism as an illness, focus on the job behavior caused by alcoholism, and provide both medical help and psychological support for alcoholics. As shown in Figure 17-3, the company demonstrates to alcoholics that it wants to help them and is willing to work with them over an extended period of time. A nonthreatening atmosphere is provided; however, there is always the implied threat that alcohol-induced behavior cannot be tolerated indefinitely. For example, if an employee refuses treatment and unsatisfactory behavior continues, the employer has little choice other than dismissal.

Following is the way that one company program operates. Assume that a supervisor named Mary Cortez notices that an employee named Bill Revson has a record of tardiness and absenteeism, poor work, an exhausted appearance, and related symptoms that may indicate alcoholism or another serious problem. She discusses only Revson's job behavior with him, giving him a chance to correct himself. When Revson's behavior continues unchanged, Cortez asks Revson to meet with her in the presence of a counselor. The supervisor presents her evidence of poor job behavior and then leaves the room so that the employee and counselor can discuss the situation privately.

In other instances medical examinations uncover alcoholism or an employee voluntarily asks for help. As soon as the problem is brought into the open, the treatment program is initiated in a supportive atmosphere. It may involve hospitalization for the employee. Throughout the procedure the company is patient but firm. Using the approach just described, the firm has achieved a recovery rate of over 50 percent.

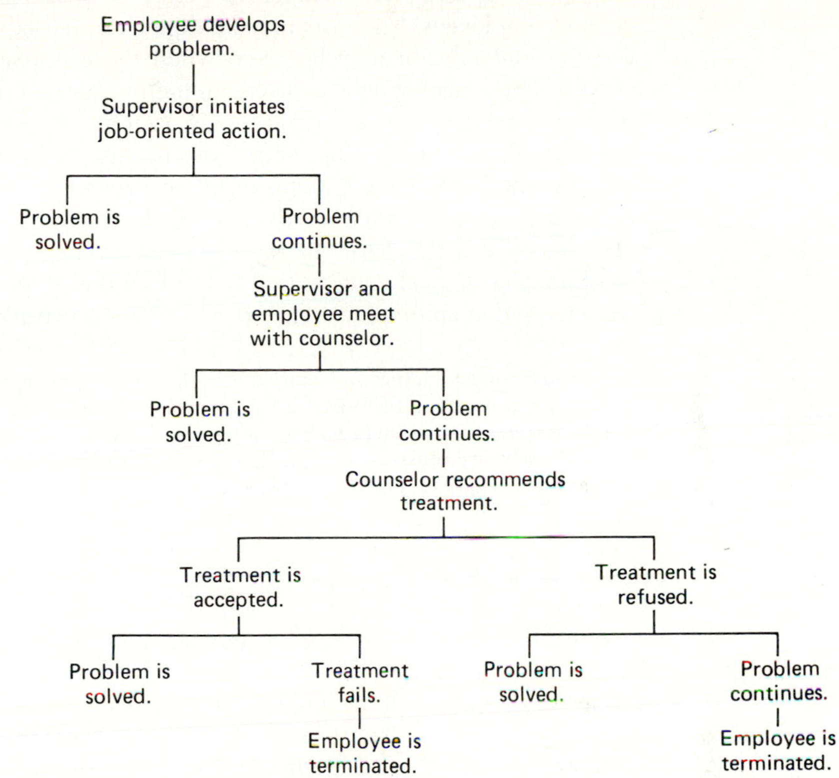

FIGURE 17-3 Program for treatment of employee alcoholics and drug abusers

Drug abuse

Abuse of drugs other than alcohol, particularly if used at work, may cause severe problems for the individual, the employer, and other employees. These drugs may include heroin, cocaine, and marijuana, or the abuse may stem from the improper use of stimulants, barbiturates, and tranquilizers. In some job situations (such as pilot, surgeon, railroad engineer, or crane operator) the direct effects of drug abuse can be disastrous.

DRUG TESTING To employers, the direct consequences of employee drug abuse are enormous.[11] Employee theft to support drug habits costs industry billions each year. Absentee rates for workers with drug problems may be as much as sixteen times higher than for nonusers, with accident rates four times as high. The lost productivity and additional health costs have been estimated to total as high as $70 billion annually. In addition, drug abuse takes a tragic toll on society.

Many companies have adopted a policy of drug testing of both new and current employees. The tests may be done on a periodic schedule, be administered randomly, or only be given when there is reason to suspect an employee. These testing policies are often highly controversial. One reason is that many of the tests are not satisfactorily accurate.[12] Tests may fail to identify some drug users, while other employees may be incorrectly identified as users because the food they ate or prescription drugs they took produced an inappropriately positive reaction. Usually, further investigation will support their innocence, but the harm to their reputation may already have occurred. Another objection to drug testing is the fear that it will reveal other medical conditions that an employee may prefer to keep private.

Methods used to detect and control drug abuse are widespread. IBM began a policy of mandatory drug testing of all potential new employees. General Motors hired private agents to uncover cocaine sellers and users in its assembly plants. Over half of the largest industrial corporations in the United States now screen their applicants for drug use, and many more have policies under review for possible implementation.[13]

TREATMENT PROGRAMS Company programs for treatment of drug abuse other than alcohol usually follow the same patterns as programs on alcoholism except that hard-drug treatment may be controlled more strictly because of the hard-drug user's greater probability of criminal behavior on the job. Most firms combine treatment of alcoholism, drug abuse, and related difficulties into *employee assistance programs* (EAPs). These programs identify and treat the problems of employees that are affecting their productivity or hindering their personal well-being. Normally the programs focus on both prevention and treatment. Figure 17-4 gives the policy statement of an insurance company on this subject.

What is an EAP?

HIRING FORMER DRUG USERS Many firms are reluctant to hire former hard-drug users. Others, recognizing a need to provide jobs for those who have

Careful supervision necessary

Our company recognizes alcoholism, mental health problems, and drug abuse as illnesses that can be successfully treated. Our people who need help in these areas will be given the same consideration as those with other illnesses. It is our goal to help those who develop such problems by providing for consultation and treatment to prevent their conditions from progressing to a degree where they cannot work effectively. . . .

The decision by management to refer an individual for evaluation, diagnosis, or treatment will be based on evidence of continuing unsatisfactory job performance. Job security will not be jeopardized by such referral. Failure by the individual to accept evaluation or to follow through on professional advice will be considered in the same manner as any factor or illness that continues adversely to affect job performance.

Medical records of those with behavioral-medical disorders will be held confidential, as are all medical records.

FIGURE 17-4
Policy statement of Employers Insurance of Wausau on its drug-abuse and mental health program
Reprinted with permission of the company.

recovered, are experimenting with carefully supervised employment programs. For example, one company employed recovered heroin addicts with the employment condition that they regularly provide urine specimens for analysis to determine that they had not resumed use of heroin or certain other hard drugs. Is this an unwarranted invasion of privacy, or is it justified because of the danger of criminal behavior if the employee returns to hard drugs?

The Equitable Life Assurance Society audited its rehabilitation program for drug users and found that the program was successful.[14] The audit covered forty-six former drug users during a rehabilitation period of nearly ten years. There was no significant difference between former drug users and other employees with regard to data such as promotions, turnover, job performance, attendance, and punctuality. The audit concluded that when former drug abusers are properly selected, placed, and supervised, their performance tends to be about the same as that of regular employees.

Genetic testing

The controversy over employee privacy rights has also emerged in the area of *genetic testing.*[15] New developments in the field of genetics allow increasingly accurate predictions as to whether an employee may be genetically susceptible to one or more types of illness or harmful substances. Positive uses of this information include transferring the susceptible employees to other work areas where they will not be exposed to the substances, providing health warnings, and developing protective measures to shield the employees from danger. A risk exists, however, in the situation in which present employees or job applicants are screened on the basis of these genetic predispositions, and the information is used to discriminate against them in an organization's attempt to minimize its future health costs. Genetic testing creates a dilemma for employers, who need to monitor the presence of harmful substances in the workplace in order to minimize or eliminate health risks to employees. The advantages must be weighed against the costs, however, as employees may feel that genetic testing is yet another invasion of their privacy.

DISCIPLINE

Two types of discipline

The area of discipline can have a strong impact on the individual in the organization. *Discipline* is management action to enforce organizational standards. There are two types, preventive and corrective.[16]

Preventive discipline

Preventive discipline is action taken to encourage employees to follow standards and rules so that infractions do not occur. The basic objective is to encourage employee self-discipline. In this way the employees maintain their own discipline rather than having management impose it. A self-disciplined group is a source of pride in any organization.

Management has the responsibility for building an organizational climate of preventive discipline. In doing so, it makes its standards known and understood. If employees do not know what standards they are expected to uphold, their conduct is likely to be erratic or misdirected. Employees are more likely to support standards that they have helped create. They also will give more support to standards that are stated positively instead of negatively, such as "Safety first!" rather than "Don't be careless!" They usually want to know the reasons behind a standard so that it will make sense to them.

Preventive discipline is a system relationship, so management needs to work with all parts of the system in order to develop it.

Corrective discipline

Corrective discipline is an action that follows infraction of a rule; it seeks to discourage further infractions so that future acts will be in compliance with standards. Typically the corrective action is a penalty of some type and is called a *disciplinary action*. Examples are a warning or suspension with or without pay.[17]

Objectives of disciplinary action

The objectives of disciplinary action are as follows:

- To reform the offender
- To deter others from similar actions
- To maintain consistent, effective group standards

The objectives of disciplinary action are positive. They are educational and corrective. The goal is to improve the future rather than punish for the past.

Discharge

The ultimate disciplinary action is *discharge*, which is separation from the company for cause. It has been said that every employee discharge is evidence of management failure, but this view is not realistic. Neither managers nor employees are perfect; so some problems cannot be solved regardless of how hard people try. Sometimes it is better for an employee to go somewhere else. There are limits to how much effort an organization can devote to retaining a poor employee, because that employee's poor performance may affect others adversely, as shown here.

> **A manager of a school lunchroom had an autocratic, incompetent supervisor of food service whom he should have fired but decided to retain in order to help her. The next fall no employees returned to this department, and no students were on the part-time employment list. During the year he fired her, and the following fall a normal number of employees and students returned to this department. In other words, by retaining her originally, he lost all the other employees!**

The lunchroom example illustrates that corrective discipline may have both positive and negative human effects, even though its purpose is positive. On the positive side, it may reform the offender and protect the interest of others. On the negative side, it may involve punishment as defined by Skinner's behavior modification, discussed in Chapter 5. This can lead to undesirable side effects such as emotional reactions, resignation, absence, and fear of the supervisor.

Due process

Corrective discipline requires attention to *due process,* which means that procedures show concern for the rights of the employee involved. Due process defines the conditions for responsible use of discipline. Labor unions and arbitrators insist on it, and it is required in decisions that relate to government regulations, such as those for equal employment opportunity.

What does due process involve?

Major requirements for due process include the following:

- A presumption of innocence until reasonable proof of an employee's role in an offense is presented
- The right to be heard and in some cases to be represented by another person
- Discipline that is reasonable in relation to the offense involved

The hot-stove rule

A useful guide for corrective discipline is the hot-stove rule, as shown in Figure 17-5.[18] The *hot-stove rule* states that disciplinary action should have characteristics similar to the consequences a person suffers from touching a hot stove. That is, discipline should be imposed with warning and should be immediate, consistent, and impersonal.

Warning

Warning is essential. It requires communication of the rules to all employees. If an employee can show that management failed to give adequate notice of rules, management will have difficulty justifying the discipline before a union or an arbitrator.

Immediate

Discipline also should be immediate. When the discipline quickly follows an infraction, there is a connection between the two events in the employee's mind and hence less probability for a future infraction.

Consistent

Consistent discipline is required because consistency is an important part of fairness. Lack of consistency causes employees to feel discriminated against. If the person receiving the more severe penalty is a minority employee, then charges of illegal discrimination may be filed, and the employer may be required to prepare a costly defense of the action.

FIGURE 17-5
The hot-stove rule for discipline

Disciplinary action should be like the penalty for touching a hot stove:

- **With warning**
- **Immediate**
- **Consistent**
- **Impersonal**

Inconsistency may imply unfairness both to the penalized employee and to others. For example, employees A and B disregarded a "no smoking" rule on numerous occasions. Then employee C disregarded it and "the roof caved in." The employee was given a severe reprimand in front of others and a three-day suspension. To other employees and to C, this action was inconsistent and unfair. Employees at this point did not know what management's real standard of conduct was, and morale deteriorated. Originally they conducted themselves on the basis of how management enforced the rule stated by the sign (instead of by the rule itself). When enforcement became erratic, they were both confused and resentful of injustice. It is evident in this example that consistent application of standards is a key to corrective discipline.

On the other hand, occasional exceptions are appropriate if they clearly have different or *extenuating circumstances*. The employer's obligation to treat all employees alike applies only when their situations are approximately alike.

Take the case of Audrey, a responsible and conscientious employee who, because of a communication error at home and a chain of unfortunate circumstances, fails to notify her supervisor of her absence until three days have gone by. Bill, on the other hand, is the devil-may-care type who has declared openly that the reason for his absence is none of management's business. On the afternoon of the third day, Bill sends a telegram from Las Vegas saying, "Car broke down. Hope to return Monday." In this instance it probably is appropriate to discipline each differently.

Impersonal

The hot-stove rule also requires that discipline be administered impersonally, just as a stove will equally burn men and women, young and old. The supervisor's like or dislike for an employee is not relevant to disciplinary action. Effective discipline separates the wrongful act from one's attitudes about the employee as a person. There is a difference between applying a penalty for a job not performed and calling an employee a lazy loafer.

Progressive discipline

Increasingly stronger penalties

Most employers apply a policy of *progressive discipline,* which means that there are stronger penalties for repeated offenses. The purpose is to give an employee an opportunity for self-correction before more serious penalties are applied. Progressive discipline also gives management time to work with an employee to help correct infractions, such as unauthorized absences.

A typical system of progressive discipline is shown in Figure 17-6. The first infraction leads to a verbal reprimand by the supervisor. The next infraction leads to a written reprimand, with a record placed in the files. Further infractions build up to stronger discipline, leading finally to discharge. However, legal restrictions on the employer's right to discharge (termination at will) have become more common in recent years. Usually the personnel department is involved by step 3 or sooner in order to ensure that company policy is followed consistently in all departments.

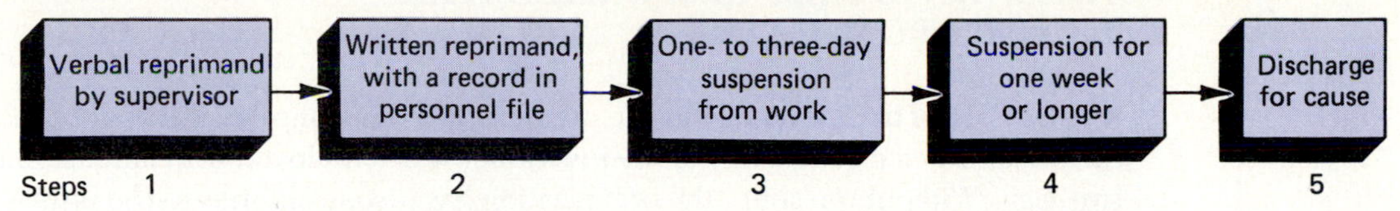

FIGURE 17-6
A progressive discipline system

Some progressive systems allow minor offenses to be removed from the record after one to three years, allowing each employee to return to step 1. Specified serious offenses, such as fighting or major theft, are usually exempted from progressive discipline. An employee who commits these offenses may be discharged for the first offense.[19]

A counseling approach to discipline

Most organizations use counseling in connection with discipline, but a few firms have moved a step further and taken a counseling approach to the entire procedure. In this approach, an employee is counseled rather than progressively penalized for the first few breaches of organizational standards. Here is how the program works in one organization.

> The philosophy is that violations are employee malfunctions that can be constructively corrected without penalty. The first violation results in a private discussion between the employee and the supervisor. The second violation brings further discussion with the supervisor, with a focus on correcting causes of the behavior. A third violation leads to counseling with both the immediate supervisor and the shift supervisor to determine the causes of the employee's malfunction. For example, does the employee dislike the job and want a transfer? Is the employee prepared to abide by the standard? The result of the discussion is given to the employee in a letter.
>
> A fourth infraction within a reasonable time, such as a year, results in final counseling with the superintendent. The offender is released from duty with pay for the remainder of the day to consider willingness to abide by standards. The offender is told that, regrettably, a further violation will result in termination because it shows that the employee is unable or unwilling to work within the standards of the organization.
>
> After a year the record is wiped clean, and any new violation starts at step 1. Certain serious offenses are exempted from the procedure and may result in immediate termination.

The focus of the counseling approach is fact finding and guidance to encourage desirable behavior instead of using penalties to discourage undesirable behavior. Emphasis is on "do this," rather than "don't do that." In this manner the employee's self-image and dignity are retained and the supervisor-employee relationship remains cooperative and constructive.

THE INDIVIDUAL'S RESPONSIBILITIES TO THE ORGANIZATION

A discussion of the individual in the organization is incomplete if it covers only the organization's obligations to the individual. The employment relationship is two-way. Without question, the organization has responsibilities to the individual, but also—and again without question—the individual has responsibilities to the organization. Employment is a mutual social transaction. Each employee makes certain membership investments in the organization and expects profitable rewards in return. The organization also invests in the individual, and it, too, expects profitable rewards.

A relationship is profitable for either party when benefits (outputs) are larger than costs (inputs) measured in a total value system. In the usual employment situation both parties benefit, just as they do in the usual social relationship. Both parties benefit because the social transaction between them produces new values that exceed the investment each makes.

The profitable relationship deteriorates if either party fails to act responsibly toward the needs of the other. The employees can fail to act responsibly, just as the organization can. If they do, they can expect the organization to respond by using tight controls to try to maintain a successful operating system.

Theft as an example

Consider the matter of theft, which was mentioned in connection with the polygraph. Overlook for the moment the legal-ethical-moral views of theft. From the point of view of the organizational system only, theft interferes with work operations. It upsets schedules and budgets. It causes reorders. It calls for more controls. In sum, it reduces both the reliability and the productivity of the organizational system. There is less output for the individual as well as for the organization. In this situation the organization must act to protect other employees as well as itself.

Organizational citizenship

As the social exchange idea is extended even further, it becomes evident that employees are expected to go beyond their job descriptions and be good *organizational citizens* in the same way that the organization is expected to be a good *citizen* in the broader society in which it operates.[20] Employees who are organizational citizens engage in positive social acts designed to help others, such as volunteering their efforts on special projects, sharing their resources, and cooperating with others. They also are expected to use their talents and energies fully to help the organization achieve its goals.

However, good citizenship does not extend to expecting an employee to support illegal activities of the organization or activities which seriously violate social standards. For example, when management disregards internal opposition to wrongful acts or fails to disclose information about defective products, an employee may become a *whistle-blower* and disclose the alleged misconduct to the public. Typical disclosures have been price-fixing, fraud, or products with inadequate safeguards for consumers.[21]

Research studies indicate which employees are more likely to be whistle-blowers in organizations.[22] They are workers who have strong evidence of wrongdoing, believe it to be a serious problem, and feel that it directly affects them. Some employees blow the whistle because they feel obligated to protect the public, while others do so in retaliation for the treatment they have received from the organization.

By going public, whistle-blowers hope to bring pressure on the organization to correct the problem. Although the legal system generally is protective of them, some employees have been the subject of employer retaliation, such as harassment, transfer, or discharge. The need for whistle-blowing can be diminished by creating a variety of ways for employees to voice their concerns inside the organization.[23] Constructive devices for this purpose include suggestion systems, survey feedback, and employee-management meetings.

SUMMARY

Some areas of individual-organization conflict are conformity, legitimacy of organizational influence, rights of privacy, and discipline. The main concern is to ensure that the employee's activities and choices are not unduly controlled by the organization. In order to protect both the organization and the worker, companies usually develop policies to guide their decisions about privacy, drug-abuse programs, and similar activities.

Both preventive and corrective discipline are important. Preventive discipline encourages employees to maintain discipline among themselves. Corrective discipline is applied when employees materially fail to meet standards. It seeks to reform the offender, deter others, and maintain standards. Due process and the hot-stove rule are useful guidelines. Most firms use progressive discipline, and some use a counseling approach.

Essentially the social transaction of employment is a two-way street with mutual responsibilities between the individual and the organization. One way by which these mutual responsibilities are clarified and maintained is through collective bargaining with unions, which is discussed in the next chapter.

Terms and concepts for review

Conformity
Learned helplessness
Legitimacy of organizational influence
Rights of privacy
Polygraph
Preventive discipline
Corrective discipline
Due process
Hot-stove rule
Progressive discipline
Individual-organization responsibilities
Organizational citizenship
Whistle-blowers

Discussion questions

1 Think of a job that you have had or now have. Discuss any conformity that was required that you felt was unfair.

2 Still considering the job in question 1, were there any ways in which you were not responsible toward the organization or took unfair advantage of it? Discuss.

3 Still thinking of the job in question 1, did you feel that the employer invaded your right to privacy in any way? Discuss. Did the employer have a policy with regard to right of privacy?

4 Assume that you are going to an interview for a job as a teller with a bank and learn that a polygraph will be used to explore your history of honesty. Describe how you would feel, and why.

5 Do any students you know exhibit learned helplessness? Describe their behavior, and explain why you think they act that way.

6 Explain the basic model of legitimacy of organizational influence. Does it seem to be a reasonable one within which you could work?

7 Form into small groups and visit a company to discuss its program for the treatment of alcoholism and hard-drug abuse. Then report the program to your classroom group and give your appraisal of its effectiveness.

8 Think of the job selected in question 1, and discuss the ways in which management applied both preventive and corrective discipline.

9 Discuss both due process and the hot-stove rule as guidelines for corrective discipline. Do you consider them fair and useful guidelines?

10 Consider your own role as a possible whistle-blower. Under what conditions would you publicly criticize your employer or another employee?

Incidents

PRIVILEGES FOR AN EMPLOYEE

Margie Wheeler, a divorcee with one child, is a bank clerk. She has had an excellent record for three years. In fact, she is so good that she has been given the added duty of instructing new employees in her department.

About three weeks ago management noticed a change in Margie's work attitude and habits. She became moody and irritable, seeming to have her mind on something else. She was absent from her work area for long periods during the day making telephone calls. She also left work early on several occasions. On two Mondays she took sick leave, reporting that she had influenza on one of the days. Her manager assumed that she had some sort of temporary personal problem; so he let her take advantage of the rules by overstaying her coffee break and otherwise not performing her work. It was rumored around the office that she was dating a married man and had been taking long breaks in order to visit him in the office of another company in the building, but her manager had no proof of this rumor.

One morning a respected senior office clerk came to the manager and reported that other employees were resentful of Margie because they felt management was making exceptions for her that it would not make for other employees. The clerk added that Margie was not performing her work and that other employees were "at the point of revolt."

Questions

Assuming you are the manager, explain what you will do and why. To what extent will you expect Margie to conform to the bank's standards? To the group's standards? To what extent will you respect Margie's rights of privacy in this situation?

TWO ACCOUNTING CLERKS

Rosemary Janis and Mary Lopez were the only two clerks handling payments from customers in the office of Atlantic Plumbing Supply Company. They reported to the owner of the business. Janis had been employed for eighteen months and Lopez for fourteen months. Both were community college graduates, about twenty-three years old, and unmarried.

By manipulating the accounts in a rather ingenious way that would not normally be detected, Janis was stealing from account payments as they were received. During her third month of employment, Lopez learned of Janis's thefts, but she decided not to tell management, rationalizing that Janis's personal conduct was none of her business. Lopez did not benefit from Janis's thefts, and the two women were not close friends. Their duties allowed them to work rather independently of each other, each handling a different alphabetical portion of the accounts.

By the time the owner learned of Janis's thefts, she had stolen approximately $5700. During investigation of the thefts the owner learned that Lopez had known about them for several months, because it was evident that the thefts could not have occurred for an extended period without Lopez's knowledge. At the time of employment, both women had been instructed by the owner that they would be handling money and that therefore strict honesty would be required of them.

Questions

1 What issues are raised by these events? Discuss.
2 What disciplinary action, if any, do you recommend for each of the two women? Why? Will the discipline be preventive, corrective, or both? What about due process? Is failure to "blow the whistle" an issue?

References

1 Suzanne H. Cook, "Privacy Rights: Whose Life Is It, Anyway?" *Personnel Administrator,* April 1987, p. 60.
2 William H. Whyte, Jr., *The Organization Man,* New York: Simon & Schuster, Inc., 1956. The idea of negative individual consequences from high levels of organizational commitment is extended in Donna M. Randall, "Commitment and the Organization:

The Organization Man Revisited," *Academy of Management Review*, July 1987, pp. 460–471.

3 Chris Argyris, *Personality and Organization: The Conflict between the System and the Individual*, New York: Harper & Row, Publishers, Inc., 1957, p. 175. See also Chris Argyris, "Personality and Organization Theory Revisited," *Administrative Science Quarterly*, June 1973, pp. 141–167. A counterargument, that individuals try to maintain at least a *perception* of control over their environment, is in David B. Greenberger and Stephen Strasser, "Development and Application of a Model of Personal Control in Organizations," *Academy of Management Review*, January 1986, pp. 164–177.

4 Mark J. Martinko and William L. Gardner, "Learned Helplessness: An Alternative Explanation for Performance Deficits," *Academy of Management Review*, April 1982, pp. 195–204. A developer of learned helplessness, Martin Seligman, is interviewed by Robert J. Trotter in "Stop Blaming Yourself," *Psychology Today*, February 1987, pp. 31–39.

5 Edgar H. Schein and J. Steven Ott, "The Legitimacy of Organizational Influence," *American Journal of Sociology*, May 1962, pp. 682–689; and Keith Davis, "Attitudes toward the Legitimacy of Management Efforts to Influence Employees," *Academy of Management Journal*, June 1968, pp. 153–162.

6 For general overviews of privacy issues and research, see Alfred Klein, "Employees under the Influence—Outside the Law?" *Personnel Journal*, September 1986, pp. 57–71; and Philip Adler, Jr., Charles K. Parsons, and Scott B. Zolke, "Employee Privacy: Legal and Research Developments and Implications for Personnel Administration," *Sloan Management Review*, Winter 1985, pp. 13–22.

7 Paul Tolchinsky et al., "Employee Perceptions of Invasion of Privacy: A Field Simulation Experiment," *Journal of Applied Psychology*, June 1982, pp. 308–313.

8 Adapted from Virginia E. Schein, "Privacy and Personnel: A Time for Action," *Personnel Journal*, December 1976, pp. 604–607; see also Donald Harris, "A Matter of Privacy: Managing Personal Data in Company Computers," *Personnel*, February 1987, pp. 34–39; and John Hoerr et al., "Privacy," *Business Week*, Mar. 28, 1988, pp. 61–68.

9 "Polygraph Testing Hit," *Resource* (American Society for Personnel Administration), October 1986, p. 13; the pros and cons are discussed in Gordon H. Barland, "The Case for the Polygraph in Employment Testing," and David T. Lykken, "The Case against the Polygraph in Employment Testing," *Personnel Administrator*, September 1985, pp. 59–65.

10 One approach, for example, is provided in Mark R. Edwards and J. Ruth Sproull, "Confronting Alcoholism through Team Evaluation," *Business Horizons*, May–June 1986, pp. 78–83. A critique of the research on alcoholism is in Richard M. Weiss, "Writing Under the Influence: Science vs. Fiction in the Analysis of Corporate Alcoholism Programs," *Personnel Psychology*, Summer 1987, pp. 341–356.

11 Brian Burrough, "How GM Began Using Private Eyes in Plants to Fight Drugs, Crime," *Wall Street Journal*, Feb. 27, 1986, p. 1; *Drug Abuse: The Workplace Issues*, New York: American Management Association, 1987.

12 Walt Bogdanich, "Labs Offering Workplace Drug Screens in New York Have Higher Error Rate," *Wall Street Journal*, Feb. 2, 1987, p. 5.

13 Arguments for and against drug testing may be found in Anne Marie O'Keefe, "The Case against Drug Testing," *Psychology Today*, June 1987, pp. 34–38; Carsten Stroud, "Do What's Fair," *Canadian Business*, April 1987, pp. 68ff; and Martha I. Finney, "The Right to be Tested," *Personnel Administrator*, March 1988, pp. 74–75.

14 "The Equitable Drug Abuse Rehabilitation Program," *Response*, May 1977, p. 10.

15 Thomas H. Murray, "Genetic Testing at Work: How Should It Be Used?" *Personnel Administrator*, September 1985, pp. 91–102; and William Pat Patterson, "Genetic Screening," *Industry Week*, June 1, 1987, pp. 45–49.

16 Eric L. Harvey, "Discipline vs. Punishment," *Management Review*, March 1987, pp. 25–29.

17 Laurie Baum, "Punishing Workers with a Day Off," *Business Week*, June 16, 1986, p. 80.

18 The hot-stove rule is attributed to Douglas McGregor, developer of Theories X and Y (discussed in Chapter 9).

19 Examples of these offenses, and guidelines for responding to them, are in Terry L. Leap and Michael Crino, "How to Deal with Bizarre Employee Behavior," *Harvard Business Review*, May–June 1986, pp. 18–22.

20 Arthur P. Brief and Stephan J. Motowidlo, "Prosocial Organizational Behaviors," *Academy of Management Review*, October 1986, pp. 710–725; and Janelle Brinker Dozier and Marcia P. Miceli, "Potential Predictors of Whistle-Blowing: A Prosocial Behavior Perspective," *Academy of Management Review*, October 1985, pp. 823–836.

21 The risks of whistle-blowing are discussed in Arvind Bhambri and Jeffrey Sonnenfeld, "The Man Who Stands Alone," *New Management*, Spring 1987, pp. 29–33; and Myron Peretz Glazer and Penina Midgal Glazer, "Whistleblowing," *Psychology Today*, August 1986, pp. 36–46.

22 Marcia P. Miceli and Janet P. Near, "Characteristics of Organizational Climate and Perceived Wrongdoing Associated with Whistle-Blowing Decisions," *Personnel Psychology*, Autumn 1985, pp. 525–544; and Janet Near and Marcia P. Miceli, "Retaliation against Whistle Blowers: Predictors and Effects," *Journal of Applied Psychology*, February 1986, pp. 137–145.

23 Daniel G. Spencer, "Employee Voice and Employee Turnover," *Academy of Management Journal*, September 1986, pp. 488–502. A case study of whistle-blowing, with four experts' responses, is in Sally Seymour, "The Case of the Willful Whistle-Blower," *Harvard Business Review*, January–February 1988, pp. 103–109.

For additional reading

Argyris, Chris, *Personality and Organization: The Conflict between the System and the Individual*, New York: Harper & Row, Publishers, Inc., 1957.

Elliston, Frederick, et al., *Whistleblowing Research: Methodological and Moral Issues*, New York: Frederick A. Praeger, Inc., 1985.

Koven, Adolph M., and Susan L. Smith, *Alcohol-Related Misconduct*, Dubuque, Iowa: Kendall/Hunt Publishing Company, 1984.

Organ, Dennis W., *Organizational Citizenship Behavior: The Good Soldier Syndrome*, Lexington, Mass.: Lexington Books, 1988.

Scanlon, Walter E., *Alcoholism and Drug Abuse in the Workplace: Employee Assistance Programs*, New York: Frederick A. Praeger, Inc., 1986.

Westin, Alan F. (ed.), *Whistle Blowing! Loyalty and Dissent in the Corporation*, New York: McGraw-Hill Book Company, 1981.

Whyte, William H., Jr., *The Organization Man*, New York: Simon & Schuster, Inc., 1956.

CHAPTER 18

Working with unions

Since the goals of the parties are to some extent incompatible, it is inevitable that there will be structurally based conflict.

MICHAEL SCHUSTER[1]

Not surprisingly, the more one moves toward cooperative and democratic relations, the more trust one finds between employer and employee.

WILLIAM WINPISINGER[2]

CHAPTER OBJECTIVES

To understand

Basic labor legislation

The collective-bargaining process

Mediation and arbitration

Problem-solving bargaining

How grievance systems operate

The postindustrial society and labor force

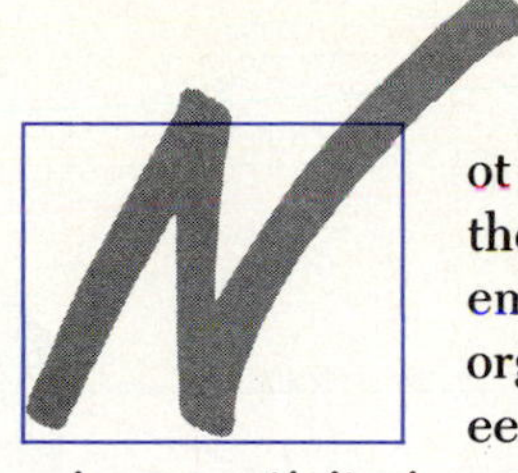

ot all employers deal with labor unions, but a number of them do. A union is a distinct organization separate from an employer. On the other hand, it is the closest of all separate organizations because its membership consists of employees, its interests concern conditions of employment, and its primary activity is representing worker interests to management. Observe in the following situation how readily the union became involved in work issues.

In an electrical company four employees worked at a table performing four identical skilled operations before passing parts to four other skilled workers at another table. Under these conditions they had a skilled artisan's pride in work and ample opportunity to engage in friendly conversation during the day. The work was then changed to assembly-line conditions where each employee was isolated along a conveyor belt and performed only a semiskilled fraction of the former skilled job. The result was unrest and constructive protest. When management failed to heed the protest, the employees appealed to their union, which made a strike issue of the incident and built union solidarity.

The subject of union-management relations is called *labor relations*, or *industrial relations*.[3] In this chapter we examine the union's role in the work environment, collective bargaining, grievance systems, and union response to the postindustrial labor force. Not all aspects of labor relations are discussed. Instead, we focus on those items that especially affect organizational behavior.

THE UNION'S ROLE IN AN ORGANIZATION

Two formal organizations

A *labor union* is an association of employees formed for the primary purpose of influencing an employer's decisions about conditions of employment. It also may engage in fraternal activities, political action, and related activities. It is a social group, and it brings to the work environment a second formal organization, as shown in Figure 18-1. The union hierarchy sits alongside the management hierarchy, and the employee becomes a member of both. Sometimes this arrangement is beneficial to workers, because when their wants are not satisfied by management, they can turn to the union for help. At other times this arrangement is stressful, because each organization makes some conflicting demands on workers.

A second formal organization greatly increases the interaction relationships that can occur, some of which are shown by the lines in Figure 18-1. Looking only at the mathematics of the situation, the introduction of a second hierarchy causes a geometric increase in relationships, which tremendously complicates human interaction. Although no more people are added, most of them are now playing two formal roles, one as union member and one as company employee.

Two informal organizations

The union also introduces a second set of informal organizations. These informal groups are built around union interests and activities, and they are

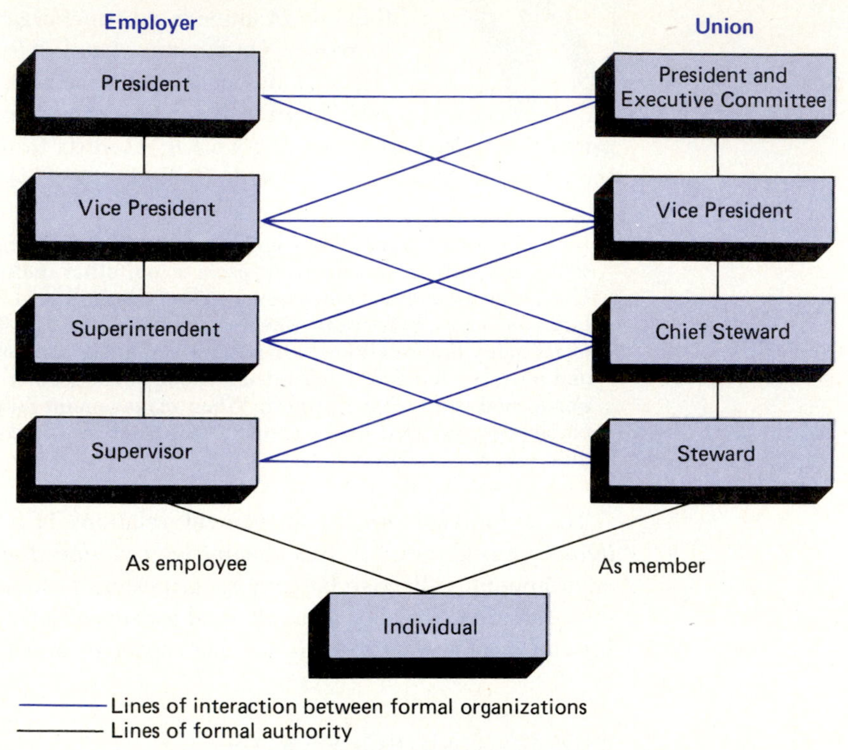

FIGURE 18-1
The union adds a second formal organization to the employment relationship.

sometimes as powerful as the union's formal structure. Take an unauthorized strike as an example. Though union leadership joins with management in demanding that workers return to work, the demand is not always successful because of informal group pressures. Informal leaders have the group emotionally worked up and are so in control of the situation that union orders are ignored.

Union membership

Labor-union membership in the United States historically has ranged between 20 and 25 percent of the total labor force. Although unions have generally grown in total membership as the labor force expanded, the *proportion* of union members in the labor force was relatively stable for several decades following the end of World War II. Since about 1970, however, their relative size has gradually declined (see Figure 18-2). This was probably the result of a decrease in manufacturing jobs and a sharp increase in service-related jobs, where unions have had a harder time organizing workers.[4] Even though the current level of union members is not a large proportion, it does represent a

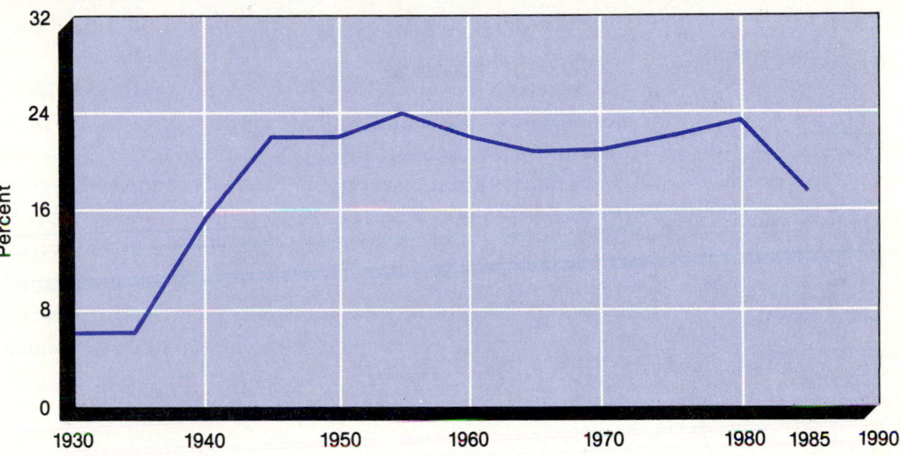

FIGURE 18-2 Labor-union membership as a percentage of the total labor force, 1930–1985

Source: *"New Data on Workers Belonging to Unions, 1986,"* Monthly Labor Review, *May 1987, p. 36.*

powerful economic, social, and political force in the work environment. Labor unions are vocal, influential, and often have a significant effect on wages, benefits, and working conditions for nonunion employees as well as union members.

Labor unions are stronger in some industries and occupations than in others. For example, only a few professional engineers belong to unions, but unions are a dominant force among automobile workers, miners, and steelworkers. A high proportion of federal employees belong to a labor organization, but the proportion of unionized state employees varies sharply from state to state.

Labor legislation

Important labor laws

Labor relations in the United States are governed by a variety of state and federal laws. Three important laws are summarized in the following paragraphs.

NATIONAL LABOR RELATIONS ACT The National Labor Relations Act (NLRA) of 1935 establishes a government procedure for union-representation elections and requires employers to bargain with a union that wins an election. The act also defines and prohibits certain unfair labor practices on the part of the employer that might discourage fair bargaining. The union can bargain with regard to terms and conditions of employment, and it bargains for all employees, both union and nonunion, in a bargaining unit.[5] The act is administered by the National Labor Relations Board (NLRB).

LABOR-MANAGEMENT RELATIONS ACT The Labor-Management Relations Act (LMRA) of 1947 defines and prohibits certain unfair labor practices on the part of unions similar to those specified earlier for employers. It also establishes a procedure for handling strikes that cause national emergencies.

THE LABOR-MANAGEMENT REPORTING AND DISCLOSURE ACT The Labor-Management Reporting and Disclosure Act of 1959 provides further controls of improper practices such as the misuse of funds by unions. Controls are applied through a number of reports that labor and management must file with the secretary of labor. The act also provides certain rights to union members, such as freedom of speech in union meetings and participation in union elections.

As a whole, the various laws provide a government-regulated system of collective bargaining. Bargainers remain free to reach their own agreements, but their activities are regulated closely to ensure fairness and good faith.

COLLECTIVE BARGAINING

Collective bargaining is the negotiation between representatives of management and labor to produce a written agreement covering terms and conditions of employment. It essentially is a compromise and balancing of opposing pressures of two social groups who have enough mutual interests to work together. Pressures at the bargaining table usually are framed in economic and technical terms; yet bargaining overall is a social process. The objective of collective bargaining is to work toward a new equilibrium of social forces and to make it easier to maintain this new equilibrium. To the extent that these pressures can be reconciled, conflict can be reduced.

Bargaining is a social process.

Though it presents difficulties, collective bargaining is a useful practice to help preserve labor-management autonomy in a free society. If we require labor disputes to be settled by third parties, labor and management freedoms will be reduced. Collective bargaining, therefore, serves long-run interests of a free society as well as the interests of labor and management.

Bargaining is permitted for federal and state civil service employees and many local government employees as well as employees in private organizations. Bargaining for government employees tends to be more limited, and it may not include the right to strike against government. Because of these limitations, government unions tend to rely more heavily on political activity and arbitration of unsettled issues.

A continuous process

People sometimes look upon collective bargaining as an affair that is conducted annually or less often and then is finished and forgotten until the next time for bargaining rolls around. This is the way they read about bargaining in the public press, so they think there is no more to it. This viewpoint is shared by some managers. As one manager put it, "Thank goodness, bargaining is finished for this year. Now we can get down to business!"

Bargaining is continuous.

Actually, this view of periodic bargaining recognizes only a part of the whole picture. From the behavioral point of view, *collective bargaining is a continuous process.* It is true that formal negotiations around a bargaining table take place only periodically; but after the contract is signed, a number of other parts of the bargaining process remain to be performed. The contract must be communicated to managers, employees, and union officers. After that, it must be interpreted. New situations, not exactly spelled out in the contract, always arise. They require management and union representatives to get together to try to interpret what the contract says or what they meant it to say. Decisions must be made concerning whether something is or is not covered by the contract.

Contract is a living document.

All the while, as these interpretations are being made, both parties are watching for flaws in their contracts so that they can introduce amendments at the next negotiation period. They also are studying local, industrywide, and nationwide labor relations developments to see how their own contract may be affected. This means that while the old contract is being interpreted (and according to the way that it is interpreted), plans for negotiating a new contract are under way. Truly, overall collective bargaining is a continuous process, and the contract is a living document.

The relationship between Shell Canada and the Energy and Chemical Workers Union illustrates this living relationship.[6] Their collective-bargaining system has three components—a traditional contract with fixed rules governing basic rights and benefits, a "good work practices handbook" that is continually developed and modified, and a consultative process that involves over 90 percent of the union members in some regular union-management committee to deal with strategic issues. With these processes in place, it was no surprise to hear one Shell Canada manager comment, "We negotiate 365 days a year."

Planning for negotiations

In planning for negotiations, management first takes stock of the present state of its labor relations, because each forthcoming bargaining period is built upon what has gone before. If labor relations are poor and the union is antagonistic, the next bargaining session will tend to be antagonistic also. However, if labor relations have matured to a state of active cooperation, bargaining should be reasonable and responsible.

In appraising the current state of labor relations, management should not overlook conditions within the union. If there is trouble here, it may spill over into the bargaining sessions. Is the union leadership competent? Are there rivalries between two or more factions? Questions like these must be considered in order to predict what kinds of attitudes the employer will face across the bargaining table.

Top management, with the guidance of other members of management, is responsible for developing the basic bargaining strategy. It then appoints the bargaining team and works with the team to develop an effective bargaining plan. Usually the top manager assigns the actual bargaining process to the labor relations director or another qualified manager.

Supervisory participation

In planning for negotiations, top management needs to encourage participation by its supervisors and middle managers. These are the people who actually live with the current contract day by day, and they know much about where it is weak and strong. Furthermore, these are the people who will administer the new contract, and they will give the contract better support if they can participate in the changes that are made. If their voice is heard—and heard in advance—they should feel more responsible for making the contract work.

For example, management in one firm asked supervisors to report three times a week what the employees were talking about in their daily work. The personnel department organized the material and placed a report about employee thinking on the negotiating team's desk the next morning before negotiations started. This quick feedback was helpful to the team.

One or more supervisors often are included on the bargaining team. If they are not, the team will lack the realistic touch with jobs that the union has, because usually most union representatives are acquainted intimately with day-to-day problems.

Constructive attitudes

The role of attitudes

Collective bargaining is a flexible, give-and-take group process. It depends upon both careful preparation and skillful maneuvering from a flexible position. If management takes extreme positions in its bargaining and consistently peppers the opposition with a categorical "No, we won't," it may have to waste much of its energy trying to withdraw itself from this unalterable position. Furthermore, this negative attitude sets the wrong emotional tone for bargaining sessions.

Some employers attempt to build constructive attitudes by having prenegotiation conferences in which no direct bargaining confrontation takes place. The parties discuss mutual problems and try to obtain agreement on facts such as current wages and job classifications. In this way some agreement on the current situation is reached before agreement on new demands is sought.

Bargaining attitudes are important.[7] If managers do not accept the union or if union leaders do not accept management, bargaining sessions are likely to be emotional and hard-fought. Each group will be defensive because it will feel that its survival is being challenged. Individuals also will be defensive and emotional if they are personally challenged, and bargaining sessions will deteriorate into personal arguments.

In one company an international union negotiator stated to the company president, "What do you know about the needs of the workers in the shop? You never did any manual labor and you're too fat to do a day's work now if you had to!" The president replied that the union representative did not have enough education to understand business anyway, so why bother to bargain. At this point bargaining ceased and personal insults began to fly from both sides. No bargaining was accomplished until the next session, several days later.

On the other hand, attitudes of cooperation and concession can be a powerful *positive* force in collective bargaining. When management makes concessions, the union is more likely to do the same. The introduction of plans for labor-management cooperation creates positive perceptions of management, and the increased trust stimulates concessions by the union. The attitudes and behaviors of top management are often as important as the economic conditions in determining the union's response in negotiations.[8]

Bargaining procedures

Procedures for bargaining sessions have a significant influence on agreement, just as attitudes do. If bargaining procedures are not clear, each party never quite understands what the other is doing, and agreement becomes almost impossible until they can begin to communicate with each other.

Who will do what?

BARGAINING ROLES For example, what is the role of a lawyer at the bargaining table? Is the lawyer speaking as a bargaining representative of the employer, or only as a legal adviser? The same question also can be asked concerning an international union representative if one is present. The question of who will attend and represent the parties in bargaining sessions is an important one. Each side will have a chief negotiator, but usually more than one person will speak across the bargaining table as a negotiator. However, it is wise to limit the size of the negotiating committee, because this reduces human relationships to a reasonable number. If the group is small, all active negotiators can get to know each other fairly well as negotiations develop.

ADVISERS AND OBSERVERS It is common practice for both sides to have present a number of nonnegotiating advisers and observers. The advisers deal only with their own negotiators rather than across the table. The observers usually listen only. They often are used as a means of communicating the current state of negotiations to those who cannot attend. Management, for example, may have its supervisors attend bargaining sessions on a rotating basis. In some cases the supervisors select their own delegates. The union may encourage stewards or rank-and-file members to attend in order to keep them informed and to assure them that their union leaders are working diligently and making no "sellout" to management.

Bargaining tactics

Four typical tactics

There are a number of tactics that bargainers use to improve their bargaining.[9] Following are four tactics that typically are used.

COUNTERPROPOSALS All negotiators use counterproposals in an effort to get the two sides closer together. A *counterproposal* is an offer suggested as an alternative to a previous proposal by the other party, in the hopes that both sides will find it more acceptable. To take an example, if the union asked for a 20-cent wage increase, management might offer a 16-cent increase to skilled workers and 8 cents to all others or offer a pension plan costing 12 cents in lieu of any wage increase. Since the union typically does most of the asking during negotiations, management will be wise to introduce whatever elements it can to reverse this one-way relationship and gain some initiative.

There are several advantages to counterproposals. First, they show to the other party an attitude of flexibility and an honest attempt to make progress. A counterproposal also gives one side the opportunity to take the initiative and shape the proposed solution in terms most favorable to it. In addition, counterproposals generally include some degree of compromise so that a series of them edges the negotiations toward resolution. Even the search for counterproposals can be useful, as it encourages the parties to be creative in how they look at and talk about the conflict before them.

TRADE-OFFS Another tactic used is the *trade-off,* which is an offer to give up on one issue in exchange for "winning" another. For example, the firm may offer an additional paid holiday if the union will agree to more flexibility in work rules. Although neither side wants to give up its item, the exchange may be perceived as favorable to each. Whereas counterproposals gradually move the two sides together, trade-offs can greatly expedite resolution of differences.

A special form of trade-off, *concession bargaining,* emerged in the 1980s when a changing balance of power forced many unions to give up some rights and conditions they had previously won.[10] In this case the trade-off became a powerful tool because severe economic conditions allowed organizations to use the threat of job loss to obtain substantial cuts in the level of wages and benefits. Unions were forced to trade part of their economic package for job security.

A RECESS One important tactical device is a *recess.* It is obviously useful when negotiators become fatigued, but more importantly, it is a means for the bargaining committee to take a break to discuss some point privately. If members of a committee show disagreement among themselves, this may indicate weakness to the other side; so when a knotty problem arises, some member may request a recess. This allows either party to work out the problem in private and return to the meeting with a united front. A recess also gives one party time to work out of a difficult position. Just as a football team calls "Time out" when the going gets tough, a negotiating committee should recess to reconsider its position, assemble more information, develop a counterproposal, or consult higher authority.

DELAY OF ITEMS When some negotiators reach an especially troublesome issue that is blocking negotiations, they request that it be tabled and then taken up in later meetings. They hope that meanwhile the situation will change to make the issue more easily resolved. In some bargaining sessions there is mutual agreement to begin negotiations with the easy or minor problems, gradually working up to the more difficult ones. Subcommittees may be used to get a difficult problem out of the mainstream of bargaining into the quieter environment of a smaller group.

PUBLICITY The parties in a negotiation sometimes find it useful to affect public opinion, in hopes of bringing additional pressure to bear on their opponents. For example, a corporation may place a large ad in a local paper explaining its position in the negotiations, especially when it feels other news coverage has been incomplete. Unions have experimented with the strategy of telling their story to focused segments of the community through various publicity campaigns.[11] By lawsuits, demonstrations, and advertising, unions bring pressure both directly on the employer and indirectly through groups with economic power such as lenders, insurance companies, and retailers. Either unions or corporations also may take their publicity campaign directly to stockholders by massive letter-writing programs. These are all potentially useful strategies to gain additional leverage in the negotiation process.

What do mediators do?

MEDIATION If an agreement cannot be reached, a *mediator* may be brought to the scene by one of the parties or by government. The mediator's role is that of an outside specialist who encourages the negotiating parties to come to an agreement. Mediators have wide experience and a fresh viewpoint, so they may be able to suggest settlements not previously considered. Mediators also help hold down emotionalism and use persuasion to try to get the parties to come to agreement.

From a human point of view, an important mediator role is that of confidential intermediary carrying messages and viewpoints from one party to the other. This enables the negotiators to sound out each other without formally committing themselves. Here is a simplified version of how this worked in one company:

> **Management hinted to the mediator that it might raise its wage offer to 24 cents if the union would drop the thorny job-security issue. The mediator, Roy Korman, hurried across the street to union headquarters and suggested that he might be able to get management to come up to 24 cents on its wage offer, but he didn't think management would accept the demand for job security. The union officers hinted that they couldn't sell that kind of package to the membership, unless it included a seventh holiday. After receiving that information, the mediator had another talk with management the next day, and so on.**

Other options

Strike

Contract arbitration

If mediation fails, two options for resolution of the impasse remain. One is a *strike,* which is a work stoppage called by a union to place bargaining pressure on management. The other alternative is *contract arbitration,* also called *interest arbitration,* which is primarily used in the public sector where the strike option is prohibited for most employees. Contract arbitration is the use of a third party to make final and binding decisions on major bargaining issues. The decision then becomes part of the labor contract.

From a behavioral standpoint, there are both merits and weaknesses in interest arbitration. On the positive side, it does provide finality to negotiations, and the threat of arbitration may produce an incentive to negotiate. However, it may also discourage negotiators from bargaining seriously, because they know that the arbitration process usually results in compromise. Clearly, there is no simple solution to the contract settlement process.

Problem-solving bargaining

Win-lose bargaining

A fundamental difficulty with the usual collective bargaining is that both management and labor approach it with a desire to win. Each prepares to do battle with the other. This is *win-lose bargaining*, because each party tries to win from the other party a favorable division of limited resources. Both parties come to the bargaining table ready to reject as unreasonable the other's demands. By expecting these things and preparing for them, they create an adversarial relationship that tends to cause the expected conduct.[12] Genuine collaboration becomes almost impossible. Since neither party wants to lose and both wish to win, either a bitter fight or a stalemate is likely to occur. If the fight gets too rough or the stalemate goes too long, the government is called in, thus restricting the combatants' freedom and making them more dependent on others. Under these conditions government control probably will expand.

Though the situation described can be eased in various ways, the machinery of conflict is still there. What is needed is a different approach to bargaining. Behavioral science theory provides a framework for a better approach, already tried successfully by employers. This new approach recognizes union-management conflict as failures in problem solving. It attempts to help the group find the causes of its failures, and it directly treats these causes to restore mature relations. This is *problem-solving bargaining*, because it takes a problem-solving approach to get joint gain for both parties.

Problem-solving bargaining can be successful.

In one small company the system worked as follows. All persons in a department met away from their work for a few days under the guidance of a behavioral scientist in order to discuss their perceptions of one another, their goals, and finally their problems. Supervisor, workers, steward, and staff were included. They presented to management a statement of their problems with desirable solutions. Each department did this separately.

Though the cost of these sessions was considerable, management and union for the first time had joint statements of needed changes from the work units themselves. These statements included items previously overlooked by both union and management, and they were developed in collaboration, not in bargaining. The result was a problem-solving climate for the customary bargaining sessions, and a new and superior contract was reached easily. This new contract had the support of employees because it came from them and fitted their needs.

Experience with problem-solving bargaining has shown that useful innovations can be made—innovations that will help the participants solve their own problems instead of depending on outside force. The theory and techniques of problem-solving bargaining should be able to improve collective bargaining. Some conflict is unavoidable, but it is questionable whether the whole bargaining process needs to have a conflict orientation, as it usually does in traditional win-lose bargaining.

One key to the success of problem-solving bargaining lies in the use of power sharing by management. This process, as used at Eastern Airlines, allows unions access to data on both operating expenses and capital investments.[13] In addition, the union participates in corporate planning and decisions regarding airfares and route changes. Since the union's influence over work procedures also has increased sharply, many employees take a much more active interest in suggesting productivity improvements.

Contract settlement and maintenance

Understanding is essential.

When agreement is reached on any issue, it should be put into writing as clearly and concisely as possible, because people with different education, interests, and backgrounds will use it. A contract clause is no good unless most readers can get the same meaning out of it. The contract is written to stabilize relationships rather than confuse them. Legal terminology should be at a minimum, because most of those who will use the contract are not lawyers. Though the contract must be correct legally, it also must command the emotional respect of the parties involved; and it will not do this if they cannot understand it. Contract clauses can be tested for meaning by having them read by supervisors and workers who have not attended negotiations and have only the written words to depend upon.

Signing the contract is only part of the job to be done. The next step is to communicate it to those who will work under its rules. Copies are usually printed for each supervisor and steward, and it is common practice to provide each worker with access to a copy. When there are major contract changes, management may decide to hold meetings with supervisors to explain the new clauses. Union leaders may do the same for their stewards. Since employer and union goals in this instance are the same—better understanding of the contract—joint meetings sometimes are held. In this way supervisors and stewards get identical instructions and are shown that management and union have mutual interests in correctly interpreting their contract. Separate meetings, on the other hand, give the impression that there are separate management and union positions regarding the contract.

Joint meetings are helpful.

Although line managers will do most of the contract interpretation, usually the human resource staff is responsible for advising managers on difficult interpretations and following up to see that interpretations are consistent. In the final analysis a collective-bargaining contract is merely a word symbol of the agreement that is in the minds of the groups involved. The same contract words can be interpreted and acted upon in many different ways depending on how people feel about them; so the participants try to build sound overall labor-management relations in order to get maximum effectiveness out of their contract.[14]

GRIEVANCE SYSTEMS

A *grievance system* is a formal system by which disputes over working rules are expressed, processed, and judged in an organization. Grievance systems are used in both unionized and nonunionized organizations. The systems provide a means by which alleged wrongs may be reasonably and fairly resolved among organizational members. Disputes will arise in any organization, and grievance systems offer a socially acceptable way for people to claim their perceived rights and occasionally to save face.

Grievances

Definition

A grievance is defined as any real or imagined feeling of personal injustice that an employee has about the employment relationship. (In some unionized organizations, a grievance is narrowly limited to mean "any protested violation of the labor agreement.") This feeling does not have to be expressed to become a grievance. Neither does it have to be true or correct. A feeling that arises from imaginary conditions or from incorrect reasoning is still a grievance if it causes a feeling of injustice. Usually, but not always, the term "grievance" applies only to one's personal feeling of injustice. If Joe feels that Mary has been treated unjustly, Joe does not have a grievance. However, if Joe feels that both he and Mary have been treated unjustly on the same matter, procedures usually permit Joe to present his grievance both for himself and as an agent of all others similarly treated. In this way one dissatisfied employee may present a grievance for a hundred others. When Joe formally expresses his grievance in the grievance system, it is said that he "files" a grievance. If he states it informally, it sometimes is called only a complaint or a gripe.

Quite often a distinction is made between a real grievance and a stated grievance. Employees sometimes do not know precisely what is making them dissatisfied. Their own feelings may set up mental blocks that prevent them from interpreting correctly what is happening. They may not have sufficient knowledge of human nature or of the many forces affecting them. Not knowing their actual grievances but still feeling dissatisfied, they tend to file grievances about something else. When management corrects this "something else," both management and the worker find to their surprise that dissatisfaction still exists because of some real grievance yet uncovered. Even when the real grievance is known, a worker may disguise it out of fear that it will not make sense to management. Here is an example:

Rudy Miles, a semiskilled machine operator, filed a grievance saying that he was not given an automatic seniority wage increase that was due him. Both the seniority and wage-increase systems were complicated, so management thought that it may have been a mistake or that Rudy justifiably could be confused. Careful investigation disclosed that Rudy was not due an increase according to the labor contract, and management spent nearly an hour at two grievance levels trying to explain the rules to him. He did not seem convinced and kept answering, "Yes, but . . ."

Finally an experienced personnel clerk who was present concluded that there was something behind this stated grievance, because Rudy kept referring to what "other workers" received. When the conversation was turned in this direction, Rudy soon disclosed that a coworker who was hired the same day had said, "I got a 2-cent seniority increase on my last check. Did you?" This was Rudy's real grievance, but he did not want to state it this way because it might embarrass his friend if it was untrue. As soon as Rudy was assured that his friend did not get the raise, his grievance vanished.

Many grievances are directed as much against other workers as they are against management. An example is a jurisdictional dispute.

In one factory semiskilled machinists claimed the right to operate certain new automated machines, but toolmakers said the machines were their responsibility. When management assigned the machines to the toolmakers, the machinists filed a grievance saying that the new machines required only semiskilled work which machinists were supposed to perform, even though they admitted that the new machine work was slightly more difficult than the work they had been doing.

Grievance rates

Typical grievance rates

A *grievance rate* usually is stated in terms of the number of written grievances for 100 employees in one year. So many factors affect grievances that a low rate is not necessarily desirable, because it may mean that grievances are suppressed. Neither is a high rate absolute evidence of poor labor relations. A typical grievance rate is 5 to 20; however, well-managed organizations with mature labor relations have developed lower rates.

Employees of all types and at all levels develop grievances. They are not some headache brought about by unions. Some of the factors affecting grievance rates are management, unions, union steward needs,[15] grievance procedures, job conditions, government rules, general social conditions, and the home environment. Management can alter some of these causes, but in other cases its job is to work out a reasonable accommodation to them.

The experience of International Harvester Company shows how grievance procedures and organizational climate can affect grievance rates. At one time it had a high annual grievance rate of 27.5 per 100 employees. It also had a high proportion of grievances going to the central level for probable arbitration. In a thirteen-year period over 100,000 grievances went to the central level!

Recognizing a serious problem, top officials of both union and company worked hard to shift attitudes toward problem solving and to install a new program calling for settlement at the local level when the grievance was first presented orally. Local settlement was attempted even if this meant calling the superintendent, labor

relations director, time-study specialist, and others to the workplace. People came to the problem, instead of having it sent in writing to them. The program was remarkably successful. Attitudes materially improved. More important, in the two years following the new program, not one grievance went to the central level, and fewer than ten were put into writing.[16]

Generally, effective contract administration tends to reduce grievances. Fair, open, and prompt treatment of problems that arise tends to reduce the misunderstandings that are the underlying causes of many grievances. Increased participation and power sharing are also effective ways to reduce grievances. When employees share in decision making about working conditions, they have fewer reasons to file grievances about their work.

Benefits of grievance systems

Open communications

Benefits of grievance systems are shown in Figure 18-3. Probably the principal benefit of any grievance system is that it encourages human problems to be brought into the open so that management can learn about them and try corrective action. The social organization of a plant is much like a complicated machine in the shop. Both need constant attention and frequent adjustment.

Grievances are symptoms that should be studied carefully to determine the real causes of this "human machine" breakdown. They signal that part of the human organization is not functioning properly and needs readjustment. It matters not that a grievance is invalid according to the technical terms of the labor contract; it is still a grievance and a symptom of social imbalance in some trouble spot somewhere. Any attempt to disregard it, smother it, or "throw it out of court" on some technicality will be largely ineffective because it still exists and will try to find expression in some other way.

Another benefit of grievance systems is that they help to catch and solve problems before they become serious. If problems are left unsolved, their collective pressure may become large enough to cause a major breakdown in labor-management relations. Or they may grow within an employee, becoming more difficult to adjust. The unhappy employee tends to communicate with others and to spread dissatisfaction.

A related benefit is grievance prevention. Almost everyone agrees that it is better to prevent fires than to try to stop them after they start, and the same

FIGURE 18-3
Benefits of grievance systems

- □ **Help make employee problems known.**
- □ **Encourage solution of problems before they become serious.**
- □ **Help prevent future problems.**
- □ **Give employees emotional release for their dissatisfactions.**
- □ **Help establish and maintain a working relationship in the group.**
- □ **Provide a check and balance on arbitrary management actions.**

philosophy applies to grievances. A good solution to one grievance may keep twenty others from arising.

Emotional release

A grievance system also is a way of giving employees emotional release for their dissatisfactions. It provides a safe procedure for an aggrieved employee to become aggressive and strike back at the controls required by an organization. Emotional release often plays an important role in individual grievance cases. Union leaders sometimes carry a losing case higher in the grievance procedure "just to make the employee happy." They hope that as the case moves upward, ill feelings will decline and the employee will become more cooperative. Even workers who do not use the grievance system for their own emotional release feel better because they know the system is there to use if needed. It gives them a sense of emotional security.

Another benefit of grievance systems is that they help establish and maintain a work culture or way of life. Each group has its own particular way of living together, and the grievance procedure helps develop this group culture. As problems are interpreted in the grievance procedure, the group learns how it is expected to respond to the policies that have been set up.

A check and balance on management

A further benefit of grievance systems—one that managers often fail to see—is the simple fact that the system's existence provides a check and balance on arbitrary and capricious management action. Managers tend to give more care to human relations when they know that some of their actions are subject to challenge and review in a grievance system. They are put on guard to make sound decisions so that they are not placed in the embarrassing position of having to defend their poor judgment in the grievance system. They are encouraged to develop effective compromises and working relationships with their groups. However, the pendulum can swing too far. Supervisors may become so aware of the grievance system that they are afraid to make decisions and hesitate to discipline employees. In this situation the supervisor's capability vanishes.

Grievance procedures

A grievance procedure is the method by which a grievance is filed and carried through different "steps" (decision levels) to an ultimate decision. Most procedures start with the supervisor and the grievant, have from three to six steps, and usually have arbitration as the last step. Other details vary greatly.

A sample procedure

Figure 18-4 shows a grievance procedure in one company. It begins when the employee or employee's representative discusses the grievance with the supervisor. This perhaps is the key step. It gives the supervisor and employee an opportunity to work out their own problems before the grievance is written down. Skills in areas such as transactional analysis and consideration, discussed in earlier chapters, can help the supervisor reduce conflict and solve the problem at this early stage.

If the grievance cannot be settled in step 1, then it is reduced to writing and presented formally to the supervisor. This gives the supervisor and employee a second opportunity to solve their own problems. Usually a written management reply is required at this step and later steps. If no settlement is reached at step 2,

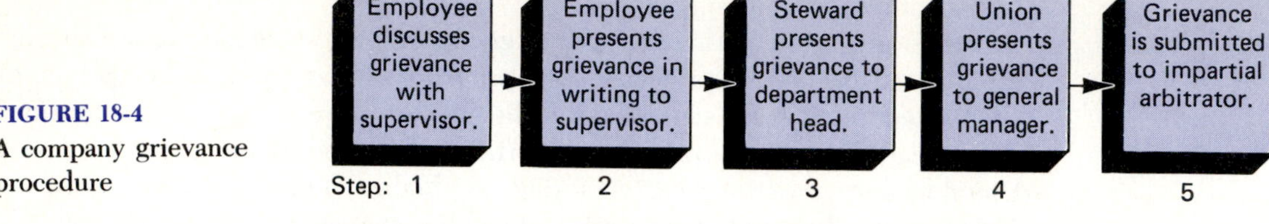

FIGURE 18-4
A company grievance procedure

then the steward as a representative of the union presents the grievance to the department head. If settlement still cannot be reached, the grievance goes to top management for a final company-union effort. If there is no agreement, either party eventually may take the grievance to arbitration.

TIME LIMITS Reasonable speed in processing a grievance is important. Most procedures establish time limits at each step so that delays cannot be used as excuses to prevent settlement. The supervisor who delays a grievance actually strengthens the grievant's cause, since the delay convinces the grievant that the grievance is a sound one that the supervisor is afraid to face.

SUPERVISORY ATTITUDES The supervisor's attitude toward grievances can be a long step toward their settlement. Some workers fear supervisory retaliation if they present a grievance, especially if they win it. It is important for supervisors to convince workers that they want to hear grievances and to settle them. Supervisors should approach grievances in a problem-solving frame of mind, rather than with the idea "This is a fight—it's either them or me." There is a need for discussion that moves rationally toward a mutual solution, instead of argument that emotionally seeks to provide a winner. All possible facts—including how people feel—should be gathered before making a decision.

Grievance arbitration

As a grievance moves to higher steps, it becomes less a person-to-person discussion and more a group problem involving several union and management representatives. If the grievance is not settled at the highest company level, labor or management may submit it to *arbitration,* which is final and binding decision by a third party or parties. The arbitrator's decision stands only until the next collective-bargaining negotiation, at which time the parties can negotiate any contract changes they wish. The arbitrator's role is merely to stabilize contract meaning during the life of the contract.

The interpretation of what the existing contract means is called *grievance arbitration.* It is distinguished from arbitration to establish new contract terms, which was discussed earlier as contract arbitration. The former is a method of grievance settlement, while the latter is a temporary substitute for collective bargaining. Management and labor generally support the former but oppose the latter because it takes settlement power out of their hands.

From the behavioral point of view, the chief benefits of grievance arbitrators are that they are outsiders who bring a fresh perspective, they are not emotionally involved in the dispute, and they can render a final decision that usually is enforceable in the courts. Their decisions, however, can be painful to an inept management, as illustrated by the following situation:

Mary Byrne was discharged for smoking on a stair landing in a dangerous chemical operation. Discharge was clearly within the rules for this offense. When the case came to arbitration, however, she claimed that the company had discriminated against her, since many employees smoked on the landing and were still doing so. She challenged the arbitrator to count the cigarette butts on the floor. True enough, when the arbitrator and the representatives of both parties went there, they found cigarette butts all over the place. Mary was reinstated immediately with back pay.

Problems with arbitrators

A weakness of arbitrators is that they usually lack personal knowledge of the organization's way of life, which may cause them to make unrealistic decisions. Another weakness is that they may overlook human values and render a legalistic decision based on technical evidence. They also lack personal responsibility for the continuing labor-management relationship because they often step out of the picture as soon as a decision is rendered. Some of these weaknesses are overcome by appointing a permanent arbitrator to arbitrate all issues for a period of time.

PEER REVIEW PANELS An innovative approach to the resolution of employee grievances lies in the use of internal *peer review panels*. These are special boards (consisting of peers of the grievant and managers not involved in the situation itself) that take informal testimony and make binding decisions. The issues most often addressed include discipline, firing, and promotions. Despite the fact that management "wins" an estimated 60 to 70 percent of all cases, the peer review panel overcomes many of the weaknesses of using external arbitrators.[17] The panels are fast, relatively inexpensive, and reduce the probability of costly lawsuits.

UNION RESPONSE TO THE POSTINDUSTRIAL LABOR FORCE

Unions have worked effectively with bargaining and grievances during the last century, and it is certain that their influence will continue. However, unions often are less effective in some organizational behavior areas such as serving the diverse and changing needs of the labor force.

A postindustrial labor force

New characteristics

The basic problem is that the postindustrial labor force has changed toward the characteristics shown in Figure 18-5, but labor unions have not always changed adequately to serve these new needs. In the postindustrial society, labor is more educated and knowledge-oriented. It also is more employed in service occupations instead of industrial ones. Higher earnings have made labor more affluent with television sets and other conveniences in most worker homes.

The postindustrial force also has changed value systems and lifestyles. There is less emphasis on the work ethic and more emphasis on leisure activities and other satisfactions. The labor force is upwardly and geographically mobile. Its white-collar, professional, and knowledge orientations cause it to be more identified with upward growth and with management than workers were a century ago.

With regard to the postindustrial labor force, one analyst comments, "Because we are living in the postindustrial era, future problems for the unions are rooted in the radically changed labor market."[18] A labor analyst explains labor-force changes in the following manner:

> *Increasing education, changing values, and the strong urge to move up the socioeconomic ladder have created a less militant worker. Unions also face serious difficulties in responding to the needs and interests of educated, upwardly mobile employees. These upwardly mobile people feel that they would lose self-esteem if they became card-carrying union members. At the same time, public attitudes toward corruption in some unions, violence on the picket lines, and the open confrontations of organizing efforts have created psychological barriers which many workers are afraid to cross. In fact, white-collar and professional workers prefer to identify with management, given half a chance to do so.*[19]

Individual needs

One issue is individual needs. The union often has bypassed individual needs in favor of standardization, uniformity, and equal treatment for everyone. What

- **Knowledge orientation, in contrast to manual-skill orientation**
- **Education**
- **Service occupations, in contrast to industrial occupations**
- **Affluence**
- **Changed value systems**
- **Different lifestyles**
- **Less emphasis on work ethic than in 1900–1950**
- **Upward and geographic mobility**
- **More white-collar and professional occupations, in contrast to blue-collar**
- **Some identification with management**

FIGURE 18-5
Characteristics of the postindustrial labor force, 1980–2000+

can be done to make the inflexible procedure, the airtight contract, and the unionwide standard apply to individual situations? Growing pressures to think in global terms have caused issues to become symbolized in statistical norms and settled in central headquarters, leaving the individual isolated on the sidelines. Union benefits are largely general, applying to the group. The individual may be overlooked or even abused, as in the "Coventry" incident at the end of this chapter.

Higher-order needs

Affluence and other developments have made higher-order needs important in a postindustrial society.[20] Can labor unions adjust their practices to serve them effectively? These higher needs are not easily served by nationwide norms. What is required is more emphasis on job enrichment, human resources, and human growth along channels that are desirable to each employee personally.

A postindustrial labor relations lifestyle

Cooperation and integration are needed.

The postindustrial society and labor force require adaptations by *both* labor and management. The trends toward computer-assisted manufacturing and the use of industrial robots require widespread retraining of workers for jobs demanding higher-level skills. To accomplish these challenging tasks, labor and management need to reexamine the value of their adversary positions and develop a new labor relations lifestyle for themselves. This new lifestyle will probably include a trend away from industrywide bargaining and settlements, the emergence of joint labor-management and problem-solving committees, and more cooperation to serve the new needs of workers, customers, and the community.[21] The frameworks of organizational behavior suggest that integrated efforts are necessary to develop a production system that better serves human needs in a postindustrial society.

SUMMARY

The union introduces additional formal and informal organizations at work. Two major union-management activities are collective bargaining and grievance systems. Collective bargaining is negotiation between representatives of management and labor to accomplish a written agreement covering terms and conditions of employment. It essentially is a social process for balancing pressures of two groups that have a mutual interest in employment conditions. It is regulated by the National Labor Relations Act and other legislation.

Grievance systems have fairness and justice as their goal. A grievance is any real or imagined feeling of personal injustice that an employee has about the employment relationship. Grievance systems help bring grievances into the open so that corrective action can be taken (1) to adjust a current grievance and (2) to prevent future grievances.

The postindustrial society presents new needs for both labor and management. There is a postindustrial labor force with stronger individual needs and higher-order needs. These new conditions probably require labor and management to move toward a more cooperative labor relations lifestyle in order to serve human needs better.

Terms and concepts for review

National Labor Relations Act
Collective bargaining
Mediation
Strike
Interest arbitration
Win-lose bargaining
Problem-solving bargaining
Grievance
Grievance rate
Grievance arbitration
Peer review panel
Postindustrial labor force

Discussion questions

1 Discuss the human implications of adding a second formal organization (the union) to the employment relationship.
2 Have you ever belonged to a union? If so, discuss with your group how it affected you and your job.
3 In what ways is it possible for labor legislation to influence human relationships at work? Discuss.
4 In what ways is collective bargaining a human problem as distinguished from an economic and a technical problem? Discuss.
5 Discuss the idea that collective bargaining is a continuous process.
6 Have you ever filed a grievance? If so, discuss in the classroom how it worked. If not, interview a worker who filed a grievance and give a classroom report about how it worked.
7 Discuss interest arbitration and grievance arbitration. How are they similar? How are they different?
8 Using library sources, read five arbitration decisions (or summaries of them) and comment on the types of problems that went to arbitration, how successful management and unions were in winning an arbitration, and your view of how fair the arbitrator's decision was.
9 Discuss the characteristics of the postindustrial labor force and how well you think labor unions are meeting its needs.
10 Review the chapter, and then summarize the behavioral issues that are dominant in labor relations (such as face-saving).

Incident

(*Note:* The following incident also relates especially to the two chapters on the individual and on the informal organization. The case is a complete news article from an Australian daily newspaper.)

A VICTIM BACK FROM COVENTRY, BY ALEX HARRIS[22]

Keith Digney, a pressure welder at the State Electricity Commission's Muja power station at Collie, has become a victim of his own convictions.

Mr. Digney's beliefs came into conflict with his unionist working mates—and he was sent to Coventry and declared [unacceptable to the group].

Men he had worked with for nearly 10 years refused to speak to him on or off the job.

They refused to touch any equipment he touched, and raised demarcation issues over actions as simple as picking up a hammer.

After six weeks he decided to call it quits because, as he said yesterday, he did not like standing around doing nothing.

He is a Christadelphian and his beliefs prevent his joining a union or a political party. Six years ago he was granted exemption from union membership by the Industrial Commission.

He had been declared [unacceptable] before, but had battled it out and avoided trouble during strikes by taking leave without pay.

About two months ago, however, the issue of his beliefs arose again when he refused to subscribe to a Metal Trades Union's fighting fund—a so-called voluntary contribution [to a political fund] which Mr. Digney claimed was not enforceable by law.

The Industrial Commission was called in to arbitrate and Mr. Digney agreed to pay an equivalent sum to a charity. But union representatives refused to compromise.

Mr. Digney said the word went out that he had to go. He is still puzzled why it took six years to decide his presence at the power house was intolerable.

He did not mind being sent to Coventry.

"What bothered me was standing 'round doing nothing all day," he said.

"I was getting paid for it but I have to work for my money; I don't like taking it under false pretences."

"The SEC didn't want me to leave and things were beginning to ease up a little at the power house but I knew they would not get better if I stayed."

"The same thing would have happened again so I got another job to make peace for all concerned."

The move cost Mr. Digney his 10 years' long service leave which would have come up this year.

"Of course I'll miss it but money is not my first concern," he said. "Money is not my god."

He and his wife do not feel bitter about the experience.

"We know what our beliefs are," Mr. Digney said.

"And men are the same everywhere."

"I suppose you could say it was a question of human rights and freedom of belief but I didn't expect these arguments to have any weight."

"If anything, I feel sorry for the men who took part in the ban. Sooner or later you reap what you sow."

Questions

1 Comment on the human relations and union-power implications of this case.
2 Discuss possible reasons why employees acted the way that they did in this case. What can management do to improve situations of this type?

References

1 Michael Schuster, "Models of Cooperation and Change in Union Settings," *Industrial Relations,* Fall 1985, p. 384.
2 William Winpisinger, "Labor Looks at 'New Management'," *Management Review,* July 1987, p. 53.
3 See, for example, E. Edward Herman, Alfred Kuhn, and Ronald L. Seeber, *Collective Bargaining & Labor Relations,* 2d ed., Englewood Cliffs, N.J.: Prentice-Hall, Inc., 1987.
4 Other factors in the attractiveness of union membership are worker dissatisfaction, the labor market, and the current public policy toward unions. See Lee P. Stepina and Jack Fiorito, "Toward a Comprehensive Theory of Union Growth and Decline," *Industrial Relations,* Fall 1986, pp. 248–264.
5 Barbara A. Lee, "Collective Bargaining and Employee Participation: An Anomalous Interpretation of the National Labor Relations Act," *Labor Law Journal,* April 1987, pp. 206–219.
6 Tom Rankin and Jacquie Mansell, "Integrating Collective Bargaining and New Forms of Work Organization," *National Productivity Review,* Autumn 1986, pp. 338–347.
7 One successful method for improving bargaining attitudes is "Relationships by Objectives," developed by the Federal Mediation and Conciliation Service. See Harvey A. Young, "The Causes of Industrial Peace Re-revisited: The Case for RBO," *Human Resource Management,* Summer 1982, pp. 50–57.
8 Forms of labor-management cooperation are discussed in Gary N. Chaison and Mark S. Plovnick, "Is There a New Collective Bargaining?" *California Management Review,* Summer 1986, pp. 54–61; and Beverly Geber, "Teaming Up with Unions," *Training,* August 1987, pp. 24–30. The difficulties are illustrated in Jacob M. Schlesinger, "Auto Firms and UAW Find That Cooperation Can Get Complicated," *Wall Street Journal,* Aug. 25, 1987, pp. 1, 14.
9 Joseph F. Byrnes, "Ten Guidelines for Effective Negotiating," *Business Horizons,* May–June 1987, pp. 7–12.
10 Gary N. Chaison and Mark S. Plovnick, "How Concessions and Cooperation Affect Labor-Management Relations," *Personnel,* November–December 1984, pp. 57–59.
11 See Peter Cappelli, "The Changing Face of Labor-Management Relations," *Management Review,* March 1986, pp. 28–30; and Aaron Bernstein et al., "The Unions Are Learning to Hit Where It Hurts," *Business Week,* Mar. 17, 1986, pp. 112, 114.
12 This is even advocated, in Barbara Reisman and Lance Compa, "The Case for Adversarial Unions," *Harvard Business Review,* May–June 1985, pp. 22ff.
13 Robert Kuttner, "Sharing Power at Eastern Air Lines," *Harvard Business Review,* November–December 1985, pp. 91–101. However, see another view in John Hoerr, "Power-Sharing between Management and Labor: It's Slow Going," *Business Week,* Feb. 17, 1986.
14 An example of effective human resource management practices in the face of significant organizational adjustments to its work force is in Leonard Greenhalgh, Robert B. McKersie, and Roderick W. Gilkey, "Rebalancing the Workforce at IBM: A Case Study of Redeployment and Revitalization," *Organizational Dynamics,* Spring 1986, pp. 30–47.

15 Steward needs for achievement, autonomy, and dominance tend to be associated with the number of grievances the steward files; see Dan R. Dalton and William D. Todor, "Manifest Needs of Stewards: Propensity to File a Grievance," *Journal of Applied Psychology*, December 1979, pp. 654–659.

16 Robert B. McKersie, "Avoiding Written Grievance by Problem-Solving: An Outside View," *Personnel Psychology*, Winter 1964, pp. 367–379.

17 Larry Reibstein, "More Firms Use Peer Review Panel to Resolve Employees' Grievances," *Wall Street Journal*, Dec. 3, 1986, p. 33.

18 Robert Schrank, "Are Unions an Anachronism?" *Harvard Business Review*, September–October 1979, p. 110.

19 Jerome M. Rosow, "American Labor Unions in the 1980s," *IRRA Newsletter* (Industrial Relations Research Association), November 1979, pp. 1, 4.

20 A comprehensive discussion of social changes is Alvin Toffler, *The Third Wave*, New York: Wm. Morrow & Company, 1980; John Naisbitt, *Megatrends: Ten New Directions Transforming Our Lives*, New York: Warner Books, 1982; and Alvin Toffler, *Previews and Premises*, New York: Wm. Morrow & Company, 1983.

21 The future of American unions is discussed in several articles in a special issue of *New Management*, Winter 1986.

22 Alex Harris, "A Victim Back from Coventry," Perth, Australia: *The West Australian*, Apr. 16, 1974, p. 1. Copyright 1974. Reprinted with permission of West Australian Newspapers, Limited.

For additional reading

Cohen-Rosenthal, Edward, and Cynthia E. Burton, *Mutual Gains: a Guide to Union-Management Cooperation*, Westport, Conn.: Frederick A. Praeger, Inc. (Greenwood Press) 1986.

Dunlop, John T., *Dispute Resolution: Negotiation and Consensus Building*, Dover, Mass.: Auburn House Press, 1984.

Elkouri, Frank, and Edna Asper Elkouri, *How Arbitration Works*, Washington: Bureau of National Affairs, 1985.

Jandt, Fred E., and Paul Gillette, *Win-Win Negotiations: Turning Conflict into Agreement*, New York: John Wiley & Sons, Inc., 1985.

Kochan, Thomas A., Harry C. Katz, and Robert B. McKersie, *The Transformation of American Industrial Relations*, New York: Basic Books, 1986.

Lax, David A., and James K. Sebenius, *The Manager as Negotiator: Bargaining for Cooperation and Competitive Gain*, New York: The Free Press, 1986.

Lewicki, Roy J., and Joseph A. Litterer, *Negotiation*, Homewood, Ill.: Richard D. Irwin, Inc., 1985.

Lipset, Seymour (ed.), *Unions in Transition: Entering the Second Century*, San Francisco: ICS Press, 1986.

Loughran, Charles S., *Negotiating a Labor Contract: A Management Handbook*, Washington: Bureau of National Affairs, 1984.

CHAPTER 19

Equal employment opportunity (EEO)

Ignoring any source of talent and motivation will unduly restrict a company.

ROSABETH MOSS KANTER[1]

With the key legal issues settled, companies can view affirmative action as an opportunity rather than a burden.

PAULA DWYER[2]

CHAPTER OBJECTIVES

To understand

Social benefits of EEO

Legal requirements for EEO

Enforcement of EEO

Protected groups and affirmative action

Company programs for EEO

Job adjustment and retirement of older workers

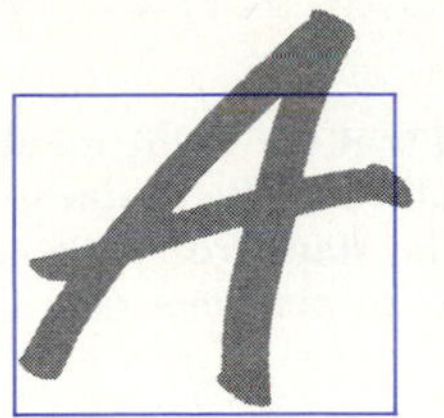

s the idea of creating and managing corporate cultures has gained popularity, every organization has wrestled with ways to manage itself so as to develop a cohesive group of employees. This can happen under conditions where employees are loyal to the organization and committed to its objectives.[3] On the other hand, employees in almost any organization are also divided into subgroups of different kinds. As discussed in earlier chapters, mutual similarities such as type of work, rank in the organization, physical proximity to each other, and social interests often encourage employees to relate to one another in all sorts of intricate subgroups.

Formation of employee groups is determined by two broad sets of conditions. First, *on-the-job* differences and similarities cause people to align themselves into groups. Throughout this text, attention is given to these on-the-job conditions that underlie the separation of workers into different interest groups, such as office and production workers. It is now appropriate to emphasize the second set of conditions—those arising primarily *off the job*—because they may relate to equal employment opportunity.

In the first part of this chapter we discuss equal employment opportunity and laws relating to it. Then we examine how it applies to various employee groups.

EQUAL EMPLOYMENT OPPORTUNITY AND THE LAW

What is EEO?

Equal employment opportunity (EEO) is the provision of equal opportunities to secure jobs and earn rewards in them, regardless of conditions unrelated to job performance. EEO is supported by federal, state, and local *equal opportunity laws*. State and local laws also may be called *fair employment practices laws*. These laws prohibit job discrimination based on specific nonjob conditions, such as race, color, religion, national origin, sex, and age. The laws also prohibit discrimination against handicapped individuals in a number of circumstances. All EEO laws prohibit discrimination with regard to both (1) securing employment and (2) terms and conditions of work after employment.

Discrimination based on job performance is permitted as a necessary and desirable employment activity. Employers can legally reward high performers and penalize inadequate performers. The law merely requires rewards and punishments to be related to performance or seniority rather than nonperformance factors such as race. Equal opportunity, therefore, implies *unequal results*, because people will differ in their skills, effort, and performance. Some will rise higher than others, but U.S. law demands that all shall have an equal opportunity to do so.

For example, a federal court upheld the dismissal of a woman flight attendant who had alleged sex discrimination. She was suspended six times for exceeding the airline's weight limits as they related to reasonable appearance and safety standards for flight attendants. When she failed to meet standards after the sixth suspension,

she was dismissed. The court concluded that the flight standards were a legitimate employer requirement related to the nature of the business and that dismissal was not for reason of the employee's sex. The standards were applied equally to male and female flight attendants and the six suspensions gave the employee adequate time to correct her deficiency.

Discrimination vs. prejudice

There is an important difference between discrimination and prejudice. Discrimination is an action, while prejudice is an attitude of mind. One may occur without the other. Discrimination may unintentionally occur without prejudice, and likewise prejudice may exist without any act of discrimination. The law focuses on an employer's actions, not feelings. If actions lead to discriminatory results, they are unlawful regardless of the employer's good intentions.

For example, the Primrose Company posted its new job vacancies on the company bulletin board so that employees could learn about them and recommend their friends for employment. It had loyal employees, so it was able to fill most of its vacancies with the bulletin board system. Finally a black applicant brought charges that the selection method involved unlawful discrimination against blacks. Subsequent investigations showed that the firm had mostly white employees who usually recommended other whites, so the result was discrimination against blacks, even though the company did not intend to discriminate.

Social benefits and problems

The social benefits of EEO are substantial. As summarized in Figure 19-1, EEO gives equal access to jobs for those who want work and are willing to develop themselves to perform a job successfully. In this way it reinforces the American dream of equal opportunity for all people. EEO ensures that more of the labor force—such as women and minority groups—can work, thus leading to higher family earnings. There also may be higher national output because a larger proportion of the labor force is working.

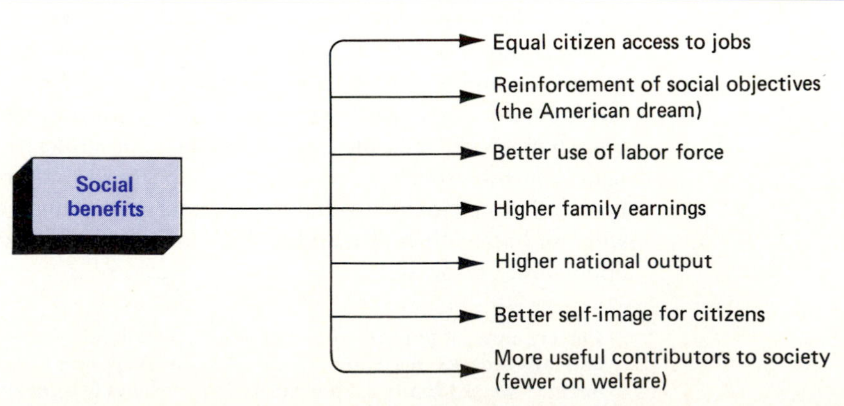

FIGURE 19-1
Potential social benefits of EEO

Equal opportunity gives more people a chance to grow toward their potential. By providing fair access to jobs, it builds the self-image of people and encourages them to be useful members of society. In some instances this process may change receivers of government benefits into useful contributors of taxes to government. Welfare can be reduced, and people can become more self-reliant. In general, when EEO can be successfully implemented, it offers many potential benefits compared with costs.

Although the social benefits have received the most attention, there is also a strong pragmatic argument for EEO practices. Phoenix-based Mountain Bell has specifically recognized the value of using a variety of diverse talents for the good of its business.[4] It endorses a pluralistic work force as "a state within the company in which a diversity of employees is nurtured to ensure that a variety of the best ideas and talents possible are utilized at all levels to provide for the growth of our business and to promote its success." It believes that the benefits of a pluralistic work force will include easier recruiting, more effective problem solving, and an improved quality of work life for its employees.

EEO has caused problems.

There have been a number of social problems associated with EEO. As individuals sought their legal rights, both they and their employers incurred tremendous legal costs; the administrative expense of fair employment programs has created an additional burden. Also, management has lost some of the autonomy it previously enjoyed in hiring decisions, as the courts laid down strict guidelines to follow. Another problem has been EEO's challenge to the seniority system in many firms. To preserve jobs for recently hired minorities when work force cutbacks are made, seniority rules have been forced to bend, thereby disrupting existing social patterns. Although the *intent* of EEO is highly positive, its net *effects* must be judged in the light of both its benefits and the problems it has caused.[5]

Federal EEO laws

The major federal laws that govern EEO are summarized in Figure 19-2. These laws are passed by Congress and enforced by the executive branch of the government. They are supplemented by executive orders of the President, which seek to ensure compliance with EEO policies in federal agencies and among certain government contractors. When conflicts arise between (1) federal laws and (2) state and local laws, usually the federal law dominates unless the state law is more stringent. As can be seen in the figure, the federal laws apply very broadly to most major employers, employment agencies, union hiring halls, and federal, state, and local governments.

Laws relevant to EEO

TITLE VII OF THE CIVIL RIGHTS ACT Title VII of the Civil Rights Act of 1964 as amended is the dominant law governing EEO. It requires employers, labor unions, and employment agencies to treat all people without regard to race, color, religion, national origin, sex, or age in all phases of employment. This includes hiring, training, apprentice programs, promotions, job assignments,

FIGURE 19-2
Major federal laws governing EEO

MAJOR EQUAL EMPLOYMENT OPPORTUNITY LAWS	OBJECTIVES	JURISDICTION
Equal Pay Act (1963)	**Equal pay for equal work regardless of sex**	**Employers engaged in interstate commerce and most employees of federal, state, and local governments**
Title VII of the Civil Rights Act (1964)	**EEO for different races, colors, religions, sexes, and national origins (as amended in 1972)**	**Employers with fifteen or more employees; unions with fifteen or more members; employment agencies; union hiring halls; institutions of higher education; federal, state, and local governments**
Age Discrimination in Employment Act (1967)	**EEO for age forty and over (as amended in 1986)**	**Employers with twenty or more employees; unions with twenty-five or more members; employment agencies; federal, state, and local governments**
Vocational Rehabilitation Act (1973)	**EEO and reasonable affirmative action for handicapped people**	**Federal government agencies and government contractors with contracts of $2500 or more**
Pregnancy Discrimination Act (1978)	**EEO during pregnancy**	**Same as Civil Rights Act**

and other personnel actions.[6] Certain exceptions are allowed, primarily with regard to employment with religious organizations and "in those certain instances where religion, sex, or national origin is a bona fide occupational qualification (BFOQ) reasonably necessary to the normal operation of that particular business or enterprise" (sections 702 and 703). An exemption also is provided to allow use of seniority for job assignments and layoff protection in many instances.

OTHER LEGISLATION Prior to the Civil Rights Act, the Equal Pay Act in 1963 provided equal pay for equal work regardless of one's sex. Practices of any type that gave men or women different pay for the same or substantially similar work were prohibited. One year later (1964) the Civil Rights Act initiated a major national effort for equal opportunity, including Title VII, which provided EEO. Several congressional acts followed.

In 1967 Congress passed the Age Discrimination in Employment Act, which (as later amended) provided EEO for people age forty and over. It was felt that younger people until age forty can compete for themselves in the labor market, but beginning with age forty and for the remainder of their expected working life they need protection to help them compete equally with others.

In 1973 the Vocational Rehabilitation Act was passed to give handicapped people EEO. It applies both to government as an employer and to government contractors with contracts of $2500 or more. Since most major employers have government contracts of one type of another, this act covers most of the job market. Then in 1978 Congress passed the Pregnancy Discrimination Act as an amendment to the Civil Rights Act. The Pregnancy Discrimination Act provides EEO to those able to work during pregnancy. Equal opportunities for medical benefits and leaves of absence are included.

EXECUTIVE ORDERS EEO also is supported by executive orders of the President. They apply to federal agencies and to most government contractors, and they have approximately the same coverage as federal EEO laws. They are enforced by the executive branch of the government.

Enforcement

EEOC

EQUAL EMPLOYMENT OPPORTUNITY COMMISSION Most EEO laws are enforced by the *Equal Employment Opportunity Commission* (EEOC). It has offices in major cities and can initiate court action against noncomplying businesses. Enforcement begins when a charge is filed by an aggrieved person, someone acting for the aggrieved person, or one of the EEOC commissioners. Charges also can be filed with an approved state agency, which is allowed a limited time to settle the case before it comes to the EEOC.

Conciliation agreement

If there is reason to believe that a violation has occurred, the EEOC seeks a *conciliation agreement*. It is a negotiated settlement acceptable to the EEOC and all aggrieved parties. If conciliation fails, court action may be initiated by the EEOC or the individual involved (or the attorney general if a public employer is involved). Remedies include back pay to injured parties and required affirmative action programs.

For example, in a court settlement, a textile company agreed to pay a settlement of $875,000 to eighteen blacks. They alleged discrimination in employment and promotion. After their complaint was filed, the case worked its way through the EEOC and the courts for a number of years while the company contested the allegation. During this period the potential liability for back pay continued to grow, so the settlement was large when it finally was made.

FEDERAL CONTRACT COMPLIANCE Enforcement against government contractors is secured through the Office of Federal Contract Compliance Programs. The office may cancel contracts or reach various types of conciliation agreements with a contractor in order to avoid contract cancellation.

For example, the Office of Federal Contract Compliance Programs made an agreement with a coal company concerning seventy-eight women who alleged employment discrimination. Coal mining traditionally has been a man's work, but under the law qualified women have equal opportunity for employment in it. The company agreed to pay the women $370,000 in order to comply with Executive Order 11246, which concerns sex discrimination by government contractors.

STATE AND LOCAL FAIR EMPLOYMENT PRACTICE AGENCIES In a similar manner state agencies can order a variety of settlements, particularly back pay. For example, the Fair Employment Practice Commission in California ordered a city to return an employee to the job and pay $80,000 in back pay. The employee, a native of India, alleged discrimination because of national origin, and the commission supported the allegation.

Protected groups

What are protected groups?

Since EEO laws are designed especially to protect certain groups of people from employment discrimination, these groups are called *protected groups*. For example, a black person typically is considered a member of a protected group but a white person is not. Similarly, women are a protected group but men are not. However, a fifty-year-old white male is a member of a protected group because of his age. A person needs to fit only one of the protected categories in order to be a member of a protected group. Because of the large number of people in certain protected categories, such as women and older employees, protected groups consist of more than three-fourths of the labor force. EEOC enforcement activities are directed primarily toward protection of the interests of these groups.

Affirmative action

Affirmative action is an employer effort to increase employment opportunity (including promotion and all other conditions of employment) for protected groups that appear to be inadequately represented in a firm's labor force. Employers are encouraged by government agencies and public pressures to examine their labor force and ensure that all groups are fairly represented. If they are not, companies may begin *affirmative action programs* as evidence that they are making a positive effort to provide equal employment.

Why create affirmative action programs?

The objectives of affirmative action programs are to remedy any alleged past discrimination and qualify employers to serve as government contractors. Employers often develop timetables by which they will accomplish certain goals, especially placement of an improved proportion of underrepresented groups in various jobs and levels of the organization.[7] The goals typically apply to minorities, women, employees age forty and over, and handicapped employees.

Affirmative action programs are common among employers. These programs have often been required by the EEOC or the courts, and they have been a business necessity for large employers who wished to qualify for government contracts. Many other firms also use them because they desire to take a more positive approach toward EEO.

The PQ Corporation, a specialty chemicals manufacturer, has experimented with making affirmative action goals part of its operating philosophy, while decentralizing hiring decisions. The company created a voluntary program, and then told its managers about demographic trends indicating strong future competition for

qualified minorities.[8] Managers also were informed about the legal effects of discriminatory decisions. As a final key element, managers were assigned the responsibility to set their own affirmative action goals and were appraised on their results. The company reports that not only have attitudes changed but also selection decisions have become more balanced than before.

Reverse discrimination

Affirmative action occasionally leads to *reverse discrimination*, by which there is discrimination against an employee not included in an affirmative action program. For example, one bank's affirmative action program required it to provide college tuition for female bank officers. If similar tuition is not available to male bank officers on an equal basis, they may consider themselves victims of reverse discrimination.

While affirmative action programs seek to accomplish desirable social goals, they also have an adverse impact on those employees who suffer reverse discrimination because of them. They want equal employment opportunity, and they argue that the way to end discrimination against some is not to begin discrimination against others—particularly those who do not bear responsibility for past discrimination. The groups favored by affirmative action reply that it is required to compensate for past discrimination and improve employment of underrepresented groups. They sometimes favor *proportional employment* or *parity employment*, which means that an organization's employees should approximately represent the proportions of different groups in the local labor force or population. For example, if the labor force has 20 percent racial minorities, then supervisors also should be about 20 percent racial minorities.

Proportional employment

The law supports EEO for all people, but the courts have sometimes interpreted the law in different ways. In one decision, the Supreme Court stated that Title VII "does not demand that an employer give preferential treatment to minorities or women," and it refused to support reverse discrimination.[9] In other instances the courts have supported it.

From the human point of view of organizational behavior, there are substantial questions of equity in affirmative action practices when they cause reverse discrimination. They can lead to employee frustration, tension, conflict, turnover, decreased satisfaction, and other negative feelings that harm work relations. In addition, a basic long-run issue is whether parity employment will be abandoned after acceptable equality in the work force is achieved, or whether it will become entrenched in law and custom, thereby making job structures rigid and reducing free job choice by workers.

EEO PROGRAMS

Basic requirements

Elements of EEO programs

An effective EEO program has a number of basic requirements, as shown in Figure 19-3. The first requirement is to develop positive policy statements.

- □ **Develop positive policy statements.**
- □ **Ensure top management support.**
- □ **Assign responsibility for applying the program.**
- □ **Gather data to identify problem areas.**
- □ **Identify and develop people in protected groups who have potential for promotion.**
- □ **Develop recruitment activities that reach protected groups as well as others.**
- □ **Communicate to maintain awareness of the program.**
- □ **Build supervisory support for the program.**
- □ **Appraise and follow up to ensure compliance.**

FIGURE 19-3
Requirements for an effective EEO program

Strong top-management support is required, and consultants and task forces may be used to provide specialized aid. Usually responsibility for developing and administering an EEO program is assigned to the personnel department, but in small firms the job may be assigned to another office as a part-time duty.

IDENTIFY PROBLEM AREAS Another requirement is to gather data to identify problem areas. Information is sought about such items as seniority, salary, education, promotions, and employment of different groups.

> **For example, there may seem to be no discrimination problem regarding women in a public school or retail store, because most of its employees are women. However, the data may show that the majority of managerial and better-paying professional jobs are held by men. In another organization the data may show that less pleasant and dirtier blue-collar jobs have been given to certain minorities, while women and nonminorities have been given more pleasant, higher-status, cleaner jobs.**

The purpose of the statistics is to help identify areas of probable discrimination, but it should not be assumed that every instance of unequal representation is proof of discrimination. There are many other reasons for unequal representation, such as education of employees. The data only provide a base for more investigation.

IDENTIFY AND DEVELOP PROTECTED GROUPS A further requirement is to identify and develop minorities and other protected groups that have potential for promotion. An important point is to assure them that EEO is available. In the past they may have felt discriminated against, so they were discouraged from developing themselves and seeking promotion. In one office, for example, when equal employment became a reality, a number of women and black employees became interested in self-development plans for possible promotion. Prior to equal employment, they showed only minor interest in self-development.

DEVELOP EQUAL RECRUITMENT An additional requirement is to be sure that there are equal recruitment activities for all types of people. Recruitment cannot be confined to familiar channels, or to contacts through friends, in a way that might perpetuate dominance of one sex, race, or ethnic group in certain jobs such as that of engineer. Recruitment should be done in ways that reach all types of potential employees, and any advertising should portray equality in all types of jobs. For example, a telephone company attracted favorable attention with a recruiting advertisement showing a woman climbing a telephone pole as part of a telephone line crew. The EEOC is encouraging both men and women to move into what is called *nontraditional employment,* or jobs not historically held by members of that sex. Examples include a woman becoming a crane operator or a man becoming a secretary. The policy is to encourage a climate in which all jobs are equally acceptable and available to all types of employees.

EEOC supports nontraditional employment.

Following are some of the affirmative action recruitment efforts made by one employer trying to meet employment goals encouraged by the EEOC.

1. **Selective recruiting in high schools having large numbers of minority students**
2. **Selective recruiting in colleges having large numbers of blacks, women, and ethnic groups**
3. **Establishment of a recruiting office in a minority neighborhood**
4. **Selective advertising in newspapers appealing to protected groups**
5. **Hiring of recruiters who are members of protected groups**
6. **Special training programs for recruits who were weak in employable skills**

COMMUNICATE ABOUT PROGRAM Another requirement is communication within the organization to maintain constant awareness of the EEO program. In many instances when a program begins, training sessions are held with all managers to explain the program to them. Supervisors are given special training to make them more aware of different work attitudes and values among protected groups.

BUILD SUPERVISORY SUPPORT Supervisory support especially is necessary because supervisors are the point of direct contact with employees. EEO and affirmative action programs may complicate their employment activities and increase their paperwork. Often EEO leads to a loss of their traditional power, because some of their decision making is transferred to the personnel department and higher management. In some instances the potential for work-group conflict is increased as new people are integrated into the work group. For these reasons, supervisory training often is essential to ensure EEO understanding and support.

One company discovered that its supervisors had built-in expectations of failure for certain minority employees who were being hired. To compound the problem, some of the new employees also had expectations that they would fail in the new environment because they lacked a background of successful employment experiences. The result of these two reinforcing sets of negative expectations was a high failure rate

for the minorities. When the company identified the problem, its solution was to train its supervisors. Now all supervisors take a special three-day training course designed to improve their attitudes and behaviors toward all protected groups.

APPRAISE PROGRAM A final requirement is appraisal and follow-up. If EEO is important, then the managerial appraisal and reward system must reflect this policy, because managers tend to emphasize the practices on which they are appraised. Follow-up also provides both a basis for correcting deficiencies in the program and evidence that EEO is being accomplished.

Application of EEO programs to various protected groups is discussed in the following sections.

Race, color, and national origin

EEO laws generally prohibit job discrimination on the basis of race, color, or national origin. The United States historically has been called a "melting pot" of people from all parts of the world, so it is important to give these people equal access to jobs regardless of their backgrounds. In this way they have a fair chance to earn their way into the mainstream of society and become self-sufficient. One of the major problems remaining is integration of minorities into professional and managerial jobs, because movement into these jobs requires substantial time for education, training, and growth. However, positive action can bring progress.

One company found that its number of minority managers was relatively low. It began a strong affirmative action program, and in five years increased its proportion of black managers from 2.2 to 5.5 percent and Hispanic managers from 0.7 to 2.1 percent. When EEOC investigated the company's compliance with EEO laws, it determined that the company's steady progress substantially complied with the law.

Sex

Job discrimination with regard to sex is prohibited. However, employers may establish job requirements that could be related to one's sex, provided the requirements clearly are necessary for the job. For example, an employer may employ only female fashion models to model women's clothing. A more complex issue is illustrated by a feed mill that requires employees to lift 100-pound bags. The company may use this as a screening criterion for new employees, but only if it provides both male and female applicants the actual opportunity to demonstrate their capacity to lift the bags. In other words, the mill managers should not assume that females cannot lift the bags, nor should they assume that females wouldn't be interested in the job. Although it is possible that the job requirement might lead to the rejection of a greater proportion of female job applicants than males, the requirement would appear to be legitimate and not discriminatory. There are, however, relatively few jobs with specialized requirements of this type.

Firms need to establish careful monitoring programs to ensure that sex discrimination does not occur, because sometimes it may happen without conscious intent or even knowledge.

A large bank was feeling the effects of a recession, so it needed to reduce its corporate lending staff. Six female lending officers were transferred to positions with less prestige in other areas. More than seventy male corporate lending officers were left in the lending office. (Can you speculate about reasons for this action? Was the selection of six women merely a matter of chance, or was it intentional? Did the selecting executives think that male lending officers presented a better image to clients? Did the executives simply have more confidence in male friends that they knew better? What were the reasons?)

When the monitoring program revealed that only women had been transferred, the bank quickly took corrective action.

Sexual harassment is discriminatory.

Sexual harassment is the process of making employment or promotion decisions contingent on sexual favors, or engaging in any verbal or physical conduct that creates an offensive working environment (see Figure 19-4). Although there is some disagreement over what constitutes sexual harassment, females responding to one survey generally included in their definition sexual propositions, physical touching, sexual remarks, and suggestive gestures.[10] Estimates of the extent of harassment indicate the problem is pervasive, with as many as 40 to 50 percent of females having experienced it.[11] Such harassment can occur anywhere in a company, from executive offices to assembly lines. From a human point of view, it is distasteful and demeaning to its victims, and it is discriminatory according to EEO laws and EEOC guidelines.

A majority of firms have developed a policy on sexual harassment, but many still have not. In the absence of a preventive program, employers may be responsible for the harassment actions of their supervisors and employees. When it occurs, employers may be liable for reinstatement of the victims if they were unfairly discharged, and may have to pay back wages, punitive damages, and awards for suffering and pain.[12] Most victims of sexual harassment are women, but there have been instances in which men were victims.

In order to provide equal opportunity regardless of sex, employers have developed policies to prevent harassment. They also have conducted training

FIGURE 19-4
EEOC definition of sexual harassment

From Equal Employment Opportunity Commission's Guidelines on Discrimination Because of Sex, *1604.11 (Sexual Harrassment), November 10, 1980.*

Unwelcome sexual advances, requests for sexual favors, and other verbal or physical conduct of a sexual nature constitute sexual harassment when:

(1) submission to such conduct is made either explicitly or implicitly a term or condition of an individual's employment,

(2) submission to or rejection of such conduct by an individual is used as the basis for employment decisions affecting such individual, or

(3) such conduct has the purpose or effect of unreasonably interfering with an individual's work performance or creating an intimidating, hostile, or offensive working environment.

programs to educate employees about the relevant law, actions that could constitute harassment (see Figure 19-4), possible liabilities, and the negative effects of harassment on its victims. For example, some victims have required psychological counseling.

Religious beliefs

Companies must attempt accommodation.

With regard to religious beliefs of employees, the law requires that employers make a reasonable effort to accommodate a worker's religious needs. Acceptable company efforts include actively seeking qualified substitutes, providing a flexible work schedule, redesigning the job, or transferring the employee to another position. If all accommodation efforts would place an undue hardship on the company or on other employees, then they are not required. For example, a company is not required to violate its seniority agreement with the union in order to accommodate an employee who wants all Saturdays off. Neither is it required to pay overtime regularly to other employees or require them to work double shifts in order to replace an employee who is absent for religious needs. As stated by the U.S. Supreme Court in a ruling concerning an airline employee, the law does not "require an employer to discriminate against some employees in order to enable others to observe their Sabbath."[13]

Employers, however, may make accommodations that go beyond the requirements of law if workers who are affected agree and have equal opportunity for similar accommodations.

Mark Jones faithfully observed his Sabbath on Saturday. When he applied for a job, he learned that Saturday work sometimes was required, so he told his potential employer about his needs. Since only a few employees were required to work on any Saturday, management arranged with other employees in the department to do Mark's work on Saturday when it was required. In turn, Mark agreed to an equal amount of Sunday work for others when it was required. The agreement operated for many years without any difficulty.

Any temporary religious absence that Mark requests, such as a day off to attend a religious conference, is handled according to the standard procedure for personal leave.

Handicapped employees

Who are the handicapped?

Handicapped employees are those with a significant disability of some type, either physical, mental, or emotional. They include people with a prison record, major obesity, or a history of heart disease, cancer, or mental illness, since others might view them as handicapped. Also included are rehabilitated alcoholics and drug abusers, as discussed in Chapter 17.

The Vocational Rehabilitation Act requires employers who are federal contractors to provide EEO for handicapped employees. Many employers, such as 3M, Control Data, and Sears, already had a long history of providing employment for handicapped people, but the law applied these types of programs to most other employers. They can require handicapped employees to meet the same productivity standards as other employees, but there must be a reasonable effort to accommodate those who are handicapped. A typical program is built on an affirmative action plan, including a variety of actions to remove physical, social, and other barriers to employment.[14]

Figure 19-5 shows the Tennessee Valley Authority affirmative action program for handicapped employees. The figure especially illustrates the complexity of an effective program. A policy statement and employment program are only the beginning. There must be education and training to prepare both supervisors and other employees. Changes may be required in building entrances, locker rooms, and other physical facilities. Job modifications frequently are required so that certain jobs can be performed by handicapped employees. In addition, much coordination is required among departments and with various external organizations.

AIDS Acquired Immune Deficiency Syndrome (*AIDS*) is a deadly viral disease of the human immune system. Because no cure for AIDS is yet known, and the number of persons diagnosed as having the AIDS virus is increasing, there is

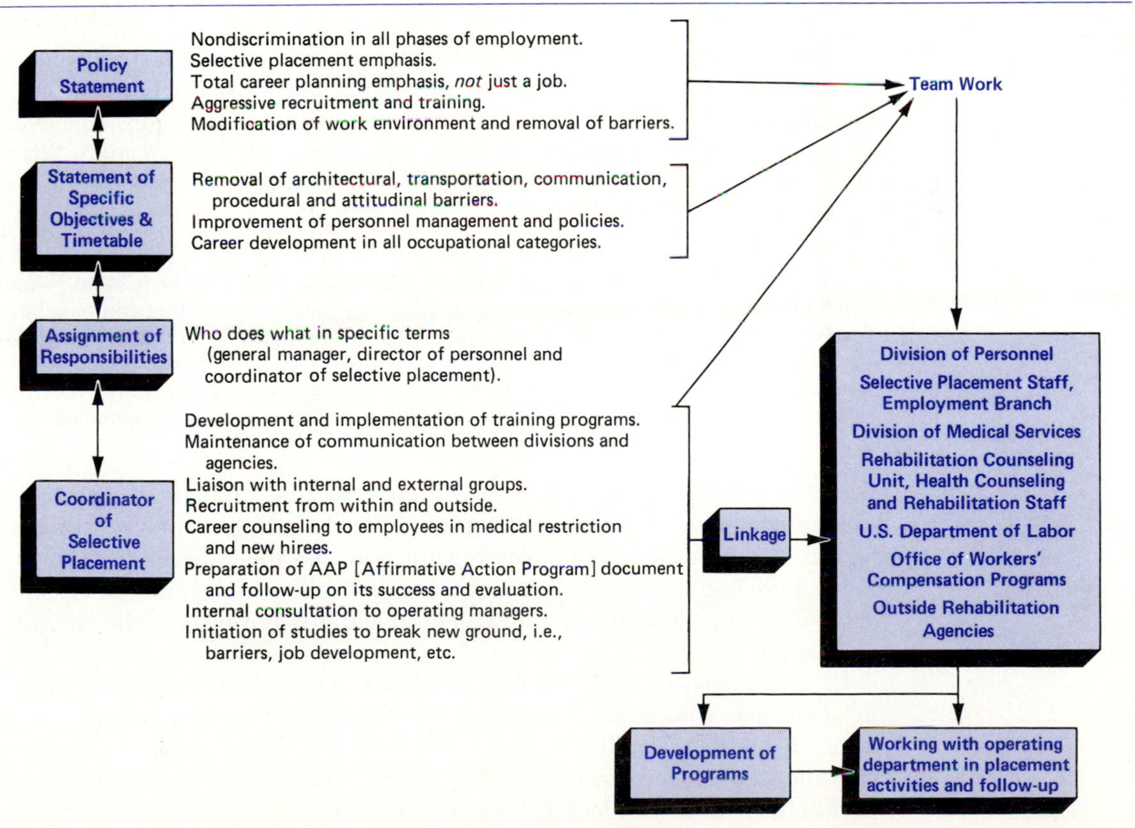

FIGURE 19-5 Tennessee Valley Authority's affirmative action program for handicapped employees

From "A Comprehensive Model for a Handicapped Affirmative Action Program" by Gopal C. Pati and Edward F. Hilton, Jr. Reprinted with permission of Personnel Journal, *Costa Mesa, Calif., copyright © February 1980.*

widespread concern about it. Employers need a large degree of knowledge and sensitivity to deal with the many fundamental issues in organizational behavior related to AIDS. Because AIDS is so new, employer responsibilities have not yet been fully clarified in the courts. Regardless of the legal status of AIDS employees, however, key behavioral issues include the following:[15]

Issues surrounding AIDS

- Can the medical privacy of AIDS employees be protected?
- What can be done to help coworkers understand AIDS, remain calm, and accept an AIDS employee into the work group?
- How might the presence of AIDS employees affect teamwork and their participation in a group?
- How can managers prevent AIDS employees from becoming socially isolated through the possible loss of normal communications with their coworkers?

Although these are difficult issues, employers need to consider them and develop their policies *before* the first case arises in their firm.[16] Awareness of emerging case law also will be essential.

EMPLOYER PROGRAMS The supportive philosophy of most employer programs is to focus on employee abilities, not disabilities. In spite of disability, nearly all handicapped people have remaining abilities to perform some jobs effectively. It is the employer's responsibility to identify those jobs, prepare applicants for them, and make reasonable modifications in the jobs so that they can be performed effectively.

A large bank in Chicago has a successful senior transcriptionist who is blind.[17] Some job modifications were made to accommodate her, such as providing additional desk space for her seven-volume braille dictionary. Employees in her department formerly performed both transcription and typing of written material. Now the job is redesigned so that the blind employee performs only transcription work, which she does virtually error-free, and other employees mostly type written material.

PERFORMANCE RESULTS Most employers find that properly placed handicapped employees can perform their jobs as well as other employees. In many instances handicapped employees compensate for their disabilities, such as being more regular in attendance or giving more effort to the job. For example, some firms report both lower absenteeism and less turnover for handicapped employees.

In some instances a handicapped employee may be better able to perform a job than one who is not handicapped because the handicap becomes a job advantage rather than disadvantage. For example, a blind employee may have an acutely developed sense of hearing that is an advantage in a certain job, or a deaf employee may be less distracted by noises.

Tony Valente was deaf. He worked in a noisy machine-shop office in a clerical job that required intense mental concentration. Prior to the time that Tony took the job, turnover in the job was high. Employees stayed from three days to six months and complained that the noise distracted them, increased their errors, and reduced the minutes of actual work that they could do in an hour. When Tony took the job, he adapted to it easily. Communication with others took more time because of his handicap, but this loss was more than offset by the gain from his ability to concentrate better on the job.

OLDER WORKERS

Employment of older workers will be discussed in more detail in order to illustrate additional behavioral issues involved.

EEO

Why protect older workers?

The Age Discrimination Act of 1967 (as amended in 1986) provides EEO for employees over age forty. The law recognizes that people now live longer, that many older people are in good health and able to work after sixty-five, and that many of them want to work beyond sixty-five. In addition, inflation reduces the real value of retirement benefits and savings for some older workers, so they need to work longer to maintain a satisfactory standard of living.

People age forty and over are a protected group, so employers need to take the usual actions to ensure that older employees actually have EEO. Areas of action include employment, training opportunities, rates of pay, promotions, reasonable adaptation to physical limitations, and eventual retirement.

For example, a manufacturing company laid off several of its middle managers who were under age seventy. It said that their work was unsatisfactory and that they were unable to keep up with the fast-moving pace of change. They filed charges of age discrimination and eventually won back pay and an opportunity for reinstatement. In a few instances the company was able to prove unsatisfactory performance, so the charges brought by these managers were dismissed.

Job adjustment of older workers

As workers grow older, they have many adjustments to make. With regard to organizational behavior, older workers tend to develop gradually into social groups that are often separate from younger workers. Their interests and even their day-to-day conversations are different. Older workers become less able to take part in active sports such as company softball. The important point is that these changes need to take place without causing older employees to feel socially isolated and insecure. They need to be accepted and understood—to be respected for what they have to offer, rather than penalized for what they cannot help. Age comes alike to all persons, so management, unions, and work groups need to recognize their responsibility to build an organizational climate that accepts and integrates older workers. In this way they can be assured of genuine EEO in their older years.

Older workers perform well.

PERFORMANCE OF OLDER WORKERS Generally the job performance of older and younger workers is about the same.[18] Although there are many variations, a typical situation is that infirmities associated with age often are offset by improvements of other types, so total performance remains about the same. For example, some older workers need to work at a slower pace, but they compensate for this deficiency by improved dependability, quality of work, attendance, and effort. Perhaps the greatest difficulty faced by older workers is job changes that upset established job patterns and may cause their jobs to become obsolete. These kinds of situations can be threatening.

JOB PLACEMENT PROFILE CHARTS Improved EEO for older workers can be encouraged by using *job placement profile charts* to match worker physical and mental abilities with a job's requirements.[19] The profile chart displays an evaluation of both job requirements and worker abilities for key features of the job so that management can easily determine how well a worker fits a job. With the aid of proper counseling for job placement, profile charts have helped older workers reduce absences and sick leave and continue effective work for a longer period of time.

Figure 19-6 displays a profile chart for an older worker in an office job. The worker is a reasonably suitable match except for eyesight. Perhaps the employee's eyesight can be corrected in some way, as with better eyeglasses. If not, perhaps the job can be changed to require less effective eyesight or the employee can be reassigned to a job with less stringent requirements. One older worker, for example, was moved from a standing job to a sitting job, and that worker's sick leave declined from an excessive amount to zero for the next sixteen months.

Easing the transition into retirement

Retirement tends to be one of life's most difficult adjustments. Suddenly a worker moves from a full-time job to no job, so a feeling of uselessness can be overwhelming.

Consider the case of Mack McGuire, whose department is holding a retirement dinner for him. There he stands at the head of the table fiddling with the watch the company just gave him. He is choked with emotion and fishing for the right words to tell how he feels inside. A month ago he was willing and able to work, but now he is seventy and about to retire. He knew retirement was coming, but he never did want to think about it before because the subject was too painful. Suddenly he realizes that retirement is upon him, and he panics at the thought of it.

PRERETIREMENT COUNSELING Retirement, like one's own funeral, is something many employees would rather not think about, so employers develop

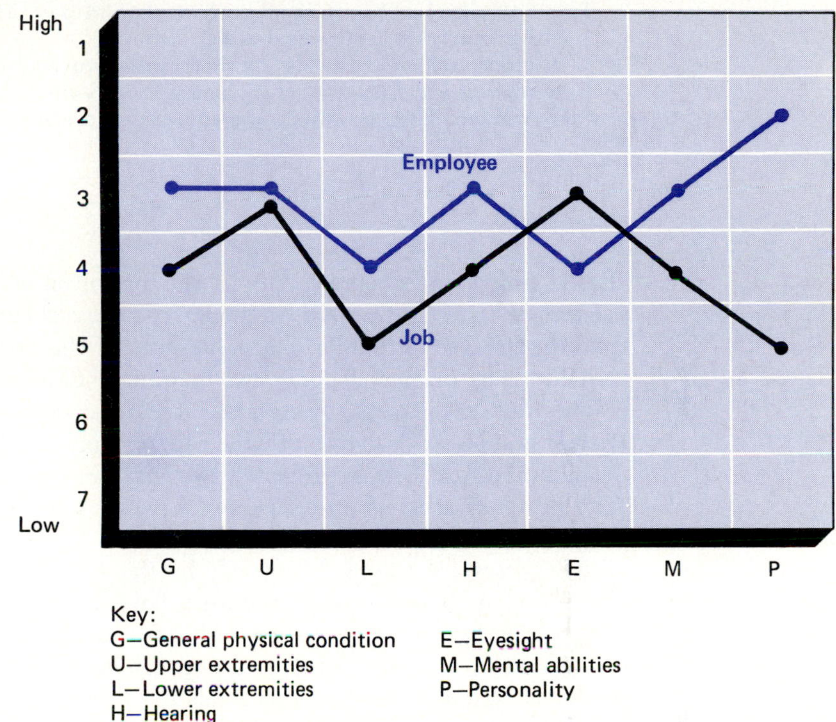

FIGURE 19-6
Profile chart for job placement of an older worker in an office job

Two programs for better transition

programs that encourage employees to think about pending retirement. These programs usually are called *preretirement counseling*. One necessary subject is pension choices and insurance benefits that will be available after retirement. Since a major concern of workers after retirement is income maintenance, they often welcome counseling of this type. Other counseling topics include financial management, possible hobbies, and emotional problems associated with retirement.

Another subject with a significant influence on retiree satisfactions is health, so firms may provide health guidance prior to retirement. Workers are encouraged to develop good health maintenance patterns so that they can maintain these patterns after retirement.

PHASED RETIREMENT Another way to soften the transition to retirement is to give workers more time off, usually with pay, in the years immediately preceding retirement. This is called *phased retirement*. It allows workers to become accustomed to being away from work and learning to enjoy other activities.

A few European firms have generous phased retirement plans.[20] One firm allows workers beginning at age sixty-one to have one-half day off each week with pay.

With each advancing year, the amount is increased one-half day, so that at age sixty-four a worker has two days off each week with pay. The worker then should be better prepared for retirement at age sixty-five.

Another company provides workers with two additional weeks of paid leave beginning at age sixty-one. This amount is increased gradually until, at age sixty-four, workers receive twelve summer weeks and eight other weeks with pay.

SUMMARY

Equal employment opportunity is the provision of equal opportunities to secure jobs and earn rewards in them, regardless of conditions unrelated to job performance. It is public policy because of the social benefits that it can provide. The primary federal laws that apply EEO are Title VII of the Civil Rights Act, the Equal Pay Act, the Age Discrimination Act, the Vocational Rehabilitation Act relating to handicapped persons, and the Pregnancy Discrimination Act. People protected by these laws are called protected groups. The principal areas of protection are a person's race, color, religion, national origin, sex, age, and handicap.

EEO laws are enforced primarily by the Equal Employment Opportunity Commission. Many major employers have adopted affirmative action programs. EEO presents many difficult behavioral issues such as social integration of minorities into work groups, group conflict, individual and group power, sexual harassment, reverse discrimination, religious freedoms, and adaptations for handicapped and aged employees.

Terms and concepts for review

Equal employment opportunity (EEO)

Equal Employment Opportunity Commission (EEOC)

Conciliation agreement

Protected groups

Affirmative action

Reverse discrimination

Proportional and parity employment

Sexual harassment

Job placement profile charts

Preretirement counseling

Phased retirement

Discussion questions

1 Survey your classroom group to determine how many of you currently are members of a protected group. How many are members of more than one protected group at the present time? Assuming that EEO laws remain the same, how many of you are likely to be members of a protected group twenty-five years from now?

2 Form into research groups to study and discuss the potential benefits and problems that appear to be associated with EEO as currently enforced.

Present your report to the entire classroom group, and discuss it compared with reports of other groups.

3 Do you think some job discrimination is justified? Consider such instances as the denial of certain jobs to people below certain ages; the hiring of relatives by the owners of small businesses; and, for certain government jobs, the giving of preference to veterans of military service. If some of this discrimination is justified, how will that which is equitable be distinguished from that which is not equitable?

4 Read current EEO information and then prepare an affirmative action program for women in an organization of your choice.

5 Contact three local organizations, and ask them what their policy on sexual harassment is. Present your findings to the class, and compare them to Figure 19-4.

6 Discuss the use of job placement profile charts for older employees. What problems and benefits do you see in their use?

7 Review the idea of phased retirement programs. What equity issues might arise when younger employees discover that some workers are receiving full pay for reduced time at work?

8 Read some additional information about affirmative action. Conduct a class debate, highlighting its strengths and weaknesses.

9 Report to the class whether you have ever felt that you were the victim of reverse discrimination. If you were, discuss the circumstances, how you felt, and how it was resolved.

10 Discuss AIDS-related issues at work. How would you feel about hiring, or working next to, an AIDS victim?

Incidents

BORDER ELECTRONICS

Border Electronics is an electronic assembly plant in a community near the Mexican border. About 60 percent of employees are Mexican-Americans, and a few others are Mexican citizens. This firm had a rush order that required steady work from all employees and no leaves of absence. This order extended through September 16, the Independence Day of Mexico. This holiday and surrounding days are elaborately celebrated by the Mexican-American community; however, the company strongly needed full attendance of all employees during this period.

To ensure attendance, department superintendent Max Ways wrote a directive, as was his usual practice with employees, stating that no leave would be granted to anyone during the holiday period because the rush order was not completed.

Another superintendent, Arleigh Watkins, called his employees together in his usual way and explained the problem in detail in both English and Spanish. He stated that he could allow leaves only to a few people who were on entertainment committees and had other special reasons for absence. He appealed for the cooperation of all employees to continue working because of the rush order.

Question

Appraise the different ways in which the two superintendents approached their employees. Discuss the probable absence rates in the two departments during the holiday period.

MARY SCROGGINS

Mary Scroggins graduated from Northwestern University in accounting. Immediately after graduation she was employed effective July 1 by the local office of a national accounting firm. During the employment process Mary was told that her normal hours of work would be 8:30 A.M. to 5 P.M., Monday through Friday, but that overtime work might sometimes be required, particularly in the months immediately preceding the income tax deadline of April 15. Mary belongs to a Christian denomination whose Sabbath is on Saturday, and she is an active and devout member of her church. At the time of employment the accounting firm did not inquire about her religion because it wished to comply fully with the Civil Rights Act concerning race, religion, creed, and national origin. Mary likewise did not mention her religion at this time.

During the following six months Mary proved to be a capable and loyal employee. Her performance was above average for her team, and her supervisor, Royce Mathis, remarked to his manager how pleased he was to have Mary in his group. He felt that, assuming she continued to grow, she had potential for promotions within the firm.

As the income tax period approached, Mary's supervisor began preparing overtime schedules for his group. Based upon past practice and consensus within the group, all overtime was scheduled on Saturdays. When Mary's supervisor discussed the tentative schedule with her, she said she would not work on Saturday because of her religious belief. In fact, her religious belief required her to stop work before sundown Friday.

Questions

1 Discuss the organizational behavior issues raised by this incident and what Royce Mathis should do to solve them.
2 Perform library research on EEO law and discuss how it might influence Royce's actions in this situation.

References

1 Rosabeth Moss Kanter, "Men and Women of the Corporation Revisited," *Management Review*, March 1987, p. 16.

2 Paula Dwyer, "Affirmative Action: After the Debate, Opportunity," *Business Week*, Apr. 13, 1987.

3 Examples of committed, cohesive employees abound. For an example in the Silicon Valley area, read the account provided in John Sculley, *Odyssey: Pepsi to Apple . . . A Journey of Adventure, Ideas, and the Future*, New York: Harper & Row, Publishers, Inc., 1987.

4 Frances C. Shipper and Frank M. Shipper, "Beyond EEO: Toward Pluralism," *Business Horizons*, May–June 1987, pp. 53–61. For a discussion of the value of internally consistent beliefs within the organization, see Buddy Robert S. Silverman, "A Litmus Test for EEO Philosophies," *Personnel Journal*, May 1987, pp. 143–151.

5 Thomas I. Chacko, "Women and Equal Employment: Some Unintended Effects," *Journal of Applied Psychology*, February 1982, pp. 119–123.

6 Three tests of discrimination in employment are evidence of adverse impact, failure to prove job relatedness, and the availability of other nondiscriminatory screening devices; see David G. Scalise and Daniel J. Smith, "Legal Update: When Are Job Requirements Discriminatory?" *Personnel*, March 1986, pp. 41–48.

7 For a review of some key decisions, see James R. Redeker, "The Supreme Court on Affirmative Action: Conflicting Opinions," *Personnel*, October 1986, pp. 8–14; and Paula Dwyer, "Clearing the Confusion over Affirmative Action," *Business Week*, July 14, 1986, pp. 26–27.

8 Jeanne C. Poole and E. Theodore Kautz, "An EEO/AA Program That Exceeds Quotas—It Targets Biases," *Personnel Journal*, January 1987, pp. 103–105.

9 "Supreme Court Rules on Title VII," *Washington Vantage Point*, April 1981, p. 1.

10 Gary N. Powell, "Sexual Harassment: Confronting the Issue of Definition," *Business Horizons*, July–August 1983, pp. 24–28.

11 Diane Feldman, "Sexual Harassment: Policies and Prevention," *Personnel*, September 1987, pp. 12–17; and David E. Terpstra and Susan E. Cook, "Complainant Characteristics and Reported Behaviors and Consequences Associated with Formal Sexual Harassment Charges," *Personnel Psychology*, Autumn 1985, pp. 559–574.

12 A landmark sexual harassment case, *Meritor v. Savings Bank v. Vinson*, was the first to reach the U.S. Supreme Court in 1986. Its ruling is discussed in Frederick L. Sullivan, "Sexual Harassment: The Supreme Court's Ruling," *Personnel*, December 1986, pp. 37–44. A review of the prior relevant case law is in Robert H. Faley, "Sexual Harassment: Critical Review of Legal Cases with General Principles and Preventive Measures," *Personnel Psychology*, Autumn 1982, pp. 583–600.

13 "Supreme Court Eases Task of Employers in Meeting Religious Needs of Workers," *Wall Street Journal* (Western edition), June 17, 1977, p. 4.

14 George E. Stevens, "Exploding the Myths about Hiring the Handicapped," *Personnel*, December 1986, pp. 57–60; and Rod Willis, "Mainstreaming the Handicapped without Tokenism," *Management Review*, March 1987, pp. 43–48.

15 For a more thorough discussion of issues, see Robert S. Letchinger, "AIDS: An Employer's Dilemma," *Personnel*, February 1986, pp. 58–63; and Dale A. Masi, "AIDS in the Workplace: What Can Be Done?" *Personnel*, July 1987, pp. 57–60.

16 Phyllis Schiller Myers and Donald W. Myers, "AIDS: Tackling a Tough Problem through Policy," *Personnel Administrator*, April 1987, pp. 95ff; and William S. Waldo, "A Practical Guide for Dealing with AIDS at Work," *Personnel Administrator*, August 1987, pp. 135–138.

17 Gopal C. Pati and John I. Adkins, Jr., "Hire the Handicapped—Compliance Is Good Business," *Harvard Business Review*, January–February 1980, pp. 14–22.

18 Survey data from human resource managers support this conclusion; see Paul L. Blocklyn, "The Aging Workforce," *Personnel*, August 1987, pp. 16–19. An alternative view, in which supervisors' performance ratings of older workers are lower than for younger workers, is reported in Gerald R. Ferris et al., "The Influence of Subordinate Age on Performance Ratings and Causal Attributions," *Personnel Psychology*, Autumn 1985, pp. 545–557.

19 The job placement profile chart is adapted from Michael D. Batten, "Application of a Unique Industrial Health System," *Industrial Gerontology*, Fall 1973, p. 41.

20 Bernhard Teriet, "Gliding Out: The European Approach to Retirement," *Personnel Journal*, July 1978, pp. 368–370. An in-depth study of phased retirement programs in seventeen European firms is reported in Constance Swank, "Phased Retirement Programs Working Well in Europe," *Management Review*, August 1983, pp. 32–33.

For additional reading

AIDS: A Manager's Guide, New York: Executive Enterprises Publications Co., Inc., 1987.

Banta, William F., *AIDS in the Workplace: Legal Questions and Practical Answers*, Lexington, Mass.: Lexington Books, 1987.

Gutek, Barbara A., *Sex and the Workplace: The Impact of Sexual Behavior and Harassment on Women, Men, and Organizations*, San Francisco: Jossey-Bass Inc., Publishers, 1986.

Humple, Carol Segrave, and Morgan Lyons, *Management and the Older Workforce: Policies and Programs*, New York: AMA, 1983.

Roberson, Cliff, *Staying Out of Court: A Manager's Guide to Employment Law*, Lexington, Mass.: Lexington Books, 1985.

Rosen, Benson, and Thomas H. Jerdee, *Older Employees: New Roles for Valued Resources*, Homewood, Ill.: Dow Jones–Irwin, 1985.

Schlei, Barbara Lindemann, and Paul Grossman, *Employment Discrimination Law*, 2d ed., Washington: Bureau of National Affairs, 1983.

Weatherspoon, Floyd D., *Equal Employment Opportunity and Affirmative Action: A Sourcebook*, New York: Garland Publishing, 1986.

CHAPTER 20

Stress and counseling

Friend (to worker with unpleasant factory job): "Doesn't your job give you a lot of trouble?"
Worker: "Bother, perhaps, but never trouble. You see, trouble is on the heart, but bother is only on the hands."

ANONYMOUS

Stress is a major cause of low productivity, high absenteeism, poor decisions, bad judgment, misallocation of resources, and poor morale.

ROBERT W. ECKLES[1]

CHAPTER OBJECTIVES

To understand

The role of stress in employee mental health

Causes of stress

The relationship between stress and job performance

Management actions that may reduce stress

Different types of counseling and their usefulness

Different counseling functions

In an insurance office, the work of a young stenographer became erratic as the result of an emotional conflict she was having with her mother. In a foundry, a skilled worker asked for transfer to a semiskilled job in another department because "I just wouldn't work for that stupid supervisor one more day." These kinds of situations illustrate stressful conditions that often can be helped by counseling. No matter how well human relationships are handled, people occasionally develop emotional problems, and a prime way to treat these difficulties is to counsel one or more of the parties involved.

In this chapter we discuss what stress is and how it affects job performance. Then we discuss types of counseling and how they are used to help employees with their problems.

EMPLOYEE STRESS

Stress

Stress is the general term applied to the pressures people feel in life. The presence of stress at work is almost inevitable in many jobs. For example, a survey by the National Association of Working Women reported that one-third of the respondents perceived their jobs as very stressful, and another 62 percent saw their work as somewhat stressful.[2] When pressure begins to build up, it can cause adverse strain on one's emotions, thought processes, and physical condition. When stress becomes excessive, employees develop various symptoms of stress that can harm their job performance and health, and even threaten their ability to cope with the environment. As shown in Figure 20-1, people who are stressed may become nervous and develop chronic worry. They are easily provoked to anger and are unable to relax. They may be uncooperative or use alcohol or drugs excessively. Although these conditions also occur from other causes, they are common symptoms of stress.

Symptoms of stress

Stress also leads to physical disorders, because the internal body system changes to try to cope with stress. Some physical disorders are short-range, such as an upset stomach. Others are longer-range, such as a stomach ulcer. Stress over a prolonged time also leads to degenerative diseases of the heart, kidneys, blood vessels, and other parts of the body. Therefore it is important that stress, both on and off the job, be kept at a level low enough for most people to tolerate without disorders.

For example, Peter Randall was transferred from a small city to a very large city where his commuting time to work was nearly one hour. He disliked city noises, heavy traffic, and crowds, and he felt he was wasting his time while commuting. His new job also had more responsibilities.

Within a few months he developed intestinal problems. When a medical examination showed no medical cause of his difficulties, he was sent to a counselor. There was only slight improvement, so finally his counselor in cooperation with his physician recommended that he transfer to a smaller city. His firm arranged his transfer, and within a short time his problems disappeared.

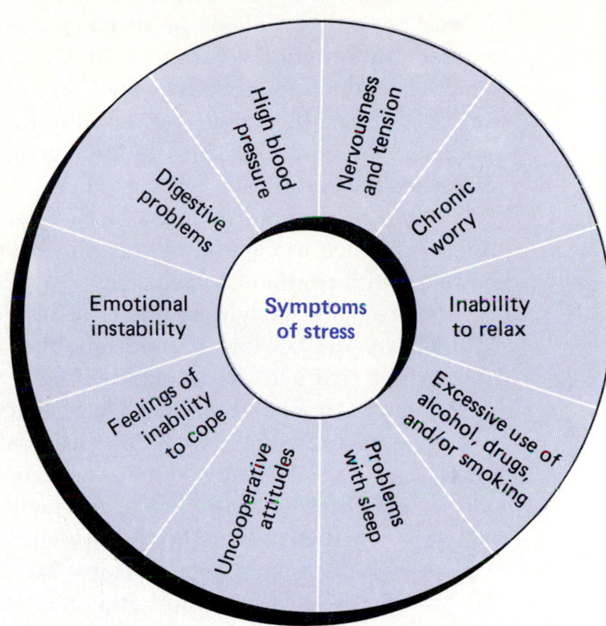

FIGURE 20-1
Typical symptoms of stress

There is emerging evidence that in some situations an organization can be held legally liable for the emotional and physical impact of job stress on employees like Peter. Poor working conditions, sustained conflicts with supervisors, traumatic events, or intentional harassment of employees sometimes results in anguish, neuroses, or even suicide. If liability is established, employees could claim benefits under workers' compensation laws, as well as sue for financial damages.[3]

Duration and intensity of stress

Stress can be either temporary or long-term, mild or severe, depending mostly on how long its causes continue, how powerful they are, and how strong the employee's recovery powers are. If stress is temporary and mild, most people can handle it or at least recover from its effects rather quickly.

Meyer Jamison, a sales representative, was transferred to a new territory after nine years in his old territory. Suddenly he found himself in a new and unknown situation with different people and job requirements. He felt frustrated, uneasy, and overloaded with work. There was too much to learn in too short a time. He developed conflicts with two or three customers and became less cooperative at home. He was in a condition of mild stress.

After a few weeks in his new territory, his stress gradually disappeared, and eventually he became as comfortable as he had been in his old territory.

In contrast to Meyer's temporary stress, some major pressures are sustained for long periods. Problems predictably arise when high-intensity stress continues for an extended duration of time. According to the theory developed by Hans Selye, the human body cannot instantly rebuild its ability to cope with stress.[4] As a result, people become physically and psychologically weakened from trying to combat it. This condition is called *burnout*—a situation in which employees are emotionally exhausted, become detached from their work, and feel unable to accomplish their goals. Some jobs, like those in the helping professions (such as counselors, health care professionals, and social workers) and those with continuous high stress (such as air-traffic controllers and stockbrokers) are more likely than others to result in burnout.

Burnout

When workers become burned out, they are more likely to complain, attribute their errors to others, and be highly irritable. The alienation they feel drives many of them to think about leaving their jobs, to seek out opportunities to become trained for new careers, and actually to quit.[5] Organizations need to identify both the jobs that lead to early burnout and the employees who exhibit some of the burnout symptoms. Sometimes it may be possible to change the parts of a job that contribute to burnout. In other cases the firm can help employees learn how to cope better with their stressful work situations. An important first step is to examine and understand the causes of stress, and these will be discussed here.

Causes of stress

Conditions that tend to cause stress are called *stressors*. Although even a single stressor may cause major stress, usually stressors combine to pressure an employee in a variety of ways until stress develops.

The experience of Walter Mathis, an automobile mechanic, illustrates how various conditions combine to cause stress. Mathis felt that he was doing well, but then he failed to get a wage increase he had expected. At about the same time, his wife divorced him. A short time later, partly because of problems leading to the divorce, he underwent a detailed audit by the U.S. Internal Revenue Service. So many different problems were hitting Mathis that he began to show signs of stress.

This example illustrates the results of an ongoing study by the National Institute of Mental Health.[6] It reports that the major sources of employee stress are evenly divided between organizational factors and the nonwork environment. These dual causes are reflected in Figure 20-2, which shows that employees may respond to these stressors with either positive stress (which stimulates them) or negative stress (which detracts from their efforts). As a result, there may be either constructive or destructive consequences for both the organization and the employee. These effects may be short-term and diminish quickly, or they may last a long time. To control stress, then, organizations usually begin by exploring its job-related causes.

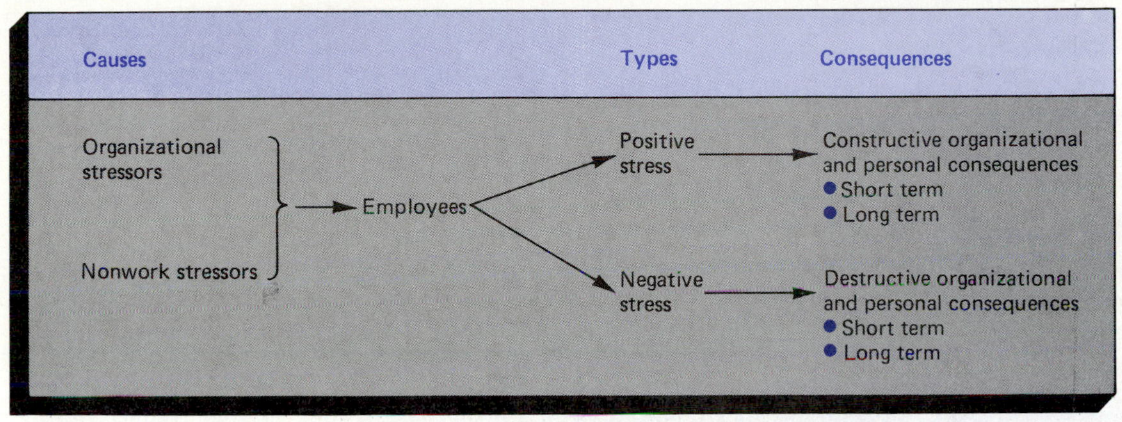

FIGURE 20-2
A model of causes, types, and consequences of stress

Source: *Parts of the model are adapted from Randall S. Schuler, "An Integrative Transactional Process Model of Stress in Organizations,"* Journal of Occupational Behaviour, *January 1982, pp. 5–19.*

Job causes of stress

Almost any job condition can cause stress, depending upon an employee's reaction to it. For example, one employee will accept a new work procedure while another rejects it. There are, however, a number of job conditions that frequently cause stress for employees. Major ones are shown in Figure 20-3.

Work overload and time deadlines put employees under pressure and lead to stress. Often, some of these pressures arise from supervision, so a poor quality of supervision can cause stress. Examples are an autocratic supervisor, an insecure political climate, and inadequate authority to match one's responsibilities.

Examples of job stressors

For example, Marsha Oldburg worked three years as a production expediter in an electronics plant. She experienced frequent emergencies, conflict, tight schedules, and pressures. She seldom had enough authority to match her responsibility. Occasionally she commented, "This job is getting me down." At about this time, she discovered during a routine physical checkup that she had high blood pressure. After discussions with a physician, she consulted a personnel counselor, who helped her transfer to a job with less pressure and a better match of authority with responsibility. Within six months her blood pressure was under control.

Role conflict and ambiguity also are related to stress.[7] In situations of this type, people have different expectations of an employee's activities on a job, so the employee does not know what to do and cannot meet all expectations. In addition, the job often is poorly defined, so the employee has no official model on which to depend.

A further cause of stress lies in differences between company values, as often reflected in the organization's culture, and employee values. Substantial differences can lead to significant mental stress as an effort is made to balance the

- Work overload
- Time pressures
- Poor quality of supervision
- Insecure political climate
- Inadequate authority to match responsibilities
- Role conflict and ambiguity
- Differences between company and employee values
- Change of any type, especially when it is major or unusual
- Frustration

FIGURE 20-3
Typical causes of stress on the job

requirements of both sets of values. The results of this conflict between individual needs and organizational characteristics are illustrated in this study:

> **Seventy-three U.S. Army and Air Force officers were surveyed to identify their perceptions of job factors causing stress for them.[8] Respondents in the highest stress group, called *achievement-centered* individuals, feared making wrong decisions, were unclear about their advancement opportunities, and didn't know what people expected of them. Another high group was labeled *organization-centered*, and these officers were unclear about their responsibilities and the basis for performance appraisals. They also felt that both the authority and information needed to perform their jobs was inadequate. Officers in a third group felt low stress on the other items, but were deeply concerned about having to make decisions on the job that were against their better judgment. Even respondents in a group that was otherwise free of stress felt substantial stress from the inconsistency between their own values and the job requirements.**

Sources vary.

Some jobs provide more stress than others.[9] Those that involve rotating shift work, machine-paced tasks, or hazardous environments are associated with greater stress. Workers who spend many hours daily in front of computer screens also report high stress levels. Evidence also indicates that the sources of stress differ by organizational level. Executive stress may arise from the pressure for short-term financial results or the fear of a hostile takeover attempt. Supervisory stressors include the pressure for quality and customer service, numerous meetings, and responsibility for the work of others. Workers are more likely to experience the stressors of low status, resource shortages, and the demand for a large volume of error-free work.

A general and widely recognized cause of stress is change of any type, because it requires adaptation by employees. It tends to be especially stressful when it is major or unusual, such as a temporary layoff or transfer. A related source of stress that affects many employees is worry over their financial well-being.[10] This can arise when cost-saving technology is introduced, contract negotiations begin, or the firm's financial performance suffers. Clearly, there are numerous and powerful forces at work that can contribute to the feeling of stress.

Frustration

What are defense mechanisms?

Another cause of stress is *frustration*. It is a result of a motivation (drive) being blocked to prevent one from reaching a desired goal. If you are trying to finish a report by quitting time in the afternoon, and one interference after another develops to require your time, then by the middle of the afternoon, when you see that your goal for the day may not be reached, you are likely to become frustrated. You may become irritable, develop an uneasy feeling in your stomach, or have some other reaction. These reactions to frustration are known as *defense mechanisms*, because you are trying to defend yourself from the psychological effects of the blocked goal.

The example given is merely a one-day frustration that probably will be overcome tomorrow, but the situation is more serious when there is a long-run frustration, such as a blocked opportunity for promotion. Then you have to live with the frustration day after day. It begins to build emotional disorders that interfere with your ability to function effectively.

TYPES OF REACTIONS One of the most common reactions to frustration is aggression. Whenever people are aggressive, it is likely that they are reflecting frustrations that are upsetting them. Additional reactions to frustration include apathy, withdrawal, regression, fixation, physical disorders, and substitute goals. We can illustrate them by continuing the story of the blocked promotion. Suppose that you think your supervisor is blocking your promotion. The blockage may be real or only a result of your imagination, but in any case it is real to you. As a result of your frustration, you may become aggressive by demanding better treatment and threatening to appeal to higher management. Or you may do almost the reverse and become apathetic, not responding to your job or associates. Another reaction is withdrawal, such as asking for a transfer or quitting your job. Regression to less mature behavior also is possible, such as self-pity and pouting.

If there is a fixation, perhaps you constantly blame your supervisor for both your problems and the problems of others, regardless of the true facts. You also may develop a physical disorder such as an upset stomach or choose a substitute goal such as becoming the leader of a powerful informal group in office politics. All of these are possible reactions to frustration. It is evident that they are not usually favorable, either to the individual or to the organization, so it is desirable in organizational behavior to reduce frustrating conditions.

SOURCES OF FRUSTRATION Although the example that was discussed concerns management as the source of frustration, management is only one of several sources. Another major source is coworkers who may place barriers in the way of goal attainment. Perhaps they delay work inputs to you, thereby delaying your work. Or their poorly done inputs prevent you from doing quality work. You also can be frustrated by the work itself, such as a part that does not fit or a machine that breaks down. Even the environment, such as a rainy day, may prevent you from doing the work you intended.

Frequency and severity of hassles

Some research suggests that it is the little things, called hassles, rather than major life crises, that produce frustration. These hassles are conditions of daily living that are perceived to threaten one's well-being. They have been found to be related to both symptoms of ill health and level of absenteeism.[11] The most frequent hassles include too many things to do, losing items, interruptions, and unchallenging work. Some of the hassles with the greatest average severity were related to both the job and the environment, such as problems with aging parents, prejudice and discrimination, and insufficient personal energy.

A source of frustration rarely recognized is you, yourself. Perhaps your goals are higher than your present abilities. You may want promotion to a job that requires mathematical ability, but you did not learn it well in school, so others are better prepared for the job. The result is that you are frustrated. A mature solution is to return to school part time and learn the mathematics that you lack. However, you may not be able to invest the time, so you remain frustrated as long as the strong drive exists.

Pamela Bond was a supervisor who did not bother to learn proper grammar in community college. As a supervisor, she had reports to prepare and knew that she did not do them well. She was frustrated, defensive, and critical of those who presented reports to her. She felt that any further promotion was blocked until she learned to write.

Management finally recognized that a number of employees had problems similar to Bond's. It developed a training course in business writing and encouraged supervisors to take it. Bond took the course and learned so much that she later took a follow-up course in a community college. Within a year her language frustration vanished and her performance improved.

Supportive management is needed.

FRUSTRATION AND MANAGEMENT PRACTICE The stronger one's motivation or drive toward a blocked goal, the stronger one's frustration will be, other things being equal. If motivation is lacking, then very little frustration is likely to develop. This means that when management attempts to motivate employees strongly, it also should be prepared to remove barriers and help prepare the way for employees to reach their goals. The required managerial role is a supportive one. For example, if precision machine work is encouraged, the machinist needs proper training, equipment, tools, and materials for precision work. Similarly if an employee is assigned a special project and motivated to do it, then a suitable budget and other support are required in order to prevent frustration. The idea is not to remove all difficulties so that the assignment loses its challenge but rather to provide enough support to make the project reasonably possible.

Counseling can help reduce frustrations by helping employees choose mature courses of action to overcome blockages preventing goal accomplishment. The counselor also can advise management regarding blockages so that it can try to reduce or remove them.

Stress and job performance

Effects of stress on performance

Stress can be either helpful or harmful to job performance, depending upon the amount of it. Figure 20-4 presents a *stress-performance model* that shows the relationship between stress and job performance.[12] When there is no stress, job challenges are absent and performance tends to be low. As stress increases, performance tends to increase, because stress helps a person call up resources to meet job requirements. It is a healthy stimulus that encourages employees to respond to challenges. Eventually stress reaches a plateau that corresponds approximately with a person's top day-to-day performance capability. At this point additional stress tends to produce no more improvement.

Finally, if stress becomes too great, performance begins to decline, because stress interferes with it. An employee loses ability to cope, becomes unable to make decisions, and is erratic in behavior. If stress increases to a breaking point, performance becomes zero; the employee has a breakdown, becomes too ill to work, is fired, quits, or refuses to come to work to face the stress.

The stress-performance relationship may be compared with strings on a violin. When there is either too little or too much tension on the strings, they will not produce suitable music. As with violin strings, when tension on an employee is either too high or low, the employee's performance will tend to deteriorate.

Stress thresholds

People have different tolerances for stressful situations, and this helps explain variations in employee performance across similar jobs. The level of stressors

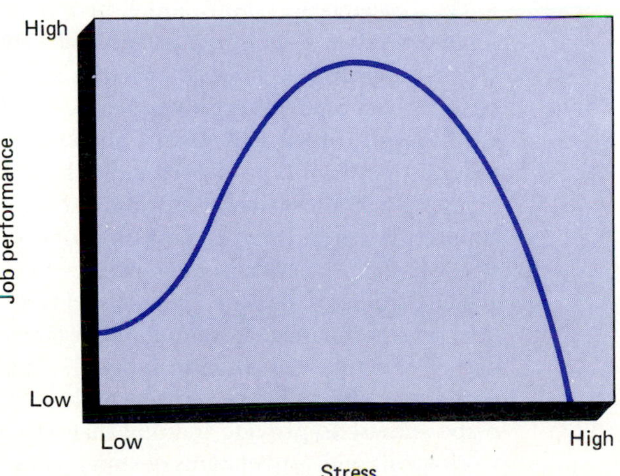

FIGURE 20-4
A stress performance model

that one can tolerate before negative feelings of stress occur and performance is adversely affected is one's *stress threshold.* Some people are easily upset by the slightest change or disruption in their work routines. Others are cool, calm, and collected under the same conditions, partly because they have confidence in their ability to cope. They have a much higher stress threshold, and their performance does not suffer unless a stressor is major or prolonged.

Marie Johnson was a cashier at a local supermarket. Every day she faced long lines, time pressures, complaints from customers about high prices, and cash register errors, but these events did not trouble her. She enjoyed meeting people. On the other hand, Antonio Valenzuela, a cashier at an adjoining counter, had difficulty with the complaints and pressures he received. He began to make errors and get into arguments. He seemed nervous. Finally, he asked to transfer to another part of the store. The two employees had different stress thresholds.

Type A and B people

Reactions to stressful situations often are related to type A and B people.[13]

Type A behaviors

Type A people are aggressive and competitive, set high standards, and put themselves under constant time pressures. They even make excessive demands on themselves in recreation and leisure. They often fail to realize that many of the pressures they feel are of their own making rather than products of their environment. Because of the constant stress that they feel, they are more prone to physical ailments related to stress, such as heart attacks.

Type B behaviors

Type B people are more relaxed and easygoing. They accept situations and work within them rather than fighting them competitively. Such people are especially relaxed regarding time pressures, and so they are less prone to have problems associated with stress.

The research on type A and B people is still accumulating.[14] For example, some of the type A behavior patterns like competitiveness and a drive for career success appear to be consistent with society's values. At the same time, the hostility and aggression these people exhibit may make it difficult for many employees to work with them. Some studies also suggest that there may be different forms of type A personalities. As a result, the type A's who are more expressive and less hostile may be less prone to heart disease. Other type A's apparently enjoy their success so much that they disregard the surrounding stress and don't suffer from heart attacks or other physical consequences.

The distinction between type A and type B people raises several challenging questions for managers. Should an organization consider the type A or type B nature of employees when making job assignments? Should it develop training programs to help change type A employees into type B persons? Does it have a responsibility to provide training that will help both A's and B's cope with the work habits and expectations of supervisors who are different from themselves? Although stress reduction at work is a desirable goal, finding the answers to these questions will require consideration of ethical, financial, and practical issues.

Approaches to stress management

There are several ways to help employees cope with stress and control its effects. Some of the approaches that have been presented in earlier chapters are improved communication, participation, organization development, and the redesign of jobs. These are just some of the positive ways in which an *organization* can reduce or eliminate the stressors for its employees. Four approaches that often involve employee and management *cooperation* for stress management are social support, meditation, biofeedback, and personal wellness programs.[15]

SOCIAL SUPPORT Some observers suggest that "much of the stress of life grows out of one's feelings of separateness from the world."[16] Some people who have a driving ambition and choose to work independently may fail to develop close attachments to friends and colleagues. To achieve their success they often sacrifice fulfillment of their social needs. This may result in anger, anxiety, and loneliness, all producing stress in their lives.

A powerful antidote to this problem lies in the presence of *social support* at work. Social support is the network of activities and relationships that provides an employee with desired social satisfaction. Its source may be supervisors, coworkers, friends, or family. Its focus may be on either work tasks or social exchanges, such as games, jokes, and teasing. Research suggests that when employees have at least one person from whom they can receive social support, they will experience lower stress.[17] This suggests that supervisors could choose to play this role for their employees, or they can simply encourage it to develop among a group of workers.

MEDITATION Meditation involves quiet, concentrated inner thought in order to rest the body physically and emotionally. It helps remove persons temporarily from the stressful world and reduce their symptoms of stress.

Transcendental meditation (TM) is one of the more popular practices. Transcendental meditators try to meditate for two periods of fifteen to twenty minutes a day, concentrating on the repetition of a word called a *mantra*. There are a number of similar practices with other names, such as yoga. Usually they all have the following common elements:

- A relatively quiet environment
- A comfortable position
- A repetitive mental stimulus
- A passive attitude

Meditation is so highly regarded that a few organizations have established meditation rooms for employee use, and many employees who meditate report favorable results.

Does meditation work?

New York Telephone Company provides a program called Clinically Standardized Meditation for its employees, and more than 300 have participated in it. A pilot study after five months showed that meditators improved more than a control group on test scores of anxiety, hostility, and psychosomatic disorders. Participants also reported feeling better about life and better about themselves.[18]

BIOFEEDBACK A different approach for working with stress is *biofeedback*, by which people under medical guidance learn from instrument feedback to influence symptoms of stress such as increased heart rate or severe headaches. Until the 1960s, it was thought that people could not control their involuntary nervous system which, in turn, controls internal processes such as heartbeat, oxygen consumption, stomach acid flow, and brain waves. There now is evidence that people can exercise some control over these internal processes, so biofeedback may be helpful in reducing undesirable effects of stress.

Preventive approaches

PERSONAL WELLNESS In general, there is a trend toward programs of preventive maintenance for personal wellness that are based on research in behavioral medicine. Health care specialists can recommend changes in lifestyle such as breathing regulation, muscle relaxation, positive imagery, nutrition management, and exercise that enable employees to use more of their full potential. Clearly, a preventive approach is preferable for reducing the causes of stress, although coping methods help one adapt to stressors that are beyond direct control. The key is to create a better "fit" between people and their environment, and alternative approaches may be useful for different employees.

EMPLOYEE COUNSELING

Definition

The goal of counseling

Counseling is discussion of a problem that usually has emotional content with an employee in order to help the employee cope with it better.[19] Counseling seeks to improve employee mental health. As shown in Figure 20-5, *good mental health* means that people feel comfortable about themselves, right about other people, and able to meet the demands of life.

The definition of counseling implies a number of characteristics. It is an exchange of ideas and feelings between two people, a counselor and a counselee, so it is an act of communication. Since it helps employees cope with problems, it should improve organizational performance, because the employee is more cooperative, worries less about personal problems, or improves in other ways. Counseling also helps the organization be more human and considerate with people problems.

Counseling may be performed by both professionals and nonprofessionals. For example, both a personnel specialist in counseling and a supervisor who is not trained in counseling may counsel employees. Company physicians also counsel employees and even an employee's friends may provide counseling.

People with good mental health—

1 *Feel comfortable about themselves.*

- Are not bowled over by their own emotions—by their fears, anger, love, jealousy, guilt, or worries.
- Can take life's disappointments in their stride.
- Have a tolerant, easygoing attitude toward themselves as well as others; they can laugh at themselves.
- Neither underestimate nor overestimate their abilities.
- Can accept their own shortcomings.
- Have self-respect.
- Feel able to deal with most situations that come their way.
- Get satisfaction from the simple, everyday pleasures.

2 *Feel right about other people.*

- Are able to give love and to consider the interests of others.
- Have personal relationships that are satisfying and lasting.
- Expect to like and trust others, and take it for granted that others will like and trust them.
- Respect the many differences they find in people.
- Do not push people around, nor do they allow themselves to be pushed around.
- Can feel they are part of a group.
- Feel a sense of responsibility to their neighbors and others.

3 *Are able to meet the demands of life.*

- Do something about their problems as they arise.
- Accept their responsibilities.
- Shape their environment whenever possible; adjust to it whenever necessary.
- Plan ahead but do not fear the future.
- Welcome new experiences and new ideas.
- Make use of their natural capacities.
- Set realistic goals for themselves.
- Are able to think for themselves and make their own decisions.
- Put their best effort into what they do and get satisfaction out of doing it.

FIGURE 20-5
Characteristics of people with good mental health

Source: Mental Health Is 1, 2, 3, *Arlington, Va.: Mental Health Association, n.d.*

Counseling usually is confidential, so that employees will feel free to talk openly about their problems. It also involves both job and personal problems, since both types of problems may affect an employee's performance on the job.

Although a few companies had employee counseling programs at an earlier date, the recognized beginning of employee counseling was in 1936 at Western Electric Company in Chicago.[20] It is believed that this was the first time a company used the term "personnel counseling" for employee counseling services. Employee job satisfaction definitely improved as a result of the counseling.

Need for counseling

The need for counseling arises from a variety of employee problems, including stress. When these problems exist, employees benefit from understanding and help of the type that counseling can provide. For example, an employee feels insecure about retirement, so counseling is necessary. Another employee is hesitant to take the risk required by a promotion, so the employee ceases growing on the job. A third employee may become unstable in the job.

Ross Callander was an interviewer in a state employment office. Within a few weeks he became unstable in his job, becoming angry easily and being rude to interviewees. His manager noticed the change and discussed it with him. When his behavior continued, he was referred to a counselor. The counselor learned that Callander's son had been arrested and in anger had accused Callander of being a failure as a parent. Callander felt angry, frustrated, and defeated, and he was transferring these feelings to his interviewees. With the help of a community agency, Callander's family problem was solved, and he quickly returned to normal job performance.

Emotions can cause problems.

Most problems that require counseling have some emotional content, such as the problem Callander had. *Emotions are a normal part of life.* Nature gave people their emotions, and these feelings make people human. On the other hand, emotions can get out of control and cause workers to do things that are harmful to their own best interests and those of the firm. They may leave their jobs because of a trifling conflict that seems large to them, or they may undermine morale in their departments. Managers want their employees to maintain good mental health and to channel their emotions along constructive lines so that they will work together effectively.

What counseling can do

The general objective of counseling is to help employees develop better mental health so that they will grow in self-confidence, understanding, self-control, and ability to work effectively. This objective is consistent with the supportive and human resources models of organizational behavior, which encourage employee growth and self-direction. It is also consistent with Maslow's higher-order needs and Alderfer's growth needs, such as self-esteem and self-actualization.

Six functions of counseling

The counseling objective is achieved through one or more of the following *counseling functions,* which are activities performed by counseling. These are shown in Figure 20-6. As will be seen later, some types of counseling perform one function better than another.

1 ADVICE Many people look upon counseling as primarily an advice-giving activity, but in reality this is only one of several functions that counseling can perform. The giving of advice requires a counselor to make judgments about a counselee's problems and to lay out a course of action. Herein lies the diffi-

FIGURE 20-6
Functions of counseling

Advice **Telling a person what you think should be done**

Reassurance **Giving a person courage and confidence to face a problem**

Communication **Providing information and understanding**

Release of emotional tension **Helping a person feel more free of tensions**

Clarified thinking **Encouraging more coherent, rational thought**

Reorientation **Encouraging an internal change in goals and values**

culty, because it is almost impossible to understand another person's complicated problems, much less tell that person what to do about them. Advice giving may breed a relationship in which the counselee feels inferior and dependent on the counselor. In spite of all its ills, advice occurs in routine counseling because workers expect it and managers tend to provide it.

2 REASSURANCE Counseling can provide employees with reassurance, which is a way of giving them courage to face a problem or a feeling of confidence that they are pursuing a suitable course of action. Reassurance is represented by such counselor remarks as "You are making good progress, Linda," and "Don't worry; this will come out all right."

One trouble with reassurance is that the counselees do not accept it. They are smart enough to know that the counselor cannot know that the problem will come out all right. Even if counselees are reassured, their reassurance may fade away as soon as they face their problems again, which means that little real improvement has been made.

Though reassurance has its weaknesses, it is useful in some situations and is impossible to prohibit. Reassurance cannot be prohibited just because it is dangerous, any more than automobiles can be prohibited because they cause accidents; but, like automobiles, reassurance should be used carefully.

3 COMMUNICATION Counseling can improve both upward and downward communication. In an upward direction, it is a key way for employees to express their feelings to management. As many people have said, often the top managers in an organization do not know how those at the bottom feel. The act of counseling initiates an upward signal, and if the channels are open, some of these signals will travel higher. Individual names must be kept confidential, but statements of feeling can be grouped and interpreted to management. An important part of any counselor's job is to discover emotional problems related to company policies and to interpret those problems to top management. Counseling also achieves downward communication because counselors help interpret company activities to employees as they discuss problems related to them.

4 RELEASE OF EMOTIONAL TENSION An important function of nearly all counseling is release of emotional tension; this release is sometimes called *emotional catharsis*. People tend to get an emotional release from their frustrations and other problems whenever they have an opportunity to tell someone about them. Counseling history consistently shows that as people begin to explain their problems to a sympathetic listener, their tensions begin to subside. They are more relaxed, and their speech is more coherent and rational. This release of tension does not necessarily solve their problems, but it does remove mental blocks in the way of solution, enabling them to face their problems again and think constructively about them. In some cases emotional release accomplishes the whole job, dispelling an employee's problems as if they were mental ghosts (which they largely were).

Emotional catharsis reduces tensions.

In a warehouse an electric-truck driver, Bill Irwin, began to develop conflicts with his supervisor. Irwin was convinced that his supervisor gave him the hardest jobs and otherwise took advantage of him. He was convinced that his supervisor did not like him and would "never" give him a raise. One day the elderly timekeeper was in the warehouse checking time records, and Irwin, being particularly upset at the moment, cornered him and began to tell about his troubles. It all happened when Irwin commented, "You don't need to worry about my time. I'll never get a rate increase, and I'll never have any overtime." The timekeeper asked, "Why?" and the conversation went on from there.

The timekeeper was a staff employee working for the warehouse superintendent and was not in the chain of command from superintendent to supervisor to Irwin, so Irwin felt free to talk. Perhaps also Irwin saw the timekeeper as a means of communication around his supervisor to the superintendent. At any rate, Irwin talked. And the timekeeper listened.

Since the timekeeper spent much of his time on the warehouse floor, he was closely acquainted with work assignments and the supervisor. Irwin knew this; and as he stated his grievances, he began to revise and soften them because he realized some of them did not agree with details of the situation about which the timekeeper had firsthand knowledge. As Irwin continued to bring his feelings out into the open, he felt easier and could discuss his problem more calmly. He realized that what he had said in the beginning was mostly a buildup of his own imagination and did not make sense in terms of the actual situation. He closed the conversation with the comment, "I guess I really don't have much of a problem, but I'm glad I told you anyway."

5 CLARIFIED THINKING The case of Irwin also illustrates another function of counseling, that of *clarified thinking*. Irwin began to realize that his emotional comments did not match the facts of the situation. He found that he was magnifying minor incidents and jumping to drastic conclusions. As his emotional blocks to straight thinking were relieved, he began to think more rationally. In this case realistic thinking was encouraged because Irwin recognized that he was talking to someone who knew the facts and was not emotionally involved.

Clarified thinking tends to be a normal result of emotional release, but a skilled counselor can aid this process. In order to clarify the counselee's thinking, the counselor serves as an aid only and refrains from telling the counselee what is "right." Further, not all the clarified thinking takes place while the counselor and counselee are talking. All or part of it may take place later as a result of developments during the counseling relationship. The result of any clarified thinking is that a person is encouraged to accept responsibility for emotional problems and to be more realistic in solving them.[21]

Reorientation requires a major change.

6 REORIENTATION Another function of counseling is reorientation of the counselee. *Reorientation* is more than mere emotional release or clear thinking about a problem. It involves a change in the employee's psychic self through a change in basic goals and values. For example, it can help people recognize and accept their own limitations. Reorientation is the kind of function needed to help alcoholics return to normalcy or to treat a person with severe mental depression. It is largely a job for professional counselors who know its uses and limitations and who have the necessary training. The manager's job is to recognize those in need of reorientation before their need becomes severe, so that they can be referred to professional help in time for successful treatment.

The manager's counseling role

Excluding reorientation, the other five counseling functions can be performed successfully by managers, assuming they have qualified themselves. They will at times perform all five of these counseling functions. On other occasions, if professional counseling services are available, they will refer employees to the professional counselors.[22] The point is that when counseling services are established, *managers must not conclude that all their counseling responsibilities have been transferred to the counseling staff.*

Managers are important counselors because they are the ones in day-to-day interaction with employees. If managers close their eyes to the emotional problems of employees and refuse to discuss them, it appears that managers are saying to employees, "I don't care about you, just your work." Managers cannot, when an emotional upset arises, say, "This is not part of my job. Go see a counselor." Emotions are part of the whole employee and must be considered a part of the total employment situation for which a manager is responsible. For this reason all managers, from the lowest to the highest levels, need training to help them understand problems of employees and counsel them effectively.

Almost all problems brought to a manager have a combination of factual and emotional content, so a manager should not spend all day looking for emotional content when a rational answer will solve the problem.

For example, if an employee asks, "Is this desk going to be moved?" it may be that she is really wondering why, is worried that it may reduce her status, and so on; but it is also possible—just possible—that she only wants to know "Is this desk going to be moved?" If you answer, "Yes, over by the window," you have solved the problem she brought you, and there is no need to try to be an amateur psychiatrist about it!

It is said that the father of psychiatry, Sigmund Freud, warned about the dangers of seeing emotional meaning in everything a person says or does. When a friend asked him what was the emotional meaning of the pipe he smoked, he replied, "Sometimes, sir, a pipe is just a pipe," meaning that it had no particular emotional interpretation.

TYPES OF COUNSELING

A continuum of counseling types

In terms of the amount of direction that a counselor gives a counselee, counseling is a continuum from full direction (directive counseling) to no direction (nondirective counseling), as shown in Figure 20-7. Between the two extremes is participative counseling. These three counseling types will be discussed in order to show how counselors may vary their direction in a counseling situation.

Directive counseling

Directive counseling is the process of listening to an employee's problem, deciding with the employee what should be done, and then telling and motivating the employee to do it. Directive counseling mostly accomplishes the counseling function of *advice*, but it also may reassure, communicate, give emotional release, and—to a minor extent—clarify thinking. Reorientation is seldom achieved in directive counseling.

Most everyone likes to give advice, counselors included, and it is easy to do. But is it effective? Does the counselor really understand the employee's problem? Does the counselor have the knowledge and judgment to make a "right" decision? Even if the decision is right, will the employee follow it? The answer to these questions is usually "No," and this is why advice may not be helpful in counseling.

Though advice is of questionable value, some of the other functions are worthwhile. If the directive counselor is first a good listener, then the employee should feel some emotional release. As the result of emotional release plus ideas that the counselor imparts, the employee also may clarify thinking. Furthermore, useful communication probably takes place. Both advice and reassurance can be worthwhile if they give the employee more courage to take a helpful course of action that the employee supports.

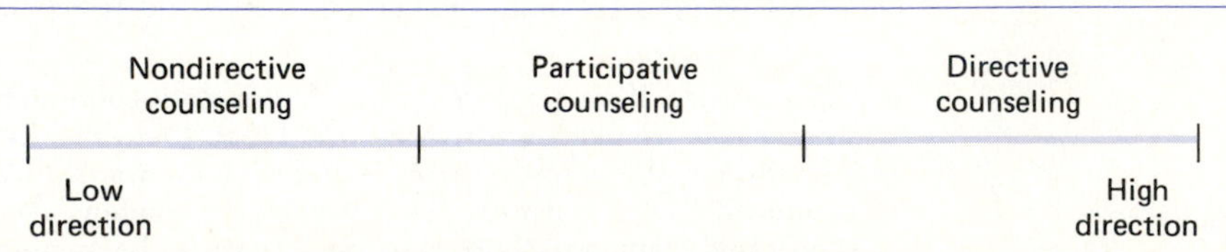

FIGURE 20-7
Types of counseling according to amount of direction that counselors provide

Nondirective counseling

Skillful listening is required.

Nondirective, or *client-centered, counseling* is at the opposite end of the continuum. It is the process of skillfully listening and encouraging a counselee to explain troublesome problems, understand them, and determine appropriate solutions. It focuses on the counselee rather than on the counselor as judge and adviser; so it is "client-centered." Managers can use the nondirective approach; however, care should be taken to make sure that managers are not so oversold on it that they neglect their normal directive leadership responsibilities.

One company gave a full two days of training to its managers on the nondirective approach. They went back to their jobs thoroughly sold on the idea and ready to put it into practice. The trouble was that they did not sufficiently understand its limitations. They refrained from stating their own opinions to employees in their day-to-day interaction. They hesitated to issue instructions and directives. Employees became confused, and their frustrations multiplied. The results were harmful rather than helpful, so finally management had to instruct its managers to return to their former ways of working with employees. They were told that if the nondirective approach was to be used to counsel, it should be a supplement along with normal directive approaches, similar to participative counseling, discussed in the next section.[23]

Nondirective counseling was developed concurrently by two groups: Mayo, Roethlisberger, and others at Western Electric Company and Carl R. Rogers and his colleagues.[24] Here is the way nondirective counseling typically works.

Assume that Harold Pace comes to a counselor, Janis Peterson, for assistance. Peterson attempts to build a relationship that encourages Pace to talk freely. At this point Peterson defines the counseling relationship by explaining that she cannot tell Pace how to solve his problem but that she may be able to help him understand it and deal satisfactorily with it.

Pace then explains his feelings, and the counselor encourages their expression, shows interest in them, and accepts them without blame or praise. Eventually the negative feelings are drained away, giving Pace a chance to express tentatively a positive feeling or two, a fact that marks the beginning of Pace's emotional growth. The counselor encourages these positive feelings and accepts them without blame or praise, just as she did the negative feelings.

If all goes well, Pace should at this point begin to get some insight into his problem and to develop alternative solutions to it. As he continues to grow, he is able to choose a course of positive action and see his way clear to try it. He then feels a decreasing need for help and recognizes that the counseling relationship should end.

Feelings need to be accepted.

Throughout the counseling relationship, it is important for the counselor to *accept* feelings—rather than *judge* them, offering blame or praise—because judgment may discourage an employee from stating true feelings. The basic idea is to get the employee to discuss feelings, to explore solutions, and to make wise decisions.

Major differences between nondirective and directive counseling are summarized in Figure 20-8. They reveal that in nondirective counseling the

Counseling method **The employee primarily controls the direction of conversation and does most of the talking.**

Responsibility **Solution of the problem is the employee's own responsibility.**

Status **The employee is equal to the counselor as a person, while the directive method implies that the counselor is superior and knows what to do.**

Role **The employee is psychologically independent as a person, choosing a solution and growing in ability to make choices in the future.**

Emphasis **Emphasis is on deeper feelings and problems rather than surface symptoms. Adjustment of a person, rather than solution of a current problem, is paramount.**

FIGURE 20-8
Ways in which nondirective counseling differs from directive counseling

counselee is the key person, while the counselor is the key in a directive approach.

USE BY PROFESSIONALS Professional counselors usually practice some form of nondirective counseling and often accomplish four of the six counseling functions. Communication occurs both upward and downward through the counselor. Emotional release takes place even more effectively than with directive counseling, and clarified thinking tends to follow. The unique advantage of nondirective counseling is its ability to cause the employee's reorientation. It emphasizes changing the *person* instead of dealing only with the immediate *problem,* in the usual manner of directive counseling.

Professional counselors treat each counselee as a social and organizational equal. They primarily listen and try to help the counselee discover and follow improved courses of action. They especially "listen between the lines" to learn the full meaning of an employee's feelings. They look for the assumptions underlying the employee's statements and for the events and feelings that are so painful that the employee tends to avoid talking about them. As shown in Figure 20-9, nondirective counselors follow an "iceberg model" of counseling in which they recognize that sometimes more feelings are hidden under the surface of a counselee's communication than are revealed. For this reason they constantly encourage the counselee to open up and reveal deeper feelings that may help solve the employee's problem.

LIMITATIONS With all its advantages, nondirective counseling has several limitations that restrict its use at work. First of all, it is more time-consuming and costly than directive counseling. Just one employee with one problem may require many hours of a counselor's time, so the number of employees that a counselor can assist is limited. Professional counselors require professional education and consequently are expensive. Nondirective counseling also depends on a capable, willing employee. It assumes that the employee possesses a drive for mental health, has enough social intelligence to perceive what problems need solution, and has sufficient emotional stability to deal with them. The nondirective counselor needs to be careful not to become a crutch for

Costliness of nondirective counseling

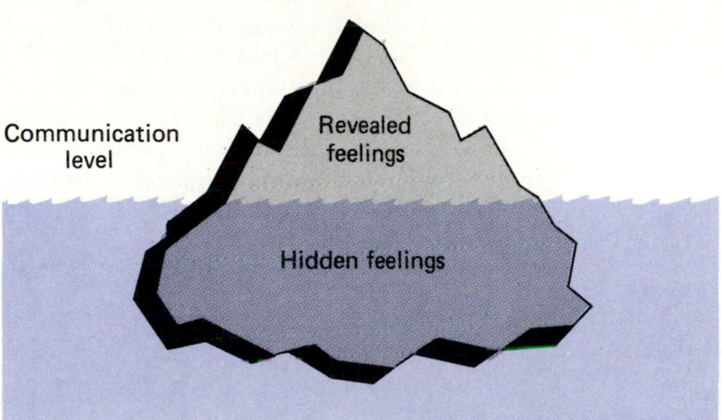

FIGURE 20-9
Iceberg model of a counselee's feelings in a counseling situation

emotionally dependent employees to lean on while they avoid their work responsibilities.

In some cases counseling itself is a weak solution because it returns the employee to the same environment that caused the problem. What is really needed is a better environment for employee psychological support. In this situation the counselor may step beyond the usual counseling role and give advice to management to take corrective action.

Participative counseling

Nondirective counseling by employees is limited because it requires professional counselors and is costly. Directive counseling often is not accepted by modern, independent employees. This means that the type of counseling typically used in organizations is between the two extremes of directive and nondirective counseling. This middle ground is called participative counseling.

How does participative counseling work?

Participative counseling (also called cooperative counseling) is a mutual counselor-counselee relationship that establishes a cooperative exchange of ideas to help solve a counselee's problems. It is neither wholly counselor-centered nor wholly counselee-centered. Rather, the counselor and counselee mutually apply their different knowledge, perspectives, and values to problems. It integrates the ideas of both participants in a counseling relationship. It is, therefore, a balanced compromise that combines many advantages of both directive and nondirective counseling while avoiding most of their disadvantages.

Participative counseling starts by using the listening techniques of nondirective counseling; but as the interview progresses, participative counselors may play a more active role than nondirective counselors would. They offer bits of knowledge and insight; and they may discuss the situation from their broader knowledge of the organization, thus giving an employee a different view of the problem. In general, participative counselors apply the four counseling functions of reassurance, communication, emotional release, and clarified thinking.

For example, Mary Carlisle was emotionally upset because she was not getting the promotions that she wanted. Although she discussed her problem with her supervisor, she was not wholly satisfied and asked to see a counselor. She and the counselor established open communication early in their discussion because at this point Carlisle was ready to open up about her problems.

The counselor did not tell Carlisle what to do (directive approach) and did not merely listen (nondirective approach). Rather, the counselor explored various alternatives with Carlisle, communicated some ideas about training, and provided reassurance that Carlisle could become fully qualified for promotion. The result was that Carlisle saw her problem more clearly (clarified thinking) and chose an appropriate course of action.

A contingency view

A manager's decision to use either directive, participative, or nondirective counseling with an employee should be based on an analysis of several contingency factors. It should not be made solely on the manager's personal preference or past experience. However, the manager's knowledge and capacity to use a variety of methods is clearly a critical factor in choosing how to proceed.

One of the key contingency elements to consider is the degree to which the employee's problem appears to be focusing on facts and the need for a timely, logical solution (implying the use of a more directive approach) versus focusing on personal feelings and emotions (implying a more nondirective approach). Another consideration is the degree to which the manager is willing to devote time and effort to the growth and development of a more independent employee. There is also evidence to suggest that counselees have different expectations for the behaviors and characteristics of their counselors, and so their preferences may need to be considered.[25] For example, some counselees prefer the nurturing role provided through participative or nondirective methods. Others are seeking someone with job-related expertise or problem-solving skills, which are more easily shared through the directive approach. Overall, an effective manager requires awareness of the alternatives available, the skills to be comfortable with each method, and the analytical ability to make a choice that fits the situation.

Cooperation with community agencies

When mental health problems arise on the job, the employer usually provides counseling, either by the immediate supervisor or through the firm's employee assistance program (discussed in Chapter 17). On the other hand, if a problem arises from off-the-job causes, employers are more hesitant to become involved. There are good reasons for this hesitancy, because employees have certain rights of privacy, and the organization should not interfere unless the employee's performance declines. When it does become aware of an employee's personal problems, a firm will often refer the individual to an appropriate community agency for more specialized help. Some companies even provide similar support when an employee's family members experience mental health problems.

SUMMARY

Counseling occasionally is necessary for employees because of job and personal problems that subject them to excessive stress. The conditions that tend to cause stress are called stressors and include work overload, time pressures, role ambiguity, financial problems, and family problems. Stress affects both physical and mental health and results in burnout when it occurs chronically. The stress-performance model indicates that excessive stress reduces job performance, but a moderate amount may help employees respond to job challenges. Type A people tend to show more stress than type B people.

Counseling is discussion of a problem that usually has emotional content with an employee in order to help the employee cope with it better. Its goal is better mental health, and it is performed by both managers and professional counselors. Major counseling functions are advice, reassurance, communication, release of emotional tension, clarified thinking, and reorientation. The most appropriate type of counseling for nonprofessionals is participative counseling. Counseling programs deal with both job and personal problems, and there is extensive cooperation with community counseling agencies.

Terms and concepts for review

Stress
Burnout
Stressors
Frustration
Stress-performance model
Stress threshold
Type A and B people
Social support
Biofeedback
Counseling
Characteristics of good mental health
Counseling functions
Directive, participative, and nondirective counseling
Iceberg model of feelings

Discussion questions

1 List and discuss the five major sources of stress in your life during the last five years.
2 Think of someone you know who suffers from burnout. What are the symptoms? What may have caused it?
3 Do you see yourself as primarily a type A or type B person? Discuss, and make a list of your five main type A characteristics and five main type B characteristics.

4 Discuss how stress and job performance are related. Is stress interfering with your performance in school? Discuss.
5 Discuss four management practices covered in earlier chapters of this book that should help reduce employee stress.
6 Discuss the six main counseling functions. Which are best performed by directive, nondirective, and participative counseling?
7 Explain major differences between directive and nondirective counseling.
8 Should professional company counselors be provided in the following situations? Discuss.
   a A large West Coast aircraft plant during rapid expansion
   b A government office in Valdosta, Georgia, employing 700 people
   c A marginal job-order foundry in Chicago having unstable employment varying from thirty to sixty workers
9 What should be the main type of counseling used in the following situations?
   a A traveling sales representative with fifteen years of seniority has become an alcoholic.
   b A newly hired engineer engages in petty theft of office supplies.
   c A receptionist receives two job offers and must make a decision over the weekend.
   d A maintenance worker's spouse files for divorce.
10 Outline a preventive program for personal wellness that you could implement for yourself over the next five years. What are its elements?

Incident

UNIT ELECTRONICS COMPANY

Unit Electronics Company produces electronic process controls for industry. The high reliability required for these controls, each designed for a specific customer, requires the production department to work closely with the test section of the quality-control department, which determines if the product meets customer specifications. For one important order it was necessary for a production representative to work in the quality-control department with the chief test engineer. Charles Able, the manager of production, assigned William Parcel, one of his capable assistants, to this job. Parcel had worked with Able for years and was well acquainted with this equipment order, since he had coordinated its production for Able. The test engineer was named Dale Short.

A week after Parcel began working with Short, he reported to Able that he was having difficulty with Short and that Short seemed to resent his presence in the test section. Able agreed that a crisis situation might be developing and said that he would visit the test section and attempt to talk with Short.

When Able visited the test section, Short immediately started complaining about Parcel. He said that Parcel undermined Short's authority by giving testers instructions that were at variance with Short's. He claimed that Parcel even contradicted him in front of the testers. After a number of other complaints he asked Able to remove Parcel from the test section and send a substitute. Short even threatened that if Able did not remove Parcel, Short would "go over his head" to have Parcel removed. Able listened and asked questions, but made no judgments or promises.

Parcel apparently saw Able talking to Short, so before Able left the test section, Parcel approached him with the comment, "Well, I guess Short has been telling you a tale of woe about me."

Able acknowledged that Short had complained, but he omitted mentioning Short's threat to have Parcel transferred.

"That's Short, all right," said Parcel. "He can't stand to have anyone try to correct him, but things were so fouled up I felt I had to do something."

Able admitted that the situation was sensitive, but he pointed out that Short was in charge of the test section. He ended the discussion with the comment, "Let's play it cool and not push."

Able, however, was upset by the situation, and during the next few days he gave much thought to it. Since Short felt the way he did, Able finally decided to remove Parcel from the test section and send another employee. As he was reaching for the telephone to call Parcel in the test section, Short walked into the office smiling.

"I want to thank you, Charlie," he said. "I don't know what you said to Parcel the other day, but it sure changed his attitude. We are getting along just fine now. Funny thing, when I spoke to you the other day, I had the impression that you weren't going to do anything for me, but I guess I had you figured wrong."

Able gulped a few times and made a few vague remarks. Then Short left in high spirits.

Able was quite curious about the whole situation; so later in the day when he happened to meet Parcel alone, he commented casually, "Well, Bill, how are things going with Short?"

"I have been meaning to tell you, Charlie," Parcel said, "Short has been much easier to work with the past few days. He actually takes some of my advice—even asks for it. I guess that talk you had with him really did some good."

Question

Analyze the events in this case in terms of counseling and communication. Did counseling occur? What type of counseling? When and by whom?

Experiential exercise

CONTRASTS IN COUNSELING

Form the entire class into pairs. Designate one person within each pair as the counselor and the other as the counselee. Ask the counselees to think of some emotional problem that is currently on their mind, and have them share it with their counselor. The counselors should attempt to play a nondirective role for the first few minutes, switch to a directive role for the next few minutes, and then conclude with a participative role for the final few minutes of interaction.

Questions

1 Ask the counselors how they felt, and how successful they were, in each of the three roles.
2 Ask the counselees how they felt, and how successful the counselors were, when they used each of the three roles.
3 Under what conditions might counselees prefer to have (*a*) directive, (*b*) participative, and (*c*) nondirective counselor roles used with them?

References

1 Robert W. Eckles, "Stress—Making Friends with the Enemy," *Business Horizons*, March–April 1987, pp. 74–78.
2 John M. Ivancevich, Michael T. Matteson, and Edward P. Richard III, "Who's Liable for Stress on the Job?" *Harvard Business Review*, March–April 1985, pp. 60–72.
3 Resa W. King and Irene Pave, "Stress Claims Are Making Business Jumpy," *Business Week*, Oct. 14, 1985, pp. 152, 154.
4 Hans Selye, *The Stress of Life*, rev. ed., New York: McGraw-Hill Book Company, 1976. Another explanation—that energy is highly expandable and therefore burnout is relatively controllable—is offered in Ellen L. Maher, "Burnout and Commitment: A Theoretical Alternative," *The Personnel and Guidance Journal*, March 1983, pp. 390–393.
5 Susan E. Jackson, Richard L. Schwab, and Randall S. Schuler, "Toward an Understanding of the Burnout Phenomenon," *Journal of Applied Psychology*, November 1986, pp. 630–640. A wide range of other consequences of burnout is identified in Ronald J. Burke, "Burnout in Police Work," *Group & Organization Studies*, June 1987, pp. 174–188.
6 Jerry E. Bishop, "Age of Anxiety," *Wall Street Journal* (Western edition), Apr. 2, 1979, pp. 1, 26.
7 See, for example, John H. Howard, David A. Cunningham, and Peter A. Rechnitzer, "Role Ambiguity, Type A Behavior, and Job Satisfaction: Moderating Effects on Cardiovascular and Biochemical Responses Associated with Coronary Risk," *Journal of Applied Psychology*, February 1986, pp. 95–101.
8 Rolf E. Rogers, Eldon Y. Li, and Abraham B. Shani, "Perceptions of Organizational Stress among U.S. Military Officers in Germany: An Exploratory Study," *Group and Organization Studies*, June 1987, pp. 189–207.
9 Kathleen Anthony and Brian H. Kleiner, "The Price of Success," *Business Forum*, Spring 1987, pp. 10–13; Saroj Parasuraman and Joseph A. Alutto, "An Examination of the Organizational Antecedents of Stressors at Work," *Academy of Management Journal*, March 1981, pp. 48–67.
10 Arthur P. Brief and Jennifer M. Atieh, "Studying Job Stress: Are We Making Mountains out of Molehills?" *Journal of Occupational Behaviour*, April 1987, pp. 115–126.
11 John M. Ivancevich, "Life Events and Hassles as Predictors of Health Symptoms, Job Performance, and Absenteeism," *Journal of Occupational Behaviour*, January 1986, pp. 39–51. Also see Richard S. Lazarus, "Little Hassles Can Be Hazardous to Your Health," *Psychology Today*, July 1981, pp. 58–62.
12 Stephan J. Motowidlo, John S. Packard, and Michael R. Manning, "Occupational Stress: Its Causes and Consequences for Job Performance," *Journal of Applied Psychology*, November 1986, pp. 618–629.
13 Meyer Friedman and Ray H. Rosenman, *Type A Behavior and Your Heart*, New

York: Alfred A. Knopf, Inc., 1974. Also see Meyer Friedman and Diane Ulmer, *Treating Type A Behavior and Your Heart*, New York: Alfred A. Knopf, Inc., 1986.

14 A meta-analysis, or quantitative review and synthesis of previous results, is provided by Stephanie Booth-Kewley and Howard S. Friedman, "Psychological Predictors of Heart Disease: A Quantitative Review," *Psychological Bulletin*, May 1987, pp. 343–362; a readable update is Joshua Fischman, "Type A on Trial," *Psychology Today*, February 1987, pp. 42–50, 64.

15 Three broad types of coping responses to stress are control, escape, and symptom management. See Janina C. Latack, "Coping with Job Stress: Measures and Future Directions for Scale Development," *Journal of Applied Psychology*, August 1986, pp. 377–385.

16 Jonathan D. Quick, Debra L. Nelson, and James C. Quick, "Successful Executives: How Independent?" *Academy of Management Executive*, May 1987, pp. 139–145.

17 Monika Henderson and Michael Argyle, "Social Support by Four Categories of Work Colleagues: Relationships between Activities, Stress, and Satisfaction," *Journal of Occupational Behaviour*, July 1985, pp. 229–239; and Daniel C. Ganster, Marcelline R. Fusilier, and Bronston T. Mayes, "Role of Social Support in the Experience of Stress at Work," *Journal of Applied Psychology*, February 1986, pp. 102–110.

18 William A. McGeveran, Jr., "Meditation at the Telephone Company," *The Wharton Magazine*, Fall 1981, pp. 28–32.

19 An excellent overview is Peter C. Cairo, "Counseling in Industry: A Selected Review of the Literature," *Personnel Psychology*, Spring 1983, pp. 1–18.

20 F. J. Roethlisberger and William J. Dickson, *Management and the Worker*, Cambridge, Mass.: Harvard University Press, 1939, pp. 189–205, 593–604; and William J. Dickson and F. J. Roethlisberger, *Counseling in an Organization: A Sequel to the Hawthorne Researches*, Boston: Harvard Business School, Division of Research, 1966.

21 A comprehensive discussion is in P. Paul Heppner and Charles J. Krauskopf, "An Information-Processing Approach to Personal Problem Solving," *The Counseling Psychologist*, July 1987, pp. 371–447.

22 Virginia Novarra, "Can a Manager Be a Counselor?" *Personnel Management*, June 1986, pp. 48–50.

23 Bruce Harriman, "Up and Down the Communications Ladder," *Harvard Business Review*, September–October 1974, pp. 143–151.

24 Roethlisberger and Dickson, op. cit.; and Carl R. Rogers, *Counseling and Psychotherapy*, Boston: Houghton Mifflin Company, 1942.

25 Sandra L. Leong, Frederick T. L. Leong, and Mary Ann Hoffman, "Counseling Expectations of Rational, Intuitive, and Dependent Decision Makers," *Journal of Counseling Psychology*, July 1987, pp. 261–265.

For additional reading

Bardwick, Judith M., *The Plateauing Trap: How to Avoid It in Your Career and Your Life*, New York: AMA, 1986.

Friedman, Meyer, and Diane Ulmer, *Treating Type A Behavior and Your Heart*, New York: Alfred A. Knopf, Inc., 1984.

Golembiewski, Robert, *Stress in Organizations: Toward a Phase Model of Burnout*, Westport, Conn.: Frederick A. Praeger, Inc., 1986.

Ivancevich, John M., and Daniel C. Ganster (eds.), *Job Stress: From Theory to Suggestion*, special edition of the *Journal of Organizational Behavior Management*, Fall–Winter 1986.

Matteson, Michael T., and John M. Ivancevich, *Controlling Work Stress: Effective Human Resource and Management Strategies*, San Francisco: Jossey-Bass Inc., Publishers, 1987.

Myers, Donald W., *Employee Problem Prevention and Counseling: A Guide for Professionals*, Westport, Conn.: Quorum Books, 1985.

Quick, James C., and Jonathan D. Quick, *Organizational Stress and Preventive Management*, New York: McGraw-Hill Book Company, 1984.

Selye, Hans, *The Stress of Life*, rev. ed., New York: McGraw-Hill Book Company, 1976.

CHAPTER

21 International dimensions of organizational behavior

Understanding a recipient country's culture enables [a person] to utilize the most effective channel in passing on the message.

FRANCIS BLANCHARD[1]

Surprisingly, many expatriates have more problems readjusting to the U.S. social and work environment than they did moving into the foreign environment.

JEFFERY M. KADET AND ROBERT J. GAUGHAN, JR.[2]

CHAPTER OBJECTIVES

To understand

How social, political, and economic conditions vary in different cultures

Ways to overcome barriers to cultural adaptation

The operation of ethnocentrism and cultural shock

Cultural contingencies in establishing high productivity

The need to adapt communications to the nation's culture

Multinational organizations

global economy is now a reality. As a result, many organizations now operate in more than one country, and these *multinational* operations add powerful new dimensions to organizational behavior. Expansion beyond national boundaries is much more than a step across a geographical line. It is also a step into different social, political, and economic environments. Communication lines are lengthened, and control often becomes more difficult. As we have pointed out throughout this book, it is hard enough to operate an organization in one language and one culture. When two, three, four, five—or twenty—languages and cultures are involved, communication difficulties are compounded, as Blanchard suggested in the opening quote for this chapter. Complex multinational organizations push a manager's behavioral skills to their limits. It proves easier to handle the technical factors of building a new plant than to handle the social factors of operating it thereafter. The following case illustrates the complexities that arise as different cultures are mixed in multinational operations.

In a South American nation, a consultant from the United States was called upon to study why the West German machinery in a cellophane plant owned by South Americans was not operating properly. (This single preliminary sentence reveals that already three different cultures were involved in the incident.) When the consultant arrived, he studied the situation for several weeks. His conclusion was that there was nothing at all wrong with the machinery. It was of excellent quality and in perfect adjustment. The raw materials and other supporting factors were entirely satisfactory.

The real problem, in the consultant's opinion, was the supervisors, who had a father image of the patriarchal mill manager and were unable (or unwilling) to make operating decisions without his approval. They deferred to him as their elder and superior. When something in the mill went wrong, they waited indefinitely for his decision before correcting the problem. Since he had other business interests and was frequently out of the mill for part of the day, or even for two or three days, they permitted the continuous-production machinery to produce scrap cellophane for hours or even days because of some minor maladjustment which they could have corrected. The mill manager tried to delegate decision making on these control matters to his supervisors, but neither he nor they were able to overcome this powerful custom of deference to authority which existed in their culture. The consultant finally summarized the situation this way: "The problem is the people, not the machines."

The cellophane machinery was built to operate in an advanced industrial culture, but in this instance it was required to operate in a less developed culture. Neither the machinery nor the supervisors could be changed quickly to meet this new situation. Reengineering of machinery would be costly and time-consuming, and, in this case, might reduce the machinery's productivity. Training of supervisors to change their cultural beliefs, even if this were possible, would likewise be time-consuming. The solution offered by the consultant was an effective compromise. He advised the manager to appoint one person as "acting director" during his absence, give the acting director an imposing office, and work to build the acting director's image of authority with the supervisors. Then there would always be someone at the plant to make decisions quickly.

This situation presents extreme contrasts, but it illustrates the cultural predicaments that often arise in modern times because much of the world is still less developed than the United States and other industrialized nations. In the more advanced countries (where cultural contrasts among them may be smaller), the issues raised in this chapter will often be less extreme in degree, but they continue to exist. Discussion here is limited to issues affecting work behavior, leaving other aspects of multinational operations to other books. In this chapter we examine the nature of multinational operations, ways for an organization to integrate social systems, and ways to improve motivation, productivity, and communications when operating in less developed cultures.

CONDITIONS AFFECTING MULTINATIONAL OPERATIONS

The people of the world are organized into communities and nations, each in its own way, according to its resources and cultural heritage. There are similarities among nations, but there are also significant differences. Some nations have a market-driven economy, while others have one that is centrally planned, and there are various shades of practice in between. Some are economically developed, but others are just now developing their natural and human resources. Some are political dictatorships; others are more democratic. Some are educationally and socially advanced, while others have minimum literacy and social development. And in each case the conditions of work are different because of different attitudes, values, and expectations from participants. To help understand these differences and how they influence international organizational behavior, key social, political, and economic conditions will be examined.

Social conditions

In many countries, the overriding social condition is poorly developed human resources. There are major shortages of managerial personnel, scientists, and technicians; and these deficiencies limit the ability to employ local labor productively. Needed skills must be temporarily imported from other countries, while vast training programs begin to prepare local workers.

A Central American nation, for example, welcomed an electronic assembly plant to its capital city. The plant was labor-intensive, so it provided many jobs to reduce the nation's high unemployment rate. Wages were above community standards, working conditions were good, and the plant was environmentally clean. In addition, the valuable and tiny product that was assembled provided needed foreign exchange because it was shipped by air to assembly plants in other parts of the world.

Perhaps most important of all, the company's agreement with the nation provided that the company would supply a cadre of managers and technicians to train local employees in all phases of operating the plant. Locals would gradually become

supervisors, superintendents, technicians, accountants, purchasing specialists, and so on. At the end of five years the company could have no more than eight nonlocals in the plant, including the general manager, engineers, and auditing personnel. In this manner the labor force of the nation would be upgraded.

Training multiplier effect

As this example shows, the lending of skilled people to a nation for training their local replacements may provide a more lasting benefit to its development than the lending of capital. The *training multiplier effect* is in action, by which the skilled people develop others, and these trained locals become the nucleus for developing still more people. There is a ripple effect of self-development, much as a pebble thrown into a pond creates an impact far beyond the spot where it landed. Just as the size and placement of the pebble dictates how far the ripples will radiate, the amount and focus of the initial training dictates its long-run impact. The occupational areas whose development will provide the greatest return are scientific, professional, and managerial personnel. International studies show that per capita productivity tends to increase as the proportion of these occupations increases in the labor force.[3]

Another significant social condition in many countries is that the local culture is not familiar with advanced technology or complex organizations. Western nations over a period of two centuries have adapted their culture to an industrial and organizational way of life, but this is not so in many other nations. The background of their employees is still largely agrarian, suggesting that they are not familiar with high-technology products and the close margin of error that they tolerate.

Fortunately, over a period of time workers tend to recognize the benefits of industrialized work and they begin to adjust to it. Figure 21-1 shows the change in attitudes of factory workers toward their jobs in one firm over a period of ten years in a less developed country that was newly industrializing. In the beginning, their views of factory work, compared with farming and shopkeeping, had been only moderately favorable. After ten years, however, a strong majority favored factory work as the most desirable of the three occupations and recognized its substantial positive impact. There was a major favorable change in their belief that factory work "provides a better family life." One reason was that good pay provided families with more necessities than they earlier en-

FIGURE 21-1
Factory workers' perceptions of factory work, compared with farming and shopkeeping, following introduction of a factory into a less developed area newly industrialized

Source: *Cynthia A. Cone, "Perceptions of Occupations in a Newly Industrializing Region of Mexico,"* Human Organization, *Summer 1973, p. 147.*

	PERCENT OF WORKERS FAVORING FACTORY WORK	
FACTORY WORK	INITIAL VIEWS	10 YEARS LATER
Provides a better family life	29	58
Provides more security	46	58
Is more useful	46	60
Requires more education	49	72

joyed, and another reason was that steady work gave workers some security that their family standard of living might be maintained. In addition, factory work provided shorter hours than farming and shopkeeping, so workers could spend more time participating in family life. They also recognized that factory work gave them more opportunities to improve themselves through education.

Political conditions

Instability and nationalism

Political conditions that have a significant effect on organizational behavior include instability of the government, nationalistic drives, and subordination of employers and labor to an authoritarian state. Instability spills over onto organizations that wish to establish or expand operations in the host country, making them cautious about further investments. This organizational instability leaves workers insecure, and causes them to be passive and low in initiative. They may bring to the job an attitude of "What will be, will be; so why try to do anything about it?"

In spite of instability, a nationalistic drive is strong for locals to run their country and their organizations by themselves without interference by foreign nationals. A foreign manager may simply not be welcome.

In Burma, for example, a visiting professor presented a group of trainees with a case study featuring a problem between a British shipmaster and a Burmese crew. Expecting the group to discuss authority, interpersonal conflict, and other behavioral issues, the professor was surprised when the class focused instead on how to train the Burmese to take control from the British master. Their reasoning—that then the crew would not have to deal with the shipmaster any longer—was a clear reflection of their nationalistic values.

Organized labor in many nations is not an independent force, but is mostly an arm of the authoritarian state. In other nations, labor is somewhat independent, but it is socialistic, class-conscious, and oriented toward political action more than direct negotiation with organizations. Employers find that the state tends to be involved in collective bargaining and other practices affecting workers. In some nations, for example, employee layoffs are restricted by law and made costly by requiring dismissal pay. Even employee transfers may be restricted. The following is an incident that illustrates how different employment practices among nations can cause employee-employer frictions for multinational companies. In this instance, both nations were economically developed.

Air France, a major international airline, provides service to Japan. It employs a number of Japanese flight attendants who are stationed in Tokyo and serve flights to and from that city. In order to provide further international training and integration of its flight crews, it transferred thirty Japanese attendants to Paris. They refused to go, so the company threatened dismissal for refusal to transfer. The attendants sought relief through the courts, and the Tokyo High Court upheld a lower-court injunction preventing Air France from dismissing the attendants. They could retain

the Air France jobs in Tokyo, because transfer to Paris would "(1) restrict their civil rights as Japanese citizens, (2) cause them the anxiety of living in a place where the language and customs are different, and (3) affect their marital situation."[4]

Several European nations have laws requiring codetermination (discussed in Chapter 10), which provides for worker representation on the board of directors (and sometimes other committees) of major companies. The idea is to increase worker participation in higher manager levels, giving the employees some voice in major policy and operating decisions. This process of expanding workers' control over their jobs, often called *industrial democracy*, tries to increase labor understanding of higher-management problems and reduce labor unrest. While codetermination may reduce unrest and improve labor responsibility, it also places additional restrictions on multinational organizations that aren't familiar with the practice in their home countries. A particular problem arises in countries of rigid perspectives, where a local, job-protecting attitude of labor representatives on the board may prevent them from understanding broader, strategic decisions involving plants in a number of nations.

Effects of codetermination

Economic conditions

The most significant economic conditions in less developed nations are low per capita income and rapid inflation. Many nations of the world exist in genuine poverty compared with the United States. A number of nations have average per capita incomes under $1000 annually.[5] With their population increasing at the same time, they are fortunate if they can increase their real per capita incomes even 1 percent in a year. Assuming that a family has an annual income of $1000, a 1 percent increase is just $10. Even if this increase is compounded across five years, the family income would barely exceed $1050, and this expected gain would not provide much motivation.

A common economic condition in many less developed countries is inflation. The United States has had moderate overall inflation reducing the value of its dollar substantially since 1940; but in other parts of the world some countries' currencies have been cut to one-hundredth or even one-thousandth of their value since 1940, as reflected in cost-of-living increases. What used to cost 1 unit of currency now costs 1000 or more. In terms of dollar currency, a 10-cent ice cream cone in 1940 would now cost 10,000 cents, or $100, in some countries!

Inflation makes the economic life of workers insecure. They must spend quickly before their money loses its value. Savings payable in fixed currency units become meaningless because they depreciate rapidly; therefore, workers often do not plan for their own security as much as workers do in the United States. They develop more dependence on the government and more anxiety about their personal welfare, and this may lead to social unrest.

Looking at social, political, and economic conditions as a whole, we see that these conditions impede the introduction of advanced technology and sophisticated organizational systems. They constrain the stability, security, and trained human resources that developing countries require to be more productive. A new plant in a less developed country usually cannot be expected to produce as efficiently as it would in a developed nation, because environmental conditions surrounding the plant do not support high productivity. The unfortunate fact is that these limiting conditions cannot be changed rapidly, because they are too well established and woven into the whole social fabric of a nation. High productivity is not achieved by such simple answers as the construction of new plants or the infusion of more capital. As explained by Peter Drucker, "A society is poor not because it has a problem, not because it has hookworm, but because it cannot organize its resources to do anything."[6]

MANAGING AN INTERNATIONAL WORK FORCE

Whenever an organization expands its operations so that its geographic boundaries span two or more countries, it tends to become multicultural and will then face the challenge of blending various cultures together. *Multiculturalism* occurs when the employees in two or more cultures interact with each other on a regular basis. Managers and technical employees entering another nation to install an advanced organizational system need to adjust their leadership styles, communication patterns, and other practices to fit their host country. In some instances these new employees are *parent-country nationals* from the nation in which the home office is located, or they may be *third-country nationals* from some other nation. In either case they are called *expatriates,* since they come from another nation. Their role is to provide a fusion of cultures in which both parties adjust to the new situation of seeking greater productivity for the benefit of both the organization and the citizens of the country in which it operates.

Role of expatriates

Barriers to cultural adaptation

PAROCHIALISM The dominant feature of all international operations is that they are conducted in a social system different from the one in which the organization is based. This new social system affects the responses of all persons involved. Managers and other employees who come into a host country in order to get a new operation established naturally tend to exhibit a variety of behaviors that are often true of citizens in their homeland. For example, many people are somewhat *parochial,* meaning that they "see" the situation around them from their own perspective. They may fail to recognize key differences between their own and other cultures. Even if they do, they tend to conclude that the impact of those differences is insignificant. In effect, they are assuming that the two cultures are more similar than they actually are.

Possible characteristics of expatriates

INDIVIDUALISM Expatriates from the U.S. and other countries also may be relatively *individualistic,* meaning that they place greatest emphasis on their personal needs and welfare. At the extreme, individualism suggests to people that their actions should be guided by the motto "Look out for number 1" (themselves) before being concerned about others. This characteristic may create conflict for expatriates, if they do not adapt to the strong group orientation that exists in some other cultures, such as in Japan. (In sharp contrast to the American motto, note the different implications of the famous Japanese proverb "The nail that sticks up gets pounded down.")[7]

ETHNOCENTRISM Another potential barrier to easy adaptation to another culture (see Figure 21-2) occurs when people are predisposed to believe that their homeland conditions are the best. This predisposition is known as the self-reference criterion, or *ethnocentrism.* Though this way of perceiving conditions is very natural, it interferes with understanding human behavior in other cultures and obtaining productivity from local employees. In order to integrate the imported and local social systems, expatriate employees need cultural understanding of local conditions. Even with this understanding, they must then be adaptable enough to integrate the community of interest of the two or more cultures involved.

CULTURAL DISTANCE In order to predict the amount of adaptation that may be required when an expatriate manager moves to another country, it is helpful to understand the *cultural distance* between the two countries. Cultural distance is the amount of difference between any two social systems, and this may range from minimal to substantial. As a citizen of one country accurately expressed the contrast, "We are only one day (geographically) but many years distant (technologically and socially) from Washington, D.C." Research has shown that some measures of cultural distance (from the United States) are greater for countries in the Mediterranean area and Asia, and smaller for Scandinavian and English-speaking countries.[8]

Whatever the amount of cultural distance, it does affect the responses of all persons to business. Expatriate managers naturally tend to be somewhat ethno-

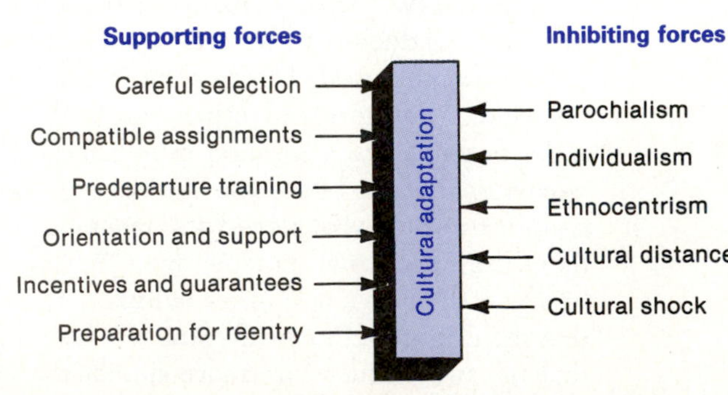

FIGURE 21-2
Forces supporting and inhibiting cultural adaptation

centric and to judge conditions in a new country according to standards of their homeland. These problems will be magnified if the cultural distance is great.[9] However, expatriates' jobs require employees to be adaptable enough to integrate the interests of the two or more cultures involved. But cultural adaptation is not easy.

For example, executives of a U.S. firm in an Asian nation were unable to adapt to the philosophy of its local partner regarding the employment of relatives (nepotism). The home office in the United States had strong rules against this practice, so the expatriate managers tried to apply the same policy in their Asian branch. The Asian partner and manager, on the other hand, saw the business as a source of jobs for family members, so he employed many of them even when they were poorly qualified. His actions were consistent with the cultural belief that as the senior male member of his family, he should help provide for the economic needs of his entire extended family. The Asian–United States differences on this issue were so great (largely because of cultural distance) that the partners finally separated.[10]

Effects and causes of cultural shock

CULTURAL SHOCK When employees enter another nation they tend to suffer *cultural shock*, which is the insecurity and disorientation caused by encountering a different culture. They may not know how to act, may fear losing face and self-confidence, or may become emotionally upset. In severe cases their surroundings appear to be social chaos, and this diminishes their ability to perform effectively. Some individuals isolate themselves, while a few even decide to return home on the next airplane. But a different culture is not behavioral chaos; it is a systematic structure of behavior patterns, probably as systematic as the culture in the employee's home country. But it is different, and these differences are a strain on newcomers regardless of their adaptability.

Cultural shock is virtually universal. It happens even on a move from one advanced nation to another. For example, many Japanese firms have established assembly plants, made substantial investments in real estate, or distributed their electronic and photographic products in the United States in recent years. When they send their managers to oversee foreign operations, these individuals suffer cultural shock; and when U.S. employees move to Japan or other countries, they also suffer cultural shock.

Similar cultural shock may develop for a spouse or children accompanying the employee. "Inability of the manager's spouse to adjust to a different physical or cultural environment" was the most important reason given for expatriate failure in one study of U.S. expatriates.[11] Spouses may have difficulty adapting to their new culture and may develop family conflicts, withdraw into their home, or experience other emotional problems. The shock can be even greater for family members than for the employee, since the latter is usually immersed in job responsibilities and perhaps not as sensitive to emerging problems. When the family's cultural shock is overwhelming, the spouse and children might decide to return home, which often causes the employee to return prematurely as well.

Some of the more frequent reasons for cultural shock are shown in Figure 21-3. Many expatriates report difficulty adjusting to different human resource

Cultural shock

- **Different management philosophies**
- **New language**
- **Alternative foods, dress, driving patterns, availability of goods**
- **Attitudes toward work and productivity**
- **Separation from friends and work colleagues**
- **Unique currency system**

Reentry

- **Loss of decision-making authority**
- **Loss of responsibility**
- **Changes in level of status and lifestyle**
- **Adaptation to technological and organizational changes**

FIGURE 21-3
Typical reasons for cultural shock and cross-cultural reentry problems

management philosophies, the strange language, the unique currency, and work attitudes in another culture.[12]

Overcoming barriers to cultural adaptation

In spite of the strong evident need for expatriate employees to understand local culture and to be adaptable, they often arrive unprepared. Their selection is typically based upon their job performance in the home country, or their need to better understand the company's international operations as a prerequisite to obtaining top-management positions. Because of their parochial, individualistic, or ethnocentric beliefs, they might not be concerned about the fact that they will be doing business with people whose traditional beliefs are different from their own. They may not know the local language and might have little interest in becoming a part of the community. They also may have been selected largely on the basis of their technical qualifications, with the employer overlooking the need for a good "fit" between the expatriate and the local culture. As one company stated its position, "Our main concern is that they can do the technical job we send them to do." However, cultural understanding is essential to avoid errors and misunderstandings that can be costly to an organization. There are, fortunately, several actions that firms can take to prevent cultural shock and reduce the impact of the other barriers discussed previously. Some of the most useful actions are the following (refer to Figure 21-2).

CAREFUL SELECTION Employees can be chosen who are low in ethnocentrism and other possibly troublesome characteristics. The *desire* to experience another culture and live in another nation may also be an important prerequisite attitude worth assessing. Potential expatriates might be screened to determine which employees are already capable of speaking the language of the nation where they will be assigned, or which ones have traveled to that region previously.[13] Learning the attitudes of the employee's spouse toward the assignment also can be important, to ensure that there is strong support for becoming expatriates.

In selecting employees for multicultural assignments, some organizations have been concerned about placing women in foreign environments with a history of discrimination. The workplace in many cultures remains a male-dominated domain, with local women systematically excluded from higher managerial roles. However, in one study of fifty-two female expatriate managers from North America, the vast majority (97 percent) were successful despite having no female predecessor for a role model in that position. The women attributed their success to their high visibility, cultural sensitivity, and interpersonal skills.[14] This should stimulate other firms to focus their selection of expatriate candidates on the identification of similar characteristics in both females and males.

COMPATIBLE ASSIGNMENTS Adjustment to new surroundings is easier if employees, especially on their first international assignment, are sent to nations that are similar to their own. This is much more possible in giant firms like Exxon and IBM that have widespread foreign operations than in smaller organizations that have only a few international offices.

A study of industrialized nations in the free world shows that most of these can be grouped into five sociocultural clusters (see Figure 21-4).[15] The Anglo-American

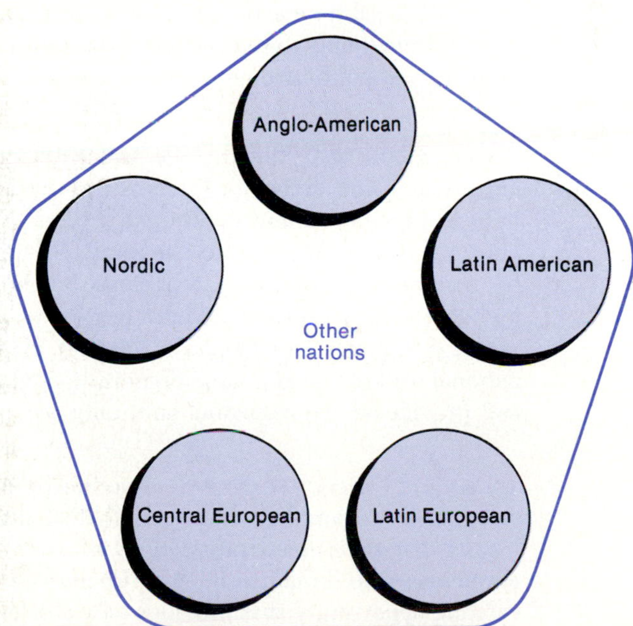

FIGURE 21-4
Primary sociocultural clusters of industrialized nations
Source: *Simcha Ronen and Allen I. Kraut, "Similarities among Countries Based on Employee Work Values and Attitudes,"* Columbia Journal of World Business, *Summer 1977, p. 94.*

Some cultures are similar; others are different.

cluster includes the United States, United Kingdom, Canada, and Australia; the Nordic group includes Norway, Finland, Denmark, and Sweden; the Latin European one has Portugal, Spain, Italy, France, and Belgium; the Latin American cluster includes Peru, Mexico, Argentina, Chile, and Venezuela; while the Central European group contains Germany, Austria, and Switzerland. Researchers found that four nations—Israel, India, Japan, and Brazil—did not fit into any of the five clusters.

Using information such as this, a firm can attempt to assign expatriate employees within their own cluster of nations, with the result being easier adjustment and less cultural shock. For example, a Canadian employee assigned to Australia is likely to adjust more quickly than a Spanish employee in the same assignment.

PREDEPARTURE TRAINING As a minimum, many organizations try to hasten adjustment to a host nation by encouraging employees to learn the local language. They offer language training prior to the assignment, and some even give pay differentials to expatriate employees who learn the local language (a form of knowledge-based pay). The added language capacity seems to be well worth its personal and organizational costs, because those who possess it can speak with local employees in their native language. This contributes to cultural adaptation in two ways. First, it helps avoid the misunderstandings that can arise when communications have to be translated by someone else. Second, it creates a better impression of the expatriate as someone who is willing to invest personal time and effort in adapting to the local environment. Predeparture training now often includes orientation to the geography, customs, culture, and political environment in which the employee will be living.[16]

ORIENTATION AND SUPPORT IN THE NEW COUNTRY Adjustment is further encouraged after arrival in the new country if there is a special effort made to help the employee and family get settled. This may include assistance with housing, transportation, and shopping. It is especially helpful if a mentor can be assigned to ease the transition. Sometimes this can be the previous jobholder who stays for a short period to share useful experiences before moving to a new assignment. Another valuable mentor would be a local national working for the same organization who is available to answer questions and provide advice regarding culturally acceptable behavior.[17]

INCENTIVES AND GUARANTEES Another problem that can arise when employees transfer to another culture is that of intensified need deficiencies. This means that their need satisfactions are not as great as those of comparable employees who remain at home. Although a move to another nation may be an exciting opportunity that provides new challenges, responsibilities, and recognition, a diminished level of Herzberg's maintenance factors can interfere with the enjoyment of these satisfiers. Specifically, an international job assignment may bring about financial difficulties, inconveniences, insecurities, and separation from relatives and friends. To induce employees to accept such assignments in other nations, organizations frequently give them extra pay and fringe benefits to compensate for the problems that they will experience.[18] They also should be assured that they will receive comparable or better positions within the organization upon their return to the homeland, which can help relieve their job insecurities.

Reverse cultural shock

PREPARATION FOR REENTRY Employees who return to their home country after working in another nation for some time tend to suffer cultural shock in their own homeland. This is sometimes called *cross-cultural reentry,* and may cause *reverse cultural shock.* After adjusting to the culture of another nation and enjoying its uniqueness, it is difficult for expatriates to readjust to the surroundings of their home country. The situation is made more difficult by the multitude of changes that have occurred since they departed. Just as philosophers suggest that a person may never step into the same river twice, it is also unlikely that one's home environment will remain the same. Not only does the actual homeland change, but expatriates are likely to idealize the positive aspects of it while they are away, only to be surprised at the reality they later find.

Furthermore, in their host country expatriates may have enjoyed higher status, better pay, and special privileges (such as servants), but back home they are merely one of several employees with similar rank in the home office. Colleagues who remained at home might have been promoted, leaving returning employees with a feeling that they were bypassed and therefore have lost valuable advancement opportunities. Returning to Figure 21-3, we see that overseas executives often report difficulty with insufficient decision-making authority and diminished responsibility after reentry. For example, 82 percent of expatriate managers in one study reported overall satisfaction with their international assignment, but only 35 percent reported being satisfied with their repatriation process.[19] As a result, companies need repatriation policies and programs to help returning employees obtain suitable assignments and adjust to the "new" environment.

PRODUCTIVITY AND CULTURAL CONTINGENCIES

Productivity is the central idea that the people of a country need to absorb and embrace in order to develop the capacity to progress. Without a devotion to productivity, conditions of poverty, inefficiency, and wastefulness of natural resources continue, while new capital inputs are dissipated. Without a belief in productivity, more education merely increases one's desire for gaining additional personal status. Without a goal of productivity, achievement motivation simply adds to the competition for resources that are not growing. Unless productivity increases, whatever one person gains is usually achieved at the expense of others.

Expatriates often find, however, that some local managers do not understand the idea of productivity. Even those who do may still have difficulty communicating it to their supervisors and workers. Despite the simple notion of productivity (introduced in Chapter 1) as an input-output measure of efficiency, local managers and employees may view it in terms of production (a net increase in output *regardless* of inputs). In contrast, the extensive publicity and educational efforts devoted to it in Europe, the United States, and Japan have resulted in a resurgence of understanding and active pursuit of productivity.

The gap in understanding productivity in other nations is widened by the fact that local managers often ignore rational methods of solving problems and making decisions.[20] They tend to treat management as a personal art, solving problems subjectively without adequate attention to whether their decisions will increase or decrease productivity. Since decision patterns like these are firmly ingrained, it is difficult to change them, regardless of the quality of communication efforts and the number of training programs provided by the home organization. Problems are further compounded when these subjective decisions are not followed with objective measures to determine whether productivity was in fact increased.

Cultural contingencies

Match practice to the culture.

Even when nations want to reduce waste of their resources and have more goods and services for their citizens, this does not occur easily. Since each nation is different, productive business practices from one country cannot be transferred directly to another country. This reflects the idea of *cultural contingency*—that the most productive practices for a particular nation will depend heavily on its culture. The ideas that work in one nation's culture must be blended with the social system, level of economic development, and employees' values in a host country. The difficult lesson for both expatriate and local managers to accept is that neither the home nation's productivity approaches nor the host nation's traditional practices are used exclusively. Instead, a third set of practices must be developed that integrates the most workable ideas from both nations. In this way both the new firm and the host nation gain benefits from the company's operation.

Cultural contingencies are illustrated by the fact that Japanese and American business practices are both quite productive, even though the cultures are different. Practices in Japan that are different from those in the United States include Japanese emphasis on lifelong employment and promotions based on seniority, avoidance of overt conflict, decision making by consensus, and teamwork. By contrast, management practices in the United States have traditionally focused more on merit as a basis for advancement, confrontation of conflict, top-down decision making, and individualism. In spite of these cultural differences, both countries are among the world's most productive.

Visible examples of cultural contingencies in action have appeared in the automotive industry. Honda, Toyota, Nissan, Mitsubishi, and other Japanese firms have all established joint manufacturing operations in the United States. They have gradually sought to instill the spirit of *kaizen* (a never-ending quest for perfection) and a goal of *wa* (harmony between people and machines). Teamwork and consensus decision processes also are stressed by the Japanese, and seem to fit with the host country's culture.[21] However, it is still too early to conclude whether or not American workers will relinquish their desires for rapid promotion or subdue their confrontational conflict resolution tendencies. In the meantime, Japanese managers in the United States must be content to blend the best of both countries' cultural practices together.[22]

Cultural contingency, then, suggests that expatriate managers must learn to operate effectively in a new environment. Although they must operate within the limits of most home office policies, managers also must be flexible enough to respond to local conditions. Labor policy, personnel practices, and production methods need to be adapted to a different labor force. Organization structures and communication patterns need to be suitable for local operation as well as coordination with the home office and other branches. There is a much greater probability of achieving productivity improvements when a business and its expatriate managers adapt to host-country conditions.

Blend technology and culture.

MANAGEMENT'S INTEGRATING ROLE Once managers are on location in a host country, their attention needs to be directed toward integrating the technological approaches with the local cultures involved. Where local practices that interfere with productivity cannot be changed, they can perhaps be bypassed or integrated into a modified production plan. If, for example, a one-hour siesta must be accepted, perhaps siesta hours can be staggered so that equipment can be kept operating and service maintained for customers.

The job of international managers is to try to retain in their management practices the essential elements of both old and new cultures so that their employees may work with the security of some old practices, but also with greater productivity than the old culture normally has accomplished. As both experience and research demonstrate, technological change is also accompanied by social change. The technological part of change usually can be aided by the tools and logical approaches of science, but the social part is dependent on effective leadership.

Managers as well as technicians need to restrain their tendency to set up complex administrative and production systems in the host country to match those in their own country. These systems may be beyond the skills or educational backgrounds of local people, and may be misunderstood and inefficiently operated. A simpler system may operate better, as the following situation shows:

A human resource management specialist on assignment in another country set up a complicated performance appraisal system having ten items just like the one used in

the Chicago home office. Local supervisors nodded their heads with an understanding "yes" as instructions were given, so the specialist thought everything was shipshape. When the completed appraisal forms were returned, however, he found that all seven supervisors had rated each employee exactly alike on all ten items.

Investigation disclosed that the supervisors nodded "yes" because they wished not to offend the specialist, who was to them a guest and a superior, but they did not understand the appraisal system concept. Furthermore, they could not culturally accept the idea of judging their employees (who were also their neighbors) in writing because neither party in this kind of situation could then save face.[23]

Lower-level needs remain important.

MOTIVATING AND LEADING LOCAL EMPLOYEES Even when employees understand productivity and accept it as a desirable goal, they may remain poorly motivated. One reason is that employees in many nations often are at a low level in their need structures. They tend to seek satisfaction of their primary (physiological and security) needs rather than their advanced needs. Therefore, some of the sophisticated motivational practices of more advanced countries (such as gain-sharing plans) may still be inappropriate in other countries. In these situations, the needs of workers may be more adequately reached by direct motivation. In some instances the employees have worked in economic systems that had little direct connection between how effectively they worked and how well they were rewarded. They also may lack trust in the new organization and its practices. Therefore, they require management to provide evidence that if they are more productive, they will receive more.[24] In other words, rewards must be designed to match workers' immediate needs, rather than providing indirect results through a complex economic or social system. Accordingly, motivational methods that would have limited effectiveness in one nation may have desirable outcomes in another nation.

Studies show that the same principle applies to the use of leadership styles. While the use of an authoritarian style is diminishing in the United States, it is not necessarily dysfunctional in many situations in developing nations.[25] This is because employees with strong security needs may readily accept autocratic and paternalistic behavior. Since they have strong role expectations for it, and it satisfies their needs, it may be a culturally correct approach in these conditions. Essentially, the most effective motivational and leadership practices are contingent on local conditions in the host nation.

COMMUNICATION Even when two parties speak the same language and share the same culture, communication problems can emerge. When a communication is expressed in one cultural context and then interpreted in another, misunderstanding is even more likely.[26] As a result, international firms find that providing language training for their expatriates is not a substitute for cultural training. Both are needed.

In one mill an expatriate manager introduced a grievance system for employees. He was amazed when workers interpreted grievances as including mostly external problems. Workers brought to the mill manager their personal problems about families, relatives, and finances, perceiving him in the role of paternalistic autocrat

who would care for them and resolve their personal disputes. They gave little thought to complaining about working conditions, because working conditions were above average (and better than they were familiar with), so complaints in this situation would be considered poor manners in their culture.

Communication practices differ.

Managers also need to make adjustments in their personal manners in dealing with people in the host country. In the United States it is the custom for people in face-to-face conversation to maintain some physical distance between them, perhaps a foot or two depending on their level of intimacy. In some cultures, however, it is the custom for people who talk face-to-face to do so quite closely, perhaps only 6 inches apart. A manager from the United States may be initially uncomfortable in interactions of this type. For example, during a short conversation one expatriate manager backed halfway across the room trying to increase the distance between himself and an employee who kept following him in order to keep the cultural distance of 6 to 9 inches with which he was familiar. Under these conditions it is difficult to achieve one's objectives because of the substantial feeling of being uncomfortable in the employee's presence.

Communication among people of different cultures is difficult enough; but when one begins talking about abstract ideas like productivity, effective communication is even more difficult. The image that an expatriate manager sends is not likely to be that which local receivers interpret, because they will tend to see the image from their cultural point of view. Communication is made even more difficult by the fact that an expatriate manager's communication with workers is usually done through local supervisors who may attach their own interpretations to what is being transmitted.

THE COMMUNITY ROLE OF EXPATRIATE MANAGERS Expatriate managers need to consider what their role will be in a local community. Although they are generally respected figures with considerable economic power, they are in a country as guests, and may not be readily absorbed into the social and power structures of a local community. Even if they speak the local language and live in a community for years, they still may not be fully accepted into its social structure. Because of their marginal role and subsequent insulation from important insights, they risk misinterpreting much of the community's value structure. As a result, they must be cautious not to overstep local customs by getting too familiar. The Spanish language and some other languages, for example, have certain "familiar" pronouns and verb conjugations that are used only among close personal friends and relatives. One manager related the following experience on this subject:

I was assigned to a country whose people spoke the Spanish language. I had been there two years, and since I speak the language fluently, I felt that I was working very well with the community. On one occasion I was particularly pleased when our top local manager asked me to his home to meet his grandmother, who was the family matriarch and revered by all of the family. When I was introduced to her in

rather formal circumstances, without thinking I spoke to her using the "familiar" form of the verb. Immediately the atmosphere in the room turned to ice, and my visit was hastily terminated. I still didn't know what had happened, but on my way home I asked our local manager, and he emotionally told me that this kind of familiarity is not accepted in his culture. It took me weeks to make the proper apologies through necessary intermediaries, and I felt I never did recover socially from this setback.

Though these kinds of cultural errors may seem minor to an outsider, they can be highly important to a local citizen. Expatriate managers must not establish the image that they are callous to local culture or desire to change it. They are more likely to succeed by maintaining a balance of respect for the local culture and its compatibility with the parent company's culture. If local culture is ignored, the resulting imbalance in the social system interferes with productivity. Likewise, if the organization submits wholly to the culture of the host country, the lack of fit with the technological system will cause loss of efficiency. Both local culture and advanced technology must be integrated.

Transcultural managers

Transcultural employees are needed.

It is evident that careful attention should be given to cultural preparation of expatriate employees. Eventually a cadre of employees with cross-cultural adaptability can be developed in organizations with large international operations. These employees are *transcultural employees* because they operate effectively in several cultures. They are low in ethnocentrism and adapt readily to different cultures without major cultural shock. They usually can communicate fluently in more than one language.

Transcultural employees are especially needed in large, multinational firms that operate in a variety of national cultures. For a firm to be truly multinational in character, it should have ownership, operations, markets, and managers truly diversified without primary dominance of any one of these four items by any one nation. Its leaders look to the world as an economic and social unit; but they recognize each local culture, respect its integrity, acknowledge its benefits, and use its differences effectively in their organization.

SUMMARY

The world of business has been transformed into a global economy. More and more multinational organizations are extending operations into other countries, and their managers encounter many different social, political, and economic environments. Among many other factors, the difficulty in understanding productivity can be a major barrier to improvement. However, when expatriate managers are effective, they help create a powerful training multiplier effect, providing skills which become multiplied many times in the host country.

Expatriate managers find that organizational behavior practices of one country cannot be transferred directly to another, especially if the host country is less developed. Models for understanding and managing people need to be adapted to the particular culture, level of development, and employee need structure of a host country. The best results occur when neither the home country's nor the host nation's traditional practices are used. Instead, a third set of practices contingent upon situational needs is developed that integrates the most workable ideas from both sets of existing practices.

Employees entering another nation may suffer from the effects of cultural shock, or they may fail to fit into the new culture because of their parochial, individualistic, or ethnocentric characteristics. Many of these problems can be prevented or minimized through careful selection, training, and counseling. Transcultural managers—those who can adapt successfully to a number of other cultures—are able to adjust their motivational, leadership, and communication practices to achieve their goals of improved productivity.

Terms and concepts for review

Multinational organizations
Training multiplier effect
Multiculturalism
Expatriates
Parochialism
Individualism
Ethnocentrism
Cultural distance
Cultural shock
Reverse cultural shock
Transcultural employees

Discussion questions

1 Select a foreign country that has recently been in the news. Class members should contribute information about key social, political, and economic factors that would collectively help a manager who is about to move there to understand it better.

2 Identify firms in your region that are multinational. In what parts of the world do they operate? How recently have they become multinational? If possible, invite a representative of one of these firms to speak to the class about policies, experiences, and problems the firm has encountered in its multinational operations.

3 Discuss the effects of parochialism, individualism, and ethnocentrism. How would employees behave if they had all three characteristics? How would you respond to workers from another country if they demonstrated these three traits? Suggest ways by which they could be reduced or eliminated in an individual.

4 Think of a time when you may have experienced cultural shock. How did you react? How could you have better anticipated and prevented it? Is it possible to experience cultural shock by just traveling across the United States? Explain.

5 Evaluate the various recommendations for minimizing or overcoming barriers to cultural adaptation. Which do you think have the greatest potential likelihood of succeeding?
6 Which person do you predict will experience the greatest amount of cultural shock upon moving to a new country, the expatriate or that person's spouse? Why?
7 Offer several suggestions for preventing or at least minimizing the problem of cross-cultural reentry (reverse cultural shock).
8 Why is the concept of productivity difficult to grasp for some host-country employees? Would it be easier to explain its necessity in an oil-rich country or in one with very limited natural resources? Explain.
9 The discussion on motivating employees in other countries revolved mostly around need structures. Review the chapters on motivation and indicate how you think the other motivational models would, or would not, be valuable tools in understanding and guiding behavior in other countries.

Incident

THE PIEDMONT COMPANY

The Piedmont Company is a major multinational manufacturer with branch operations in several nations around the world. Its home office is in the United States, but it has sent expatriate managers to work in its various branches. The company recently conducted a survey of its middle managers to determine their relative levels of need satisfaction in their jobs. The results of the survey are reported in the following table:

APPROXIMATE NEED SATISFACTION LEVELS OF MIDDLE-LEVEL AMERICAN MANAGERS IN U.S. OPERATIONS VS. OVERSEAS BRANCHES

SURVEY ITEMS	MANAGERS IN U.S.	EXPATRIATE (U.S.) MANAGERS IN BRANCHES
Satisfaction with		
Job security	**High**	**Moderate**
Opportunity for friendships	**High**	**Low**
Feelings of self-esteem	**High**	**Moderate**
In-company prestige	**Moderate**	**Moderate**
Community prestige	**Moderate**	**High**
Opportunity for autonomy	**Moderate**	**High**
Level of authority	**Low**	**High**
Feeling of accomplishment	**Moderate**	**Moderate**
Feeling of self-fulfillment	**Low**	**Moderate**

Questions

1 Analyze the results shown, and give your interpretation of the kinds of problems that exist. Offer possible explanations for them.
2 Prepare a set of recommendations for resolving or diminishing the problems that you have identified.
3 Speculate what the results might look like if the nonsupervisory employees in each country had been surveyed. What is the basis for your conclusions?

Experiential exercise

ADAPTABILITY TO A MULTICULTURAL ASSIGNMENT

1 Assume that you have been hired by a firm with extensive operations in many different countries around the world. Your first job assignment will take you out of the United States for approximately three years, and you will depart about thirty days from now.
2 Review the text discussion of parochialism, individualism, ethnocentrism, and cultural shock. Think about the degree to which you would be likely to exhibit each of these barriers to cultural adaptation, and record your responses on the following scales. Then indicate the degree to which you would honestly expect to experience difficulty adapting to each of the five sociocultural clusters.

FACTOR	PROBABLE LEVEL						
	(LOW)						(HIGH)
Parochialism	1	2	3	4	5	6	7
Individualism	1	2	3	4	5	6	7
Ethnocentrism	1	2	3	4	5	6	7
Cultural shock	1	2	3	4	5	6	7
RELATIVE DIFFICULTY ADAPTING TO AN ASSIGNMENT IN EACH OF THE SOCIOCULTURAL CLUSTERS							
Anglo-American	1	2	3	4	5	6	7
Latin American	1	2	3	4	5	6	7
Latin European	1	2	3	4	5	6	7
Nordic	1	2	3	4	5	6	7
Central European	1	2	3	4	5	6	7

3 Share your personal assessments with the rest of the class. (Create a frequency distribution of the responses.) Explore why differences exist among students, and what the overall pattern implies regarding the capacity of class members to become transcultural employees. What could you, or your employer, do to improve the likelihood of your success in view of the above characteristics?

References

1 "Developing Nations Offer New Challenge to HR Management," ASPA's *Resource*, October 1986, p. 9.

2 Jeffery M. Kadet and Robert J. Gaughan, Jr., "Oversee Expatriate Returns to Curtail Taxes," *Personnel Journal*, July 1987, p. 71.

3 P. R. G. Layard and J. C. Saigal, "Educational and Occupational Characteristics of Manpower: An International Comparison," *British Journal of Industrial Relations*, July 1966, pp. 222–266, especially Fig. 1, reporting studies of census data in twenty nations.

4 "Court Invalidates Airline's Policy for Transfers to Foreign Cities," *Japan Labor Bulletin*, Nov. 1, 1974, p. 7.

5 *The World Almanac and Book of Facts*, New York: World Almanac (Pharos Books—a Scripps-Howard Company), 1988.

6 Peter F. Drucker, "What Have We Learned about Economic and Social Development?" *Proceedings, Annual Conference on International Management*, New York: Council for International Progress in Management, 1966, p. 6.

7 Discussions of individualism versus collectivism are in Richard E. Dutton, "The Japanese Manager: A Coordinator of the Network," *Business Forum*, Spring 1987, pp. 21–24; and Richard S. DeFrank et al., "The Impact of Culture on the Management Practices of American and Japanese CEOs," *Organizational Dynamics*, Spring 1985, pp. 62–76.

8 Geert Hofstede, "Motivation, Leadership, and Organization: Do American Theories Apply Abroad?" *Organizational Dynamics*, Summer 1980, pp. 42–63; an extension of Hofstede's findings to identify specific OD interventions compatible with the values in various cultures is in Alfred M. Jaeger, "Organization Development and National Culture: Where's the Fit?" *Academy of Management Review*, January 1986, pp. 178–190; an application of Hofstede's clusters to managerial roles in different cultures is in Ellen F. Jackofsky, John W. Slocum, Jr., and Sara J. McQuaid, "Cultural Values and the CEO: Alluring Companions?" *Academy of Management Executive*, February 1988, pp. 39–49.

9 A study contrasting the different ideologies of Japanese and British managers is Ritsuko Miyajima, "Organisation Ideology of Japanese Managers," *Management International Review*, vol. 26, no. 1, 1986, pp. 73–76. In contrast, a study of work-related reward preferences among MBA candidates in the United States, Australia, Canada, and Singapore revealed surprisingly few differences; see G. E. Popp, H. J. Davis, and T. T. Herbert, "An International Study of Intrinsic Motivation Composition," *Management International Review*, vol. 26, no. 3, 1986, pp. 28–33.

10 John I. Reynolds, "Developing Policy Responses to Cultural Differences," *Business Horizons*, August 1978, pp. 28–35.

11 Rosalie L. Tung, "Expatriate Assignments: Enhancing Success and Minimizing Failure," *Academy of Management Executive*, May 1987, pp. 117–125.

12 "When the Overseas Executive Comes Home," *Management Review*, August 1982, pp. 53–54; the troublesome lack of foreign-language fluency of U.S. managers is noted in Arthur M. Whitehill, "America's Trade Deficit: The Human Problems," *Business Horizons*, January–February 1988, pp. 18–23.

13 "Living with Stress," *First Class* (a publication of International Airline Passenger Association), vol. 9, no. 10, 1988, pp. 21–22.

14 Mariann Jelinek and Nancy J. Adler, "Women: World-Class Managers for Global Competition," *Academy of Management Executive*, February 1988, pp. 11–19.

15 Simcha Ronen and Allen I. Kraut, "Similarities among Countries Based on Employee Work Values and Attitudes," *Columbia Journal of World Business*, Summer 1977, p. 94.

16 Research on the effectiveness of training is in P. Christopher Early, "Intercultural Training for Managers: A Comparison of Documentary and Interpersonal Methods," *Academy of Management Journal*, December 1987, pp. 685–698. Twelve guidelines for teaching in another culture are in Lennie Copeland, "Skills Transfer and Training Overseas," *Personnel Administrator*, June 1986, pp. 107–109ff.

17 An intriguing article providing guidance on culturally acceptable behavior is Jeffrey A. Fadiman, "A Traveler's Guide to Gifts and Bribes," *Harvard Business Review*, July–August 1986, pp. 122–124ff; also see Diane Wagner, "The Global Guide to Executive Etiquette," *Republic*, March 1986, pp. 18–21. Maintaining a supportive connection between the expatriate and the home office is recommended by Philip R. Harris, "Employees Abroad: Maintain the Corporate Connection," *Personnel Journal*, August 1986, pp. 107–110.

18 An article focusing on incentives for expatriates is Michael A. Conway, "Manage Expatriate Expenses for Capital Returns," *Personnel Journal*, July 1987, pp. 66–70.

19 Luis Gomez-Mejia and David B. Balkin, "The Determinants of Managerial Satisfaction with the Expatriation and Repatriation Process," *Journal of Management Development*, vol. 6, no. 1, 1987, pp. 7–17. An excellent discussion of reentry is in Nancy J. Adler, *International Dimensions of Organizational Behavior*, Boston: PWS-Kent Publishing Company (Wadsworth), 1986, chap. 8.

20 Anant R. Negandhi, "Comparative Management and Organization Theory: A Marriage Needed," *Academy of Management Journal*, June 1975, pp. 334–344.

21 Representative articles on Japanese practices in the United States are Robert Rehder, "Japanese Transplants: A New Model for Detroit," *Business Horizons*, January–February 1988, pp. 52–61; and Stanley J. Brown, "The Japanese Approach to Labor Relations: Can It Work in America?" *Personnel*, April 1987, pp. 20–29. Suggestions on cultural contingencies for employees working in Asian countries are in Milton Pierce, "25 Lessons from the Japanese," *New Management*, Fall 1987, pp. 23–26; and John A. Reeder, "When West Meets East: Cultural Aspects of Doing Business in Asia," *Business Horizons*, January–February 1987, pp. 69–74.

22 The importance of blending two countries' practices is discussed in James S. Bowman, "The Rising Sun in America (Part Two)" *Personnel Administrator*, October 1986, pp. 81–91.

23 Face-saving in Asian cultures is discussed in John A. Reeder, "When West Meets East: Cultural Aspects of Doing Business in Asia," *Business Horizons*, January–February 1987, pp. 69–74.

24 Jiing-Lih Farh, Philip M. Podsakoff, and Bor-Shiuan Cheng, "Culture-Free Leadership Effectiveness versus Moderators of Leadership Behavior: An Extension and Test of Kerr and Jermier's 'Substitutes for Leadership' Model in Taiwan," *Journal of International Business Studies*, Fall 1987, pp. 43–60.

25 Negandhi, *loc. cit.*

26 Advice for avoiding such problems in dealing with the Japanese is provided by Mayumi Otsubo, "A Guide to Japanese Business Practices," *California Management Review*, Spring 1986, pp. 28–42.

For additional reading

Adler, Nancy J., *International Dimensions of Organizational Behavior*, Boston: Kent Publishing Company, 1986.

Condon, John C., and Fathi Yousef, *An Introduction to Intercultural Communication*, Yarmouth, Maine: Intercultural Press, Inc., date unknown.

Copeland, Lennie, and Lewis Griggs, *Going International: How to Make Friends and Deal Effectively in the Global Marketplace*, New York: Random House, Inc., 1985.

Furnham, Adrian, and Stephen Bochner, *Culture Shock: Psychological Reactions to Unfamiliar Environments*, New York: Methuen, Inc., 1986.

Harris, Philip R., and Robert T. Moran, *Managing Cultural Differences: High-Performance Strategies for Today's Global Manager*, Houston, Tex.: Gulf Publishing Company, 1987.

Kohls, L. Robert, *Survival Kit of Overseas Living: For Americans Planning to Live and Work Abroad*, Yarmouth, Maine: Intercultural Press, Inc., date unknown.

Sethi, S. Prakash, Nobuaki Namiki, and Carl L. Swanson, *The False Promise of the Japanese Miracle: Illusions and Realities of the Japanese Management System*, Marshfield, Mass.: Pitman Publishing Company, 1984.

Tung, Rosalie L., *The New Expatriates: Managing Human Resources Abroad*, Cambridge, Mass.: Ballinger Publishing Co. 1987.

PART  Conclusion

CHAPTER

22 Organizational behavior in perspective

Instead of worrying about the future, let us labor to create it.

HUBERT HUMPHREY[1]

CHAPTER OBJECTIVES

To understand

How models of organizational behavior relate to other ideas

Human resource accounting

Dangers of behavioral bias

The law of diminishing returns

Importance of ethical leadership

The role of theory and research in organizational behavior

This book has been about people as they work together. They are the great potential in organizations, a potential that can be developed better than it is now. This subject is called organizational behavior. It is the study and application of knowledge about how people act within organizations. It helps people, structure, technology, and the external environment blend together into an effective operating system. The result is a triple-reward system that serves human, organizational, and social objectives.

In this last chapter we review basic models and ideas about organizational behavior. Then we discuss its limitations and conclude with a note about its future.

MODELS OF ORGANIZATIONAL BEHAVIOR

As we learn more about human behavior at work, we apply improved models of organizational behavior. Modern organizations are increasing their use of supportive, collegial, and Theory Y models. In order to provide review and perspective, Figure 22-1 presents the four models of organizational behavior from earlier in the book and then relates them to other ideas on the subject. By reading the figure, one can determine that McGregor's Theory Y is related to the supportive and collegial models. Similarly, Herzberg's maintenance factors apply mostly to the autocratic and custodial models.

What are the trends?

As shown in Figure 22-2, the trend of each subsequent model of organizational behavior is toward more open human organizations.[2] Generally there is also movement toward a wider distribution of power, more intrinsic motivation, a more positive attitude toward people, and a better balance of concern for both employee and organizational needs. Discipline has become more a matter of self-discipline instead of being imposed from the outside. The managerial role has advanced from one of strict authority to leadership and team support.[3]

Much progress has been made during the last few years, and we can expect further progress. Through the application of organizational behavior knowledge, *we are building a better quality of work life.* For U.S. firms to prosper in the face of strong global competition, however, that high-quality work life must result in a more productive work force. This is more likely to occur if management discards the values and practices of the autocratic and custodial models and moves deliberately toward the supportive and collegial ones. Although management approaches vary widely from firm to firm, we can conclude that the greater awareness of effective practices has doubled the good and halved the bad in human relationships at work during the last generation. More and more pieces are falling into place in the complex puzzle of excellent people-organization systems.

FIGURE 22-1 Models of organizational behavior related to other ideas on the subject

	AUTOCRATIC	CUSTODIAL	SUPPORTIVE	COLLEGIAL
Basis of model	**Power**	**Economic resources**	**Leadership**	**Partnership**
Managerial orientation	**Authority**	**Money**	**Support**	**Teamwork**
Employee orientation	**Obedience**	**Security and benefits**	**Job performance**	**Responsibility**
Employee psychological result	**Dependence on boss**	**Dependence on organization**	**Participation**	**Commitment; self-discipline**
Employee needs met	**Subsistence**	**Security**	**Status and recognition**	**Self-actualization**
Performance result	**Minimum**	**Passive cooperation**	**Awakened drives**	**Enthusiasm**
		RELATION TO OTHER IDEAS		
Maslow's hierarchy of needs	**Physiological**	**Security**	**Middle-order**	**Higher-order**
Alderfer's need levels	**Existence**	**Existence**	**Relatedness**	**Growth**
Herzberg's factors	**Maintenance**	**Maintenance**	**Motivational**	**Motivational**
Motivational environment	**Extrinsic**	**Extrinsic**	**Intrinsic**	**Intrinsic**
McGregor's theories	**Theory X**	**Theory X**	**Theory Y**	**Theory Y**
Leadership style	**Negative**	**Mostly neutral on job**	**Positive**	**Positive**
Blake and Mouton's managerial grid	**9,1**	**3,5**	**6,6**	**9,9**

Emphasis on higher-order needs

One reason for emphasis on improved models of organizational behavior is the evolution of employee need structures. Postindustrial nations have reached a condition wherein higher-order (growth) needs are the prime motivators for many employees.[4] Consequently, managers of these workers must seek to design organizational behavior systems that provide a greater probability of satisfying those needs than was possible in the past. In addition, the emergence of a knowledge society requires more use of intellectual abilities across a wide range of employees, and advanced organizational behavior systems tend to be

From	To
□ Closed systems	□ Open systems
□ Materialistic orientation	□ Human orientation
□ Centralized power	□ Distributed power
□ Extrinsic motivation	□ Intrinsic motivation
□ Negative attitudes about people	□ Positive attitudes about people
□ Focus on organization needs	□ Balanced focus on employee and organization needs
□ Imposed discipline	□ Self-discipline
□ Authoritative managerial role	□ Managerial role of leadership and team support

FIGURE 22-2 Trends in organizational behavior

more effective with knowledge workers. A manager cannot *make* employees think; they must be internally motivated to do so.

Organizational behavior unlocks human potential.

The key that unlocks this combination of higher-order needs and intellectual abilities in order to make the system productive is improved organizational behavior. The human mind is encouraged to be more creative by positive motivation. This is a unique energizing force wholly unlike the application of physical energy to a machine. A machine has a rated capacity beyond which it cannot go, no matter how much energy is applied to it. It can produce only so much and no more. But a person can produce unlimited amounts through better ideas. The promise of better organizational behavior is that it motivates people to produce better ideas. There is no apparent limit to what people can accomplish when they are motivated to use their potential to create new and better ideas. The key thought is: Work smarter, not harder.

A systems approach

We need to view changes toward improved organizational behavior in terms of a total system. Effective change is complex and takes a long time to effect. Any new practice such as participation treats only part of the whole system, so it often fails to achieve its full potential for improvement. There are too many unchanged intervening variables that restrict its success. What is needed in organizational behavior is gradual enrichment of entire socio-technical systems to make them more suitable to people. This is a large task, but a challenging one.

A contingency approach

Organizational behavior is applied in a contingency relationship. That is, not all organizations need exactly the same amount of participation, open communication, or any other condition in order to be effective. With regard to participation, some situations *permit* more extensive participation than others, and some people *want* more participation than other people. The most effective organizational behavior system will tend to vary according to an organization's total environment.

Different environments must be considered.

For example, let us compare the two variables of a stable environment and a changing one and then relate these variables to different approaches discussed in this book. Effective practices in these two environments are likely to vary in the directions shown in Figure 22-3. The figure represents only probable tendencies, not absolutes. For example, all that it implies regarding structure is that an effective organization in a stable environment may give more emphasis to hierarchy than a comparable organization in dynamic surroundings. Similarly, a stable-environment firm probably gives more emphasis to vertical communication than a firm in a changing environment does. In other words, there is some evidence of the need for organizational differences between stable and changing environments. This is especially significant in view of the fact that many firms will face increasingly competitive conditions in the remainder of this century and beyond.[5]

It should be understood that contingency theory and goals that seek more human organizations exist side by side as joint ideas. They do not cancel out each other. Both stable and changing organizations, for example, need a more human environment for people (such as more job enrichment and consideration), and in the next generation both will have it. However, even then, contingency ideas predict differences in practice between stable and changing organizations.

A social approach

Two-way influence

A social approach recognizes that what happens outside the firm will influence organizational behavior practices within the firm. Also, what happens inside the firm will influence society. Management must be constantly aware of and responsive to this external environment, because it is an important influence on internal operations.

ORGANIZATIONAL CHARACTERISTICS	ENVIRONMENT STABLE	 CHANGING
Structure	**More rigid hierarchy**	**More flexible (some project and matrix)**
Production system	**More specialization**	**More job enrichment**
Leadership style	**More structure**	**More consideration**
Communication	**More vertical**	**More multidirectional**
Model of organizational behavior	**More autocratic**	**More supportive**
Performance measure	**More management by rules**	**More management by objectives**

FIGURE 22-3
Application of contingency ideas to stable and changing environments

MACROMOTIVATION The external environment has a substantial influence on how employees think and feel. In addition to critical elements of the internal (micromotivational) environment such as the organizational culture, reward system, and social cues, management needs to be aware of forces outside the firm. It must operate within the constraints of the external (macromotivational) environment, and adapt to it.

> **For example, today's labor force has a different set of values than workers had a quarter century ago. These changing values are no myth. They must be faced by all organizations during the next decade.**
>
> **Some of the changes in the labor force are as follows: There has been a decline in the work ethic and a rise in emphasis on leisure, self-expression, fulfillment, and personal growth. The automatic acceptance of authority by employees has decreased, while desires for participation, autonomy, and control have increased.[6] At the same time, several major factors are affecting the work force. Skills become obsolete due to technological advances, and manual workers must either be retrained for knowledge-oriented jobs or be displaced. Chronic inflation has blunted the usefulness of money as a motivator, because any gain is quickly neutralized by inflation.**

Indeed, there is a new labor force, so management's leadership practices must change to match the new conditions. These fast-moving developments have given new emphasis to leadership ability. One study of effective companies reported that a sense of caring, a management which listens to employees, and executives who are concerned with both competence and relationships are among the keys to the motivation of the present work force.[7]

SOCIAL RESPONSIVENESS A social approach also implies that society expects firms to operate in ways that show social responsiveness and social responsibility to the broader social system.[8] An example is society's values of social justice in the employment of women and minorities. These external values are translated into legislation that governs the employment activities of firms. Employment, promotion, supervision, wage administration, and other activities must, as a whole, be responsive to these expectations of society.

Another major area that is only indirectly related to organizational behavior is environmental pollution. It has forced both managers and employees to rethink their practices within the firm. Both groups must be sure that their actions do not cause pollution or even the appearance of it. The company truck driver who drives in a way that increases truck exhaust pollution and who tosses rubbish outside the vehicle's window is polluting the environment in the same way that the company smokestack may be.

Human resource accounting

Human resource values are stressed.

In an effort to give more emphasis to people in a language that management understands—the language of accounting—*human resource accounting* has received some attention.[9] It is an attempt to attach financial values to human

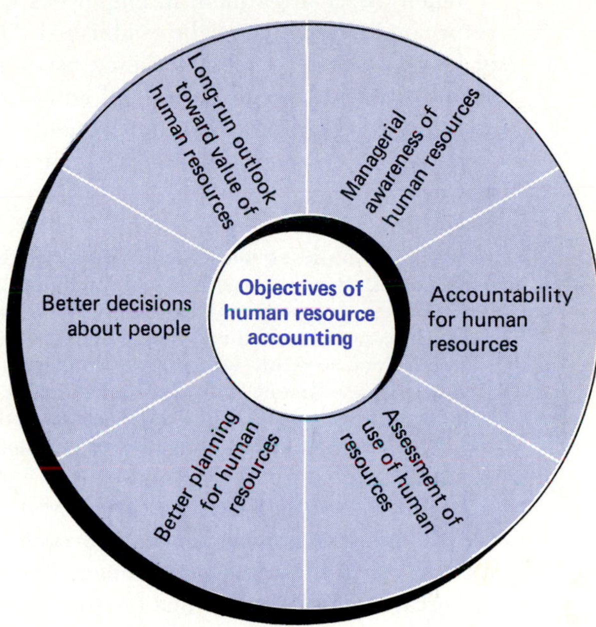

FIGURE 22-4
Objectives of human resource accounting

data for use in the regular accounting system. Although a few firms have experimented with it, it is not widely used.

The basic objectives of human resource accounting are shown in Figure 22-4. It seeks to make managers more aware of the importance of people as valuable resources and to hold managers more accountable for these assets. One of its objectives is to provide a means for assessing management performance in the use and development of human resources. The increased attention would predictably encourage better planning for human resources and better decisions whenever they involve people. Another objective of human resource accounting is to encourage managers to take a long-run outlook toward the value of people, rather than a short-run, quick-profit outlook that ignores human resources.

There are several approaches to human resource accounting, and two principal ones will be discussed in the following paragraphs.

Costs are capitalized.

THE INVESTMENT APPROACH One approach, often called the *investment approach*, seeks to account for the amount that an organization has invested in human resources. Costs such as recruiting and training, rather than being treated as current expenses, are capitalized as an investment to be depreciated during an employee's expected employment. There is no attempt to theorize about how much an employee is worth but only how much has been directly invested in each employee.

When direct investment in employees has been determined, a measure of return on investment may be established. This measure gives an improved idea of how human resources are being used. For example, assume that five research scientists resign because of an autocratic manager. Their resignations will appear as an immediate investment loss, thereby giving strong financial emphasis to the need for better organizational behavior in order to reduce turnover.

One of the earliest firms to experiment with this type of human resource accounting was R. G. Barry Corporation of Columbus, Ohio. Beginning in 1968, this firm established an investment accounting system to provide human resource accounting for its managers, and this system was later extended to office and factory personnel. The system accounts for genuine employer costs that should provide a regular return on investment and which, for human reasons, should not be wasted through underemployment. This investment figure is then used to compute return on assets, return on investment in human resources, and similar accounting values.

Climate surveys are used.

THE ORGANIZATIONAL CLIMATE APPROACH Another approach, which may be called the *organizational climate approach,* uses periodic surveys to determine ways in which the organizational climate has improved or deteriorated. Based on research, it is assumed that changes in these human resource variables will affect future performance. Established formulas are used to convert the human gain or loss into cost increases or decreases in the future. In this way management is encouraged to look beyond short-range economic results to longer-range results. For example, a manager may use autocratic methods to cut costs and show a higher economic profit for the year. A survey of climate may reveal, however, that the manager reduced resources so greatly that future costs will be greater than present savings.

Human resource accounting has its limitations, but has also made a contribution to organizational behavior. It may be demeaning to treat human beings in economic terms on accounting statements. Further, it has proven difficult to translate human data into accounting figures, in terms of both the cost and the accuracy of doing so. In spite of these practical limitations, the *philosophy* underlying human resource accounting is consistent with emerging models of organizational behavior. Experiments with the method have helped emphasize the value of socioeconomic data in decision making.

LIMITATIONS OF ORGANIZATIONAL BEHAVIOR

Problems exist in its nature and use.

This book has been written from a specialized point of view that emphasizes primarily the human side of organizations and the kinds of benefits that attention to it can bring. Nevertheless, we always recognize the limitations of organizational behavior. It will not abolish conflict and frustration; it can only reduce them. It is a way to improve, not an absolute answer to problems.

Furthermore, it is but part of the whole cloth of an organization. We can discuss organizational behavior as a separate subject, but to apply it we must tie it back to the whole of reality. Improved organizational behavior will not solve unemployment. It will not make up for our own deficiencies. It cannot substitute for poor planning, inept organizing, or inadequate controls. It is only one of many systems operating within a larger social system.

Behavioral bias

Tunnel vision restricts objectivity.

People who lack system understanding may develop a *behavioral bias,* which gives them a narrow viewpoint that emphasizes satisfying employee experiences while overlooking the broader system of the organization in relation to all its publics. This condition often is called *tunnel vision* because viewpoints are narrow, as if people were looking through a tunnel. They see only the tiny view at the other end of the tunnel while missing the broader landscape.

It should be evident that concern for employees can be so greatly overdone that the original purpose of joining people together—productive organizational outputs for society—is lost. Sound organizational behavior should help achieve organizational purposes, not replace them. The person who ignores the needs of people as consumers of organizational outputs while championing employee needs is misapplying the ideas of organizational behavior. It is also true that the person who pushes production outputs without regard for employee needs is misapplying organizational behavior. Sound organizational behavior recognizes a social system in which many types of human needs are served in many ways.

Behavioral bias can be so misapplied that it harms employees as well as the organization. Some people, in spite of their good intentions, so overwhelm others with care that they are reduced to dependent—and unproductive—indignity. They become content, not fulfilled. They find excuses for failure rather than taking responsibility for progress. They lack self-discipline and self-respect. As happened with scientific management years ago, concern for people can be misapplied by overeager partisans until it becomes harmful.

Employees as well as managers can handicap a fellow employee through unrestricted concern and care. These conditions are illustrated by the following events.

Edna Harding was a clerk in a government office. Her elderly father was growing mentally unstable, and plans were being made to have him placed in an institution within a few months. Her worry over this matter was compounded by the fact that he frequently came to the building where she worked and waited in the corridors for her before lunch and in the afternoon. His appearance was not pleasant, and he often mumbled. Sometimes he followed her into other offices, creating embarrassing situations. She received much sympathy and attention from her associates, and some of them began doing her work for her while she was upset. Since this problem was reducing her productivity, her supervisor finally arranged with her and the building guards not to admit her father, thus keeping him out of the building entirely. The supervisor allowed Edna's associates to continue performing some of her work, pending placement of her father in an institution.

Even after her father was placed in an institution, Edna continued letting others do her work. It soon became apparent to both her associates and her supervisor that they had sympathized with her and carried her load so long that she was depending on them as she would on a crutch. She relished their sympathy and help and seemed incapable of doing the job she had once done. She became "handicapped," as surely as if she had a physical handicap, because of too much care and good intentions from others. Seeing these negative results, her supervisor wisely insisted that her associates reduce both their help and sympathy. Slowly and painfully, Edna's performance then returned to normal.

The law of diminishing returns

A limiting factor

Overemphasis on an organizational behavior practice may produce negative results, as indicated by the law of diminishing returns.[10] It is a limiting factor in organizational behavior the same way that it is in economics. In economics the *law of diminishing returns* refers to a declining amount of extra outputs when more of a desirable input is added to an economic situation. After a certain point, the output from each unit of added input tends to become smaller. The added output eventually may reach zero and even decline when more units of input are added.

For example, a farmer who has a laborer working on 20 acres of land may double the output by adding another laborer. Similar results could occur by doubling the work force to four people, but soon a point will be reached where the increase in output from adding workers is smaller and smaller. Eventually production will decline as the field becomes overcrowded with workers, coordination deteriorates, and crops are trampled by the crowd.

How does the law work in organizational behavior?

The law of diminishing returns in organizational behavior works in a similar way. It states that at some point increases of a desirable practice produce declining returns, eventually zero returns, and then negative returns as more increases are added. The concept implies that for any situation there is an optimum amount of a desirable practice, such as participation. When that point is exceeded, there is a decline in returns. In other words, the fact that a practice is desirable does not mean that more of it is more desirable. More of a good thing is not necessarily good.

The diminishing returns associated with various incentives for enlisting in the U.S. Navy were studied in interviews with 1700 civilian males. Substantially different levels of incentives were offered: $1000 versus $3000 bonuses, two years versus four years of free college, and 10 versus 25 percent of base pay for exceptional performance. None of the three larger incentives produced more favorable dispositions to enlist. In fact, the respondents found the 10 percent bonus more attractive, leading the researchers to conclude that not only is more not necessarily better but it "can be worse."[11]

Diminishing returns may not apply to every human situation, but the idea applies so widely that it is of general use. Furthermore, the exact point at which an application becomes excessive will vary with the circumstances; but an excess can be reached with nearly any practice.

Why does the law of diminishing returns exist? Essentially, it is a system concept. It applies because of the complex system relationships of many variables in a situation. The facts state that when an excess of one variable develops, although that variable is desirable, it tends to restrict the operating benefits of other variables so substantially that net effectiveness declines. For example, too much security may lead to less employee initiative and growth. This relationship shows that *organizational effectiveness is achieved not by maximizing one human variable but by working all system variables together in a balanced way.*

EMPLOYEE AUTONOMY AS AN EXAMPLE Employee autonomy is a higher-order need that is frequently emphasized. Some observers speak of autonomy as an ideal, implying that if employees could have complete autonomy, then the ideal state would be achieved. But this kind of reasoning ignores the law of diminishing returns. As shown in Figure 22-5, effectiveness tends to decline when too much autonomy occurs. One reason probably is that excess autonomy prevents coordination toward central goals. Different units of the organization cannot work together, so the labor of employees is wasted.

At the other end of the continuum, the lack of autonomy also is ineffective. When autonomy declines below an appropriate level, the organization fails to develop and use the talents of employees. The result is that effectiveness declines with both excessive use and miserly use of autonomy. Most success is gained in the broad middle ground of use. This relationship produces a humpback curve for autonomy when it is charted with effectiveness.

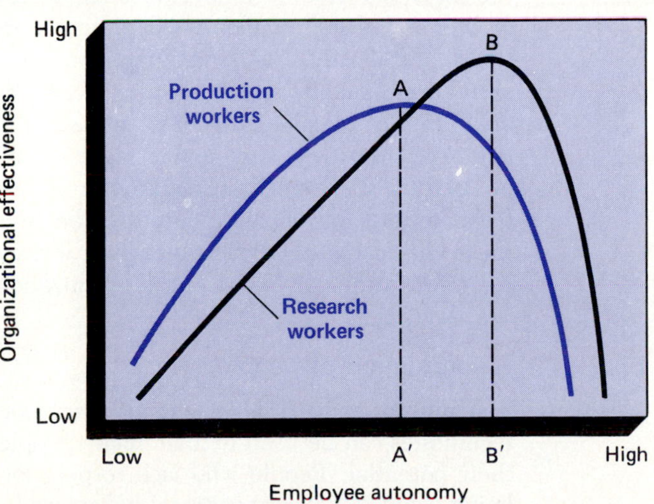

FIGURE 22-5
Assumed application of the law of diminishing returns to employee autonomy

Optimum levels differ and may change.

The humpback curve may vary somewhat with different situations, but the basic curve persists. Figure 22-5 shows a colored curve as it might exist for a group of production workers. Line *AA′* shows the amount of autonomy that produces maximum effectiveness. The black curve shows how diminishing returns might apply to workers in a research unit in the same organization. Line *BB′* shows that much more autonomy can be provided for the research workers before a point of maximum effectiveness is reached. Ten years from now, the curves for both probably will be different because of different conditions. However, whatever the situation, the humpback curve persists and a point of diminishing returns is reached.

The law of diminishing returns serves as a warning that although increases in desirable practices can be beneficial, an excess of any of them will be counterproductive. Moderation is required. People obsessed with building only autonomy or creating maximum employee security will not be contributing to organizational success. There can be too much of a good thing just as there can be too little of it.[12]

OTHER PROBLEMS One problem that has plagued organizational behavior has been the tendency for business firms to have short time horizons for the expected payoff from behavioral programs. This search for a "quick fix" sometimes leads managers to embrace the newest fad, to address the symptoms while neglecting underlying problems, or to fragment their efforts within the firm. The emergence of organizational development programs that focus on systemwide change and the creation of long-term strategic plans for the management of human resources have helped bring about more realistic expectations concerning employees as a productive asset.

Immediate expectations are not realistic.

Can organizational behavior adapt to change?

Another challenge that confronts organizational behavior is to see whether the ideas that have been developed and tested during periods of organizational growth and economic plenty will endure with equal success under new conditions. Specifically, the environment in the future may be marked by some shrinking demand, scarce resources, and more intense competition. When organizations stagnate, decline, or have their survival threatened, there is evidence that stress and conflict increase. Will the same motivational models be useful in these situations? Are different leadership styles called for? Will the trend toward participative processes be reversed? Since no easy answers to these and many other questions exist, it is clear that there is still tremendous room for further development of organizational behavior.

Manipulation of people

A significant concern about organizational behavior is that its knowledge and techniques can be used to manipulate people as well as to help them develop their potential. People who lack respect for the basic dignity of the human being could learn organizational behavior ideas and use them for selfish ends. They could use what they know about motivation or communication to manipulate people without regard for human welfare. People who lack ethical values could use people in unethical ways.

Ethical managers will not manipulate people.

The *philosophy* of organizational behavior is supportive and oriented toward human resources. It seeks to improve the human environment and help people grow toward their human potential. However, the *knowledge and techniques* of this subject may be used for negative as well as positive consequences. This possibility is true of knowledge in most any field, so it is no special limitation of organizational behavior. Nevertheless, we must be cautious that what is known about people is not used to manipulate them. The possibility of manipulation means that people in power in organizations need to be people of high ethical and moral integrity who will not misuse their power. Without ethical leadership, the new knowledge that is learned about people becomes a dangerous instrument for possible misuse. *Ethical leadership* will recognize such guides as the following:[13]

- *Social responsibility* Responsibility to others arises whenever people have power in an organization.
- *Open communication* The organization shall operate as a two-way open system with open receipt of inputs from people and open disclosure of its operations to them.
- *Cost-benefit analysis* In addition to economic costs and benefits, human and social costs and benefits of an activity shall be considered in determining whether to proceed with it.[14]

What is the difference between genuine motivation and manipulation of people? Basically the conditions of use need to be examined. If people understand what is happening and have substantial freedom to make their own choices, they are not being manipulated. But if they are being covertly directed and/or lack free choices, they are being manipulated. This is true whether the manipulator is a social scientist, another employee, or a manager.

As the general population learns more about organizational behavior, it will be more difficult to manipulate them, but the possibility is always there. That is why society needs ethical leaders. But ethical leaders cannot succeed unless there also are ethical followers.

THE FUTURE OF ORGANIZATIONAL BEHAVIOR

Interest in the four goals of describing, predicting, explaining, and controlling human behavior at work has increased throughout the twentieth century. This evolving interest in organizational behavior stems from both a *philosophical* desire by many people to create more humanistic workplaces and a *practical* need to design more productive work environments.[15] As a result of these forces, organizational behavior is now a key part of business school, engineering, and medical school curriculums. Furthermore, its role in both academic programs and corporate management development seminars is expected to increase further as a response to endorsements such as the one described below.

A call for major redirection of the learning objectives for management education and development has been announced by leading educational groups in both the United States and Europe.[16] They began their report by accepting the important need for cognitive knowledge and analytical skills as a basis for competence in functional specialties (such as marketing and finance). In addition, they called for new emphasis on development of noncognitive (affective) skills. These include skills in leadership, communication, organizational change, and negotiation. In effect, managers in the twenty-first century will need to examine their attitudes and values, develop their creativity, and apply their interpersonal skills with enthusiasm to the solution of organizational problems. Organizational behavior provides a strong foundation for these emerging skills.

Theory, research, and practice

The field of organizational behavior has grown in depth and breadth, and it will continue to mature. The keys to its past and future success revolve around the related processes of theory development, research, and managerial practice.

Theory

Theories offer explanations of how and why people think, feel, and act as they do. Theories identify important variables and link them together to form tentative propositions that can be tested through research. Good theories are also practical—they address significant behavioral issues, they contribute to our understanding, and they provide guidelines for managerial thought and action.

Research

Research is the process of gathering and interpreting relevant evidence that will either support a behavioral theory or help change it. Research hypotheses are testable statements connecting the variables in a theory, and they guide the process of data collection. Data are generated through various research methods, such as case studies, field and laboratory experiments, and surveys.[17] The results of these research studies, as reported in various journals, can affect both the theory being examined and future managerial practices.

Neither research nor theory can stand alone and be useful, however. Managers apply the theoretical models to structure their thinking; they use research results to provide relevant guides to their own situations. In these ways, there

Practice

is a natural and healthy flow from theory and research to *practice,* which is the conscious application of conceptual models and research results with the goal of improving individual and organizational performance.

There is also a vital role for managers to play in the other direction—the development of theory and conduct of research. Feedback from practitioners can suggest whether theories and models are simple or complex, realistic or artificial, and useful or useless. Organizations serve as research sites and provide the subjects for various studies. As shown in Figure 22-6, there is a

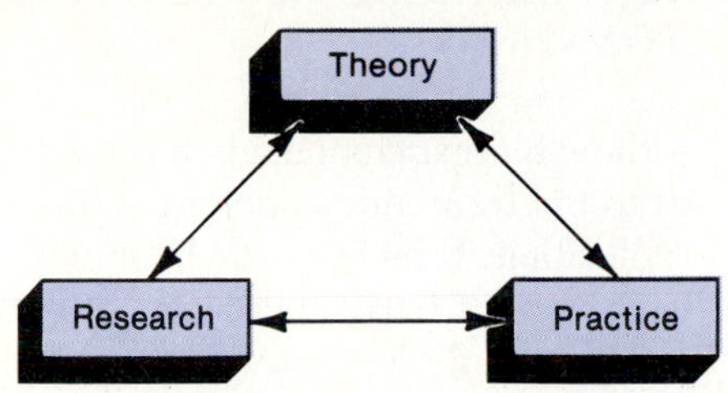

FIGURE 22-6
Theory, research, and practice are closely interrelated and necessary in organizational behavior.

two-way interaction between each pair of the processes, and all three are critical to the future of organizational behavior. Better models must be developed, theory-based research needs to be conducted, and managers need to be receptive to both sources and apply them in their work.

As an example, the development of Vroom's leadership model introduced in Chapter 9 illustrates this interactive process. The authors began with the (contingency) idea that some factors are more important than others in the selection of a leadership approach. Then they identified some of these dimensions, such as the quality and commitment requirements, problem structure, importance of time constraints, and so forth. Through initial research, they classified a number of different approaches that could best be used to deal with different problems. When Vroom and his colleagues observed managers as they used the original leadership model, they found it necessary to revise the theory by modifying the contingency factors, the major approaches recommended, and the relationships between the two. As a result, they now have a newer model which is based on a combination of their original thinking, a series of research studies, and observations of managers. Yet they recognize that this model also will undergo further change.

The point of the illustration is that research is an *ongoing* process through which valuable behavioral knowledge is continually uncovered. Examining a stream of research is like exploring the Mississippi River from its gentle source in northern Minnesota to its powerful ending in the Gulf of Mexico. Just as a trip down the entire river allows us to better appreciate its growth and its impact, so does a review of research help us to better understand how the major ideas in organizational behavior evolved over time.

Fortunately, one of the major trends today is the increasing acceptance of theory and research by practicing managers. This explains why the eighth edition of *Human Behavior at Work* includes more theory and research results than earlier editions. Managers today are more receptive to new models, they support related research, and they experiment more with new ideas. Examples of this increasing dialogue between the world of science and the world of practice abound, as seen in the experiments with sociotechnical systems and autonomous work groups. These illustrate the kinds of organizational practices which, when coupled with theory development and research, will continue to produce improved organizational performance.

THE PROMISE OF A BETTER TOMORROW

Although organizational behavior does have limitations, these should not blind us to the tremendous potential that it has to contribute to the advancement of civilization. It has provided and will provide much improvement in the human environment.[18] By building a better climate for people, organizational behavior will release their creative potential to help solve major social problems. In this way organizational behavior may contribute to social improvements that stretch far beyond the confines of any one organization. A better climate may help some person make a major breakthrough in solar energy, health, or education.

Improved organizational behavior is not easy to apply. But the opportunities are there. It should produce a higher quality of life in which there is improved harmony within each person, among people, and among the organizations of the future.

Terms and concepts for review

Human resource accounting

Investment and organizational climate approaches to human resource accounting

Behavioral bias and tunnel vision

Law of diminishing returns

Manipulation of people

Ethical leadership

Theory

Research

Practice

Discussion questions

1 Now that you have completed the book, discuss basic philosophical differences among the four models of organizational behavior.

2 Compare some of the contingency relationships in stable and changing environments.

3 Form into groups of a few people, and discuss current trends in the macromotivational environment that may have an important influence either positively or negatively, for motivation on the job. If you are employed full time, discuss whether the external environment has influenced your job motivation during the last year. If you are not employed, has the environment influenced your drives to seek a job or to work in particular jobs?

4 Explain the relationship between the various models of organizational behavior and the philosophy behind human resource accounting.

5 Interpret some of the limitations of organizational behavior, including the law of diminishing returns. Discuss application of the law to employee autonomy and one other item.

6 Assume that you work for a firm that suffers a severe economic decline. What behavioral practices might change?

7 Form into research groups, and develop by means of research a list of guides, such as the three given in this chapter, that an ethical leader might follow. Report your list to your entire classroom group, and discuss reasons for each item on your list. Can the manipulation of people be completely stopped?

8 On the basis of library research, prepare a five-minute talk on "What Organizational Behavior Will Be Like Twenty Years from Now."

9 Create a personal action plan indicating how you will contribute to, and continue to learn about, organizational behavior in the future. Include comments about theory, research, and practice.

10 Without reviewing the text or your notes, explain what organizational behavior means to you now. How does this definition differ from your understanding of the term before you read this book?

Incident

THE NEW CONTROLLER

Statewide Electrical Supply, Inc., is a wholesale distributor of electrical supplies serving a population area of 3 million persons. Business has expanded gradually, and during the last eight years the number of accounting clerks has grown from one to twelve. The first clerk employed was Berta Shuler, who was middle-aged, had completed two years of college, and had taken two accounting courses. She proved to be a loyal and capable clerk, so when the department expanded to three people she was promoted to chief accounting clerk with supervisory duties over the other two clerks. She reported to the firm's general manager, Charlie Pastroni, and depended on him to handle accounting decisions that were more than routine.

As the business grew larger, the existing accounting arrangement became inadequate, so Charlie decided to employ a controller to handle all financial and accounting functions of the firm. Berta recognized that she was not qualified to handle accounting and financial affairs of this magnitude, and she did not seek promotion to this job. She did, however, welcome the idea of a controller, because she was overloaded with work and felt that the new controller might help relieve her of some of her more difficult responsibilities.

An additional factor in the firm's decision to establish the position of controller was that there were many complaints about Berta's supervisory ability. She appeared to be effective with the first two or three clerks when the department was small and duties were less complex, but she was unable to handle the larger department and the more complex duties. Her problems seemed to be confined mostly to internal supervision in her department. Other departments in the firm reported that she worked effectively with them, and they expressed some fear that the new controller might upset this favorable working relationship.

Charlie is not sure how to handle the problem of integrating the new controller into the organization. He wants to retain Berta because she is a valuable employee, but he is concerned that if he demotes her from supervisory duties at the time the controller is employed, she may resign.

Questions

1 How do you recommend that the new controller's department be organized?
2 What can be done to improve this situation?

Experiential Exercise

PUTTING ORGANIZATIONAL BEHAVIOR IN PERSPECTIVE

Divide the class into groups of three to five persons each. Have each group address one of the following questions. Each group should select a spokesperson, who will report to the class on the group's conclusions.

1 What are some examples of the most progressive applications of organizational behavior ideas that the group members are familiar with? (Examples may be drawn from personal experience, study of business periodicals, and other sources.)
2 What are the topical areas within organizational behavior that need the most significant development in the next few years? (In other words, where are the present weaknesses in terms of theory and research?)
3 Which of the various models and principles presented in this book do the group members feel will have the greatest immediate personal benefit for them?
4 What are the major issues and critical concerns facing the field of organizational behavior today?

References

1 Richard A. Cosier and Dan R. Dalton, "Search for Excellence, Learn from Japan—Are These Panaceas or Problems?" *Business Horizons*, November–December 1986, pp. 63–68.
2 One analyst sketched out four different scenarios of possible work environments in 1995; all four show some elements of more humane organization. See James O'Toole, "How to Forecast Your Own Working Future," *The Futurist*, February 1982, pp. 5–11.
3 See, for example, Charles Manz and Henry P. Sims, Jr., *SuperLeadership: Leading Others to Lead Themselves to Excellence*, New York: Harper & Row Publishers, Inc., 1988.
4 See, for example, Kenneth A. Kovach, "What Motivates Employees? Workers and Supervisors Give Different Answers," *Business Horizons*, September–October 1987, pp. 58–65.
5 This position is persuasively presented in Tom Peters, *Thriving on Chaos: Handbook for a Management Revolution*, New York: Alfred A. Knopf, Inc., 1987.
6 ". . . On Productivity: A Conversation with William B. Werther, Jr.," *Quarterly Business Reports*, Fall 1987, pp. 7–9. Also see George S. Odiorne, "Human Resource Strategies for the Nineties," *Personnel*, November–December 1984, pp. 13–18.
7 Fred K. Foulkes, "How Top Nonunion Companies Manage Employees," *Harvard Business Review*, September–October 1981, pp. 90–96.
8 Social responsiveness is discussed extensively in William C. Frederick, Keith Davis, and James E. Post, *Business and Society*, 6th ed., New York: McGraw-Hill Book Company, 1988.
9 Further details are available in Eric G. Flamholtz, *Human Resource Accounting:*

Advances in Concepts, Methods, and Applications, San Francisco: Jossey-Bass Inc., Publishers, 1985. A critique of the method is William D. Campbell, "A Note on the Utility of Human Resource Accounting," paper presented at the National Academy of Management Conference, Boston, August 1985.

10 This discussion is adapted from Keith Davis, "A Law of Diminishing Returns in Organizational Behavior?" *Personnel Journal*, December 1975, pp. 616–619.

11 Abraham K. Korman, Albert S. Glickman, and Robert L. Frey, Jr., "More Is Not Better: Two Failures of Incentive Theory," *Journal of Applied Psychology*, April 1981, pp. 255–259.

12 A discussion of the "myth of optimization" is in Neil Agnew and John Brown, "Limited Potential: Human Relations Then and Now," *Business Horizons*, November–December 1986, pp. 34–42.

13 Adapted from Keith Davis, "Five Propositions for Social Responsibility," *Business Horizons*, June 1975, pp. 19–24. A current perspective on social responsibility, social responsiveness, and social rectitude is William C. Frederick, "Toward CSR_3: Why Ethical Analysis Is Indispensable and Unavoidable in Corporate Affairs," *California Management Review*, Winter 1986, pp. 126–141.

14 A comprehensive resource on this topic is Wayne F. Cascio, *Costing Human Resources: The Financial Impact of Behavior in Organizations*, 2d ed., Boston: PWS-Kent Publishing Company, 1987.

15 One author has suggested that more emphasis needs to be placed on the role of employees in creating the work environment, and less on the impact of structure, processes, and technology; see Benjamin Schneider, "The People Make the Place," *Personnel Psychology*, Autumn 1987, pp. 437–453.

16 These were some of the conclusions of a joint project of the American Assembly of Collegiate Schools of Business (AACSB) and the European Foundation for Management Development (EFMD), as reported in Clarence C. Walton (ed.), *Managers for the XXI Century: Their Education and Development*, Washington: AACSB, 1981.

17 For a discussion of one method, see Allen Lee, "The Scientific Basis for Conducting Case Studies of Organizations," *Academy of Management Proceedings '85*, Boston: Academy of Management, 45th annual meeting, August 1985, pp. 320–324.

18 A research example providing moderate support for this contention is Dennis M. Daley, "Humanistic Management and Organizational Success: The Effect of Job and Work Environment Characteristics on Organizational Effectiveness, Public Responsiveness, and Job Satisfaction," *Public Personnel Management*, Summer 1986, pp. 131–142. However, a warning that we should have realistic expectations from behavioral approaches is in Barry M. Staw, "Organizational Psychology and the Pursuit of the Happy/Productive Worker," *California Management Review*, Summer 1986, pp. 40–53.

For additional reading

Flamholtz, Eric, *Human Resource Accounting: Advances in Concepts, Methods, and Applications*, 2d ed., San Francisco: Jossey-Bass Inc., Publishers, 1985.

Manz, Charles, and Henry P. Sims, Jr., *SuperLeadership: Leading Others to Lead Themselves to Excellence*, New York: Harper & Row, Publishers, Inc., 1988.

Odiorne, George S., *The Human Side of Management: Management by Integration and Self-Control*, Lexington, Mass.: Lexington Books, 1987.

Rosenzweig, Mark R., and Lyman W. Porter (eds.), *Annual Review of Psychology*, vol. 38, Palo Alto, Calif.: Annual Reviews, Inc., 1987. (Especially see "Organizational Behavior: Some New Directions for I/O Psychology.")

Schneider, Benjamin, and F. David Schoorman, *Facilitating Work Effectiveness: Concepts and Procedures*, Lexington, Mass.: Lexington Books, 1986.

PART 7 Case problems

INTRODUCTION

Case problems provide a useful medium for testing and applying some of the ideas in this textbook. They bring reality to abstract ideas about organizational behavior. All the case problems that follow are true situations recorded by case research. Certain case details are disguised, but none of the cases is a fictional creation. All names are disguised, and any similarity to actual persons is purely coincidental.

These cases have a decision-making emphasis in the sense that they end at a point that leaves managers and/or employees with certain decisions to make. Most of the cases emphasize decisional problems of managers. One decision often is: Do I have a further problem? If that decision is in the affirmative, then further analysis must be made. What problems exist? Why are they problems? What can be done about them within the resource limits available (i.e., what alternatives are available)? Finally, what *should* be done to solve this particular problem in this specific organization? This is the reality that every manager faces in operating situations. There is no escaping it.

Even a person who does not plan to be a manager can gain much from analyzing these cases, because all employees need to develop their own analytical skills about human behavior in order to work successfully with their associates and *with management* in organizations. Placing yourself in the employee role in a case, you can ask: Why do my associates act the way they do in this situation? Why is management acting the way it is in this instance? Was there something in my behavior that caused these actions? How can I change my behavior in order to work more effectively with the organization and my associates and thereby reach my goals more easily?

Since these case problems describe real situations, they include both good and bad practices. These cases are not presented as examples of good management, effective organizational behavior, bad management, or ineffective organizational behavior. Readers may make these judgments for themselves. However, the primary value in studying cases lies in the development of analytical skills and the application of organizational behavior knowledge to solve challenging problems.

CASE 1

Dudley Lodge

Professor Henry Ellis taught management in a large Midwestern state university. On August 5 of last year, at about 6:30 P.M., he received a long-distance telephone call from the factory town of Corbin, 30 miles distant. The caller was Dudley Lodge, a student in his course called "Organizational Behavior" during the previous spring. After the necessary exchange of pleasantries, Lodge said that he had gone to work for the Roanoke Company and was having trouble. Lodge reminded Professor Ellis that he had told the students of his class he would be glad to help them when they were in business, and Lodge wanted help. He wanted to visit Professor Ellis that night because he had to have an answer to his problem by the next morning. Professor Ellis encouraged the visit and made an appointment for 8 P.M.

While he was waiting for Lodge to arrive, Professor Ellis recalled that he did not know Lodge very well, but Lodge had impressed him as a young, friendly, intelligent student. Lodge made an A in the course, although he was not a business major.* Professor Ellis also remembered that near the end of the course he had told his students, "Your formal education and training will not provide you with all the answers in your job. If I can help you any time, please call on me. Your education does not end at graduation." When Lodge arrived, he appeared emotionally upset and exhausted. He was impatient to describe his problem. He agreed to let Professor Ellis record his comments on a tape recorder which had been used for role playing in the class he attended. Professor Ellis mostly listened, occasionally asking a question or interjecting a remark such as "Tell me more about that." Lodge's description of his problem was as follows.

*Lodge's placement file, which Professor Ellis examined the next morning in the Placement Office, College of Engineering, showed that Lodge had no business experience. He had a farm background. He did not work any of his way through college. He was captain of artillery in Army ROTC during his senior year and program chairman of the student chapter of the American Society of Mechanical Engineers. He made above-average grades. Letters of reference from his professors, a banker, a doctor, and a minister stated that he was honest, sincere, deeply religious, hard-working, and somewhat retiring in nature.

LODGE'S DESCRIPTION OF HIS PROBLEM

I believe this case will be clearer if I present some of the background of my experiences with the company before I relate the facts in the immediate problem. I was accepted for employment with the Roanoke Company through one of its regular application forms without a personal interview. This was an irregular procedure for the company, and I do not know why it was done in this case; however, I had no reason to be concerned about this until after my arrival in Cleveland.

When I reported to the central company offices in Cleveland on June 15, I was interviewed by both Mr. Sharp, the director, and Mr. Thomas, the assistant director of the student training course. This interview seemed quite routine. These men had my written application before them with all my personal data, yet they both seemed somewhat surprised by two facts: first, that I was married, and secondly, that I was a mechanical engineer. I was not married when I made out the application, and thus this fact did not show on the form. The second fact, that I was a mechanical engineer, was shown quite plainly on the application, and I cannot understand why it was such a surprising fact unless it was an important consideration in the Cleveland plant where only electrical equipment was manufactured. There was no serious discussion over any of my qualifications, and after a few humorous remarks about my being newly married, I was assigned to Department W-3, small motor and generator winding.

At this interview I made a special point of informing Sharp that I was interested in steam turbine design and testing, as stated in my application, that I had specialized in this work in college, and that I should like assignment to this work in the Corbin plant of the company* where this type of research and testing was done. My request was casually and carefully avoided at this time; but when it was repeated to Sharp in a short talk with him about two weeks later, he informed me that there was no student opening available in Corbin. Thomas suggested that I might be interested in transformer work, but I could see no mechanical problems involved in this, so I requested to remain in motive power if I could not be transferred to Corbin.

The day after this second interview, Sharp called me into his office at the end of the day and asked me if I would like to teach a course of physics and trigonometry to the apprentice machinists. I accepted this offer and was enjoying the work to such an extent that I had about made up my mind to be satisfied with the work in Cleveland when, on July 13, Sharp again called me to his office and told me there was an opening in steam turbine work at Corbin if I wanted it. As a result of this conference I reported to the plant in Corbin on July 15.

*The company had several large plants located in various parts of the United States. The Corbin plant was located about three hundred miles from Cleveland.

When I arrived in Corbin, I was received quite cordially by Mr. Barry, director of student training at this plant, who called my wife into the office and then conducted both of us on a short tour of the plant. He suggested that I take two or three days to find a place to live, look around the plant for a day, and then report back to his office for assignment.

Two days later when I reported to Barry's office, he took me around to the many shops and offices and introduced me to the shop supervisors and department heads. He made a special visit to the production control department, supervised by a Mr. Schmidt, and there told me that I would not be placed immediately on the student training course but would be assigned temporarily to this department to relieve some of the employees who were going on vacation. Barry then left me with Schmidt, who took me immediately to the desk of a Mr. Langner, a production expediter, whose place I was to take while the latter was on vacation for a month.

The production control department, including Schmidt's desk, was all together in one large room. Langner spent the rest of the day with me in an attempt to familiarize me with the work involved in "chasing" an order through the intricacies of design, machining or purchase, testing, inspection, storage, and shipment. It seemed to me that the details involved would be impossible to grasp in several months, and yet I was to take over this job on the following day.

Frankly I was scared. I had never seen the inside of a large manufacturing plant before. I had hardly seen the working parts of a steam turbine, and here I was to have the responsibility of expediting the manufacture of a 190,000-kilowatt turbogenerator with all auxiliaries for the National Utility Company. I went home that evening a very bewildered and "sick" production expediter, or "chaser," as the employees in the shops sneeringly called us.

The next weeks passed almost as a nightmare. In my own confusion it seemed that there was no order, no scheme to follow, and that everyone was too busy to realize that I was a green country kid who hardly knew one end of a turbine from the other. I tried conscientiously to memorize shop orders, purchase orders, delivery dates, promise dates, the names of parts, the names of shop supervisors, and a few other details all at the same time, and it seemed like a hopeless task.

The other expediters were all very friendly and helpful, but Schmidt seemed to assume that I was a "full-grown expediter" and expected me to replace Langner in all respects. He told me that he would expect me to know the exact status of my order at all times and that I should keep a large progress chart on my wall up to date by making daily changes each morning. To be sure that I understood this, he called me to his desk each morning for a complete report. If I was uncertain as to the exact status of some operation, he was very impatient. His loud-talking manner and his habitual and routine use of profanity irritated me. These morning interviews took on the aspects of an inquisition. I confided in another of the expediters who seemed sympathetic, and he told me to come to the office early, to get the progress chart up to date, and to spend most of the rest of the day out in the shops away from Schmidt. None of the expediters liked him, and they avoided him as much as possible.

Acting on the advice of the other expediter, I began spending most of the day in the shops. I made friends with the shop supervisors and found that I was enjoying the time spent in discussing their work with them; I also found that they were more willing to give me the information that I required relative to my order.

I also learned that the shop employees had a contempt for the production control department and refused to cooperate with the time-and-motion-study specialists when they came through to study machine operations. This association gave me a different view of shop relations, and I found myself sympathizing with the shop attitude. This contact made it more difficult for me to conscientiously put the "pressure on" the shop supervisors to make them meet promise dates on the machining operations for my job.

In spite of this tactic of remaining out of the office as much as possible, I managed to keep my progress chart up to date by getting to the office early. I reported to work on the regular student schedule of 7:30 A.M. and left work at 4:18 P.M. In this way I was in the office well ahead of the regular office staff. My order was keeping reasonably well to its schedule, and I had no serious complaints from Schmidt. From time to time during the day I would meet him in one of the shops, and on occasion he would stop me and discuss the progress of the work. On these occasions I noticed that he was much more friendly and talked in a much more casual and less "official" tone of voice. He never criticized me for not spending more time in the office.

Late yesterday afternoon, however, just before quitting time, I learned from the engineering department that there had been a mistake made in the machining of the flange bolts for the low-pressure turbine casing. I was on my way to the automatic screw machine shop to stop production when I met Schmidt in one of the shops. He stopped me rather abruptly and the following conversation took place:

Lodge, what's the status of the shaft-centering plugs for the low-pressure turbine?

I am not certain, Mr. Schmidt, but I don't think any work has been done on them. The shaft forgings are not due in the shops for nearly two weeks yet.

Damn it, I told you that I wanted to know the exact status of that entire job at all times. I happen to know that those plugs have not even been put on production order yet, and by damn, I want them done tonight and on my desk tomorrow morning. Put them on overtime for tonight.

Yes sir, I'll see Hill in the light-machine shop about it right away.

After this conversation with Schmidt, I made arrangements with Hill, the light-machine shop supervisor, to have the centering plugs placed on overtime order and to have them finished by morning when I would pick them up. I saw Hill make out the order and place it in the overtime work basket. The operation was simple and would require about two hours of work on a power cutoff saw and a lathe.

By the time I had finished in the light-machine shop, the automatic screw machine shop, which was working only one shift per day, was closed, and I was unable to stop production on the flange bolts. I had, however, secured one of the bolts and back at my desk had confirmed the fact that they were ½ inch too short. I planned to stop production on them the first thing the next morning. While at my desk I checked my production schedule and found that the turbine shaft, for which the centering plugs were so urgently needed, was not due from the foundry and forge shop until August 21. I then went home feeling that the day had gone very well.

When I arrived at the office this morning I brought the progress chart up to date, made a few notes for the work for the day, and started out to the shops. I took the flange bolt along with me and was going to the automatic screw shop right after I went by the light-machine shop to see about the centering plugs. The time must have been almost 8 A.M., and as I passed through No. 2 shop, I met Schmidt and the following discussion took place:

Lodge, are those centering plugs finished?

I'm on my way to see about them right now, but I have an urgent stop order for these flange bolts and—

Damn it, I told you to have those plugs on my desk when I came in. By damn, Lodge, when I give you an order I expect it to be obeyed. (He grabbed me roughly by the arm.) Come on, we're going over to the shop to see about those plugs.

(I jerked away from Schmidt's grasp.) Keep your hands off me and stop cussing me, or I'll beat your damn brains out with this bolt! I'm going to put a stop order on those bolts, and then report you to Mr. Ball (the plant superintendent). Those plugs are not needed for nearly another month anyway.

After the above conversation Schmidt turned and walked hurriedly toward his office. I was, by this time, very nervous and upset. I did, however, regain enough composure to place the hold order on the flange bolts and then went to the light-machine shop to see about the centering plugs. I had, by this time, decided it best to talk to Barry about the whole thing before going to the plant superintendent with the matter.

However, upon my arrival at the light-machine shop I learned from talking to Hill that the centering plugs had not been finished because after I talked with Hill yesterday afternoon, Schmidt had come in and given a special order for overtime work that involved all the available lathes and operators for the entire night shift. This made it impossible for work to be done on the centering plugs, and I found them cut off of bar stock, but no more work done on them. This information "made me see red," and I headed for Schmidt's office.

By the time I had arrived at Schmidt's office, I had become rather nervous, wrought up, and very angry about the whole state of things. I went directly to Schmidt's desk and told him, in something of a loud voice, I'm sure, that he was "the double-crossing so-and-so" that had stopped work on the centering plugs, that it was a dirty frame-up of me on his part; and that as of now he could get someone else to take over the job of expediter; that it was a job for a stool pigeon, anyway; and that I refused to do any more of his dirty work; and that I would not take any more of his cussing.

The effects of these remarks were somewhat awe-inspiring in the office, to say the least. Schmidt jumped from his desk and started toward me; but a very calm, quiet, purchasing agent, Mr. Andrews, intervened and restored a bit of order before things got completely out of control. Schmidt got in several "air-burning" profane remarks and told me that he was going to report me to the plant superintendent.

Andrews went with me to my desk, advised me to go immediately to see Barry, and offered to go along with me as a witness. I gladly accepted his offer, and we went over to Barry's office and told him the whole story. He talked to us for about half an hour and then wanted me to go with him back to Schmidt's office to talk to him. This I refused to do, and both Barry and Andrews left to talk to Schmidt.

After talking to Schmidt for a long time, Barry returned and told me that Schmidt admitted that both of us "acted like fools" and that he was ready to forget the matter, if I would, and he would like me to continue in the work until Langner returned. Barry told me that if I would go with him and apologize to Schmidt, work for him until Langner returned, and "keep my nose clean," he would transfer me to the regular student training course just as soon as I could be relieved. I told him that I would not do so, the way I felt at the present time, but that I would think it over during the night and would give him an answer tomorrow. That is why I need your help, Professor Ellis. I am all mixed up and don't know what to do. I shall appreciate your advice and shall let you know the outcome.

Study guides

1 Why do you think Lodge came to Professor Ellis for help?

2 What mistakes did the "company" make in "training" Lodge? Who made these mistakes? Explain.

3 Why do you think Schmidt acted the way he did? Why do you think Lodge reacted the way he did? Did the two people "understand" each other?

4 What are the primary problems existing at the end of the case?

5 What action should be taken to help solve the main problems of the case? By Lodge? Barry? Schmidt? Others? Give specific behavioral reasons for proposed actions.

6 Discuss this case in terms of basic organizational behavior ideas that you have covered to this date, such as social systems, organizational climate, the psychological contract, expectancy theory, equity theory, and models of organizational behavior.

Role-playing situations

1 Assume that you are Professor Ellis, and then continue the conversation with Lodge.
2 Role-play the meeting of Lodge and Barry on August 6.
3 Role-play the meeting, if any, of Lodge, Barry, and Schmidt on August 6.

CASE 2

The Consolidated Life Company*

PART I

It all started so positively. Three days after graduating with his degree in business administration, Mike Wilson started his first day at a prestigious insurance company—Consolidated Life. He worked in the Policy Issue Department. The work of the department was mostly clerical and did not require a high degree of technical knowledge. Given the repetitive and mundane nature of the work, the successful worker had to be consistent and willing to grind out paperwork.

Rick Belkner was the division's vice-president, "the man in charge" at the time. Rick was an actuary by training, a technical professional whose leadership style was laissez-faire. He was described in the division as "the mirror of whomever was the strongest personality around him." It was also common knowledge that Rick made $60,000 a year while he spent his time doing crossword puzzles.

Mike was hired as a management trainee and promised a supervisory assignment within a year. However, because of a management reorganization, it was only six weeks before he was placed in charge of an eight-person unit.

The reorganization was intended to streamline workflow, upgrade and combine the clerical jobs, and make greater use of the computer system. It was a drastic departure from the old way of doing things and created a great deal of animosity and anxiety among the clerical staff.

Management realized that a flexible supervisory style was necessary to pull off the reorganization without immense turnover, so they gave their supervisors a free hand to run their units as they saw fit. Mike used this latitude to implement group meetings and training classes in his unit. In addition he assured all members raises if they worked hard to attain them. By working long hours, participating in the mundane tasks with his unit, and being flexible in his management style, he was able to increase productivity, reduce errors, and reduce lost time. Things improved so dramatically that he was noticed by upper management and earned a reputation as a "superstar" despite being viewed as free spirited and unorthodox. The feeling was that his loose, people-oriented management style could be tolerated because his results were excellent.

*This case was prepared by Joseph Weiss, Mark Wahlstrom, and Edward Marshall, and is used with permission of the authors and the publisher, Elsevier Science Publishing Co., Inc.

A chance for advancement

After a year, Mike received an offer from a different Consolidated Life division located across town. Mike was asked to manage an office in the marketing area. The pay was excellent and it offered an opportunity to turn around an office in disarray. The reorganization in his present division at Consolidated was almost complete and most of his mentors and friends in management had moved on to other jobs. Mike decided to accept the offer.

In his exit interview he was assured that if he ever wanted to return, a position would be made for him. It was clear that he was held in high regard by management and staff alike. A huge party was thrown to send him off.

The new job was satisfying for a short time but it became apparent to Mike that it did not have the long-term potential he was promised. After bringing on a new staff, computerizing the office, and auditing the books, he began looking for a position that would both challenge him and give him the autonomy he needed to be successful.

Eventually word got back to his former vice-president, Rick Belkner, at Consolidated Life that Mike was looking for another job. Rick offered Mike a position with the same pay he was now receiving and control over a 14-person unit in his old division. After considering other options, Mike decided to return to his old division feeling that he would be able to progress steadily over the next several years.

Enter Jack Greely; return Mike Wilson

Upon his return to Consolidated Life, Mike became aware of several changes that had taken place in the six months since his departure. The most important change was the hiring of a new divisional senior vice-president, Jack Greely. Jack had been given total authority to run the division. Rick Belkner now reported to Jack.

Jack's reputation was that he was tough but fair. It was necessary for people in Jack's division to do things his way and "get the work out."

Mike also found himself reporting to one of his former peers, Kathy Miller, who had been promoted to manager during the reorganization. Mike had always "hit it off" with Kathy and foresaw no problems in working with her.

After a week Mike realized the extent of the changes that had occurred. Gone was the loose, casual atmosphere that had marked his first tour in the division. Now, a stricter, task-oriented management doctrine was practiced. Morale of the supervisory staff had decreased to an alarming level. Jack Greely was the major topic of conversation in and around the division. People joked that MBO now meant "management by oppression."

Mike was greeted back with comments like "Welcome to prison" and "Why would you come back here? You must be desperate!" It seemed like everyone was looking for new jobs or transfers. Their lack of desire was reflected in the poor quality of work being done.

Mike's idea: supervisors' forum

Mike felt that a change in the management style of his boss (Jack) was necessary in order to improve a frustrating situation. Realizing that it would be difficult to affect his style directly, Mike requested permission from Rick Belkner to form a Supervisors' Forum for all the managers on Mike's level in the division. Mike explained that the purpose would be to enhance the existing management-training program. The Forum would include weekly meetings, guest speakers, and discussions of topics relevant to the division and the industry. Mike thought the forum would show Greely that he was serious about both his job and improving morale in the division. Rick gave the O.K. for an initial meeting.

The meeting took place and ten supervisors who were Mike's peers in the company eagerly took the opportunity to "Blue Sky" it. There was a euphoric attitude about the group as they drafted their statement of intent. It read as follows:

TO: Rick Belkner
FROM: New Issue Services Supervisors
SUBJECT: Supervisors' Forum

On Thursday, June 11, the Supervisors' Forum held its first meeting. The objective of the meeting was to identify common areas of concern among us and to determine topics that we might be interested in pursuing.

The first area addressed was the void that we perceive exists in the management-training program. As a result of conditions beyond anyone's control, many of us over the past year have held supervisory duties without the benefit of formal training or proper experience. Therefore, what we propose is that we utilize the Supervisors' Forum as a vehicle with which to enhance the existing management-training program. The areas that we hope to affect with this supplemental training are: a) morale/job satisfaction; b) quality of work and service; c) productivity; and d) management expertise as it relates to the life insurance industry. With these objectives in mind, we have outlined below a list of possible activities that we would like to pursue.

1. Further utilization of the existing "in-house" training programs provided for manager trainees and supervisors, i.e., Introduction to Supervision, E.E.O., and Coaching and Counseling.
2. A series of speakers from various sections in the company. This would help expose us to the technical aspects of their departments and their managerial style.
3. Invitations to outside speakers to address the Forum on management topics such as managerial development, organizational structure and behavior, business policy, and the insurance industry. Suggested speakers could be area college professors, consultants, and state insurance officials.
4. Outside training and visits to the field. This could include attendance at seminars concerning management theory and development relative to the insurance industry. Attached is a representative sample of a program we would like to have considered in the future.

In conclusion, we hope that this memo clearly illustrates what we are attempting to accomplish with this program. It is our hope that the above outline will be able to give the Forum credibility and establish it as an effective tool for all levels of management within New Issue. By supplementing our on-the-job training with a series of speakers and classes, we aim to develop prospective management personnel with a broad perspective of both the life insurance industry and management's role in it. Also, we would like to extend an invitation to the underwriters to attend any programs at which the topic of the speaker might be of interest to them.

cc: J. Greely
Managers

The group felt the memo accurately and diplomatically stated their dissatisfaction with the current situation. However, they pondered what the results of their actions would be and what else they could have done.

PART II

An emergency management meeting was called by Rick Belkner at Jack Greely's request to address the "union" being formed by the supervisors. Four general managers, Rick Belkner, and Jack Greely were at that meeting. During the meeting it was suggested the Forum be disbanded to "put them in their place." However, Rick Belkner felt that if "guided" in the proper direction the Forum could die from lack of interest. His stance was adopted but it was common knowledge that Jack Greely was strongly opposed to the group and wanted its founders dealt with. His comment was "It's not a democracy and they're not a union. If they don't like it here, then they can leave." An investigation was begun by the managers to determine who the main authors of the memo were so they could be dealt with.

About this time, Mike's unit had made a mistake on a case, which Jack Greely was embarrassed to admit to his boss. This embarrassment was more than Jack Greely cared to take from Mike Wilson. At the managers' staff meeting that day Jack stormed in and declared that the next supervisor to "screw up" was out the door. He would permit no more embarrassments of his division and repeated his earlier statement about "people leaving if they didn't like it here." It was clear to Mike and everyone else present that Mike Wilson was a marked man.

Mike had always been a loose, amiable supervisor. The major reason his units had been successful was the attention he paid to each individual and how they interacted with the group. He had a reputation for fairness, was seen as an excellent judge of personnel for new positions, and was noted for his ability to turn around people who had been in trouble. He motivated people through a dynamic, personable style and was noted for his general lack of regard for rules. He treated rules as obstacles to management and usually used his own discretion as to what was important. His office had a sign saying "Any fool can manage by rules. It takes an uncommon man to manage without any." It was an approach that flew in the face of company policy, but it had been overlooked in the past because of his results. However, because of Mike's actions with the Supervisors' Forum, he was now regarded as a thorn in the side, not a superstar, and his oddball style only made things worse.

Faced with the fact that he was rumored to be out the door, Mike sat down to appraise the situation.

PART III

Mike decided on the following course of action:

1 Keep the Forum alive but moderate its tone so it didn't step on Jack Greely's toes.

2 Don't panic. Simply outwork and outsmart the rest of the division. This plan included a massive retraining and remotivation of his personnel. He implemented weekly meetings, cross training with other divisions, and a lot of interpersonal "stroking" to motivate the group.

3 Evoke praise from vendors and customers through excellent service and direct that praise to Jack Greely.

The results after eight months were impressive. Mike's unit improved the speed of processing 60% and lowered errors 75%. His staff became the most highly trained in the division. Mike had a file of several letters to Jack Greely that praised the unit's excellent service. In addition, the Supervisors' Forum had grudgingly attained credibility, although the scope of activity was restricted. Mike had even improved to the point of submitting reports on time as a concession to management.

Mike was confident that the results would speak for themselves. However, one month before his scheduled promotion and one month after an excellent merit raise in recognition of his exceptional work record, he was called into his supervisor's, Kathy Miller's, office. She informed him that after long and careful consideration the decision had been made to deny his promotion because of his lack of attention to detail. This did not mean he was not a good supervisor, just that he needed to follow more instead of taking the lead. Mike was stunned and said so. But, before he said anything else, he asked to see Rick Belkner and Jack Greely the next day.

The showdown

Sitting face to face with Rick and Jack, Mike asked if they agreed with the appraisal Kathy had discussed with him. They both said they did. When asked if any other supervisor surpassed his ability and results, each stated Mike was one of the best, if not *the* best they had. Then why, Mike asked, would they deny him a promotion when others of less ability were approved. The answer came from Jack: "It's nothing personal, but we just don't like you. We don't like your management style. You're an oddball. We can't run a division with ten supervisors all doing different things. What kind of a business do you think we're running here? We need people who conform to our style and methods so we can measure their results objectively. There is no room for subjective interpretation. It's our feeling that if you really put your mind to it, you can be an excellent manager. It's just that you now create trouble and rock the boat. We don't need that. It doesn't matter if you're the best now, sooner or later as you go up the ladder, you will be forced to pay more attention to administrative duties and you won't handle them well. If we correct your bad habits now, we think you can go far."

Mike was shocked. He turned to face Rick and blurted out nervously, "You mean it doesn't matter what my results are? All that matters is how I do things?" Rick leaned back in his chair and said in a casual tone, "In so many words, Yes."

Mike left the office knowing that his career at Consolidated was over and immediately started looking for a new job. What had gone wrong?

Study guides

1 This case can be treated as a three-part predictive exercise.

   a Read only Part I, and stop. How do you think the supervisors' "statement of intent" will be received by top management at Consolidated Life?

   b Read Part II. What do you think Mike will do now? What do you recommend that he do?

   c Read Part III. Should Mike try to continue his career with Consolidated Life, or find a job elsewhere? How does the self-fulfilling prophecy affect this situation? If he leaves, do you think he can be successful in another organization?

2 Was Mike wise to attempt to change the behavior of his boss? Was it ethical? What methods have you read about that he could have used? What would you have done differently?

3 How do you think that Mike would describe the organizational culture at Consolidated Life? What is an employee's responsibility for "reading" a firm's culture, and for adjusting to it?

4 Evaluate the memo that Mike wrote. Now assess the fairness and motivational impact of the feedback that Mike received. Will it be useful in changing his behavior? What advice could you have given Rick and Jack prior to the meeting with Mike?

CASE 3

The Video Electronics Company

Frank Simpson, president and controlling stockholder of the Video Electronics Company, now in its tenth year, was faced with the problem of gearing his plant to meet both increased production demands brought on by the expanding electronics industry and also increased competition from other producers of his line of products. The plant tripled its employees during the past year, but production per worker decreased nearly 20 percent and costs rose nearly to the break-even point. For the preceding quarter, profit on sales was less than 1 percent and profit on invested capital was under 3 percent. This was one-fourth of what Simpson considered normal.

The company employed mostly unskilled labor who were trained by the company. Employees were not represented by a labor union. All employees were paid hourly wages rather than incentive wages.

The company was founded by Simpson and a few investor friends for production of a narrow line of specialized small electronics parts that were sold to other manufacturers. It grew slowly and had a labor force of only 105 workers at the beginning of last year. Its reputation for quality was excellent. This reputation of quality was the primary reason for a flood of orders from new clients in the spring of last year, requiring the firm to triple its labor force by July. Simpson remarked, "I didn't seek those orders. *They* came to us. I didn't want to expand that fast, but what could I do? If you want to stay in business, you can't tell your customers you are too busy to sell them anything."

The company was located in a manufacturing town of 15,000 people in rural New York, about 60 miles from any large town. Enough untrained people were available locally for hiring for the expansion, which required the operation of two shifts instead of one. Management forecasts indicated that the expansion would be permanent, with the additional possibility of moderate growth during the next five years or longer.

Simpson, in consultation with the board of directors, concluded that he needed to establish the new position of general manager of the plant so that he (Simpson) could spend more of his time on high-level work and less of it ironing out production difficulties. He also concluded that under present conditions he needed to build an industrial engineering staff that could both cope with present production problems and give his company the developmental work that was needed to stay ahead of his competitors.

Almost all his present supervisory personnel had been with the company since the year it was founded. They were all skilled people in their particular phases of the operations, but Simpson felt that none of them had the training or overall insight into company problems to take charge as general manager.

After much thought, Simpson decided to employ a general manager from outside the company. This person would report directly to him and would have full responsibility for production of the product and development of a top-notch industrial engineering department. Simpson called a meeting of all his supervisory personnel and explained his decision to them in detail. He described the need for this plan of action and stressed the necessity for the utmost in cooperation. The older supervisors did not seem to be pleased with this turn of events but promised that they would cooperate fully with the new manager.

About four months after his meeting with his supervisors, Simpson found a suitable general manager, John Rider. Rider, age thirty-six, was a mechanical engineer who had been a general supervisor in a large Philadelphia electronics plant. One of his first jobs as general manager was to find a qualified person to develop the industrial engineering function. Paul Green, an industrial engineer thirty-one years of age, was hired from the industrial engineering department of a large steel company in Pittsburgh. Green had an M.B.A., a good academic record, and two years of experience.

Green and Rider both felt that the company was in bad condition in relation to machine utilization, employee utilization, waste, and reject rates. On the basis of their first impressions of the production facilities they estimated that production management and industrial engineering changes might be able to increase productivity at least 25 percent and reduce unit costs 35 percent.

Green wanted time to get acquainted with the processes and the supervisory personnel before recommending major improvements. Rider granted this wish, so Green spent two months getting acquainted with the supervisors. During this period he recommended to Rider only minor changes that the supervisors seemed to go along with except for minor disagreement. However, after this period Simpson, Rider, and Green felt that major steps had to be taken to improve both production and quality. They decided that the first industrial engineering project should be a study of production processes, department by department. This study was to cover every operation done on the products. All processes were to be put in writing, since many of the processes had developed without anyone ever writing down just how they were to be performed. Several of the supervisors were the only ones who understood how certain operations were to be set up and performed, and any supervisor who left the company often took valuable knowledge that was difficult to replace.

At the next supervisory meeting (of all management personnel), Simpson announced the plan for the production study. No estimated completion date for the study was given. No comments were made by the production supervisors, but it was plain to Rider and Green that several of the older supervisors were not happy about the idea. Simpson tried to get across the idea that full cooperation was required and that the company had "to meet its competition or go out of business."

Green started the survey the following week. There was outward rebellion in some cases, but he smoothed this over by discussing with the supervisor the reasons for the survey and then leaving that department alone for a few days. Green thought he was convincing the people who objected, so he proceeded with the study without comment to either Rider or Simpson about the resistance.

About five weeks after Green started the study, he and Rider left town together on a business trip that kept them away from the plant for two days. On the night of the second day one of the second-shift supervisors telephoned Simpson, who happened to be working late at the office. The supervisor said that a group of them would like to talk to Simpson. Since many of these supervisors had known Simpson for a long time and called him by his first name, he did not object and told them to "come on up."

The group that arrived consisted of all supervisors with more than one year's company seniority. First-shift supervisors were there, even though they had been off duty for three hours. As soon as the group arrived, it was apparent to Simpson that they were troubled about something and that this was no social call. All the supervisors entered his office, and one older man who had been supervisor for nine years, Charles Warren, acted as speaker for the group.

"Frank," he said, "all of us here have been in this game for a good many years. We know more about this business than anyone else around here, and we don't like people standing around in our departments watching what we are doing. We also don't like the idea of some young guy telling us that we should do this and that to improve our production and quality. This industry is different, and those new ideas about industrial engineering just won't work for us. We want you to tell that new guy, Green, that his ideas won't work for a company like this." Warren then paused to give Simpson a chance to answer. The other supervisors stood there quietly.

Study guides

1 If you were Simpson, what would you do now? What would you do later, if anything? What behavioral models and ideas are involved in your decisions?

2 Should Simpson have permitted the supervisors to see him, since they now report directly to Rider?

3 What kinds of changes are taking place in this case? What are the effects of these changes? What ideas about change will help you in dealing with this situation?

4 Does the learning curve for change apply in this case? Discuss.

Role-playing situations

1 You are Simpson. Reply to Warren and the other supervisors gathered in your office.
2 Have people play the roles of Simpson, Rider, and Green in a meeting in Simpson's office to discuss this situation on the day Rider and Green return from their trip.
3 Role-play the supervisory meeting in which Simpson announces to his supervisors the production process study. Include people in the roles of Rider and Green.

CASE 4

Elite Electric Company*

Elite Electric Company is a moderately small manufacturing subsidiary of a large European conglomerate. The company manufactures electric components supplied to its parent company for sale to consumer retail outlets as well as commercial distribution. Sales five years ago were approximately $10 million and grew to $35 million last year. Elite Electric Company has two plants, one in Pennsylvania and the other in Massachusetts. The plant in Pennsylvania is relatively new and can manufacture three times the amount of units as the Massachusetts plant. The Massachusetts plant was established in the early 1920s and is on a large, beautifully manicured estate. The buildings are quite old, and the machinery is antiquated. However, the company headquarters is at the Massachusetts plant, and the company's president is insistent upon keeping both plants active. (See Table I for the five-year production history of both plants.)

In order to cope with the growth of the company administratively, additional staff were hired. However, there was no organized plan to establish systems and procedures for training, mechanization, etc., in anticipation of the increased work load and specialization of activities and functions that would eventually arise. People who had been with the company for a long period of time knew their assignments and, by and large, carried the company through its day-to-day activities. When many of these people left suddenly during a personnel reduction, an information void was created because there was little in the way of written procedures to guide those who remained and the replacement staff who were hired.

Another significant factor in the company's history was employee turnover. An administrative employee organization chart shows that 40% of the people employed as of just two years ago are no longer associated with the company. Of those remaining, 90% have different assignments today. Many of the losses in staff were in important positions, and all levels were affected. (Figures 1 and 2 show the organization charts for the company and the Massachusetts plant, respectively.)

*This case was prepared by Barry R. Armandi, and is used with permission of the author and the publisher, Elsevier Science Publishing Co., Inc.

	YEAR 1	YEAR 2	YEAR 3*		YEAR 4		YEAR 5	
			MASS.	PENN.	MASS.	PENN.	MASS.	PENN.
Transistors (K)	**800**	**600**	**500**	**400**	**475**	**535**	**452**	**629**
Large integrated circuit boards (K)	**475**	**479**	**325**	**201**	**300**	**227**	**248**	**325**
Small integrated circuit boards (K)	**600**	**585**	**480**	**175**	**250**	**212**	**321**	**438**
Large-capacity chips (millions)	**1.2**	**1.1**	**0.7**	**0.5**	**0.6**	**0.7**	**0.6**	**0.9**
Small-capacity chips (millions)	**1.8**	**2.0**	**0.5**	**1.3**	**0.2**	**2.0**	**0.3**	**2.7**
Cathode-ray tubes (K)	**325**	**250**	**210**	**22**	**126**	**46**	**147**	**63**
Percent with defects	**0.1**	**0.15**	**0.9**	**4.2**	**1.6**	**2.5**	**2.5**	**1.2**

***New plant begins operations.**

TABLE 1
Five-year production history for Elite Electric Company (in units)

THE MASSACHUSETTS PLANT

The president of the company, Mr. William White, originally came from LTV, which is located in Dallas, Texas. From there he was recruited to be Plant Operations Manager in Massachusetts. When the original owners sold out to the European concern, Mr. White was made President. The next year, he opened the Pennsylvania plant.

As president, Mr. White developed an extensive operational philosophy. The components of this philosophy are listed below:

1 Make product quality and customer service a top priority

2 Foster a human-oriented working atmosphere

3 Maximize communication, interaction, and involvement

4 Minimize the layers of organizational structure and control the growth of bureaucracy

5 Value and respect our form of company organization

6 Strive for excellence in our business performance

Upon being appointed president, White promoted Peter Johnson to the position of Plant Operations Manager from his previous position of Production Manager. White told Johnson that he (Johnson) had a lot to learn about running a plant and to go easy with changes until he got "his feet wet." He also indicated that with the projected operation of the new plant the following year, Johnson should expect some reduction in production demand, but White felt this would be temporary. Further, White emphatically reminded Johnson of the company's operational philosophy.

While Mr. White was Plant Operations Manager, he initiated daily operations meetings with the following people: the Purchasing Manager (Paul Bar-

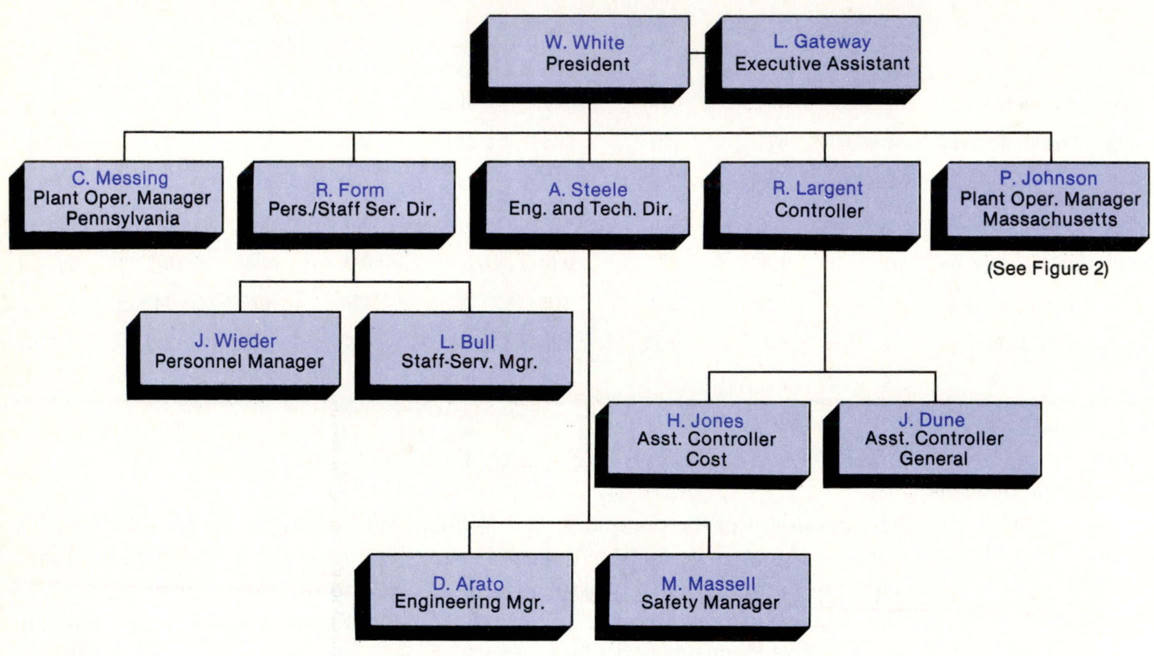

FIGURE 1 Elite Electric Company organization chart

bato); the Production Manager (Brian Campbell); the Quality Control Manager (Elizabeth Schultz); the Engineering Manager (David Arato); the Safety Manager (Martin Massell); the Personnel Manager (Jane Wieder); a representative from Customer Service (Michael St. John); and an Accounting representative (Harvey Jones).

When Mr. Johnson took over, he decided to continue the daily meetings. One day, after discussing problems of the company at an open meeting, it was decided that individuals from various other line and staff areas should attend the daily meetings. The transcript of a typical meeting is given below.

PETER JOHNSON O.K. everybody, it's 9:00, let's get started. You all know what the agenda is, so let's start with safety first.

MARTIN MASSELL (Safety Manager) Well Peter, I have a number of things to go over. First, we should look into feedback from maintenance. The other day we had an incident where the maintenance crew was washing down the walls and water leaked into the electrical wiring. Nobody was told about this, and subsequently seepage began Friday and smoke developed.

PETER JOHNSON O.K., we will have maintenance look into it and they will get back to you. What else, Marty?

MARTIN MASSELL We found out that the operators of the fork lifts are operating them too fast in the plant. We are sending out a memo telling them to slow down.

DAVID ARATO (Engineering Manager) Why don't we just put some bumps in the floor so they can't speed over them.

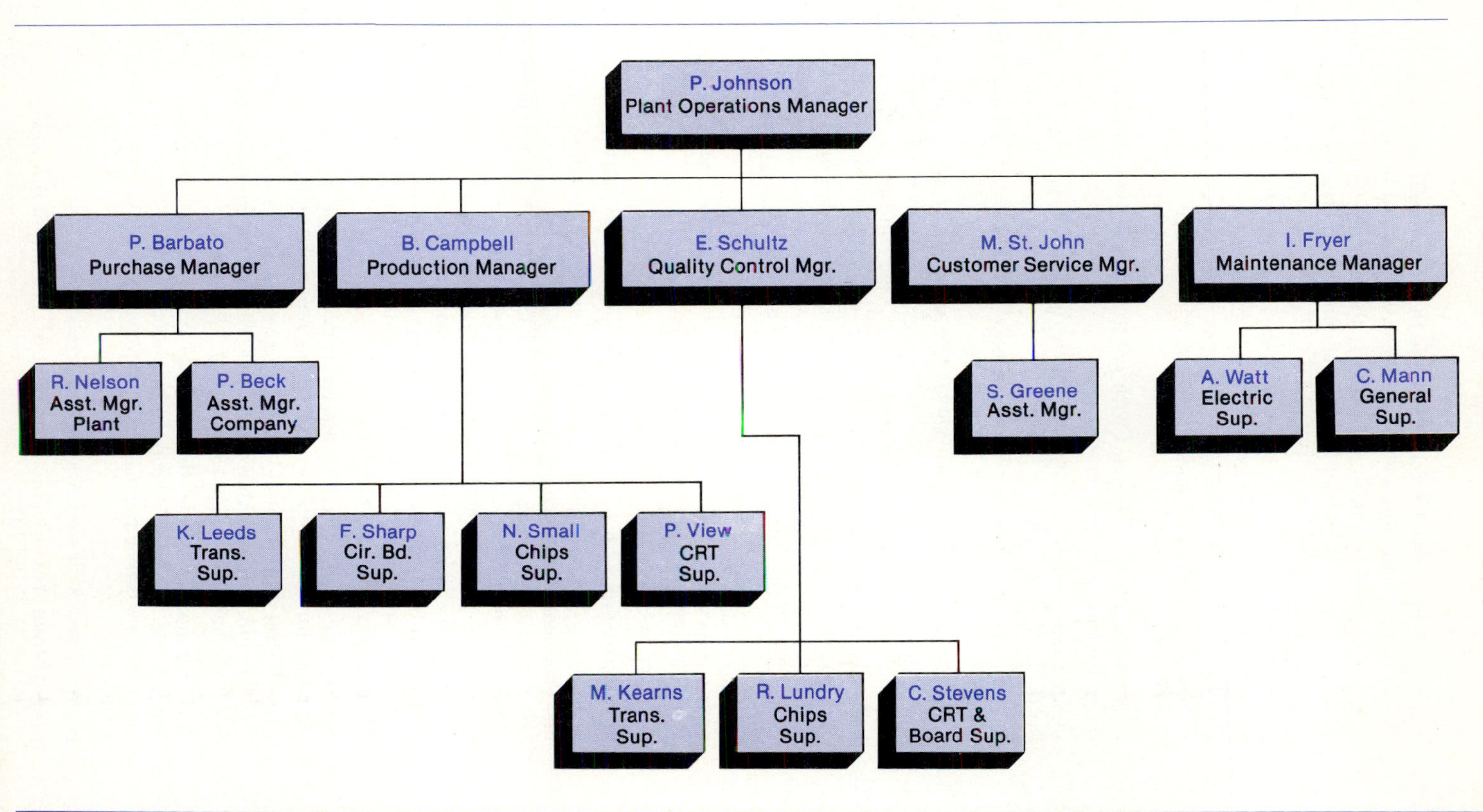

FIGURE 2
Massachusetts' plant organization chart

MARTIN MASSELL Well, we are looking at that. We may decide to do it, but we have to get some cost estimates and maintenance will have to fill us in.

PETER JOHNSON By the way, where is the representative from Maintenance . . . well, I will have to contact Irving (Maintenance Manager). Anything else, Marty?

MARTIN MASSELL Oh yeah, I forgot to tell you yesterday the entire loading dock has been cleaned. We shouldn't be having any more problems. By the way, Brian, make sure you contact Irv about the spill in the area.

BRIAN CAMPBELL Oh, I forgot to tell you, Peter, but Irv said that we would have to close down machines 1 and 6 to get at the leak that is causing the oil spill. I have already gone ahead with that.

PETER JOHNSON Gee, Brian, I wish you would clear these things with me first. How badly will this affect our production?

BRIAN CAMPBELL Not badly, we should be able to get away with a minimum of overtime this weekend.

PETER JOHNSON Customer Service is next. Mike, how are we doing with our parent company?

MICHAEL ST. JOHN (Customer Service) Nothing much. We are starting to get flack for not taking that Japanese order, but the guys at the parent company understand. They may not like it, but they can deal with it. Oh, Paul, are you going to have enough transistors on hand to complete that order by next Tuesday?

PAUL BARBATO (Purchasing Manager) Sure, Mike, I sent you a memo on that yesterday.

MICHAEL ST. JOHN Sorry, but I haven't had a chance to get to my morning mail yet. I was too busy with some visitors from Europe.

PETER JOHNSON Are these people being taken care of, Mike? Is there anything we can do to make their stay here more comfortable?

MICHAEL ST. JOHN No, everything is fine.

PETER JOHNSON O.K., let's move on to Employee Relations, Jane.

JANE WIEDER (Personnel Manager) I would like to introduce two guests from Training Programs, Inc. As you know, we will be embarking upon our final training program shortly. The grievance with Al Janow has been resolved. At the Management/Employee Meeting last week, an agreement was reached that a representative from each department would attend. As you are aware, this meeting is once a month. It's funny, the biggest complaint at the meeting was an extra chair for the conference room (laughter). The Interview Workshop memo is done, Peter, and here it is. Also, Peter, we have to work on a posting of dates for the Annual Family Get-Together. I don't know if July will work out.

MICHAEL ST. JOHN July does not look that good. We have a great deal of overtime since that Australian order is due the beginning of August. Can we push it up to June?

HARVEY JONES (Accounting Representative) Don't forget that in June, revised budgets are due. (The meeting continues to discuss the best date for the Annual Family Get-Together for another 15 minutes.)

JANE WIEDER One more thing, please notify us of any changes in marital status, address, etc. We have to keep our records up to date. Also, please be advised that the company cars can be purchased by employees. Sales will take place through a lottery system.

DAVID ARATO Will we get a memo on this?

JANE WIEDER Yes, I will have one out by the end of the week.

PETER JOHNSON Let's move on to Quality Control. Elizabeth?

ELIZABETH SCHULTZ (Quality Control Manager) Our number 1 and 8 machines have been throwing out bent transistor leads. Over the weekend, these two machines will be down. Irv and Brian are aware of this. We have to straighten out this problem before we do the order from IBM. I have also noticed that the last gold shipment had some other metals in it. Paul, can you check this out to see what was the problem?

PAUL BARBATO What amount of extraneous metals was present?

ELIZABETH SCHULTZ We didn't do complete tests of the material, but it seems 5 ounces per 100 pounds.

PAUL BARBATO That doesn't seem to be a significant amount.

ELIZABETH SCHULTZ Well, it is according to our estimates, and I would like it to be checked out.

PETER JOHNSON O.K., Elizabeth, Paul will look into it. Now let's turn to production.

BRIAN CAMPBELL Last Monday we manufactured 3,000 transistors. Machines 1, 2, and 8 did 300, machines 2 and 4 were down, and the rest of the production was done by the remaining machines. On Tuesday we had to change to produce the larger integrated circuits that were needed by Control Data. We had two hours of down time to change the machines. Machines 6 and 7 did 20% out of the total production run of 5,000 boards. Machine 1 continued to manufacture the small transistorized chips, with machines 2 and 5 completing the rest of the integrated circuit board runs (at about this time, two people got up and walked out of the room as Brian was talking). Wednesday we switched back to the transistor runs on all machines. Unfortunately, machine 2 was down for the entire day, and machine 7 was up for preventive maintenance. We manufactured 2,700 transistors. Machines 4, 5, and 8 did approximately 60% of the work (a number of people started yawning). Thursday we produced only 1,000 transistors and had to ship part of our run to the cathode-ray tube production for Digital Equipment Corp. We produced 500 units for Digital. Machines 3, 4, and 5 were used for the DEC run, and machines 1, 2, and 8 were kept on the transistor production. Machine 7 was down. On Friday we had half a day and in the morning we had a blackout and were only able to get 100 transistors and 22 cathode-ray tubes done.

PETER JOHNSON Brian, do you think you will be able to make up the rest of the order this week without much overtime?

BRIAN CAMPBELL I don't know. I think we should talk to Harry (Harry Brown was the union representative).

PETER JOHNSON That may be difficult since Harry is on vacation, but I will try to get in touch with him. If I can't, let's go ahead with it anyway and we will take the consequences. All right, let's go around the room and see what anybody has to say.

PAUL BARBATO Nothing.

BRIAN CAMPBELL Dave, I want to talk to you about the machine changeover and also if we can design a better ramp.

ELIZABETH SCHULTZ Peter, can I see you after the meeting to discuss a personal matter?

DAVID ARATO Nothing.

MARTIN MASSELL I just wanted to let everyone know that we had a problem in one of the machine wells. It appears that while they were pouring some concrete around the well, some slipped in and it took us a couple of days to get it cleaned up.

JANE WIEDER Paul, see me on Mary Bernstein's problem.

MICHAEL ST. JOHN Just wanted to let you know we may be getting a very big order from Grumman.

HARVEY JONES The following people have not reported their exempt status to payroll (he lists about 12 individuals). Remember this was from Jane's memo about three weeks ago.

PETER JOHNSON Brian, I want to take a tour with a couple of people from the university next week. I will call you and set something up. O.K.? Good meeting. See you tomorrow, same time, same place.

Study guides

1 Comment on Mr. White's operational philosophy, from the standpoint of:
 a The motivational impact of the six goals
 b The overall type of organizational culture that probably exists there

2 Assess the nature and quality of the communications that took place in the meeting conducted by Mr. Johnson, indicating what strengths and weaknesses were illustrated there. Does anyone exhibit assertive communication? What transactional analysis ego states are apparent?

3 Examine some of the group dynamics present in Mr. Johnson's meeting. What task and social leadership roles were used by participants? How could the meeting have been improved?

4 Why do you think that Mr. Johnson concluded that it was a "good meeting"? Do you agree? Explain.

CASE 5

The Patterson Operation*

BACKGROUND

Carrington, Inc. is an international company engaged in the production and distribution of pharmaceuticals, proprietary drugs, and cosmetics and toiletries. In its worldwide operations, Carrington employs over 15,000 people and has sales of over $500 million annually.

At the Mid-South plant of Carrington, Inc. management was faced with problems of low productivity, low employee morale, and high unit costs in the section responsible for the assembly of various kinds of packages containing assortments of different products made by the company. These "prepaks" or "deals," as they are referred to within the organization, are specifically prepared to the specifications of the individual customer. Each package may contain from 24 to 480 items, and the total number of packages for a customer may range from 10 to 1500 units. Most of these packages are prepared in such a way that the retailer can set them up as freestanding, point-of-sale promotional displays. From Carrington's standpoint, the objective of using these product displays was to create additional shelf space for Carrington's products. In the stores these displays could be placed in aisles or used as shelf extenders. Assembling the deals is essentially a job-shop type process, and prior to last year the "assembly room" was located in a part of the main plant known as Section 10.

The employees in Carrington's manufacturing and assembly operations are unionized and the firm uses a Halsey 50–50 Incentive Plan, a time-saved bonus plan. Under the Halsey Plan, if a worker can do his job in less than the standard time, he receives a bonus of 50 percent of the hourly wage rate multiplied by the time saved. For example, an employee who completed 10 standard hours of work in 8 hours would be paid for 8 hours plus 1 of the 2 hours saved. Thus, if the hourly pay rate were $8.50, the worker would earn $76.50 for the day.

PROBLEMS WITH SECTION 10

The assembly of prepaks in Section 10 utilized roller-type conveyor belts which supplied each worker with the products to be included in a particular package.

*This case was prepared by James M. Todd and Thomas R. Miller, and is used with permission of the authors and the publisher, *Journal of Case Studies*.

The working conditions were outstanding in that the work area was very clean, well-lighted, and air conditioned. An attractive cafeteria for employee use was available in the same large building.

In spite of good working conditions and the chance to earn extra pay through the company's incentive system, the operation in Section 10 had encountered a marked trend of increases in unit costs and decreases in output per labor hour. In fact, during the last three years cost figures revealed that the section was below the break-even point. Contributing to this deteriorating situation was low productivity and failure of employees to meet the work standard. This latter problem was made particularly evident by the fact that no employees were able to earn a bonus under the incentive plan.

Discipline in Section 10 was poor and supervisors were constantly having problems. A number of grievances had been generated. Morale was not helped by the fact that any employee quite often found himself being moved from one assembly line to another. This tended to increase production costs because the employees had little chance of moving down a particular learning curve before being moved to another operation. Another factor indicative of low morale was the employees' attitudes. There was no spirit of mutual cooperation and the attitude of "that's not my job" was prevalent.

All in all, working in Section 10 was considered an unpopular work assignment. The work required manual labor and was perceived as relatively hard work compared to the automated lines in the other work areas. Also, word had spread that no one could "make bonus" working there. Eventually, through the bidding system used by the organization, the work force in Section 10 came to consist, in large part, of young inexperienced employees, problem workers, and malcontents. As one manager described the situation, "Section 10 had the pits of the work force."

A NEW OPERATION

Early last year management at Carrington was confronted with a severe space problem for its expanding manufacturing and assembly operations. Several alternatives were considered, but none seemed to offer a solution to the space problem that was economically feasible. In a sense of near desperation, a brainstorming session of managers led to a decision to move a large part of the assembly of the deals to a facility already leased by the company, presently used as a warehouse. This facility was located on Patterson Street and for this reason the new deal room became known in the company as the "Patterson Operation."

The new facility fell far short of providing work space and conditions comparable to those in Section 10. The building was located in an entirely separate area approximately 3 miles from the main plant in a neighborhood of run-down, low-income housing and other warehouse operations.

The building housing the Patterson operation had been thought to be acceptable only for warehouse use. It was an older brick structure with a number of large open bays for shipping and receiving. The building was dark, poorly ventilated, not air conditioned, and inadequately heated. It was poorly suited for use by workers involved in assembly operations. Temperatures averaged approximately 50 degrees during the winter months and well over 90 degrees in the summer. There was no cafeteria or food service, and employees either brought their own lunch or went to a small neighborhood grocery in the vicinity and bought food. Other worker facilities such as restrooms and break areas were poor. In summary, working conditions contrasted sharply with Section 10 and its clean, air-conditioned, well-heated facilities in a good neighborhood and with a first-class company cafeteria available.

Despite these tremendous obstacles and seemingly against their best judgment, management, pressed for manufacturing space, had decided on the move to the Patterson warehouse. Little money was spent on modifications of the Patterson facility.

RESULTS OF THE MOVE

Moving to Patterson involved the transfer of approximately 40 employees from the main plant, most of whom were blacks with low seniority. Under the new structure, all of these workers were managed by Fred Hammond, a black first-line supervisor.

As foreman, Fred made some drastic changes in the assembly operation. He set up the assembly line so that individual workers could work on the same job until that particular order was completed. The situation was entirely different from Section 10 where an employee could work on as many as three different assemblies during a day's time. Of course, the repetition of working on the same line enabled workers to develop speed, which facilitated their earning bonuses.

The new foreman introduced some other innovations. He allowed employees the opportunity to influence decisions concerning their work hours and the times of their rest breaks. While at the main plant the playing of radios in a production area was not permitted, at Patterson it gradually became acceptable to have radios tuned to "disco" or "soul" music, usually playing at a high volume level. Other "non-standard" conditions existed at Patterson. Unlike Section 10, employees did not have to observe dress codes, wear bonnets, or refrain from wearing jewelry on the job. Because of the rather remote location of Patterson off the main plant site, managers or supervisors from the plant visited the new facility rather infrequently. Where violations of certain company policies existed, a somewhat liberal attitude was taken by management.

In order to have some place to eat or to take a break the employees got together and furnished a small room with enough tables and chairs to modestly equip a rather austere dining and rest break area. Eventually this room was air conditioned. At the time the case was written the employees were attempting to get the company to furnish some paint so that they could repaint the room.

With these and other changes a shift in worker attitudes began to evolve. Employees came to view Patterson as their own "company." A feeling of mutual cooperation became prevalent as evidenced by the willingness of individual workers to assist others when possible. An esprit de corps developed among the Patterson workers. Productivity increased to such an extent that employees were receiving bonuses which had very seldom been the case in the old location. The jobs at Patterson became more popular and the composition of the work force there gradually changed from one of inexperienced and dissatisfied workers to one in which older and better qualified people (black and white) began to actively bid for the jobs. Since the Patterson operation was opened, there has been only one grievance filed and during the first year of operation there was a 32.8% increase in productivity over Section 10.

Since the inception of the Patterson operation, Fred Hammond, the first-line supervisor initially in charge, has been promoted and was replaced by May Allison, who has continued to run the operation in the same manner as Hammond. To an outside observer it is rather amusing to watch this young lady, who stands less than five feet tall and weighs approximately 100 pounds, in her supervisory relationship with the work force, particularly the burly male employees and the older women workers. It is apparent that she has been able to earn the respect and admiration of the employees and has developed effective work relationships with them. Recent data indicates higher productivity and more bonuses at Patterson than in comparable work in the main plant. May is well-liked personally as evidenced by employee contributions of about $75.00 for her birthday gift.

May has continued to get the employees to participate in decision making as, for example, the decision to change work hours at Patterson during the summer months from 5:30 A.M. to 2:00 P.M. rather than 7:30 A.M. to 4:00 P.M. in the other plant areas. This was initiated because of the nearly unbearable heat of the late afternoon in the warehouse. This change in work schedule, in actuality, was not in accordance with company policy, but has been tolerated by management. The workers at Patterson really preferred an even earlier work day, but this was not feasible due to coordination problems in receiving goods from the main plant.

Another interesting development at Patterson is the formation of their own softball team called the "Patterson Warriors." At the time of this writing, the team was in second place in a city-wide tournament. Normally, the company will field a team composed of players from all units instead of from one particular section. Again, Patterson employees did this independently without reference to overall company personnel policy.

Work records at the Patterson operation concerning absenteeism, tardiness, and turnover are not better than in the main plant. In a few cases they are slightly worse, although this difference is not considered to be significant by management. However, the very low grievance rate, the high level of worker morale, and the better productivity at Patterson are pleasant surprises to management.

The activities of the Patterson operation are fairly well-known among the managers at the Mid-South plant of Carrington. Management reactions range from positive to negative with some managers ambivalent about Patterson. All, however, seem to agree that it is, at least, interesting.

Study guides

1 Is the Patterson operation successful? To the degree that it can be judged a success, what factors contributed to it?
2 Identify the leadership styles of Fred Hammond and May Allison. Apply several of the leadership models to the case, such as Fiedler's contingency model and the Hersey-Blanchard situational model. What do they imply?
3 Comment on the informal organization at Patterson. In what ways did the employees create their own "company"?
4 Review Herzberg's maintenance and motivational factors. Why didn't the change in physical working conditions (a deterioration of a maintenance factor) have a negative effect on productivity? What *did* cause the workers to be productive?

CASE 6

TRW—Oilwell Cable Division*

It was July 5, and Bill Russell had been expecting the phone call naming him general manager he had just received from the corporate office of TRW in Cleveland. Bill had been the acting general manager of the Oilwell Cable Division in Lawrence, Kansas, since January when Gino Strippoli left the division for another assignment. He had expected to be named general manager, but the second part of the call informing him that he must lay off 20 people or achieve an equivalent reduction in labor costs was greatly disturbing to him. It was now 8:00 A.M. and at 8:15 A.M. Bill had called a meeting of all plant personnel to announce his appointment and, now, to also announce the impending layoffs. He was wondering in his own mind how to handle the tough decisions that lay before him.

TRW

TRW is a diversified, multinational manufacturing firm that has sales approaching $5.5 billion. Its roots can be found in the Cleveland Cap Screw Company, which was founded in 1901 with a total investment of $2,500 and employment of 29. Today, through a growth strategy of acquisition and diversification, the company employs 88,000 employees at over 300 locations in 17 countries. The original shareholders' investment has grown to over $1.6 billion. As quoted from a company publication, "This growth reflects the company's ability to anticipate promising new fields and to pioneer in their development—automotive, industrial, aircraft, aerospace, systems, electronics, and energy. We grew with these markets and helped create them."

OILWELL CABLE DIVISION, LAWRENCE, KANSAS

The Oilwell Cable Division is part of the Industrial and Energy Segment of TRW. This segment of TRW's business represents 24% of its sales and 23% of

*This case was prepared by Michael G. Kolchin, Thomas J. Hyclak, and Sheree Deming, and is used with permission of the authors and the publisher, Elsevier Science Publishing Co., Inc.

its operating profits. The pumps, valves, and energy-services group, of which the Oilwell Cable Division is a part, account for 30% of the Industrial and Energy Segment's net sales.

The Oilwell Cable Division had its beginning as the Crescent Wire and Cable Company of Trenton, New Jersey. When TRW acquired Crescent, the company was losing money, occupied an outmoded plant, and had significant labor problems. In order to improve the profitability of the Crescent division, TRW decided to move its operations out of Trenton. The first decision was to move oilwell cable production to Lawrence, Kansas, about ten years ago. The line was moved into a new building and all new equipment was purchased. Only Gino Strippoli, the plant manager, and three other employees made the move from Trenton to Lawrence.

The reason for choosing Lawrence as the new site for Crescent division was fourfold. Most importantly, Lawrence was considerably closer to the customer base of the division, which was in Northeast Oklahoma. Second, Kansas was a right-to-work state and, given the labor problems of the Trenton plant, TRW was looking for a more supportive labor environment for its new operations. Third, the wage rates for the Lawrence area were very reasonable compared to Trenton. Finally, there was an already existing building that could house the oilwell cable production line in an industrial park in North Lawrence. In addition to the building, there was considerable acreage next to the building that would allow for future expansion.

By just moving the oilwell cable line to Lawrence, TRW hoped to be able to focus in on this product and make it more profitable before moving the other products from the Crescent plant in Trenton. Soon thereafter, when the Oilwell Cable plant had reached division status, no further consideration was given to moving the rest of the Trenton plant. The remaining operations in Trenton were sold.

Team management at Lawrence

When Gino Strippoli was given the task of starting up operations in Lawrence, he saw a great opportunity to establish a new management system. With a new plant, new equipment, and almost all new employees, the time seemed perfect to test the value of team management. Gino had long been a supporter of team management, and now a golden opportunity was being presented to him to set up an experiment to test his ideas.

Team management is a form of worker participation whereby team members are responsible for task-related decisions concerning their areas of responsibility. Teams are formed along functional lines. In the case of the TRW-Lawrence plant, 11 teams exist ranging in membership from 4 to 17. The title of the teams and brief descriptions of their make-up are shown in Table 1. Figure 1 depicts the current organization of the Oilwell Cable Division.

The five production teams are formed around the production process in use at TRW-Lawrence. Each of the teams meets on a weekly basis or as needed

TABLE 1
Team Structure

TEAM	NUMBER OF TEAMS	COMPOSITION
Management	1	Members of management
Resource	1	Management information systems, design engineering, process engineering, employment, accounting, chemists, etc.
Technical	1	Nonexempt laboratory personnel
Administration	1	
Maintenance	1	Boiler, electrical, mechanical
Shipping and receiving	1	
Production	5	Extruding, armoring, braiding

with exception of the resource team, which meets every two weeks. The typical meeting lasts an hour and a half to two hours. There is no formal structure for the team meeting, but most meetings adhere to an agenda similar to the one described below:

1 Scheduling labor hours and overtime
2 Round-robin discussion/reporting from various plant committees (e.g., safety, gainsharing, etc.)
3 Area manager's comments regarding scrap, labor efficiency, and any new information since the last meeting

FIGURE 1
Organizational structure at the Oilwell Cable Division
Note: An organizational chart for the Oilwell Cable Division does not exist. The chart below represents the casewriters' depiction of the structure existing at TRW-Lawrence based on discussions with division personnel.

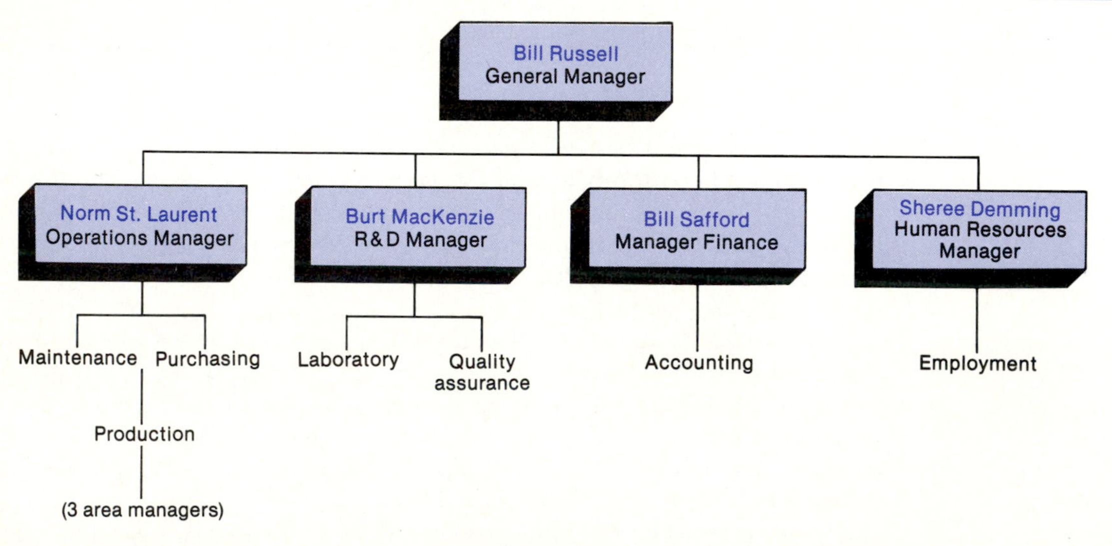

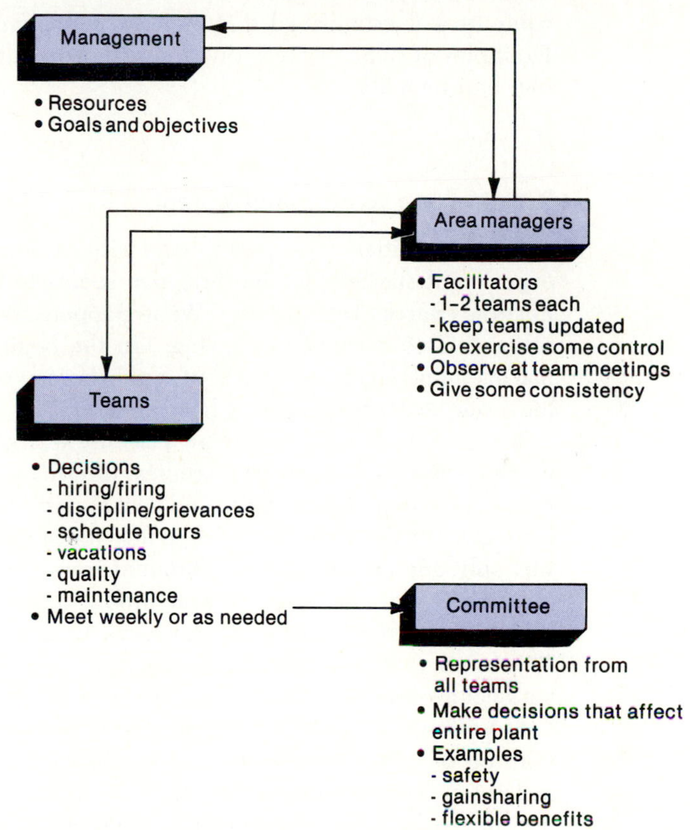

FIGURE 2
Relationships between the various levels in the team management concept

Other decisions made by the team are listed in Figure 2, which illustrates the roles of the various levels of management at the Oilwell Cable Division. Figure 2 also shows the relationships between levels. For instance, management has the responsibility for setting overall divisional goals and objectives and providing the resources necessary to the teams in order to attain these targets.

The role of the area managers is that of an intermediary. They are present at most team meetings to act as facilitators and to provide the teams with information necessary to carry out their scheduling functions. In addition, the area managers fill a coordination function by meeting twice a week to discuss mutual problems and to discuss other items that should be presented at the weekly team meetings.

As can be seen in Figure 2, the teams are filling managerial roles, and the decisions they make are more typical of those made by supervisory levels in more traditional plants. In essence, they, the team members, are given control over their work areas.

For decisions that affect the entire plant, a task force or a division-wide committee is established that includes representatives from all of the teams. Examples of some of these division-wide committees include safety, gainsharing, and benefits.

Results from team management

After some initial start-up problems with the team management concept, the experiment started by Gino Strippoli seems to be a success. In an article in *Fortune* (Burck, 1981) titled, "What Happens When Workers Manage Themselves," Gino is quoted as saying: "In the beginning we considered it (team management) an experiment, but somewhere along the way we said, 'This is no longer an experiment; this is how we operate.'"

The success of the experiment not only was written up in *Fortune* but also was the subject of several case studies. But this success was not achieved easily. In the beginning, there was a good deal of mistrust among employees regarding management's motives. Also, when first starting up the Lawrence facility, there was only one union employee brought from Trenton. The rest of the people hired had little experience with the production process involved in making wire cable. As a result, there was a lot of frustration with a high level of turnover. The turnover rate of 12% in the first two years of operations compared to a national average of 3.8% at this time (U.S. Department of Labor, p. 180).

But Gino was not to be deterred from seeing his experiment succeed. He realized that he was concentrating too heavily on team involvement concepts and not paying enough attention to technical concerns. A compensation scheme was developed that encouraged employees to master the various pieces of equipment in the plant. This action seemed to have the desired effect, for the division became profitable for the first time two years after his arrival.

By that time, employment had dropped from a high of 132 to what seemed to be a more optimal level of 125. Turnover dropped from in excess of 12% to a range of 2–4%, which was more in line with the national average for manufacturing firms. More impressive was the absentee rate, which hovered in the range of 2.5–3% for several years. The national average during this period was closer to 6.5% (U.S. Department of Labor, p. 136). Productivity was improving steadily as well. The Oilwell Cable Division now enjoyed the highest productivity of any plant in the oilwell cable industry.

It was not only the objective data that indicated that team management was succeeding but comments from employees at the Oilwell Cable Division seemed to confirm this as well. By and large, all employees rated TRW-Lawrence as a good company and preferred the team management concept to more traditional methods of management.

Some sample comments from the various levels of "management" verify this conclusion.

Team Members

". . . an excellent place to work."

"Team management gives employees a good deal of responsibility."

"Now at least we have some control over scheduling."

"The company gains as much as the employee because of the flexibility. Now there is little idle time."

"Team management gives the employee a feeling of equality."

"System allows for the maximum contribution of each member of the team."

Area Managers

"The plant is not a Utopia but I do feel better at the end of the day."

"Decision making is more difficult but team management results in easier implementation and better understanding by team members."

Management

"System allows for crossing over lines of responsibility. There is not the turf issue that exists in traditionally structured plants."

"Team management concept has resulted in an excellent labor climate. TRW-Lawrence is a good place to work and the workers here are receptive to change."

"The major benefit of the team management concept is flexibility while maintaining goal orientation."

This last statement is one of the real keys to team management—flexibility. Under such a management system idle time is greatly reduced, as is the involvement of the plant manager in day-to-day operating problems. As noted by Strippoli, "I really feel for the first time that I am managing rather than putting out fires. The teams are putting out the fires way down in the organization" (Burck, p. 69).

From the worker's point of view, the major benefit of team management is their ability to control their job. This control has resulted in a high level of commitment by the employees, as evidenced by the numerous suggestions made by the teams that have resulted in significant improvement in quality and productivity.

Of course, the team management concept is not without its difficulties. As noted earlier, there are numerous problems with start-up. It takes awhile for participants to become comfortable with the system and to accept the responsibility of managing themselves. In this case, it took a period of two years. However, after the settling-in period, productivity improved dramatically and has been maintained at that level. This achievement is illustrated in Figure 3.

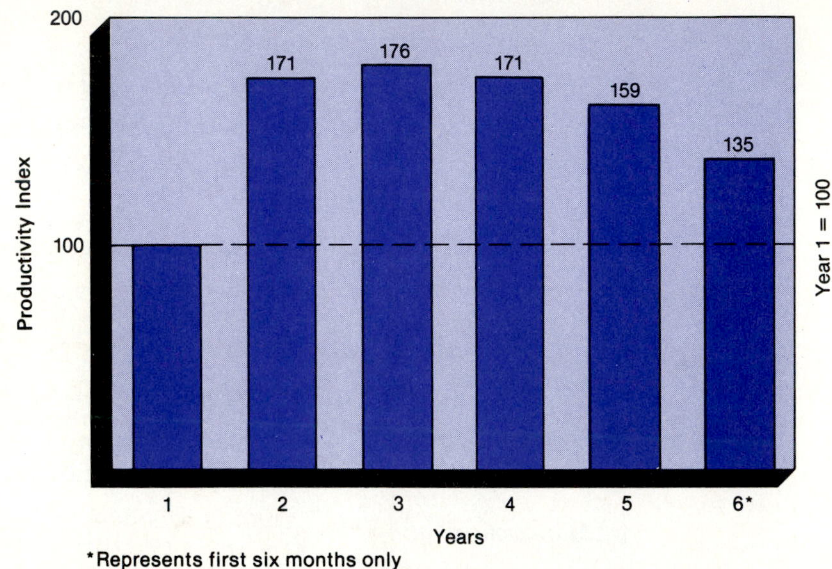

FIGURE 3
Productivity at TRW-Lawrence

In addition to start-up problems, the people who filled middle-management positions had great difficulty in adjusting to their new roles as facilitators as opposed to being bosses in the traditional sense. This is an area that is often overlooked in implementing participation schemes in factories. In the case of the Oilwell Cable Division, this inability to adapt to a new system resulted in four area managers leaving their positions. Plant management tried to deal with this problem by providing facilitator training for area managers. Although the current area managers still express some frustration at not being able to simply "tell" workers what to do, they do feel the team management concept is a much more effective system than traditional supervisory systems, and they would not want to go back to a traditional system.

All in all, Gino was very pleased with the experiment. After five years, he left the Lawrence facility for another assignment and Bill Russell, who had been Gino's operations manager, replaced him as the acting general manager.

THE OILWELL CABLE DIVISION'S MARKET

The basic product produced by the Oilwell Cable Division is wire that provides power to submersible pumps used in oil drilling. As a result, the demand for its product is directly dependent on the demand for submersible pumps, a demand that is a function of the price of crude oil. As the price of oil increases, the demand for pumps increases as it becomes economically feasible to drill deeper wells.

Drilling deeper wells also produces a need for cables that are able to withstand the harsher environments found in such wells. For example, these wells often require the use of lead jackets to protect the cables from the corrosive effects of hydrogen sulfide.

With the Iranian oil crisis and the resultant increase in oil prices, cable producers were able to sell almost all they were able to produce. Prices were determined on the basis of quality and delivery. Now, however, with the advent of an oil glut, demand for submersible pumps had dropped and the competitive factors in the market were determined more on the basis of price.

In all, TRW had ten competitors in the cable market. TRW was the market leader with a significant share of the market but it was now facing strong competition from both domestic and foreign producers.

Location was also a competitive factor that foreign competitors enjoyed, especially with regard to oil and gas drilling in Southeast Asia and the Middle East. As the production of cable was basically a semicontinuous process, economies of scale were important. With this in mind, it was infeasible to build smaller plants nearer to a customer base that was widely dispersed. As noted earlier, one of the reasons for moving to Lawrence was so that TRW could be closer to its primary customers in Oklahoma.

By the end of June the market for cable had declined dramatically. As Bill Russell reviewed the quarterly financial data and he observed the idle equipment and employees in the plant, he knew he had to do something soon if he were to maintain market share and profitability.

THE LAYOFF DECISION

As Bill Russell prepared to meet with all personnel at the Lawrence facility, he wondered how he would handle the process of laying off 16% of the current workforce of 125. Two things particularly troubled him. First, his predecessor, Gino Strippoli, had implied to the employees that there would never be a layoff at the Oilwell Cable Division. Second, and perhaps more importantly, he had to decide whether the decision as to how to reduce labor costs was a decision he should make alone or one that the teams should undertake as their responsibility.

It was now 8:15 A.M. and Bill headed out to meet his employees.

References

Burck, Charles G. (1981) "What happens when workers manage themselves," *Fortune*, July 27, pp. 62–69.

U.S. Department of Labor (1983) *Handbook of Labor Statistics*, Washington, D.C.: Bureau of Labor Statistics.

Study guides

1 Evaluate team management at TRW's Lawrence plant. What organizational behavior system is it most similar to? Does it reflect Theory X or Theory Y assumptions?

2 Examine the results from team management at Lawrence. Do they support a "satisfaction causes productivity" or a "productivity causes satisfaction" relationship? Explain.

3 Assume the role of Bill Russell at the end of the case. Prepare to make your announcement regarding the layoff to the Cable Division's employees. What do you expect their reactions will be, and how will you respond to them?

4 Can participative and team management approaches work equally well during times of organizational crisis as well as during normal times? Explain.

CASE

7

United Mutual Insurance Company

The United Mutual Insurance Company was organized in 1939 by Paul and James Taylor. Since its organization, these two men have maintained active personal direction of the company. The company is located in Kansas City, Missouri, and writes all forms of automobile and general casualty insurance. At the present time United Mutual is represented by more than 2000 agents located in Wisconsin, Illinois, Iowa, Missouri, Kentucky, and Colorado, and it has thirty-two field managers and eighty claims adjusters working out of forty-seven offices. The company has grown steadily since it was founded.

The home office of United Mutual has about 425 employees. Annual labor turnover is 25 to 30 percent, and it has been difficult to replace this turnover because of a mild labor shortage in Kansas City the past few years. Of the 425 people in the home office, about 100 are supervisory employees. The term "supervisory employees" or "supervisors" in this company refers to those who do not have to punch time clocks and do not receive overtime pay. It includes people who direct the work of others and also some technical and professional people such as lawyers and underwriters. An organizational chart of the people primarily involved in this case is shown in Figure 1.

This case began about five years ago. At that time the company allowed one coffee break of fifteen minutes in the morning and a similar break in the afternoon. Employees went to the cafeteria for their break. At this time both Gorman and Townsend had some responsibility for the coffee break. Gorman had general responsibility for control of the break, because he was in charge of general operations in the home office. Townsend had responsibility for the cafeteria and payroll. He also acted unofficially as personnel director.

Gradually many of the supervisory employees started taking advantage of the coffee break and overstaying their time in the cafeteria. When the nonsupervisory employees saw what was happening, they also started to take longer coffee breaks than were authorized. Before many months had passed, most all the employees were taking longer breaks than were allotted. When Townsend and Gorman questioned several of the supervisory employees as to why they spent so much time during coffee breaks when they knew that only fifteen minutes were authorized, the standard reply was "We were discussing business problems of United Mutual" or "We were having a meeting, so we actually were working."

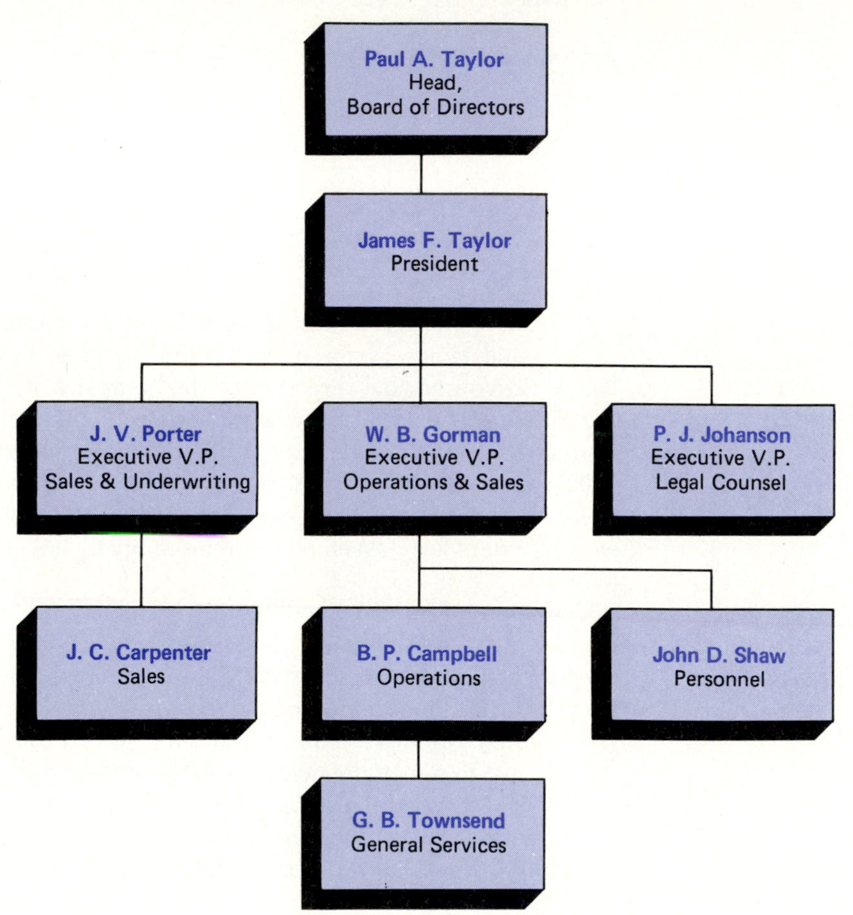

FIGURE 1
Current organizational chart showing top positions in United Mutual Insurance Company

It is probable that many overstayed coffee breaks actually were informal business meetings, because most of the supervisors were either underwriters, claim adjusters, or operations supervisors, and daily meetings of some of these people were common to discuss their business problems. There was, of course, no way to prove which discussions were social and which were informal business meetings.

One thing seemed sure. It was almost impossible to get nonsupervisory employees to believe that supervisors actually were working during coffee hour; therefore Gorman told the supervisors that they had to keep within their fifteen minutes in order to set an example for the rest of the employees. They failed to heed his word, and the coffee break continued to be violated. To add to the complication, too many employees were coming to the cafeteria at the same time, which resulted in much congestion and waiting for coffee.

In an effort to keep the coffee break limited to fifteen minutes, Townsend started staying in the cafeteria during the complete coffee hour, and watching for offenders who stayed over the time limit. He, in turn, reported the offenders to department heads, who were supposed to take the action necessary to ensure that their employees obeyed the coffee-period time limit. For the next few months their employees observed the fifteen-minute coffee period very closely with few exceptions. Then the department heads again became lax, and nonsupervisory as well as supervisory employees began exceeding the time limit on coffee periods.

Again Gorman and Townsend went into consultation, and this time they came up with the idea of installing bells in the cafeteria. The bells were installed and were adjusted to ring every ten minutes. Considering that it took a few minutes for employees to go from their offices to the cafeteria, Gorman and Townsend felt that ten minutes in the cafeteria was the maximum time that could be allowed in order to stay within the limits of the fifteen-minute coffee period. Schedules were set up by the department heads so that the employees were supposed to arrive at the cafeteria when the bells rang and they would stay until the bells rang again, at which time they were supposed to leave.

Townsend noted that the bells did keep some employees in the cafeteria for only ten minutes, but it was very difficult to synchronize the various groups. People were drifting into and out of the cafeteria all the time and not according to the schedule for which the bells were adjusted. Also, when one group was leaving the cafeteria, another group was scheduled to enter, which added to the congestion. The general opinion among some employees was that the bells made them feel "like they were in prison cells" and could not get out until the bells rang. Others thought the bells very irritating and said it was impossible to enjoy the coffee period. It was soon evident that the bells were not solving the coffee-period problem, but since no better solution was offered, the bells remained, and employees continued to complain about them.

Three years ago top management realized that United Mutual was expanding to the extent that there was definite need for a personnel director to handle the coffee-break problem as well as the increasing number of other personnel problems existing within the home office. Therefore, in July of that year John Shaw was hired as personnel director of United Mutual. Shaw had sixteen years' experience in personnel work and was highly regarded in local personnel circles.

Soon after Shaw arrived at United Mutual, Gorman explained the current personnel problems to him. Of course, one of these problems was the coffee break. Shaw soon found out for himself that employees were taking more than their allotted time during coffee periods. The president wanted something done to remedy the situation, and this problem was given to Shaw.

He tackled the problem rapidly and directly. In his own words, "I made periodic checks with all the department heads concerning the coffee break and found out what their reactions were. I told the department heads to keep check on their employees and to try to keep the coffee break confined within the fifteen-minute period."

Shaw soon found that the bells were ineffective and unpopular. He had them removed from the cafeteria. A few executives approached Shaw and suggested that the coffee periods be discontinued. He countered with the following argument: "The labor shortage in our city is critical at the present time. We have twenty-five vacancies within the company, and yet you want me to discontinue a practice that other employers have and, as a result, perhaps lose more employees."

In December of Shaw's first year top management asked him to justify his stand that the coffee break was necessary and, if he could justify it, to provide a remedy to the problem. Shaw gave the following reasons why the coffee periods should be continued:

1 A coffee break helps new employees make friends with people in their own and other departments. United Mutual has a 25 to 30 percent labor turnover each year, so several new employees are coming to the company every week.
2 By having a coffee break, there is a cross-pollination of ideas, and this prevents stratification and cliques.
3 A coffee break will give renewed vigor to the employees, and this will result in greater productivity.
4 The nature of detailed work and mental activity is so confining that people need a break from their routines.

After much deliberation and consultation, Shaw prepared a solution for the coffee-break problem and submitted it to top executives. They approved it, including his proposal that coffee be furnished free to employees. Free coffee was first given on March 23 by means of a routine announcement in the cafeteria. The remainder of Shaw's proposal was put into effect by a memorandum issued on March 31 by Shaw to all home office employees of United Mutual, as shown in Figure 2.

The memorandum was well received by most of the employees. The workweek was cut from thirty-nine hours, thirty-five minutes, to thirty-eight hours, forty-five minutes. Shaw believed that everything would have turned out all right if United Mutual had not been remodeling and adding to its building at that time (see Figure 3).

As can be seen from the diagram, this construction meant that all employees from the North Building had to walk outside and around the center building in order to get to the cafeteria for the coffee period. Employees on the third floor took as long as six to seven minutes to reach the cafeteria, which caused their break to extend beyond the fifteen-minute limitation. In the next few months, department heads became slack in enforcing the memorandum issued by Shaw, and employees again started taking more time than was allotted to them.

Most department heads had their departments split into two sections. One section was to go for their coffee, and the other section was to wait until the first

UNITED MUTUAL INSURANCE COMPANY
MEMORANDUM

Subject *Changes in Working, Lunch, and Rest Period Schedules*
To *All Home Office Department Heads and Employees*
From *Personnel*

Effective April 4, the working schedule of the office will be as follows:

8:00 A.M. to 12:00 noon.
Forty-minute lunch periods will be scheduled at five regular intervals.
Fifteen-minute morning rest periods will be scheduled at five regular intervals.
The working day will end at 4:25 P.M.

This new working schedule reduces the workday by ten minutes and makes an overall workweek of 38.75 hours. We feel sure that employees will welcome this change since it will help to avoid further the evening traffic congestion and facilitate bus connections.

The morning rest periods will be scheduled from 9:30 A.M. through 10:25 A.M. Departments will be scheduled at ten-minute intervals. Fifteen minutes will be allowed for each employee, which includes travel time to and from the cafeteria. *It is important that employees adhere to the schedules listed below since the principal reason for scheduling is to eliminate confusion and congestion and to improve service in the cafeteria. It will be the responsibility of department heads to make certain that employees follow the assigned schedules. Following is the morning rest period schedule for all departments.*

[The schedule is omitted.]

Where stand-by telephone service is required, department heads will exercise discretion in keeping their operation staffed during the morning rest and lunch periods.

With the reduction of the workweek by fifty minutes, we feel that the afternoon rest period is unnecessary. The cafeteria will be closed after the last lunch group has been served.

3/31/—

JDS:RG

FIGURE 2 Memorandum to employees

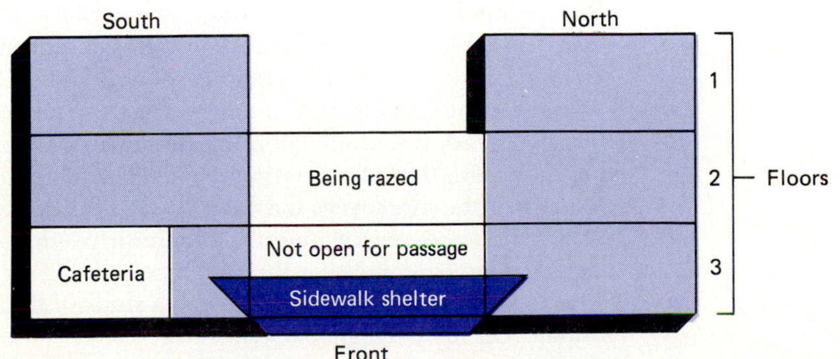

FIGURE 3 United Mutual building during remodeling

section returned. The only trouble was that the second section was not waiting for the first section to return before they left. The result was mass confusion in the cafeteria. Groups did not come on the regular schedule, and when they did come, they stayed over fifteen minutes. Shaw conferred with all the department heads and told them if the practice of long coffee breaks continued in the future, there was a strong possibility of not having any coffee breaks at all.

One department head realized the seriousness of the problem and issued a memorandum to all his employees explaining why time limits must be observed by everyone. Gorman liked the memorandum and had Shaw send copies to all supervisors.

Early last year United Mutual's management decided that an opinion survey might help solve some of the personnel problems encountered by the company. In this survey approximately sixty employees complained about the coffee period. Many of them didn't drink coffee and wanted to know why coffee was free while the rest of the liquid refreshments were not. There were some complaints about not having an afternoon coffee break in addition to the morning break. Shaw conferred with Gorman, and they decided to offer free tea and cocoa as well as free coffee to employees, but the practice of only one coffee break each day was continued. Shaw informed all department heads that the coffee break was still only fifteen minutes and in the morning only, but that cocoa and tea were free to employees beginning June 1. He also mentioned that this free coffee, tea, and cocoa would cost United Mutual $400 a month, and in order for this coffee break to be continued, employees would have to restrict their coffee break to the time mentioned in the memorandum, which was fifteen minutes.

In October of last year the building was finished and employees could walk through the building again to get to the cafeteria. A new middle section had been added to the building, and there was considerably more space for all employees.

The coffee break in the morning continued, and employees seemed to like the free coffee, tea, and cocoa. In fact, they liked it so much that most of them started taking second cups and overstaying their allotted fifteen minutes. In an effort to remind employees that the coffee period was still only fifteen minutes, Shaw had table napkins printed showing a friendly clock tapping two employees on their shoulders and reminding them, "Coffee break is fifteen minutes."

The printed napkins were removed from the tables once or twice a week so that employees would not get a "routine feeling" about them and would know that they were there for a purpose. The napkins served a very useful purpose, as many of the employees did limit their coffee break to fifteen minutes, but there still were several (mostly supervisory employees) who continued to disregard the time limit on the coffee period.

Recently the case interviewer began a study of the coffee problem at United Mutual. On his first random visit to the coffee period he made the following observations:

1 Although the coffee break wasn't scheduled to start until 9:30, approximately thirty-five persons were in the cafeteria prior to that time.
2 At 9:35 A.M. there were approximately two hundred employees in the cafeteria when there should have been only seventy-five to one hundred. There was much congestion, and when the 9:45 group came to get coffee, there weren't enough clean cups due to the overflow at 9:30.
3 At 9:45 when the first group of employees was supposed to leave the cafeteria, approximately 25 percent remained.
4 On the basis of spot checks, it appeared that about 90 percent of the clerical employees obeyed the fifteen-minute coffee-break rule and the other 10 percent were just a few minutes over the limit. Spot checks of several supervisors showed that they spent anywhere from fifteen minutes to over an hour in the cafeteria. Typical examples included one supervisor who stayed in the cafeteria for twenty-two minutes and another who stayed approximately thirty minutes. One supervisor spent an hour and ten minutes in the cafeteria.
5 A check of two departments revealed that in each the second section left for coffee break before the first section returned.

Shaw feels that a problem still exists at United Mutual concerning the coffee period. The current action that Shaw is taking is to revise the coffee-break schedule in order to prevent congestion and achieve better control. Neither Gorman nor Shaw is sure what else should be done, if anything.

Study guides

1 Appraise management's handling of the problems that developed in this case. What behavioral ideas were overlooked or misapplied?
2 At the end of the case, what are the key problems, if any? What are the alternatives to choose from? What would you do in the role of Gorman? What would you do if you were Shaw? What organizational behavior ideas would you apply?
3 Would any of the following be useful in interpreting this case?
   a Behavior modification theory
   b Models of organizational behavior
   c Maslow's need hierarchy
   d The law of diminishing returns
   e Herzberg's motivational-maintenance theory
   f Organizational culture

Role-playing situations

1 In the role of Shaw, arrange to discuss this case with Gorman.
2 In the role of Gorman, call in Shaw to instruct him to improve the coffee-break situation.

CASE

8

The Palmer Export Site*

The Palmer export site is a large port for shipping iron ore mined by the Flick Company, a major international mining company. Ore is brought to the site by rail from mines some 150 miles distant. Irvin Corporation, which holds a construction and maintenance contract at the site, operates worldwide in the construction of heavy, technical engineering projects. The Palmer site is in an extremely isolated desert area over 700 miles from the nearest city of as many as 50,000 people.

Information in this case is presented only concerning the relationship of Irvin management with Flick management at the Palmer site. Two consultants who studied the situation described it as follows.

COMMENTS OF CONSULTANTS

Our comments concerning the investigation must be viewed against the background of the physical and social conditions in which work is conducted at Palmer. Above all, Palmer exists solely as a port for the export of iron ore. There are no other reasons for the town to be located there. Palmer is a company town; all the facilities, and to a large extent the way of life, are dependent on Flick. Similarly, it is quite evident that Irvin's situation in Palmer is dominated by its contractor-client relationship with Flick. Much of what we saw happening is a direct result of this relationship.

In contrast to its usual operation, Irvin in Palmer is performing a service function mainly consisting of maintaining, servicing, and altering a wide range of activities for Flick. The work varies from substantial modifications of port and plant facilities all the way to gardening.

This type of work is not typical for Irvin, which normally has been engaged in major construction. On a major project a job has a beginning, middle, and end. In comparison, while Irvin's contract with Flick obviously had a beginning, it has no clearly discernible end. The difference between these two types of work should be expressed in more than time, because it is evident that the lack of a clearly defined terminal objective has important psychological effects on Irvin managers.

*This case is adapted with permission from comments prepared by T. A. Williams and G. G. Watkins.

The nature of Irvin's task evidently runs counter to the construction way of life. Employees building a major facility from start to finish are able to recognize clearly what they have accomplished, the specific contributions which different work roles have made to the outcome, and the relationships between these contributions. They claim that there is a sense of challenge associated with working to a quoted price on the job and a sense of satisfaction in seeing something built and operating. The lack of this attitude was clearly evident from our interviews with Irvin staff, during which they expressed dissatisfaction with the role they see themselves performing in Palmer.

It is apparent that Irvin people in Palmer are engaged in a rather different kind of business from that to which they have become accustomed. It is clear that the basic nature of the present contract compares unfavorably with the type of work that Irvin normally does. There are also certain drawbacks with respect to the way in which Flick uses Irvin in this contract.

The work is initiated for Irvin on a continuing basis by Flick. While this may appear to be a sensible arrangement as far as the client is concerned, it places Irvin in a position of having constantly to adapt to Flick initiatives. Flick's plans continually change in a large number of areas in which Irvin is engaged, and this makes the problem of adaptation more difficult. Irvin's difficulties are further compounded by the tendency for Flick requirements and changes to be initiated for Irvin at all levels of the respective organizational structures. Together, these factors place Irvin's staff in a relationship of second-class citizens with respect to the Flick staff. This has consequences for both the work roles and the social status of the Irvin people.

First, it is a classic example of the frustrations which are generated when one party to the work relationship is continually initiating activity on the other party. The most common example of this problem is the traditional relationship between production and maintenance in industrial organizations. Initially in such a relationship, it seems normal for the parties to cooperate with each other as much as possible. However, as problems arise, the relationships often go sour, with production (in this case the client Flick) using its authority to make increasing demands on maintenance (Irvin). Such action even extends to overt intimidation. In turn, the recipient of this initiation may attempt to protect itself by using the fact that the initiator depends on it for task performance. In other words, the Flick staff may be using the client relationship to give vent to their own feelings of aggressiveness toward Irvin people. The latter might well respond by withholding effective task performance or by carrying out their tasks less than enthusiastically.

It would appear that Irvin and Flick are laboring under confusions and contradictions concerning the nature of company objectives. Irvin's formal task seems to be one of ensuring the continued efficient operation of Flick's facilities and adaptation of these facilities to meet changing needs. One might have supposed that Flick's final task is to export iron ore with a degree of efficiency which approaches maximization of export volume, given a reasonable rate of return. To some extent we gained the impression that Flick was concerned with this objective. However, there were signs that the "real" objectives of Flick management, as implied by their actions, are the product of psychological pressures caused by the sight of empty ships sitting in the harbor.

During the period we were in Palmer, Flick was loading at a rate of approximately 2000 tons per hour. The maximum possible rate is 6000 tons per hour. Over a period of time, it might be more efficient to stop the conveyor for necessary repairs and modifications to be carried out in order to continue at a more efficient rate. However, Irvin managers cited numerous examples of being unable to get in to carry out work because of Flick's insistence on keeping the conveyor belts running.

In the particular case of the Flick-Irvin relationship in Palmer, the above problems may have been compounded by the circumstances under which Irvin went into Palmer as a contractor. It appears that initially Flick staff resented the contract. Before the signing of this contract, the work which Irvin now performs was contracted to a number of firms on the basis of bids. This procedure enabled Flick staff to obtain certain free services from the contractors who were competing, such as boat repairs and garden maintenance. The nature of the Flick-Irvin contract requires Irvin to charge Flick on a cost-plus basis. This means that Irvin must submit detailed accounts justifying its expenditures. Hence there is little, if any, scope for Flick staff to improve their private well-being through the manipulation of contractual relationships.

Second, the situation illustrates the difficulty of trying to carry out rationally planned work when Irvin has little control over both the circumstances which create the need for work and the resources needed to carry out that work. Weekly work schedules are drawn up every Thursday afternoon at a meeting attended by both Flick and Irvin management. While we were in Palmer, there were some 171 open work orders on Irvin. The official purpose of the weekly planning meeting is to assign priorities among the work orders. By the Monday of our visit, the priorities laid down the previous Thursday had been substantially changed by Flick. Presumably the involvement of Irvin managers in the meeting is intended as a means of enabling them to participate in the planning of work for which they are responsible. However, it is clear that after the meeting the power to veto any decisions reached rests with Flick, and that this right is frequently and constantly exercised.

To this extent, Irvin managers would appear to have little real control over the events with which they are required to cope. Moreover, their lack of control over the work situation extends to use of the resources for performing work. While Irvin has some equipment on site, it is required to use Flick equipment when it is "available." However, frequently the equipment is not available. First, the equipment may be required for use by Flick. Second, Flick may not actually be using the equipment but may wish to hold it in reserve in order to gain flexibility in its own operations. Either way this reduces the flexibility that Irvin requires in order to cope with a rapidly changing work situation. Two outstanding examples of this are related to the paint shop and the fitting of a down pipe. Irvin is now involved in painting ore cars and is not allowed to use a paint shop specially built to repaint rolling stock. The shop is at present unused. With regard to the down pipe, a job that would have taken a day with a crane was still unfinished after several weeks.

Irvin's situation in Palmer is curiously paradoxical. Its people are subject to Flick's planning. To the extent that Flick plans its work efficiently, Irvin's profitability is increased due to the cost-plus basis of the contract. However, Irvin may be suffering a less obvious cost in this situation. Its management people are used to working with greater self-determination than they are allowed in Palmer, where their work plans are subject to weekly Flick initiatives and daily Flick alterations. Over a period of time, this may lead to an erosion of the managerial capacity of Irvin people, whether this be expressed in resignations or loss of confidence and competence. The continued exposure of Irvin managers to the Palmer situation may result in the withering away of its most valuable asset, human resources.

Study guides

1 Analyze the events in this case, using frameworks, ideas, and professional terms from this book, in order to determine what is happening at the Palmer site and why it is happening.

2 If you were a member of Flick top management and became aware of how the conditions in this case may be costing your firm money, what would you do? Explain why, using frameworks, ideas, and professional terms from this book.

3 If you were Irvin top management and became aware of how the conditions in this case may be damaging your human resources, even though they may be giving higher earnings at the moment, what would you do, if anything? Explain why, using frameworks, ideas, and terms from this book.

4 Do any of the ideas you have expressed in any of the preceding three questions apply to typical management-worker relationships in your nation? Explain.

Glossary

ABSENCES Employees who fail to show up for work as scheduled.

ACCEPTANCE THEORY OF AUTHORITY Belief that the power of a manager depends on the willingness of employees to accept that authority.

ACHIEVEMENT MOTIVE Drive to overcome challenges and obstacles in the pursuit of goals.

ACTION RESEARCH Method of improving problem-solving skills by discussing data-based system problems.

AFFILIATION MOTIVE Drive to relate to people on a social basis.

AFFIRMATIVE ACTION Employer effort to increase employment opportunity for protected groups that appear to be inadequately represented in a firm's labor force.

AGE DISCRIMINATION ACT Law (as amended) that provides EEO for employees age forty and over.

AIDS Acquired Immune Deficiency Syndrome.

ALIENATION Feeling of powerlessness, lack of meaning, loneliness, disorientation, and lack of attachment to the job, work group, or organization.

ALLOCATIVE VALUES Resources that must be given up by someone in order for another to have them.

APPRAISAL See *Performance appraisal.*

AREA OF JOB FREEDOM Area of discretion after all restraints have been applied.

ASSERTIVENESS TRAINING Program that teaches people to be more direct, honest, and expressive as a means of dealing with anxiety-producing situations.

ATTRIBUTION Process by which people interpret the causes of their own and others' behavior.

AUTOCRATIC LEADERS Leaders who centralize power and decision making in themselves.

AUTOCRATIC MODEL Managerial view that power and formal authority are necessary to control employee behavior.

AUTONOMY Policy of giving employees some discretion and control over job-related decisions.

BEHAVIOR MODELING Method of teaching skills to handle commonly encountered behavioral problems.

BEHAVIOR MODIFICATION Theory that behavior depends on its consequences; therefore, it is possible to control a number of employee behaviors by manipulating their consequences.

BEHAVIORAL BIAS Narrow viewpoint of some people that emphasizes satisfying employee experiences while overlooking the broader system of the organization in relation to all its publics.

BENEVOLENT AUTOCRAT Autocratic leader who chooses to give rewards to employees.

BIOFEEDBACK Approach by which people under medical guidance learn from instrument feedback to influence symptoms of stress, such as increased heart rate.

BODY LANGUAGE Way in which people communicate meaning to others with their bodies in interpersonal interaction.

BOUNDARY ROLES Positions that require an ability to interact with different groups in order to keep a project successful.

BOUNDARY SPANNERS Individuals with strong communication links within their department, with people in other units, and often with the external community.

BRAINSTORMING Group structure that encourages creative thinking by deferring judgment on ideas generated.

BUREAUCRACY Large, complex administrative system operating with impersonal detachment from people.

BURNOUT Condition in which employees are emotionally exhausted, become detached from their work, and feel helpless to accomplish their goals.

CAFETERIA BENEFITS See *Flexible benefits.*

CHAIN-REACTION EFFECT Situation in which a change (or other condition) that directly affects only one or a few persons may lead to a reaction from many people, even hundreds or thousands, because of their mutual interest in it.

CHANGE AGENT Person whose role is to initiate change and help make it work.

CLUSTER CHAIN Grapevine chain in which one person tells several others, and a few of those tell more than one person.

CODETERMINATION Government-mandated worker representation on the board of directors of a firm.

COGNITIVE DISSONANCE Internal conflict and anxiety that occurs when people receive information incompatible with their value systems, prior decisions, or other information they may have.

COGNITIVE THEORIES OF MOTIVATION Motivational theories based on thinking and feeling (i.e., cognition) of the employee.

COHESIVENESS Degree to which employees stick together, rely on each other, and desire to remain members of a group.

COLLECTIVE BARGAINING Negotiation between representatives of management and labor to produce a written agreement covering terms and conditions of employment.

COLLEGIAL MODEL Managerial view that teamwork is the way to build employee responsibility.

COMMITTEE Specific type of meeting in which members in their group role have been delegated authority with regard to the problem at hand.

COMMUNICATION Transfer of information and understanding from one person to another person.

COMMUNICATION CIRCUIT Two-way flow of information from sender to receiver and back to the sender.

COMMUNICATION LOOP See *Communication circuit*.

COMMUNICATION OVERLOAD Condition in which employees receive more communication inputs than they can process or than they need.

COMMUNICATION PROCESS Steps by which a sender reaches a receiver with a message and receives feedback on it.

COMPETENCE MOTIVE Drive to do high-quality work.

COMPLEMENTARY TRANSACTION Communicative action in which the ego states of the sender and receiver in the opening transaction are reversed in the response.

COMPLETE PAY PROGRAM Comprehensive reward system that uses different bases of pay to accomplish various objectives (e.g., retention, production, teamwork).

CONCEPTUAL SKILL Ability to think in terms of models, frameworks, and broad relationships.

CONCILIATION AGREEMENT Negotiated settlement (of a discrimination charge) that is acceptable to the EEOC and all aggrieved parties.

CONDITIONAL STROKES Strokes offered to employees if they perform correctly or avoid problems.

CONFLICT Disagreement over the goals to attain or the methods used to accomplish them.

CONFORMITY Dependence on the norms of others without independent thinking.

CONSENSUS Agreement of most of the members of a group.

CONSIDERATION Leader's employee orientation.

CONSULTIVE MANAGEMENT System of management in which employees are encouraged to think about issues and contribute their own ideas before decisions are made.

CONTEXT Environment in which words are used.

CONTINGENCY APPROACH TO O.B. Philosophy that different environments require different behavioral practices for effectiveness.

CONTINGENCY MODEL OF LEADERSHIP Model that states that the most appropriate leadership style depends on the favorableness of the situation, especially in relation to leader-member relations, task structure, and position power.

CONTINGENCY ORGANIZATIONAL DESIGN Use of different organizational structures and processes that are required for effectiveness in different kinds of environments.

CONTRACT ARBITRATION Use of a third party to make final and binding decisions on major bargaining issues.

CORE DIMENSIONS OF JOBS Five factors of jobs, including task variety, task identity, task significance, autonomy, and feedback.

CORRECTIVE DISCIPLINE Action taken to discourage further infractions so that future acts will be in compliance with standards.

COST-REWARD COMPARISON Process in which employees identify and compare personal costs and rewards to determine the point at which they are approximately equal.

COUNSELING Discussion of a problem that usually has emotional content with an employee in order to help the employee cope with it better.

COUNSELING FUNCTIONS Six activities that may be performed by counseling, including advice, reassurance, communication, release of emotional tension, clarified thinking, and reorientation.

COUNTERPROPOSAL Offer suggested as an alternative to a previous proposal by the other party.

CROSS-COMMUNICATION See *Lateral communication*.

CROSSED TRANSACTION Communicative action in which the stimulus lines in an opening transaction are not parallel to those in the response.

CULTURAL DISTANCE Amount of difference between any two social systems.

CULTURAL SHOCK Feeling of confusion, insecurity, and anxiety caused by a strange new environment.

CULTURE Social environment of human-created beliefs, customs, knowledge, and practices that define conventional behavior in a society.

CUSTODIAL MODEL Managerial view that security needs are dominant among employees.

DELEGATION Assignment of duties and authority to others.

DELPHI GROUP Group structure in which a series of questionnaires are distributed to the respondents for their response, but they do not need to meet face-to-face.

DEMOCRATIC MANAGEMENT System of management in which opportunities to make major decisions are given to employee groups.

DESCRIPTIVE SURVEYS Format in which employees respond in their own words to express their feelings, thoughts, and intentions.

DEVELOPMENT LEVEL Task-specific combination of employee competence and motivation to perform that helps determine which leadership style to use.

DIRECTIVE COUNSELING Process of listening to an employee's problem, deciding with the employee what should be done, and then telling and motivating the employee to do it.

DISCHARGE Separation of an employee from the company for cause.

DISCIPLINE Management action to enforce organizational standards.

DOUBLE-LOOP LEARNING Process of using current information about a change to prepare participants to manage future changes even more effectively. See also *Single-loop learning.*

DUAL-CAREER COUPLES Situations in which each spouse has a separate career.

DUE PROCESS Disciplinary procedures that show concern for the rights of the employee involved.

DYSFUNCTIONAL ACTION Change that creates unfavorable effects for the system.

ECOLOGICAL CONTROL Alteration of the surroundings so as to influence another's feelings and behavior.

ECONOMIC INCENTIVE SYSTEM System that varies an employee's pay in proportion to some criterion of individual, group, or organizational performance.

EGO STATES Psychological positions of Parent, Adult, and Child that form the basis for social transactions.

ELABORATING Adding one's own strong feelings and reasoning to a communication.

ELECTRONIC GRAPEVINE Transmission of informal messages by the use of computers.

ELECTRONIC MAIL Computer-based communication system that allows messages to be sent to multiple parties simultaneously.

EMPLOYEE ASSISTANCE PROGRAM Program to identify and treat the problems that are affecting employee productivity or hindering the personal well-being of employees.

EMPLOYEE OWNERSHIP PLANS Programs for employees to provide the capital to purchase control of an existing operation.

EMPLOYMENT ENRICHMENT Situation in which jobs, work teams, and work systems have all been enriched to create a balanced environment.

ENCOUNTER GROUP Unstructured small-group interaction under stress in a situation that requires people to become sensitive to one another's feelings.

ENRICHED SOCIOTECHNICAL WORK SYSTEM System in which a whole organization or major part of it is built into a balanced human-technical system.

EQUAL EMPLOYMENT OPPORTUNITY (EEO) Provision of equal opportunities to secure jobs and earn rewards in them, regardless of conditions unrelated to job performance.

EQUAL EMPLOYMENT OPPORTUNITY COMMISSION (EEOC) Federal agency charged with enforcing EEO laws.

EQUAL EMPLOYMENT OPPORTUNITY LAWS Federal, state, and local legislation to support EEO.

EQUITY SENSITIVITY Recognition that employees have different preferences for overreward, equity, or underreward.

EQUITY THEORY Tendency of employees to judge fairness by comparing their inputs and rewards on the job with those of other relevant people.

ESCALATING COMMITMENT Act of persevering to advocate a course of action, and possibly allocating additional resources to a project, despite rational evidence that it will result in a failure.

ETHICAL LEADERSHIP Recognition and use of guides such as social responsibility.

ETHNOCENTRISM Predisposition to use oneself as the criterion for judging others.

EXISTENCE NEEDS Physiological and security factors.

EXPATRIATES Employees who work in a nation (and culture) different from their own.

EXPECTANCY Strength of belief that work-related effort will result in successful completion of a task (performance).

EXPECTANCY MODEL Theory that motivation is a product of three factors: valence, expectancy, and instrumentality.

EXPERIENTIAL LEARNING Process in which participants learn by experiencing in the training environment the kinds of human problems they face on the job.

EXPERT POWER Power that arises from a person's knowledge of and information about a complex situation.

EXTINCTION Lack of a significant consequence accompanying behavior.

EXTRINSIC MOTIVATORS External rewards that occur apart from work.

FACT PREMISES Science-based views of how the world behaves.

FEEDBACK Information from the job itself, management, or other employees that tells workers how well they are performing.

FEEDBACK LOOP See *Communication circuit*.

FILTERING Reducing a communication to a few basic details that can be remembered and passed on to others.

FLEXIBLE BENEFITS Systems that allow employees to select their individual combination of benefits.

FLEXIBLE WORKING TIME System in which employees have some autonomy to adjust their work schedules to fit their lifestyles or to meet unusual needs.

FLEXTIME See *Flexible working time*.

FOLLOWERSHIP SKILLS Behaviors that help a person to be an effective subordinate to a leader.

FREE-REIN LEADERS Leaders who avoid power and responsibility.

FRUSTRATION Result of a motivation (drive) being blocked to prevent one from reaching a desired goal.

FUNCTIONAL ACTION Change that is favorable for the system.

FUNCTIONALIZATION Division of work into different kinds of duties.

GAIN SHARING Policy of giving employees a substantial portion of the cost savings produced when their jobs are improved.

GAIN-SHARING PLAN Program that establishes a historical base period of organizational performance, measures improvements, and shares the gains with employees on some formula basis.

GENETIC TESTING Process of predicting whether an employee may be genetically susceptible to one or more types of illness or harmful substances.

GOAL SETTING Establishment of targets and objectives for successful performance, both long run and short run.

GOOD MENTAL HEALTH Condition in which people feel comfortable about themselves, right about other people, and able to meet the demands of life.

GOSSIP CHAIN Grapevine chain in which a person tells many others.

GRAPEVINE Communication system of an informal organization.

GRIEVANCE Real or imagined feeling of personal injustice that an employee has about the employment relationship.

GRIEVANCE ARBITRATION Final and binding interpretation of what the existing contract means, as judged by an arbitrator.

GRIEVANCE RATE Number of written grievances for a hundred employees in one year.

GRIEVANCE SYSTEM Formal system by which disputes over working rules are expressed, processed, and judged in an organization.

GROUP DECISION SUPPORT SYSTEM Use of computers, decision models, and technological advances to remove communication barriers, structure the decision process, and generally direct the group's discussion.

GROUP DYNAMICS Social process by which people interact face-to-face in small groups.

GROUPTHINK Tendency of a group to bring individual thinking in line with the average quality of the group's thinking.

GROWTH NEED The desire for self-esteem and self-actualization.

HANDICAPPED EMPLOYEES Those employees with a significant disability of some type, either physical, mental, or emotional.

HAWTHORNE EFFECT Concept that the mere observation of a group tends to change it.

HIDDEN AGENDA Private emotions and motives of group members.

HIERARCHY OF NEEDS Philosophy that different groups of needs have a specific order of priority among most people, so that one group of needs precedes another in importance.

HIGHER-ORDER NEEDS Need levels 3 to 5 on the Maslow hierarchy of needs.

HOLISTIC O.B. Philosophy that interprets people-organization relationships in terms of the whole person, whole group, whole organization, and whole social system.

HOMEOSTASIS Self-correcting mechanism in a group by which energies are called up to restore balance whenever change threatens the group.

HOT-STOVE RULE Disciplinary action with characteristics similar to the consequences a person suffers from touching a hot stove.

HUMAN RELATIONS Term applied to organizational behavior early in its history, and especially applied to practices that were less sophisticated, shallow, and faddish.

HUMAN RESOURCE ACCOUNTING Process of converting human data into money values for use in the regular accounting system.

HUMAN SKILL Ability to work effectively with people and to build teamwork.

HUMANISTIC VALUES Positive beliefs about the potential and desire for growth among employees.

IMPOSTOR PHENOMENON Belief that personal capabilities are not as great as other people believe them to be.

INCENTIVES Environmental factors that are established for the purpose of motivating a person.

INCREMENTAL VALUES Resources that a person may receive without the necessity of another person's giving them up (for example, education).

INDIVIDUAL DIFFERENCES Idea that each person is different from all others and that these differences usually are substantial rather than meaningless.

INDIVIDUALISM Process of placing greatest emphasis on one's personal needs and welfare.

INDIVIDUALIZATION Process through which employees successfully exert influence on the social system around them.

INDUSTRIAL DEMOCRACY Government-mandated worker participation at various levels of the organization with regard to decisions that affect workers.

INDUSTRIAL RELATIONS See *Labor relations.*

INFERENCE Interpretation of symbols that is based on assumptions, not facts.

INFORMAL ORGANIZATION Network of personal and social relations not established or required by the formal organization, but arising spontaneously as people associate with one another.

INITIATION OF ACTION Process of sending work and/or instructions to another person.

INSTITUTIONAL TEAM Companywide group of people.

INSTRUMENTALITY Belief that a reward will be received once a task is accomplished.

INTEREST ARBITRATION See *Contract arbitration.*

INTRAMANAGEMENT COMMUNICATION See *Management communication.*

INTRINSIC MOTIVATORS Internal rewards that a person feels when performing a job, so there is a direct connection between work and reward.

INVESTMENT APPROACH Policy of treating certain human resource costs as an investment to be depreciated during an employee's expected employment.

JOB CONTENT Conditions that relate directly to the job itself and the employee's performance of it, rather than conditions in the environment external to the job.

JOB CONTEXT Job conditions in the environment surrounding the job, rather than those directly related to job performance.

JOB DIAGNOSTIC SURVEY (JDS) Instrument used to determine the relative presence of the five core dimensions in jobs.

JOB ENLARGEMENT Policy of giving workers a wider variety of duties in order to reduce monotony.

JOB ENRICHMENT Policy of adding motivators to a job to make it more rewarding.

JOB PLACEMENT PROFILE CHARTS Visual displays that match worker physical and mental abilities with a job's requirements.

JOB SATISFACTION Set of favorable or unfavorable feelings with which employees view their work.

JOB SATISFACTION SURVEY Procedure by which employees report their feelings toward their jobs and work environment.

KEYSTONE ROLE OF SUPERVISORS Behavior pattern in which the supervisor is seen as the element that connects both sides (management and workers) and makes it possible for each to perform its function effectively.

KNOWLEDGE-BASED PAY See *Skill-based pay.*

KNOWLEDGE SOCIETY Society in which the use of knowledge and information dominates work and employs the largest proportion of the labor force.

LABOR RELATIONS Subject of union-management relations.

LABOR UNION Association of employees formed for the primary purpose of influencing an employer's decisions about conditions of employment.

LABORATORY TRAINING Situations in which the trainees experience through their own interactions some of the conditions they are talking about.

LATERAL COMMUNICATION Communication across chains of command.

LAW OF DIMINISHING RETURNS Principle that a declining amount of extra outputs are received when more of a desirable input is added to an operating system.

LAW OF EFFECT Tendency of a person to repeat behavior that is accompanied by favorable consequences and not to repeat behavior accompanied by unfavorable consequences.

LEADER-MEMBER EXCHANGE Idea that leaders and their followers exchange information, resources, and role expectations that determine the quality of their interpersonal relationship.

LEADER-MEMBER RELATIONS Degree to which the leader is accepted by the group.

LEADER-POSITION POWER Organizational power that goes with the position the leader occupies.

LEADERSHIP Process of encouraging and helping others to work enthusiastically toward objectives.

LEADERSHIP STYLE Total pattern of a leader's actions, as perceived by the leader's employees.

LEARNED HELPLESSNESS Condition in which employees continue to act in a dependent manner even after organizational changes make greater independence possible.

LEGITIMATE POWER Power that is delegated legitimately from higher-established authorities to others.

LEVELING EFFECT See *Groupthink.*

LIAISON INDIVIDUALS Persons who are active communicators on the grapevine.

LIFE POSITION Dominant way of relating to people that tends to remain with the person for a lifetime unless major experiences occur to change it.

LINKING PIN Managerial role of connecting the group with the remainder of the organization.

LOOSE RATE Payment at a rate that allows employees to reach standard output with less-than-normal effort.

LOWER-ORDER NEEDS Need levels 1 and 2 on the Maslow hierarchy of needs.

MACROMOTIVATION Conditions outside the firm that influence employee performance (type B).

MAINTENANCE FACTORS Conditions that tend to satisfy workers when they exist and to dissatisfy workers when they do not exist, but their existence tends not to be strongly motivating.

MANAGEMENT BY OBJECTIVES (MBO) System in which managers and subordinates mutually agree on the employee's objectives for the next year and on the criteria that will be used to measure accomplishment of the objectives.

MANAGEMENT COMMUNICATION Communication within the management group.

MANAGERIAL GRID Framework of management styles based on the dimensions of concern for people and concern for production.

MANIPULATION OF PEOPLE Disregard for the basic dignity of the human being by learning and using organizational behavior ideas without regard for human welfare.

MATRIX ORGANIZATION Overlay of one type of organization on another so that there are two chains of command directing individual employees.

MECHANISTIC ORGANIZATIONS Organizations characterized by the use of hierarchy, centralized direction, certainty of task assignments, and strict definition of roles.

MEDIATOR Outside specialist who encourages the negotiating parties to come to an agreement.

MEDITATION Quiet, concentrated inner thought in order to rest the body physically and emotionally.

MENTOR Person who serves as a role model to help other employees gain valuable advice on roles to play and behaviors to avoid.

MICROMOTIVATION Conditions within the firm that influence employee performance (type A).

MODELS OF ORGANIZATIONAL BEHAVIOR Underlying theories that act as unconscious but powerful guides to managerial thought and behavior.

MORALE Level of job satisfaction within a group.

MOTIVATING POTENTIAL SCORE (MPS) Index that indicates the degree to which a job is perceived to be meaningful, foster responsibility, and provide knowledge of results.

MOTIVATION Strength of the drive toward an action.

MOTIVATIONAL FACTORS Conditions that tend to motivate workers when they exist, but their absence rarely is strongly dissatisfying.

MOTIVATIONAL PATTERNS Attitudes that affect the way people view their jobs and approach their lives.

MULTIPLE MANAGEMENT Middle-management committees to improve the participation of managers below top organizational levels.

MULTIPROFESSIONAL EMPLOYEES People who are trained in two or more professions or intellectual disciplines.

MUTUAL INTEREST Idea that people need organizations and organizations need people, which gives them a superordinate goal of joint interest to bring them together.

NATURAL WORK MODULE Job designed so that a person performs a complete cycle of work to make a whole product or subunit of it.

NATURAL WORK TEAM Group of employees whose task is to work together to produce an entire unit of work.

NEEDS, PRIMARY Basic physical needs.

NEEDS, SECONDARY Social and psychological needs.

NEGATIVE LEADERSHIP Leaders who emphasize penalties to motivate people.

NEGATIVE REINFORCEMENT Removal of an unfavorable consequence that accompanies behavior.

NEIGHBORHOODS Centers of related individual offices to encourage the formation of social groups.

NETWORK Group of people who develop and maintain contact to informally exchange information, usually about a shared interest.

NETWORKING Being active on a network.

NOMINAL GROUP Group structure that combines individual input, group discussion, and independent decision making.

NONDIRECTIVE COUNSELING Process of skillfully listening to and encouraging a counselee to explain troublesome problems, understand them, and determine appropriate solutions.

NONLOGICAL Based on feelings rather than logic.

NONTRADITIONAL EMPLOYMENT Jobs not historically held by members of that sex.

NONVERBAL COMMUNICATION Actions (or inactions) that people take that serve as a means of communication.

NORM Informal group requirement for the behavior of its members.

NORM OF RECIPROCITY Principle that two people in a continuing relationship feel a strong obligation to repay their social "debts" to each other.

O.B. MOD. See *Organizational behavior modification.*

OBJECTIVE SURVEYS Format using highly structured response categories for gathering job satisfaction data.

OPEN-DOOR POLICY Statement encouraging employees to come to their supervisor or higher managers with any matter that concerns them.

OPERANT CONDITIONING Any type of reinforcement to modify behavior by its consequence.

ORGANIC ORGANIZATIONS Organizations characterized by flexible tasks and roles, open communications, and decentralized decision making.

ORGANIZATION DEVELOPMENT (OD) Intervention strategy that uses group processes to focus on the whole culture of an organization in order to bring about planned change.

ORGANIZATIONAL BEHAVIOR (O.B.) Study and application of knowledge about how people act within organizations.

ORGANIZATIONAL BEHAVIOR MODIFICATION (O.B. MOD.) Behavior modification used in organizations.

ORGANIZATIONAL BEHAVIOR SYSTEM Integrated framework of elements that portrays how behavior is guided toward achievement of organizational goals.

ORGANIZATIONAL CITIZENS Employees who engage in positive social acts designed to help others, such as volunteering their efforts, sharing their resources, or cooperating with others.

ORGANIZATIONAL COMMITMENT Degree to which an employee identifies with the organization and wants to continue actively participating in it.

ORGANIZATIONAL CULTURE Set of values, beliefs, and norms that is shared among an organization's members. Also called *organizational climate.*

ORGANIZATIONAL GAMING Group exercise in sequential decision making under simulated organizational conditions.

ORGANIZATIONAL LEARNING CURVE FOR CHANGE Period of adaptation that follows change and typically shows a decline in effectiveness before a group reaches a new equilibrium.

OUTPUT RESTRICTION Situation in which workers choose to produce less than they could produce with normal effort.

OVERPARTICIPATION Condition in which employees have more participation than they want.

PARITY EMPLOYMENT See *Proportional employment.*

PAROCHIALISM Condition in which people "see" the situation around them from their own perspective.

PARTICIPATION Mental and emotional involvement of persons in group situations that encourage them to contribute to group goals and share responsibility for them.

PARTICIPATIVE COUNSELING Mutual counselor-counselee relationship that establishes a cooperative exchange of ideas to help solve a counselee's problems.

PARTICIPATIVE LEADER Leader who decentralizes authority by consulting with followers.

PATH-GOAL LEADERSHIP Model that states that the leader's job is to create a work environment through structure, support, and rewards that helps employees reach the organization's goals.

PEER REVIEW PANEL Special board that takes informal testimony and makes binding decisions in grievance cases.

PERCEPTION Individual's own view of the world.

PERCEPTUAL SET People's tendency to perceive what they expect to perceive.

PERFORMANCE APPRAISAL Process of evaluating the performance of employees.

PERFORMANCE-SATISFACTION-EFFORT LOOP Flow model that shows the directional relationship between performance and satisfaction.

PERSONAL POWER Ability of leaders to develop followers from the strength of their own personalities.

PERSONAL WELLNESS Programs of preventive maintenance that help individuals reduce the causes of stress or cope with stressors that are beyond their direct control.

PHASED RETIREMENT Programs that give workers more time off, usually with pay, in the years immediately preceding retirement.

PIECE RATE Reward system that pays employees according to the number of acceptable pieces produced.

POLITICAL POWER Ability to work with people and social systems to gain their allegiance and support.

POLITICS Ways that leaders gain and use power.

POLYGRAPH Instrument (lie detector) that measures the physiological changes when a person tells a significant lie.

POSITIVE LEADERSHIP Leaders who emphasize rewards to motivate people.

POSITIVE REINFORCEMENT Favorable consequence that accompanies behavior and encourages repetition of the behavior.

POWER Ability to influence other people and events.

POWER MOTIVE Drive to influence people and change situations.

PRACTICE Conscious application of conceptual models and research results with the goal of improving individual and organizational performance.

PRERETIREMENT COUNSELING Programs that encourage employees to think about and prepare for impending retirement.

PREVENTIVE DISCIPLINE Action taken to encourage employees to follow standards and rules so that infractions do not occur.

PROBLEM-SOLVING BARGAINING Approach that tries to get joint gain for both parties.

PROCEDURE Organization of work based on its flow from one operation to another.

PRODUCTION SHARING Incentive program that pays employees for improvements in labor costs that are better than standard.

PRODUCTIVITY Ratio that compares units of output with units of input.

PROFILE CHART Graphic display of the scores of the five core dimensions of jobs.

PROFIT SHARING System that distributes to employees some portion of the profits of business.

PROGRESSIVE DISCIPLINE Policy that provides stronger penalties for repeated offenses.

PROPORTIONAL EMPLOYMENT Belief that an organization's employees should approximately represent the proportions of different groups in the local labor force or population.

PROTECTED GROUPS Groups of employees who are protected from employment discrimination by EEO laws.

PSYCHIC COSTS Costs that affect a person's inner self or psyche.

PSYCHOLOGICAL CONTRACT Unwritten agreement that defines the conditions of each employee's psychological involvement with the system.

PSYCHOLOGICAL COSTS See *Psychic costs.*

PSYCHOLOGICAL STRESS EVALUATOR Instrument that analyzes changes in voice patterns to determine whether a lie is being told.

PSYCHOLOGICAL SUPPORT Condition in which leaders stimulate people to want to do the job.

PUNISHMENT Unfavorable consequence that accompanies behavior and discourages repetition of the behavior.

QUALITY CIRCLES Voluntary groups that receive training in statistical techniques and problem-solving skills and then meet to produce ideas for improving productivity and working conditions.

QUALITY OF WORK LIFE (QWL) Favorableness or unfavorableness of a job environment for people.

RATE SETTING Process of determining the standard output for each job.

READABILITY Degree to which writing and speech are understandable to receivers.

REALISTIC JOB PREVIEWS Employment process in which job candidates are given a small sample of organizational reality.

RECESS A break taken by the bargaining committee to discuss some point privately.

RED TAPE Procedure that appears to be unnecessary to those who are following it.

REFERENCE GROUP Group whose norms a person accepts.

REFREEZING Term applying to situations involving change and referring to a person's acting to integrate what has been learned into actual practice.

REINFORCEMENT Behavior consequence that influences future behavior.

REINFORCEMENT, CONTINUOUS Reinforcement accompanying each correct behavior.

REINFORCEMENT, FIXED-INTERVAL Reinforcement after a certain period of time.

REINFORCEMENT, FIXED-RATIO Reinforcement after a certain number of correct responses.

REINFORCEMENT, VARIABLE-INTERVAL Reinforcement after a variety of time periods.

REINFORCEMENT, VARIABLE-RATIO Reinforcement after a variable number of correct responses.

REINFORCEMENT SCHEDULES Frequency with which reinforcement accompanies a desired behavior.

RELATEDNESS NEED Desire of an employee to be understood and accepted.

RELIABILITY Capacity of a survey instrument to produce consistent results.

RESEARCH Process of gathering and interpreting relevant evidence that will either support a behavioral theory or help change it.

RESISTANCE TO CHANGE Desire not to accept a change or to accept it only partially.

RETRAINING Providing opportunities to learn new skills to those employees whose jobs are replaced by technological change.

REVERSE CULTURAL SHOCK The difficulty experienced by expatriates in readjusting to the surroundings of their home country upon their reentry.

REVERSE DISCRIMINATION Discrimination against an employee not included in an affirmative action program.

RIGHTS OF PRIVACY Freedom from organizational invasion of a person's private life and unauthorized release of confidential information about a person.

ROBOTICS Design and use of programmable, mechanical devices to move parts and perform a variety of tasks.

ROLE Pattern of actions expected of a person in activities involving others.

ROLE AMBIGUITY Feeling that arises when roles are inadequately defined or are substantially unknown.

ROLE CONFLICT Feeling that arises when others have different perceptions or expectations of a person's role.

ROLE MODELS Leaders who serve as examples for their followers.

ROLE PERCEPTIONS How people think they are supposed to act in their own roles and others should act in their roles.

ROLE PLAYING Spontaneous acting of a realistic situation involving two or more people under classroom conditions.

RULE OF FIVE Steps in communication taken by a receiver—receive, understand, accept, use, and provide feedback.

RUMOR Grapevine information that is communicated without secure standards of evidence being present.

SANCTIONS Rewards and penalties that a group uses to persuade persons to conform to its norms.

SCALAR PROCESS Division of an organization into levels on the basis of authority and responsibility.

SCANLON PLAN Highly successful production-sharing plan that emphasizes teamwork and active participation.

SELF-ACTUALIZATION Need to become all that one is capable of becoming.

SELF-APPRAISAL Process of asking individuals to identify and compare their strengths and weaknesses.

SELF-EFFICACY Belief that one has the necessary capabilities to perform a task, fulfill role expectations, or meet a challenging situation successfully.

SELF-FULFILLING PROPHECY Probability that a manager's expectations for an employee will cause the manager to treat the employee differently, and that the employee will respond in a way that confirms the initial expectations. Also known as the *Pygmalion effect*.

SELF-LEADERSHIP Act of leading oneself to perform naturally motivating tasks, and managing oneself to do work that is required but not naturally rewarding.

SELF-MANAGING TEAMS Groups that are given a large degree of decision-making autonomy and expected to control their own behavior and results.

SEMANTICS Science of meaning.

SENSITIVITY TRAINING See *Encounter group*.

SEXUAL HARASSMENT Process of making employment or promotion decisions contingent on sexual favors, or exhibiting any verbal or physical conduct that creates an offensive working environment.

SHAPING Successive reinforcement as behavior comes closer to the desired behavior.

SHORT-CIRCUITING Situation in which people skip one or more steps in the communication hierarchy.

SINGLE-LOOP LEARNING Process of adapting to changes which are imposed on employees.

SKILL-BASED PAY A system that rewards individual employees for what they know how to do. Also known as *knowledge-based pay*.

SOCIAL CUES Information that employees receive from their social surroundings.

SOCIAL EQUILIBRIUM Dynamic working balance among the interdependent parts of a system.

SOCIAL LEADER Person who helps restore and maintain group relationships.

SOCIAL LEARNING THEORY Belief that employees gain substantial information about how to perform by observing and imitating those around them.

SOCIAL LOAFING Lessening of output by employees when they think their contributions to a group cannot be measured.

SOCIAL RESPONSIBILITY Recognition that organizations have significant influence on the social system, which must be considered and balanced in all organizational actions.

SOCIAL SUPPORT Network of activities and relationships that satisfies an employee's perceived need to be cared for, esteemed, and valued.

SOCIAL SYSTEM Complex set of human relationships interacting in many ways.

SOCIALIZATION The continuous process of transmitting key elements of an organization's culture to its employees.

SOCIOECONOMIC MODEL OF DECISION MAKING Model in which social costs and benefits, as well as economic and technical values, are considered in the decision-making process.

SOCIOGRAM Diagram of the feelings of group members toward each other.

SOCIOMETRY Study and measurement of feelings of group members toward one another.

SOCIOTECHNICAL SYSTEMS Relationship of technology to people at work.

SPAN OF MANAGEMENT Number of people a manager directly manages.

SPECIALIZATION Process of becoming adept at a certain function as a result of concentrating efforts upon it.

STATUS Social rank of a person in a group.

STATUS SYMBOLS Visible, external things that attach to a person or workplace and serve as evidence of social rank.

STRESS THRESHOLD Level of stressors that one can tolerate before feelings of stress occur.

STRESSORS Conditions that tend to cause stress.

STRIKE Work stoppage called by a union to place bargaining pressure on management.

STROKING Performing any act of recognition for another person.

STRUCTURE Leader's task orientation.

SUBSTITUTES FOR LEADERSHIP Characteristics of the task, employees, or organization that may reduce the need for leadership behaviors.

SUGGESTION PROGRAMS Formal plans to encourage individual employees to recommend work improvements. A monetary award frequently is offered for acceptable suggestions.

SUPERORDINATE GOAL Goal that integrates the efforts of individuals or groups.

SUPPORTIVE APPROACH TO O.B. Philosophy of working with people in ways that seek to satisfy their needs and develop their potential.

SUPPORTIVE MODEL Managerial view that leaders should support employees in their attempts to grow and perform their jobs.

SURFACE AGENDA Official task of a group.

SURVEY FEEDBACK Communication of job satisfaction information to managers and others as a basis for action.

SYSTEMS 1 THROUGH 4 OD framework developed by Rensis Likert that uses four systems of management to describe organizations, with System 4 as the most participative.

TASK IDENTITY Practice of allowing employees to perform a complete piece of work.

TASK LEADER Person who helps the group accomplish its objectives and stay on target.

TASK SIGNIFICANCE Amount of impact, as perceived by the worker, that the work has on other people.

TASK STRUCTURE Degree to which one specific way is required to do the job.

TASK SUPPORT Condition in which leaders provide the resources, budgets, power, and other elements that are essential to get the job done.

TASK TEAM Cooperative small group in regular contact that is engaged in coordinated action and whose members contribute responsibly and enthusiastically to the task.

TEAM BUILDING OD process of developing integrated, cooperative groups.

TECHNICAL SKILL Person's knowledge and ability in any type of process or technique.

TECHNOPHOBIA Emotional fear of all technology regardless of its consequences.

TELECOMMUTING Process of accomplishing all or a part of an employee's work at home through computer links to the office.

TERRITORY Space that employees can call their own and in which they can control what happens.

THEORIES Explanations of how and why people think, feel, and act as they do.

THEORY X Autocratic and traditional set of assumptions about people.

THEORY Y Human and supportive set of assumptions about people.

THEORY Z Model that adapts the elements of Japanese management systems to the U.S. culture and emphasizes cooperation and consensus decision processes.

TRADE-OFF Offer to give up on one issue in exchange for "winning" another.

TRAINING MULTIPLIER EFFECT Process by which skilled people develop others, who then become the nucleus for developing still others.

TRANSACTIONAL ANALYSIS (TA) Study of social transactions between people, so as to develop improved communication and human relationships.

TRANSCULTURAL EMPLOYEES Individuals who have learned to operate effectively in several cultures.

TRIPLE-REWARD SYSTEM Term applied to practices that jointly benefit the needs and objectives of three groups: people, organizations, and the whole social system.

TUNNEL VISION See *Behavioral bias*.

TURNOVER Rate at which employees leave an organization.

TWO-FACTOR MODEL OF MOTIVATION Motivational model developed by Frederick Herzberg, which concludes that one set of job conditions primarily motivates an employee while a different set primarily reduces dissatisfactions of the employee.

TYPE A PEOPLE Individuals who are aggressive and competitive, set high standards, and put themselves under constant time pressures.

TYPE B PEOPLE Individuals who are relaxed and easygoing and accept situations readily.

UNCONDITIONAL STROKES Strokes presented without any connection to behavior.

UNDERPARTICIPATION Condition in which employees want more participation than they have.

UNFREEZING Term applying to situations involving change and referring to a person's casting aside old ideas and practices so that new ones can be learned.

VALENCE Strength of a person's preference for receiving a reward.

VALIDITY Capacity of a survey instrument to measure what it claims to measure.

VALUE PREMISES Personal views of the desirability of certain goals.

VARIETY Policy of allowing employees to perform different operations that often require different skills.

VISION A long-range image or idea of what can or should be accomplished.

WAGE INCENTIVE Reward system that provides more pay for more production.

WHISTLE-BLOWER Employee who discloses alleged misconduct to the public.

WIN-LOSE BARGAINING Negotiation in which each party tries to win from the other party a favorable division of limited resources.

WORK COMMITTEES Groups of workers and their managers that are organized primarily to consider and solve job problems.

WORK ETHIC Employee attitude of viewing work as a central life interest and a desirable goal in life.

"X" CHART Model in the form of an "X" showing how attitudes affect responses to change. (Originally developed by F. J. Roethlisberger.)